Winifred Wagner

Winifred Wagner

A Life at the Heart of Hitler's Bayreuth

BRIGITTE HAMANN

Translated from the German by Alan Bance

HARCOURT, INC.
Orlando   Austin   New York   San Diego   Toronto   London

www.HarcourtBooks.com

This is a translation of *Winifred Wagner oder Hitlers Bayreuth*.

First published in English in the UK by Granta Books.

Library of Congress Cataloging-in-Publication Data
Hamann, Brigitte.
[Winifred Wagner. English]
Winifred Wagner: a life at the heart of Hitler's Bayreuth/Brigitte Hamann;
translated from the German by Alan Bance.—1st U.S. ed.
p.   cm.
1. Wagner, Winifred. 2. Opera producers and directors—Germany—
Bayreuth—Biography. 3. Bayreuther Festspiele. 4. Hitler, Adolf, 1889-1945—
Friends and associates. 5. Music and state—Germany—History—20th century.
I. Title.
ML429.W136H3613 2006
792.5'023092—dc22 [B]   2006011372
ISBN-13: 978-0-15-101308-1   ISBN-10: 0-15-101308-X

Printed in the United States of America
First U.S. edition
A C E G I K J H F D B

PREFACE

This is the kind of life story you only find in novels. In 1907, a nine-year-old English orphan called Winifred Marjorie Williams was packed off, on account of a medical condition that refused to heal, to stay in Berlin with distant relatives, Karl and Henriette Klindworth. They were complete strangers to her. The elderly pianist Klindworth was one of Richard Wagner's closest disciples, and so the girl grew up as a passionate Wagnerian and German nationalist.

In 1915, in the middle of the World War, the tall blonde eighteen-year-old married Siegfried, Richard Wagner's only son. At forty-six, he was a rather unsuccessful composer, and head of the Bayreuth Festival. After years of resistance, this 'man's man' finally gave in to family pressure to marry. It was his duty to produce the heirs who were so desperately needed. At the time of his marriage, Siegfried was living in his father's house, Villa Wahnfried in the small Franconian town of Bayreuth, which he shared with his mother Cosima, then seventy-seven and suffering from chronic ill-health. She was venerated by Wagnerians throughout the world as head of the Wagner clan. After Wagner's death in 1883, it was Cosima who had truly established the Bayreuth Festival, conducting it with great energy, and handing over the reins to Siegfried in 1906. When Winifred moved to Wahnfried, a famous compatriot of hers was also living there: Houston Stewart Chamberlain, the writer and race theorist, who at the age of sixty was already seriously ill. He had married Wagner's daughter Eva, and was the intellectual leader of the nationalist and anti-Semitic movement in Germany, to which Wagner's devotees had many links. Because of the war, the Germanophile Chamberlain would only talk to Siegfried's English bride in German.

Between 1917 and 1920, at the rate of one a year, Winifred presented the Wagners with four healthy children, the heirs they desperately needed, and her resourcefulness and energy pulled the ageing, ailing family through the hungry war years. But her union with Siegfried became a marriage of convenience as he turned back to his male friends.

In 1923 the 34-year-old politician Adolf Hitler, heralded as the future 'saviour of Germany', paid his first visit to Bayreuth. He revealed himself to be a knowledgeable Wagnerian, whose political principles accorded with the ideology of Wagner: extreme German nationalism, anti-Semitism, anti-liberalism and racism. In a fervent letter of 7 October 1923, Houston Stewart Chamberlain bestowed his blessing upon the young man.

At the time of this visit, Winifred, at twenty-six, was a frustrated wife – and she fell in love with Hitler. But he did not need a wife; he needed political support from the Wagner family, and from the Wagner Societies, an effective network. Shortly afterwards, Siegfried and Winifred Wagner travelled to Munich to witness the putsch that was supposed to bring Hitler to power, only to see it fail. Winifred in particular now worked harder than ever on behalf of the allegedly victimized and wrongly imprisoned Hitler. Her relationship with him in the 'years of struggle' before 1933 became easy and familiar, a rarity with Hitler. Röhm, Hess, Goebbels, Hans Frank and many other friends of Hitler came and went at Wahnfried.

In 1930, the newly widowed Winifred became head of the Festival, which by 1933 was practically bankrupt. But her friend Hitler, now Reich Chancellor, showed his gratitude for the long years of support by buying up large numbers of unsold seats, thereby ensuring the survival of the Festival. Moreover, he made a yearly official visit, as head of the German government, and stayed for a whole cycle – about ten days. He enjoyed the family and artistic atmosphere at home with the Wagners, playing the kind uncle to the Wagner children, and fancied himself as a friend of the arts.

Every summer, from 1933 to 1939, Bayreuth became the centre of European politics. A field was turned into a landing strip for ministers, ambassadors, military personnel and secretaries. Events such as the Röhm massacre, the murder of Dollfuss, the Spanish Civil War, the Sudetenland crisis and the *Kristallnacht* pogrom loomed large there.

'Winnie and Wolf' held court together on Festival Hill before and after the performances, surrounded by thousands of cheering onlookers. Later, Hitler slipped away to join the intimate Wagner family circle along with the singers, and with conductors such as Wilhelm Furtwängler and Richard Strauss.

Winifred used her contacts to intercede ever more frequently with Hitler and others in high places for those who were being persecuted, including many Jews – although she was notoriously anti-Semitic. Many previously unknown statements and reports by witnesses describe these rescue operations, which were for the most part very lengthy and difficult. They reveal the vast spectrum of everyday brutality under the Nazis, but they also demonstrate the considerable effort Winifred put into trying to end what she thought of as irregularities. As the decade progressed, Hitler made himself less and less accessible to Winifred.

In the summer of 1939, Winifred overestimated her influence. Stressing her English origins, she supported the peace overtures of the British ambassador Nevile Henderson, who had travelled to Bayreuth specifically for this purpose. But Hitler refused Henderson an audience and, in a rage, he forbade any attempt to interfere in his policies. He wanted war. Winifred's star waned further when her daughter Friedelind decided to emigrate, and disseminated anti-Hitler propaganda from abroad. 'Winnie' met 'Wolf' for the last time in person, very briefly, in the summer of 1940. From now on Hitler avoided Bayreuth, and invited only Winifred's children, above all his declared favourite, Wieland, to Berlin or Munich.

The 23-year-old Wieland, a member of the Nazi Party and an ardent admirer of Hitler, entirely exempt from military service, tried from this point on to deprive his weakened mother and her colleagues of power in Bayreuth, and take over as head of the Festival himself. But Hitler hesitated to transfer the direction of the Festival to such an inexperienced young man. None the less, even during the 'total war' phase of hostilities, the effort was made to create a 'research institute' in Bayreuth, officially run as a concentration camp, in order to give Wieland a leading role in it and thereby continue his exemption from military call-up. The Wagner family fell into furiously competing factions.

In 1945, Villa Wahnfried was destroyed by bombing. Wieland fled as early as the end of April 1945 to evade arrest. When he returned to Bayreuth after some years of silence, he played the part of a long-standing opponent of Hitler; a phenomenon typical of the post-war era in Germany.

Winifred, by contrast, openly declared her friendship with Hitler during the de-nazification process. She passed the leadership of the Festival to her two sons, and from this point on worked behind the scenes to preserve the Wagner heritage.

Winifred was no 'grand lady' like Richard Wagner's widow, Cosima, another powerful head of the Festival: she was more earthy; overbearing, anything but intellectual, yet also infinitely helpful, energetic and generous. However, the naïve pride – increasing steadily with the obstinacy of old age – of her boasts about Hitler's friendship was hardly calculated to arouse sympathy, even though she naturally condemned and regretted Hitler's crimes. She occasionally took some pride in playing up to her reputation as 'the last unre-constructed Nazi'. She looked down with scorn upon 'those turncoats', among whom she always included her son Wieland, who from May 1945 onwards had suddenly lost all recollection of ever cheering for Hitler.

This biography of Winifred Wagner, whose life-span was almost coexten-sive with the twentieth century, may help us to understand this extremely complex period a little better. For example, it shows the powerful grip, long before Hitler, that nationalist and racist ideology – in cultural terms, too – had on the upper echelons of German society. This was true, above all, of the Bayreuth circle around Chamberlain and Cosima. Their ideology was based on Richard Wagner's, but it was a more extreme and more dogmatic version of his thinking. Certainly, as early as the 1920s Wahnfried was a meeting place for Hitler supporters, including the most radical.

On the other hand, it is an unusual side of Hitler that Bayreuth brings out. Here, he was the charming art-lover, the family's nice uncle, the financial saviour of the Festival, and the patron of a long-overdue modernization who aroused genuine enthusiasm among the Bayreuth artists and public alike. Unseen even by the Wagners, however, were the important political strings he was pulling from Bayreuth, especially after the murder of the Austrian chancellor Dollfuss in 1934 and the Spanish Civil War in 1936, and before the outbreak of war in 1939.

What Winifred and her son Wieland exemplify is how impossible it is to pronounce a clear-cut verdict on Hitler's contemporaries. Careers full of contradictions, lies and reinvented personal histories were the norm, and later generations have had to accept them as such. For none of us can say whether, in such dangerous but also seductive times, we would have been able to sustain our resistance.

This book is based on a wealth of newly discovered sources, and would have been impossible without Winifred Wagner's lifelong habit of writing copious and candid letters to a huge circle of correspondents. In addition to archives all over the world, private lenders, particularly the daughter of Winifred's best friend Lenchen Roesener, made many unpublished letters available to me. This help was needed, because certain members of the still warring Wagner family continue to keep all the papers of Winifred, Siegfried and Wieland Wagner under lock and key.

Brigitte Hamann
Vienna, October 2004

NOTE ON CURRENCY REFERENCES

There are many references in this book to sums in German marks across a very wide time-span. While there are methodological problems about interpreting the worth of these amounts in today's terms, a rough idea of values can be gained by glancing at the rate of conversion of marks into pounds sterling at any given time, and then at the purchasing power of the pound at that time in today's money. So, for example, in 1900 the mark stood at 20.72 to the pound, and a 1900 pound would have the equivalent purchasing power of £56.49 in 2004.

Figures for roughly each decade are as follows: in 1910 £1 = **20.71 marks**; **£1 in 1910** = **£56.49** in 2004.

In 1920 £1 = **404.59 marks**; £1 = **£21.00** today.

Bearing in mind the inflationary period up to 1923, when the mark rate against hard currencies eventually ran into the billions, stabilization by 1930 produced a rate of £1 = **20.38 marks**. £1 then bought the equivalent of **£33.09** today.

In the last full peacetime year of 1938, £1 = **12.17 marks**; £1 = **£33.43** today.

In 1953 (with the Deutschmark newly established), £1 = **11.70 DM**; £1 = **£18.36** today.

In 1960, £1 = **11.71 DM**; £1 = **£15.15** in 2004.

In 1970, £1 = **8.736 DM**; £1 = **£10.18** in today's prices.

In 1980, £1 = **4.227 DM**; £1 = **£2.82** today.

In 1988, £1 = **3.124 DM**; £1 = **£1.76** today.

CHAPTER 1

An Orphan from Sussex

(1897–1915)

FROM ENGLAND TO BERLIN

On 8 April 1907 a nine-year old English orphan, Winifred Marjorie Williams, entered the orbit of Richard Wagner. The child was very sickly, and the staff of St Margaret's Orphanage in East Grinstead, Sussex, looking for someone to put her up for a few weeks' holiday, hit upon a distant relation of her mother: Henriette Klindworth, née Karop, aged seventy, who lived in Berlin. Although Winifred was a total stranger to them, Henriette and her 77-year-old husband Karl agreed to look after her for six weeks. Winifred later came to see her arrival there that April as the beginning of a new life.[1]

A childless couple, the Klindworths had lived for decades in Berlin. They were German nationals, but they spoke English at home and, as her letters demonstrate, Henriette Klindworth had only a limited command of German. Klindworth himself, a pianist and piano teacher, and the founder of the Karl Klindworth Music Conservatory in Berlin, was a star pupil of Franz Liszt. But what he regarded as his true life's work was transcribing for the piano excerpts from the works of his friend Wagner, particularly *The Ring of the Nibelung*. It was only for financial reasons that he still gave piano lessons.

In April 1907 Klindworth wrote to Wagner's widow, Cosima, the daughter of his revered teacher Liszt: 'At our advanced age, we have now taken upon ourselves something else to worry about – the care and education of a nice young girl of ten [sic], who is completely without means and all alone in the world. She is a little English girl, a distant relation of ours – and now we must hope to live long enough for the little creature to achieve sufficient independence to make her own way.'[2] It quickly became clear that the Klindworths wanted to keep the child permanently.

They were founder partners in the fruit-growing colony 'Eden' in Oranienburg near Berlin, a commune they shared with a variety of land reformers and vegetarians, physical culture enthusiasts and Simple Lifers, freethinkers and opponents of industrialization and speculation in land. Most of the members were nationalist and anti-Semitic, and championed the idea of 'Blood and Soil', free of 'capitalist' aims. They successfully grew fruit, vegetables and flowers on the poor soil of the Mark Brandenburg, and enjoyed a good social life. Klindworth regularly sent Cosima samples of produce from his fruit garden.

The healthy country air, so the old couple thought, would do the child good and alleviate her severe skin complaint. With her raw and bleeding skin, Winifred cannot have been an attractive sight. She said later: 'I immediately felt very good there. With exceptional love and kindness' the Klindworths had 'taken in the orphaned child, who spoke nothing but English'.[3] Her skin healed under the care of the old couple and in the idyllic summer setting of the 'Eden' colony.

No one had previously looked after Winifred for long. She had been born on 23 June 1897 in Hastings, Sussex, the only child of the second marriage of the 54-year-old John Williams, who worked in the tropics as an engineer but was also a writer and theatre critic, and the actress and painter Emily Florence, née Karop, twenty-five years his junior. 'My mother ran away from home as a young girl to become an actress. And my father came across her on the stage – as a critic of her art.'[4]

When the little girl was less than a year old, her father died of a liver disease he had contracted in India. A year later the young mother fell victim to a typhoid epidemic. Winifred had no memory of her parents, and not so much as a picture of them. Much later she found out that her father had 'sunk £12,000 into literary enterprises alone . . . There had also been a fine house, but so laden with mortgages that there was nothing in it for me!' And she added: 'This reckless tendency is something I've inherited from my father.'[5]

The orphaned infant was sent to relatives, but they did not keep her for long, 'so that as a child I was passed from hand to hand'. Finally she ended up in the orphanage, a terrifying place. It was here that her skin complaint broke out and became so bad that the doctors urgently advised that she needed a Continental climate – probably in part so as to be rid of a complicated case. Now at last she had found a settled home. She learned German from Klindworth: 'He sat down at the piano and played folksongs and nursery rhymes for me. And I had to try to recite and sing the text.' He also gave the girl piano lessons and a basic musical training, and introduced her gently to the works of his idol, Wagner. 'Every day I heard the tones of Wagnerian music', initially from The Flying Dutchman, which Klindworth was then transcribing for the piano.[6] The story of Senta, the girl who falls in love with the picture of a stranger who almost hypnotically spellbinds her, and for whose redemption she ultimately sacrifices herself, made a lasting impression on the growing Winifred.

When it was time for Winifred to go to high school, her foster-parents made an astonishing decision. They chose 'for my sake to give up their rural idyll near Oranienburg and move to Berlin, so that I could go on living with them'. Klindworth wrote to Cosima's daughter Eva: 'Leaving my nice little house and the lovely things growing in the garden will make tomorrow a hard day to bear, but later perhaps the development of our little girl will give us some happy years.'[7]

And so in September 1908 they moved into the 'rather more modest circumstances' of a rented apartment in Berlin, living there quite isolated at first, in contrast to the sociable life of the settlement, but 'our little one, wild as she was, provided noise and life in plenty'.[8] The child enjoyed living with her beloved 'grandparents' and the ever-present music of Wagner. She loved the invitations from the rich Bechstein family to their country estate in summer, and in winter to the elegant Berlin villa standing in the grounds of their piano factory. The Bechstein villa had a wide marble staircase, leading to the first floor and the piano display rooms, and then to thirty-six private rooms, wood panelled and filled with luxurious furniture, silver, rugs and valuable paintings, including a Velásquez. Helene Bechstein ran a popular salon, where Berlin society – including industrialists and politicians, and international artists passing through the city – gathered. The Bechstein salon was considered nationalist-conservative in tone, but, if only for sound business reasons, it was also cosmopolitan.

The Klindworths soon had plenty of visitors: 'All the best-known conductors and performers frequented the Klindworths' home in Berlin.'[9] In particular, Winifred later recalled Feruccio Busoni and Eugen d'Albert, a pair of modern composers, about whom Klindworth was disparaging, especially if they were enjoying any success. According to Klindworth, the appropriate reaction to the music of Busoni 'and similar members of a foreign race' was disapproval.[10] Opera was 'being buried more and more beneath the subversive influence of Jewry'. But 'Bayreuth lives, so that there is still a temple for those who yearn . . . a sacred place of edification and the holy enjoyment of art.'[11]

The 'little one' grew up venerating the Bayreuth circle and angry about the supposed outrages committed by 'Jewish' Modernism, which desecrated the memory of Richard Wagner, the 'Master', and dragged it through the mire. In terms of ideology and aesthetics there was an ever-increasing gulf between the unchanging, emotionally charged and solemn Bayreuth style, with its old stage sets and costumes, and the enthusiastically experimental modern staging of Wagner in Berlin, Munich, Dresden or Vienna, rejected as 'Jewish' and 'un-German'. For Klindworth, conductors such as Gustav Mahler, Bruno Walter, Leo Blech, Felix von Weingartner and Otto Klemperer were 'the Jewish-appreciation-society rabble'.[12] Klindworth's loathing of the contemporary musical life of Berlin was so great that he never took Winifred to a Wagner opera there. Her first great experience of Wagner was to be in Bayreuth.

Klindworth's party-political orientation followed the line of his friend Heinrich Class, the powerful leader of the Pan-German League and editor of the *Alldeutsche Blätter* (Pan-German Journal) and the *Deutsche Zeitung* (German Newspaper). With his 1912 publication *Wenn ich der Kaiser wär* (If I were the Emperor) Class became a much-quoted authority among nationalists and anti-Semites. In it he sketched out his idea of a strong 'Pan-Germany', including Austria and German Bohemia, according to the principle of 'one people, one empire'. To enable this Pan-Germany to gain world-wide respect, he demanded an active colonial and ship-building policy directed against the world power, England. Domestically, he called for a strong dictatorial government that would deprive Parliament of power, prevent universal suffrage, and neutralize 'Reds' and Jews alike. For him, since the Jews were responsible for 'devastating and ruining our public life', the 'gift of emancipation' should be taken away from them. Only this would give the Germany they had 'led astray' the power to renew itself. Class thought the best way to realize these aims would be war at the earliest possible opportunity.[13]

Klindworth adopted these articles of belief as his own, and as early as 1907 he was writing to Evan in Bayreuth: 'I believe that only a terrible world war can release the tension, and only the most awful misery can bring our people back to prudence and moderation, faith and moral aspiration.'[14] Such ideas were also propagated by the *Bayreuther Blätter* (Bayreuth Journal), which was read as a kind of bible in the Klindworth household. It mixed scholarly essays on Wagner's music with articles on national politics, modern race theories and nationalistic poems by its editor, Hans von Wolzogen. Klindworth wrote in 1913: 'I firmly believe that our group will one day lend a powerful hand to liberating our misguided people from the degrading chains of their enemies within.'[15]

When Henriette Klindworth fell dangerously ill and could no longer run the household, the thirteen-year-old Winifred was sent away to boarding school. But this was not without its problems. Winifred was a spirited child, and on one occasion she deliberately disrupted the crocodile of schoolgirls by repeatedly changing her pace, until the teacher, Ethel Scott, lost her temper and boxed her ear. The girl instantly retaliated in kind. After lengthy discussions, the school authorities concluded that this retaliatory blow was a reflex action, and decided not to expel her. 'Scotty', the recipient of the box on the ear, was to become a lifelong friend.

In 1913 Klindworth described Winifred's achievements at sixteen: 'Our foster child finishes high school this Easter, with a very pleasing report – she has turned out handsomely, has a lively spirit, moves energetically, and always tries hard to be one of the best in the class . . . if we are spared long enough for her, she is likely to be well prepared to enter life's fray.'[16] A tall, attractive girl, Winifred had no particular career ambitions; she was good at drawing and watercolours, but first of all, in Berlin she took the 'finishing' training in household management that was customary for girls in bourgeois circles. The training school, only five years old, was part of a large educational establishment that offered everything from a kindergarten to a humanities-based grammar school. Every day the girls in the domestic-science school prepared a four-course lunch and served it to the teachers, at tables laid by the pupils, in a variety of formal styles. The syllabus included infant care, French and civics, the last taught with the aid of the *Kreuzzeitung*, a nationalist-conservative newspaper. For dancing classes they were joined by cadets from the military academy.

SCANDAL AT WAHNFRIED (THE HOUSE OF WAGNER)

In the summer of 1911, when she was fourteen, Winifred witnessed a 'smear campaign' in the press, as she later described it, against Siegfried Wagner, the 'son of the Master'. She had never met him, but he was highly regarded by Klindworth. Seventy years later she still remembered 'the paper sellers on the Berlin streets shouting: "Siegfried Wagner versus Richard Strauss"'.[17] Siegfried had attacked his former close friend Strauss in an interview. He said it was 'profoundly sad' that Wagner's *Parsifal* should be staged in theatres 'which had been defiled by the disastrous works of Richard Strauss', on 'boards which had been crossed by the revolting Salome, and also by Elektra, who could only be called a mockery of Sophocles, a profanation of the whole of classicism. My father would turn in his grave if he could see the decline evident in the operas of Richard Strauss . . . since when has art been synonymous with filth?' Strauss was speculating 'upon his audience's most impure and base instincts and exploiting them to make money'. He compared Strauss to a 'stock exchange speculator', and declared: 'But let the demi-monde keep to itself, and not try to serve up at a respectable table dishes crawling with bacilli and full of the worst kind of poison.'[18]

In his criticism of Strauss Siegfried revealed his own problems: 'He moves for ever in the light! The conquering hero! His fame knows no bounds! What are the likes of us compared to him? I am satisfied if I'm allowed to light my little oil-lamp here and there and present my operas to the small company of those who take pleasure in folk-sagas and German-ness. It's a kind of catacomb existence!'[19]

Siegfried loudly lamented the failure of his operas *Der Bärenhäuter* (The Idler), *Herzog Wildfang* (Duke Wildfang), *Der Kobold* (The Goblin), *Bruder Lustig* (Brother Lustig), *Sternengebot* (The Command of the Stars), *Banadietrich* (Banadietrich) and *Schwarzschwanenreich* (Kingdom of the Black Swans). They were composed in the style of his teacher Engelbert Humperdinck, with texts he had written himself, printed at his own expense and sometimes performed with the aid of rich sponsors. He ascribed his choice of themes from German folk-tales to his need 'to draw closer to the soul of the German people, the only antidote to the pestilence of the metropolis'.[20] Among the 'Modernists' Siegfried's composing and poetic talents aroused a good deal of scorn and derision. Karl Kraus, alluding to Siegfried's 'unnatural likeness' to his father, foisted upon him the words: 'Even if I can't write music, at least I look the part.'[21] And Claude Debussy wrote in 1903 about *Duke Wildfang*: 'Decent music, nothing more; a bit like an exercise by a pupil who has studied under Richard Wagner – one whom his teacher did not consider very promising.'[22]

Artistically, Wagner's son could not hold a candle to Strauss, unanimously favoured by the Berlin liberal press. Conscious that Siegfried's aggression could only have positive results for him as the target of the attack, Strauss stayed out of the public arena. Only later did he counter Siegfried's accusation of writing for money with the remark: 'But the difference is that I live off the takings of my own shop, not from Daddy's business.'[23]

According to Siegfried, and in the old tradition of Bayreuth, it was 'the Jews' and their hatred for Wagner that were to blame for the malicious reviews he received: 'If my father had never written his "Judentum in der Musik" (Jewishness in Music) I would be better off!'[24] Klindworth backed him up, and cursed the 'stupidity and brutalization of an audience that rewards such circus tricks with rapturous cheers. Things are very bad with us, our whole culture is becoming a caricature of rampant Semitism, and I'm afraid that we're sinking down irretrievably into a morass of general sensuality.'[25]

The House of Wagner was always good at providing headlines, especially in the 'Wagner Year' of 1913, 100 years after the composer's birth and thirty after his death. In the 'Valhalla' hall of fame near Regensburg a white marble bust of Wagner was put on display. Monuments and statues to the composer proliferated throughout the world, including the USA. As 'the son of the Master', Siegfried was made a Freeman of the city of Bayreuth.

It was also in 1913 that the hitherto richly endowed Wagner family lost its income. By law the copyright on Wagner's works, which had earned his heirs millions of marks in royalties, lapsed thirty years after his death. He was, after all, the most performed opera composer of the day. Cosima had fought in vain for a long time to have the copyright period extended by at least twenty years, to 1933. When this turned out to be a hopeless cause, she petitioned the Reichstag to at least grant Bayreuth exclusive performance rights to *Parsifal*. But the Reichstag, with the Liberals and Social Democrats voting against, rejected any special legislation ('Lex Cosima' [law on behalf of Cosima]). This reinforced Cosima's wrath against Parliament, the Left and, later, against democracy itself. As a result of the lifting of copyright, the 'stage-consecrating festival drama' *Parsifal* was performed in all the great opera houses of the world. There were even new dedicated Wagner opera houses built. As a protest against the 'theft of Parsifal' no festival was staged

at Bayreuth during the 'Wagner Year' of 1913. There was not even a ceremony to mark the day of his death. In every interview Siegfried, the Festival's
director, repeated his mantra for the jubilee year: 'We are celebrating by
working.'[26]

Siegfried concentrated on finishing the opera *Der Heidenkönig* (The
Heathen King), and began on his vocal work *Märchen vom dicken fetten
Pfannkuchen* (Tale of the Big Fat Pancake). He conducted a few concerts,
including one at the Berlin Philharmonie, which Klindworth described to
Cosima in high-flown language: as a conductor Siegfried had 'proved himself a true hero'. The audience had been enthusiastic about his
compositions, he said, and it was scandalous that the Berlin opera 'is so
unbelievably banal, concerned with satisfying the frivolous desires of the
general public, and ignoring true, high German art – that of the "young
Master", in fact'.[27]

The Wagner clan provided plenty of copy for the newspapers once more
in 1914, when a legal inheritance action that had been running for years in
the Bayreuth provincial court reached its final stage. Wagner's oldest daughter, Isolde, was suing her mother, Cosima. The background to the story was
this: Isolde and her husband, the conductor Franz Beidler, had stormed out
of Bayreuth in 1906 after a quarrel with Cosima and Siegfried. Isolde had
been Wagner's favourite, but she was born while Cosima was still married to
her first husband, Hans von Bülow. Now divorced and suffering from tuberculosis, Isolde staked a claim to the Wagner inheritance on behalf of her
twelve-year-old son Franz Wilhelm Beidler, Wagner's only grandchild to
date. Further successors were hardly to be expected, since Siegfried had
made no move to get married. Wagner's 47-year-old daughter, Eva
Chamberlain, was childless. Cosima's older daughters, Daniela Thode and
Blandine, Countess Gravina, were unambiguously offspring of the Bülow
marriage and not in line for the Wagner inheritance. Isolde's son was therefore the only candidate for the succession to Bayreuth.

For years Isolde had vainly begged her mother for a heart-to-heart talk.
When Siegfried obstinately prevented this, his sister, in her despair, threatened that she knew 'how serious the charges against you are'. She was
referring to his homosexuality, a criminal offence at that time. Unmoved,
however, Siegfried replied: 'There was ugly gossip about Frederick the Great,
too, the greatest king of all time, and he made Prussia great and strong! So
don't worry! I won't defile the House of the Festival.'[28]

In June 1913 Siegfried informed his sister via a lawyer that because royalties were drying up the 'voluntary subsidy' paid to her by Cosima was to be reduced to 8,000 marks a year. In response, Isolde threatened to go to court with a paternity case, but hoped that Cosima would be deterred by the prospect of having to air intimate details in public. Against her expectations, the threat had no effect, and Isolde was left with no option but to go to law.[29]

So the sensational case passed into the hands of the lawyers. The old lady, Cosima, supported by Siegfried and her son-in-law Houston Stewart Chamberlain, contested Wagner's paternity of Isolde in writing, and though she knew otherwise, asserted that her daughter was the child of her former husband, Bülow. In the process, she let it be known that during the period in question she had had sexual relations with both men – the height of disgrace in the prudish Wilhelmine era.

The legal position was unambivalent. Since there was no biological test of paternity available at that time, Isolde could not prove Wagner was her father. Legally speaking, she had been conceived and born within the marriage to Bülow, Bülow had acknowledged her as his daughter, and she had inherited from him. In the verdict delivered on 19 June 1914, her claim was duly dismissed. Isolde had to bear the legal costs. Wagner's beloved 'Soldchen' retreated embittered and humiliated, and died four years later. 'It was a most miserable fate that had thus ended,'[30] commented Siegfried, who enjoyed the greatest benefit from the 'de-Wagnering' of his sister. But the price was high: the details of the case were revealed in the world press and damaged the reputation of the family.

During the Festival rehearsals, on 27 June 1914, Maximilian Harden published a long, destructive article in his Berlin publication *Die Zukunft* (Future), with devastating effect. Using the material of the Beidler action, and under the heading 'Tristan and Isolde', Harden meticulously argued that both Wagner's widow and her son had lied in court. This majestic Bayreuth of 'wahnfriedian sacred-festival nobility' was dominated, according to Harden, by greed, lies, perjury, adultery and 'dynastic delusions'.

Wahnfried was appalled by Harden's allusion to Siegfried's homosexuality, even if it confined itself to the brief statement that 'Herr Siegfried Wagner, who cannot wish for too much exposure to the public eye', was a 'saviour of an altogether different hue'.[31] A brilliant journalist, Harden was infamous and feared for ruthlessly outing homosexuals. His most prominent victim until then, Prince Philipp Eulenberg, the cultivated, high-ranking diplomat and friend of Kaiser Wilhelm II, had forfeited his reputation, career and health as a result of such a campaign and the subsequent court action.

Cosima and her daughters, now in a genuine panic, went on the hunt for a wife for the reluctant Siegfried. It was imperative to produce an heir.

It seems unlikely that Winifred, just seventeen at the time, was informed about the background of the ongoing Bayreuth scandal. In accordance with the moral code of the day, girls of good family were kept away from indecent reading-matter. But day after day she heard her 'grandfather' cursing the rabble of the Jewish press, which had supposedly dragged the noble family of the Master down into the dirt. But the uproar about the article was over-shadowed the very next day by an item of political news: the heir to the Austrian throne, Franz Ferdinand, and his wife, Sophie, had been assassinated in Sarajevo.

LOVE AT FIRST SIGHT

Cosima invited the Klindworths to the dress rehearsals for the Bayreuth Festival in July 1914. Friends of Wahnfried had access to these rehearsals, not yet open to the general public, and they sat in the front rows of the empty Festival Theatre. The 84-year-old Klindworth was particularly look-ing forward to Siegfried's new production of The Flying Dutchman, due to be performed in Bayreuth for the first time since 1902. Since this was Winifred's favourite opera, it is easy to imagine how hard she begged to be taken along.

And so she was, for since Henriette Klindworth was too ill to travel, and the shortsighted, somewhat deaf old gentleman felt it too unsafe to go by himself, he asked Cosima 'that I might be permitted to bring our foster-child along as my support and companion'. Winifred had 'in the meantime grown into a tall, slim young woman of seventeen, certainly too young and spirited for the seriousness of the highest art. But what she would experience there would make a powerful and unforgettable impact on her lively and receptive mind'.[32] Shortly afterwards Klindworth was thanking Cosima for permission 'to bring the child along with me. Still completely immersed in the innocent years of school discipline, with fitting modesty and keen atten-tion she will simply be completely absorbed by the wonders of the Festival. O happy youth!'[33] The seventeen-year-old wrote to her friend Lenchen: 'I'm as pleased as Punch.'[34]

The journey was arduous, for the small Upper Franconian provincial town of Bayreuth was a long way from main-line train routes. This remote-ness had been one of the reasons why Wagner had chosen the place to found his deliberately plain Festival Theatre. For *The Ring of the Nibelung*, performed for the first time as a complete tetralogy in the house on the hill especially built for it and financed by King Ludwig II, was not meant to be any ordinary opera, to be attended in an evening in some big city. People who came to Bayreuth were supposed to detach themselves from the everyday world as though on a pilgrimage, and devote themselves entirely to the *Gesamtkunstwerk*, the Total Work of Art, without any urban distractions.

The morning after their arrival Klindworth took the young girl up to Wahnfried to see Cosima: 'Then the two old people went off for a walk. Meanwhile I was sat down in the hall, and my future sisters-in-law, Frau Eva Chamberlain, Countess Gravina, and Daniela Thode, took it in turns to look after me and chat with me.'[35] The marked attention paid by Cosima's daughters to this unsuspecting girl from Berlin indicates an exceptional degree of interest, underlined by the way that Cosima soon preoccupied herself so intensively with her. Winifred was allowed to keep 'the Master's Lady' company on her daily walks – the highest mark of favour.

After the Master's death, Cosima had energetically and devotedly continued the Bayreuth Festival he had founded, but also changed it. In Richard's day it had been a mecca of Modernism and the avantgarde, where musicians and students could experience the most innovative musical theatre in the world, Wagner's *Gesamtkunstwerk*, and his much admired and much reviled 'music of the future'. Cosima's task was to preserve carefully what Richard had staged. This daughter of Countess d'Agoult made the little Upper Franconian town into a rendezvous for an elegant public, for aristocrats and the rich and beautiful people of the German Empire. For reasons of ill-health she had transferred the direction of the Festival to her only son, Siegfried, but among Wagnerians she continued to be the revered central figure of Wahnfried.

Winifred, who could not have been better prepared, enjoyed six evenings in the Festival Theatre: the four parts of the *Ring of the Nibelung, Parsifal* and *The Flying Dutchman* with Barbara Kemp as Senta. Siegfried Wagner was conducting. Since the Festival Theatre had a partly covered orchestra pit, the 'mysterious abyss', the conductor could not be seen by the audience.

It was the usual custom to invite people backstage during the intervals, and that was how the young woman was introduced to the 45-year-old Festival director. 'For me this meeting with Siegfried meant love at first sight. It was his lovely warm voice that most impressed me, his whole appearance; his wonderful blue eyes captivated me . . . For me, Siegfried was the unattainable ideal of my dreams.'[36] He had a quiet, high, somewhat sing-song voice, which Winifred was later to describe as a 'chirping voice'.[37] His style was that of an almost too elegant, perhaps even eccentrically dressed gentleman of the old school, and in familiar company he was genial and humorous. 'Every day I sat at the Wagners' tea-table during the first interval, and it was Siegfried Wagner with his cheerfulness and kindness who helped me to get over my shyness and awkwardness. It was then that the first threads were spun to and fro between us.'[38]

Those days at Bayreuth were 'overwhelming for my receptive and youthful spirit', and 'from now on nothing else existed for me but Wagner and the world of Bayreuth'.[39] Back in Berlin, Klindworth thanked 'the Master's Lady' for the invitation and 'the kindness and attentiveness shown to me and my wild companion', who was 'still revelling in all the glories of Bayreuth that she had enjoyed, with a heart full of gratitude for all the favour and goodness'.[40]

From 22 July onwards Bayreuth was not only caught up in the turmoil of the Festival, but was preparing itself for the visit of King Ludwig III of Bavaria and Queen Maria Theresa which was planned to last several days: there were to be torchlight processions, parades and concerts. Amidst all the long newspaper reports about the visit it was easy to overlook a brief announcement of 24 July: the Austrian government had issued an ultimatum to the Kingdom of Serbia, four weeks after the assassination in Sarajevo. By 25 July the 'Austro-Serbian conflict' was filling page 5 of the newspaper, and by 26 July it had reached the front page.

Siegfried Wagner said later: 'Even during the performances of the *Ring*, disquieting rumours were already spreading up the hill to the Festival, where it was usually more like the Isle of the Blessed: we avoided talking about politics. After the performance of *Siegfried*, all the Hungarian visitors left, followed soon afterwards by the Austrians . . . Still not believing in the war, we tried to play on.'[41]

On 27 July the headline ran: 'Austria's War against Serbia'. The multinational Habsburg state had ordered a partial mobilization. Bayreuth saw the first contingent of musicians from Austria and Bohemia depart for home. The King's visit was cancelled. On 28 July the Austro-Hungarian Empire officially declared war. The question now was how the German Empire would react, as the ally of Austria-Hungary.

On 1 August – before the third act of *Parsifal* – the German Empire announced its mobilization against Russia. The depleted orchestra played on until the end. The next afternoon, shortly before a performance of *The Flying Dutchman*, a sergeant and a drummer made their way through the streets of Bayreuth proclaiming in the name of the King of Bavaria that war had been declared. The oft-cited 'Nibelung loyalty' (the Nibelungs' legendary loyalty unto death) of the Austro-German alliance held good. On the other side, too, alliances were invoked. One declaration of war followed another. Europe had 'stumbled' into a great war.

Only eight of the twenty performances planned for the 1914 Festival took place. Since contracts did not include any escape clauses to cover such an eventuality, the returned tickets, performers' salaries, and other fees all had to be funded. Without any income at all, these expenses added up to a loss of 350,000 marks.[42] This spelt total ruin for the Festival's finances. There was now no capital left for future festivals, regardless of the outcome of the war.

Nevertheless, at Wahnfried and in the Klindworths' home in Berlin as everywhere in Germany there was patriotic enthusiasm for the war. At the weekly religious services at Winifred's domestic-science school the girls now sang not only hymns but 'Deutschland, Deutschland über alles' and 'Ich bin ein Preusse; kennt ihr meine Farben?' (I am a Prussian; do you recognize my colours?) The English girl Winifred Williams was especially patriotic about Germany.[43]

Siegfried, who had never done military service, wrote to the Viennese journalist Ludwig Karpath: 'The unity of Austria and Germany is glorious! How pleased everybody is for your dear Kaiser, who has lived to see this after all his tribulations!'[44] Everyone who returned from the front was welcome at Wahnfried and was invited to dine. The empty Festival restaurant soon became a military hospital.

All troubles faded into insignificance at the end of August 1914 in the light of the victory of General Paul von Hindenburg, already sixty-seven years old, and the Chief of his General Staff, Erich Ludendorff, over the Russians at the Battle of Tannenberg. The liberation of East Prussia which followed unleashed a storm of national enthusiasm. The two generals were celebrated as national heroes. Among the many congratulatory telegrams that Hindenburg received was one from Cosima Wagner. Contented, the 77-year-old wrote: 'War seems to suit us Germans far better than peace, where everything un-German was taking hold.'[45]

Siegfried composed an *Oath on the Flag* for male choir, organ and large orchestra, and dedicated it to 'The German Army and its leaders in keen gratitude'. He invited the Klindworths to its première at a charity concert in the Berlin Philharmonie in October 1914. It was here that Winifred first saw the object of her veneration conducting. His style was not spectacular, but somewhat sober and static; for outsiders, it was often tedious. One of his admirers even thought that 'Siegfried completely neglected to make any effort to impress his audience.' 'His movements were a little too calm, almost tiring in their lack of variety, and he conducted the orchestra more with his eyes than with the baton.'[46] His stiff style of conducting may have derived from the fact that he was left-handed, and had had to train himself with great effort to conduct with his right hand, in order not to confuse the orchestra.

As Winifred wrote to 'Lenchen' [Lene], she had sat in the director's box opposite Siegfried's half-sister Countess Blandine Gravina, her son Gil, and Siegfried's long-standing friend, the Art Nouveau painter Franz Stassen: 'they were terrifically amused by my enthusiasm'. But 'Fidi' had carried it all off 'in masterly fashion (conducting from memory)'. They then went off to the green room: 'as soon as my old lady appeared, Fidi came up to us and was very sweet once more. He introduced me to several people as Klindworth's youngest daughter, remarking: "a lucky old man, eh? To have such a daughter at 84!"' And 'then we looked at each other in silence for at least 1½ minutes – Fidi's look was so searching, but so charming – my old lady was most amused by us!'[47]

Siegfried accepted an invitation to the Klindworths' for the next day. After his departure, Stassen, who lived in Berlin, appeared several times at the Klindworth house to sketch the old man – surely in order to reconnoitre on Siegfried's behalf. This increasingly close relationship was reflected in Klindworth's letters to Cosima, which talked more and more about 'the child' and her great difficulties with officialdom as an 'enemy alien'. 'Our foster-child was suddenly placed under the closest surveillance by the authorities. It was only with great difficulty that we secured permission for her to continue going to school.' For this reason, he had decided to adopt the girl: 'after legal confirmation the child has now become Winifred Klindworth – officially; but we call her Senta'.[48] Klindworth made arrangements for the care of Senta in the case of his death, and asked the Bechsteins to be her guardians.

After her adoption Senta no longer needed to report constantly to the police, but as she was not yet a naturalized German she could not leave the area of Greater Berlin, and could not travel to Bayreuth. But there was a lively correspondence between Siegfried and Senta, now a dedicated student of his works. She even involved her fellow-pupils, getting them to write essays for her about themes from Siegfried's operas, as Stassen was later to recall.[49]

On 23 May 1915 the Kingdom of Italy declared war on Austria-Hungary. Great indignation was directed at this perfidious member of the Triple Alliance, and Klindworth complained about 'the heinous and nasty Latin race': 'it pains my heart to have grown too old to help, to take part in the fight, to punish our enemies, to liberate the Fatherland, to rescue Germanic culture and art'.[50] Cosima was particularly upset by the news, because her daughter Blandine lived in Italy, and three Italian grandsons were now in danger of having to fight against the Central Powers. However, one of them, the pro-German flautist Count Gilberto Gravina, immediately enlisted in the German army.

ENGAGEMENT AND MARRIAGE

In June 1915 the love affair between Siegfried and Senta became serious. The girl wrote Siegfried a supportive letter on his forty-sixth birthday: she had read his new libretto for The Angel of Peace, and it had been painful for her. It had given her the feeling of 'how alone he . . . must have been inwardly' to have created such a work.[51] 'That made him sit up,'[52] was the later comment of Siegfried's friend Stassen. The libretto had been written during the difficult time of the Isolde case, and it is a dreadful tale about the secret burial of a suicide in a Christian cemetery and an unofficial court that insists the body must be disinterred. When the peasants get to work with pickaxes in the cemetery, a saint appears to redeem the dead man. Siegfried's taste for the macabre and the supernatural, the constantly recurring motif of a secret guilt that cries out to be expiated, are stamped upon this work.

On 23 June Senta turned eighteen and was therefore of marriageable age. It was precisely now that Siegfried travelled to Berlin with a long screed in his pocket by Eva Chamberlain with the title 'Observations for the journey, from your almost fifty-year-old sister'. It was a forceful injunction to look around for a wife, and it reveals the great pressure Siegfried was under. Eva's first instruction read: 'For once, do not rush this journey, please! Take all the time you need to find the maiden that you, Wahnfried, and our cause require.' Then she pulled out all the stops, reminding him that as Mama Cosima was already in her seventy-eighth year, 'what a joy and comfort it would be for her to know that Wahnfried's future was secured!' Chamberlain was almost sixty, and she, Eva, wanted to devote herself more to him than hitherto. So 'a young, strong support was what the family wanted'. The most important thing was that Siegfried should now fulfil his 'highest duty'. Then she produced Isolde as a warning: 'Don't let Loldi's frightening, triumphant words, "Fidi won't marry", come true! If you do, you play into the hands of the evil people, what we call the "un-German devils". Everyone who loves and respects you is concerned about the future and shares with us the profound wish that you may find the right one!' She went on: 'You have all the qualities you need to be the genial and glorious father of a family; a pity to waste them on Tommy and Flossy' (his dogs). She even mentions that she and Chamberlain were sad not to have an heir for their inherited family treasures, such as 'my lovely jewellery I got from Mama; Papa's letters to Mama, Mama's diaries' and so forth. She closes with the appeal: 'so find your Katherlieschen and bring some young life into our beloved Wahnfried! It's high time.'[53]

Mother and daughters alike knew who was the sole candidate for the role of Katherlieschen from Siegfried's opera *An Allem ist Hütchen Schuld* (It's All Hütchen's Fault): Senta Klindworth. According to first-hand reports, on arriving at the station in Berlin Siegfried was greeted by the sight of 'the slim, beautiful high-school girl in the company of her teacher, as they had joined in with a welcoming group from the Berlin University Wagner Society. The girl was full of anticipation and 'only regretted that in the preceding domestic science class she had got a fruit stain on her immaculate white blouse'. Siegfried got off the train, greeted the students – and then turned to the girl.[54]

Soon afterwards he and Stassen went to tea at the Klindworths'. When 'Fräulein Senta' showed the two gentlemen her watercolours, Stassen noted that there were no fewer than nine photos of Siegfried on a small table. On this occasion Klindworth spoke very earnestly with Siegfried and asked him to take care of the girl should anything happen to him.[55] There followed a visit together to Potsdam and then, with a larger group, an outing to the Havel lakes. On the long walk back to the station Siegfried bought a punnet of cherries to nibble. Stassen recalled: 'As we walked up the steps to the Kaiser's Pavilion [at Wannsee station] the punnet of cherries swayed in front of my eyes, carried by Siegfried and Senta, their two little fingers entwined around the handle.'[56]

Senta got out at Lichterfelde-West, and Siegfried followed. When an over-eager student made to accompany him, the singer Barbara Kemp forcefully intervened, threw herself upon the lap of the too-devoted follower and hissed at him: 'You silly ass, just you stay sitting there!'[57] So the tête-à-tête went ahead undisturbed. It really did take a great deal of effort on the part of many well-disposed friends to bring Siegfried close to the haven of marriage at last.

Siegfried made his proposal in a letter: 'He didn't say it in simple words, though, but wrote: "My wish is that you wish what I secretly wish".'[58] Senta's reply on 5 July 1915 was already completely Wagnerian in style:

Most honoured, dearest Master, how may I interpret your gladdening words? If I may read them as I would like to, then I am the happiest soul beneath God's glorious tent of Heaven! Master, I am really still an over-grown child, but if you love me just a little as I am – then your wishes have surely long been fulfilled? And if it depended on me they would all, all be fulfilled! Good night! Tonight I won't dream of lizards! Your Senta Klindworth.[59]

Siegfried wrote to Bayreuth: 'A shooting star appeared as I took my leave of Winifred – These are all good signs! We love each other from the heart! Her story is a remarkable one. Klindworth told me some details . . . I would like to marry soon.'[60] As was right and proper, Siegfried now formally submitted his suit in writing to Klindworth. The latter saw a 'wonderful stroke of divine providence in the fate of this good child, who flew into our house eight years ago like an unfathomable enigma', and was pleased that the son of the Master saw 'the longing of his heart fulfilled by a union with the little imp'.[61] For Klindworth this engagement was the high point of his long life.

When everything had been settled, the eighteen-year-old wrote as she thought a Wagner fiancée ought:

Siegfried, my beloved, words cannot say how happy I am! A sweet dream, which I never dared hope would come true, is now reality! I am so proud, so full of bliss, so glad – how can I bear it all! . . . I entrust myself body and soul to you, guide me through life – shape me as you would have me! . . . I can scarcely comprehend this joy! Good night, my dearly beloved Siegfried – a thousand blissful greetings from your Senta.[62]

Immediately after Siegfried had left, his older half-sister Daniela Thode appeared on behalf of Cosima to buy the impecunious bride a trousseau.

Daniela was a powerful, austere woman who acted as wardrobe mistress at the Festival. Only the year before she had been divorced from her husband, the art historian Henry Thode, and she was going through a period of intense depression. Without consulting the girl, she bought napery and bedlinen by the dozen, and nightwear and lingerie for Senta, right down to brassières, all in keeping with her own severe, old-fashioned taste.

Senta wrote to Lenchen: 'Today we are having a rest from shopping, because I'm half dead . . . We've done the lingerie, and we've also got shoes, gloves, coats, dresses, and hats, though we've still got masses to do . . . I look so funny in very long skirts and hats with veils.'[63] Daniela's three and a half week stay laid the foundations for Winifred's deep aversion to her sister-in-law. Even in old age, Winifred would still relate how she was not allowed to express a will of her own at all, and had not dared to contradict the much older, stony-faced Daniela. She was obliged to be grateful for everything, however hideous she found it.[64]

Klindworth on the other hand revelled in his happiness, and wrote to Siegfried: 'the poor child will be so well off when she comes to you that she will seem like a stranger. But her youthful high spirits have done poor suffering Daniela good, she's calmer, and occasionally she even quite enjoys a glimpse of the frivolous, unwarlike activities of ladies in the capital.'[65]

Bureaucratic difficulties dragged on. Senta's application for naturalization, submitted as long before as March, was turned down: the 'enemy alien' was allowed neither to travel nor to marry. Klindworth's angry comment was: 'what has the war or the difference in nationality got to do with it? After all, there's nothing to stop the sons of this country from marrying Negresses from South West Africa.' He begged Siegfried to 'try to espy a way out of the labyrinth created by this State petty-mindedness'.[66] The way out consisted in Siegfried having himself appointed as his fiancée's guardian. This was also the occasion for Senta to be changed back to Winifred, which her fiancé shortened to 'Winnie'.

In her joy, Cosima sent the bride 'princely gifts', and reported the great news to a friend with whom she corresponded: 'No choice could suit me better than the one he has made!' The girl had been 'brought up in strict morality and seclusion, and given a select education . . . It does no harm, it seems to me, that the eighteen-year-old child is also charming and beautiful. So we may see divine providence in this event and give devout thanks for it.'[67]

It was to Stassen that the honour fell, 'on a gloriously sunny September day', of escorting Wagner's fiancée by train to Bayreuth. Wagnerians waited at many stations along the route to congratulate her. Stassen wrote: 'In Leipzig she had been given a mass of flowers, and as the journey continued all the carriages were full of our men in field-grey uniforms. She went from one compartment to another and distributed the flowers, and the warriors laughed with pleasure at this beautiful benefactress.'[68]

At Neuenhof station, according to Stassen 'Siegfried was already running down the platform as the train drew in, and he took his fiancée that same evening to see his mother.'[69] There was a festive banquet in the hall of Villa Wahnfried. Afterwards, Siegfried sang arias from his new opera, *An Allem ist Hütchen Schuld*, to his fiancée.

It pained the Klindworths immensely that they were too ill and too weak to accompany their 'little child' to the wedding at Bayreuth. Klindworth wrote to Cosima: 'now our loved one has left us, and fate did not grant us the favour of letting us place her in your arms ourselves'.[70] And to the bride-groom he wrote: 'Now the enchanted princess of Bayreuth has been claimed, and rejoicing she departs for the arms of her dearly beloved.'[71] He exhorted Winifred constantly to think of him, in letters that mentioned her virtues – 'talent, purity of spirit, seriousness of intent, ambitious striving' – but a 'stiff obstinacy' as well. Repeatedly he lamented 'the agony of parting', but com-forted himself with 'the glorious knowledge . . . that what they had lost they had offered up for people they loved and for the son of the Master, whom he had to thank for everything that had given his life any value'.[72]

On the morning of 22 September 1915 the civil and religious ceremony of a wartime marriage between the 46-year-old Siegfried Wagner and the eighteen-year-old Winifred Klindworth took place among a very intimate circle at Wahnfried. Religion presented no problem, since Winifred's Anglican faith was compatible with the Lutheranism of the Wagner family. Stassen recalled: 'Frau Cosima was seated in an armchair in a grey silk dress, her hands raised and clasped . . . the bride was in plain white with a long, full veil.' Apart from the registrar, the dean and the witnesses – Stassen and Siegfried's former guardian Adolf von Gross – only the Chamberlains and the servants were present. After the wedding ceremony the couple, 'greeted on the way to the station by many inquisitive Bayreuthers', travelled to Dresden, where Siegfried conducted his opera *Bärenhäuter*. Following the performance there was a celebratory supper for nearly a hundred guests. Winifred told Lene: 'I still haven't got everything straight in my head – can't yet grasp that it's all supposed to be true.'[73]

The marriage of Wagner's son to an English girl made the news internationally, and inspired in the *Musical Courier* the headline: 'Siegfried Wagner Finds his Real Brünnhilde among the Britons'.

The Master's Lady was content: 'I sometimes think I'm dreaming when I see a graceful young creature walking by his side, one brought up in exemplary fashion by our friend Klindworth, and who brings with her all the qualities that suit his nature and harmonize with our house. A great happiness, therefore, for which I thank Heaven every day.'[74]

CHAPTER 2

The Newly-weds

(1915–22)

EVERYDAY LIFE AT WAHNFRIED

The honeymoon trip to Bad Homburg lasted only a few days. Siegfried cut it short on the grounds that his musical director, Karl Kittel, had just been given leave from the army, and he urgently needed to do some work with him on a piano score.[1] So Winifred started her new life sooner than she had anticipated.

The married couple did not maintain a separate household at Villa Wahnfried, but were part of a feudal extended family with established rituals into which the young wife was expected to fit. In the background there was the massive presence of the late Master, Richard Wagner, whose testament was now embodied in the person of his 78-year-old widow, Cosima, venerated by all. She was the one who prescribed the strictly regulated daily routine described by Winifred to her girlfriend Lies:

'Get up, half past seven. Breakfast, eight o'clock, then read the paper to Fidi, then stroll in the garden till nine.' (She often accompanied her mother-in-law on a short walk into town, with Cosima using a small parasol to protect her sensitive eyes from the light. Contrary to what has often been asserted, Cosima was not blind, 'She was simply too vain to wear glasses.'[2] In wet weather Siegfried stood ready on the Wahnfried steps with woollen shawls for his mother, and always had aconite pills handy for her, a trusty prophylactic against colds.)

'At nine, off to the kitchen. Make arrangements for the day etc.' (Every morning Cosima made the young wife do the dusting in the main hall: 'At the time, that was really the job of our servant. He used to stand in the corner grinning while Mama was checking whether I'd done everything properly.'[3])

'Then from half past ten to half past eleven, time for a chat or reading aloud with Fidi – half past eleven to twelve, Mama reading aloud, with Fidi present. From twelve to half past twelve, Fidi, reading aloud from the newspaper, and a stroll in the garden – half past twelve lunch, half past one to three [. . .] any activity you liked, three to five a drive and a walk with Mama, Fidi usually going with us.' (The outing would be by horse and carriage to Lake Röhren, or to the rococo palaces, the 'Hermitage' or the 'Fantaisie', of Margravine Wilhelmine of Bayreuth, or other favourite spots.)

'At five, time for tea, usually with company.' (Cosima's faithful old followers would visit; the conductor Hans Richter, Cosima's financial advisor Adolf von Gross, and the writer and editor of the *Bayreuther Blätter*, Hans von Wolzogen.)

'From half past five until seven, dealing with Fidi's correspondence and reading aloud. At seven we go and chat to Mama until half past.' (That was when Cosima retired to bed, assisted by her nurse: 'she had a parrot in the next room, and the parrot had noticed exactly what went on, I mean the ceremony of going to bed, and she [Cosima] always had an extra bottle of beer in bed to help her to sleep, and the parrot imitated this beer-gulping sound. And when she had finished her beer the parrot always said good night, good night, to which my mother-in-law responded with good night cock-a-doodle, good night cock-a-doodle.' Cosima 'was very fond of a drink'; Siegfried 'often wagged his finger at her because of it and said "you little Noah".'[4]*)

'From half past seven to a quarter to eight, discussion of the day's news, a quarter to eight supper. From a quarter past eight until half past, a little stroll down the road with Fidi. From half past eight to ten, we read in the company of the Chamberlains, who also share our meal. At ten it's time for bed.' Winifred's friend Lies copied this timetable out for her other girlfriend Lene with the comment: 'Dividing the day up like this is not my idea of happiness.' She just hoped that Winifred 'would go on enjoying what she thinks of as happiness'.[5]

---

*After the Flood, Noah cultivated a vineyard and became drunk on his own wine.

This rigid daily routine was interrupted only by 'strangely cheery yet boring rounds of visits to friends and acquaintances of very mature years'.[6] Now and again singers came to give a recital, and 'I learned a lot from listening as well as from Siegfried's opinions and advice.'[7]

After breakfast, while Siegfried retreated to his bachelor establishment next door, Cosima worked on Winifred's French by dictating letters and making her read to her. As the illegitimate daughter of the Hungarian Franz Liszt and the French Countess Marie d'Agoult, Cosima was a highly educated polyglot – an enthusiast for 'Germania' who certainly read more than just the German classics.

Eva Chamberlain took it upon herself to instruct her young sister-in-law in household management, much to the annoyance of Winifred, who after all had only just left her domestic-science school: 'I was convinced that I knew more about housekeeping than my sister-in-law, who couldn't even thread a needle.'[8] Siegfried settled the dispute by suggesting that Eva should run the household as long as she lived in Wahnfried. But with Eva's imminent move to her own house, Winifred would take over.

Eva decided who should be allowed to visit Cosima, who should accompany her on walks, what she should eat, and what medicine she should take. She sent regular reports to Cosima's doctor, Privy Councillor Ernst Schweninger in Munich. Cosima suffered from convulsions that brought on loss of consciousness and severe headaches as well as making her hear music in her head, mostly noisy military bands. Winifred was present at such an attack during her first days at Wahnfried, and reported to Lene: 'she suffered loss of consciousness three nights running and needs the utmost consideration and tenderest care, which I've now taken over almost completely'.[9]

Nothing had been changed at Wahnfried since the days of Wagner. His armchair, notes, books and spectacles were still where he always left them; nothing could be touched. In every room there was a historic grand piano that nobody was allowed to play; some were Wagner's, others had belonged to Liszt. The holy of holies was the settee on which the Master had died in Venice in 1883. It was now in Cosima's bedroom, and of course nobody was allowed to sit on it.

Winifred, not initiated into all these mysteries, was spontaneous and impetuous by nature, and initially shocked her mother-in-law by plumping herself down on the nearest free seat, including even the Master's famous armchair. It had never been occupied since his death, for it was there that Wagner sat every evening to read to his family and chat. 'But nobody had told me anything about it being a sacred chair.' She continued: 'People at Wahnfried tended to make fun of my youth. They laughed at me a lot.' Above all, her Berlin idiom was somewhat out of place in the house.[10]

Wahnfried was extremely spacious and 'wildy impractical'. In the basement were the utility rooms and the kitchen, while the ground floor housed the reception rooms, including the great hall, the 'ballroom' and the mauve drawing room. Spiral staircases led to the mezzanine floor with its dressing rooms and bathrooms, and further spiral staircases up to the bedrooms. 'My mother-in-law lived at the top of the house, and if she wanted something, for example, the staff had to trudge up all three flights of stairs . . . I was really alarmed at the number of servants.' Cosima had a nurse and an 'old maid', Dora Glaser, 'but gradually she too became an invalid, and needed help herself. In the kitchen lived a cook with a scullery maid.' Siegfried had a servant who doubled up as a coachman and helped serve at table; then there were two chambermaids and a gardener with an assistant.[11]

Cosima gave allowances to her daughters Daniela, Eva and Blandine, as well as to her son, whose income from his compositions was nowhere near enough to live on. Winifred received pocket-money of 150 marks a month for her private expenses, which included a clothing allowance.[12] But the cancellation of the Festival for the duration of the war deprived the family of its sole source of income. To support the costly life-style of Wahnfried, Cosima had to fall back upon her capital, which was reduced by the War Loans she pledged year after year. Signing up to these loans was a patriotic duty, offset by the promise of repayment with compound interest after an assured victory.

Without a festival to prepare for, the usually hospitable life at Wahnfried became monotonous, and on grey winter days the mood was particularly dreary. Eva observed that the weather 'really put one's patience to the test, but when you thought of our brave men enduring life at the Front you couldn't complain about it'.[13] Daniela had 'completely reverted to her depressive moods, apathetic and brooding'.[14] Winifred had 'a difficult time' with her sister-in-law. Siegfried would not acknowledge that Daniela's 'fixed ideas' were the product of her psychological condition. 'Fidi is the only one who is blind to it – she's his favourite sister, and she idolizes him so much that any normal person would notice how unhealthy it is.' Daniela pulled herself together in his presence, but 'when she's alone with me she gives me hell'. Once, when the Chamberlains were away travelling, leaving her to spend her days with Daniela and Cosima, she complained: 'I was the poor kid left holding everything by myself – for 14 days.'[15] Her other sisters-in-law hardly made any impression on Winifred's life. Blandine lived in Italy and rarely came to Bayreuth. No meeting ever took place between Winifred and Isolde, banished by Cosima.

The state of Siegfried's nerves was also giving serious cause for concern. Eventually Dr Schweninger advised him to cancel all his concerts and stop composing, in order to avoid over-excitement. As a famous naturopathic healer, the doctor prescribed air baths, mineral water, walking and lavish daily bathing of the head. Eva remarked: 'the little wife has already become expert at this treatment'.[16]

Retrospectively, Winifred confessed to a woman friend that in this period she had been 'a poor mite', isolated among these old people, intimidated by the venerable air of the place, full of homesickness for her 'grandparents', and irritated by all the attempts to educate her.[17] Still bewildered, she wrote to Lene a month after the wedding: 'It's a joke, really – an 18-year-old creature like me as mistress of Wahnfried!'[18]

According to Winifred, this is how her first Christmas at Wahnfried went: Cosima sat in the hall in front of the candle-lit Christmas tree, while 'Eva, Houston and Siegfried gathered around her – I was at the piano – and the servants came in. Eva recited a poem by Hans von Wolzogen, "Christ in the War" . . . and then I played the carol "Vom Himmel hoch" [From Heaven on High]. Finally, Wolzogen read out a piece he'd just written for Carnival, based on the Grimms' tale "The Jew in the Thorn Patch".'[19]

This is a story about a mischievous serving-lad and 'a rich Jew with a long quivering beard'. The serving-lad tricks the Jew, lures him into a thorn patch and then, with the aid of a magic fiddle, forces him to dance. 'You've bled people for long enough, and now the thorn bush can do the same to you.' The tortured and exhausted Jew begs for mercy and gives the lad a sack of gold, whereupon the latter puts an end to his torment. Put on trial, the serving-lad is condemned to death, but is saved from the gallows by his magic fiddle, which forces the judge and the hangman to dance and settles the dispute: it is the Jew who is hanged, not the lad. So the story has a 'happy ending'.

Read out in wartime and under the Christmas tree, the story was meant to inspire confidence that the supposed 'war of survival' against the Jews would end with the death of the adversary. In this process, music was allocated the function of a deadly weapon, putting the opponent in a state of intoxication and making him helpless.

HOUSTON STEWART CHAMBERLAIN

The intellectual leader of Wahnfried was the writer Houston Stewart Chamberlain, recently turned sixty, and married to Wagner's daughter Eva since 1908. An Englishman brought up in France, he had been converted to a love of Germanic culture by Wagner's music, and since that time wrote only in German. As a private scholar he had written well-known biographies of Wagner, Kant and Goethe, and had become world-famous with his book *Die Grundlagen des 19. Jahrhunderts* (The Foundations of the Nineteenth Century). The book acclaimed the 'white', 'Nordic' or 'Aryan' race as superior to all others, although admittedly it had been seriously harmed by the influence of the Jews and its tolerance of them. In order to survive, 'Aryans' needed to restore the 'purity of Aryan blood', particularly through careful 'selective breeding' – successfully practised since Charles Darwin in the case of plants and animals – and through the strict separation of 'Aryans' and Jews. He gives short shrift to assimilation: a Jew remains a Jew, and neither conversion nor assimilation can alter that fact.

As Chamberlain wrote: 'If you have learnt to understand what miracles can be achieved by selection, how a race-horse or a dachshund or a luxuriant chrysanthemum is gradually produced by screening out all that is inferior, then you will recognize the effectiveness of the same phenomenon among human beings.' 'Abandoning feeble infants to the elements' had proved to be 'one of the most beneficial laws of the Greeks, Romans, and Teutons' for strengthening the race. 'Hard times, which only a sturdy man and a hardy woman could survive, had a similar effect.'[20]

Eugenics at the time was regarded as a modern science; it was taught at universities and much discussed. Chamberlain's simple tenets, explaining world history in black-and-white terms, moulded a whole generation, from William II to Cosima and the Bayreuth circle, right down to Adolf Hitler, who by then had already encountered and internalized Chamberlain's theories in Vienna.

According to Franz Stassen, Siegfried Wagner took 'a passionate interest in the question of race; it was constantly with him, and he scrutinized all new acquaintances from that point of view'. Winifred wrote to Lene after reading the *Grundlagen*: 'Never in my life have I grasped anything with such effortless ease and speed . . . But you need plenty of time for it; it's 1,200 pages long!'[21]

Chamberlain liked talking to his young sister-in-law; he 'enjoys my logical mind', wrote Winifred to her girlfriend Lies, 'he gives me a lot of interesting reading matter and occasion for fierce debates, which amuse everybody very much'.[22] But the pair never spoke English to each other.

When Britain unexpectedly declared war on Germany in August 1914, Chamberlain, the son of an English admiral, was so shocked that he fell ill with a severe nervous complaint. At least, so the story goes. He felt that Britain's entry into the war was a betrayal of the 'Aryan race' the two countries had in common, and in a flood of war-essays, distributed as cheap pamphlets among the populace at government expense, he incited hatred against Britain. Winifred read these publications with great enthusiasm and recommended them to her friend Lene: 'it's a little pamphlet for 1 mark. So far 60,000 of them have been sold, and the 5th edition is already being printed'.[23]

Kaiser William II valued Chamberlain's services as a propagandist, and as an eager disciple wrote in response to the latter's essay 'The Will to Victory':

War is a struggle between two world-views; the Teutonic-German one representing morality, justice, loyalty and faith, against . . . the service of Mammon, the power of money, indulgence, greed for land, treachery, deception, and, not least, cowardly murder! These two world-views cannot be 'reconciled' or 'get on with each other', one must be victorious, the other must go under! Until then, the fight must continue![24]

In the hall at Wahnfried hung a huge war map, upon which Chamberlain kept track of troop movements. Through him the house of Wagner became a centre for German war propaganda. Field Marshal Paul von Hindenburg was mentioned with great pride: 'In him we have found a splendid comrade-in-arms.'[25]

On account of this anti-British agitation his British relatives regarded Chamberlain as a traitor. He was deprived of his British nationality and the funds he held in Britain were seized. In Germany he officially came under the category of 'enemy alien', so he applied for German nationality, and when he obtained it in 1916 he was very proud to be a 'proper German'. However, his Germanness did not prevent him from being subjected to suspicious surveillance in Bayreuth. Because his house had an observatory, it was even said at one point that Chamberlain was sending secret signals to his fellow-countrymen from there.

In 1915 Chamberlain brought out a third, revised edition of his little book *Arische Weltanschauung* (Aryan World-view), in which he set out the significance of race theory in wartime: 'We have sacrificed a whole century to the notion of unlimited tolerance . . . We're heading towards chaos. It is high time we came to our senses: not to reduce the freedom of others, but so that we can be masters in our own house, which today we are not.'[26] He was writing all this at a time when some 100,000 Jews were fighting in the war; 12,000 of them died for the German Empire.

In his publication *Zuversicht* (Confidence), Chamberlain described the Jews as a

> ring of completely soulless, heartless, shameless business jobbers intent on subjugating the whole of humanity to one god, Mammon; Germany is blocking their path; they have made deep-laid plans to push Germany out of their way . . . and driven almost all the nations of the world to madness. It falls to Germany to be the warrior of God and oppose this devil's brood: Siegfried versus the monster, St. George the dragon-slayer.[27]

In the Wagner family it was accepted as more or less scientifically proven that only pure race counted, and that nothing good could be expected from 'half-breeds'. Winifred's comment after reading Gerhart Hauptmann's *Weisser Heiland* (White Redeemer) shows that she shared this conviction: 'He [the hero] always has two souls – an attractive Germanic one, and a repellent Jewish one (he's a half-breed).'[28]

Chamberlain's nervous complaint persisted, accompanied by severe convulsive attacks. In October 1916, as he could no longer write, his publisher, Bruckmann, sent him the ultra-modern '"Parlograph" dictation-machine'. A few months later he lost his voice, too, and relied upon his wife, Eva, to read and write down the words he mouthed silently. The government continued to commission, print and distribute essays by Chamberlain, intended to encourage the Germans to hold out and to convince them of their forthcoming great victory.

In 1917, together with Heinrich Class and others, Chamberlain founded the journal *Germany's Renewal* as a focus for German nationalist and anti-Semitic writers, many of them from the Bayreuth circle. Its aim was the 'salvation' of the German people through 'renewal instead of degeneration', whereby Chamberlain created a link with Wagner's doctrine of regeneration. To achieve 'salvation' from the threat of decline, he believed the German people had to free themselves from the Jewish racial admixture and find their way back to 'pure blood'. For Wolzogen, too, known at

Wahnfried as 'the apostle' or 'our Knight of the Grail', Wagner with his doctrine of regeneration had created nothing less than a new religion. This mentality caused many of his Jewish admirers, from Gustav Mahler to Bruno Walter and Arnold Schönberg, to turn away from Bayreuth in disgust. They cultivated Wagner's music from afar and in opposition to Bayreuth and 'the Cosimans'.

AN HEIR IS BORN

At the end of April 1916 the eighteen-year-old Winifred found she was pregnant at last. The married couple travelled immediately to see Dr Schweninger in Munich, accompanied by the good wishes of the family. The joy of the 'grandparents', the Klindworths, was particularly great. But Karl Klindworth did not live to see the birth of an heir for Wahnfried. He died at the end of July 1916.

The domestic situation was eased after 1 May 1916, when the Chamberlains moved into their own house, next to Villa Wahnfried. It meant that Winifred became 'the mistress of the household'.[29] To the great astonishment of the family, subject as it was to every conceivable kind of ailment, the young wife was visibly blooming. She wrote happily to Schweninger that 'apart from the baby's movements I don't, so to speak, feel my condition at all'. She then asked if she was allowed to drink wine, and declared: 'I feel completely like a fish in water!'[30] Her main worry was on behalf of her husband. He was suffering from neuralgia in his head, which needed daily bathing.

In addition to running the household and looking after her mother-in-law, Winifred made herself useful as Siegfried's secretary. At first he dictated his letters to her. Very soon she was handling routine letters independently, had taken over correspondence dealing with the various Wagner Societies, and was giving brief and succinct answers to the often long-winded questions of Wagner admirers. There is a clear difference when we compare letters by Winifred and Siegfried to the same correspondent, as in the case of the Viennese writer Max von Millenkovich. Siegfried wrote elaborately, and he loved joking and complaining, above all about 'the Modernists', 'the Jews', and 'the Reds'. Winifred on the other hand, was mainly concerned to get through the post, concentrated on essentials and never entered into personal matters. She addressed this influential leading light of the Vienna University

Wagner Society simply as 'Herr Mallenkovitch', simultaneously misspelling his name and leaving out the 'von'; a mortal sin in Vienna. Her thanks on receiving the most lengthy accounts of Viennese Wagner concerts were brief. She used postcards because the postage was cheaper, and her response to a deferential but indecisive letter from Vienna was unadorned: 'As soon as everybody in Vienna is in agreement, then my husband will certainly come and conduct.'[31] Initially she signed herself 'Frau Siegfried Wagner', but soon cheerfully adopted the style 'Siegfried Wagner', something that has been causing confusion in the autograph market ever since. Before long, Siegfried was also confidently entrusting to his industrious young wife the onerous job of correcting the proofs of his scores: 'Fidi is overjoyed that I am able to take so many clerical tasks off his hands . . . I have asked for lessons in theory to improve my reading and writing of scores, so that later I can help Fidi with that as well.'[32]

The military situation in the summer of 1916 was grave. In the west, the murderous stalemates of the Allied offensive on the Somme and the German assault at Verdun dragged on. According to Winifred, Chamberlain was so incensed 'by the pathetic feebleness of the Government towards England and America concerning the U-boat and Zeppelin campaigns that it has made him ill!!!!!! Incidentally, Fidi would cheer up too if we could conduct the war with better prospects!' While the family dreamed of an expansion of the war, even from Bayreuth the practical young woman saw that human resources were becoming scarce: 'I'm afraid that everything will have to be thrown in now – it seems that the reserves are getting used up, because the military are no longer based in the Festival Theatre and in a big school here in Bayreuth, which can only mean that manpower is becoming more limited.'[33]

The food situation worsened all the time, and the amounts of fat, sugar, and bread obtainable against ration coupons became ever smaller. In the park at Wahnfried, roses had long since yielded to potatoes and other vegetables. Laboriously bottled foodstuffs were strictly rationed, stocks sharply monitored by the municipal authorities. Heavily pregnant, Winifred struggled energetically to feed the Wagner family, who were capable of soaring to empyrean heights but were hopeless when it came to survival. In the process, she showed great resourcefulness. For instance, in order to protect their store of eggs from requisitioning, in October 1916 she turned to Dr Schweninger: 'We have pickled 500 eggs – and have been ordered to hand over 265 of these 500 – because with the supply of eggs available at present there is one egg per person every week until 31 March. That means for us with 9 people 245 eggs up to 31 March 1917. We don't get ration coupons to buy fresh eggs.' She wanted to submit a claim to keep the pickled eggs, citing Cosima's invalid diet as the reason, and: 'Perhaps I'll need eggs after the birth, I don't know – maybe that could be given as a reason, too.' She requested medical confirmation from Schweninger.[34]

The nationalists could see only one way to end the war quickly and victoriously: Paul von Hindenburg and Erich Ludendorff, the heroes of the Battle of Tannenberg in 1914, must take control. On 29 August 1916 William II transferred supreme command to them, thus largely relinquishing power himself.

In December 1916 the battle that had raged at Verdun for ten months had to be broken off without a victory. The strategy of 'bleeding our French adversaries to death' had not succeeded: on the contrary, the 'hell of Verdun' claimed the lives of 700,000 soldiers altogether – German, French and British. The German public was never properly informed of the scale of the disaster. Cosima's opinion was that 'this little set-back at Verdun surely won't bother Hindenburg too much, although the 10,000 prisoners of war must be a serious matter for us'.[35]

In the meantime, Winifred's pregnancy was reaching term. Her Bayreuth doctor had two or three hundred wounded men to look after single-handed in the town hospital, and had no time to attend a home delivery at Wahnfried. So Winifred had to give birth in the same hospital, by now in effect a military one. On 5 January 1917 the Master's grandson and heir was born: Wieland Adolf Gottfried, named after Richard Wagner's composition *Wieland der Schmied* (Wieland the Smith), his godfather Adolf von Gross, and Gottfried, the infant heir to Brabant in *Lohengrin*. The circumstances of the birth were dramatic, as it was some time before the baby could be induced to cry. Only after some anxious minutes, when the doctors were almost on the point of giving up, did the child's lungs begin to function.[36] Wieland was to suffer from lung problems all his life.

Proudly Winifred described her son: 'he's got terribly long arms and legs (from Liszt and Mama), an impressive head – unmistakably the Master's shape, a face like Fidi'.[37] And in euphoric mood Siegfried wrote to Franz Stassen: 'You can imagine Mama's bliss: yes, Heaven itself sent little Winnie to me . . . How good this Winifred-idyll feels in these dreadful times! My prayer for this year is "God preserve my little wife and the baby!"' Another prayer was 'May God inspire our Kaiser so that there may be a German peace': a victorious peace (*Siegfrieden*) with great territorial gains, that is, and not the 'compromise peace' which the Chancellor, Bethmann Hollweg, and the Left thought was the only realistic resolution. Siegfried complained in the same letter about his lack of success as a composer: 'I never get any-where! The hatred of Judah and the German couldn't-care-less attitude make sure of that! In the end, my progeny will only be physical, not brain-children!'[38]

The reception of mother and child at Wahnfried was theatrical. As the two arrived a friend played a passage from the second act of *Lohengrin*: 'Es gibt ein Glück, das ohne Reu' (There is a happiness without remorse).[39] Cosima sat in her festive Japanese gown in the middle of the hall. The young mother walked towards her with the newborn baby and laid him cere-monially in her lap. Thus Wieland, the crown prince of the Wagner dynasty, made his entry into Wahnfried and thereby displaced Isolde's son from the succession.

At the christening, for the first time since Wagner's death thirty-three years earlier, Cosima brought the sacred *Parsifal* piano to life again, playing a few bars from the 'Siegfried Idyll'. Shortly afterwards Siegfried, Winifred, the baby and his thirty-year-old nurse, Emma Bär, moved into Siegfried's house, because the high-ceilinged rooms of Wahnfried were impossible to heat any longer. The female staff were accommodated in the gardener's house. The manservant, Paul, was in the army. Only Cosima remained in her accustomed room, with her nurse, sitting close to a stove.

On 31 January 1917 the German Empire put an end to all plans for peace and declared the unlimited submarine war that the Pan-Germans had long been demanding. Siegfried's reaction was 'Thank God, at last! A year too late!'[40] 'Unlimited' warfare included attacking merchant ships, even neutral ones, so that conflict with the USA became inevitable. On 6 April 1917 America declared war on Germany. The exhausted German troops now had to face fresh troops and the massive resources of the United States. But the Pan-Germanists and Wahnfried still believed in a 'victorious peace'.

The winter of 1916–17, which has gone down in history as the 'turnip winter', was especially long and cold. Many people died of cold and starva-tion. Siegfried wrote to Stassen on his birthday: 'We'd love to have sent you some eatables. But there's nothing to be found anywhere except starving crows and jackdaws!'[41] Winifred lamented: 'If only we had more coal – we can only heat three rooms altogether, which is not much for 10 people.'[42] The sugar shortage was so acute that she made syrup out of sugar-beet, a highly laborious and time-consuming procedure. When she ran out of sugar-beet, she asked Lene in Berlin to get hold of some seeds so that she could plant them out in the spring.

Nursing mothers received a higher milk ration only for the first three months, which forced Winifred to give up breastfeeding quite soon: 'if I only get ¼ of a litre of milk a day, how can I be expected to produce a whole litre'.[43] From then on her biggest worry was rustling up milk for the baby. In August 1917 she asked Schweninger: 'According to a decree of 22.6, production of baby cereal is no longer allowed. So I can't get Nestle's any more for the baby – is it all right for him to have goat's milk for his 6th meal, and how prepared? Or would it not go with the other cow's milk? . . . There are so many shortages that you really don't know what to do for the best.'[44]

Winifred was pregnant again. Years later they were still telling the story in Bayreuth of how the young lady suffered badly in the early stages from bouts of sickness, and how Siegfried would follow her to the WC with the refrain: 'But Winnie, all that good food!'[45]

Despite all these trials the Wagner family were still far better off than most Germans, because they received many presents from abroad, especially from Switzerland. From the Basel Wagnerian and goldsmith Adolf Zinsstag, Winifred ordered a present for her husband for Christmas 1917, 'a kind of lockable box with two pots inside that can hold about 1–1½ pounds'. The jeweller was mystified, and Winifred admitted it was 'a wild idea' of hers, but went on to spell out the point of the arrangement: 'with a lock and key – so that the wrong people don't dip into it'.[46] It turned out to be a lockable jampot-holder.

When the left-wing parties protested against Great Power politics and staged a debate in the Reichstag about a peace resolution without territorial demands, Siegfried was enraged: 'So, the German simpleton puts up with this! We're far too spiritless, incapable of anger and true patriotism!'[47] On 19 July 1917 the impotent Reichstag adopted the motion by a large majority, and was thereupon accused by the Right of treason. Winifred expressed her anger in a real Siegfried-style outburst: 'so, out of the frying pan into the fire – it's a fine state of affairs here in this country – it drives you crazy to see one stupidity being committed after the other and everything getting into a deeper mess'.[48]

Parliament's desire for peace was countered by the nationalists behind Tirpitz and Classen with the founding of a 'German Fatherland Party', and the clarion call: 'There is a danger that this war that has been forced upon us

may end in a peace that will do the utmost harm to our people. All our sacrifices would then have been for nothing, all our victories in vain. That must
not be allowed to happen.' There followed an appeal to the starving population to hold out: 'If we are willing to endure hardship and deprivation, the
German people will enjoy a Hindenburg peace that will deliver the spoils of
victory in return for our massive sacrifices and strenuous efforts.' All the
members of the Wagner family, including Cosima and Chamberlain, joined
the German Fatherland Party.

By then the war was making a visible impression in the garrison town of
Bayreuth. In April 1918 Cosima described her impressions of 'a troop of
wounded men, then a group of prisoners of war' whom she had encountered
in the town park, the Hofgarten. 'A few steps further on they were holding
a memorial service for an airman who had crashed; and when I reached the
town church, I saw that one of the big windows had been smashed in and the
pipes of the burnt-out organ strewn across the square.' But, with her trust in
the revered Hindenburg, she remained 'confident and full of hope'.[49]

As an afterthought she mentioned that Dr Schweninger was in Bayreuth
and had driven her to the hospital at six in the morning. A second child,
Friedelind, was born on Good Friday, 29 March 1918, named after the pro-
tagonist of the opera Siegfried was currently working on, Der Schmied von
Marienburg (The Smith of Marienburg).

In March 1918 the Central Powers imposed the humiliating peace settlement of Brest-Litovsk upon the revolutionary Soviet government. Great
hopes were attached to the German offensive on the Western Front that followed. But there was a great shortage of matériel, and the troops were
exhausted. By April the offensive was already petering out, having cost
about 230,000 German lives. 'The standstill in France weighed heavily upon
him all that summer,' reports Stassen of Siegfried.[50]

REVOLUTION AND 'SHAMEFUL PEACE'

Despite the bad military situation, nobody at Wahnfried in October 1918 was
prepared to countenance any talk of peace. As Winifred said: 'Well – this is
a really lousy time – that's all you can say. Every right-minded German is
beside himself over all this disgraceful whining about peace!, and the arch-
crooks in the Government – they should all be sent to the stocks – This is a
really terrible time! All that sacrifice for this – It's shameful – scandalous!'[51]

In the late autumn of 1918 two new operas by Siegfried were premièred: *Sonnenflammen* (Flames of the Sun) in Darmstadt, and *Schwarzschwanenreich* (Kingdom of the Black Swans) in Karlsruhe. During the dress rehearsal in the Hoftheater in Darmstadt on 29 October the Wagners were profoundly shocked by an 'eerie omen': 'When the arrogant Byzantines hurled on to the pyre the dolls representing the Emperor, the Pope and the Frankish princes, the Kaiser-doll was wearing not the crown of the Holy Roman Empire, but the Imperial crown of William II. Our hearts stood still.'[52] Like his friend Stassen, the superstitious Siegfried saw in this a sign that the end of the German Empire was at hand.

On 5 November 1918 Siegfried conducted in Karlsruhe the first performance of his grisly opera *Schwarzschwanenreich*. The plot concerns a young woman, Hulda, who, before she marries, has a relationship with a 'Black Knight', and gives birth to a 'changeling', which she strangles and buries in the forest. She is betrayed and burnt as a witch, and her husband throws himself on to the flames. When the little arm of the buried child reached out above the soil, as prescribed in Siegfried's stage instructions, a number of people in the audience left the theatre in disgust. After a single repeat performance, the piece disappeared from the programme.[53]

The Wagners drove back to Darmstadt for *Sonnenflammen*, where they learned on 8 November that King Ludwig III of Bavaria had renounced his throne the day before and a Bavarian Republic had been proclaimed. During the performance the red flag of the revolution was hoisted over the grand-ducal palace in Darmstadt. Then 'the racket started up immediately, and there was shooting the whole night long. Next morning, 9 November, we set off for home as fast as we could . . . During the journey there were 7 air-raid warnings!'[54]

By the time the exhausted Wagners arrived back in Bayreuth on 9 November, there was no longer an Empire. Germany had become a republic, with the Social Democrat Friedrich Ebert as provisional Chancellor: 'My God, who would have thought that such a turn of events was possible! How proud we were of our German fatherland, and how ashamed we are that a worm at the core could produce such degradation!! – We still can't believe that things can stay like this, and hope for a turn for the better.'[55] The republicans and the Left were the 'worm at the core'.

In Bayreuth, too, a 'Workers', Peasants' and Soldiers' Council' was formed, its seventy-five members under the leadership of Georg Hacke, editor of the SPD (Social Democrat) newspaper. However, the Council did not set up in opposition to the local government, but collaborated with it. Both were interested in preserving peace and good order in the town and avoiding bloodshed.[56]

The harsh conditions of the Armistice on 11 November 1918 came as a shock. As well as requiring German troops to pull out of areas they were still occupying, they demanded that the left bank of the Rhine should be relinquished to French occupation. To make further military action impossible, the Germans must surrender all their U-boats, 2,000 warplanes and other *matériel*. Siegfried's reaction was: 'We deserve to be ruined. Well, we are anyway, totally and for all time. I wish I were a Swiss, because I'm ashamed to be German! . . . These soldiers slouching about with cigarettes in their mouths, red cockades, slovenly gait, bone idle, vacant look – they're getting on our nerves so much that I am desperate to avoid going into town altogether.'[57] 'Because of anger and pain at the German collapse', according to Stassen, he stopped work on a hymn to peace that he had begun.[58] The agitation now brought on Winifred's old skin complaint; she had no idea how to cope with it, and had to turn to Dr Schweninger for advice.[59]

The 'stab in the back legend' began circulating in Bayreuth at this time, as it was throughout Germany. It asserted that the revolution, the 'worm at the core', the 'red' and 'Jewish' 'enemies of the Fatherland', had treacherously fallen upon the rear of a German army that was 'still undefeated on the field of battle', and for selfish and cowardly reasons had destroyed the German Reich in order to gain power themselves. Anti-Semitic propaganda made a great deal of capital out of the fact that many of the leaders of the revolution in Bavaria were Jews. It was at that time that Siegfried wrote to a Jewish woman acquaintance in Berlin: 'It must be painful for all right-minded Jews to know that the people who have brought this misery of revolution upon Germany are members of your race.'[60] For Cosima, too, there was no room for doubt 'that as always and everywhere it is the Semitic element that is responsible for agitation and subversion. My son jokes that Robespierre and Marat were really called Rubinstein and Marx.'[61] After all, hadn't the revolution in Russia also been the work of Jews?

At the 'celebration of the revolution' on 17 November 1918 in Munich, Bruno Walter conducted the Munich Philharmonic and thereby declared himself a man of the Left. This appearance by the 'non-Aryan' Walter, who was disliked by the House of Wagner though he was a brilliant Wagner conductor and supporter of modern music, served to reinforce anxieties that, in the aftermath of the revolution, 'the Jews' might take over the 'German

'Master' Wagner and alienate him from 'the true German way'. The Wagners lamented not only the end of the German Reich, but also the end of 'German art', brought about by 'alien conductors and directors'. This anxiety was further strengthened by rumours that Heinrich Mann had written in a newspaper that it was high time that Wagnerian heroes 'danced off' and left the stage.[62]

The spirit of the revolution brought with it new ideals, a new style of life without court hierarchies, without an aristocracy and without an educated bourgeoisie. The spirit of the age was left-wing and democratic. The Minister-President of the Bavarian Republic, Kurt Eisner, pushed through new welfare laws and labour regulations, in a move that was perceived in bourgeois circles as a declaration of war. Winifred grumbled that 'because of Eisner's law' she had to give her staff more time off: one afternoon a week and every other Sunday.[63]

The spectre of the Bolshevik revolution now haunted Germany, too, as the newly founded German Communist Party (KPD) attempted to grab political control in Berlin with its 'Spartacist uprising'. The SPD government crushed the revolt by military force, and the leaders Rosa Luxemburg and Karl Liebknecht were murdered by Freikorps soldiers (far-right army veterans formed into irregular troops).

On 19 January, amidst serious civil disturbances, the elections to the National Assembly took place. Women had the vote for the first time in German history. As the voting age had been reduced from twenty-six to twenty-one, Winifred too was able to cast her ballot. The turn-out was 90 per cent in Bayreuth, and the SPD was the clear winner with 53.7 per cent of the vote.[64] The nationalists lost badly. Siegfried wrote to his teacher Engelbert Humperdinck: 'So, that is Germany finished for all time. Jehovah has led his people to victory, and we are enslaved! . . . Shame on Germany! It fills you with disgust and revulsion! – You throw yourself into work to numb your senses, so as to see nothing, to hear nothing!'[65]

On 21 February Eisner, called by Cosima 'the Galician Semite', was shot dead on a Munich street. The killer was the 22-year-old former lieutenant Count Anton Arco, conscious of support from nationalist circles. Cosima declared: 'In my eyes Count Arco is a martyr.'[66] The murder of Eisner precipitated chaos and civil war. This highly explosive situation led on 7 April 1919 to the proclamation of a Communist soviet republic in Bavaria. The fear that the atrocities of the Russian Revolution might be repeated in Bavaria, with the murder, plunder and expulsion of property owners, led to the formation of citizens' militias throughout Bavaria. In Bayreuth on 29 August 1919 the mayor proclaimed: 'A horde of irresponsible non-Bavarian elements in Munich has brought Russian conditions to Bavaria. Russian Bolshevism, Communism, the dictatorship of the proletariat are endangering all kinds of property, and even women.' Now it was a case of 'all hands on deck'.[67]

Rich nationalists financed and equipped the Freikorps units being formed everywhere which consisted of unemployed soldiers, who fought in the Baltic states and in Upper Silesia for 'Germanness', and undertook to oppose the Communists throughout Germany. In May 1919 the Bayreuth Freikorps helped to put down the Munich soviet republic.

On 28 June 1919 the treaty drawn up by the Allies at Versailles, without consulting the Germans, was signed, or 'dictated'. The terms were tough: the German Reich had to accept sole responsibility for the war, and was sentenced to go on making reparations for all war damage until 1951. Larger merchant and fishing vessels were to be handed over, factory machines dismantled; overseas communications cables, tractors, building materials, coal, even horses, cows and pigs were forfeit.

There was no further mention of the self-determination of peoples proposed by US President Woodrow Wilson: the union with Germany that Austria desired was ruled out. The German-speaking Sudeten territories, previously a part of the Austro-Hungarian Empire, were assigned to Czechoslovakia. The Saar area nominally become a League of Nations responsibility for fifteen years, but in fact fell to France. The German army was limited to 100,000 professional soldiers, deprived of heavy weapons and an air force. Winifred's opinion of this 'shameful peace' was that: 'I wouldn't have believed it possible to get signatures for it! – it's sickening – what have the Germans come to. – No sense of honour! No sense of shame! – Terrible – that we've sunk so low in 40 years'[68] (since the victorious Franco-Prussian war of 1870–71).

The 'shame of Versailles' became the most significant slogan of the Weimar Republic's enemies and of the anti-Semites, who blamed the new republic, democracy, the Left and, above all, the Jews for this 'scandal'. Propaganda maintained that 'international Jewry' wanted to force Germany to its knees.

On 8 October 1919 the new Deutschvölkischer Schutz- und Trutzbund (German Nationalist Protection and Shelter League), an anti-Semitic pan-German association, held a gathering in Bayreuth. Commenting on the inflammatory speeches it produced, the SPD newspaper wrote: 'There is no wickedness that has not been perpetrated by the Jews. From the lost war to the despoiling of the true German race – everything is the fault of the Jews. And the speakers see nothing but Jews wherever they look; in the press and the banks, in the Army and the judiciary, among university lecturers – nothing but Jews everywhere.' The Jewish lawyer Berthold Klein had protested emphatically against these insults, and sworn an oath of loyalty to Germany. The atmosphere in the hall had been so tense that 'all it needed was hand grenades'.

The paper did not omit to mention that before their appearance the speakers had enjoyed the hospitality of the Chamberlain and Wagner households.[69] Winifred must have been at the event, because she reported on Klein to Lene, mentioning how he had defended 'his racial community': he 'opened his address with the words: Gentlemen, I am a Jew. Thereupon there was a general uproar: shame, shame!'[70] How widespread anti-Semitism was in Bayreuth was indicated by the admonition that Mayor Albert Preu felt obliged to issue: the almost daily attacks on Jewry were 'a threat not only to those involved, but also to the public peace'.[71]

As far as anti-Semitism was concerned, Winifred shared the opinions of the Wagner family. She was proud to be personally acquainted with the nationalist writer Adolf Dinter, the author of the novel *Die Sünde wider das Blut* (The Sin against the Blood): 'he is a terrifically original chap and a fanatical anti-Semite . . . His main activity consists in anti-Semitic lectures and court cases involving rabbis – so far he hasn't lost a single one, because he's so terrifically knowledgeable – knows the Talmud inside out etc. etc.'[72] In the same letter she asked her friend: 'Do you know Wagner's *Judentum in der Musik* (Jewishness in Music)?', that little 1850 publication of the Master's which was the touchstone of the Wagner family's anti-Semitism. In her diary Cosima mentioned a conversation with 'Richard' in 1879 about the Jews: 'R. wants them all deported. We laugh about the fact that his essay appears to be the beginning of such a campaign.'[73]

Anti-Semitism was a constant feature of everyday life at Wahnfried. Thus Winifred explained why they had not congratulated the singer Carl Clewing on getting married: 'That's what these fine fellows are like. First of all they boast about their student duelling fraternity etc. etc., and then they go off and marry some full-blooded Jewess. Ugh!'[74] One visitor, who arrived twelve hours too late for lunch at Wahnfried, explained that on the express train at Breslau 'a whole Jewish family' had got into his carriage, and 'he was so annoyed by this that he got out, travelled to Leipzig, caught a slow train and only arrived here at 9 in the evening!' Winifred commented to Lene: 'You can imagine how pleased I was to see all my menu-planning going to waste.'[75]

Like those in nationalist circles, the only way that the House of Wahnfried could see to avoid the misery of 'Jewish' domination was through an authoritarian government. As Cosima remarked after reading General Ludendorff's memoirs: 'Ah, if only Ludendorff could be our dictator and liberate us from mediocrity!'[76]

The most important right-wing putsch attempt against the Berlin government was that led by Wolfgang Kapp in March 1920, which was defeated only by a general strike. Here too Winifred was a faithful echo of her husband's opinions: 'a pity Kapp didn't have enough force to succeed – it would have been the saving of us – the German people are just too pathetic, and the so-called people for the most part deserve their dreadful fate – they prefer to tear each other apart rather than unite and go on fighting the enemy for another ¼ of a year back in 1918.'[77]

The Kapp putsch had significant political consequences in Bavaria. The new Minister-President, Gustav Ritter von Kahr, instituted a move to the extreme right, which made Bavaria into 'the law and order centre of the Reich' and attracted nationalists and right-wing radicals from other parts of Germany. Ludendorff, a Kapp sympathizer, was one of those who came to Munich, where he gathered his supporters around him. The Right in Bavaria could rely upon the protection of the Kahr government. Police charges were dropped, and right-wingers convicted of violent assault were released early, while those on the Left were treated harshly. Count Arco, Eisner's assassin, was one of those who benefited: his death sentence was commuted to imprisonment for life, and he was a free man by May 1924.

One new demagogue in Munich who enjoyed the protection of the Bavarian authorities was the thirty-year-old Austrian Adolf Hitler. This 'simple man of the people' was an expert at addressing the fears of an insecure public, painting their supposed enemies for them in drastic colours: the Jews, the Left, the democrats, the Versailles powers. He had after all enlisted in the German, not the Austrian, army in 1914, and as a corporal had been decorated with the Iron Cross First Class. His audience were convinced of his fanatical love for Germany.

Hitler's reputation as a gifted speaker and potential saviour from all evils reached Wahnfried as early as 1919 via two Munich Wagnerians, the writer

Michael Georg Conrad and the music critic Josef Stolzing-Cerny, who was soon to become editor of the new (Nazi) newspaper, the *Völkischer Beobachter* (Nationalist Observer).[78]

The centrality of the Wagners in the German nationalist web is demonstrated by this early awareness of Hitler. Traditionally – and supposedly in line with the will of the Master – the Wagners stood firmly in the nationalist camp. They were supporters of the Pan-Germans, belonged to nationalist associations, sympathized with the anti-democratic Freikorps, and campaigned for the 'old German values' and 'order' in art and the state. The leaders of the Freikorps billeted in Bayreuth were always welcome guests in Wahnfried: 'For a few days now the "Iron Horde" – 1,000 men under the magnificent air force captain Berthold – have been billeted here. They all look splendid. Berthold is boiling over with rage at the present state of affairs, and immediately very nicely made a friend of Siegfried, who completely shares his outlook.'[79] Rudolf Berthold was a highly decorated and much-wounded First World War pilot who had become a member of the Freikorps in the Baltic. Seven months after his visit to Wahnfried he was killed in Hamburg fighting against the Weimar Republic during the Kapp putsch.

As both the revolution and the Republic were held to be 'Jewish', Jewish representatives of the Weimar Republic were in great danger. The Freikorps fighters, inured to killing after years at the front, thought of themselves as continuing the war, this time against the 'enemy within', the Left and the Jews. The song of the Rossbach Freikorps, for example, was a pure incitement to murder: 'Strike all the Jews down dead,/Smash all the Jews to death,/Strike them down dead,/ Ebert and Scheidemann/ They're going down the pan,/Strike all the Jews down dead/Strike them to death.'[80]

On 26 August 1921 the Centre Party Member of Parliament Matthias Erzberger, who had supported a compromise peace during the war, was murdered in broad daylight. On 24 June 1922 the Foreign Minister, Walther Rathenau, representing the government policy of 'fulfilment' towards the victorious powers (the tactic of appearing to try to meet reparations payments), was shot dead in his car. On 3 July the journalist Maximilian Harden barely survived an assassination attempt; badly wounded in the head, he lived on as an invalid. As the scourge of homosexuals he had many enemies, including Siegfried Wagner.

Those who controlled and financed the assassinations remained in the shadows. But everything pointed to the 'OC' (Consul Organization), a network of nationalist fanatics, prepared to use force, keen to destabilize and destroy the hated Republic. The head of the OC was Freikorps leader Captain Hermann Ehrhardt, highly esteemed in nationalist circles. Protected by the Munich chief of police Ernst Pöhner, he organized a nation-wide, clandestine group of fighters against the Republic. After Rathenau's murder, parts of this network of OC conspirators were unmasked by the police and immobilized by arrests. But Ehrhardt remained active, although outside Munich he appeared on 'wanted' posters.[81] Ehrhardt too was a wel-come guest in Wahnfried, according to Winifred 'a dashing, splendid fellow, who is re-forming his brigades everywhere. But please keep this quiet.'[82] These indications of the political contacts enjoyed by Wahnfried are neces-sarily incomplete. There must be a great deal of material among the sealed effects of Siegfried Wagner.

FAMILY WRANGLES AND MONEY WORRIES

On 30 August 1919 Winifred gave birth to her third child. Wolfgang Manfred Martin was named after Goethe, his cousin Manfredi Gravina and Martin Luther. Siegfried said of Cosima: 'Her greatest joy is my married happiness . . . so at least within Wahnfried we have peace without delu-sions'[83] (*Wahn* = illusion/delusion, *Fried* = peace).

In reality, though, this picture of domestic bliss was often knocked badly askew. Winifred had begun to resist Cosima's dominance. Superficially the causes were trivial. Winifred asked Dr Schweninger to 'most strictly' warn her overwrought mother-in-law that she must calm down.[84] Cosima took her revenge by complaining to the doctor about her daughter-in-law: 'My grand-son, who is 2 years old, is already wearing shoes with heels, although a doctor in Berlin once told me that this was unhealthy and also caused poor posture. I would be grateful for your opinion on this so that we can act accordingly.'[85] Four days later Winifred again turned to Schweninger and sent him by registered post a small boot for his evaluation, accompanying it with a ten-page letter: 'please – take a look at the boot – and write and tell me whether it could distort his pelvis'.[86] Evidently the small pair of shoes was a gift from America, where they were beginning to manufacture such orthopaedically correct shapes and abandoning soft, flat children's footwear.

At twenty-one, Winifred was starting to break away from Cosima's shadow. She resolutely defended her power base and expanded it step by step.

When she became pregnant once more, for the fourth time in her four-year marriage, Siegfried remarked: 'I always call little Winnie Mrs Globus now! The girls from the Bayreuth alleys are getting very worried because they never see the poor thing in town any more!'[87] On 2 December 1920 Verena was born in Siegfried's house, named after Siegfried's Swiss nursemaid Verena Stocker.[88]

On account of the coal shortage, the little house built just for Siegfried's use was now accommodating a family of seven, including Emma Bär. The lack of space and the children's noise increased Siegfried's despair. He had lost both his accustomed freedom and his ability to concentrate on composing. He made clear to his wife, who had always happily declared that she wanted a dozen children, that he wished to have no more. She was bitterly disappointed.

To make some money, in ever shorter supply due to inflation, Siegfried went on frequent concert tours, as far as the extreme north of Norway: 'I'm conducting away like a wild man to earn money, since our budget (with a staff of seven!!!) is in ruins, and on top of that there are the sh . . . tty government securities!' In Sweden he had 'stuffed himself to his heart's content!'[89] But despite the need for money he declined an invitation from Warsaw 'because of the vicious attitude of the Poles to us Germans'.[90] Many of his concerts took place within a clear political context; for example, a private Berlin concert in early February, in aid of the National Association of German Officers. This was a 'mutual protection organization' of ex-officers who helped each other to find employment and were politically active on the extreme Right.

These efforts and his lack of success imposed a heavy toll upon Siegfried, the scion of a rich family now forced to earn money: 'God forbid that my children should want to be artists! Better that they should become town clerks rather than suffer the disappointments I am going through!'[92] Winifred explained that the reason he almost always travelled without her, but with old friends, was that 'if he took me with him, he'd bring nothing at all home with him, so to speak!'[93] But she looked after him, even from a distance: 'This evening I've sent you some eatables by express mail – a sandwich loaf, half a sausage, which I hope isn't too fatty for you, send it to Stassen otherwise, the remains of a cake and a tin of jam.' She continued: 'We've had a warning from the electricity company that we keep too many lights burning; so I've unscrewed a few more bulbs.' And furthermore: 'If you have any sausage left over, bring it back with you – we can do with it here, too!'[94]

It was because his energetic wife dealt with the day-to-day chores, including correspondence, that Siegfried was able to travel with an easy mind. She
backed him loyally whatever he did. She was tactful and discreet, always prepared to overlook any foibles, or simply not to notice them in the first place.
She never gave the slightest indication of being aware of her husband's
homosexual leanings. Tough and unperturbed, she fought her way through
life, as she had been forced to do since childhood. Ultimately, for her
Siegfried was the 'son of the Master', entitled to his freedoms.

Obviously restless, she used Siegfried's periodic absences to have
improvements and renovation work done, and to rearrange the furniture.
There were always tradesmen in the house. Shortly before Christmas she
declared to their man of business Adolf von Gross: 'please make sure you're
sitting down – bills amounting to 1,578.11 marks!!! – Please make
arrangements for the bank to cover them.'[95] Before the move back into
Wahnfried, gas heating replaced the seven coal-burning stoves in the old
house. In the bathrooms Winifred got rid of the oversized washstands with
their jugs and bowls, had running water put in, and installed 'enormous
baths that you needed a little ladder to get into!'[96] Debts piled up: 'I've got
a tailoring bill of 4,740 marks (!), too, which I can't pay.'[97] Permanently
short of money, both Siegfried and Winifred trespassed on Gross's professional territory, withdrawing cash or receiving payments without telling
him. The old gentleman lost his grasp of their finances, was no longer in a
position to draw up orderly accounts, and was finally unable to cover tax
liabilities.

Siegfried reproached Gross for not having converted government securities into material assets in good time before the war. These previously solid
investments were visibly losing their value with inflation, and were soon as
worthless as War Loan bonds. The Wagner family fortune was dwindling,
and had practically disappeared by 1923. Embittered, Gross resigned, and left
Siegfried and Winifred to look after their own financial affairs. His exhorta-
tions to thrift had no effect. A warm and friendly relationship now turned to
enmity.

Siegfried blamed the 'Left' and their supposed hatred of the property-
owning classes for the plight of the bourgeoisie. Used to living off their
investments and annuities, they were becoming ever more impoverished
due to massive inflation; initially creeping, and then at full gallop. It made
Siegfried furious that people who lived by working were at first not affected
by these concerns. He thought that 'nobody is doing well in Germany except

our friends the factory workers and the black marketeers'.[98] In fact, inflation suited the government because it made reparations payments easier to meet.

In the meantime friends of Bayreuth were pressing for the Festival to be reopened. But Siegfried listed the obstacles: 'First of all the coal shortage and everything that goes with it: travel by train, lighting, running machines etc. Secondly the housing shortage': all Bayreuth houses were full to bursting point with lodgers quartered upon them. The biggest hindrance, however, was the shortage of money. 'So just let us wait until the mood calms down and reason and order return to our poor, shattered country.'[99]

In May 1921 he invited some close friends, together with Mayor Albert Preu, to a meeting to discuss a fund-raising campaign for the Festival. The German Bayreuth Festival Foundation was constituted on 21 June 1921, and it was decided to follow the pattern set by the first Festival in 1876 in offering sponsorship certificates for subscription at 1,000 marks each. The inheritable certificates guaranteed each subscriber four Festival tickets at a reduced price.

The subscription appeal was saturated with the spirit of nationalism, and began by invoking 'the old dream of German unity' from 1871: 'Violent external forces, and sad to say also internal ones, have laid waste the proud structure built by our fathers.' Bayreuth offered salvation from this gloom: 'what wonderful opportunities to rally Germans once more in shared emotion around a high ideal, to reawaken brotherly feelings in the happiness of shared devotion to art and pilgrimage to Bayreuth, to raise and strengthen consciousness of Germanness in the pure atmosphere of a German work of art'. Foreigners would have to pay 'an appropriate currency surcharge', except for German-Austrians.[100]

The Leipzig Wagnerian Richard Linnemann advertised for subscriptions to the certificates by offering only non-Jews the right to apply. Even 'descendants of Jews' were excluded unless they could prove 'that all family members had been baptized for the past fifty years'. This seems to have brought in substantial amounts of money.[101] August Püringer, editor-in-chief of the newspaper published by Class, the *Deutsche Zeitung*, demanded that members of the Festival Foundation should have Aryan credentials, as was usual in many German societies.

When Jewish Wagnerians protested and threatened to end their support, Siegfried felt obliged to contradict Püringer in an open letter to the *Deutsche Zeitung*: 'We have a good many loyal, honest, and selfless Jewish supporters, who have given us numerous proofs of their friendship. Do you really want us to close our doors to all these people and turn them away, simply because they are Jews? Is that human? Is that Christian? Is that German? No!' His letter also stated that: 'We want our work on Festival Hill to be positive, not negative. Whether people are Chinese, Negroes, Americans, Red Indians or Jews is a matter of complete indifference to us.' The Germans 'could learn from the Jews how to stick together and to help each other'. He added: 'If I were a Jew, my operas would be performed in every theatre. But as things stand, we'll have to wait until we're dead for that to happen.'[102]

There were obvious reasons for Siegfried to distance himself from anti-Semitism, a move that was often cited in later years: Siegfried knew that he had to be careful in public. He had an urgent need for money, that of the Jews included. But this did not prevent him from making anti-Semitic remarks in private.

By September 1922 5 million marks had already flowed in. Added to this there were the collections of the Richard Wagner Award Foundation, which themselves brought in 750,000 marks by 1921.[103] Siegfried also planned an American tour with concerts and fund-raising talks, to obtain foreign currency.

Photos of the blond Wagner children, distributed as postcards to the Wahnfried flock, turned out to be very useful for campaigning purposes. Like royalty, the Wagners were proud to show how splendidly the grandchildren of the Master were developing, thus projecting themselves as a model family and promoting loyalty to the dynasty. Donations in kind were forthcoming, such as children's clothes, groceries, offers of hotel accommodation or the sponsoring of performances of Siegfried's operas. Liszt's former pupil Albert Morris Bagby sent dollar cheques from New York. The Swiss jeweller Adolf Zinsstag in Basel showed as much generosity as the descendants of Eliza Willes, patroness of the Master. A few theatres paid Wagner's widow complimentary royalties of 1 or 2 per cent.

In the spring of 1923 an American journalist who had known Bayreuth before the war compared it to the state it was now in and opened the floodgates for donations. German and Swiss newspapers took up the topic. The Wagners presented their tax assessments, showing that Cosima and Siegfried had annual incomes of just 174,000 and 128,000 marks respectively. 'The pay of any mechanic or whatever comes to the same for a month as our income for a year – but he has not got the responsibility of maintaining a house or such a crazy number of relatives to consider! . . . A school writing slate costs 2,000 marks!!! . . . A school satchel was supposed to cost 35,000 marks, but I made one out of an old travelling rug! In every other country' Siegfried would have 'an income from his work', but he was 'completely silenced in Germany by the Jews'.

As to the food parcels they received, Winifred's view was that 'many people would definitely have sent them sooner, but were put off by the lies about our wealth spread by the Jewish press!'[104] Benefit concerts in Buenos Aires and Rio de Janeiro in July 1923 yielded some 10,000 Swiss francs for Cosima, a veritable fortune at the height of the inflation.[105]

Cosima, at the age of eighty-five, was no longer taking much part in events. Whenever she had one of her attacks and was plagued by the awful music in her head, Winifred deployed her children as therapy. They soon made Cosima forget her sufferings. While friends and family alike would approach the old lady only with deference, she willingly lent herself to her grandchildren's wild games. They had moved into the room next to Cosima's drawing room on the top floor of Wahnfried, and 'loved Cosima's room with its deep chintz-covered armchairs and the bust of Richard Wagner on the mantelpiece', as Friedelind was later to write. They were even allowed to turn the delicate old lady into one of their patients when they played at being doctors: 'Wieland took her temperature with a pencil, I measured her pulse, Wolfgang held a spoon over a glass and tried to fill it drop by drop with water, and Verena, the two-and-a-half-year-old baby, played on the floor with a few cushions.'[106]

This idyll at Wahnfried was set amidst hunger, homelessness, unemployment and inflation. The inhabitants of the spa resort of Bad Berneck near Bayreuth forced all tourists to leave within twenty-four hours on the grounds that such food as there was should be reserved for the locals.[107] The authorities particularly had their sights on the Eastern European Jews who had arrived only since 1914. 'In Bayreuth ten Nagods* have been deported by Kahr so far.'[108]

As Siegfried wrote in June 1923:

Everything is getting much worse. The yawning abyss is just about to open up! – And we're supposed to hold a festival! The word is an irony in itself! . . . How many people are wandering around alone, have lost

*Winifred's private word for Jews.

everything in Russia, are staying alive by taking the most menial jobs; how many artists are obliged to play in cinemas and nightclubs! Misery wherever you look! I've completed umpteen things that are just lying in a drawer, I can't get them printed, just like a painter who can't get any more paints![109]

He had composed a scherzo on the line from Luther, 'Und wenn die Welt voll Teufel wär' (Even if the world were full of devils), and had written on the score: 'Bayreuth/completed on 9 November (!), of all dates! 1922',[110] that is to say, on the fourth anniversary of the hated revolution. He distinguished two types of devil among the many who pursued their evil business in his operas: the German and the un-German. The German devil tended to be easy-going, while the un-German one was 'the devil of discord, of slander', always ready 'greedily to destroy our joyful work'.[111] He was working on an ancient Germanic subject, *Die Heilige Linde* (The Sacred Linden Tree). Stassen commented: 'This time it was Rome with its Assyrian-Semitic cults, its cruel circus games, its despicable politics, to which he opposed plain old Germanic customs, loyalty, courage, and the nobility of women.'[112]

In the summer of 1923, when the first rehearsals were beginning at Wahnfried, the money so laboriously collected to relaunch the Festival was almost completely lost through inflation. Emmy Krüger, engaged for the roles of Sieglinde and Kundry and travelling in 1923 from Zurich, noted in her diary when she arrived in Munich: 'already frozen with horror on the journey at the sight of the horrible chaos in our country, I shared out all my Swiss money among friends and at the orphanage – there is so much hardship written on every face!' And somewhat later: 'I am suffering greatly – because of the death-struggles of my country, too!' And then: 'Bought a pair of slippers for 70 billion – the misery is indescribable!'[113] But when she set foot in Wahnfried for the first time, 'the house where the Master lived, loved, suffered, created, a great sense of sanctity came over me, and I felt strangely "at home"!'

The rehearsals took place in the hall at Wahnfried. The children watched. Cosima too put in an appearance, as reported by the Danish singer Lauritz Melchior, hired to play Parsifal and Siegmund: up in the gallery 'sat a lady dressed in white like a ghost. She was pale, wan, with a veil . . . As we were working down below, Siegfried and I, we heard a coughing and rustling. Siegfried went straight up to the gallery. When he came back, he said:

"Mama wants . . ." And they weren't at all bad suggestions.'[114] Winifred was present at all the rehearsals, according to Emmy Krüger: 'She sits quietly with the piano score in a corner, makes a careful note of all the Master's remarks, as explained and demanded by Siegfried, and follows every detail with the most lively interest.' The atmosphere was one of 'a rare, quick intellectuality, but at the same time an agreeably healthy, light-hearted calm and cheerfulness, expressed in down-to-earth humour, especially at meal times. – They are not just artists, but artists of life!'[115]

Winifred attached herself that summer to the 39-year-old English author Hugh Walpole, who had come to Bayreuth as Melchior's companion and patron. She clearly enjoyed the opportunity to speak English. He observed Chamberlain, whose reputation extended to England, being pushed in his wheelchair through the Hofgarten park, and Siegfried, who was 'to be seen everywhere, like a ponderous white bird, already going forward to meet decline'. He met Winifred, 'very tall . . . straightforward, sweet', for the first time at tea in Wahnfried, and she had 'most spiritedly aired her thoughts about some totally impossible problems'.[116] She led her amusing fellow-countryman to Wagner's grave, and mentioned the forthcoming trip to America, and her plans to give fund-raising talks in aid of Bayreuth in the USA. Walpole was ready to help, and offered her a letter of recommendation to an American friend of his. He left after ten days, amazed to find he had only spent three shillings during his whole stay.[117] You could live well with foreign currency in Germany in 1923.

Without a doubt Winifred had fallen head over heels in love with the writer, thirteen years her senior. She wrote him many letters, and read his novels: 'His books are charming. So serious, true, sensitive, humorous, and the opposite of limited in all his views. I've now read all 5.' Elsewhere she wrote: 'Hugh is so pleased with my appreciation that he's sending all his books to me one by one. I hope he'll bring them himself.'[118]

She was noticeably on edge, hectic and anxious, and felt lonely and isolated in Bayreuth. She was occasionally bad-tempered with her sisters-in-law, and then had to sheepishly apologize to them. 'It's my own fault, but my position here is completely isolated . . . Fidi can't stand by me for ever – and one day it will turn out that I'm utterly superfluous here.' In Wahnfried she was playing 'the part of an outcast: you have taken from me every feeling of happiness, every sense of being at home here and belonging to you – all I have left is Fidi – but for how long? Almost every day there are complaints about my behaviour etc. etc.' Moreover: 'Because of my temperament, because of circumstances a happy person has become isolated, a cheerfully active one has become bitter and worried – an open, honest soul has shut herself off.'[119] At twenty-six, Winifred felt she was no longer needed. The Wagners had got from her what they wanted: an heir, and three other children besides.

CHAPTER 3

Hitler in Bayreuth

(1923–4)

THE NATIONALIST NETWORK

The Wagner family had been following the rise of Adolf Hitler from a distance since 1919, and were very well informed about him through the *Völkischer Beobachter* and through many mutual acquaintances. In November 1922 a branch of Hitler's party, the National Sozialistische Deutsche Arbeiterpartei (NSDAP) was founded in Bayreuth; within four months it had more than 300 members.[1] The Wagners did not join the party, but it was a blatant understatement when Winifred declared after 1945: 'At first we had no connections with the party, although as the town was small we knew one or two of the members.'[2] For the fact was that a close friend of the Wagners and the Chamberlains, Christian Ebersberger, was the leader of the Bayreuth branch of the new party.

It is safe to say that the party did not interest the Wagners particularly, since in bourgeois circles it had a reputation for street fighting, and was always drawing attention to itself through some brawl or other. What did attract them was Hitler's personality, and in this they were far from unique among their friends. The most important link between the Wagners and Hitler was the Bechstein family, Winifred's former 'substitute parents'. They initially financed Dietrich Eckart's nationalist periodical *Auf gut Deutsch* [In Good German]. The writer Eckart was a Wagnerian, and very proud that his essay on *Parsifal* had been printed in the handbook for Festival visitors in

1911.[3] He introduced his protégé Hitler to the Bechstein household in June 1921, probably with his customary announcement: 'This is the man who one day will set Germany free.'[4] At this point Hitler was already filling the Circus Krone* in Munich with audiences of 5,000, who were even prepared to pay for the privilege. He was currently heading a popular protest against the payment of reparations.

For the elegant, artistic Helene Bechstein, Hitler's appeal lay in his zeal for the nationalist cause. But she was also interested in Hitler as a 'simple man of the people' who was able to inspire the masses. His claim to be an artist helped him to make an impression on her, as did the way he convincingly demonstrated his knowledge of architecture, Chamberlain's writings and the works of Wagner. Helene Bechstein conceived a motherly liking for this awkward young man from provincial Austria, thirteen years her junior. In his worn-out blue suit and threadbare trench coat, he hardly seemed ready for polite society. She provided him with a suitable wardrobe, showed him how to appear relaxed in evening dress with starched shirts and patent-leather shoes, and coached him in table manners and etiquette. Hitler perfected the art of kissing a lady's hand, which soon earned him a reputation for old-world Viennese charm. By 1922 one of his friends noted with astonishment that Hitler was elegant, in a frock-coat with pressed trousers and a black felt hat: 'A complete copy of Mussolini.'[5]

Thus groomed, Hitler soon became a star of the elegant receptions held by Helene Bechstein in the Four Seasons Hotel in Munich. She saw it as her mission to introduce him to influential and wealthy personalities. In the Bechsteins' Berlin villa, so familiar to Winifred from her youth, Hitler persuaded many a nationalist to switch to the NSDAP. Hitler's patroness gave him financial support and sometimes jewellery, which, when the need arose for ready money, might spend a short time at the pawnbroker's. Winifred remarked in 1923 that the Bechsteins were 'passionate friends of Hitler's'.[6]

Apart from Helene Bechstein, the Wagner family were also kept informed about Hitler by Heinrich Class, leader of the Alldeutscher Verband (AV) (Pan-German League). Hitler had visited Class in 1921 in Berlin, acknowledged him as leader of the Right in Germany, and received

*The Krone family circus was and still is the largest circus in Europe, and was the first to have a permanent base, 'Circus Krone', which was and still is in Munich (rebuilt after the war). It was used as a venue for Nazi meetings.

substantial sums from him for the NSDAP. He said of Class in 1923: 'Politically we all stand on the shoulders of the A.V., and there's only one thing we have against it: although it has the right views, and has existed for decades as a very influential organization, it has not yet achieved any practical object whatsoever. Using its funds, we can now make up for that.'[7] Since his time in Vienna, Hitler had been very familiar with the aims of the Austrian Pan-Germans under Georg von Schönerer: the merging of Austria with the German Reich, and a new 'racist' interpretation of civil rights.[8]

As money lost its value in Germany, Hitler needed access to stable foreign currencies, above all Swiss francs. Among other things, he worked hard at his contacts with the Wille-Schwarzenbach family in Zurich, who had had a long association with the Wagners, and were generous benefactors of Bayreuth. The Wille family, related to Bismarck, Tirpitz and Eulenburg, were at the centre of Swiss Germanophile circles. The link with Hitler was made by Rudolf Hess, who studied in 1922–3 in Zurich and was invited to lunch every Thursday at the Willes' magnificent house. In this company, still influenced by the impact of the short-lived Swiss soviet republic, Hess talked about Hitler and his party, and represented them as the only effective counterweight to Communism in Germany.

On 1 November 1922 Hess, Eckart and Hitler's fund-raiser Emil Gansser signed the guestbook at the Wille family's country house near Zurich. Entering the date, Eckart referred to 'this decisive year' (note that the year in question was 1922) and quoted from his poem 'Storm' with its closing lines: 'Rage, rage in the thunder of vengeance,/ Sound the dead from out of their graves,/ Germany awake!'[9] It was not a tone calculated to win friends and benefactors in the highly cultivated atmosphere of this house.

Out of growing curiosity, 74-year-old General Ulrich Wille Senior, commander-in-chief of the Swiss army during the World War, attended a Hitler rally in Munich in December 1922. He got to know Hitler personally, and subsequently wrote to Admiral Tirpitz that Hitler and his party must be regarded as highly significant for the future of the country.[10] Wille shared the Germans' opinion that Versailles had treated them too harshly, and therefore held the German struggle for justice to be legitimate – especially as far as France was concerned. But he gave Hitler no Swiss francs.

In urgent search of funds, and after thorough preparatory work by Hess, on 31 August 1923 Hitler visited the house of Wille's son in Zurich. He was greeted by an affluent Swiss circle, a kind of German nationalist club. Clara

Wille noted in her diary entry for that day: 'Hittler [*sic*] extremely appealing. His whole body shakes when he speaks. He talks wonderfully well.'[11]

At his trial in 1924,* Hitler denied ever having been in Switzerland. But in 1942 he said over lunch one day: 'I went once to Switzerland, in 1923, had dinner in Zurich and was completely perplexed by the number of dishes. What kind of life-ideology can such a small state have?'[12] There was a powerful contrast between a rich Swiss household and the miserable state of affairs in Germany.

The next day Hitler was received by General Wille. The topics discussed must surely have included Wagner and Mathilde Wesendonck, whom the general had known as a close friend of his mother Eliza. Contact between the two men was made easier by Hitler's ability to present himself as a knowledgeable Wagnerian, although this did not completely overcome the general's scepticism. When Hitler declared as he was leaving: 'I shall strike in the autumn!' the general counselled him: 'Not so violent, young man!' And when Hitler announced: 'And the Jews have got to get out!', Wille's response was: 'If you do that, everything will start to go wrong.'[13]

His party comrade Gansser, who as usual after Hitler's appearances was supposed to collect the funds that had been pledged, was certainly able to confirm that 'Hitler's appearance at the nationalist club . . . had been an event with enormously far-reaching consequences.' But he complained bitterly about problems with the intended donors. In General Wille's case he had not been able 'to unlock funds in desirably large amounts'. For the dreadful impression made by other comrades sent to Switzerland had ruined everything! 'Their swaggering behaviour provokes people here.' Gansser felt that: 'People like D. E[ckart], H[ermann] E[sser] or S[treicher] should not be showing up here at all . . . On Swiss soil you need sophisticated types to get anywhere at all.' 'Visitors like that' had 'offended against Swiss political feelings'. 'The equation of Reich-German and Swiss-German has a most irritating effect here.' Gansser continued: 'We would have won people over almost completely to our new idea, if D. E[ckart] hadn't had one over the eight and started banging his fist on the table and behaving like a bull in a china shop. These Bavarian methods are out of place here.'[14] This kind of observation explains why Hitler so urgently needed to build up contacts

*Hitler's trial for staging the attempted 'Beerhall Putsch' in Munich in November 1923.

with 'better circles'. The failure of his Swiss visit may have been what finally impelled him to approach the Wagner family. He would be able to get at the rich yield of Switzerland (and elsewhere) only with the aid of the right class of intermediary and foreign contacts.

In times of unemployment, hunger and massive loss of capital, the radical nationalist groups always shouted louder, calling for the advent of a 'strong man' and the overthrow of the hated Weimar Republic. Hitler was well aware of these links, and in 1922 he remarked to his supporter Ernst Hanfstaengl: 'People are still having it much too good. They'll only come to us when things get really bad.'[15]

Meanwhile, almost all building work had been halted because of inflation, and factories and businesses closed. Producers were charging 10 million marks for a litre of milk; and shortly afterwards, a billion. There was not enough paper to keep up with the demand for new banknotes. Local authorities issued vouchers or printed emergency notes. Even minimal support for the starving and homeless was beyond the means of the impoverished state, and had to be abandoned.

In this climate, the previously feuding nationalist paramilitary groups and Freikorps banded together in the Deutscher Kampfbund (German Combat League) and prepared to fight the 'red' government in Berlin. On 1 and 2 September 1923 they appeared before their supporters, in the presence of Ludendorff and Prince Ludwig Ferdinand of Bavaria, at the first 'German Day', held in Nuremberg.

Soon afterwards Hitler took over political command of the Combat League, at thirty-four a big step forward in his career. Promising rumours began to circulate about the imminence of a right-wing putsch along the lines of Mussolini's, starting in the 'centre of law and order', Bavaria, and ending with a 'march on Berlin'. As a tribune of the people, the 'saviour from Communism', legitimated by the cheers of the people, Hitler was already encouraging his followers to call him 'the Führer' or 'our Duce'. Opposed to the hunger and misery of the 'red democracy', the ideal of a nationalist, 'German' Führer-state was proclaimed, and was well received in Wahnfried. Cosima thought that the Italians seemed to 'possess a statesman-like personality in Mussolini. Everything you hear about him indicates strength, and he will surely remember what Germany has done for Italy.'[16]

Further 'German Days' followed, including one in Bayreuth. Hitler gave an address on the evening of 17 September to local functionaries, among them no doubt the head of the Bayreuth Nazis, Ebersberger (factotum at Villa Wahnfried), in the party's regular public house. Hitler stayed at the Hotel Anker, where he signed the guestbook, went for a walk in the as yet unfamiliar town, was driven out to the Hermitage Palace, and, according to the *Oberfränkische Zeitung* (Upper Franconian Newspaper), was the object of general attention and expressions of appreciation. Everywhere he went he was greeted with cries of 'Heil'. When he departed at 9 p.m. a 'large crowd' had gathered in front of the hotel. 'Accompanied by tumultuous greetings of "Heil" and flowers thrown by the crowd, Hitler drove in an open car down Richard Wagner Street, which was lined with a guard of honour, towards Nuremberg.'[17] He did not go to Wahnfried.

Meanwhile, inflation continued apace: by 24 September 1923 one gold mark was worth 35 million paper marks.[18] On 26 September passive resistance to the French occupation of the Ruhr had to be broken off, 'because to continue would undoubtedly have led to total collapse'. It was painfully humiliating for Germany, and a confession of impotence. Right-wing parties seized upon the opportunity of this 'surrender' to further inflame popular feelings. However, the mass meetings that Hitler planned to hold in Bavaria under the slogan 'down with the Ruhr traitors!' were banned by the government. A state of emergency was declared throughout the Reich.

On the day when the newspapers were full of the news of the end of the Ruhr action, the nationalistic *Oberfränkische Zeitung* exhorted the citizens of Bayreuth to welcome the participants in the 'German Day': 'Come on then, Bayreuthers . . . revive once more the spirit of 1914 . . . fly the black, white and red flag [of imperial Germany], for which your sons gladly went to their deaths.' The great objective must be a proud Greater Germany, in place of this land brought low by the 'shameful Treaty of Versailles'. 'In the hour of national need' it was up to Bavaria to spearhead the country's fight for freedom. On that day, 28 September 1923, a dollar was worth 142 million marks.[19]

On the eve of the 'German Day', the paramilitary units assembled to hear the opening speeches. Mayor Albert Preu assured them that, 'especially for Bayreuth, an old town with a world reputation as a centre of art and the home of Wagner', it was an honour to be chosen for this 'German Day'. 'It is the spirit of Siegfried that we need, so that, like our Master, Richard Wagner, who triumphed over all hostile forces, we can once more achieve respect in the world.'[20] The Bechsteins had travelled from Berlin for the occasion.

During that night, the nationalistic Bavarian government under Gustav von Kahr ordered the disbanding of all Social Democratic security units, and confiscated all weapons belonging to SPD members, even when they held gun-licences. The police carried out dawn searches of Social Democrats' homes, and of the editorial and printing premises of the local SPD newspaper. Its reaction was to ask bitterly: 'why are these units being disbanded, when they exist only to resist attacks on the national and Bavarian constitutions, in other words to defend the constitutions, while other organizations are ignored although their aim is the opposite?'[21] The Bavarian government acted as the protector of the 'German Day'. The nationalists were free to stoke up hatred of the Republic without fear of a backlash from the SPD. The prohibited black, white and red flag of the Republic's opponents flew above the town hall.

Hitler arrived shortly before midnight at the station, where his supporters awaited him, and shook the small town out of its slumbers with a band accompanied by raucous bawling. Supporters gathered in front of the Hotel Anker: 'But,' reported the disappointed Bayreuth nationalist newspaper, 'hopes that Hitler might appear at the window and address the crowd were not fulfilled.'[22]

On the Sunday morning all participants marched 'briskly . . ., mostly wearing smart uniforms and medals, decorated with flowers and oak leaves', to an open-air church parade. 'Siegfried Wagner stood at the foot of the drive at Villa Wahnfried, and was greeted with vigorous "Heils",' as was the ailing Chamberlain, 'who sat at the open ground-floor window of his villa and waved at the passing procession'. By now, if not before, it was clear that the doors of the Houses of Wagner and Chamberlain stood wide open to Hitler.

Then the pompous ceremonial unfolded, beginning with the consecration of nationalist flags. In the afternoon about 6,000 men marched through the town with flags flying, accompanied by others on horseback. They were 'greeted with cheers and shouts of "Heil", and flowers strewn from windows'. By the Spitalskirche (Church of the Infirmary), with bells tolling, there was an act of remembrance for the dead of the World War. At the parade on Palace Square a girls' detachment from the 'Young Bavarian' movement, dressed in blue and white (Bavarian colours) and in black, white and red, provided a guard of honour.

The high point of the evening was Hitler's first public address in Bayreuth, held in the overfull former riding hall of the margraves. In the account given by the *Oberfränkische Zeitung*: 'He described the depths of Germany's misfortune, and why we had fallen so low. Everywhere, he said, you heard: "It cannot go on like this"; everyone was waiting for the day of redemption. The only thing that made it possible for us to continue was the hope of liberation.' The way to deliverance was 'replacing the system of parliamentary majorities with the authority of a personality . . . Nobody should be a German citizen except those who are and feel German, and everyone else should go to Moscow.' 'What we need in Germany,' he said, 'is not 10 million academics or diplomats, but 10 million soldiers!'[23]

The SPD newspaper expressed surprise that on this occasion Hitler did not fulminate against the Jews, but left that entirely to his comrade Julius Streicher. As recently as March 1923, an aggressively anti-Semitic speech by Streicher had caused a fracas between Right and Left in Bayreuth. The clash had almost reached civil war proportions, raging on for six hours before motorized police with machine guns had managed to restore order.[24] The commotion created a good deal of publicity for the NSDAP. But many citizens were repulsed by the inflammatory speeches and the fighting, among them Winifred Wagner, who for the rest of her life never concealed her loathing of Streicher. In the town of Richard Wagner, then, Hitler struck the pose of the passionate, idealistic champion of his Fatherland, thus bringing out a positive contrast between himself and his aggressive, uncouth and thuggish party comrade.

The SPD newspaper angrily described the side-effects of the 'German Day'. Onlookers wearing republican badges had been beaten up by Nazis, and 'instead of arresting the aggressors, the police had taken the victims into custody'. The paper exhorted its readers: 'Do not follow gamblers like Ludendorff and Hitler . . . Do not fall for mass suggestion.'[25]

After his speech Hitler rushed straight off to see Chamberlain, with Ebersberger following on close behind. It is a myth that he knelt to kiss the hand of the man he had idolized since his early years in Vienna. But there is no doubt that Hitler made an overwhelmingly good impression on the invalid. From then on, Chamberlain spoke enthusiastically about him, calling him, in a long letter of 7 October 1923, 'the awakener of souls from sleep and lethargy', and stressing that after Hitler's visit he had for once enjoyed 'a long, refreshing sleep', such as he had not known since his illness had begun in August 1914, for 'the real awakener is also the bringer of repose'. He wrote: 'You are not at all the fanatic I have had described to me'; in fact, he was the opposite, for 'you warm people's hearts', and he proclaimed that 'with you all parties disappear, consumed by the flame of love for the

Fatherland'. He even resorted to a Goethe allusion, telling Hitler that 'in the sense of cosmos-forming powers, he counted Hitler among those who build and not among the violent'.

Chamberlain went on to vilify the parliamentary system: 'I hold its prevalence to be the greatest misfortune; it can only lead again and again to a morass.' Hitler had given him new hope for 'Germanness': 'Bringing forth a Hitler at its greatest hour of need is a sign that Germany is alive.' He closed with: 'May God protect you!'[26] Stolzing-Cerny wrote to Eva Chamberlain: 'Hitler was childishly pleased by the letter.'[27]

From then on, the Nazis cast the meeting in the mould of a historic moment: 'Adolf Hitler and Houston Stewart Chamberlain clasped hands. The great thinker, whose writings went with the Führer on his journey and laid the intellectual foundations of the Nordic German world-view, the genius, seer and herald of the Third Reich, felt that through this simple man of the people Germany's destiny would achieve a glad fulfilment.'[28]

HITLER'S BID FOR POWER

Siegfried and Winifred had not heard Hitler's speech, but learned about it from Ebersberger, and they knew how enthusiastic Chamberlain was about the visit. Thus prepared, the 26-year-old Winifred went the same evening – without Siegfried, who was otherwise engaged – to the Anker, where the Bechsteins were holding a reception in Hitler's honour. 'My youthful enthusiasm knew no bounds at that time, and A.H. must have really enjoyed it, because he accepted my invitation to breakfast the next day at Wahnfried.'[29]

So it was that on 1 October 1923 Hitler, 'full of awe' as Winifred put it, set foot for the first time in Villa Wahnfried. The Chamberlains were present, too, and of course the children: Wieland six, Friedelind five, Wolfgang four and Verena just three years old. Hitler met Siegfried, the son of the Master, and according to Winifred 'was moved by the sight of everything that had a direct connection with R.W. – the downstairs living-rooms with his desk, the grand piano, pictures, library etc. etc.' The 'saviour of Germany', celebrated by the masses the day before, appeared in Wahnfried in the guise of a reverential and knowledgeable Wagnerian. He was modest, had good manners, and showed how deeply impressed he was. He recalled his youth in Linz and what a great impression *Lohengrin* at the Linz Landestheater had made upon him as a boy. At the time he had even wanted to become an opera singer.[30]

Unusually for him, he did not just hold forth in monologues, but took an interest in the Wagner family's problems, its concerns about the 'theft of *Parsifal*', the forthcoming tour of America, the laborious revival of the Festival. Winifred recalled that finally, 'after an extraordinarily lively conversation . . . in his spontaneous way', and with a cordial laugh, Siegfried had put his hands on the shoulders of Hitler, twenty years younger than himself, exclaiming (and using the familiar 'du' form of address): 'Do you know, I like you!'[31] Like Chamberlain, Siegfried was 'taken with A.H., in that extremely modest but very definite way of his, and soon offering to be on 'du' terms with him'.[32]

The Wagners then escorted their guest down to the grave of the Master and left him there alone. When he came back to the house, he reportedly promised: 'If I should ever have any influence over events, I shall ensure that Parsifal is returned to Bayreuth.'[33]

Hitler had carefully staged his visit to Wahnfried. It came at a moment when he was thought of as somebody special, the future 'saviour of Germany' that everyone craved, and had a leading position among the German nationalist paramilitaries. There was an element of consecration of his plans in his timing: he came to Wahnfried just before his putsch attempt and the expected breakthrough to power. As the faithful will go on a pilgrimage before making some momentous decision, so Hitler obtained the blessing of Chamberlain and of the dead Master. It is entirely credible that he was still enthusing in 1942 in his 'Wolf's Lair' wartime headquarters: 'When I entered Wahnfried for the first time, I was so moved!'[34]

Even after 1945, Winifred still constantly stressed her recollection that Hitler had made a 'very cultivated impression', and had shown himself to be a 'highly gifted personality with wide interests, and above all a Wagner enthusiast and connoisseur'. The family hoped that 'he would one day turn out to be a keen and powerful sponsor of the Festival'.[35] In retrospect, Winifred tried to explain the enormous impact of Hitler's visit by reference to conditions at the time: 'But, dear God, you'd have felt just the same.' She cited the great misery after 1918: 'Such a depression had descended on the whole of Germany, and then there were these really extreme left people, real radicals, the Spartacist group . . . And then the soviet republic in Munich. That was pure anarchism.' So it had been quite natural 'that German-minded people should try to close ranks and that they somehow looked for leadership. And when this completely unknown Hitler appeared in Munich and gave his really fiery speeches and more or less promised to try to save us by creating a new national community, so that [sic] you were ready in every sense to join him.'[36]

Later on she was also fond of reading out in self-vindication Chamberlain's letter of homage to Hitler, as a 'description of Hitler with all his charisma, the way he was at the beginning of his career . . . it was during this beginning and in this state that we all got to know him at that time'. Her 26-year-old self had not been the only one to succumb to this 'absolute fascination', and 'if an old and, after all, a sick man could be so impressed, then you ought to show some understanding for the fact that much younger and far . . . less inhibited people were very strongly influenced by him'.[37] Siegfried was as enthusiastic as his wife, and wrote at the time (1923): 'Thank God there are still German men! Hitler is a splendid person, the true soul of the German people. He's got to bring it off!'[38] To Stassen he said: 'When the Führer first came to Bayreuth, as a man and a German Helferich [the name of the tenor in Siegfried's opera *Sternengebot*] he won all our hearts.' According to Stassen, Siegfried was 'from the very beginning . . . an enthusiast for the movement, expecting it to bring about Germany's awakening and renewal'. In 1923 'a pact of friendship was concluded between Hitler, Wahnfried, and Chamberlain's house'.[39]

Stolzing-Cerny, reporting on the Bayreuth 'German Day' for the *Völkischer Beobachter*, gave prominence to Hitler's visit to Wahnfried and 'the intimate melding together there of the nationalist freedom movement and the Bayreuth ideal of culture; the practical fulfilment of the renewal of the German people in the spirit of Richard Wagner'.[40]

Hitler was soon looking for an opportunity to return to Wahnfried. On one occasion he was travelling through with his party comrade Ernst Hanfstaengl, and made a stop in Bayreuth, staying overnight at the Hotel zur Post. As the Wagners were away, the visitors used the time to look around the abandoned Festival Theatre. In this 'building filled with a ghostly half-light' there still stood the set for the *Flying Dutchman*, just as it had been left nine years before when the war broke out. In the midst of this 'dusty theatrical splendour from a bygone era, and under the spell of Richard Wagner', Hanfstaengl experienced 'a strangely transformed Hitler': 'the windbag whose annoying "superior" knowledge had sometimes got on my nerves in Berlin, to my surprise had changed into a grateful, attentive listener, who could not get enough of whatever I could tell him about the early years of Richard Wagner as director of the court orchestra in Dresden'. Hanfstaengl's great-grandfather Ferdinand Heine had been the costume designer for the première of the *Flying Dutchman*, and for *Rienzi*, 'facts that Hitler absorbed with profound and almost devout emotion'.[41]

Rumours of a putsch grew ever louder. There was also talk of Bavaria seceding from the Reich and restoring the monarchy under the Wittelsbachs,* a story that Winifred vigorously denied to her friend Lene, who lived in Prussia: 'a pity that you people in Berlin always see things through the wrong spectacles!' The Bavarians were

> loyal to the Reich right down to their bones, there's no word of truth in any talk of Kahr or Hitler being separatists! – It's just that they don't intend to obey *this* Reich – everything here is absolutely fine – you feel good and safe – we're not going to let Berlin spoil any of it – on the contrary, we want to give Berlin the same security! – Since yesterday, Hitler's SA [Sturmabteilung, Storm Detachment] have been under military oath – so the two things go hand in hand, and anything else you hear is a lie! – We are in a state of feverish anticipation. But I really believe everything is going to be different and better![42]

The putsch was planned to take place on the eve of 9 November 1923, the fifth anniversary of the hated Republic. The Wagners had devised something special for the following day. To celebrate what they confidently expected to be Hitler's successful seizure of power, they had arranged a concert in Munich at the Odeon near the Feldherrnhalle, officially under the auspices of the German Women's Richard Wagner Association. Winifred commented twenty years later: 'November 8 was supposed to be the prelude to the national revolution and revival.' To celebrate the victory, 'a big gala concert had been planned for Munich'.[43] She said elsewhere that Siegfried was supposed to 'conduct the concert, and went with me to the rehearsals in Munich'.[44]

It was, of course, only the initiated who could work out what the programme was intended to celebrate. The high point of the evening would have been the first performance of Siegfried's symphonic poem *Glück* (Luck/Happiness). By way of explanation he intended to read out a long

---

*The Wittelsbachs were the former ruling house of Bavaria, which came to an end in 1918 when King Ludwig III of Bavaria fled at the outbreak of revolution.

text, whose content was as follows (although this is a highly simplified version): the goddess Fortuna flies down to Earth in order to bestow her favours on the most worthy. She rejects the first contenders because they desire minor blessings such as wealth, comfort, love or wisdom. And then at last 'she spies warriors riding out into the world on fiery steeds. She calls out "Hail, bold fellows! Whither does your path take you?" "We are riding forth to do battle! The enemy wants to steal from us what we hold most sacred! He shall not succeed!"' Thereupon 'the goddess rejoices: "Hail to you! You are the chosen ones! . . . To him who thinks not of himself, but lives and fights for ideals, shall my blessing be given."'[45] Amidst trumpet fanfares the piece concludes with the message that 'true happiness' is 'the deed that brings blessings to mankind'.

Glück was intended as a tribute to the triumphant 'redeemers of Germany', Ludendorff and Hitler, and their 'seizure of power'. To remove any doubts about the interpretation of the piece, Siegfried had noted in the score the significant date on which he finished one particular section: '20.4 (!)', that is Hitler's birthday.[46] A further confirmation was supplied by Siegfried's remark to his admirer Rosa Eidam in 1923: 'My *Glück* fits Hitler and his followers so well, it's like a premonition.'[47]

The preparations for the concert were very difficult. Because of the political uncertainty, many singers cancelled their engagement. Winifred therefore wrote on 20 October to Hugh Walpole on Siegfried's behalf, asking him to persuade Lauritz Melchior to appear in the concert. Naturally, she thought privately that 'if M. is willing to perform, then perhaps he (Walpole) might come along too . . . Fidi is gradually becoming very reasonable about our friendship and has agreed to let me stay on a few days longer in Munich than him, if I want to . . . Now I'm just crossing my fingers that Hugh will come.'[48] Her hopes were to be dashed. Melchior accepted, but came without Walpole.

On 8 November Siegfried and Winifred set off for Munich. They stayed with friends, and passing through the Maximilianstrasse next morning they were astonished to be asked for identification papers. They were told that the national revolution had just been proclaimed in the Bürgerbräukeller (Beer Hall). Winifred later recalled that 'public buildings had been occupied without incident, and law and order prevailed everywhere'.[49] Swastika flags hung from many windows. The putsch seemed to have succeeded.

On the evening of 8 November Hitler with his armed troops had broken up an address to the nation by Kahr and the Bavarian government in the

Bürgerbräukeller. He declared that both the Bavarian and the Reich governments had been removed, and 'the army and the regional police are already coming out on our side, flying the swastika flag', which clearly was not true. He invited Kahr to become head of state in place of the Wittelsbachers; Ernst Pöhner was to be Minister-President with dictatorial powers, and Hans von Seisser Minister of Police. Ludendorff was designated to command the 'national army' in the 'march on Berlin'. Hitler reserved for himself the office of Reich Chancellor.

Kahr agreed to these demands, giving his word of honour, and Hitler felt that victory was his. The SA were already wrecking the premises of the SPD newspaper, the *Münchner Post*. In the town hall the SPD mayor and all SPD and Communist councillors had been taken hostage. Above the town hall on the Marienplatz Hess ran up the swastika flag. But, as Winifred described it, 'when we went out into the street, we noticed a strange tension everywhere. Big yellow posters had been put up, saying that Kahr, Lossow and Seisser had only pretended to go along with the announcement from the Bürgerbräukeller, and that Hitler and his followers were guilty of high treason.'[50] There was great uncertainty.

Nevertheless, on 9 November at about 11.30 a.m., 2,000 putschists in lines twelve abreast, flags waving, singing 'Deutschland über Alles', and led by Ludendorff and Hitler, set out from the Bürgerbräukeller along the Isar Heights into the city, accompanied by supporters shouting 'Heil', to move upon the district army headquarters in the Ludwigstrasse, and join up with their colleagues there under Ernst Röhm. They brushed aside the first police barrier, and arrived at the Marienplatz and the town hall, where speakers were addressing the crowds. Winifred remembers: 'On the ninth we found ourselves in the crush around the Feldherrnhalle – A.H. told us later that he had spotted us both from the Town Hall.'[51]

Kahr had ordered heavily armed police to be posted in the narrow Residenzstrasse close to the Feldherrnhalle to suppress the putsch by force. In an exchange of fire lasting a minute, sixteen putschists and three policemen died, and two other putschists were killed simultaneously in shooting at the army headquarters.[52] 'Towards noon we got . . . into a mass of people that was being broken up with rifle butts. Early in the afternoon we got news of the events at the Feldherrnhalle, together with the rumour that Ludendorff was dead and Hitler seriously wounded.'[53] There was no reliable information. All public events were cancelled, including the Wagners' concert. Winifred recorded later: 'I had never seen a crowd like that before or experienced such agitation. And I could not understand how a National Assembly could be announced on 8 November, and the next day Hitler and Ludendorff denounced as traitors and the events of the previous evening seen as treason.'[54]

From then on, Kahr's 'betrayal' made him the object of frenzied hatred among all Hitler supporters, including Siegfried Wagner:

> On 8 and 9 November we saw all the events in Munich at first hand. Cheering to heaven, then utterly cast down. There has never been such a shameful betrayal! Of course, pure people like Hitler and Ludendorff are not immune to this kind of contemptible act. It is impossible for a German to grasp! – And this split in the ranks of the nationalists. It makes you despair. Vanity and stubbornness, but never harmony. It plays right into the hands of the Jews and the clerics.[55]

The Wagners knew many of the putschists personally, not just those from Bayreuth, but also Röhm, Hanfstaengl, Eckart, Leu Du Moulin Eckart, the Freikorps leaders Hermann Ehrhardt and Gerhard Rossbach, Ulrich Graf and others. Looking back, Winifred thought that 'Kahr, Lossow and Seisser had deceived him [Hitler] dreadfully, and I think that whole business at the Feldherrnhalle in Munich . . . the shooting etc., all that just drove us to take his side, because we thought that was an unacceptable . . . reaction, at that time.'[56]

While Siegfried travelled to Berlin, Winifred returned in a highly agitated state to Bayreuth. The police there had already closed the Nazis' public-house meeting place on the morning of 9 November and arrested their local leaders. None the less, until the police stepped in, the Bayreuth Nazis staged a demonstration in the Marktplatz, wore swastikas, shouted 'Heil', and cheered their hero Hitler.

In Wahnfried there was much activity. Many visitors wanted to hear first-hand reports of the putsch: 'At the time the post-office was occupied, and there was no press reporting; a state of siege had been declared, so to speak . . . wild rumours were reaching Bayreuth.'[57] On 11 November came the news that the fugitive Hitler had been tracked down to the Hanfstaengls' house in Uffing on Lake Staffel (south of Munich), arrested and taken to Landsberg Fortress. Many of the putschists, including Hermann Goering, escaped over the nearby Austrian border. For obvious reasons, this option was not open to the Austrian Hitler: he could not expect the kind of toler-ance from his fellow-countrymen that the Bavarians had shown. It gradually emerged that two putschists from Bayreuth had been killed, one seriously wounded, and seven others were under arrest.[58]

As the party chronicler Benedikt Lochmüller noted, on 12 November the Bayreuth branch of the NSDAP asked Winifred to supply a first-hand report, and she had uttered the 'positively prophetic words': 'Believe me, in spite of everything, Adolf Hitler is the man of the future, and he will still pull the sword out of the German ash-tree'[59] – an allusion to Siegmund in *The Valkyrie*.

Winifred reported to Lene on her appearance:

> to the cheers of everybody present, I went this evening to meet the Hitler people at their pub, and when they asked me to report on the Munich events . . . I did so straight away, stood up and sounded off with my soprano trumpet!! The complete Rosa Luxemburg!! This naturally caused the greatest consternation among the *haute volée* [higher authorities], and next morning I got a mass of warnings about arrests.[60]

Later, at the de-nazification hearings, Winifred gave the evening a more innocent slant: 'Relaxing over a glass of beer I told a small number of Bayreuthers (because not many people use that bar anyway) our impression of the Munich events.'[61] And after all, she had been only twenty-six at the time, and 'a real little nobody . . . no one paid any attention to me at that time. I stood quite modestly in the background at the time, just a wife and mother.'[62] Later still, by contrast, in a letter written in old age to her political soulmate Gerdy Troost, she saw the whole episode as positively bathed in glory, and described the evening 'in the local party pub, Lieb's in the Kanzleistrasse, where I stood on the table to report!!!!! During the day I had been out distributing leaflets in the streets! It was just that I was young and keen then, and Siegfried gave me his approval.' He had given her *plein pouvoir*.[63]

In truth, the young woman who had so far remained in the background now stepped forward into public view, and wrote enthusiastically to Lene: 'For me the 9th of November opened up a completely new field of activity; passionate commitment to Hitler and his ideas.'[64] From then on, she had kept in contact with Hitler's supporters 'and, wherever I could, made people aware of Hitler and his significance'. He had been 'silenced with the greatest terror, but he can never be eradicated, his roots go too deep'.[65] She was extremely angered by critical reports, like the leading article in the politically more or less neutral *Bayreuther Tagblatt* on 12 November. It compared the failed putsch to 'a bandit farce' set in the Abruzzi mountains, and carried out 'by children or by childish minds'. 'For it is mad to think that from Munich you could displace the Reich government in Berlin and establish a new one there. Only political infants could get up to such a prank.'[66]

That evening Winifred happened to meet the author of these words, Georg Spitzer. Going up to him, she asked him 'in a conspicuously loud voice', 'Herr Spitzer, why is your attitude to Hitler always so hostile?' Spitzer was taken aback, since he did not know of any links between Wahnfried and Hitler. As he later recollected, Winifred even turned up in his office the next day and tried to persuade him 'that Hitler's programme really was the right one for Germany, and I would be wrong to go on . . . opposing this man'.[67] But as the editor remained unconvinced, she never again had a good word to say for the paper, and even years afterwards she held that 'the *Bayreuther Tagblatt* pretends to be right-wing, is run by a Centre Party man, subsidized by Jews, and trims its sails before the wind. (In November 1923 they were particularly nasty!)'[68]

On the same day, 12 November, new rates of unemployment benefits came into force: men over twenty-one got 135 billion marks a week, women 48 billion, and children 40 billion. A newspaper cost 13 billion.[69] Many local authorities could no longer afford to pay even this meagre rate of subsistence. Starving people besieged the inadequate soup kitchens; bakeries and butchers' shops were broken into. More and more died of starvation, especially children. On 14 November 1923 a dollar was worth 837,900,000,000 marks.

Winifred's commitment to Hitler was given such prominence that rumours soon started circulating about an affair between the two. She defended herself in an open letter, and in doing so made herself the spokesperson of the Wagner family: 'for years and with ever-increasing involvement and sympathy we have been following the constructive work of Adolf Hitler, this German man who, full of a burning love for his Fatherland, subordinates his life to his idea of a purified, united Greater Germany'. She continued:

Everyone in Bayreuth knows that we enjoy friendly relations with Adolf Hitler . . . His personality has made a profound and moving impression on us, as it does on everybody who meets him, and we have come to understand how such a simple, physically slight person should be capable of commanding such power. That power is rooted in the moral strength and purity of the man, who works tirelessly and selflessly for an idea that he knows is right, and that he attempts to put into action with all the fervour and humility of a divine mission. Such a man, who stands so unconditionally for what is good, must be able to inspire people, captivate them, and fire their imagination with self-sacrificial love and devotion to his person. I admit frankly that we too are under the spell of this personality, and that we too, who were behind him in happier times, will now stand by him in his hour of need.[70]

At this point, when Winifred was penning such encomiums for Hitler, she had met him in person only twice: once at the Bechstein reception in Berlin, and the second time when he visited Wahnfried. The sudden political commitment of Richard Wagner's daughter-in-law caused such a sensation that the head of the Upper Franconia regional government called in the leader of the Bayreuth NSDAP, Ebersberger, and gave him 'the directive' that 'if Frau Winifred Wagner continued to make anti-government pronouncements at public meetings, he would have to take her into custody'. But, as Ebersberger proudly put it, 'Winifred went on declaring in public that the day would come when everyone would believe in Hitler.'[71] The government were putting the Wagners under police surveillance for 'announcing their loyalty and support for the leader of the NSDAP, Adolf Hitler, and thereby giving sufficient grounds for suspicion of anti-state activity'.

According to Ebersberger, Siegfried was of one mind with Winifred: 'nothing could prevent them both from openly and courageously professing their faith in Hitler and his movement'. Siegfried had 'recognized in Hitler the future saviour of Germany from the most profound degradation . . . So we can justifiably call Siegfried Wagner one of the earliest champions of the Führer . . . He remained faithful to him until his death.'[72] Neither Siegfried nor Chamberlain had any notion of reining Winifred in. On the contrary; Siegfried said 'my wife fights like a lioness for Hitler! Magnificent!'[73]

Shortly after the Hitler putsch, by 15 November 1923, the first stage of the currency reform was at last producing some stability in an economy that was, admittedly, extremely feeble. One billion in the old currency now became one new 'Rentenmark'. For Cosima this devaluation of the currency put the final seal on the loss of her considerable fortune. The laboriously collected donations to the Bayreuth German Festival Foundation had also practically disappeared with depreciation. But despite all his worries, Siegfried visited the badly wounded Goering in hospital in Innsbruck and lent him a significant sum of money, against a promise of repayment as soon as possible.[74]

To finance the 1924 Festival, Siegfried once again had to motivate Wagnerians to contribute. Immediately after the currency reform he undertook a month-long fund-raising tour to Czechoslovakia and Austria, organized by the local Wagner societies. In these societies outside Germany the tight inter-meshing of Wagnerian ideology, aggressive German nationalism and anti-Semitism was particularly apparent. It was precisely in those German-speaking territories banned by the Versailles Treaty from merging with Germany that the Pan-German idea, invoking Wagner, was very much alive, offering a vision of uniting all Germans in a Pan-Germany or Greater Germany.

'Richard Wagner's only son', as the newspaper announcements always called him, gave lectures on this tour. He talked about his father, his mother and his grandfather Liszt, and showed slides of the Festival Theatre, Villa Wahnfried and his four children. In these circles he naturally also had to report on the events of the Munich putsch. 'I spent three weeks in Czechoslovakia,' he wrote to Rosa Eidam, 'i.e. naturally among the Bohemian Germans, who are much better Germans than most Germans in the Reich. I gave lectures in 12 different places and finished with a concert in Karlsbad ... The local National Socialists gave me a wreath with a swastika! People are showing their colours openly now.'[75]

The next stop was Graz, whose municipal theatres were soon to become notable for demanding proof of 'German descent', and a certificate of bap-tism, when advertising for a new director.[76] The most prestigious Wagner Society in Austria was the University Richard Wagner Society in Vienna, which perceived its aim as 'to free German art from adulteration and Judaizing'. As early as 1883 the founder of the society, the Pan-German leader Georg Ritter von Schönerer, venerated like a prophet by Hitler, deliv-ered a eulogy for the recently deceased Wagner in which he justified excluding Jews from membership on the grounds that 'We German national-ists regard anti-Semitism as a basic pillar of the nationalist outlook, and therefore as the greatest national achievement of the century.'[77]

One of these combative Austrian Wagnerians was the writer Max von Millenkovich, who declared that 'a man like Adolf Hitler, whose strivings and destiny we have been following, became for us more and more the embodiment of everything that we ourselves, between presentiment and insight, have yearned and striven for'. According to Millenkovich, who also wrote for Hitler's *Völkischer Beobachter*, there was 'no chattering about art and poetry' at the meetings of the Wagner Society, 'there were more serious things to think about . . . As in a secret order', every member was 'imbued with a sense of his duty, not just at the inn table but day and night, to strive for and contribute to the realization of our lofty aim: the realization of the Greater German concept, which for us could no longer be distinguished from allegiance to national socialism.'[78] With his personal connections to the House of Wagner, Hitler could always call upon the network of Wagner societies when necessary.

HITLER IMPRISONED

Two weeks after the putsch, on 23 November 1923, both the NSDAP and the KDP were banned and dissolved. The next day Chamberlain publicly declared himself for the prisoner Hitler: the *Oberfränkische Zeitung* reprinted his tribute of October, which, with its final sentence originally referring to the forthcoming putsch, had now acquired a new relevance: 'May God protect you.'[79] On 1 December a cover organization for the NSDAP was founded, called the Bayreuth German Block, also known as the German League, officially an alliance of all right-wing parties with the declared object of 'the internal and external liberation of German people of Aryan-Teutonic descent'.[80] Ebersberger was elected chairman. It is said that members of the Wagner family took part in the founding ceremony; probably Eva Chamberlain and Daniela Thode.[81]

On the same day Winifred sent out copies of another Chamberlain letter for like-minded friends and acquaintances to sign. It consisted of a declaration of solidarity addressed to the prisoner Hitler, awaiting trial:

> We cherish more keenly than ever our love for you, our trust in the purity of your being and our faith in the power of your cause to triumph; and we recognize it as a sign from God that both you and our other leader, the noble hero Ludendorff, strode unscathed through the fire aimed at you; with this almost miraculous protection Providence has clearly shown that it still has need of you both for great things!

It appears that the letter was ultimately signed by some 1,000 Hitler sympathizers; the first signatures were those of the Chamberlains, Siegfried, Winifred and Hans von Wolzogen.[82]

On the same day, 1 December, Winifred also wrote a personal letter to the prisoner. She addressed him as 'Verehrter, lieber Herr Hitler' (that is, first formally, then more familiarly). She encloses the libretto of Siegfried's opera *Schmied von Marienburg*: 'If this little book can help you through some long hours, then it will have done its duty.' In Berlin, she continued, she and Siegfried would be staying 'with our mutual friends B[echstein] – you know that you will be present with us in spirit! Devotedly, Your Winifred Wagner.'[83]

Der Schmied von Marienburg was set in the time of the greatest crisis of the Teutonic Order, after its defeat in the Battle of Tannenberg against Poland and Lithuania in 1410, followed by a struggle for survival on the part of the Knights of the Order under Heinrich von Plauen, and the fight to shore up their dominance in the east. When Heinrich is arrested and imprisoned, their decline begins. Aside from the embellishment of a love story foregrounded in the opera, the parallels with Hitler's imprisonment are evident.

On 6 December Winifred told her friend Lene that she had already written the prisoner of Landsberg three letters, and had sent him 'a fantastic parcel with a woollen blanket, a jacket, socks, foodstuffs, books etc.'. She had received first-hand information about Hitler from two visitors to Landsberg: the author Count Richard Du Moulin Eckart and Josef Stolzing-Cerny. Hitler had been made 'so apathetic and depressed by all these terrible events . . . that he believed only his death could breathe new life into the movement. That is why he drank only water for fourteen days.' But Ludendorff had uttered powerful advice, 'to hold out in spite of all the forces against him'.[84]

As a matter of fact, the prisoner of Landsberg was doing splendidly. With his friend and secretary Hess, he occupied a suite of rooms which, according to Hanfstaengl, 'were more like a shared apartment'. The warders treated him with 'extreme respect, some of them even secretly greeting him with a "Heil Hitler", and allowed him every possible privilege, including the unrestricted receipt of all kinds of charitable gifts'. His quarters looked like a delicatessen: 'There were fruit and flowers, wine and other alcohol, hams, sausages, cakes, boxes of pralines and many other things.'[85]

The Wagner women tried to outdo each other in their display of loyalty to Hitler. After Winifred's performance in November, 'Frau Privy Councillor Daniela Thode' appeared on 17 December in Lieb's, the party's regular public house – by then under police surveillance – to report on her trip to Munich, where she had visited her fellow-Bayreuther Max Sesselmann, wounded in the putsch and now in hospital. The Upper Franconian authorities recorded that: 'Apart from Bayreuth, where in particular the female members of "Wahnfried" indulge in what is nothing less than a Hitler cult, in Bamberg "loyal German" ladies had been organizing so-called tea parties, to cultivate among themselves a mood hostile to the present state order, and to nourish their enthusiasm for Hitler and his supporters.'[86] The most generous patroness was Helene Bechstein. She provided Hitler with a gramophone which had 'a softened, subdued' tone, together with records: waltzes, military marches and 'Schmerzen' (Suffering) from Wagner's *Wesendonck Lieder*.[87]

Elsa Bruckmann, née Princess Cantacuzène, the aesthetically minded spouse of Chamberlain's publisher, had never previously met Hitler, whom she revered. All the same, she caught a train from Munich to Landsberg, taking three exhausting hours to complete the journey. 'And my heart was pounding at the thought of thanking face to face the man who had awakened me and so many others, and shown us once more the light in the darkness and the path that would lead to light.' She had to wait two hours in the prison corridor, until the warder let her in to see the prisoner for twelve minutes. When Hitler, 'in Bavarian costume and with a yellow linen jacket', came forward to greet his genteel, mature lady visitor, he was 'simple, natural, a cavalier, with a clear gaze!' Elsa Bruckmann went on to say: 'He knew me through my letters, and through books and pictures I had sent to him in that desert of a fortress.' And now she brought greetings from students who had fought for him in the putsch, but also from their mutual friend Chamberlain. She assured the prisoner that 'deep loyalty awaited him upon his release – loyalty to the last breath'.[88] She made the arduous journey three times. As he did during his days in Vienna, Hitler once again exhibited his talent for winning over older ladies from the upper echelons of society with his courteous, respectful manner – and for setting them to work on his behalf.

Winifred, on the other hand, did not travel to Landsberg. She wrote a good many letters to Hitler, and kept his memory of her fresh by sending him 'thoughtful gifts', as Hitler's half-sister Angela Raubal reported: 'The loyalty shown to him at this time especially was touching. Just ahead of me, for example, there was a Count with him, who gave him a Christmas packet from Villa Wahnfried.'[89] This was Du Moulin Eckart, whose son had also taken part in the putsch.

Before Christmas 1923 Winifred set up 'a collecting point for presents to send to Landsberg'. Being practical, she asked the prison director what the prisoner particularly wanted. It turned out to be writing-paper, and she later tried to defend herself on this account: 'so I sent him masses of writing-paper. And, for goodness sake, now people accuse me of supplying him with paper to write *Mein Kampf* . . . More or less accusing me indirectly of being responsible for the writing of *Mein Kampf*.'[90]

At a time when preparations for the reopening of the Festival in 1924 had imposed the utmost frugality upon Wahnfried, Winifred sent Ludendorff a $100 cheque, a small fortune in the crisis year of 1923. It had been signed 'by an old, loyal friend of the family, Albert Morris Bagby in New York . . . with instructions to buy something nice with it on his behalf for my four children at Christmas'. But since her children were well off, she had decided 'without a second thought' to 'send the cheque to Munich to relieve people's misery . . . with the request to give the proceeds to the suffering babies and children of those arrested'.[91]

At New Year 1924 Chamberlain published a long article in the *Grossdeutsche Zeitung* (Greater German Newspaper), once again publicly declaring his support for Hitler: 'he loves his people, he loves his German people with a passionately intense love'; he had the courage of a Martin Luther,* and drew the logical conclusion from his ideas: 'For example, it is impossible for him to share the convictions we all hold about the pernicious, indeed the deadly influence of Jewry on the life of the German people, without acting upon them. If you see the danger, then you've got to take urgent measures against it, everybody recognizes this, but nobody dares express it, nobody dares to act upon their thoughts; nobody except Adolf Hitler.' In contrast to the confusion of current politics, Hitler was 'a great simplifier . . . The simplest person can follow him all the way, he's winning the people over like a storm.' He concluded with: 'May God who sent him to us preserve him for many years to come as a blessing for the German Fatherland.'[92]

When, against expectations, the Munich Archbishop Cardinal Faulhaber failed to come out in favour of Hitler, Siegfried raged: 'The Jews paid for a new roof for Herr Faulhaber's Church of our Lady, to ingratiate themselves with him.' The Protestant Church too had failed miserably: 'there's not a single prominent minister who has raised his voice in the nationalist cause . . . Oh, if Luther were to come back now and see his feeble followers,

---

*The implication is that Hitler has the courage of his own convictions, like Martin Luther, who instigated the religious reformation of Germany in the early 16th century. Luther is famous for his saying, 'here I stand, and can do no other'.

he'd tear his hair out.' Furthermore, 'perjury and treason are declared holy, and Jews and Jesuits go forward arm in arm to eradicate Germanness . . . If the German cause should really go under, then I'll start believing in Jehovah, the God of vengeance and hatred.' Then he asked his old confidante Rosa Eidam: 'Hopefully, or surely, you too are a friend of Hitler. We got to know this glorious man here in the summer during the German Day, and we'll stay faithful to him, even if it lands us in gaol. We in Wahnfried have never been time-servers.' He apologized for the length of the letter, but 'my heart simply beats too strongly for the German cause'.[93]

A letter written by Winifred at New Year 1924 exemplified the almost religious devotion to Hitler that gripped Villa Wahnfried: 'No other man has ever played such a role in our lives as Hitler does – he must be a powerful personality – for how else can you explain such passionate reverence and dedication? Either he will rescue us, or they will allow him, delicate as he is, to perish miserably in his prison-house! But if they do – then woe to Germany!!!'[94]

CHAPTER 4

American Journey

(1924)

Siegfried Wagner needed 6–7 million marks to carry out the necessary technical and structural modernization to bring the Festival back to life. However much effort the Wagnerian money-raisers put into it, there was no way that this sum could be raised in an impoverished Germany. The only hope lay abroad, 'and particularly with the Americans, who used to be so much in evidence and who understood the significance of the Festival for the entire cultural world'. Even before the war, and then increasingly after 1921, Siegfried had a concert tour of the USA in mind. Now it seemed to be the only way out of his dilemma. Winifred's feelings were ambivalent: 'Oh dear – in one way it gives me the creeps, in another I'm drawn to it!'[1]

In preparation for the journey, and for the sake of the fee, Siegfried wrote his *Erinnerungen* (Memoirs) for an American publisher, a slim, rushed little volume lacking any clear thematic concept. A German edition appeared in 1923. Most of the book is taken up with a description of the round-the-world tour that Siegfried undertook with his friend Clement Harris in 1892. Hoping to fire American enthusiasm for Bayreuth, he did his utmost to stress the international nature of the Festival. He even criticized the 'hyper-Wagnerians' with their Germanicizing fervour, and expressed his gratitude to Wagnerians abroad for 'undertaking the pilgrimage to Bayreuth at a time when the German public was still more conspicuous for its absence than for its presence'. He singled out the Parisian *Revue Wagnérienne*, the London Wagner Society and similar societies in Bologna, Barcelona and New York.[2]

He was hoping to raise 2 millions marks from his American tour, and 'something besides for my private funds',[3] that is, conductor's fees and royalties for his works, which were on the programme at every concert. The 'family programme', with pieces by Franz Liszt, Richard Wagner and Siegfried Wagner, was called 'Music of Three Generations' in the USA. Winifred expected to be paid a fee of $2,000 a time for her talks on Bayreuth.[4] Initially planned to last three months, the American tour was to take them from the East Coast to San Francisco: 'May America provide the indispensable basis for Bayreuth, and may the German spirit triumph over Ignatius Loyola!'[5] The name of the Jesuit saint was a shorthand allusion to the usual catalogue: Jesuits, Freemasons, the *Internationale*, Jews and so on.

In autumn 1923 a contract was signed with the New York music agent Jules Daiber. There were far-reaching plans for appearances not only in the USA but also in Canada, Cuba, Mexico and South America. It was the agent's job to take care of the organization of concerts: hiring venues, seeing to the soloists' commitments, ticket sales and publicity and arranging travel and high-grade accommodation for the Wagners. He also had to hire and pay for a first-rate orchestra of sixty to ninety musicians in every venue. For this considerable undertaking he would receive a percentage of the proceeds. The firm of Steinway supported the tour and appointed a representative, Ernest Urchs, in New York, to collect and administer donations received.

To start with, twenty concerts were set up in as many cities in four weeks. If things went well they could be extended from week to week. Siegfried agreed to two hours of rehearsal per day with the orchestra of the moment.[6] He, too, admitted to having 'really mixed feelings . . . Different orchestras everywhere, hence daily rehearsals, a terrible grind. But there's nothing else for it, otherwise there'll be no Bayreuth.'[7] He complained: 'I'm suffering badly from being away from home for so long! If only we were back there already!'[8]

Winifred commented:

I'm going with him – to spare him everything that would cost him time and nerves – all the interviewers – visitors – his correspondence – the constant packing etc. etc., he's got to have someone doing the work for him, after all, and that seems the right place for me to be – to take care of him, too – in case he gets ill etc. etc. I wouldn't be able to relax for a single minute here anyway. If it comes to it, children can be looked after by somebody else – but not a husband![9]

Most of all, her perfect English would be a great help to Siegfried.

Hugh Walpole gave her advice about her talks, and provided her with a recommendation to an agent he knew. Winifred copied out his flattering reference for her friend Lene: 'In my humble opinion, Frau Wagner will make a marvellous lecturer. The moment you get to know her, you too will be enchanted by the charm and the strength of her personality. Furthermore, she is an Englishwoman raised in the traditions of Bayreuth. I may say that she is a great friend of mine, but I am not biased on that account.' She had been 'terrifically pleased with it', wrote Winifred to Lene. 'I sat down . . . and worked flat out on the lecture. It's a terrific amount of work and effort . . . It will be a ton weight off my mind when I finish it.'[10]

To save on expenses, Winifred dissolved the Bayreuth household for the duration of her long absence. The four children, aged six, five, four and three, were placed with friends and affluent Wagnerians. Only Cosima and her retinue remained in Wahnfried. Daniela Thode was to be responsible for important decisions and issuing information.

On 15 January 1924 the comfortable liner *America* set sail from Bremen. As 'the only "celebrities" on board', Winifred wrote in a letter home, the Wagners sat at the captain's table and were served with delicacies not seen for years in Germany. There was some socializing, and even a fancy-dress ball, as well as storms and sea-sickness, moonlit strolls on deck, and – for the first time ever – a jazz band. Winifred's comment was: 'There are about 10 musicians [Negroes from the Philippines]. One plays the piano, one a violin, another one a kind of flute, 6 pluck lute-like instruments of different sizes. One of them, plucking strings himself, jumps around like a monkey to mark the beat. The whole thing sounds really nice – not much tune, but a lovely rhythm. The Europeans do blasé, boring dance steps to it.'[11] Siegfried, on the other hand, was capable of holding forth over many pages about this demonic music, from which he sought to protect German youth: 'Are we so decadent that a Johann Strauss waltz doesn't appeal to our youth any more? . . . If this is what our youth are really like, then we deserve Versailles!'[12]

On 26 January 1924 the Wagners landed on Ellis Island, where they were met by friends: Wolfram Humperdinck, who was then working as assistant director for Max Reinhardt, and the singer Maria Petzl, who was giving a guest performance in New York. Their agent had meanwhile worked overtime on the publicity. Advertising leaflets spoke fulsomely of the 'musical religion of Richard Wagner'. Bayreuth, offering the best musicians and singers in the world, was no ordinary opera house, but more like a festival celebration on the Acropolis, to which visitors climbed to immerse themselves in another world, as though in 'a spiritual ecstasy'.[13]

Their arrival on American soil was a shock for the Wagners. They were astonished to find themselves facing a crowd of journalists and photographers, and headlines like: 'Winifred embezzles Festival donations for political purposes'. It was only then that they discovered what had been happening during their voyage. Bagby's $100 cheque, sent on by Winifred to Ludendorff, had been intercepted by the police and passed to the Bavarian Minister of Justice. At a session of the regional parliament in January 1924 he had produced the cheque as proof that the Wagners were handing over to the banned Nazi Party donations intended for the restoration of Bayreuth. The German newspapers had picked up the story, and the American ones had followed suit.[14] Certainly, the powerful US press was extremely well informed about the connection between the Wagner family and Hitler. Ludendorff, too, was (as Winifred told Lene) 'a red rag for the Americans, who were still very hostile to Germany and infected with pacifism'.[15]

It was reassuring to have their friend Bagby warmly welcoming them to the Waldorf Astoria, and paying the hotel bill. This must be where the short film footage was shot that shows Winifred and Siegfried signing the agent's contract. She is laughing and joking in centre-shot, and is much prettier in motion than in still pictures, while Siegfried by her side looks strained, old and tired.[16]

The first thing to do was confer with Bagby and the agent to work out a strategy for dealing with the bad press reports. In the end Bagby issued a statement that he had given Winifred the $100 for her own use and not as a contribution to the Festival. She could do what she liked with it. Then a press release was composed to appear on 2 February 1924 in the *Staatszeitung*, a German-language newspaper appearing in the USA, under the heading 'An Open Word about Bayreuth'. Contrary to all accusations, it asserted, the Wagner family had never enriched themselves through donations, for the two accounts had been kept strictly separate, and all income had reached the Festival account intact. The Wagner family had therefore never profited, but had only ever made sacrifices. War and inflation had consumed their fortune. Their hope was that America, where millions had been earned through Wagner's works, would be prepared at least in part to repay its great debt of gratitude to Richard Wagner and his Bayreuth. What was needed now was a fund-raising campaign on a suitably large scale. Siegfried did not fail to make his typical observation that a labourer in Germany today could earn in two weeks the equivalent of the annual income of the admirable Frau Cosima and the son of the Master.[17]

Bagby, the immensely rich former pupil of Liszt, invited the Wagners to his 'Bagby concert', attended every Monday morning at eleven in the Waldorf Astoria, with lunch to follow, by the most distinguished members of New York society. Siegfried found it 'deadly, but necessary in order to make contact with society'. Later they visited the Metropolitan Opera for two acts of *Der Rosenkavalier*, which elicited a sour comment from Siegfried: 'You've got to take part in everything, in order to gain support . . . Naturally, we're as sweet as honey.'[18]

In the midst of all this bustle, a traveller from Germany secretly joined up with the Wagners. Thirty-three-year-old Kurt Lüdecke was an adventurer who had made a fortune in currency dealings and who for the past two years had been organizing fund-raising for Hitler. He showed the Wagners a formal letter of accreditation from Hitler, drawn up in Landsberg on 4 January 1924. In it he was charged with 'promoting the interests of the German free-dom movement in North America, and especially raising money on its behalf'. He was asked 'initially to receive this money personally and where possible also bring it back in person'.[19] Lüdecke had previously already made contact with Mussolini on Hitler's behalf, and had also been busy in Switzerland. In short, he was acting as something like the personal foreign minister of the prisoner of Landsberg. Now, with the Wagners as intermediaries, the plan was for him to gain personal access to the automobile king Henry Ford and his money. On a previous visit to America he had got only as far as the editor-in-chief of Ford's newspaper, the *Dearborn Independent*.

Detroit was the first stop on Siegfried's concert tour, and Daiber had set up an invitation to Mr and Mrs Ford's country house there. The Wagners hoped for a healthy contribution to their funds. Admittedly, Ford was not interested in classical music, least of all in Wagner, and according to Lüdecke his taste was 'at best for hillbilly fiddlers'[20] and other kinds of folk-music. It was his wife Clara's weakness for celebrities from 'old Europe' that promised the Wagners an entrée.

At the time Ford, at sixty-three, was not only the leading car manufacturer, but one of the world's leading patrons, sponsors of art and benefactors. With a world-wide reputation as the most prominent self-confessed anti-Semite, he was an admired model for the German Right, including the

National Socialists. His book *The International Jew*, based on the fake *Protocols of the Elders of Zion*,* was already available in several editions in German translation. In the book Ford conjured up the danger of 'Jewish world dominance', and according to advertising material, painted 'a grandiose but frightening picture of the total financial enslavement of every nation on earth. This was the key to understanding the World War, the Revolution, the Peace Treaty, the League of Nations, the Dawes Plan, etc.', namely as the supposed machinations of 'world Jewry'.[21] Newspaper advertisements in Germany promoted Ford's book as a 'guide through the political confusion of our time'.[22]

Ernst Hanfstaengl held that Ford was the only American Hitler was interested in. Rudolf Hess had been deputed to make an initial contact with Ford in 1922, but did not go about it very skilfully. He began his letter: 'I am reluctant to write to a member of a nation that helped to plunge my people into misfortune, through force of arms and still more through the lying words of President Wilson. If I do write none the less, it is with the conviction that basically you no more wanted the war than the majority of Americans did, and that behind the scenes our common adversary, the Jew, brought about your enmity towards us.'[23]

A reference to Ford's book was the cue for Hess to 'point to the most successful and active anti-Semitic movement in Germany', the NSDAP, and to its Führer, who, as 'perhaps the best orator in Germany', regularly attracted between 3,000 and 7,000 people to his anti-Semitic addresses in Munich. 'That is why the Jewish press hate Munich more than any other city in Germany'. For even greater success, money was needed, a few thousand dollars to expand the *Völkischer Beobachter*, 'because that is the only way to neutralize the influence of the Jewish-Marxist daily press'. But even a few hundred dollars would be enough to 'flood the country with leaflets and organize on an even larger scale. It really is high time! With the help of emergency laws and emergency courts based on the Russian model, the Soviet Jews working behind the scenes in Berlin were getting ready to launch their final attack'.

The Protocols of the Elders of Zion were a vicious forgery originating in Russia in 1897, and purporting to be the minutes of a secret meeting of the 'Learned Elders of Zion', allegedly plotting Jewish world domination. Henry Ford believed in the authenticity of the 'protocols' and drew on their anti-Semitic slanders in his own book. The 'protocols' are still in circulation today among anti-Semitic groups.

In return for his help, said Hess, the NSDAP would distribute Ford's book in German factories: 'Perhaps you could provide us with an appropriate number of copies of the translation', for 'you know as well as we do that the Jew must be fought internationally'. Hess told Ford that he 'was not approaching you as a supplicant, but as a man facing the same enemy as you are'.[24] In fact, Ford and his campaign against the 'Hebrew kings of finance' were praised to the skies by the *Völkischer Beobachter*.[25] In autumn 1923 Hess proposed that a pamphlet issued under Ford's name should be printed for the benefit of German workers, together with excerpts from Ford's book.[26]

Now the Wagners were expected to explain to Ford, in the private surroundings of his home, the significance of Hitler's party for forging an international alliance against the Jews, and to smooth the path for generous donations. Together with Lüdicke, they took the sleeper train to Detroit on the evening of 29 January 1924. Later, whenever Winifred talked about America, she never failed to mention the shocking impact on her of Detroit, the first American city she visited after New York. It must have been particularly dismal, noisy and dirty on that January morning. However, they did find waiting for them in Statler's Hotel an invitation to an early supper at the Fords' the following day, before the concert.

First, though, Siegfried was busy with interviews. The *Detroit News* described him as a pleasant person, small in stature, who smiled a lot, smoked cigarettes, wore a bow-tie and made a rather 'un-heroic' impression. Siegfried spoke little, and about innocuous things, such as how much he liked America and the orchestra in Detroit, and so forth. He firmly refused to talk about politics: 'It's a very unpleasant topic, and I'd rather not think about it.'[27]

In the evening he was confronted by an irritating medium that was a complete novelty for him: the radio. Although Siegfried was later able to laugh about it, the interview got off to a bad start. The director of the Detroit Museum had accompanied him to the studio, firing off one witticism after another: 'Not suspecting that the microphone was already switched on, I called out to this joker, "Please go away – you're making me nervous." This exclamation was heard by 100,000 unseen listeners.' A lady wrote him an 'indignant letter' afterwards, saying 'she was very astonished that the son of Richard Wagner . . . should be nervous about broadcasting. It hardly seemed compatible with the name Siegfried.'[28]

On the afternoon of 31 January, the Wagners drove out to the Fords' country estate at Fair Lane. At first the conversation ranged over the weather and the attractions of the house, and then music, Wagner, Bayreuth, the miserable economic and social state of things, and the Communist threat in Germany. And then it turned to the question of the Jews. Henry Ford and Winifred conducted the conversation almost entirely between them. Siegfried was content to put a word in now and again.[29]

Ford repeated the constant propaganda message of his newspaper, that 'the Jews' had enormous power in America and that their influence was growing by the day. Through the *Dearborn Independent* he was trying to enlighten the American people about the 'Jewish conspiracy'. Then they talked about a favourite subject they had in common: the power of the press, by which they meant the 'Jewish' press. Ford said that if he were a politician and a crisis arose anywhere in the world, he would ban all information about it. That way, he thought, 'there could not be any more wars, because nobody would know what it was actually all about'. Without the press there would be no revolutions and no citizens' revolts, and 'politicians could carry out everything they thought was good for the people'.[30]

The subject of the Versailles Treaty was broached, no doubt in the Wagners' usual version: it was an instrument of destruction employed by international Jewry against Germany. Raising the spectre of Communism led on smoothly to the topic of Hitler, the future 'saviour of the German people' and opponent of the 'Red Menace'. Winifred was astounded that the automobile king was so well informed about events in Germany and 'knew everything about the National Socialist movement . . . The philosophy and ideas of Ford and Hitler were very similar.'[31] She was obviously unaware of Hess's energetic spade-work.

When it came to the question of contributions to Hitler, Ford forestalled Winifred; he had already supported him financially by supplying Ford cars and trucks for Hitler to sell to raise funds. When Winifred indicated that Hitler needed more funding, Ford smiled and said he was happy to go on supporting him, since he was working to free Germany from the Jews. That was the cue to mention Lüdecke, and Ford agreed to see him the next day.[32] It is not clear whether, with all this politicking, the subject of an equally impoverished Bayreuth cropped up. The Fords and the Wagners drove back together into town to the concert. Shortly before it began, Lüdecke turned up in Winifred's box: 'Her charming smile told me she had been successful.'[33]

The next day Ford received Hitler's ambassador in his office for a private discussion. The latter employed all his eloquence to persuade the potential benefactor that the Nazis were giving him the chance to earn a place in history, and that it would be worth every penny it cost him. He portrayed Hitler's eventual 'seizure of power' as a certainty. When he came to power, the first thing he would do was to implement the policies of the *Dearborn Independent*; in other words, take action against the Jews. The Nazi movement must be supported, said Lüdecke, 'not just for Germany's sake, but for that of the whole world'. He invoked the solidarity of the 'white man', read out long quotations from the *Dearborn Independent*, and asserted that the Nazis were the only really important active group in the world who had a positive programme for bringing about a new world order no longer run by Jews. All they needed was money.

But Ford did not respond to this, as Lüdecke told the Wagners. They believed it, but were very disappointed, according to Lüdecke. He praised them, as true 'Hitlerites', for having shown a sincere and unselfish desire to speed up Hitler's progress. Lüdecke saw the couple once more in New York, entering a restaurant and deep in conversation with 'two rich Jewish ladies well known for their patronage of the arts'. 'We did not speak to each other,' said Lüdecke; 'it was clearly not the right moment to take up our conversation again where we left off.'[34]

Some kind of relationship between the Wagners and Ford continued; in 1927, for example, Winifred was still hoping – in vain, as it happened – that he would make her a present of her favourite car, a two-seater Ford convertible.[35] But meanwhile Ford had begun to retreat from his anti-Semitic position, once the *Protocols of the Elders of Zion* had been proved to be a fake, and he was faced with some unpleasant lawsuits and a Jewish boycott of Ford cars. On 27 July 1927 he asked the press to publish a long apologetic article, in which he begged the Jews to pardon him, and assured them of his 'unbounded friendship'. It had a powerful effect on the public when he ordered the burning of five truck-loads of his book, *The International Jew*. The amount he paid out in compensation settlements is still unknown today.

Ford also reclaimed the copyright of the book from foreign publishers.[36] However, that did not prevent the German editor Theodor Fritsch of Hammer Publishing from constantly reissuing this popular volume in new editions. After 1933, prefaced by pictures of Hitler and Ford, it was even distributed free to schools and interested parties.[37]

Ford must secretly have continued to support, not Bayreuth, but certainly the NSDAP, on a significant scale. This could easily be disguised by supplying cars and trucks in lieu of funding. The Party newspapers paid tribute to

Ford in the most ringing tones. In October 1924 Alfred Rosenberg wrote a series of articles on the topic of 'Henry Ford as a National Socialist'. Relations were so good that on the automobile king's seventy-fifth birthday, on 30 July 1938, Hitler bestowed on him the Grand Cross of the German Order of the Eagle, 'in recognition of his pioneering achievement in making automobiles accessible for the masses'. This was the highest decoration available to foreigners. Ford was the fourth person to be so honoured; Mussolini had been the third.

Left-wing US newspapers criticized Ford sharply for accepting a decoration from Hitler. The Jewish star Eddie Cantor called Ford 'a damned fool for allowing the biggest gangster in the world to bestow an honour on him'. Ford was undaunted: 'They [the Germans] sent me this ribbon. They [the critics] say I should return it, or I'm no American. I'm going to keep it.'

Some weeks later, however, Ford felt obliged by persistent protests to make a public declaration to the effect that accepting an honour from the German people did not mean, as many seemed to think, that he was a Nazi sympathizer. Everybody who knew him knew that he loathed everything that provoked hatred.[38] But the Ford company kept up lively trading relations with the German Reich. They took out whole-page advertisements in German newspapers. In Bayreuth, however, there was disappointment over Ford's unwillingness to contribute to their cause. For example, Max Wiskott, a friend of Wahnfried, remarked that 'If Ford had come to the aid of Bayreuth in proportion to his wealth, he would have made a more lasting name for himself than one based on cars.'[39]

The Wagners knew that the success of their trip depended above all upon the great Jewish families of New York, and gladly accepted invitations from them. Among the Jewish Americans who received them most warmly and supported them was M. Baruch, who also organized the American aid agency for German children.[40]

However, Siegfried was blind to the fact that, since the headlines that had connected them to Hitler, he and his wife had been under critical observation. Affected by alcohol and fatigue, he forgot about diplomatic caution and went on saying exactly what he had always said and thought. According to an eyewitness, the journalist Joseph Chapiro, at a big dinner in New York Siegfried had lost no opportunity – and this in the democratic USA – 'to vilify the German Republic and especially Ebert, its [Social Democratic] head of state'. Furthermore, he had made 'the most scornful comments' about German artists. Of Gerhart Hauptmann, for example, regarded in

America as the greatest living German writer, he said he had no further interest in him 'since he had become the acknowledged writer of the Republic'. Chapiro continued: 'It would never end if I tried to report all the value-judgements I had the pleasure of hearing from Herr Wagner's lips in a single evening.'

Bruno Walter, at the time a visiting conductor in America, had put in a brief appearance at this dinner given in Siegfried's honour. Chapiro reported: 'No sooner had he left than Herr Wagner turned to me, as I had been sitting next to Bruno Walter, and asked me if Walter was still such a keen admirer of Kurt Eisner.' When Chapiro brushed the question aside, Siegfried remarked – forgetting his Jewish host – 'that in Munich they'd made short work of Eisner and his "Jewish-Communist gang of swine"'. When Chapiro, referring to Hitler, observed that 'in Bavaria one gang followed another', Siegfried had turned pale and asked: 'Gang? What gang are you talking about?' On being told 'the Hitler gang', the son of Wagner replied heatedly: 'You call an organization of which General Ludendorff is a member a gang?'

'That really set him off,' said Chapiro, 'it was all the fault of the "Jewish press".' He, Siegfried, happened to be present during the Hitler putsch in Munich: 'the Hitlerians had behaved impeccably and had been set upon without warning by the government troops etc. etc. Everything the National Socialists were accused of, their violence and their attacks on Jews in Nuremberg and Munich, was all invented – in short, Bavaria and Hitler's people were the victims of slander by the "Jewish press".' Finally, Siegfried regretted that the American patron Otto H. Kahn was not prepared to do anything for Bayreuth as long as the threat of pogroms was still in the air: 'If only he could be made to see that's all slander on the part of the "Jewish press".'

News of this kind of table-talk, there and elsewhere, spread like wildfire through the New York music scene. And since, according to Chapiro, '30 per cent of the New York population are Jewish, so Jews form 80 per cent of concert audiences; and that's the percentage that stayed away from the concerts.' The tour became a fiasco, and this 'in a country where people love music more than anything else, worship Richard Wagner, and put up monuments to him!' Chapiro's conclusion was that every cultured person would be glad to contribute to the preservation of Bayreuth. 'But,' he went on, 'Herr Siegfried Wagner with his swastikas and swastika-wearers was not appropriate.' Only an independent artist such as Bruno Walter, Wilhelm Furtwängler or Richard Strauss would do. The American journey of Wagner's son had done no service to Bayreuth: 'On the contrary, it has done harm to the name of German art and the reputation of German artists, whose representative he claimed to be while over there.'[41]

Looking back, Siegfried was still wondering why it was that, although they had often frequented 'Jewish circles' in America, and had been treated 'with extraordinary friendliness and courtesy . . . whenever you raised the topic of the Bayreuth Festival, they became negative'. He heard one lady ask another if she, too, was giving a donation to Bayreuth, to which the second replied: 'Can you forget your Jewish father? I can't!' Siegfried continued: 'Another prominent personality said to my wife that the Jews were maintaining an unspoken boycott of Bayreuth.'[42] To outsiders, the Wagners spoke not so much about a 'Jewish boycott' as about 'hostile propaganda' aimed at Germany, the former enemy. Winifred wrote from New York: 'On the whole we have met with a good deal of kind and friendly treatment. But it's shocking to see how hostile propaganda still fuels and sustains the anti-German mood; back in Germany, you wouldn't think this was possible.'[43] Siegfried, too, covered up the real problem and pretended there were other reasons: 'We know very well from wartime what methods are employed to prevent something that doesn't suit you.'[44]

However, the tour enjoyed some success among a different section of the population: the German societies of Baltimore, Chicago, Pittsburgh and Cleveland. Siegfried wrote proudly about St Louis: 'A big reception, all Germans (there are 300,000 Germans here with 176 societies) . . . The choral society here (1,000 singers) is taking part, singing excerpts from *Tannhäuser*, *Mastersingers*, *Flying Dutchman*, *Rienzi*. The concert is in a vast hall that holds an audience of 10,000.'[45] Donations were gladly received, but came in only sparingly.

Siegfried's health was hard pressed to cope with the rigours of the average day: long train journeys; rehearsals with new, not always very good orchestras; constant confrontations with a critical press. The orchestra players had great difficulty with Siegfried's compositions, which, unlike the popular Liszt and Wagner pieces, were completely unknown to them. They were not very willing to learn this music just for one concert, and with only one two-hour rehearsal. It did not help that there were not enough scores to go round, and that they often had to work with handwritten copies. At first the agent was prepared to make the effort to coax them along, but his interest waned at the sight of the emerging financial deficit. Only ten concerts actually took place, instead of the planned thirty or forty.

The high points of the laborious journey were two concerts in New York: one at the Metropolitan Opera that brought in a profit of $2,200, the other in the Carnegie Hall on the anniversary of Wagner's death, 13 February.[46] Altogether, the financial return on the trip was disappointing. Instead of the anticipated $200,000, only $9,552 had been deposited in the account at the Bank of Manhattan.[47] Siegfried blamed this on the 'lack of solidarity among Germans': 'Only yesterday I was saying to an acquaintance of mine that if the cause of Bayreuth had been a Jewish one, millions [of dollars] would have been forthcoming from Jews!!!!'[48] But on the other hand, 'we have eaten well, enjoyed ourselves, gained many dear friends . . . and received lots of gifts of clothes and shoes for the children'. And he added: 'Winnie is packing; she has been absolutely indispensable and invaluable to me.'[49] Siegfried was exhausted, and glad when it was all over.

On 28 March they boarded ship, heading for the Mediterranean. Winifred reported home to Bayreuth about her feelings as Ischia and then the Gulf of Naples hove into sight: 'We were as pleased as children to be back in Europe and to have left America far, far behind us.'[50] Ever since he had accompanied his father on his last Italian journeys, Siegfried had had a great sentimental affection for Italy. He spoke good Italian and loved Verdi, especially *Rigoletto*. As Winifred recalled, 'On the way back from the Festival Theatre after *Parsifal* or the *Ring* he always whistled tunes from Verdi. Naturally, everyone was surprised by that.'[51]

In Rome they met up with Siegfried's favourite nephew, Count Manfredi Gravina, and many friends. The high point of their visit was Siegfried's invitation to lunch with Prime Minister Mussolini in the Palazzo Venezia. This was probably organized by Lüdecke, more or less in return for the introduction to Ford. On the difference between Mussolini and Hitler, Siegfried said: 'It is all a matter [with Mussolini] of will, strength, brutality almost. A fanatical gaze, but without the power of love as with Hitler and Ludendorff. Latin and Teutonic! We talked mainly about ancient Rome. He has something Napoleonic about him. A wonderfully true breed!'[52] Stassen, on the other hand, said that while Mussolini had made a great impression on him, 'he liked Hitler with his blue eyes even better'.[53]

Hardly was Siegfried back in Bayreuth before he was expressing anger again at the state of affairs in Germany, and thinking that America was really not so bad after all: 'America appealed to me greatly, and I am finding it hard to adjust to the German atmosphere of pettiness, spitefulness, envy, joylessness! No generosity!' He even maintained that he was treated better by the American press than the German: 'Over there they've simply got better manners and more respect for artistic achievement. I've had enough of Germany! If it weren't for Wahnfried and the Festival, there would be nothing to stay here for. – Still, you've just got to stick it out and do what you can to save the German spirit from total destruction.'[54]

Winifred kept up her new contacts overseas through a lively correspondence.[55] From the USA came many gifts in kind: coffee, chocolate, sugar, preserves, children's clothes and toys, and not least the cigarettes that both Siegfried and Winifred loved so much. As a result, the extended family were able to live relatively well, despite hard times.

CHAPTER 5

The Festival under the Swastika

(1924–7)

HITLER'S LOYAL ELECTIONEERS

Even while they were still in Italy, the Wagners made an effort to inform themselves about Hitler's trial. Winifred wrote to Lene from Rome: 'we're reading the proceedings of the whole Hitler trial, which have now appeared in book form. What splendid people he and Ludendorff are!'[1] The verdict had been announced on 1 April 1924, and it was amazingly lenient. On the charge of high treason Hitler received a sentence of only five years' imprisonment, and even then, with a period of probation, he would be released as early as the end of 1924. Above all, he would not be deported from Germany, since the Austrian authorities refused to accept him.*

Politically, the trial had done him no harm at all; in fact, he had profited from it. The judges had given him ample opportunity to make propaganda speeches, and the nationalist papers had published them. A plethora of new Hitler books appeared; for example, a posthumous volume by Dietrich

---

*Presumably, he was viewed simply as a troublemaker, not wanted in Austria. The Austrian Federal Chancellor, Ignaz Seipel, personally refused to take him back, arguing that Hitler's service in the German army incurred loss of Austrian citizenship. These legal grounds were dubious. Hitler did not finally relinquish his Austrian citizenship until 30 April 1925, but did not become a German national until 1932. In the meantime, he was stateless.

Eckart, *Der Bolschewismus von Moses bis Lenin* (Bolshevism from Moses to Lenin), the record of an alleged dialogue between Hitler and Eckart. In 1924 Ernst Hanfstaengl brought out a *Hitler Song Book*, with five *völkisch* (nationalist) songs written and composed by himself, with scores for voice and piano, including 'Germany First' or 'The Hitler-Medicine' and '*Völkisch, völkisch, völkisch* you must be!' Hitler's 'personal photographer', Heinrich Hoffmann, and his Bayreuth party comrade Max Sesselmann put out *Deutschlands Erwachen in Bild und Wort* (Germany's Awakening in Words and Pictures), a history of the NSDAP so far. What the Wagners read about the trial served only to reinforce their admiration for Hitler.

When they returned to Bayreuth six weeks before the start of rehearsals for the Festival, the campaign for the Reichstag elections set for the beginning of May 1924 was in full swing. Siegfried was constantly away recruiting musicians and singers. He was usually accompanied by his friend and fellow-repetiteur Walter Aign, son of the Reformed Church minister in Bayreuth. Winifred meanwhile offered her services to the cover organization of the banned NSDAP, the Völkischer Bund (Nationalist League) under Christian Ebersberger. So even in the run-up to the Festival, 'new Bayreuth' was a citadel of anti-republicanism and the prohibited NSDAP, whose 'Führer' was currently sitting out a sentence for high treason.

The small town had never seen so many political rallies as during the 1920s. This was attributable to the new star of the *völkisch* groups, Hans Schemm. This attractive, blond and ambitious schoolteacher, a talented speaker, had been a member of the Epp Freikorps, involved in the 'liberating' of Munich in 1919. At weekends he worked his way through the Upper Franconian villages drumming up support for Hitler. He assembled a dedicated troop around himself, and disguised the events he organized, which were banned, along with the Nazi Party, as 'gatherings for the purpose of leisure outings'. From Landsberg, Hitler gave the Schemm group permission to wear brown shirts.

Schemm said he would not rest 'until all German people think in the same *völkisch* way, develop a *völkisch* will, organize themselves along *völkisch* lines, work and celebrate in *völkisch* style', on the basis of the 'purity of our race and the maintenance of its purity against other races, particularly the Semitic'. He derived his racial information from beekeeping, and his chief tenet was 'alien protein is poison', which he explained to villagers as follows: the previously pure strain of German bees had been bastardized in the last hundred years by crossbreeding with alien bees, and hence they were now showing higher mortality rates, less resistance and more disease. Only consistent pure-race breeding could restore health and the highest yields to the German 'black-brown' bee.[2] Even during the rehearsals Schemm appeared frequently at the Festival Theatre, made contacts there, and recruited new party members from among the artists. Soon the humble Ebersberger had to make way for his dynamic younger colleague as head of the Nationalist League.

On 26 April 1924 Ludendorff, the most prominent nationalist speaker, gave a speech at a large patriotic rally in Bayreuth. He polemicized against further reparations payments, quoting the words of Frederick the Great: 'Only craven cowards bow beneath the yoke, drag their chains obediently and suffer the oppressor patiently.' Naturally, he also quoted Wagner, who shows us 'the heroic German'.[3]

The war hero and putschist, acquitted at his trial, paid a visit to Villa Wahnfried. Winifred reported to the absent Siegfried: 'we are still feeling quite uplifted and inspired today. A truly royal person (in fact he is descended from a king, Eric XIV of Sweden!), tall, kindly, straightforward, with perfect manners, and yet somehow unapproachable.' Seven-year-old Wieland had greeted Ludendorff with a bouquet; Winifred had escorted him to see Cosima and Chamberlain, and then accompanied him to the Hermitage. 'Silently we sped along, I looked at him from the side; he was grimly sunk in thought. The sky full of a blood-red setting sun: twilight of the gods, the last hero! – At the Riding Hall, music, inspection of the guard of honour . . . 4,000 people, shoulder to shoulder.' When she commented on the wonderful enthusiasm of his listeners, the old gentleman had replied drily: 'Yes, sometimes they shout "Heil" and at other times "crucify him!".' Over dinner at Wahnfried Ludendorff expressed himself on the 'Jewish question, about which he brooks no compromise'. And 'then our gaze followed him out into the night, still with the distant cries of "Heil" in our ears'.[4] No less enthusiastic was Chamberlain, who reported the following day to Hitler on Ludendorff's visit. The great commander had 'been so very kind as to spend half an hour by my bedside. What a man it was who thus honoured me!' Ludendorff was a 'Siegfried', while 'Hitler had the nature of a Parsifal'. The letter ends with 'Hitler, I congratulate you on "your friend" Ludendorff . . . To judge by this friend, you are at home among the highest peaks of humanity!'[5]

The election results brought gains for the anti-democratic parties. The Communists received 3.7 million votes, the Nationalist Block nearly

2 million.* The SPD suffered heavy losses, as did the other 'pro-Weimar' parties. Ludendorff, Streicher, Frick, Gansser and other prominent National Socialists now went off to Berlin as Nationalist Block members of the Reichstag. In Bayreuth the nationalists achieved a record 7,045 votes against the SPD's 6,141.[6]

The day after the election Hitler wrote from Landsberg one of the longest letters of his life, a letter of thanks to Siegfried. This electoral success was 'owed first and foremost to you and your good lady . . . I was overcome by proud delight to see a *völkisch* victory precisely in the town where that sword we fight with today was forged, first by the Master and then by Chamberlain.' He expressed his 'profound thanks' to 'you, Herr Wagner, and especially to your admirable wife, for having lent your name to the *völkisch* movement, above all after the ill-fated 9 November. It was easier to do so while things were going well, but after 9 November it required a sacrifice on a scale I am all the more able to appreciate since I myself in the last four years have been engulfed in a rising flood of hatred and calumny.'

Regarding the election result, 'for all his pleasure he was also gravely worried. The movement is still so young that this great success will also put it seriously to the test.' In Landsberg he had at any rate had 'more time and leisure' to read and to learn, and also to draw up a 'thorough reckoning with those gentlemen . . . who on 9 November had been shouting enthusiastic "hurrahs", only to attempt on the 10th, just about a day later, with as much "wise perception" as actual lying duplicity, to demonstrate the "rashness of this mad enterprise"'. These people were not worth fighting for: 'there would be more point in sweeping the streets than in struggling on behalf of such worthlessness'. Hitler was referring to the writing of *Mein Kampf*.

It was 'a great sorrow' to him that he could not be present for the reopening of the Festival: 'What I always had in mind from my thirteenth year onwards, the fantasy of a desire not attainable before now, seemed about to become reality in this year. Sadly, fate does not yet appear to think me worthy or mature enough.' Then he expressed his thanks for the 'charming and touching drawing' that the 'sweet little ones' had sent him 'in the winter days that had been so dismal for him', and signed the letter 'with very best wishes from your truly devoted Adolf Hitler'.[7]

---

*The Nationalist Block consisted of right-wing parties opposed to the Weimar Republic, allegedly 'imposed' on Germany in the Treaty of Versailles. It was primarily left-wing parties, especially the SPD, that supported the Weimar constitution.

Hitler often repeated later how indebted he was to the Wagner family for supporting him at a difficult time. Even in the winter of 1942, in his Wolf's Lair headquarters, he said: 'It wasn't just the others, but Siegfried too who stood by me in my worst hour. Chamberlain's letter came while I was in prison! I was on "du" terms with them, I love those people and Wahnfried!'[8]

In the run-up to the Festival, the political affinity of Villa Wahnfried to Hitler's party, the aggressively anti-Semitic tone of Bayreuth, and the ubiquity of swastikas, alarmed the Left, the republicans and above all the Jews. Cancellations piled up and gave rise to the fear of a Jewish boycott. In an already precarious financial situation, this was dangerous for Bayreuth. But Winifred was unperturbed by the public criticism of Wahnfried's close association with Hitler. Villa Wahnfried simply cared more about Hitler and Ludendorff 'than whether fewer Nagods come to the Festival . . . Anyone who really feels and thinks like a German, will come anyway . . . If we became completely free of Nagods here, we would practically have achieved the impossible without even trying.' Many thought 'that Bayreuth does more justice to Wagner than all the little Nagod directors with their stylizations of him etc. etc., and that the revival of Bayreuth might put a curb on the genius of their productions. The break of ten years has allowed all these weeds to grow unchecked, and however much people pour scorn on the ruins of Bayreuth, they are worried all the same.'[9]

However, in June 1924, when rehearsals were already in full swing, Siegfried wrote a long letter to the Rabbi of Bayreuth, Falk Solomon, to try to curry favour with 'the Jews'. But he did so in the clumsiest way possible, his cliché-ridden ideological style showing how limited his intellectual powers were: 'We are against the spirit of Marxism because we see it as the cause of all our misery. We have absolutely nothing against right-thinking, nationalistically minded Jews.' To demonstrate that Wagner was no anti-Semite, he pointed to his father's Jewish friends and the involvement of Jewish musicians in the Festival. But then he went on to marginalize the Jews as supposed outsiders in Germany, and even represented anti-Semitism as a bulwark against a supposed Jewish 'anti-Germanism': 'Just assume that a foreign people had settled in the old Kingdom of Israel, that the Jews had given them civic privileges, and let them take part in everything. What would the Jews have said if they observed the immigrants mocking and undermining their own religion, their priesthood, their army, and other institutions? They would have defended themselves.'

The final section, clearly meant by Siegfried to express friendliness towards the 'pure-bred' rabbi, equally betrayed the influence of Chamberlain's diction: 'What I think is a misfortune for the German people is the intermixing of the Jewish and the Germanic races. The outcome so far has shown that it has pro-duced human beings who are neither fish nor fowl. I for one would much rather have thoroughbred Jews to deal with than these half-castes.' Then he asks the rabbi to distribute the letter among his circle.[10]

The rabbi was not convinced by this collection of standard racist senti-ments. Two weeks later he replied, in an amiable but distant tone, stressing right from the start that Jews were not 'outsiders' in Germany and that many of them 'had offered a good and loyal reception . . . to the works of your late father . . . If one wanted to differentiate between people in the German lands according to how much respect they have for high art, and whether – to quote the Mastersingers – they "honour their German masters" – then German Jews would have nothing to fear from the verdict.'

Then he addressed racist anti-Semitism: 'A tendency has gained much ground in recent years, though, to value people not according to their inner worth, their spiritual or moral aspirations, but according to their "blood", their "race" or whatever you like to call it.' The rabbi most deeply deplored this mentality, as a Jew, as a German and as a cleric who knew 'that God had created every person in His image'. The anti-Semitic hate campaign of the nationalists was 'linked to the greatest humiliation and abuse of Jews and Judaism. The plan was to reduce the Jews more or less to the status of the niggers in America.' And if this campaign was not based on conviction, but was only 'a means to the end of winning people over . . . then it was all the more despicable'.

As far as the Wagner family was concerned, he had to be frank:

There is a widespread view that your house is a stronghold of this völkisch movement. Herr Chamberlain is the typical representative of anti-Semitic race theory. Members of your family wear swastikas. Your family . . . is said to support the völkisch parties with substantial funding. Is it any surprise that decent men and women of the Jewish faith here and abroad exercise caution regarding things Wagnerian, and are not willing to offer contributions that they fear may indirectly go to benefit the völkisch movement?

He believed Herr Wagner was sincere in wanting a rapprochement, but his letter made clear to my regret, how little comprehension you have of Judaism and the thinking of German Jews . . . Can you not see that people who have been rooted in Germany for untold generations, families whose sons have fallen in battle for our German Fatherland, must feel that your distinction between Germans and Jews is intolerable? Jews have resided in Germany for nearly 2,000 years, and have indisputably earned their right to participate in German culture.

He rejected 'most emphatically' Siegfried's comparison with the foreign people who migrated to the Land of Israel. And contrary to Siegfried's assertion, never had the German Jews mocked and undermined 'the religion, the priesthood, the army and other institutions' of Germany. Marxism and internationalism were not at all characteristic of German Jews; 'on the contrary, from my experience and in my sincere conviction our old-established German Jews were a force for conservatism', and certainly not 'anti-national' as Siegfried claimed. The rabbi went on to declare that Siegfried's serious charges were not derived from his own experience, but had been 'drawn from his reading of biased writers'. He enclosed a few informative brochures about Judaism, and closed with the words: 'We Jews, too, admire the work of Richard Wagner, and we find it painful when someone tries to destroy this admiration. A House of Wagner . . . that does not serve the parties of the day will be placed above all parties and will encounter no enemies.'[11]

Siegfried's attempts at appeasement fizzled out in any case within a very short time. For the *Bayreuther Blätter*, edited by Wolzogen, took up a clear political position: it recommended in its review section not only the new journal *Der Weltkampf* (The World Struggle) – 'We leave it to our readers to guess what power the struggle is against' – but also the *Swastika Calendar*,* and headed its 1924 spring issue with a Hitler slogan: 'The outer struggle must be preceded by an inner one. Ours is a struggle to achieve a sacred content.'

Stassen's design for the cover of the *Official Guide to the Bayreuth Festival* showed, against the backdrop of the Festival Theatre, a fist grasping the hilt of a raised sword. Around the border of the cover ran the lines: 'Nothung! Nothung! New and rejuvenated! I awakened you once again to life!' Somewhat tucked away inside was the key to the message of the cover:

*In the German, 'Hakenkreuz-Jahrweiser', a special calendar presumably containing the main events of the Nazi year, accompanied by propaganda material.

'Only if we ride forth as Knights of the Grail with such heroism in our hearts to the great struggle for German liberation, whenever it shall come, will we pull the Nothung-sword from the trunk, and no world-god will be able to shatter us! We will gain the strength we need from Bayreuth.'[12] Only a few weeks earlier Hitler had praised Bayreuth as the town 'which forged the spiritual sword with which we fight today'.

Although 'German' visitors from Czechoslovakia or Austria were welcomed, they were also told bluntly that 'it cannot be denied that foreigners, especially if they are not racially aware or not very Nordic in their outlook, often have a rather alien, or at least not an authentically Bayreuthian relationship to the art of Richard Wagner'. Reading was recommended that would promote 'knowledge of the Aryan', including Hans Günther's *Rassenkunde des deutschen Volkes* (Racial Anthropology of the German People) ('a standard work'), and Count Gobineau's 'work on race' in Ludwig Schemann's translation.[13]

In his essay on 'Richard Wagner and Bismarck' August Püringer summed up this world-view. Bismarck's Reich was 'doomed to decay' because, 'alongside the clear German spirit, to which it was dedicated, it was inhabited, "on terms of equality", by riff-raff of all sorts and a rabble of traders alien to the German people; finally they were even allowed to arrogate to themselves rule by the majority, and to indulge in shameless acts of agitation'. The Kaiser's Reich had gone under because Bismarck had neglected to collaborate with Wagner, instead 'exposing the German idea to racially alien agitators, phrase-mongers and destroyers'. Püringer dreamed of a German state where 'Wagner's cultural spirit . . . would have the state's authority behind it, and would be enclosed and shielded by the construction of a Nationalist Reich with Bismarckian instincts for size and power . . . Wagner's and Bismarck's spirit; only the two together can offer us Germans salvation!'[14]

Everyone on Festival Hill knew which politician was supposed to be the longingly awaited new Bismarck. In the regular postal exchanges between Bayreuth and Landsberg Hitler was sure to have received a copy of the *Festival Guide*, to reinforce the alliance with Wahnfried.

THE 1924 FESTIVAL

The resumption of the Festival was a risky venture, since, according to Winifred, the funds stood at only 30,000 marks. But Siegfried held that a start must be made sooner or later. The urgently needed modernization of the lighting system would have to wait. The old stage-sets and costumes from the days of the Master and the Master's Lady were repaired and put to use. The singers and orchestra worked without pay, receiving only expenses, which explained Siegfried's difficulty in finding musicians. Winifred later suggested that all the big theatres and orchestras had put up opposition to Bayreuth at that time, and were unwilling to give their members leave to perform there: 'We were considered to be absolutely reactionary and undesirable.'[15]

None the less, a prominent and, naturally, 'non-Jewish' conductor was successfully appointed. Siegfried had previously tended to regard Fritz Busch, director of the Dresden Opera, as his enemy, since he had made his mark with premières of Strauss operas. Politically, too, as a confirmed democrat, Busch hardly fitted in with Bayreuth, but he was also a great Wagner devotee, and accepted the offer with pleasure. Hans Knappertsbusch, too, wanted to conduct at the Festival and maintained that he had already accepted a firm offer from Siegfried. Later, he attributed the final discussion to Winifred, and was bitterly resentful towards her for the rest of his life.[16] If Knappertsbusch was right, there is only one explanation for the choice of Busch: he was Hitler's preferred candidate. Hitler had a very high opinion of the blond Westphalian conductor, and even in 1942, years after Busch had gone into exile, he opined ruefully that 'After Krauss and Furtwängler, Busch would have been the best German conductor.'[17]

Busch certainly served as a democratic fig-leaf for an event that was thoroughly *völkisch* in nature. But he, too, was concerned about the quality of the Festival, in view of the great need to economize. He pointed out 'that the fate of Bayreuth for the next few years, if not for decades' was in the balance, and suggested postponing the reopening for a year if no first-class singers and musicians could be found.[18] But Siegfried did not agree.

During the frequent absences of her husband, the 26-year-old Winifred had taken over practically the whole organization of the Festival. Helping her in the Festival office were only the administrative director, Wilhelm Schuler, a secretary and a caretaker. Winifred contributed youthful energy, a great appetite for work and an immense talent for organization, but officially she remained in the background. Whenever Siegfried was at Bayreuth, she shielded him carefully, as the author Erich Ebermeyer described: 'In these years, if a visitor comes to Wahnfried to talk to Siegfried, he is directed towards the house next door, the small bachelor house . . . and here in a little anteroom leading to Siegfried's study sits his young wife, radiating happiness

and harmony, and, before she announces the guest, explains with a laugh
that she is the Cerberus guarding the threshold of her master.'[19]

Siegfried particularly preferred to employ his forceful wife whenever he
could not trust himself to carry out unpopular measures; he had a horror of
arguments. While he played the 'kind and friendly' part, Winifred's role was
to take the tough decisions, thereby drawing down all the rancour upon her
person. She had to be at home, wrote Winifred to a friend, because a high-
ranking office-bearer of some Wagner Society was due to come, 'and
Siegfried needs me there to do the shouting – facing it alone makes him a
wreck'.[20] Increasingly often it happened that she drove Siegfried to see
friends, to Leipzig for example, because he wanted 'to feel light-hearted and
cheerful just for once'. Then she drove on alone; as far as Magdeburg, on one
occasion, to discuss casting with the conductor of *Parsifal*, Carl Muck.[21]
Winifred's swashbuckling way of destroying structures that had become a
hindrance, or at least trying to do so, reinforced the reservations that the traditionally minded 'Cosimans' had about the young woman, so at odds with
the solemn mood of Bayreuth. In reality the way the married couple operated
amounted to a perfect combination of two complementary and mutually
dependent characters. Since Siegfried was averse to conflict, it was Winifred
who carried out his wishes.

There was a great argument, for example, over the 'patrons', the members
of the Festival Foundation. By January 1924 they had signed up for 5,210
sponsorship certificates at 1,000 marks each, and thereby acquired the right
to 20,840 reduced-price Festival tickets between them. Although the money
collected had been reduced by inflation to a fraction of its former value, the
tiny Festival office now received a veritable flood of letters from patrons
demanding four discounted tickets each. They thus precipitated, as Winifred
put it, 'endless unpleasant exchanges' about individual wishes, and an
'immeasurable increase in work for the office', quite apart from the expense
of postage. Furthermore, much to Winifred's ire, there were only 7,000 ordinary tickets left for sale.

When a few of the Foundation members even wanted a say in the casting
of the singers, she exploded: 'The retention of these rights until doomsday'
was really too much. The sponsors had gone so far as to ask to look at the
accounts, and wanted to 'interfere wherever they could'. It was logical to dis-
solve the foundation, because it had done its job: 'we are now standing
entirely on our own two feet'. She asked her friend Margarethe Strauss to
mediate, apologized 'if I have expressed myself too sharply now and again',

but added self-confidently: 'that's the way I'm made'.[22] Indicating that her husband was on a concert tour allowed her to keep him out of the argument and deflect any ill-feeling towards herself. Conflict with the obstructive Festival Foundation lasted until 1931.

The artists arrived in June to a rousing welcome from the director. It was true that this was hardly the right time to hold a Festival, but he regarded it as 'a Festival to strengthen the German spirit'. Everyone had to help to ensure that 'the spirit was restored to purity'.[23] Winifred was overjoyed that Lauritz Melchior brought Hugh Walpole with him again. She must have attached herself so firmly to her adored Englishman that in the end they became the focus of 'town gossip'.[24]

At the rehearsals, as Winifred still recalled decades later, she had been 'Siegfried's shadow'. 'He never wanted me to leave his side. I didn't dare say a word during the rehearsals, and of course I never interfered.' Then she added with a laugh: 'In those days I thought everything Siegfried did was perfect.'[25] He had a very quiet voice, and he had used her as his 'soprano trumpet': 'Since there was no technical address system available, he always asked me to convey his instructions from the viewing box to the stage.' Aside from that, she also functioned as Siegfried's 'lighting director'[26] with the special task of looking after difficult artists.

General Ludendorff appeared as a guest of honour at the rehearsals. To mark his visit the Festival Theatre flew the old Reich flag, in other words the flag of the Republic's opponents. The Festival restaurant was decorated with black–white–red braid. Around Villa Wahnfried swastika stickers had been placed on fences and walls. Busch, who had never seen a swastika in his life before, was deeply disturbed. When Siegfried invited him to Wahnfried to meet 'the greatest German', he declined, much to Siegfried's surprise.[27]

From the first rehearsals onwards Busch had his differences with Muck, who had been Bayreuth's star conductor as far back as the days of Cosima, and now plagued his self-confident young rival with his jealousy and his superior knowledge. Busch criticized the artistic quality of both singers and orchestra players, but Muck simply smiled at all suggestions for improvement and, 'being senior in years and in experience of working at Bayreuth',[28] insisted on retaining tried and trusted artists. The most important thing about Bayreuth was that 'those called to work there agreed with the Bayreuth idea; that they had absorbed the teachings laid down in the artistic writings of the Master as they had the scores of his works; and that they should bring to their work in the Festival Theatre the humility and the zeal of believers'.[29]

Siegfried backed up Muck, and held that the audience at Bayreuth was not to be compared with regular big-city audiences; he was alluding to the opera house in Dresden. As 'the complete musician' Busch could not understand the uniqueness of Bayreuth; 'beautifully singing throats' were not so important. 'We've also got to bear in mind the drama, the credibility of the characters.'[30] And about Elisabeth Rethberg, who sang all the great roles in Dresden and had been suggested by Busch, he declared: 'Certainly Frau Rethberg has the most beautiful voice, but do I want to spend 4 hours in the theatre watching such a boring and lifeless Eve?'[31]

When Busch then suggested inviting Toscanini, who liked coming to Bayreuth, to conduct *Tristan and Isolde* in 1925, Siegfried declined: 'A foreigner is not suitable for Bayreuth!' The maestro was unyielding in his demands, impossible to work with; in short, according to Busch's bitter comment, 'he would disturb the peace of the Bayreuth atmosphere . . . The result of my mentioning the great Italian was that I was suspected of "lacking nationalist conviction".'[32] Emmy Krüger, who sang Kundry and Sieglinde, noted: 'Fritz Busch curses Bayreuth from morning to night! The Wagners don't like him! I can see why! Although he's right about a lot of things.'[33]

After a nine-year break the Bayreuth Festival was reopened on 22 July 1924 with the *Mastersingers*, conducted by Busch, in the old production, décor and costumes of 1911. To celebrate the occasion, even 86-year-old Cosima occupied her box for the first act – for the first time since 1906, when illness had forced her to hand over the direction to Siegfried. It was to be the last time.

No official representatives of the government were present. Of the old Festival habitués, the former Czar Ferdinand of Bulgaria had come, as well as Crown Princess Cecilie and Prince August Wilhelm of Prussia, the Duke and Duchess of Saxe-Coburg, the Grand Duchess of Oldenburg, the grand-ducal family of Mecklenburg, industrialists such as Siemens, Thyssen, Sachs and Bahlsen, and many high-ranking military men.

The *Frankfurter Zeitung* recorded a drop in the numbers of foreign visitors, and a corresponding increase in the German element. The newspaper also noted

that the seekers after freedom had almost completely disappeared from among the German contingent in the Wagner-temple . . . So this is what has become of the heritage of a genius who knew how to encompass lands and hearts! This is the change of mentality that Bayreuth has undergone since 1914. Is it still worthwhile for any independent thinker to make the pilgrimage to the Green Hill?[34]

The conductor Kurt Singer was blunter: 'The stalls – dignified, formally dressed, tails, glittering evening dress, nationalist and conservative to the (Nazi) core, cheering uncritically . . . hardly the audience that Wagner wanted. Scarcely ten non-Aryans in the house . . . a hidden hand has ensured that the aura of the Festival shifts from the artistic to the political.'[35]

Among this politically homogeneous audience, the last scene of *Mastersingers* with its colourful procession on the Festival meadow aroused nationalist emotions that led to a sensation. When Hans Sachs proclaimed: '. . . even if the Holy Roman Empire were to vanish into the mists, we would still possess holy German art!', the audience got to its feet, silent at first, but finally bursting into a loud and enthusiastic rendition of the three verses of 'Deutschland über Alles', which had been adopted as the national anthem two years earlier. With the lines from the first verse that run 'from the Maas to the Memel, from the Adige to the Belt' it became a nationalist statement.

Wagnerians like Prince Heinrich Reuss XLV were irritated: 'We saw Wagner and his work of art desecrated by a non-artistic demonstration . . . Wahnfried should beware the spirits who have invoked this demonstration. Perhaps they do not know what they are doing. But they are the enemies of the artist Wagner, and they are digging the grave of the Bayreuth idea.'* He concluded his newspaper review with: 'Despite individual highlights, the overall impression was shattering and depressing.'[36]

In view of the protests, Siegfried attempted to limit the damage; he had leaflets distributed with the text: 'Please refrain from singing, however well meant; here we serve art!' Even Winifred, experiencing the Festival for the first time (in 1914 she had attended only the dress-rehearsal) found herself in conflict with the nationalist spirit. Talking in English with English guests in her box, she was rebuked with the demand to 'speak German'. Her justification was that 'I had done so out of politeness; it seemed to me that if they were in England and did not know English, they would be pleased if somebody spoke German to them'.[37] It is quite possible that the guest in her

---

*Prince Heinrich conceived of the 'Bayreuth idea' as high art, above nationalism and beyond mere politics.

theatre box was Walpole. It was because of this powerful anti-English feeling that Winifred did not teach her children English, something they very much regretted later on.

Walpole caused domestic difficulties, not with Siegfried, but with his suspicious sisters. By the end of the Festival the quarrel became so bad that Siegfried suggested to Daniela that she should move out, whereupon Winifred wrote with relief to Lene: 'I find it strangely touching that Hugh should have brought about this liberation [from Daniela's presence] after nine years; he's done me the greatest favour.'[38] The reason why Siegfried was not worried about his wife's relationship with Walpole was that he could hardly overlook the writer's sexual orientation. Even if the rapturous Winifred missed it, the fact was that Walpole was gay.

The emotionally charged nationalist mood became ever more intense, and exploded in anti-Semitic outbursts. Victims of abuse included the university professors Max Koch in Breslau, Arthur Prüfer in Leipzig and Richard Sternfeld in Berlin, who had all been doing successful Wagner research at their universities for decades, had inspired a love of Wagner in many students, and were firm German nationalists. 'Outrageous things'* had happened, reported Winifred indignantly to Lene: 'Jews have been spat at here, mocked; poems . . . have been circulating with lines like "throw them out" etc. etc.; in the so-called official guide Püringer talks about the Jews as "riff-raff".' The völkisch groups, among whom she included the Pan-Germans led by Class, had regarded Bayreuth 'as something that belonged solely to them', and Siegfried was being made responsible for this. And 'I'm angry . . . more with fellow nationalists than with the Jews.'[39] One of these defamatory poems, for example, ran: 'For who comes here with his flat feet/With crooked nose, and frizzy hair/It's not for him to enjoy the Festival/He's got to go, he's got to go.'[40]

These scandalous events provoked protests. In reply to a newspaper questionnaire on 'the future of Bayreuth', Thomas Mann said: 'Wagner will never cease to interest me . . . but Bayreuth as it now presents itself interests me not at all, and I cannot help thinking that neither will it ever interest the world again.'[41] Siegfried had to deal with many critical letters from Jewish Wagnerians. Fearing a boycott, he refuted all accusations in an open letter to

---

*Although anti-Semitic herself, Winifred was repulsed by physical expressions of anti-Semitism.

the *Centralvereinszeitung deutscher Staatsbürger jüdischen Glaubens* (Central Society Newspaper of German Citizens of the Jewish Faith). He maintained that he had known nothing about any of it – including the official *Festival Guide* – and promised that from then on the Festival would be 'free of any political slant' and 'Nobody needs to fear that any events of an unpleasant kind would occur.' He asked the newspaper to tell this 'to all its friends'. The newspaper responded in a conciliatory tone and hoped that Bayreuth as 'a great centre of German culture, freed from *völkisch* dross, will once again serve the great ideals of humanity, pure art and true love of the Fatherland'.[42]

The artistic presentation of the Festival also drew criticism. While Emmy Krüger's Sieglinde and Lauritz Melchior's Parsifal were enthusiastically applauded, the problem lay with the veteran singers, of whom there were far too many, and whose great days lay in the past. It was the same with the orchestra. The stage-sets from the days of the Master, panoramas painted on canvas, were antiquated and dusty like the hangings and curtains, which, pulled up and down and to and fro, formed the movable wings. The old costumes had undergone only essential repairs. The lighting technology dated from the turn of the century. Bayreuth could not compete with the modern staging of Wagner in Vienna, Berlin, Dresden and Munich.

But still, the festival brought in a surplus of 200,000 marks,[43] enough to extend the rear of the stage, which nearly doubled the stage area. The town of Bayreuth was pleased with its increased tax income. As well as the hotels, 700 private individuals profited from letting rooms to Festival visitors.

HITLER'S RETURN

Hitler was released on probation from Landsberg and received enthusiastically by his supporters. Helene Bechstein presented him with a big new Mercedes, and even paid the chauffeur's wages of 200 marks a month. This early release served only to increase Hitler's scorn for the Republic's mild treatment of him. Winifred commented: 'Hitler always accused the soft democrats of being too lenient on their enemies. He derided democracy's penal methods.'[44]

Immediately after his release Hitler went to express his gratitude to his patronesses. On 23 December he visited Elsa Bruckmann for the first time at No. 5 Karolinenplatz in Munich. In a drawing room formerly graced by Nietzsche, Rilke and Hofmannsthal, Hitler now monopolized the conversation, ranging across his war experiences, his youth, and 'the first great impact on me of monumental architecture in my days in Vienna'. He presented himself as an artist and connoisseur of literature, and showed his extensive knowledge of the writings of Chamberlain, the most important writer in Bruckmann's canon. He wrote in the guestbook: 'Anyone broken by sorrow deserves no joy.'[45]

Hitler planned to visit Wahnfried in person on 3 January 1925 to express his thanks. This was precisely at the time when the newspapers were being highly critical of the political involvement of Bayreuth. Winifred reported to Lene: 'Fidi has laid down the law to me and forbidden me to play any active public role in the movement from now on. You can imagine how difficult it will be for me. But actually he's right. Hitler will understand that immediately.' She went on: 'The Jews have succeeded in trumpeting it about to the whole world that artists are exploited here for political purposes, and they prove it by pointing to our friendship with Hitler etc.' The Festival depended upon theatres making musicians and singers available to them: 'So in public we must be careful . . . Poor Fidi has been getting one nasty letter after another on this subject.'[46]

The Bayreuth police learned about Hitler's intended visit, 'and Villa Wahnfried was immediately put under police surveillance . . . My husband has had enough of it, and I wrote a letter to Hitler telling him how he would cause trouble for us. So I put him off.'[47] It was therefore pointless for the municipal authorities to post four pairs of policemen around the grounds, 'and an army of detectives to keep watch on us'. Winifred told Lene: 'It's our President who's responsible for all this . . . and the Jewish Commissioner for the town, Reichart. Please be careful with this letter, or I might get into trouble for my impudence. Fidi won't put up with being so badly treated for much longer.'[48]

By way of compensation, the Wagners received from Hitler an invitation to his first big political speech, in the Bürger Beer Hall in Munich on 27 February 1925. At a mass meeting in the very place where he had hoped to start a successful putsch in November 1923, he relaunched the NSDAP. Although he was still on probation and was not supposed to be engaging in political activity, his faith in the Bavarian authorities encouraged him to risk this appearance.

Siegfried could not accept the invitation, because he was preparing to stage *Schwarzschwanenreich* in Plauen at that time. So Winifred travelled by herself to Munich, and – in an overcrowded hall with an audience of more than 3,000 – she saw Hitler again for the first time since 1 October 1923. He spoke for nearly two hours, repeated his attacks on the Jews, who were responsible for all of Germany's misfortunes, and urged unity upon his supporters and unconditional loyalty to him, the Führer. The evening ended with shouts of 'Heil' and the singing of 'Deutschland über Alles'.

Winifred was deeply honoured by the decision of Hitler, thus acclaimed and at the end of a day that was so significant for him, to take her and an adjutant to Plauen, in his new chauffeur-driven Mercedes, to see Siegfried's opera and thank him personally for his help during his imprisonment. Since Bayreuth lay on their route, Winifred invited Hitler to spend the night at Villa Wahnfried, and continue to Plauen the next morning. Under cover of darkness, he could avoid attracting attention. Friedelind wrote later: 'Nobody knew this secret apart from Wieland,'[49] who was eight at the time.

The following morning, 28 February, as Winifred and Hitler were already on their way to Plauen, came the news of Reich-President Ebert's sudden death. Hitler had one powerful enemy the fewer. The proclamation of national mourning meant that all theatres closed down, including the one in Plauen. Hitler broke off his journey, delivered Winifred to Bayreuth, and went back to Munich. Paul von Hindenburg became the new president in April 1925.

Siegfried and Winifred soon made up for the aborted meeting, visiting Hitler in his small flat at No. 1 Thierchstrasse in Munich. Half a century later Winifred could still recall it in detail: 'The bed beneath the window, a piano [presented by the Bechsteins] on one side, and outside the trams ran until 4 in the morning.' She liked telling her grandchildren: 'There in that room Wolf [a nickname for Hitler] suffered from insomnia.'[50] In the bookcase, next to volumes by Ludendorff, Treitschke, Clausewitz and a biography of Frederick the Great, stood Chamberlain's Wagner biography.[51] It was on this occasion that Hitler agreed to attend the Festival in 1925.

Siegfried had his work cut out to defend himself against a rising tide of resentment and the accusations of anti-Semitism. During February 1925 he wrote another letter – intended for public consumption – to Bruno Weil, chair of the Central Society for German Citizens of the Jewish Faith, and declared: 'It is extremely important to me that this year's festival should take place, and that it should be completely free of political controversy.'[52]

In the *Berliner Tagblatt* (Berlin Daily News), Joseph Chapiro recalled Siegfried's assurances [that Bayreuth would not be affected by anti-Semitism] in 1923–4, 'when he came to America to raise money for Bayreuth among rich, mostly German-Jewish, Americans'. Despite this, the Festival in 1924 had turned into 'a *völkisch* celebration in honour of General Ludendorff, at the expense of unsuspecting Bayreuth devotees'. So how could one believe this new promise? There was a barely disguised demand that Siegfried should step down as Festival Director, in order to save Bayreuth.[53] Once again the papers were full of claims and counter-claims by Siegfried, who was torn between, on the one hand, efforts to keep affluent Jewish Wagnerians on board and on the other, the wish not to offend the *völkisch* groups.

Afraid that his pro-Jewish declarations would arouse Hitler's disapproval, he got Winifred to explain the awkward situation to her friend when she sent him good wishes for his birthday on 20 April. Winifred's letter ran: 'You are sure to have heard certain rustlings in the newspaper jungle' about the letter that Siegfried 'had written for the sake of a few long-standing Jewish supporters of Bayreuth'. She mentioned the anti-Semitic excesses committed against Professors Koch, Prüfer and Sternfeld, and the Püringer article in the *Festival Guide*. Siegfried had been held to account for all of this. He had written letters to defend himself 'against these exaggerations', and to deny all responsibility for them. Winifred stated firmly that it was inexcusable for 'highly respected German-minded men and others of their ethnic [Jewish] group' in Bayreuth 'to be jeered at by barbarous people, in one case even spat at'. 'For the sake of sheer human decency,' Siegfried had been obliged to declare, 'that there should be no such provocations in future. And anyway, those who came to Bayreuth are not the Jews who deserve to be treated like this. The attitude of Jews as a whole to Bayreuth will never change . . . but the Jews who were here last year must have felt hurt, because they are precisely the ones who had earned a right to Bayreuth with their life's work.'

The *völkisch* movement, still inexperienced, did not understand 'that Bayreuth stood above politics and must not be made into a tool of the movement. That is what happened last year, and it gave the enemy new ammunition to use in his diabolical campaign against Bayreuth, which represented for him the embodiment of a hateful idea.' Bayreuth must, 'so to speak, be regarded as a sacrosanct symbol, as a shrine. People would make the pilgrimage to it, draw new strength from its source, but not drag it with them into the struggle . . . They [the *völkisch* groups] should be content to know that the custodian', that is Siegfried, 'is one of your own . . . Our friends still do not understand' that a distinction had to be made between the cause and the person, 'and they thereby make Siegfried's already difficult position even worse'.

Winifred continued: 'We could not bear it if you thought badly of us. So please excuse these long-winded explanations.' She begged for Hitler's indulgence, and closed with the assurance: 'My thoughts and wishes are with you always and with your work. Your grateful, loyal Winifred Wagner.' She even wrote on the envelope: 'with the urgent request that you should not feel obliged to answer this! It would be dreadful for me to think I had taken up a moment of your valuable time!'[54]

Meanwhile, Siegfried was continuing his goodwill action directed at the Bayreuth Rabbi, asking him to write an article for the *Central Society Newspaper* to recommend Bayreuth. Salomon did so, albeit cautiously, shortly before the dress rehearsals in 1925. It was true that Siegfried lacked 'a proper understanding for the thinking and outlook of German Jewry', but what mattered about the Festival was not 'the political views and outlook of Richard Wagner's son, but Richard Wagner's work'. If Bayreuth was going to stand for 'pure art' once more, German Jews could take pleasure from that.[55]

The 1925 Festival repeated the programme of the previous year, but with the rebuilding and technical improvements it was no longer as old-fashioned, especially since young assistant directors, such as Kurt Söhnlein and Wolfram Humperdinck, were more in evidence, and Siegfried took his first steps towards a new production of the *Ring of the Nibelung*. To avoid giving offence, instead of the black–white–red flag a plain white one bearing the letter W was flown, the new household standard.

Three weeks before rehearsals began, Busch resigned from his role in the Festival. On the face of it, the reason was the failure to meet his demand for better singers, but in reality it was all to do with Muck's plotting and the uneasy political atmosphere. Winifred was furious, and probably also concerned that Hitler might be disappointed at this resignation.

At the rehearsals morale among the performers was low, and there was gossip around Siegfried, in addition to annoyance with the agents in America. Winifred seems to have poured all her troubles into the no-longer-so-willing ears of Walpole. 'According to Winifred, the Rhine maidens were giving a lot of trouble; the *Parsifal* scenery had a nasty habit of sticking on its way up or down; she was worried about her husband's health, and about the future of the Festival if he were to die.' Walpole had heard, too, about the political attack on Bayreuth.[56] Winifred was very nervous because it was not yet clear whether Hitler would be coming to Bayreuth. The Bechsteins, in whose private lodgings he was supposed to stay, were equally in the dark, and could not make any plans. In the end, as Lotte Bechstein related, Hitler arrived unexpectedly and so late that her parents were already asleep; and late in the evening Lotte had to give up her room for him.

Helene Bechstein was so besotted with Hitler that she even envisaged him marrying her only daughter, Lotte. However, an approach on the part of the young lady must have gone wrong. 'He was no good at kissing!' was the reason the Bechstein heiress, fifteen years younger than Hitler, later gave for the failure of the relationship to flourish. From then on she limited her admiration entirely to Hitler the politician.[57]

Years later, Hitler recalled the first visit he made to the Bayreuth Festival: 'In 1925 the Bechsteins invited me to stay with them in Bayreuth; they lived in the Liszt Strasse . . . just around the corner from Wahnfried . . . I didn't actually want to go, I thought it would only increase Siegfried's difficulties, he was rather in the power of the Jews. I arrived in Bayreuth about eleven at night, Lotte was still up, but the old Bechsteins had gone to bed . . . The next day,' he went on, 'Frau Wagner came, and brought me a few flowers. Then things got very lively!'[58]

Hitler allowed the Bechsteins to spoil him, attended a whole cycle of operas – the *Ring*, the *Mastersingers* and *Parsifal* – and enthused: 'For me there was a luminous beauty about Bayreuth! It was a sunny time, I was thirty-six, had no worries yet, and the air was full of violins! I had reached that pleasant level of popularity where everybody was nice to me without expecting anything from me; I was left in peace. By day I wore Bavarian Lederhosen, and I went to the festival in a dinner-jacket or tails.'

After the performances 'we sat with the artists in the Festival Theatre or in the Anker, or went out to Bube's at Berneck . . . We went on outings to Luisenburg, another time to Bamberg, often to the Hermitage.' For the first and only time Hitler's name cropped up in the Bayreuth visitors' register: 'Hitler, Adolf, writer, Munich, staying with Rudolf Bayerlein, Lisztstrasse 16/I'.[59] Accompanying Hitler were the Wagnerians Franz von Epp and Ernst Röhm. However, Röhm expressed himself disparagingly to Siegfried about Hitler: he was just the 'drummer', and no statesman; the latter had yet to appear.[60] Röhm, who had reorganized the SA during Hitler's internment and turned it into a powerful small private army, pulled out in 1925 after a quarrel with Hitler and emigrated to Bolivia, where he was military adviser to the government for a few years.

It was no surprise that Hitler took offence at 'the Jew' Friedrich Schorr singing Wotan, and he was still holding forth about it in 1942: 'it made me so angry; to me it was racial sacrilege! Why didn't they bring in Rode from

Munich? They had another top-rate man, too, the "Kammersänger" [Austrian title for outstanding singer] Braun.'[61] Both Wilhelm Rode and Carl Braun were not only 'German' artists, but early supporters of Hitler. In the intervals Hitler waxed enthusiastic over the blonde Emmy Krüger, and invited her to his table for high tea. When she came in, he got up, went to meet her, kissed her hand and invited her to sit next to him. Emmy Krüger said later: 'He immediately began to talk about my performance, picking out details that astonished me, and I clearly remember thinking "en passant" – well, this man knows a thing or two about art!'[62]

Walpole, on the other hand, has a colourful description in his memoirs of how Hitler hid himself away at Bayreuth, appearing only after dark, popping up in the Wagner box, and generally behaving like a stage conspirator. It was Walpole who just happened to be sitting in the box next to Hitler and so was well placed to observe how, while Melchior sang, 'the tears poured down Hitler's cheeks'. At that moment he had looked like 'a poor fish quite certain to be shortly killed'. Hitler had expressed to the author his admiration for Britain, and the need for an alliance. Walpole found him 'fearfully ill-educated and quite tenth-rate. When Winnie Wagner said that he would be the saviour of the world I just laughed . . . I thought him silly, brave and shabby – rather like a necromantic stump orator.'[63]

But since Hitler's name did not occur at all in Walpole's original diary for 1925, the suspicion arises that it was only later, in 1940 when Hitler had become Britain's greatest enemy, that he added some graphic touches about him at Bayreuth. It is true that as a former political internee Hitler was under police surveillance in Bayreuth, but far from trying to hide, he appeared quite openly in the Bechsteins' box – and without Walpole. We also have to ask what language this supposed conversation took place in, since Walpole spoke no German, and Hitler could not speak English.

Winifred's ardour for Walpole had cooled off considerably. She was now passionate about Hitler. Walpole left Bayreuth early, on 8 August, and he never returned.

The Wagners were not the main focus for Hitler on this occasion; he was the Bechsteins' guest, and was more in need of his patroness's substantial donations than of Winifred's less material support. Winifred was reasonable about this; as she wrote to Lene: 'The Bechsteins no longer have any stake in the firm, they've been paid off. I believe they got 3 million. If it's true, then I'm pleased for Hitler, because he'll get some of it straight away, of course.'[64] Helene Bechstein took great care not to be disturbed in her social circle by the presence of any other female Hitler-admirers; especially Winifred. The formerly very close relationship between the two women became so strained that in the end Winifred did not dare speak to Hitler in Helene Bechstein's presence: 'that would only give rise to a lot more chatter from Frau B., and then perhaps her jealousy would drive her to make a scene to W. [Wolf], and he would curse me along with all other women'.[65]

During the Festival Winifred kept her distance from Hitler, especially as she was busy from morning to night. Ernest Urchs, the steward of the funds raised in America, was in Bayreuth for the first time, along with his family, and had delivered urgently needed dollars. Lene sang for the first and only time at the Festival in 1925, in the role of Freia; she needed comfort and support, particularly as she was about to be married, to the lawyer August Roesener, a nephew of Heinrich Class. Not until the seventh day of the Festival, when there were no performances, did Winifred meet up with Hitler to show him around the Festival Theatre: 'That's to say, the way everything was constructed, the stage, the auditorium, all the acoustic conditions, the sight-lines. So, that took a whole morning.'[66] During the tour Hitler had talked 'about the painful experiences he had had with others since he was released from Landsberg . . . People who previously couldn't show enough enthusiasm were now cutting him dead.' Since he had seen that his presence was creating political difficulties for the Wagners, he promised Winifred 'that he wouldn't come back to Bayreuth again until he was in a position to help rather than harm us'.[67]

Hitler's visit to the Festival was no secret, and soon attracted renewed hostile criticism. Appalled, Thomas Mann complained of 'the attempt to restore Bayreuth' in which Wagner was being exploited as 'the protector of a cave-bearish Teutonizing tendency'. Wagner's work was falling prey to 'a cruder kind of populism by the day'.[68] Among the disappointed visitors was Foreign Minister Gustav Stresemann, who wondered: 'Has people's taste changed? Or are those who run the Festival foolishly confusing politics with music, and dressing up that old democrat Wagner as a modern swastika-man?'[69]

Finally, Hitler handed Winifred a freshly printed copy of the first volume of *Mein Kampf*, with a handwritten dedication. In order to be able to evaluate the significance of this gift, it is worth noting that Helene Bechstein received not only a signed book, but the original manuscript as well, though the latter had in fact for the most part been typed by Rudolf Hess. Much to the grief of her heirs, in an emotional scene Helene Bechstein was later to hand these papers back to Hitler.[70]

Winifred, ever practical, immediately noticed the printing errors in the new book: 'I pointed these howlers out to him, and he thanked me and did actually change a few things. But I don't believe I induced him to make any textual changes – only through discussion, perhaps. So it would be silly to try to claim that changes of that kind were prompted by me.'[71] Winifred greeted the second volume of Mein Kampf, which appeared in 1926, as 'a real improvement – even Fidi is reading it!!!!!'[72]

It was during this time that Hitler and Winifred agreed to go on familiar, 'du' terms, calling each other 'Winnie' and 'Wolf', the latter being Hitler's cover-name in the early twenties. Hitler was already used to calling Siegfried 'du'. The children, too, were smitten with Wolf and looked upon him as 'a kind uncle . . . He really acted like one here with us. It was quite touching to watch him with the children . . .' Hitler's big supercharged Mercedes was 'terrific fun . . . it made a most diabolical noise when it was put into gear and driven uphill'.[73]

In the meantime, Winifred had become the first woman in Bayreuth to get her driver's licence, and she also learned to service their unreliable new car, called 'Presto'. She had a pit specially dug in the garden of Wahnfried so that she could clamber down in her mechanic's overalls and change the oil or the tyres or carry out repairs. Fellow-passengers would describe how, when they suffered one of their frequent punctures, Siegfried would calmly pace to and fro on the road smoking his 'Senoussi' cigarette, while Winifred 'undismayed, in fact enjoying herself', was changing the wheel, having confirmed with a laugh that the other passengers were 'not much good at giving her a hand', either.[74]

Siegfried's poor physical and mental condition gave rise to concern, as well as to speculation about the succession. For Winifred, however, this was not in doubt: 'My biggest test will come one day with Bayreuth. God give me strength!!'[75] Daube wrote in his diary in 1926 that 'the future of Bayreuth lies with her'. He was sure 'that she will be the right successor one day'.[76] Siegfried's sisters Eva Chamberlain and Daniela Thode took a different view. Daniela, the head of the Festival's wardrobe department, felt that ever since her youth she had been picked out by Cosima for the succession. Following the row in the spring, she had now moved back into Wahnfried, where she was continuing to wage her domestic war against Winifred. In Bayreuth, carefully crafted rumours were circulating to the effect that none of

Siegfried's four children was his own, but had been sired by Winifred's lovers. Carl Muck, Albert Knittel and Franz von Hoesslin were all being proposed as putative fathers. Daniela, in particular, liked to remonstrate with the exuberant and unruly children: 'I really don't know where you all come from – what kind of children are you?' To which they would reply: 'But we know – we're Richard Wagner's grandchildren!' Their aunt would then retort: 'You're no grandchildren of Richard Wagner's, for goodness sake!'[77]

As the children got older, the family resemblances grew ever more pronounced, especially the dominant Wagner nose. There could be no doubt that Siegfried was their father. To quote Hitler: 'You can see it in the children; if ever children had a particular "face", then this is a case in point.'[78] In time, the rumours died down, but the war of nerves against Winifred went on. The Wagner offspring, nine, eight, six and five years old in the spring of 1926, developed into extremely self-confident children who would not listen to anybody. Siegfried as an elderly father was putty in their hands, and never punished them. The humble Emma Bär, more a second mother than a governess, was under their thumb. Winifred was the only one who was strict with them when their behaviour was exceptionally bad, and as a result was the main target for her children's criticism.

The domestic war between Daniela and Winifred was a strain on Siegfried's weak nervous system, and forced him to take action, because

> they are both domineering characters. Of course they can't stay under the same roof for ever. The difficult conditions of the times on the one hand, and the unsuitability of the building for dividing into two separate dwellings on the other, made these frictions inevitable . . . The constant tensions wiped me out completely, and as a matter of sheer self-preservation (because I need to save my energies for better things!) I was the one who insisted that Lulu should live separately.[79]

Daniela was obliged to move out of Wahnfried into a separate establishment, which served only to increase her fury against Winifred.

The Wagners' relationship with Hitler, now more than ever carefully concealed from the public eye, became especially close just at this time. He regularly stopped off in Bayreuth on his journeys between Munich and Berlin, staying overnight in the Hotel Bube in nearby Bad Berneck, and being picked up from there by Winifred, mostly after dark, and driven to Wahnfried:

So there I was, sitting behind the steering wheel with him next to me, which seemed extremely odd to him at first, because when he was on the road he always used to call out whenever he met a woman driver: "Watch out, woman at the wheel!" . . . But for the sake of getting here unrecognized and without arousing attention, he was actually prepared to get into my car, and even found some words of approval for my driving.[80]

Friedelind remembered that 'Late as it was, he never failed to come into the nursery and tell us horror stories about his adventures. The four of us squatted on our pillows in the semi-darkness and listened with shivers running down our spines.' According to Friedelind, all the Wagner children loved Wolf, as they too called him, 'because we were excited by his stories about the adventures he had while travelling through Germany . . . His life was fascinating for us because it was so different – like something out of a fairy-tale; his arrival so late at night, his stories about his dangerous life.' Even the Wagners' dogs, 'these big wild animals, who would never go to anybody except the family', immediately made friends with Hitler; 'he attracted them with no effort through his hypnotic power'.[81]

This period is no doubt the setting for a 'nice joke' by Wieland, then eight, later noted down by Winifred's secretary. 'Travelling by car once with Wolf and his mummy . . . Wieland put his arms around Hitler's neck and said: "Know what – you should really be our daddy and daddy should be our uncle!"'[82] Wieland, who was close to his mother but distant with his father, adored Hitler, who, for his part, clearly had a soft spot for the boy, but, as Winifred said, 'basically only because the blood of Richard Wagner ran in his veins'[83], and as the oldest child he was already regarded as the heir.

On one of his night-time visits to Wahnfried Hitler discovered that neither Siegfried nor Winifred were members of the NSDAP. The reason Winifred gave was that 'the party interested me much less than the personality of Adolf Hitler'.[84] At Hitler's request, however, on 26 January 1926 she joined, with membership number 29349.[85] Siegfried 'declined to join the party, out of consideration for his position as Director of the Bayreuth Festival, but he had no objection to my becoming a member, purely as a private person'.[86]

Sometimes Hitler telephoned when passing Bayreuth en route, to ask Winifred to meet him at a rendezvous in the area, because he was in a hurry. Winifred described such a scene to her friend Lene: 'So I jumped into the car as fast as I could, and away . . . We met at the top of the hill . . . and walked for a while, and in great haste he described to me the latest events in Munich, which, I'm afraid, are looking disastrous for him.' The matter in question concerned 'an accusation brought against Hitler by the state prosecutor of having broken up a recent meeting of the People's League . . . If Hitler were to be found guilty, he would have violated his probation, and would have to go back to prison for at least 5 years. You can imagine what that would mean for him, but also for me . . . It would be horrible!!!', and then, in the following sentence: 'I've lost three pounds in two days from sheer worry that Hitler might be jailed again!!!!!!!!'[87]

Five years' incarceration – that is to say, until 1931, but with the forfeited period of probation added, actually until 1933 – would have spelt the end of Hitler's political career. But instead of (with every justification) revoking his probation, which ran until 1 October 1928, and arresting him, the Munich provincial court decided to reduce the rest of his sentence by two years, to run until 1 October 1926.[88] Hitler, regarded by many in Bavaria as the future 'saviour of Germany', continued to benefit from the protection and support of Bavarian justice. Hence Winifred was able to enjoy a trip to Stuttgart on 19 April 1926 to hear Hitler speak, and she 'was naturally once again placed right at the front. Wolf was fabulous, especially as he dealt so brilliantly with a heckler who kept on interrupting'. She had not talked to Hitler; there was 'a sort of unspoken understanding between us on such public occasions'.[89]

At this time she was musing about Hitler's relationship with women, inspired by a biography of Mussolini she was reading. There she found the theory

that in their inner life people who are destined for such great things naturally had to become totally solitary – their mission placed them above others and therefore on the outside – a relationship with a female represented the only bridge and contact to connect them with the rest of humanity, and was therefore immeasurably significant for such men – unique in fact for their character and their development, formed and directed almost exclusively in the case of such men by the mother (true of W[olf] and of M[ussolini]) and unconsciously [signifying] for such men their longing for their late mother. I had never previously understood the importance of such a relationship – and I couldn't help thinking of myself and W. – and as I did so finding, I believe, the truth of this assertion confirmed.[90]

Almost the only interpretation this permits is that Winifred thought of Hitler's feelings for her as those of a son for his mother, although she was eight years younger than him, and her euphoric adulation of him certainly suggests other feelings on her part.

Winifred angrily rejected rumours that her marriage had been wrecked by Hitler. She wrote to Lene:

> Broken marriages look rather different from ours . . . you know how much I would like Fidi to be more manly, more assertive – for a while I was naïve enough to believe that I could change Fidi . . . Fidi knows my outlook, and I know his present one, but also his *true* one, and I'm waiting for it to come back to the fore. Fidi too plays a different part in my life from the one he would like – how often he slips into expressing admiring words for Hitler's personality and the sincerity etc. etc. of his aims. Such words make up for everything he says to the contrary because I can sense the kernel of truth in them . . . If all marriages were as harmonious as ours, there would be no divorces.[91]

Villa Wahnfried's doors were also wide open to other prominent Nazis, for example the 28-year-old Goebbels, who visited in May 1926: 'Bayreuth. The town of Wagner. I feel elevated.' About Winifred, almost the same age as himself, he wrote in his diary: 'A woman of fine race. That's how they should all be. And fanatically committed to us. Lovely children. We all become friends straight away. She tells me her troubles. Siegfried is so feeble. Ugh! The Master should make him ashamed of himself . . . Feminine. Good natured. A bit decadent. Something of a cowardly artist . . . I like his wife. I'd like her as a friend.' Winifred showed him to his room, and then to the grave of the Master: 'A young woman crying because the son is not what the Master was.' His parting thought was: 'I've grown fond of this sweet young woman!'[92]

A 'GERMAN FESTIVAL' IN WEIMAR

The year 1926 was the fiftieth anniversary of the Bayreuth Festival. Siegfried was opposed to any celebrations, and decided to observe the usual closed year after two years of festivals, as in the 'Wagner Year' of 1913; in other words, not to hold a Festival: 'celebratory meals, celebratory speeches, celebratory

articles etc.! In such serious and gloomy times there is no reason to celebrate.'[93] He never tired of pointing out that the first Festival in 1876, with
the first complete performance of The Ring of the Nibelung, was such a total
failure that Wagner did not have enough money to put on a Festival for the
following six years. He, Siegfried, preferred not to reawaken these memories
and would rather use the closed year to work on the new Tannhäuser
production.

In view of Siegfried's poor health, his friends made an effort precisely in
the jubilee year to honour the son rather than the famous father. Otto
Daube, highly active in cultural politics, suggested holding a 'Siegfried
Wagner Festival' [German Festival], featuring at least two of his operas, in
Weimar, the city of Goethe, Schiller and Nietzsche. In order to create an
audience, Daube arranged for the proposed Festival to coincide with the
national meeting of the Bayreuth League of German Youth, founded the
year before. It was an organization dedicated to educating German youth in
the spirit of Wagner and building up a future force to campaign against
'degenerate art', in accordance with the slogan 'regeneration not degeneration'.[94] Two superannuated völkisch writers, Hans von Wolzogen from
Bayreuth and Friedrich Lienhard from Weimar, were to be honoured on the
same occasion. The venue for the 'German Festival' was to be the German
National Theatre; that is to say, the very place that in the eyes of the
nationalists had been desecrated by the 'red' Republic. It was there that the
hated Weimar constitution had been put together. The object now was to
seize 'German' Weimar back from the hands of the democrats and republicans.

When, soon after the first announcements, the Central Society Newspaper
reacted critically to their scarcely veiled anti-Semitism, Siegfried denied
the charge angrily, writing to the Viennese journalist Ludwig Karpath: 'It is
the right of the Bayreuth League to stand up for the German spirit. Is the
German spirit a crime? But things seem to have come to such a pass now that
if you say you are a German you become a notorious "anti-Semite". A pecu-
liar country!'[95]

The nationalistic effect of the German Festival was embarrassingly com-
pounded by the staging shortly before it of the first great NSDAP rally, in
Weimar, from 4 to 7 July. Many friends of Wahnfried were involved in the
rally as well as in the German Festival; for example, the Gauleiter of
Thuringia, Artur Dinter, and his representative Hans Severus Ziegler.
Ziegler, born in 1893, had supported the Kapp putsch in 1920, and by 1924
had already founded the first weekly journal of the NSDAP, originally called

Der Völkische, and from 1925 *Der Nationalsozialist*. Ziegler had close connections with Bayreuth: his maternal grandparents, proprietors of the New
York music publishing house Gustav Schirmer, had been patrons of Franz
Liszt and Wagner, and visited the first Bayreuth Festival in 1876. Ziegler
moved frequently between Weimar and Bayreuth, and was a welcome guest
in Wahnfried, as was Dinter.

Like Elsa Bruckmann, Prince August Wilhelm and other Wagnerians,
Winifred attended the rally in Weimar and heard Hitler's speech in the
German National Theatre, which inspired Dinter to wax enthusiastic: 'On
that spot where Ebert sat, stands and sits Adolf Hitler today . . . This is the
beginning of a new era!'[96] Goebbels reported that supporters of the party
from Berlin had stood in front of Hitler's hotel singing 'Hitler will one day
lead us out of this plight.' Goebbels wrote in his diary: 'The Third Reich is
under way . . . Germany awakes!'[97] Around the fringe of the rally there were
brawls, and slogans were chanted such as 'We shit on the Jewish Republic!',
'Chuck them out, the Jewish gang, from our German Fatherland!'[98] Abuse
was shouted at passers-by because they looked Jewish, and girls were sworn
at because they wore their hair in a fashionable short bob, which was anathema to the Nazis.

Memories of the Nazi rally were still fresh in Weimar when the German
Festival began on 18 July, in the same German National Theatre. The language of the Official Festival Programme was pretentious: 'If we all stand
together, with a single mind and a single will, then we will work for that
"German Renaissance" which must surely come if the German way and
German culture, and with them our faith in the greatness and purity of our
most sorely tried people, are not for ever to be shattered.' Daube held that
the festival was the touchstone that would show 'whether we can still believe
in a German people'. Goethe was pressed effusively into service: 'O Weimar!
Yours was a special fate! Like Bethlehem in Judah, great and small.'[99]

Compared with the powerful mass parades of the Youth SA, the event
seemed extremely old-fashioned. Assembled around the most illustrious
guests, ex-Tsar Ferdinand I of Bulgaria and ex-Princess Sophie of Albania,
were notables from the Kaiser's day, along with *völkisch* artists and professors.
Hitler was invited, but to Winifred's great disappointment, did not appear.
'He's probably run out of cash,' was her comment.[100] The performances were
poorly attended, and the financial loss was devastating. Winifred had to
help out again; in a very short time, says Daube, she had found sponsors to
send money by telegram, so that at least there was enough to pay for the

technical and workshop staff, the orchestra, singers and actors (including Emmy Sonnemann, who later married Hermann Goering), and the materials. 'We are bombarding everybody with requests for money,' wrote Winifred, 'we've got to get it together somehow. We've got wonderfully German-minded people around us, who really are helping this time – the other sort has automatically dropped out – and indirectly I'm hoping that all this will really help to stiffen Fidi's backbone.'[101]

The high point of the Weimar Festival was supposed to be the 'historic' reconciliation of the houses of Wagner and Nietzsche.* Nietzsche's 80-year-old sister Elisabeth Förster, the administrator and falsifier of his writings, invited the Wagner family and Siegfried's sisters to Villa Silberblick to celebrate their reconciliation over breakfast. They held hands around the table, and Elisabeth Förster read from Siegfried's *Commandment of the Stars*. Count Harry Kessler's comment was:

> Thus the great, world-shattering Wagner–Nietzsche feud has petered out at the coffee-table in an atmosphere of social cosiness and in a manner appropriate to the latter-day imitators on either side . . . The whole business is infinitely petty-bourgeois and removed in sentiment by several thousand miles from the closing chords of the *Götterdämmerung*, let alone the end of *Zarathustra*.

Politically the Wagner and Nietzsche clans and their hangers-on were in agreement. Kessler said of the Nietzsche Archive in Weimar: 'Inside the Archive everyone, from the door-keeper to the head, is a Nazi.' And with reference to Winifred: 'this whole stratum of German intellectuals, whose background is really Goethe and the Romantic Movement, is Nazi-contaminated without knowing why . . . It is enough to make one weep to see what has become of Nietzsche and the Nietzsche Archive!'[102] Many said something similar of Bayreuth.

At the end of the Weimar event the Wagners were left with a mountain of debt. Even by 1928 there was still a shortfall of 40,000 marks, repaid over many years with the help of donors. Siegfried remarked bitterly: 'For that

---

*From early reverence for Wagner, Nietzsche developed a strong antipathy, saying that 'Wagner had made music sick'. Nietzsche also accused Wagner of appropriating many of his original ideas about classic Greek culture. His criticism culminated in the great tirade of 1888, *The Case of Wagner*.

much money I could have had the three operas printed that will now lie
unprinted in my desk drawer until I die. God protect me from such festivals.'[103] The failure of a well-meant event that was intended to honour him
was deeply humiliating for Siegfried. As he told Daube, at this time he suffered from or, as he maintained, was amused by a recurring dream:

> He is standing in front of the orchestra at the Berlin Philharmonie and is
> supposed to be conducting Richard Strauss's 'Tod und Verklärung' [Death
> and Transfiguration]; suddenly he notices that he's only wearing a shirt,
> and that it's a very short one that exposes his rear to the audience sitting
> behind him. So he keeps on trying in vain to pull his shirt down. In a box
> sits Richard Strauss, who jumps up sympathetically, hurries to the ros-
> trum and takes over the conducting of his symphonic poem himself.[104]

Once more Siegfried complained of 'the malice of the usual people': 'Any
other country would be proud to have a Bayreuth! It's only in this miserable
run-down land of black-marketeers and horse-traders that you get muck and
poison thrown at you! First it was my father's turn, then my mother's, and
now it's mine . . . It will be an enormous pleasure to take my leave of this
Germany!'[105]

To try to raise Siegfried's spirits, Winifred decided they would both go on
a restorative trip to Switzerland. The problem was that Presto had given up
the ghost. But Heinrich Bales, owner of a thriving Cologne painting and
decorating firm, stepped in and donated 10,000 marks. Amid all their financial difficulties the Wagners bought a Mercedes.[106] The journey may have
had something to do with Hitler, who was in urgent need of money. What is
certain is that Elsa Bruckmann was also working hard in Zurich in 1926 to
raise funds on behalf of the NSDAP.[107]

In Lucerne the Wagners met up with Siegfried's nephew, the top Italian
diplomat Count Manfredi Gravina. He had just come from Geneva, where,
as Winifred put it, he 'had to attend the farcical League of Nations'.[108]
Heinrich Class, at the Pan-German Association's meeting in Bayreuth, was
one of those who called for 'ruthless nationalist opposition' to Gustav
Stresemann's intention of taking Germany into the League. The League of
Nations was 'the crowning touch of an internationally imposed Marxist
policy of fulfilment [of the Versailles Treaty]', and membership for the
Germans would mean the 'voluntary recognition of the Versailles diktat' and
'renunciation of German territory in the north, west, east and south'.[109]

Once again the black–white–red flags were run out, impotently observed by the Social Democrats. The Bayreuth parish priest Stoss and Dean Wohlfarth refused to go so far as to ceremonially bless these flags.[110]

The Bayreuth SPD newspaper quoted Class's promise to 'carry on working for a dictatorship and against the constitution', and commented that it threw a 'strange light' on Siegfried's promise that the Festival would be kept free of all nationalism, when Class and other 'top Pan-Germans' were constantly in and out of Wahnfried. Like Class, the 72-year-old Baron Konstantin von Gebsattel, leader of the deeply anti-Semitic German Shelter and Protection League, was living in Wahnfried.[111]

Independently of the Pan-Germans, but at the same time, the National Socialists held a 'Tannenberg celebration' with a procession, ceremonial consecration of flags and an 'act of dedication over the German sword'. The chief speaker was Julius Streicher. Shouts of 'Heil Hitler' and 'Heil Streicher' echoed through the town. Anyone wearing a republican badge or countering Nazi sloganizing with a 'Long live the Republic!' was attacked verbally and physically.

Even in Siegfried's and Winifred's absence, Goebbels had family access to Wahnfried: 'I love playing with the Wagner children. The oldest is the cleverest. The oldest girl is the lively one. And the two little ones are so charmingly sweet . . . And then I romp around in the hay with the whole tribe for an hour. Such lovely little rascals . . . I'm a bit in love with the Wagner tribe.' His comment on the appearance of the Pan-Germans was: 'Mr Justice Class speaks at the graveside of Richard Wagner. Around him stand 20 Germanic men with long beards. It's distressing: so much insight into the way things are, and so little practical experience.'[112] Meanwhile, Pan-German supporters were flocking into Hitler's camp, especially the younger ones. Class became more and more isolated. The Wagner family, too, soon distanced themselves from their old friend.

The Wagners were supplied by their friends, the publishers Lehmann and Bruckmann, with plenty of *völkisch* and racial-anthropological reading-matter. Winifred was fired by Paul Schultze-Naumburg's book *Kunst und Rasse* (Art and Race), and sent the author an appreciative letter: the book was 'fabulously well written and gripping, right up my street'.[113] Like many others, Schultze-Naumburg described modern art as 'degenerate', sick and insane. As an architect, Schultze-Naumburg later became a prominent opponent of the Bauhaus movement and spokesman for 'the German dwelling' and 'racially orientated art'. His friendship with Winifred lasted all his life.

The Wagners were also friends of the Konopackis, a married couple who helped to found the Nordic Ring, an anti-Modernist cultural society of disappointed and unsuccessful 'German' artists, in which Franz Stassen was also active: 'Cultural conditions in the Republic developed in an ever more catastrophic direction; an unbelievable amount of criticism was poured out upon us; exhibitions were almost completely out of the question!' The Nordic Ring was a 'ray of hope', bringing together Germanic-minded people once a month for a lecture.[114]

Hanno Konopacki had distinguished himself in 1926 with his publication *Ist Rasse Schicksal?* (Is Race Destiny?) From 1928 the couple edited the national naturist magazine *Die Sonne* (The Sun). According to Winifred Marie Konopacki, née Princess zur Lippe, conducted 'a Nordic exchange for job-seekers, people in need of rest and recreation, those seeking marriage partners etc. etc.', a kind of 'Aryan' contact agency.[115] The Konopackis soon changed their Polish name to Konopath.

The Bayreuth spirit – a mixture of reactionary, monarchist, *völkisch* and anti-Semitic elements with a constant regurgitation both of Chamberlain's theories and those of his imitators – was later described by Erich Ebermeyer in these terms: 'Anyone who had any kind of contact with Wahnfried in those years would have been shocked by the narrowness of its political horizons, more appropriate to an Eastern Pomeranian farmyard than to the successors of Richard Wagner.'[116]

CHAPTER 6

The Older Generation Gives Way

(1927–30)

THE DEATH OF CHAMBERLAIN

In its struggle with the Weimar Republic, the nationalist, anti-Semitic and anti-democratic Right still looked to Houston Stewart Chamberlain as its ideological centre. The astute publisher Bruckmann kept alive the legend of the great writer, who had been fading for years, by reissuing excerpts from his earlier works in paperback. Permission was rarely given to anyone to visit the sick man, and it was a great honour. The paralysed old man's eyes still beamed when Hitler made a bedside visit. Winifred commented: 'Last time he even managed to breathe out a "Heil".'[1]

In May 1926 Joseph Goebbels wrote in his diary after a visit to Chamberlain: 'A painful scene; Chamberlain on a day-bed. Broken, mumbling, tears in his eyes. He holds on to my hand and won't let go. His big eyes glow like fire. Greetings, father of our spirit. Path-breaker, pioneer! I am moved to the depths of my soul.'[2] During the winter of 1926 the sick man's life flickered on in a semi-conscious and hopeless state. On 4 January 1927 Goebbels again visited the dying man, almost certainly to discuss the funeral arrangements with his party comrade Eva Chamberlain.

Chamberlain died on 9 January 1927. The *Völkischer Beobachter* had described him as the 'pioneer of a new era, the coming Third Reich'. His works were 'an inexhaustible arsenal of intellectual weapons for our battle'.[3] Winifred looked after the distraught widow, as Siegfried proudly reported:

'Winnie was really terrific, actively helpful and caring in a way that truly did Eva good.'[4]

Bayreuth flew flags of mourning as the hearse, drawn by horses draped in black, halted in front of the Chamberlain house. But the town undertakers were obliged to retreat without carrying out their function, after all, for SA men in uniform were able to produce written confirmation from the widow of their right to carry the coffin out of the house to the hearse; they were observed by a large congregation of mourners. A myth later developed that they had seized the coffin by force. The letter of permission they displayed was no doubt the outcome of Goebbels's earlier visit.

SA men in brown uniforms with black, white and red swastika armbands and stormtrooper caps escorted the hearse on its journey to the railway station, from where the coffin was to be taken to Coburg for cremation. Other SA men carried a huge mourning wreath with a swastika motif. Members of the Bavarian government and the Bayreuth town council were obliged to fall in behind them. 'It is hard to imagine a more ignominious funeral procession than this,' complained the SPD newspaper *Volkstribüne* (People's Tribune). Many taking part had angrily left the funeral procession at the sight of the Nazis, said the newspaper. And since a news agency had reported the activities of these 'twelve National Socialists', the world would now 'conclude that the town of Bayreuth was controlled by the Nazis'.[5]

In Coburg, too, the funeral procession was escorted by Nazis and by other nationalist paramilitaries in uniform carrying flags, including members of the Pan-German League and the Viking League. Apart from the Wagner family, mourners at the funeral included Hitler, Hess, ex-Tzar Ferdinand of Bulgaria and Prince August Wilhelm. The former German Emperor William II had sent a wreath from his place of exile in Holland. Hitler, 'his voice trembling with grief', gave one of the many funeral orations.[6] The ceremony presented the NSDAP with a good propaganda opportunity. The fame that Chamberlain enjoyed, especially among nationalist bourgeois intellectuals, was reflected back upon Hitler. It became a matter of universal knowledge that the world-famous writer had been a member of Hitler's party.

'WOLF' STAYS AWAY

The fiasco in Weimar put the 1927 Festival in jeopardy, especially as a general shortage of money crippled ticket sales. Embittered, Siegfried had to cancel his proposed new production of *Tannhäuser* and put on *Tristan and Isolde*, which could be managed with simpler sets and needed neither a chorus nor a corps de ballet. Again he had to go off on tour giving concerts, and failed to raise enough money. In the end he laid on a concert at his own expense in Berlin, and appealed to his assistant there, Evelyn Faltis: 'I'm financing this concert! . . . Please drum up an audience, pull people in off the street, so that it's not a flop.'[7] But that event too ended up with a loss.

Finally, Siegfried turned to Ernest Urchs in New York 'with the monumental confession: "we've got no money"', and pleaded with him to sell tickets and collect donations: 'We must have an American audience. Germany has become so poor that many people who used to come can no longer afford it.' The new lighting installation cost 200,000 marks, 'but where to find the money?' He needed half of the dollar reserves held in New York since the American tour: 'damned lousy money! The cinemas are all awash with money! But when it comes to real art, then there's no money!!'[8] When the answer was slow in coming, he pressed further: 'here in Wahnfried we've got debts like dogs have fleas!!'[9] The $4,500 eventually transferred yielded just 19,000 marks, a drop in the ocean. With the transfer of the last tranche of about 25,000 marks[10] in May 1927 the funds were exhausted.

To try to get hold of some money, Winifred played the lottery, and negotiated with a brewery and a cigarette manufacturer over exclusive contracts with the Festival restaurant. '"Necessity knows no law" really applies to us.'[11] She organized a big advertising campaign: '40,000 brochures have been . . . printed (so far). In England, France, America etc. etc. all the exclusive agents have been appointed and we have arranged for the press to be used at intervals – the first big announcement has already appeared.' She asked Otto Daube to distribute posters and programmes in the course of his travels. Every local group of the Bayreuth League was supposed to put up posters in highly visible places, in 'bookshops, music shops, hotels, public houses, newspaper offices – barbers etc. etc. – The advertising on express trains is going to start in December; things are moving along well.'[12] The town of Bayreuth helpfully paved the approach to Festival Hill, so that guests would no longer complain about having to drive through dust or mud to get there. But ticket sales remained sluggish.

Despite all her frantic activity Winifred at this time felt 'terribly sad and depressed', and cried on Lene's shoulder. 'I'm going to turn into a real horror – if I have to stifle all the love and all the trust that is in me and have to wear a miserable conventional mask for the outside world.' Fidi had no time, and the rest of the family 'were more or less hostile – too many duties – and no pleasure.' When in addition Lene cancelled her visit, she was 'totally mournful and bewildered'. The reason for her sadness was 'that the only really great pleasure that I always looked forward to and that kept me going – Wolf's presence here – has now been completely and hopelessly destroyed for me'. Hitler had declined to attend the 1927 Festival on the grounds

> that while Wotan is being sung by a Nagod, he considers Bayreuth to have been defiled, and cannot get over the fact that precisely a member of the race that is ruining us racially, politically, morally and artistically, and against which his entire struggle is directed, is singing Wotan and has been found worthy to do so. As long as this sacrilege lasts, he won't be able to come.[13]

Winifred made an effort to find a non-Jewish 'father of the gods' at least to alternate with Friedrich Schorr. In summer 1926 she was happy to report that the voice of the Dresden singer Josef Correck had developed so well 'that he could sing Wotan in the middle performances at Bayreuth – then all the anti-Schorr people could come to *that* cycle of the *Ring*'.[14] But this did not change Hitler's mind. He remained wary, but no doubt also wanted to save the Wagners unpleasantness: 'And then I didn't go there for years, which I personally regretted. Frau Wagner was quite unhappy, wrote twelve times and phoned twenty-five times!'[15]

Columbia Films from Britain were filming for seven weeks at Bayreuth that year, which made the rehearsal period particularly stressful. There was filming on the stage in the Festival Theatre, and of the family life of Wagner's heirs and successors in Wahnfried. A favourite motif for the cameras was the children and dogs romping about in the garden. Furniture was moved around every day, and all sorts of devotional objects associated with Wagner rearranged for the cameras, which incensed Siegfried's sisters. In addition, an English gramophone company was making recordings at very favourable rates, negotiated by Winifred. 'No Nagods, thank goodness, just decent Englishmen!'[16]

Even Winifred's strong nerves were strained to breaking point. When, in the presence of the film crew, the rehearsals for *Tristan*, sung by Emmy Krüger and Gunnar Graarud, made an unexpectedly auspicious start, Winifred's reaction was highly emotional, according to Emmy Krüger's report: 'Everyone enthusiastic – but the biggest thing of all was that Frau Wagner threw herself into my arms without a word, sobbing uncontrollably in front of the whole orchestra and everybody listening – she was so stirred up, so deeply moved!'[17]

At this time some business brought Hitler to Bayreuth. Winifred wrote to Lene: 'I had lunch with him at the Anker – but there were 4 other people there, too. You know that's not the right thing at all.'[18] In order to see Wolf alone, she even made the journey to Munich in this hectically busy period. Her excuse was that she wanted to buy a schnauzer at a dog show. Hitler was going to meet her at the station, she wrote on 7 July to Lene, and she was 'as pleased as Punch and had palpitations whenever she even thought about it'. If Hitler happened to be free for the evening, she would send a telegram to Bayreuth saying, 'I can't buy the dog until Monday' – and then simply stay. 'I'll be so pleased if everything works out! And if that were not to be the end of it, either.'[19]

The opening of the Festival on 19 July was filmed, with the elegant crowd in the interval gathered around Ferdinand of Bulgaria, splendid in his many decorations.[20] But the opening performance of Tristan was marred by cancellations. Graarud had a cold and was replaced by an understudy, and Carl Muck insulted the singer Barbara Kemp by grimacing furiously at her from his rostrum for missing notes. She left Bayreuth immediately, never to return.

During the Festival the SPD staged a popular demonstration against the 'Siegfrieds' who 'exploit Wagner and his work for political purposes that were alien to the great man himself'. The chief speaker was the workers' leader and Wagner expert Wilhelm Ellenbogen, who had travelled up from Vienna to talk on his favourite subject, 'Richard Wagner and the Working Class'. In his speech, he demanded that poorer people should be introduced to Wagner's works, as the Master had wished.

As a Member of Parliament before 1914, Ellenbogen had represented the Viennese working-class district of Brigittenau, where Hitler had spent four down-and-out years living in a men's hostel; something unknown both to the public and to the Wagners. Hitler was very well acquainted with Ellenbogen's Wagner lectures. In Mein Kampf Ellenbogen is briefly mentioned as an example of supposedly Jewish-tainted Social Democracy.[21]

Winifred's infatuation with Hitler – as before with Hugh Walpole – was another expression of her need to escape from the frustrating everyday life of Wahnfried. She sought every opportunity to see him. The lengths to which she went emerged from a letter to Lene: she had been 'daydreaming' through

Munich and found herself standing 'suddenly in the administrative office of the NSDAP . . . Hardly had [she] arrived there than, horrors, Hess had spotted [her]'. She left her address behind, with the hoped-for outcome that Hitler invited her to lunch in a Munich restaurant. 'Generously', she took Siegfried along with her to this meeting, but 'touchingly, he went off all alone to some other eating-place. He pretended he was doing so out of generosity, but actually of course he was scared of being seen together with W[olf]!!!'[22] The meal lasted for three and a half hours and drove away Winifred's low spirits.

Shortly afterwards she travelled 'without any opposition from family members' to a speech by Hitler in Nuremberg. 'At 5.30, when I arrived, the hall was full, and I had to stand all evening. Hitler came at 8, and it ended at 10.45. It was splendid. What I'm most proud of is my self-discipline. I made a vow to myself that I would never bother him in public. Even though he passed very close to me twice and we were staying at the same hotel, I didn't make contact.' None the less, he found out that she was there. Winifred then longingly anticipated the arrival of a messenger with an invitation: 'but I can't afford to act too keen! Damn and blast it – stupid convention!'[23]

In October she drove to a Hitler speech at Hof: 'I controlled myself so well that I didn't exchange a single word with Wolf, despite a number of opportunities – I didn't even let him get a glimpse of me.' But he let her have a glimpse of *him* when driving through Bayreuth. 'Naturally I only saw him in the Anker, but he was very jolly and cheerful. The movement has doubled in size in a year, and everything is going as he wants.'[24]

In November Hitler had time only for a quick greeting at the gates of Wahnfried, and then drove straight on: 'He's got an amazing amount to do. Came from a discussion with industrialists in Chemnitz, drove on to a speech in Ulm – is speaking tomorrow in Munich to students – is in Brunswick on the 25th, in Weimar on the 27th – on 10 December he's talking in Hamburg.' Whenever possible, she travelled to his big speeches. While her sisters-in-law 'were always sniffing around and [keeping] a close eye on my whereabouts', Siegfried was 'much more broad-minded'.[25] Only in Bayreuth did Siegfried forbid his wife to meet openly with Hitler: 'Hitler is speaking here on the 25th – and I'm already scared about it, because Fidi won't let me go, and I'm going anyway!!!!'[26]

Despite the empty coffers at Wahnfried, Winifred was always open-handed with Wolf, as she was at Christmas 1927: 'I've scraped together my last few pennies for Wolf and given him sheets and a quilt he really wanted.

I'm looking forward to his face when he comes to thank me!!!'[27] Hitler sent a long letter in return. Following the political set-backs of that year, he had once again taken heart: 'I simply have to rely on the future. And now, at the end of this year, I happily place my faith in it again. I now know once more that destiny will take me back to where I hoped to be four years ago [i.e. before the putsch of 1923]. Then the time will come when pride in your friend will be my return for everything I cannot repay you for today.'[28]

Winifred soon established a reliable go-between for contact with Hitler, his private secretary and friend Rudolf Hess. Hess gave a speech in Bayreuth on 14 April 1928, and was invited to Villa Wahnfried with his young wife, Ilse. He then helped Winifred to convert a projected concert tour of Austria into a pilgrimage in Hitler's footsteps. She was absolutely set on getting to Munich with Siegfried on 20 April, Hitler's birthday. 'The later we get to Munich, the less time there will be for Wolf, of course!!! – Fidi has no idea at the moment that the date coincides with his birthday.' And she did indeed meet Hitler on 20 April, not in Munich but in Berchtesgaden, from two in the afternoon till nine in the evening: 'we spent almost the whole day on the Königssee [lake], first of all on a boat trip, and then walking'.[29] Siegfried knew about the meeting, but did not take part in it.

The car journey then continued on to Linz, Hitler's beloved home town, where the *Tages-Post* (Daily Post) reported with astonishment that Winifred was driving her husband in her own car.[30] Winifred wrote to Hess: 'By the way, Linz is not at all "boring"! – For a start, its situation by the Danube is the opposite of boring. And despite their great simplicity, the city buildings have quite a monumental effect – there's no poor taste anywhere, as there so often is with us! The sun is shining brilliantly, too, and we have friendly people for company.'[31]

There was only a small audience for Siegfried's concert. The Wagners twice went up the Pöstling mountain, which Hitler had often told them about. They made an excursion to the nearby monastery of St Florian, where in their honour the organist improvised upon themes from *Parsifal* on the great Bruckner organ; and of course they visited Anton Bruckner's grave. Their next stop was the border town of Braunau am Inn – 'Wolf's birthplace!' exclaimed Winifred.[32] Admittedly, Hitler had no memories of the town, which he had left as an infant. But in *Mein Kampf* he celebrates his place of birth on the German-Austrian border as 'a happy stroke of fate', linking it to his 'life's task, to be pursued with all possible means', of reuniting Germany and Austria.[33]

With not entirely selfless intentions, Winifred made an effort to raise some money for the poverty-stricken Hess, 'You know, Wolf's private secretary and constant companion'. As she wrote to Lene, she wanted to do him a favour. Hess had married young, she said; 'his wife, whom I've known since 1913, was really nice to me that time in Berchtesgaden'. Hess now had a chance to get hold of a flat, but no money: 'I wondered if I could help – Wolf had immediately offered to give him an advance, but he (Hess) knew what a sacrifice that would be for him – and if Hess could raise the money in some other way, both he and Wolf would naturally be pleased.'

She asked rich patrons for help, but Heinrich Bales declined. The Schwarzenbachs in Zurich said they were prepared to give money to Winifred personally, but not to Hess or Hitler. On the other hand, they did not actually mind what Winifred did with their money, although 'Hess must not know where it came from . . . Isn't that extraordinarily decent of them? – And Hess is childishly thrilled – Wolf is relieved of the problem, and I'll be able to accept favours from Hess in a way I couldn't have done otherwise . . . Wolf is so attached to Hess, he's always singing his praises to me.'[34] Hitler's lack of money was a constant topic of discussion for Winifred, who joked to Lene: 'Wolf is unbearable; he's always saying he needs 2–3 million – and I haven't got it.'[35]

From then on, a grateful Hess kept Winifred fully informed about Hitler's well-being and day-to-day activities. 'Wolf is in Berchtesgaden writing a new book – which I'm supposed to be getting as a birthday present. Hess, who knows what he's talking about, thinks highly of it.' This was Hitler's *Second Book*, which was not published until after the war.[36] Hess also wanted to give her the original manuscripts of Hitler's speeches, if the latter agreed.[37]

As ever, for the sake of the Festival, Siegfried avoided being seen in public with Hitler and his supporters. At the end of May 1928 the Wagner family happened to run into Goebbels in Thuringia, who wrote about the meeting in his diary: 'We meet Winifred Wagner. And those 4 lovely children. Siegfried is a cowardly dog. Grovels to the Jews!'[38]

Winifred worked tirelessly for Hitler and his party. She recruited subscribers for the *Völkischer Beobachter*, 'because at the moment that's the best way to help W.',[39] and publicized the Fighting League for German Culture, founded the previous year by Alfred Rosenberg. This association pretended to be apolitical, but was in fact a subsidiary of the NSDAP. It recruited its members only by personal invitation, and in this way developed a network of like-minded cultural workers to counteract the great hate-object: the 'international', 'Jewish' and 'left-wing' culture of the Weimar Republic.

In October 1928 Elsa Bruckmann, wife of the publisher, asked Winifred to solicit recruits to the Fighting League among the artists at Bayreuth; she was especially interested in enlisting the conductor Carl Muck, who was hesitant about joining. Winifred replied: 'I'll certainly try to persuade Muck that he can join without endangering himself or his employees.' She added that she 'would get in direct contact with Elmendorff (he's very keen on anything like this), and then I can get access to Graarud via Elmendorff – that would be the easiest and most natural way. If I'm involved everybody always suspects something "compromising"!!'[40]

When she failed to convince Muck, Winifred asked Elsa Bruckmann to modify the text of the Fighting League's statement of aims: 'We've got to be able to show him there's absolutely nothing political behind it, otherwise he'll just have nothing to do with it, and given his critical mind I'd like the statement to make the best possible impression on him.'[41] She also made an approach to Lene Roesener: 'Why not just join the Fighting League? It's a reasonable thing to do.'[42] At Fighting League concerts Bayreuth artists appeared, such as Emmy Krüger, who noted that 'Elsa Bruckmann is recruiting like mad for Hitler.'[43]

Hans Severus Ziegler,* closely connected with the Wagners, organized a recruiting evening for the Fighting League under the title of 'The Final Battle for German Culture'. This culture was in need of rescue from its 'decline into international decadence' by a war against the 'alien racial' menace. 'You see everywhere the decay of the spirit openly and shamelessly displayed, especially in the theatre, in painting and in architecture [the Bauhaus style]. A ruthless struggle to resist is the duty of all Germans.' Ziegler singled out for mention as destroyers of 'German culture' names that would feature again in the book-burnings of 1933: Heinrich Heine, Ludwig Börne, Ernst Toller, Lion Feuchtwanger, Berthold Viertel, Carl Zuckmayer and others.[44] There was a perfect match between these notions and those of the Bayreuth circle and the organizers of the German Festival in Weimar. The NSDAP's Fighting League needed to do no more than adopt these slogans wholesale.

---

*Hans Severus Ziegler was an early supporter of Hitler, based in Weimar, who aimed to 'cleanse' Jews from German art. He became a leading figure in Third Reich cultural politics.

In order to open up access to youth, in 1929 the Gauleiter and school-teacher Hans Schemm founded the National Socialist Teachers' League, with its headquarters in Bayreuth, 'a band of activist teacher personalities', which 'conducts a determined and ruthless struggle against all the forces prepared to see even the future of our people, our German youth, sink down into the morass of internationalism, pacifism and democracy'. The Bayreuth town council commented: 'for activity and the ruthless will to fight, the National Socialist Party in Bayreuth is second to none. Its meetings are always full to overflowing'.[45]

The former Freikorps leader Gerhard Rossbach also set about educating youth. In December 1928 he brought his 'Ekkehard' children's stage company to Bayreuth. Dressed in archaic 'Germanic' tunics, the children sang folksongs and performed mystery plays and folk-dances. The profits went to the Schill Youth Movement, founded by Rossbach and dedicated to national pre-military training for young people. Rossbach was keen to create a network of like-minded *völkisch* families throughout Germany, which is why he billeted the children in private homes. Eva Chamberlain and the Wagners took in children, too.

The Wagner family appeared at the performance with four children and two aunts. Siegfried, who had drawn upon folk art for inspiration in his operas, was 'unrestrained' in his enjoyment of the evening, according to Rossbach. The latter came to lunch at Wahnfried the next day, was even taken to see Cosima, and was invited to the Festival.[46] Winifred liked him because he had taken part in the Munich putsch: 'In November 23 he handed over the infantry training school in Munich to the NSDAP!!!!'[47]

SETTING THE COURSE FOR THE FUTURE

In 1928 Hitler once again declined to attend the Festival. But according to the visitors' list, among those present were the farmer Heinrich Himmler, the chemist Robert Ley, the lawyer Hans Frank and other party comrades.

The Wagner children, used to money worries, showed enterprise that summer: they fitted out the gardener's big wooden hand-cart with little seats and for ten pfennigs offered to take Festival guests from the gates of Wahnfried to Wagner's grave, and throw in a visit to the graves of the Master's parrot and dog. Very few visitors turned down the chance of this bit of fun with the cash-hungry Wagner grandchildren.

In a side-room at Wahnfried they put together an exhibition for the Dürer quatercentenary year of 1928, consisting of postcards and reproductions. Once again they asked for ten pfennigs, but expected to get twenty. Daube said that 'Friedelind complains about business being poor, not many customers . . . Although Wieland is director of the exhibition, he says nothing, stands around silently, simply present, that's all. His line at the moment is boxing and wrestling!'[48] However, if the children were pestered too often with the question: 'You are Richard Wagner's grandchildren, aren't you?' they would all chorus back: 'No, we are cows!'[49] Thus they confirmed their reputation as the wild, ill-bred Wagner clan.

The social position of the family was highlighted in a diary entry by Lotte Warburg, recently moved to Bayreuth:

> They are the uncrowned royalty of the town. People tell stories about the children as they do about royal princes; the tradesmen recommend their wares and services not by saying 'his Majesty has the same thing, or ordered it from me', but 'we installed the same thing in Villa Wahnfried' (wall-fitted wash-basins), or: 'Frau Wagner always buys her sausages or her corsets from me'. Or if it's a matter of finding a school for your child, you will hear 'that's where the Wagner children go'. And even 'my boy had a terrible fight with little Wagner today'.[50]

In Bayreuth Wieland, the Wagner crown-prince, came across as a self-confident, but also solitary and sullen boy. His behaviour was exemplified by the story told by a girl who was at school with him: Wieland turned up at school one day with an American scooter, equipped with a horn and other trimmings. When other children pleaded for a turn with it, he refused abruptly and just scooted round and round, silent and defiant.[51] Wolfgang was enterprising; he sold eggs from his chicken-coop and got paid to work on his Aunt Eva's garden every morning.[52] He was good at crafts and technical things, and he was sociable.

Seven-year-old Verena filled the role of the sweet little sister, while ten-year-old Friedelind was attracted to artists. That year her enthusiasm attached itself to Frida Leider, singing the part of Kundry. The singer recalled:

> During my last appearance in Parsifal – it was unbearably warm in my dressing room, and I was lying on a chaise-longue trying to get a rest – when a small girl with long blonde plaits appeared, sat down opposite me with her

hands folded in her lap, and looked at me inquisitively, without a word. It was Friedelind Wagner, known as Mausi . . . After a while we developed a rapport, until . . . gently but firmly I had to ask Mausi to leave.[53]

Out of this unequal relationship there grew a long friendship, although Winifred had reservations about Frida Leider, jeering about her to Lene Roesener: 'The synagogue is filling up!!!!!!!!'[54] But contrary to all the rumours, Frida Leider was not Jewish, though she was married to a Jew, the leader of the orchestra at the Berlin State Opera, Rudolf Deman. It was highly significant for Friedelind's later development that her enthusiasm for Frida led her to mix in 'Jewish circles'.

For the Festival, 1929 was a closed year. Siegfried, then aged fifty-nine, was bad tempered: 'I earn well with concerts, but I can't feed 15 people. It's scandalous, the way the theatres treat me! Well of course, I'm not a Jew, I'm not even half-Jewish, and I'm not married to a Jewess. There's no place for anyone like that – I even think up tunes! That's the one thing you mustn't do. What a pleasure it is to be German! – Ugh, sickening!'[55] He indulged in fantastic conspiracy theories, telling Bayreuth acquaintances 'that a committee was being formed, headed by "Jerusalem", that wanted to take over the running of the Festival; so he would have no money worries ever again!' He also said 'that he knew exactly how it would be: they'd begin with the *Magic Flute* and end with *Jonny spielt auf!* (Jonny strikes up!), and they'd be dancing to jazz on the grave of R.W.!!! He would rather shut the Festival Theatre until the German people asked him to re-open it!'[56]

Once again Siegfried was forced to look on as younger competitors achieved success, such as the 28-year-old Ernst Křenek with his jazz opera *Jonny spielt auf*. Siegfried was enraged about the performance of this 'negro music' on an opera stage hallowed by Wagner, and sneered at the Dresden première at the despised Fritz Busch's theatre: 'What bliss for the Dresdeners! Now they know what German art is! And Parsifal and Siegfried and Tristan can be proud to breathe the air in the same space as Jonny!'[57] Although with less vehemence, he reacted in much the same way to the success of Leoš Janáček's *Jenufa* in Munich.

Next to his young and active wife, Wagner's son appeared rather soft and undynamic. Lotte Warburg had 'the impression of a quite harmless, kind-hearted and childlike person, humorous and educated, with a childlike smile . . . He carries the burden of inheriting from a genius, but only being endowed with a meagre talent. There is something honest and natural about him; no empty phrases, no affectation.'[58]

Although he had been suffering for a long time from shortness of breath and asthma, Siegfried did not consult a heart specialist. Instead, he worked on the conditions of his will with a lawyer friend, Fritz Meyer. On 8 March 1929 he asked his wife to accompany him to sign a joint testament. The 32-year-old Winifred had expected him to name her as his successor as director of the Festival, but she had not suspected he might impose conditions. Suddenly confronted with these in the presence of the notary, she did not dare to object. So it was that she signed up to an agreement that, in the event of Siegfried's death, she would initially be the heir of his entire estate. But 'if Frau Wagner marries again . . . she will be entitled only to the compulsory portion prescribed by law', and lose the directorship of the Festival. The second surprising point in the will was that Siegfried laid down no special position for his oldest son Wieland, but made all four children joint heirs after Winifred. Wieland, who until then had seen himself as the undisputed heir to the throne, was thus deposed. The question of the succession in the next generation remained open.[59]

At the time of Siegfried's will the children were between eight and twelve years old. It was unclear as yet what talents they possessed. But it was precisely Wieland who showed no gift for music, in contrast to Friedelind, who, bright and rather forward, idolized her father. As a loving father Siegfried did not want to bar the younger children from the chance of inheriting. Winifred was in a state of distress when she returned home from signing the will, as Wieland's school-friend Gertrud Reissinger later reported, having been in Wahnfried at the time. It was very clear how deeply 'shocked' Siegfried's young wife was 'by his posthumous act of violence'.[60]

Since the question of the immediate succession was now settled, however, Siegfried, Winifred and their close friend Albert Knittel set to work to create the best possible conditions for the handing over of the Festival. While it was clear that Winifred would bear ultimate responsibility for the overall direction, she needed both a business and an artistic director. Knittel became honorary financial director, so there remained the most important and difficult question of finding a suitable artistic director.

In the meantime, Siegfried's condition had deteriorated as the result of a car accident. The extensor tendon of his right thumb was torn and needed stitches; there was also inflammation. Conducting was impossible. Already somewhat tired of living, Siegfried was further depressed by the loss of income from cancelled concerts. Before his sixtieth birthday he lamented to Evelyn Faltis: 'I'll have to do the decent thing and be at home for my birthday, although I'd much rather run away.'[61]

But Winifred, remembering Siegfried's complaint that nobody had taken any notice of Wagner's sixtieth birthday, was preparing a big celebration. For months she had worked hard together with Knittel on the birthday surprise, which was to be a 'Tannhäuser fund' of 100,000 marks to enable Siegfried at last to realize his ambition of a new production of his beloved *Tannhäuser*. With her typewriter in the car she had been driving to and from Knittel's home in Karlsruhe and had written hundreds of begging letters to rich Wagnerians. The list of donors grew impressive, from ex-Kaiser William II and Ferdinand of Bulgaria down to friends of Wahnfried such as Bales, Bagby, Bechstein, Bruckmann, Class and Schwarzenbach.

Siegfried's birthday on 6 June 1929 began with an early morning serenade by the children for their still half-asleep father. At half past seven Rossbach's theatre group sang a Bach chorale in the hall. Then came a procession of friends to offer their congratulations, and from ten o'clock onwards deputations from the town council, schools, societies and theatres. There was lunch for twenty-nine members of his inner circle. The theatre group put on a performance in the afternoon in the open-air theatre at the Hermitage. In the evening the park at Wahnfried, decorated with lanterns, welcomed 180 guests. Heavy rain put paid to the planned firework display, but there was a Franconian evening with beer and grilled sausages, with the four Wagner children serving the guests.

With the doors of the house thrown open, Cosima participated from within. When Siegfried read out his pre-prepared speech of thanks and came to the point 'where his thoughts turned to his aged mother above in her quiet retreat, his voice failed him, and it was a minute or so before he could continue'.[62] In his diary he wrote about the celebration: 'A brilliant achievement by Winnie.'[63] Spurred on by the donations, Siegfried immediately got to work on *Tannhäuser*. The first piano run-throughs took place in the hall in Wahnfried, with children, sisters and staff looking on from the balcony.

Modernization was afoot in Bayreuth. Siegfried had previously made only faltering attempts to move beyond artistic tradition, but was now preparing the way for his successor to introduce fundamental reforms, with new artists, although naturally only non-Jewish ones.

A triumphant guest appearance by Arturo Toscanini in Berlin, attended by the Wagners in spring 1929, made Siegfried reconsider his previous rejection of 'the Italian'. He decided to invite Toscanini to conduct at the 1930 Festival; he had in mind the new *Tannhäuser* and *Tristan and Isolde*. Toscanini leapt at the invitation, declining any payment, since he regarded working at Bayreuth as the fulfilment of a sort of religious vow;[64] and he generously offered Siegfried in turn, initially in secret, the chance to appear at La Scala in Milan as director and conductor of a new Italian-language production of the *Ring of the Nibelung* in two cycles, that is to say on eight evenings altogether. This was the most glittering engagement of Siegfried's life, and presumably a lucrative one.

In autumn 1929 the Wagners went to the première of a *Lohengrin* production at the Berlin City Opera, staged and directed by its artistic director Heinz Tietjen, with Wilhelm Furtwängler conducting and designs by Emil Preetorius. Tietjen represented the moderate Modernist tendency, and developed the greatest possible coordination of the visual with the musical. Siegfried, usually so critical of Berlin, was highly enthusiastic about this *Lohengrin*, above all about the musical and visual impact of the choruses and crowd scenes, for which Tietjen had assembled all three Berlin opera choruses. In the interval Tietjen invited the Wagners backstage. Winifred saw the then 48-year-old for the first time.

Tietjen was born in 1881 in Tangier as the son of a German diplomat and an English mother. He grew up in Constantinople until he was ten, when he came to Germany for the first time. As his mother was a friend of Cosima's, it was not long before he visited Bayreuth, and he attended most Festivals from 1898 onwards.[65] At the age of twenty-five, as artistic director of the City Theatre in Trier, he directed and conducted his own production of the *Ring of the Nibelung*, and then gravitated via Saarbrücken and Breslau to Berlin, where he became a great champion of Wagner.

Siegfried was particularly impressed by Tietjen's triple function in Berlin, as it corresponded to the Wagnerian ideal. He recommended him to his wife as a future artistic director of Bayreuth, if possible in collaboration with Furtwängler and Preetorius. Following the engagement of Toscanini, this represented a further significant step towards the modernizing of Bayreuth. Siegfried was aware how risky every step towards 'modernity' was, particularly since he had to expect bitter resistance from his sisters, and he was not fit enough to face a tough argument with them. But he was relying on his wife, whose *Tannhäuser* fund had given him the courage to engage with reform.

Winifred, meanwhile, was drumming up interest in the 1930 Festival: 'It's going to be really different here for the first time – modern-ish – with all the publicity and ticket-selling – Unfortunately we're going to have to concentrate on earning money for a year or so, and then work all the harder on the artistic side and on presenting ourselves in that light.'[66]

By this time, July 1929, her workload as wife, mother, husband's secretary and organizer of the Festival was so heavy that she alleviated it by employing a secretary-assistant. Lieselotte Schmidt, who had been active even as a schoolgirl in Stuttgart in the Bayreuth League of German Youth,[67] commended herself to the Wagners by being a Hitler supporter, and soon became an intimate at Wahnfried. Her main duty at first was to supervise the children's school homework and stand in for Winifred, who was often away. Every week Lieselotte sent a long letter to her parents. Written in her spontaneous, guileless style, these letters give a picture of the day-to-day life of the Wagner family, and represent a rich historical source.

On 3 August 1929 Winifred set off with the children, the governess, Emma Bär, her secretary, Lieselotte Schmidt, and Eva Chamberlain with her maid, to attend the NSDAP rally, taking place for the first time in Nuremberg, the town of the *Mastersingers*. The oldest and therefore the most respected party comrade among them was Emma Bär.[68] The Wagners stayed at the Deutscher Hof Hotel. Lieselotte wrote: 'We're staying in no. 55. Hitler's in no. 57!' They met him promptly in the hotel corridor at ten o'clock as he was returning from his first engagement. 'He talks to Verena in the corridor,' wrote Lieselotte, 'really sweet and nice.' Then they go 'off to the Hauptmarkt [market square], grandstand and everything completely full. But we fight our way through . . . and find a good place, actually the best, right next to Hitler's car.'

In places of honour on the stand sat Prince August Wilhelm and leading military men from the World War. Otto Wagener was next to Winifred, and this was his first impression of her: 'She was tall, she seemed strikingly vigorous and confident, to judge by her dress and bearing undoubtedly a woman of the world. She had two charming children with her, a boy and a girl between 10 and 14.'[69] The children were in fact Wieland and Verena. Ten-year-old Wolfgang was taking part in the procession, while Friedelind was at the ceremony of consecrating the standards.

It was the first time that Wagener had listened to Hitler speak, though he heard him incompletely since there were no loudspeakers as yet:

His words and gestures were full of great enthusiasm and solemn conviction . . . He talked about the right of a people to live, the right of people to fight for their chance in life, and about the injustice of others trying to make slaves of them and keep them in subjection. Freedom, the community of the people, the will to live, inner conversion to a sense of community, these were the words that recurred and aroused passion. Time and again Hitler was interrupted by the tumultuous shouts of 'Heil' that swept over the wide field and the massive crowd.

Wagener was impressed: 'What power this man has over his men and supporters! And how he manages to bring others, who have only just joined him, under his spell.'[70]

The following day Winifred and Lieselotte attended the congress of the Fighting League, whose theme was 'The Jewish Culture Society!', and where Rosenberg and Hitler were speaking. Towards noon they watched a parade of party members that lasted four hours and included many Austrians and Sudeten Germans. There was particular applause for the Palatinate contingent, appearing in white shirts because the Rhineland Commission, as the occupying power, had outlawed the wearing of brown shirts, associated with the SA. Somewhere among the many thousands was ten-year-old Wolfgang, 'carried on the shoulders of a giant SS man [Geuse] for the full four hours'. In Lieselotte's words: 'Indescribable; the enthusiasm gigantic – the heat as well; the first-aid workers are kept busy, and our Emma too collapses and is caught by an SS man, after holding out for three hours.' She adds that 'meanwhile outside the Reds are provoking a riot, the SS are called in, two wounded (two dead at the station). Hitler quietens the mood in a few seconds with steely calm and compelling power . . . and the congress runs on in perfect peace to its close.'[71] It was reported in the Bayreuth SPD newspaper that next to St Lawrence's Church in the market square Jewish business premises and restaurants had been smashed up. 'The Nazis behaved like mad dogs! . . . In Nuremberg they were like an army of organized terrorists who are beyond the law.'[72]

Years later Winifred still recalled Nuremberg with pride: 'the many meetings with A.H. in the Deutscher Hof, and above all the year 1929 when he appeared before the crowd at a first-floor window with both my sons'.[73] The next time they met, Hitler conferred with Winifred about setting a date for the party rally that would not coincide with Bayreuth. She said that 'out of respect for the Festival he did not want to set any date before the end of Bayreuth', which would mean fixing a date after 24 August. The city of Nuremberg vetoed this proposal because the new school term would have begun by then, but 'Wolf in his stubborn way would not let go'. He had calculated how much the rally was worth to Nuremberg. In 1929 250,000 to 300,000 people had visited the city over two days. If every one of them spent only 10 marks per head, that represented a sum running into millions. The straw alone, for filling straw mattresses, had cost 30,000 marks.[74] From then on the Nazi Party rallies did in fact follow on from the Bayreuth Festival.

Winifred was keener on Hitler than ever: 'With this man as its leader, something great must come out of this movement, despite so much that may shock the average comfortable citizen at first sight.'[75] When she was asked whether there was a women's organization in the NSDAP, she replied proudly: 'There is no subordinate women's movement under Hitler – we women play our part with him, and as a woman I am a full and equal member of the party.'[76]

THE DEATH OF COSIMA

At ninety-two, Cosima was no longer conscious of what was happening around her. The family had even concealed from her at Christmas 1929 that she had reached her ninetieth birthday, to avoid making her too agitated. As Siegfried said, she was 'incredibly clear about the past, but forgetful about the present, thank goodness! (what is worth noticing in *this* Germany, anyway!!), always has her family around her, and is not aware that we have become completely impoverished and can't avoid getting into debt! A serene old age, therefore.'[77] The family behaved towards Cosima 'as though they were standing in front of an altar'.[78]

Visits from strangers, or even conversations with them, were beyond her. As a mark of favour to a particular guest, the Wagners evolved a special procedure: they would lead him into the darkened room where Cosima lay on her sofa, and while they conversed with the old lady, the guest enjoyed the high honour of observing the Master's Lady from a safe distance. Since there was such curiosity about the legendary Cosima, Winifred, deep in debt as she was, even hit upon the idea of offering an American woman journalist the chance of 'sitting quietly in a corner of the nursery and listening to a conversation with Mama. If this works out, I'll get 1,000 marks.'[79]

The international economic situation was becoming worse all the time, and culminated on 25 October 1929 in the New York bank crash, which also ruined many other banks throughout the world. The German banks were unable to honour their liabilities. Tough government austerity measures, raising taxes and other deductions while reducing social benefits, aggravated social conflicts and political unrest. More and more Bayreuth craft businesses, the spinning mills and the porcelain workshops were forced to release workers. Many businesses closed for lack of customers. Crippled Bayreuth war veterans were left with no choice but to beg on the streets, 'under the guise of selling matches, sticking plasters, shoe-laces etc.'. Finally, they staged a protest against the reduction of payments to war victims with a sit-down strike in the middle of the road, and were dragged away by the police.[80] Hitler's party benefited from the desperate situation, winning at a stroke nine out of the thirty seats contested in the election to the Bayreuth Town Council on 8 December 1929. Gauleiter Schemm acquired a voice in the deliberations of the council.

Despite his poor health, Siegfried was forced by lack of funds to make a concert trip to England. Winifred went with him, partly in order to install the eleven-year-old Friedelind, who had been expelled from the grammar school in Bayreuth after a stupid prank, in York to learn English under the wing of Winifred's former teacher Ethel Scott. Winifred then hurried to Bristol, where Siegfried gave a concert for an audience of 4,500: 'jam-packed, and the English response rapturous . . . Fidi was given a laurel crown by the mayor in full regalia, and I got a flower arrangement, to the applause of the entire hall'.[81] Even at the beginning of this long concert tour Siegfried was suffering from health problems; first a bout of influenza which left him greatly tired and weak, and then his first heart attack. He went on with the tour, performing with unfamiliar orchestras in Bournemouth, London, Cologne and Hanover.

Immediately after this strenuous tour, Siegfried had to go to Milan for rehearsals. Winifred let him travel by himself at first, and played down Cosima's condition for his sake. The Milan rehearsals went smoothly, not least because Siegfried spoke such good Italian. As for the old-fashioned stage-sets, he consoled himself with the thought that 'at least there is none of the revolting cultural bolshevism you find in Germany these days'.[82]

Cosima's condition deteriorated during his absence. When Winifred arrived in Milan, she did not let her husband know that the end could come any day. His concentration must not be disturbed. After the conclusion of the second *Ring*, and with more bad news from Bayreuth, they cancelled the Greek holiday they had planned and rushed homewards. They learned of Cosima's death on 1 April, while they were still on their way.

When they got to Bayreuth the next morning, Cosima's body was lying on a catafalque beneath laurel trees, in front of the portrait of the Master and her favourite picture, *The Holy Family*, painted by a friend, Paul von Joukowsky. It depicts Daniela as the Madonna, Blandine, Isolde and Eva as angels playing instruments, and Siegfried as the child Jesus. After a private funeral service the coffin was carried one last time around the Festival Theatre, and then driven to Coburg for cremation. Siegfried's deathly white face shocked everybody present. The urn with Cosima's ashes was interred at the head of Wagner's grave.

Winifred insisted they should take a holiday immediately to try to restore Siegfried's health before the Festival rehearsals began. They set out for Italy by car on 9 April, but stopped off in Munich first. Hitler had invited them for 9.30 on 10 April to his new quarters at no. 16 Prinzregentenplatz, to offer them his condolences in person. Hitler's palatial apartment with its nine large rooms had a Wagnerian atmosphere. From one window he could see the Prince Regent Theatre, whose architectural style was heavily influenced by the Bayreuth Festival Theatre, and which opened in 1901 as the Richard Wagner Festival Hall. The large Wagner monument stands in a small park next to the theatre. Hitler was 'beaming like a child' about his new apartment, as Winifred wrote to Knittel. His housekeeper and her husband lived in a two-roomed annexe. There was plenty of space to accommodate his 21-year-old niece Geli Raubal, whom Hitler had taken in. There was no doubt that he suddenly had a good deal of money.

From Munich the journey continued to cities 'that one rarely visits, such as Mantua, Ferrara, Urbino, Camerino, Modena, Parma, Piacenza, where there are the most wonderful buildings and pictures, especially the Corregios in Parma, an unforgettable impression'. Siegfried recorded his reaction to the Italians in his diary: 'A likeable, healthy, good-looking people, who deserve their Mussolini, being patriotic, industrious, moderate, good-natured and naïve.' And, turning his gaze back towards Bayreuth: 'Time to get down to work! I hope it all works out!'[83]

Siegfried returned to find that Eva had thoroughly cleared out their mother's suite, and had appropriated important papers for herself. When Siegfried, the sole heir, saw Eva's close friend Ebersberger taking away more family documents, he intervened angrily: 'You'll be taking away the last chair from under my bum next!' His protest had little effect, since, as Ebersberger said later, 'after 2 days Frau Chamberlain had won!'[84] Siegfried was incapable of asserting himself against his elder sister. This conflict over the precious archives absorbed family energies for decades.

At the next local party rally in Bayreuth, banners proclaimed 'Germany awake!', and Hitler gave a speech. The SA band played the song 'Victoriously we will strike at France'. The economic situation was so bad, and the numbers of the needy so great, that the Bayreuth community could barely afford to give them any support.[85] These great hardships brought Hitler more votes. In the regional parliamentary elections in Saxony on 22 June 1930, the NSDAP increased its share of seats from five to fourteen, and became the second largest party after the SPD. Schemm commented that the party was no 'longer travelling forward at the pace of a stopping-train, but at express speed'.[86]

THE DEATH OF SIEGFRIED

With renewed vigour Siegfried got down to work on *Tannhäuser*. Press reports of Toscanini's invitation to Bayreuth made headlines all around the world and ticket sales took off. But there was a mixed reaction from Wagnerians to the engagement of an Italian in 'this seat of patronage of German art'. Muck, having seen off Busch, stirred up opposition to his rival among the orchestra, and took his anger out on the already harassed Siegfried. Winifred, who was obviously not well informed about Toscanini's massive reputation as an artist, inveighed against 'the music snobs through-out the world who were ecstatic' about Toscanini's acceptance of the Bayreuth invitation.[87] She thought this fuss over the maestro was demean-ing for the three other conductors that year: Muck, Karl Elmendorff and Siegfried, who was proposing to lead the second *Ring* cycle.

On 26 June 1930, in the presence of Siegfried, Winifred, Daniela, Eva and the assembled musical directors and assistants, Toscanini took his first rehearsal. It turned out to be something of a shock. The maestro demanded the highest virtuosity, and was angry when he did not find it. Instead of being grateful, as a 'non-German', for being allowed to conduct on the 'hallowed' soil of Bayreuth, he complained – and in Italian, to boot. Lieselotte recorded that 'when he did not like the way the second violins played a particular pas-sage, he brought his baton down so hard that it broke in half, and he threw the broken halves over his shoulder and stamped his foot . . . the musicians are already grumbling about his intensive rehearsals. He sings, or rather croaks, loudly along with every part.'[88] His frequent beating out of the time, accompanied by a furious 'no, no', earned him the nickname 'Toscanono'.

It was embarrassing for Bayreuth that he corrected a number of mistakes that had crept into the orchestra's performance over the years, and that in doing so he referred them back to the score, which he knew by heart. Suddenly the fossilized and barren Bayreuth tradition stood exposed. It was only two days before Lieselotte was writing: 'Toscanini is becoming unbearable! He rehearses the orchestra day after day and makes no progress, because he stops them at every bar. The musicians are already on edge.'[89]

But when the hallelujah chorus in *Tannhäuser* turned out well, Toscanini went up to the veteran chorus-master Hugo Rüdel, and 'first of all pressed his right hand between his own two hands, then took hold of his head and kissed him on the forehead. A massive storm of applause broke out.'[90] Rüdel was hostile: 'All right, it was a kiss, but I've had nearly a hundred of those from Muck, and they were meant sincerely!' And when somebody remarked that the orchestra sounded wonderful under Toscanini, Rüdel replied: 'The music is by Wagner, not by Toscanini.' We should not permit 'a cult to grow up around the maestro'.[91]

As usual there were problems with the singers, in this case with Frida Leider, who pulled out. Siegfried groaned: 'The trouble such a damned J-wife [wife of a Jew] can make for you! I hope as a true Christian that she really has placed herself between two stools!'[92] And as usual Daniela created difficulties. She put together the costumes without consultation, and showed them to Siegfried as director only at the very last rehearsal, using the fragility of the precious garments as an excuse. Winifred knew that 'in reality she was making it impossible for Siegfried to suggest any changes. Daniela's costumes succeeded in ruining certain effects that Siegfried had developed in his lighting rehearsals.' As usual Siegfried opted for a quiet life, and acquiesced.[93]

On 16 July, after an argument over the casting of *Tristan*, Muck openly attacked 'the Italian', who thereupon threatened to leave immediately. In a panic, Siegfried sent Winifred to talk to Muck: 'She's the only one who can get anywhere with him.'[94] Friedelind records that her mother 'pampered' Muck, keeping him company at breakfast, stayed at his side during the intervals, and bought 'him a pound of caviar at a time . . . at seventy marks a pound'.[95] Muck remained hostile, but went on with rehearsals. Winifred also openly took Muck's part, in order to temper his aggression towards Siegfried. For the fact was that in this particularly hot summer, the constant agitation and the pressure to succeed were visibly too demanding for a man with a heart condition. Many who saw him commented on his wan, greyish complexion.

On 16 July Siegfried wrote out the last of his humorous rehearsal plans, in this case for the cast of the bacchanalia scene in *Tannhäuser*, which he conceived as a particularly ambitious undertaking in the spirit of his father; a 'summoning up of antiquity', featuring the bull that abducts Europa, as well as Leda's swan, and carried out by the avant-garde choreographer Rudolf von Laban and his troupe. As a special attraction he brought a few horses on to the stage, together with a pack of thirty-two dogs. All this added to the disquiet.

There was a disturbance during this hectic period of work when a dancer from Laban's troupe was arrested for handing out Communist leaflets. When his lodgings were searched, the police found an army revolver with seventy rounds of ammunition, and they began to look for other Communists in the Festival Theatre. Strict surveillance was imposed on the entire personnel.[96]

On 18 July 1930, at lunchtime, Siegfried suffered a heart attack, but would not be deterred from appearing a few hours later at the rehearsals of *Götterdämmerung*. After the third act, shortly before five o'clock, he collapsed on the stage. It was a cardiac infarction.

At the hospital Winifred took over the care of her husband and stayed at his side day and night. She barred all visitors without exception, a move aimed especially at Siegfried's sisters. Knittel took over the management of the Festival together with Ludwig Fries, director of the Festival office. Winifred was kept in touch with them by Ebersberger, who came over three times a day. Dress rehearsals began.

Winifred recalled only one of her children back to Bayreuth from their holidays: Friedelind, who was in England. In sending for her, Winifred 'touchingly pinned her last hopes on his condition improving because he would be so pleased to see me unexpectedly'. When mother and daughter met in the hospital, Friedelind wrote, 'she leaned on my shoulder and broke into tears; we had never been so close to each other'. But the doctors thought that seeing his daughter again would worsen his condition, and they made her wait in vain for days. 'Neither Mother nor I ever forgave them for that.'[97]

Toscanini opened the Festival on 22 July 1930 with *Tannhäuser*. It was an unparalleled success for the maestro, but also for the director, Siegfried Wagner. The dream he had fought hard for throughout his life had been realized at last. But he was not to see this first great success – any more than Winifred did, keeping her vigil by his bedside.

It soon became apparent that, thanks to Toscanini, the Festival was going to be the most successful ever, both financially and artistically. Busch recorded a veritable 'Toscanini mania' that knew no bounds.[98] With all that was happening, it went unnoticed that Helene Bechstein had introduced a special protégée of hers to the Festival: Hitler's niece Geli Raubal, for whom he had arranged training as a singer.

On 2 August, the lawyer Fritz Meyer sought Winifred out at the hospital, and begged to be allowed urgent access to Siegfried. He needed to discuss his will once more with him and get him to agree to an alteration. But although it was in her interest to comply (the change concerned the clause about her remarrying), she refused for Siegfried's sake; he must not suspect that he was dying.[99]

Siegfried died on 4 August 1930, according to the death certificate 'a casualty of preparations for this year's Festival, carried out by him personally'.[100] He left a 33-year-old widow and four growing children: Wieland thirteen, Friedelind twelve, Wolfgang just eleven and Verena nine years old. Siegfried had left orders that the Festival should go on even if he died. Winifred was worn out by her long vigil, but in public she showed no sign of weakness. 'At eight in the morning after father's death, my mother sat at his desk in the Festival Theatre and took over his work.'[101] In so doing she carried out Siegfried's testament and his express wish.

Taking place in the middle of the Festival period, his funeral was attended by all the artists and employees, and by many visitors, as well as high-ranking Wagnerians such as Prince August Wilhelm. Rossbach's acting troupe in their uniforms accompanied the hearse on its way to the cemetery in Bayreuth. Hitler offered Winifred his condolences by telephone, but explained 'that because he knew his presence would cause more difficulties for us, he would not be taking part in the funeral'.[102]

The day of the funeral ended in the evening with a musical tribute to Siegfried in the Festival Theatre. Toscanini opened it with the 'Siegfried Idyll'. After the encomium, delivered by *Kammersänger* Carl Braun, Elmendorff conducted the overture to Siegfried's *Angel of Peace* and the entr'acte, 'Faith', from his *Heathen King*. Finally, with the entire audience on its feet, Muck conducted 'The Death of Siegfried' from the *Götterdämmerung*. As a mark of recognition, Winifred invited her two most loyal assistants, Emma Bär and Christian Ebersberger, to join her and the children in the family box.[103] Toscanini proved himself a good friend of the family in these few days. He took a kindly interest in Winifred and the children. In her distress Friedelind, having been denied access to her father at the end of his life, now attached herself devotedly to Toscanini and made him a surrogate father.

As usual after every Festival performance, the management invited both guests of honour and artists to the Festival restaurant for a shared meal. When Winifred entered the hall in mourning dress, sat down at the Wagner table with the singers, and thereby, for all to see, took Siegfried's place, the thousand or so people present remained silent for a good quarter of an hour. Then the meal commenced. Winifred mingled with the guests, thus imme-diately launching herself into her work, and was not prepared to parade her mourning in the traditional Wahnfried show of emotion. This triggered off an angry reaction among the old Wagnerians ranked around the 'aunts'. Emmy Krüger aligned herself with them, too, astonished that after the funeral: 'The widowed Winnie felt able to be with us all in the restaurant – and drink and drink until after midnight! – I and hundreds of others just couldn't fathom it!'[104]

Overnight Siegfried's widow had become an outsider, a foreigner who ought to clear out of the hallowed Villa Wahnfried: 'Even before father was buried, my mother was being pressed by the mayor and the corporation of Bayreuth to hand Wahnfried over to the town as a Wagner museum; they had even found her alternative accommodation already.' Furthermore, the town had sent the widow all the bills for the funeral, even though a freeman like Siegfried was entitled to an honorary burial.[105]

The scene was a re-enactment of what had happened in 1883 after Wagner's death, when Cosima inherited from him. Siegfried had often mocked 'certain hyper-Wagnerian types' who at that time had pushed them-selves to the fore, and 'who were almost more unpleasant than our enemies', people who talked from dusk till dawn in Wagner quotations. 'For these supporters my mother was not Teutonic enough.'[106]

And yet on the day after Siegfried's funeral, chorus-master Rüdel greeted Winifred, in the name of all his fellow-artists, as the new head of the Festival, and pledged his loyalty and unconditional allegiance.

CHAPTER 7

Winifred, the New Boss of Bayreuth

(1930–33)

TIETJEN AND FURTWÄNGLER

Though hard pressed, Winifred took time off for a short visit to the Nuremberg Rally. She talked to Hitler about Siegfried's will; he thought the ban on her remarrying was right. It is a groundless rumour that he ever entertained the idea of marrying Winifred himself in order to become 'the master of Bayreuth'. But the gossip is said to have become so widespread that the Wagner children were asked at school whether it was true there would soon be a wedding. Friedelind's alleged reply, in broad Franconian, has cropped up in the popular press ever since: 'Me mother'd like to – but me Uncle Wolf, he don't wanna do it.'[1]

During this Festival summer Hitler conducted an extremely aggressive campaign in the run-up to the Reichstag election. In a closing electioneering address on 13 September 1930 before a crowd of 5,000 in Bayreuth, Hans Schemm stressed 'that the National Socialists are the deadly enemy of democracy, and they're only entering the Reichstag in order to gain power by legal means'.[2] The elections took place in the shadow of a poor economic situation, high unemployment and another reduction in public sector salaries. More than ever, the political climate was characterized by violence and terror.

The election was a triumph for Hitler's party, which took 107 seats, against only twelve in 1928. Above all, it was now attracting younger voters. The NSDAP, the explicit opponents of the Weimar Republic, had become the second biggest parliamentary party after the SDP. Hermann Goering became president of the Reichstag. The success of the Communists (KPD), gaining seventy-seven seats against a previous fifty-four, indicates the polarization of politics.

In Bayreuth, with its roughly 35,000 inhabitants, the NSDAP's success was proportionally greater than in the Reich as a whole. With 8,209 (previously 3,700) votes it was almost as strong as the SPD with 8,310 votes. The big losers were the bourgeois parties. The Deutschnationalen (German National Party) shrank from 3,780 to 965 votes.[3]

The mutual hostility of the two largest parties to each other erupted on 22 September 1930 in the Bayreuth City Council during a speech by Schemm, whose biographer reported:

> The chamber looked like a chaotic battlefield. Broken tables, chairs, glasses, ashtrays lay strewn around, and blood spattered all over the place, from head-wounds and cuts from splintered glass – the Social Democrat councillors had to escape along the street from the excited mob, and one of them had to be taken home under police protection.

The subsequent disciplinary hearings against elementary-school teacher Schemm made him a martyr.[4]

Since firearms were banned, the Bayreuth Social Democrats fought with rubber truncheons, while the Nazi weapon of choice was the dog-whip.* The mayor complained in vain about 'the degrading of political morality'.[5]

Under the terms of Siegfried's will, Winifred was entitled to appoint her own collaborators. While the Festival was still in full swing, on 12 August 1930, she contacted the man Siegfried had recommended as a potential artistic adviser, Heinz Tietjen. He had been promoted shortly before to the post of Intendant-General of the Prussian State Theatres, and in Berlin was in charge of the State Opera on Unter den Linden, the Kroll Opera House, the Theatre on the Gendarmenmarkt and the Schiller Theatre, as well as theatres in Kassel and Wiesbaden. He had become the most powerful man in German theatre.

---

*By 1930, something close to civil war conditions prevailed in Germany. Civil politicians were at the mercy of paramilitaries, especially the Nazis, and police had a constant struggle to maintain law and order.

As she had met Tietjen only fleetingly in Berlin the previous year, and needed to sound him out, she used a current Wagner dispute to make contact with him. She asked Tietjen to support a petition, initiated by Richard Strauss and addressed to the German Theatre Association, to secure voluntary, honorary royalties for Cosima's financially distressed daughters, such as she had enjoyed up to her death.[6] There was no reply for four weeks. In the meantime, the Festival ended with record takings of 1,053,000 Reichsmarks, and with a substantial profit.[7]

On 1 September 1930 Carl Muck unexpectedly resigned from any further participation in the Festival, explaining that 'I no longer fit into the new machinery in any way, of course – my artistic outlook and convictions being rooted in 19th century Bayreuth.'[8] The euphoria surrounding Toscanini had always deeply irritated his jealous rival. But he bowed to Winifred's request to hold back any announcement until she could find a replacement conductor for *Parsifal*. Winifred immediately set off by car for Milan to see Toscanini. Although he had already been appointed to conduct at the Salzburg Festival, the two quickly came to an agreement: 'After our last discussions, no drivel in the press, however malicious, can sow discord between Toscanini and us.'[9]

At last Winifred heard from Tietjen. He apologized for the delay in replying, saying he had been away on a long official journey; and he wrote very cordially. Regarding the honorary royalties he promised: 'Please believe me when I say that, as an old Wagnerian and in memory of Siegfried Wagner, I will do everything in my power to preserve the Work.'[10] As they corresponded from then on, the understanding between them deepened.

By the end of October, collaboration with Tietjen had developed to the point where Winifred was able to send him a long list of orchestral parts that needed filling and ask him for advice about doing so. She also asked him what sort of title he wanted her to give him: 'Artistic adviser? Please think about this a bit – and let us hope that next year's adviser will become a future colleague!'[11]

Tietjen replied with a long letter: 'The thought that my childhood dream of assisting with the work of Bayreuth might be fulfilled, puts all trivial worries out of my mind.' He declared himself 'totally devoted to you, most respected and honoured lady, and the work of Bayreuth'. He asked her not to name him as her collaborator just yet, 'even though I am completely yours from this moment on'.[12] Winifred's reply was: 'I regard you from now on as my silent comrade in the struggle.'[13]

On the afternoon of 14 November Hitler dropped in at Wahnfried for three hours. Winifred told him her worries, and wrote to Lene: 'he's beside himself over Muck, and wants to go and confront him straight away – but he won't get anywhere!!!'[14]

The never-ending negotiations with singers had to be tackled next. Signing up performers involved numerous journeys. Lieselotte Schmidt never ceased to be amazed: 'all the offers and negotiations, from the soloists down to the lowest novice ballerina, all come from Frau Winnie, who needs a brain that really is a first-class control centre, not to mention a heart and a sense of humour as well . . . without her, absolutely nothing happens'.[15]

To secure a fundamental improvement in the quality of the Festival, Winifred wanted to attract another big-name conductor in addition to Toscanini. She had in mind Wilhelm Furtwängler, then heading the Berlin Philharmonic Orchestra. When consulted, Tietjen replied that he was 'completely in agreement . . . that he is the only one to entrust with the musical side of Bayreuth in the future. Please leave his "education" to me; I want to relieve you of all these things that are not easy for a lady and not agreeable.' He reported that Furtwängler was imposing conditions: 'He's stuck on the prima donna-ish notion that he must come up with a new production for Bayreuth.' He, Tietjen, had made it clear to Furtwängler 'that Bayreuth is not about the individual and his particular wishes, but that everybody, and especially the conductors, must take second place to the Work . . . in other words, I took him down a peg or two; that's what the good fellow needs when you start on some new venture with him'. But then he becomes 'a splendid, overgrown boy, keen to join in with anything for the sake of the Work'.[16]

Winifred and Tietjen met on 12 December 1930, in great secrecy, in the flat of the theatre agent Luise Reuss-Belce, to discuss tactics in their negotiations with Furtwängler. Winifred, wearing mourning dress, left the discussions relieved to have found an energetic helper in Tietjen. He was a man of the world, an accomplished linguist, cosmopolitan, highly educated, a lady's man and cavalier of the old school. He spoke polished German and could be scintillatingly witty when he chose. Above all, he was a man of the theatre through and through. His appearance was unprepossessing, but he made a great impact on Winifred.

To avoid alerting the press, the first discussion with Furtwängler took place on private premises, too, in the home of Furtwängler's manager and closest collaborator, Berta Geissmar. Furtwängler, who lauded Bayreuth as 'the dream of every musical director in the opera world', agreed to conduct *Tristan and Isolde*. Geissmar was surprised by Winifred's reaction: 'Frau Wagner is usually a strong, self-possessed person, but at that moment she broke down in tears of relief – the fate of Bayreuth evidently weighed heavily on her.'[17] In return, Furtwängler demanded the musical directorship of the Festival, which he was granted. Friction with both Tietjen and Toscanini was therefore written into the script from the very beginning.

But only a week later the notoriously difficult Furtwängler cried off, 'for personal reasons'. With zealous energy, Winifred finally managed to get him to agree to come and talk to her in Bayreuth. There she showed Furtwängler and Geissmar the Festival Theatre and the original scores of the Master, and they went on an excursion into the countryside around Bayreuth. She wrote to Tietjen: 'I can't help feeling that even a stone would melt, and that it wouldn't take much to get a "yes" out of him! If only he weren't influenced by Dr G[eissmar]; he's told me openly that she does not think it right for him to come on these terms. Damned women everywhere!' Furtwängler had asked for time to think it over. 'Perhaps my stubborn insistence that I want him and no one else will triumph in the end.'[18]

At another meeting, in January 1931 in Berlin, Furtwängler accepted. Winifred felt indebted to Tietjen: 'I know that I have you alone to thank for the happy outcome with Furtwängler – and that your high aims with regard to Bayreuth give me a feeling of absolute confidence and inner calm.'[19] In order not to upset the sensitive Toscanini, Winifred sent him a telegram straight away assuring him that he would be conducting *Parsifal* and *Tannhäuser* in 1933. 'Parsifal is yours,' she wrote (in English). His telegram of confirmation closed with 'warmest love' (also in English).[20] Tietjen's reaction was: 'I'm very happy about Toscanini's reply. Hats off to the great magician; and it bodes well for the future that he has such a strong sense of inner belonging in Bayreuth.'[21]

On 19 January 1931 Winifred as head of Bayreuth put out a press release to 650 newspapers. There were four news items, including Tietjen's appointment as artistic director, Furtwängler's as musical director and Toscanini's acceptance of the invitation to Bayreuth. It was not by chance that, among these sensations, Muck's resignation, the fourth item, went almost unnoticed. The press reaction was mostly positive. Hardly any of the papers failed to stress the modernization implicit in these decisions, made under the aegis of the Festival's new female director.

But Berta Geissmar was in contact with the press, too, and naturally her version gave Furtwängler pride of place. It took an effort on Tietjen's part to calm Winifred's anger: 'I shall deal firmly with the person in question, and will have no problem in curbing her excessive activity.'[22]

Winifred wrote to Tietjen: 'Thank goodness you and I have the same attitude to the press: make use of them when necessary; don't take them too seriously when they are indiscreet; and tell yourself that in our age of short-lived news interest, everything is quickly forgotten. I'm convinced that F. would not feel so dependent if G. were not always agitating and busying herself unnecessarily.'[23] Relations between the two powerful women were difficult from then on, which also placed a strain upon Winifred's relationship with Furtwängler. For Geissmar (known to Winifred only as 'the Jewess'[24]) was naturally present at every meeting with him, and often had a conclusive effect on his decision-making. Toscanini, too, was annoyed by the press acclaim for his rival. The first rumours that the maestro intended to step down began to circulate.

The new Festival director plunged into a frightening whirl of activity. She persuaded the Reich railway system to make the trip to Bayreuth less arduous for her visitors by successfully negotiating a daily express service between Munich and Bayreuth throughout the Festival, and even an express overnight service with *wagons-lits* on the route from Berlin to Bayreuth via Leipzig. The profits from the previous year were invested in large-scale rebuilding and modernization projects. The Festival Theatre acquired a new balcony box exclusively for the press, as well as new cloakrooms and offices. The theatre restaurant, still the old wooden structure dating from 1876, was enlarged and provided with new access points, and a new manager was appointed. Meanwhile, Siegfried's old bachelor home was converted into a house for guests. She bought a holiday home in Nussdorf on Lake Constance, and put in an extension and a terrace. She painted the window-frames light blue herself.

The vast Wahnfried library was put in order by Lieselotte Schmidt. Most of all, however, Winifred concerned herself with the famous Wahnfried archive, which had been compiled by Cosima and contained scores, manuscripts and letters to and from the Master. Winifred started with a thorough review of the material. Everything previously kept in chests and boxes was placed in new fireproof archive cabinets. From May 1932 she engaged the town archivist, Otto Strobel, whom she had known for some time. The extent of the Wagner archive can be estimated from Strobel's statement in 1948 that after sixteen years' work on the collection he had only processed two-sevenths of it.[25]

Winifred went from negotiations with Festival artists to dealing with builders, and then to her household chores. At the beginning of February she reckoned that 'my dashing about seems to have reached a high point; on Tuesday I was in Berlin, Thursday in Nussdorf, Saturday in Munich – the day after tomorrow I'm going to Milan, and next Thursday I'm going back to Berlin to sort things out with Furtwängler and to see the *Dutchman*! . . . I feel like some sort of small-scale industrialist with all my negotiating.' Ticket sales were going brilliantly. She didn't know 'how I'm going to cope with everything, but somehow I'll manage!'[26]

High-ranking Nazis continued to come and go at Wahnfried. If Winifred was away, Lieselotte acted as hostess. In March 1931, for instance, Hans Frank addressed an audience of 1,200 in Bayreuth on the subject of 'The German Revolution'. As Hitler's lawyer he was close to the leader, and commanded Lieselotte's fervent admiration: 'he's a good man, subtle and sensitive. He was here recently with Schemm from 11 till 1, took a look around Wahnfried, and relaxed . . . in its peaceful and beautiful surroundings.'[27] The good-looking Frank, a married man, father of two and well-known philanderer, became a friend of the family, and Lieselotte's lover.

Hitler's party was keeping a very close watch on events in Bayreuth. Among all the changes in the management of the Festival since Siegfried's death, one name stood out with unwelcome prominence: Heinz Tietjen. Since he had so easily secured the approval of the Prussian SPD Minister of Culture for his appointment, it was thought he must be 'on the Left'. His many connections with 'non-Aryan' artists, his multilingualism, and his international career history all aroused further suspicion.

In April 1931 Alfred Rosenberg, editor in chief of the *Völkischer Beobachter*, sent Winifred a registered letter warning her that Tietjen was 'without a doubt' a Social Democrat. He enclosed an unpublished article by the left-wing Berlin conductor Kurt Singer as 'proof'. Furthermore, Rosenberg accused Tietjen of disloyalty to the house of Wagner, citing obscure informants: 'a certain lady is, regrettably, still the secretary of the editor of a Jewish film magazine in Berlin. This editor is a very good friend of Herr Tietjen. The latter had said in the presence of the secretary that he knew very well why he was going to Bayreuth: to protect Wagner from the Wagnerians.' He was very sorry, said Rosenberg, 'if this letter should raise doubts in your mind about the rightness of your decision to appoint Tietjen to Bayreuth'.[28] This was a clear demand that the director of the Festival should dispense with Tietjen. The gossip mentioned by Rosenberg indicates how ubiquitous NSDAP informers already were.

In a long reply, Winifred fought back in defence of Tietjen. Naturally, she had not appointed him because he was an SPD man, 'which, by the way, I still do not believe', but because he was the right man for Bayreuth. She even maintained that Tietjen's alleged statement about 'protecting Wagner from the Wagnerians' was justified. For she too thought of this as 'my primary duty. What we mean are all those people who cannot bear to see Wotan's beard trimmed by a single millimetre, or Brünhilde represented by a lithe and lissom figure rather than a lady of the usual heroic proportions; people who perhaps demand that Kundry should wear an 1882 style of corset etc. etc.'

She was speaking as a National Socialist, she said, and had nothing against criticism. But she thought it was a mistake to attack Tietjen 'simply because he's supposed to be a member of the SPD. That would put our party on a par with the others, who say "show me your party card, and then you can have a job".' Tietjen had made himself unpopular among Berlin theatre staff by cutting evening pay rates, and that was why he was under attack. The writer of the article was a 'pathological plotter . . . and has the lowest character imaginable . . . In my view, the standard is simply not worthy of our Party publications.' Moreover, she could not understand how 'with this article the NSDAP could side with the Jew Singer against the Bremen Hanseatic Tietjen'. Winifred asked Rosenberg not to publish the article, 'not for Tietjen's sake, but because of the dubious character of its author', and signed herself: 'with a German greeting [Nazi salute], Your Winifred Wagner'.[29]

So Tietjen stayed on. But the attacks on him continued.

The tone of Winifred and Tietjen's relationship rapidly became more familiar. The Wagner children made fun of the new director, whom they knew only from blurred newspaper photographs; they thought he looked like an orang-utan. Tietjen immediately sent them a picture of himself in the hope of 'rehabilitating [himself] in the eyes of the children'.[30] The Wagner family thanked him: 'But one of the children still maintains that the dogs are better looking than you! Which one it was, you can ascertain on closer acquaintance.'[31] Tietjen fired back: 'The child who thinks the dogs are better looking will get extra praise from me, because that's correct.'[32] The cheeky child was Friedelind.

There could be no doubt that something more than a business relationship was burgeoning. Winifred was in a fevered state, obviously in love, and asked her friend Lene and her husband to be discreet. It would 'really endanger my whole future' if anything should slip out. 'At the moment it's all so terribly complicated and opaque that the slightest external hint could destroy everything.'[33]

Furtwängler announced that he was coming to Wahnfried at Easter 1931. Tietjen offered Winifred some advice: 'You've got to make it absolutely clear to Furtwängler from the start where he stands. Your manner with F., dear lady, must be firm from the beginning and remain so.' And she must not put up with constant interference from Berta Geissmar.[34] With this he expressly reinforced her reservations about Furtwängler's collaborator.

The guests were accommodated in Siegfried's house, newly extended, and found it 'extremely cosy'. They praised the tasteful furnishings, and the view of the old-fashioned garden of Wahnfried. Geissmar remarked that 'everything was provided for the guests' comfort; there was even some light reading in English in the library'. Winifred was a 'skilful and relaxed' hostess.[35] The children were not allowed to take part in mealtimes on this occasion, partly, according to Lieselotte, 'because they were too noisy, and also because they would have told Geissmar to her face how ugly she is'. They enjoyed being given two Easter eggs painted with swastikas instead, but could not agree 'on what to do with them; the boys wanted to eat them, and the girls wanted to keep them to look at'.[36]

Lieselotte's opinion of Furtwängler, as usual not differing much from that of her Mistress, was that

he's very straightforward, natural, not affected or conceited (though he would be if the revolting Geissmar, dead clever, skilful and 100 per cent Jewish, had her way) . . . That's the one thing none of us can understand about him, but the unpredictability of the artistic temperament has got to come out in him somewhere. But he talks quite openly and pretty scornfully about the Jews, and so does she, in fact, but with her it's hypocrisy when she keeps on stressing that he's the *German* master, and harshly rejecting Bruno Walter and all the others who belong to 'her tribe'.

But Tietjen would soon have Geissmar 'under his thumb', thought Lieselotte.[37]

There was discord already during the preparations for the Festival when Furtwängler changed almost half the orchestra, bringing in many musicians from the Berlin Philharmonic – from his own orchestra, in other words.

Toscanini, on the other hand, disagreed about singers. Winifred later angrily declared, arguing in her idiomatic style, that he 'had put at risk the livelihood of a good German singer . . .' and imposed 'what I regard as an incompetent substitute'.[38] Emmy Krüger was the singer in question, who cursed 'that foreign so-and-so', Toscanini.[39] Like Siegfried the previous year, Winifred could not get on with Frida Leider: 'That wretched Leider has cancelled again, although at last I'm now able to offer her the first Brünhilde – I've no idea what I'm going to do about Kundry, because Toscanini wants to take on the most impossible females!!!!!'[40]

Muck was agitating furiously against Winifred and spreading, according to Lieselotte, 'the lowest kind of gossip, you hardly dare repeat it, it's so disgraceful . . . Tietjen, Furtwängler, he's tried to turn them all against her in this nasty way.'[41] Winifred defended herself by sending out a refutation of Muck's slanders to her friends.

Winifred blamed Muck's rumour-mongering for the long silence from Hitler. She tried in vain to restore contact with him, and thought of going to one of his speeches, in Stuttgart. But the chances of meeting him in person at such a large-scale event were remote. Lieselotte commented: 'She doesn't want to run the risk of being turned away again, as happened to her once in Munich when the police were blocking the entrance to the Bürger Beer Hall, and she couldn't get in despite having a pass.'[42]

'THE FOREIGNER' TOSCANINI AT THE 1931 FESTIVAL

The Festival rehearsals literally began with a bang; Furtwängler was flying from Berlin to Bayreuth in a private plane that developed an engine problem, was forced to make an emergency landing midway through the journey, and turned over. Despite some minor injuries he hurried on by car, and arrived, 'covered in scratches and still half dazed with shock', half an hour late in Bayreuth.

Geissmar records that

the beginning of rehearsals was always a solemn state occasion in Bayreuth. The orchestra waited expectantly in their places, and the 'Musical Assistants', all the young co-repetiteurs and trainees, sat with their scores at the ready. And now something unheard of in the annals of Bayreuth happened – the principal figure himself, the new musical director, was not there. This was a crime, in the light of which the fact that he had almost lost his life flying to Bayreuth counted for nothing.

The press picked up on the sensation, and soon there was a rumour going around in Bayreuth that Furtwängler's manager had 'pulled off a particularly crafty publicity stunt' for him. Geissmar said that 'from this moment on I constantly had problems with my work in Bayreuth, right through the summer'.[43]

The tension between Furtwängler and Winifred stemmed above all from the fact that Berta Geissmar was Jewish: 'Herr Dr Furtwängler has once again provided proof for the whole world of the assertion that he is pro-Jewish. For about 16 years Dr Geissmar – a thoroughbred Jewess – has been his mainstay, and our first serious dispute during the 1931 Festival was caused by our differences over the Jewish-run press.'[44]

In May 1931, shortly before the start of rehearsals, there was a political scandal in Bologna. When Toscanini refused to open a concert with the fascist anthem 'Giovinezza', he was attacked by Mussolini supporters, hit in the face several times and injured. In a long letter to Mussolini he complained about his treatment and swore that he would never back down. Like many others, Winifred lost no time in sending the maestro a telegram expressing her sympathy. But Toscanini's firm political convictions, known world-wide and now reinforced, were bound to lead to conflict in Bayreuth, since the head of the Festival was in Hitler's camp and her husband had been an admirer of Mussolini.

To prevent friction between Furtwängler and Toscanini, Winifred had housed them far apart. Furtwängler stayed in an out-of-the-way, romantic house with a garden and a horse for riding, which according to Geissmar was 'one of the greatest attractions of his stay in Bayreuth', and one of the conditions laid down in his contract.[45] Toscanini and his wife, Carla, on the other hand, were back in Siegfried's house, where they spent as much time as possible on the permanently overheated, glass-covered veranda, known to the children as 'Toscanini's Turkish bath'.

In order to assert her credentials as director of the Festival, Winifred must have taken it upon herself to form judgements that were far beyond her artistic competence. This was unacceptable to Furtwängler as 'artistic director', and he expressed his misgivings in a private letter sent from Bayreuth. 'I too must admit, seeing things as they are here, that the opposition to Wagnerism (not to Wagner himself) is all too understandable, and that for all the colossal genius of Wagner's work it contains elements that inevitably force sensitive souls to defend themselves against it.' Then he expressed doubts about 'whether and to what extent I'll want to be involved here in the long run'.[46]

Toscanini for his part was annoyed when Furtwängler, the newcomer to Bayreuth, enjoyed enormous success on the opening night of *Tristan*, picking up rapturous reviews. On 18 August 1931 'Fu' celebrated another triumph when his *Tristan* went out on air as the first broadcast in the history of radio to be relayed by 200 stations worldwide. There was no question that it was Furtwängler who stole the show at this Festival, not Toscanini.

Moreover, Toscanini had another really tricky task on his hands. *Parsifal* had been conducted for thirty years at Bayreuth by Muck, and his support-ers took a jaundiced view of 'the foreigner'. Toscanini overrode the tempi established by Muck, chose a much slower pace, and to the horror of the vet-eran Wagnerians, exceeded Muck's performance time by twenty-three minutes. Although all other performances were sold out, for the last few evenings of *Parsifal* there were unsold tickets.[47]

This was exactly the time when Winifred should have taken special care of Toscanini, especially as she was indebted to him for his help the previous year. The maestro was hampered by a painful arm, annoyed by the prima-donna airs Furtwängler gave himself as director, and was therefore particularly sensitive. But in this first year of her era, Winifred's manner was far too forceful; she showed little real control, and no sensitivity at all when it came to artists like Toscanini and Furtwängler.

Much later, Toscanini confessed to Friedelind that he had been 'madly in love' with Winifred at the time. Every morning in Bayreuth he had been glad to see her, and had almost forgiven her enthusiasm for the Nazis. Late in life he still 'regretted not having had the courage to have an affair with her'. Friedelind replied drily that she regretted it just as much, or perhaps even more . . . And anybody would have been better than Tietjen.[48]

Neither were the comings and goings of well-known Nazis at Wahnfried, under the eyes of the international press, conducive to a good atmosphere. Lieselotte was pleased that Frank was around: 'I spend a lot of time with him, and he tells me lots of things.'[49] Schemm gave his usual Festival speeches, in which he acclaimed the importance of Wagner for the NSDAP. Ludendorff's supporters attempted to exploit the Festival too, by opening a bookshop selling their newspaper, *Ludendorffs Volkswarte* (The Ludendorff People's Standpoint), the sale of which was banned along with a pamphlet entitled

'Behold, a Saint'.[50] The celebrated hero of the World War had been bypassed by history. He had broken with Hitler. Winifred too had lost interest in her erstwhile hero Ludendorff.

The big row was provoked by general rehearsals for a commemorative concert for Siegfried on 4 August. Furtwängler wanted to be the sole conductor, with only Beethoven being played. However, Winifred insisted that all three Bayreuth conductors of that year – Toscanini, Furtwängler and Karl Elmendorff – should take part, and she wanted a 'family programme' with music by Franz Liszt, Richard Wagner and Siegfried Wagner. Furtwängler, or 'his Lordship' as Lieselotte called him, 'simply declared he wasn't going to conduct any "dynastic programme" – he has no idea!!!!! I never cease to be upset by him.'[51] Disputes about rehearsal times ensued, with Furtwängler always getting first choice, so that Toscanini raged about having too little time to rehearse. Winifred's version was that 'Toscanini couldn't fit into the regular rehearsal schedule, altering his arbitrarily chosen times at the last minute and then being surprised that nothing worked out.' Apart from that, he had an incompetent assistant who had lost his score and cost him another half hour of rehearsal time. 'It was this loss of half an hour that led to the disaster on 4 August.'[52] Enraged, Toscanini smashed his baton, abandoned the rehearsal and left the building. Many members of the orchestra, in their annoyance, followed his example. While Furtwängler attempted to bring the musicians back, Berta Geissmar rushed off to Siegfried's house to intercede with Toscanini, but he had just driven off 'with his chauffeur and his adored lapdog'.[53]

'He managed to offend the best German orchestra,' said Winifred, 'and show me up by cancelling the evening, and all without a word of explanation.' She had been able to persuade the orchestra to go ahead with the concert, under Furtwängler's direction, only 'by using means that were personally humiliating for me'. An attempt at open discussion had been abandoned because of Toscanini's vehemence 'and insulting words to me and my colleagues ("idiots" was the most flattering of them)'. Polemically, she asked herself in the manner of Siegfried: 'What would happen if a German abroad were to indulge in abusing a national shrine in this way? Everybody would rise up to a man against him.'[54]

Although Toscanini returned for his last performances, he left Bayreuth disgruntled, remarking that 'he had thought he was coming to a temple, but instead he had come to a completely ordinary theatre'.[55] He sent back a letter from Winifred unopened, and likewise would not accept a present from her, a 'manuscript of the Master's'.

Altogether, in spite of everything, the 1931 Festival was an enormous artistic and financial success. The town of Bayreuth was pleased to record nearly 20,000 visitors, who stayed an average of 5.6 days, almost as many as in the whole of the rest of the year. However, the visitors showed 'a marked tendency to economize'. 'As a result of the general economic crisis', moreover, this meeting-place of the *beau monde* attracted a good many thieves.[56] At any rate, the *Textil-Einzelhandel-Zeitung* (Journal of the Retail Textile Trade) called Bayreuth 'an economic bright spot'. The town was one of the few places in Germany with an international tourist trade: 'That commands special respect.'[57]

But then news came of Toscanini's interviews in New York, where he quoted passages from his last letter to Winifred, and declared he was never going back to Bayreuth. Winifred was livid with rage about his indiscretions, especially as the papers painted a vivid picture of political differences as the basis for the rift. The maestro declined

> to make Wagner's genius amenable to Hitler propaganda. In spring this year he had turned his back on Italy after being attacked for refusing to make obeisance to Mussolini. He had sought sanctuary in Richard Wagner's Bayreuth, only to discover to his great dismay that Wagner's daughter-in-law was eagerly engaged in promoting National Socialism.[58]

The Bayreuth SPD newspaper wanted to add its two-pennyworth, arguing that it was her own private affair if Frau Wagner was friendly with Hitler, but it was not a private matter if it had an impact on the Festival. The music critic of the *Volkstribüne* had been treated roughly by Nazis in the Festival Theatre: 'These people feel safe because, precisely where distance is required, the management does not always distance itself clearly enough from them.'

The newspaper did not mind if Schemm placed his people in the Festival administration and workshop. 'But it is strange, to say the least, to boast about this influence, especially since even when their work is poor . . . the people concerned are never sacked. Not to speak of the liquid life enjoyed under the swastika after the show, going on until first light next morning.' When art-loving but impoverished citizens failed to obtain Festival tickets, one wag had advised them 'to apply for a complimentary ticket in the

Brautgasse. And indeed the people there do boast of this influence.'[59] The Brautgasse was the street where the head of the Bayreuth NSDAP lived.

The public dispute became so heated that Tietjen stepped in and begged Daniela Thode to intervene; he wanted her to persuade the maestro to make a public declaration that he had not given the interviews. 'Otherwise, I can see us losing the last opportunity to win him over again for Bayreuth, because in these chaotic times the German press are already trying to politicize Bayreuth, and if they succeed, our work will be ruined.'[60]

Old habitués of Bayreuth raised the question of whether a non-German like Toscanini was not out of place there. His way of conducting allegedly demonstrated that 'stylistically speaking a Latin, however accomplished technically, cannot bring out the last ounce of what is there in the work of a German genius'.[61] However, the Wagnerian Paul Pretzsch defended Toscanini in the *Oberfränkische Zeitung* by making an 'Aryan' of him; his art was 'racially and in terms of the blood Nordic in origin, and therefore closely allied to masterly German art'. Toscanini could not be expected to subordinate himself to another conductor, 'even if it were Furtwängler'.[62]

In a five-page letter Winifred angrily forbade Pretzsch to publish this article in the journal of the Richard Wagner Society. The article was an offence to Furtwängler and a vote of no confidence in her. Then she gave vent to her fury with Toscanini: 'I think of him as a real pied piper of Hamlin. Everybody follows him blindly without even possessing the ability to consider the other side of the argument for once.'[63]

THE CHILDREN REVOLT

Since Winifred barely had any time at all to be with the children, she engaged a tutor, in addition to Lieselotte. He was a scion of the aristocratic house of Blücher, and with 'his pronounced North German officer's jargon' he was not popular either with his charges or with Lieselotte, and they drove him off the premises even before he had completed his probation.[64] Lieselotte therefore took upon herself responsibility for the children's education. She had acquired a humanities training as well as a teaching qualification, and played the piano well. She was also well connected with party officials in Bayreuth, and as a Hitler admirer she enjoyed the complete confidence of her Mistress. Thus she was able to carve out a position of considerable power within the family.

But the children, especially Friedelind, were not prepared to accept this. Once the Festival was over they rebelled against their preoccupied mother. They expressed their complaints in a long letter to Lene Roesener, and asked her to mediate. Lene wrote forcefully and with concern to Winifred: 'I may be one of the few people who talk to you openly.' The children were isolated and not in good hands with Lieselotte, who interposed herself between mother and children: 'She seems to me like a fawning courtier who does everything she can to maintain her influence, but serves you in a really pernicious way . . . Lieselotte's spying and her tale-telling all seem so undignified for you.' The children thought Winifred was nicer to Lieselotte than to them.

Very cautiously, Lene brings Tietjen into the picture. The children liked Tietjen, even though he was taking up yet more of their mother's time, 'because your emotional life is completely self-contained and absorbed by him, so that you would make any sacrifice, do anything for him etc., things you would surely not do for your children'. Finally she asks Winifred 'to keep Lieselotte just for yourself, but look for someone better for the children'.[65]

By return of post Winifred replied, defending Lieselotte and asserting that she cannot permit the children to have their way and treat the young woman 'like a skivvy'. She was quite clear that Lieselotte was not an employee, but a confidante. She asked Lene to come and visit and advise her, 'because I'm full of plans for the future, but can't put them all into effect yet. I'd like to break free, but I don't dare. I have to be reasonable all the time, and you know how well that suits me!' She revealed openly how much she needed Tietjen: 'I'm looking forward to Berlin – from somewhere or other I've managed to find some new appetite for life – I feel like a dry sponge that needs to be soaked and swell out again – I've been too solitary in the last 13 months.' She closed with the lines: 'make the best of everything [original in English] and don't think too much about the future – it just goes wrong!'[66]

Winifred did not go into the children's problems, even the very serious ones of thirteen-year-old Friedelind, a highly talented, sensitive girl at a difficult age. Unlike her siblings, she could not come to terms with the death of the father she idolized. She set out to oppose her mother and the new man at her side, and became aggressive, strident and very overweight. Winifred had no solution but to send her for slimming treatments.

Things became even worse when Tietjen started to take a hand in the children's education. There were problems, for example, with the fifteen-year-old Wieland's rather too close friendship with Gertrud Reissinger. Winifred decided that 'I'll have to end things with Gertrud – it's all got a bit out of hand. Heinz has stepped in and talks affectionately and sympathetically to him. I'm sorry for him – but there are certain things you just can't permit.' On the topic of Friedelind, she said: 'Mausi is behaving so outrageously that Heinz insists on sending her to a very strict boarding school after the holidays.'[67] So it was that Friedelind was sent in 1932 to Heiligengrabe in Brandenburg, to a Protestant convent school for daughters of the Brandenburg aristocracy. The school was politically conservative, nationalistic and 'loyal to the Emperor'. Friedelind felt rejected and abandoned, understandable enough feelings if one reads Lieselotte's comments: 'The little vixen hasn't been easy to deal with, and she's madly rebellious over this coup against her, which she never thought could happen. But it's the right course to take, and there's already been a positive effect on the others from the absence of the little trouble-maker.' Since 'that little she-goat' had been out of the house, 'things had not been half so difficult'.[68] The unruly Friedelind adapted only reluctantly to the firm regime of the convent school, and her enthusiasm for Hitler made her enemies. Her relationship with her mother was deeply disturbed.

Contrary to the intentions of Siegfried in his will, Winifred made no effort to ensure that her children enjoyed similar schooling, so that all of them would have an equal opportunity to take over the Festival. She insisted instead on Wieland's privileged position as sole heir, and he was the only one who took the *Abitur*, the university qualifying examination. The girls, by contrast, took only the lower leaving certificate, and to prepare them for marriage they were subsequently sent to domestic-science schools, and to learn languages abroad. However, it was precisely Friedelind who took a special interest in the Festival, had a close relationship with the artists from her earliest years onwards, and acquired a self-taught appreciation of music not confined to an understanding of Richard Wagner's work.

In her opposition to her mother, Friedelind formed closer bonds with Eva and Daniela. When Winifred deployed Tietjen as her defender and champion, the divisions within the family deepened. He had told Eva 'some bitter truths . . . about the inexcusable attitude of the family to me'. Daniela was relieved of her job as wardrobe-mistress: 'a new one has already been appointed. For the first time in her life, finally someone has told Eva the truth. Apparently she was sobbing and making notes for Daniela.'[69] Furthermore, Winifred cancelled the allowances to the cantankerous aunts

that Siegfried had been paying voluntarily. Daniela above all, now dependent upon donations from Wagnerians, became a dangerous enemy.

Despite their conflicts, on one point the whole family as well as the staff
were united: their support for Hitler and his imminent accession to power.
The Wagners had last seen him on Siegfried's birthday, 6 June 1931, when he
had surprised them by phoning after a long silence and inviting Winifred
out, 'with or without children', to the Beringersmühle inn, a local destination for outings. Lieselotte described the meeting in minute detail: after
about an hour's drive, towards three o'clock they had 'arrived at the great
moment and reached the even greater man; he was sitting with an escort of
5 (SS) men waiting for us in the garden. One glance from his wonderful
violet eyes was enough to make you feel his whole heart and soul.' What was
clear was that 'above all, seeing the children once more, who worship him
and to whom he is deeply attached, was almost moving for him. At one point
we had to let a serenade by 3 Nazi trumpeters wash over us, and the children
photographed the good-natured Wolf from every angle.'

After an hour and a half Hitler's chauffeur took the children and
Lieselotte back to Bayreuth, and Winifred finally had a chance to confide
her worries about the Festival to Hitler. The two of them arrived at about
eight in the evening at Wahnfried. 'Wolf and Winifred, the heroic couple,'
enthused Lieselotte, 'and what a joy it was to have "him" entirely to ourselves. He's just immensely straightforward, no airs and graces at all, and
terrifically nice and kind and he's got a great sense of humour . . . he spent
over an hour upstairs with the children, sat on Wieland's bed, and all of us
crowded in close so as not to miss a word or a look.'[70]

If Lieselotte is to be believed, the Wagner children thought about nothing
but Hitler. For their confirmation classes, Wieland and Friedelind were
assigned to the Reverend Wohlfarth, who they knew was an SPD sympathizer, and Friedelind conspicuously wore her swastika necklace in order to
make clear her political allegiance.[71] During the confirmation examination in
church, Lieselotte thought 'more about the Hitler rally tomorrow than about
the catechism. Today Hitler is in Nuremberg. It's almost unbearable to know
he's so near, and yet not to see him.'[72] At Christmas 1931 Wieland was pleased
to get a special present: a piano-score excerpt, handwritten by Pretzsch, from
the prelude to Siegfried's opera *Das Flüchlein* (The Little Curse). Admiringly,
Lieselotte records that 'in all the places where there should have been a
double-sharp [literally a 'double cross' in German, while a swastika is literally
a 'hook cross'], he has put in a little swastika; it looks very jolly'.[73]

Hitler's Christmas greetings that year were sent on black-edged postcards. On 18 September 1931 his 23-year old niece Geli Raubal had shot herself with his revolver in his Munich apartment. He lamented to his 'dear Winnie' that 'this has been a very sad time. I will have to come to terms with this great loneliness'. On Christmas Day he had driven through Bayreuth, 'and could not bring myself to come and see you. You should not take away the joy of others just because you are sad yourself.' He would soon make up for it. 'Kind regards once more from your Wolf H.'[74]

No court ever pronounced on Geli's death. The Bavarian Justice Minister prevented the legally prescribed post-mortem, or a forensic investigation, from taking place, and released the body for burial in Vienna. Rumours were flying. Winifred knew the girl, and often had to listen to Hitler's complaints about the temperamental and often subversive Geli. She was convinced that Geli's death was neither suicide nor murder, but the result of an accident. The girl had wanted to warn her uncle, and apply emotional blackmail to make him consent at long last to her marrying his former driver Emil Maurice. While carelessly handling his revolver, she had triggered the fatal shot shortly after he left the apartment. Winifred thought her theory was confirmed later by Eva Braun, who had twice wounded herself with a firearm while trying to put Hitler under pressure.[75]

While Hitler was grieving for Geli, his supporters were getting ready for the imminent 'seizure of power'. Franz Stassen was enthusiastic: 'The situation in politics and the state was becoming more confused all the time. This only served to strengthen our belief in the saviour, Adolf Hitler, who would put an end to this unaesthetic horror.' In the Society of Berlin Artists there had been many arguments 'with the permanently benighted'.[76]

The Wagner children did their bit for Nazi propaganda, and commissioned Hans von Wolzogen to write the script for a 'Kasperle' play (roughly equivalent to a Punch and Judy show). It should be 'as Nazi as possible, with a Jew in it', reported Lieselotte. Wolfgang had already acquired 'a Jewish doll with a glorious conk'. Wieland painted the scenery, and Verena played the female roles. Wolfgang directed. The play was called *Princess Bulette*, and Lieselotte said, 'there really is a Jew in it and Kasperle [the hero] is a Nazi'. The audience was welcomed with a verse that ran: 'But do not fear: this princess-play/ does not offend against the Republic; / (quietly) although I know, before the play begins, / that we're all good Nazis here.'

The plot was as follows: Kasperle kicks and cuffs two troublesome admirers of the princess to keep them away from her: one is the rich farmer Protz (braggart or toad), the other is 'a commercial traveller in perfumes (a Jew)'. The princess thanks Kasperle with a kiss. The closing verse declares: 'It truly is a scandal: these toads and perfumers / in our German land / they make you ashamed. / So you strike out – in a noble cause. / The whole lot of them make you sick.' The play ended with Kasperle stretching out his arm in a Nazi salute: 'Kasperle is silent and knows what he thinks / and at the end just shouts "Heil Hitler!"'[77]

Even to the rehearsals Emma Bär proudly brought along 'relatives and acquaintances, all Nazis'. The première took place in the presence of the author, several friends of the family and Wieland's school-friends. After a special performance in honour of Schemm, the delighted Lieselotte wrote: 'And in his honour we decorated the inside and outside of the theatre with all the swastikas we could muster.'[78]

On another occasion Schemm brought his mother with him and 'a never-ending procession of wife-and-children', as well as the office staff of the *Gau* (Nazi administrative region). At the end the audience broke out into 'three Heils' for Schemm. Lieselotte asked: 'How long must these men wait before they can put all their strength and knowledge to work for the salvation of our people?'[79]

CAMPAIGNING FOR POWER

It was only the later Kasperle performances that Winifred saw, because she was in Berlin with Tietjen. As she told Lieselotte, the political mood was buoyant, 'Hitler is in a strong position; most of the German People's Party is NSDAP.' Lieselotte commented on Hindenburg's declaration on 16 February of his intention to seek election for a second presidential term: 'I wouldn't have thought it possible that he'd lend himself once more to misuse; well, it'll be a murderous election campaign. Will we win? Or are we not miserable enough yet for the Third Reich, or not worthy enough?' Schemm asserted that 'every true Nazi ought to be a stranger to his bed in those few weeks'.[80]

On 22 February Goebbels announced that Hitler would stand for President. He had no realistic chance of becoming Reich-President, since both the SPD and the Zentrum (Catholic) Party were supporting Hindenburg, but for Hitler his candidature meant the chance to gain publicity from intensive campaigning, and to unite the fragmented nationalist vote around him.

The Bayreuth National Socialists used some clever ploys to attract new members. For example, they set up a kitchen in party headquarters, run by the minister's widow Sophie Brand, where 'unemployed party members' could get free midday and evening meals.[81] Many starving people joined the NSDAP in order to have a regular hot meal.

On 2 March 1932 Lieselotte thought: 'we do the sums again and again and always come to the conclusion that we can't really hope to make it in the first round of voting'. Winifred and Lieselotte were hoping for 'up to 14 million' votes. 'But as there are about 36 million voters, we'd have to get over 18 million, and dare we hope for that many???'[82]

The first round of voting on 13 March gave Hindenburg 18.6 million votes, but Hitler did poll 11.3 million, far more than in the Reichstag election of 1930. The other two candidates together racked up 7.7 million votes. Hindenburg's vote had therefore fallen short of an absolute majority, and he had to enter a second round, of which Hitler and the NSDAP were the main beneficiaries.

The election campaign descended into mud-slinging after a Munich newspaper published revelations about Ernst Röhm's homosexuality. Röhm had been called back from South America by Hitler in 1930, and had been Chief of Staff of the SA since January 1931, quickly expanding its numbers and turning it into a superbly organized paramilitary army. Hitler now defended his friend against all attacks: 'Lieutenant-Colonel Röhm will remain my Chief of Staff, now and after the election. This fact will not be altered, in spite of the opposition's utterly filthy and revolting campaigning methods, which do not shrink from distortion, illegality and abuse of office.'[83]

Wahnfried supported this declaration most emphatically. Röhm was an old friend of the family, a frequent visitor to the Festival, and even had the privilege of staying overnight in Siegfried's house with his friend Franz von Epp.[84] The Wagners had always known about his homosexuality, and had never held it against him.

Banned from using the radio for party propaganda, Hitler took to the air. His 'flights over Germany' were a completely novel campaign tactic. Thanks to his three-engined D 1720, piloted by Flight Captain Hans Baur, and bearing the name 'Hitler' on its pale-coloured wings, he could address several mass rallies in various cities in one day. His chauffeur, Julius Schreck, always followed on with the car in order to take him from airfield to rally. The photographer Heinrich Hoffmann flew with him, to supply the Nazi press with fresh photos. Millions of leaflets were dropped.

On a typical campaign day, 3 April, Hitler flew from Munich to Dresden, where there were 80,000 people waiting for him at the cycle-racing stadium, then to Leipzig with 70,000 at the trade fair centre, Chemnitz with 100,000 on the Südkampfbahn site, and in the evening to Plauen, to the biggest hall in the city and a specially erected tent. And so on, day after day until the election on 10 April 1932. This all gave the NSDAP the image of a modern, mobile, dynamic party, which presented a positive contrast to the ageing Hindenburg. Winifred was more inclined to see the campaign from a health point of view: 'I'm afraid that Hitler might not make it. My God, is that man wearing himself out. And anybody who knows his dislike of flying will know what he's been putting himself through!'[85]

In the second round of voting, Hindenburg was confirmed as President. But every child in Germany now knew Hitler's name.

Two weeks later there were elections for regional parliaments, including Prussia and Bavaria. The election campaign continued. On 13 April, worried by conditions close to civil war, with Hindenburg's agreement Brüning's government banned the SA and SS. The atmosphere was so highly charged that a *coup d'état* by Hitler was feared.* But he maintained his policy of seizing power by legal means, and on 16 April began a new series of flights over Germany, to Breslau and Königsberg, among other places.

During this important election period, Winifred sent her friend Wolf a very special birthday present: an autograph by Richard Wagner, in fact a page from the orchestral outline of *Lohengrin*. Lieselotte exclaimed: 'precisely the passage with King Heinrich's prayer. Highly significant, almost made for him!!!'[86] The passage comes in the first act, before the battle between Lohengrin and Telramund, where the King appeals to God to decide between them: 'Give a hero's power to the arm of the pure man, /and sap the false one's strength! / Help us, God, at this time, / for our wisdom is mere simplicity!'

Four days later Hitler was celebrating his triumph in the polls. In Lieselotte's words, again: 'Here's to the 24th! . . . And in Prussia up from 9 to as much as 164; the world has never seen anything like it; I think it surpasses Hitler's wildest dreams . . . This success, which we owe entirely to the unique personality of the Führer, is particularly important to our dear Frau Winnie,

---

*By this time Hitler was effectively beyond the control of the civil authorities, both law and order and democracy were breaking down, and the Chancellor was attempting to rule by increasingly ineffectual presidential decree.

who has been so close to him, and lived through and suffered everything with him since the very beginning.'[87] In Bayreuth the NSDAP polled more than 50 per cent, while the SPD vote collapsed to 33.3 per cent.[88]

Winifred's impatiently anticipated meeting with Hitler at the beginning of May came about in a complicated way. Before he left Berlin to travel to Berchtesgaden, Hitler got Goebbels to telephone and announce his plan to visit Bayreuth. But as it turned out that Winifred was in Berlin, he rang her there, probably at Tietjen's place, and asked her to drive with him from Berlin to Berneck. She was happy to accept, because 'on the long car ride she would be able to spend time quietly with him once more and to discuss many things'. She telephoned Lieselotte en route to say 'that "we" – she named no names, but our hearts told us straight away who she meant – would get to Berneck at 9 o'clock this evening; and she asked whether one or other of the children might like to come with us'. Lieselotte should bring her some of her things, because important deadlines meant she would have to take the night express straight back to Berlin.

From nine o'clock onwards the Wagner children waited with Lieselotte in Berneck, thirteen kilometres from Bayreuth, 'in pouring rain but the highest of spirits', and 'at half past nine two cars tore up, containing the following exalted group: the Führer, Goebbels and wife, Frau Winnie, Schreck, Schaub, Hanfstaengl and two other unknown Nazis . . . Once again, he was completely absorbed by the sight of the children, as we were by him.' They had a meal 'in relative privacy and undisturbed', where the children dominated the conversation. 'But that was the point of the expedition, for Wolf to see them again after a break of almost a year, and he couldn't believe how tall Wieland had grown.' Lieselotte thought that 'despite his tiredness' Hitler looked good: 'His eyes gleam with firm calmness and confidence, and he's full of hope, for the immediate future too . . . With heavy hearts, and yet too happy for words', the Wagners took their leave at a quarter to eleven. 'Hitler went to his car,' says Lieselotte, 'after saying goodbye to each of us twice over, and even standing to attention for the children!! It makes you weep to think that we Germans have been sent this man, and we have not yet unanimously placed the destiny of the people in his hands.'[89]

The account of the meeting given by Goebbels in his diary was as follows: 'We talk to Frau Winifred Wagner about the Bayreuth Festival. Next year they are putting on the *Mastersingers*. Hopefully, by then we will be in power. Then we can stage it in a way that suits our own taste and spirit.' The next day they had driven through Bayreuth: 'In Bayreuth the streets are black with people. The news that he is driving through has spread like wildfire ahead of us. We drive past the Wagner house. Behind it in the park rests the Master. Silent greetings and thanks.'[90]

Winifred must have discussed her most pressing problem with Hitler: she no longer wanted to work with Furtwängler, Hitler's favourite conductor. She seized the opportunity to explain her position to Hitler and to win him over. The outcome of this conversation quickly became known in Bayreuth, as was shown by a private letter from a Bayreuther:

> A prominent personality at first strongly criticized Furtwängler's non-appearance at the Festival, but after a personal discussion with Frau W., arrived at a quite different standpoint, and is now very definitely on her side. It seems that Herr Furtwängler wanted to recruit all the artists himself, without consulting Frau W. In addition, he is said to be quite pro-Jewish.[91]

The plan was for Toscanini to conduct in place of Furtwängler; he could not be expected to put up with any repetition of the messy competitive situation of the previous year. It was still only May when Winifred went to see him on Lake Maggiore. Toscanini agreed to conduct five performances of *Parsifal* and eight of the *Mastersingers*. 'He was just so sweet,' said Winifred, 'took all the blame for the problems of last year, and was completely his old self – if not even nicer!' She celebrated her success with Tietjen, although for the moment it had to remain confidential, 'because Fu is bound to kick up a stink in the press, since he's been dropped'. And 'there will now be a terrible shindig with Fu. He's so furious and his artist's vanity is so injured that he'll do his utmost to wreck Bayreuth . . . If I didn't have Heinz to deal with all this mess for me, I'd be driven crazy by people's wickedness!'[92]

Furtwängler, having indeed declared his resignation, gave his version of events to the *Vossische Zeitung*,* and it received an enormous amount of press coverage. Another step he took in his defence became known to Winifred only when she met Hitler in Leipzig in June: 'Fu had the cheek to ask for an audience with Hitler, and tried to mobilize the entire National Socialist press against me – but he went to the wrong person. Wolf described him brilliantly

---

*A liberal paper, the 'Voss' (or 'Auntie Voss', as it was nicknamed) was founded in 1721, but ceased publication in 1934 because of Nazi censorship.

to me in all his mendacity and nastiness and vanity.' The Pan-German papers had defended Bayreuth against Fu, 'no doubt thanks to Class'. Winifred explained: 'My tactic is deliberately to stay silent, and let Fu use up all his ammunition – when he's had his say, he'll have to give it a rest.'[93]

Many Wagnerians were annoyed that, in Bayreuth of all places, the 'Italian' Toscanini was given preference over the 'German' Furtwängler.

CONCERN ABOUT TIETJEN

As ever, the NSDAP had Tietjen in its sights. Anticipating the imminent 'seizure of power', in January 1932 the NSDAP representative assigned to the Berlin theatres sounded out Winifred, 'in his official party capacity', as to whether she thought that 'Herr Tietjen could maintain under the Third Reich the position he had held on to so far with such alarming cunning'.

Winifred's answer to this question was 'yes', and she went on to justify it in a long hymn of praise. Very adroitly, she mentioned only those facts of Tietjen's life that the party would look upon favourably, such as his active service in the World War, and his descent from a 'line of Bremen Hanseatic ancestors'. (She did not mention his English mother.) In the 'severely endangered Saarbrücken theatre', he had conducted a model defence of 'the interests of German art against the constant onslaughts of the French'. And 'when it came to sustaining Breslau as a bulwark of German art in the East, there could have been no better choice than Tietjen, who had once again proved himself splendidly'. After 1918, when the 'Berlin theatres had been hopelessly run down by the mismanagement of the post-war period', he had been appointed to Berlin and had created 'orderly conditions' there.

With regard to the criticism of Tietjen's 'cunning', she declared:

> He has been able to assert himself in a tough struggle with the current system. For example, since he took office, not a single un-German work has been premièred; the programme has been cleansed . . . Since the emergency decrees came into force, and ruined all of German artistic life, it is Tietjen who has tried to ward off the worst effects, who has remained at his post in order to save what could be saved.

And finally, Tietjen hoped 'that in the Third Reich he would one day be honourably released from his present life-long contract, in order to commit himself with all his strength to the service of Bayreuth'.[94] It is highly unlikely that Tietjen would have given up his position as General Intendant of Prussian State Theatres in favour of the Bayreuth Festival and settled down in Bayreuth, but it is clear that Winifred believed in this possibility for a while. It would have enabled her, she seemed to think, to marry him and hand over the directorship of the Festival to him until the children came of age.

During the summer of 1931 or 1932 Winifred arranged a first meeting, in Bayreuth, between Tietjen and Hitler, who was making one of his incognito visits to Wahnfried. Tietjen later supplied two different versions of this first encounter. The first was produced in 1936 for the official proclamation of the Berlin State Opera celebrating three years of Nazi rule: Hitler had been 'the first National Socialist who ever discussed the Prussian state theatre with me'. He, Tietjen, would 'never forget' that first meeting. On a 'turbulent summer's night, during a thunderstorm' he had been called to Bayreuth by Winifred, and 'there he was, face to face with Adolf Hitler'. It had been during the time when the Führer had to move around under cover of darkness, because the order of the day was 'arrest Hitler on sight'. The Festival had been in grave danger, since the government (the SPD government, that is, which had appointed Tietjen) disliked Wagner's music. Hitler had discussed 'the Bayreuth question' with him, and then enquired about the situation of the theatre in Germany and the Prussian state theatres in particular. 'At the end he said just one thing: "hold on".'[95]

The need for scepticism about eyewitness statements, however harmless, is clear from the contrasting version Tietjen gave to the denazification tribunal in 1947: 'Frau Wagner made the introductions: Herr Hitler – Herr Tietjen. He then asked an inconsequential question, I can no longer remember what it was. The whole business was over in half a minute. It was an awkward affair on both sides, just some embarrassed stuttering. Outside there was a storm and the rain was streaming down, and he disappeared just as he had appeared.'[96]

After the war Winifred, who for years had tried in vain to create good relations between Tietjen and Hitler, regretfully mused that 'an insurmountable distrust, if not open dislike, prevailed on both sides, Hitler's and Tietjen's, and caused me many difficult times and many a hard struggle'.[97] In fact Tietjen cautiously avoided meeting Hitler in private, even after 1933. But he could not afford to ruin his relationship with him, either, and he felt the need to have some insurance back-up. That was why he cultivated contacts with Nazis on the Festival staff before Hitler came to power, as he proudly reported in 1936. He said that when he had visited Bayreuth in the summer of 1931, privately and in no official capacity as yet, an unknown young man had spoken to him and asked him to take him on at the Berlin State Theatre. 'Then he went on to whisper something in my ear.' He had indeed taken the man with him to Berlin, where the latter had 'immediately set up an NSDAP cell' based in the organization.

The illegal Nazi in question was the soloists' repetiteur Karl Köhler: 'In the very first few days he found some brave and active men . . . to throw their weight behind him.'[98] In this way Tietjen, suspected of leftward leanings, provided himself early on with solid contacts on the Right. However, his most important supporter was Hermann Goering, who in 1932 had already assured him of his protection when the 'seizure of power' took place.

The balancing act that Tietjen was able to maintain until 1945 is a testimony to his immense skill and high intelligence, but also to the stubbornness and energy of Winifred in protecting him, through Hitler, right to the end, despite all his personal problems and the political hostility directed at him. Her love for the somewhat inscrutable Tietjen, who kept back so many secrets even from her, made Winifred a bundle of nerves. She complained to Albert Knittel that 'she had not sorted herself out'. In Bayreuth she suffered from 'moments of terribly painful loneliness' and sometimes just had to 'cry her head off' because 'I miss so much the love, kindness and care that I should have. What are you for? – that's the question that constantly arises. I'm uselessly frittering away the best years of my life – no amount of willpower and distraction can get around that. I'll try as hard as I can to be reasonable . . . but it's hard!!!' Going for a walk, 'reading, writing letters, watching Kasperle theatre etc. etc.: what sort of occupation is that for a woman of my ability? But – for the moment there's nothing for it, and I'll just have to come to terms with it.'[99]

As usual when times were difficult, she sought refuge in frantic activity. She employed a whole horde of workmen to dust, clear out and redecorate Wahnfried. She did not shrink from tackling 'the sacred rooms of the Master', the mauve drawing room and the 'hall', preserved as veritable museum pieces with the Master's original furnishings and everything he used allocated a fixed place ever since his death. In the corners and behind the furniture, more or less valuable objects had accumulated, which were now brought out. 'Everything superfluous, with no value for the children later on', was passed on to the new Richard Wagner Memorial Centre which the Wagnerian Helena Wallem was in the process of creating in the New Palace.*

Winifred loaned a few items to the new Wagner Museum in Tribschen. The Érard grand piano lent by Winifred, lovingly called 'my swan' by Wagner and used when he was composing *Siegfried* in Tribschen, is still a prize exhibit at the small museum there. Winifred also returned some furniture to Tribschen, although with unfortunate results. The Swiss were not happy with these historic upholstered pieces, because 'according to experts, it is not possible to halt the continuing destruction of the furniture, as moths have been established for too long in the fabric'.[100]

After a thorough clear-out, the mauve drawing room became a reception room with modern furniture and new silk wall coverings. In the 'hall' and in the large dining room the furniture was re-upholstered in light colours, and the walls were painted. Lieselotte found it in no way impious to 'sweep the place out thoroughly, because there must be dust from the year 1876 behind the sideboards!!!! The furnishings won't be changed, of course, but stripped and brightly painted with designs and patterns by Bales-Köln, probably very opulent! And the gloomy and uncomfortable north room has also become a bit lighter and more welcoming!'[101] All these changes were a shock for the aunts. Winifred tried to take the edge off some of their indignation by making Daniela a present of 'the dining-room furniture used by the Master and his Lady in the Festival Theatre'.[102]

Simultaneously with the modernizing of Villa Wahnfried there were further changes to Siegfried's house: internal spaces were reorganized, and a separate telephone line installed. The house was meant to accommodate guests, but Lieselotte also reported another purpose for it: 'Besides, Frau Wagner is thinking ahead to when Wieland is married and takes over Wahnfried, and as a sensible mother she will not want to be breathing down his neck, so she'll retire there.'[103] In fact, Winifred was preparing a home for Tietjen and herself. For the time being she was keeping all her options open, and considering 'first of all what rooms Heinz needs – that is – while we're not yet married, and maybe we won't want to live in Wahnfried any more'.[104]

Her old friends were concerned about Winifred's total dependence on Tietjen. She threw herself into the great love of her life like a completely

---

*The New Palace in Bayreuth is the former seat of the Margraves of Brandenburg–Bayreuth, built in 1735 after the old palace burned down.

inexperienced girl. As a connoisseur of women, and sixteen years older, Tietjen unleashed previously unknown feelings in her that went far beyond her intense but platonic crushes on Hugh Walpole or Hitler. When Knittel urged caution, she reacted fiercely, defended Tietjen, and then apologized, filled with remorse: 'Forgive me for imposing so heavily on you – I don't understand it myself – but our feeble natures are helpless against a force of nature!' Then she complained about the lack of news from Tietjen once more: 'Being keyed up like this is destroying me. Even when you school yourself not to worry, you are angry about the thoughtlessness behind it all.' One glance at the scales reinforced her despair. She told Knittel that, 'in spite of massages', she had gained weight again, and now weighed 187 pounds (about 93 kilos)*: 'I am beside myself.'[105]

Once again she could not bear to be in Bayreuth and went to Berlin, but she faced more problems there. Tietjen had been separated from his wife for years, and he had agreed to a divorce. However, he did not live alone, but with a former girlfriend, Nena, who had psychological problems, acted nominally as his housekeeper, and whom he did not want to abandon. Winifred said she had written to Tietjen 'that, if he had insurmountable problems with Nena, I would have to give him up. He was terrifically irritated, and yesterday he phoned to say the exact opposite'. She rejected anything Knittel had to say about Tietjen. All the same, she asked her old friend to go on telling her the truth, even if she thought him wrong: 'I'm sure I understand Heinz, with all his faults – it's an understanding you frequently lack, which is only natural.'[106] She poured her heart out to her friend Lene, too: 'For the rest, the outlook is as bleak as ever – and yet we're happy all the same! Crazy people, eh?', and with regard to the divorce: 'Heinz has not got a single step further with his personal affairs.'[107]

The emotional roller-coaster continued. Tietjen was a very busy man, and as a powerful theatre director, he was surrounded by beautiful women. He made himself scarce, plunging Winifred into new depths of despair. Lieselotte noted that 'Frau W. feels hemmed in and not as much at home here as you would wish her to, or as she did before . . . What can we poor people do to prevent her being miserable about Bayreuth and about coming home? We can only go on being fond of her!'[108]

---

*Although the metric system had been adopted throughout Germany by 1875 (beginning with Prussia in 1816), the pound (*pfund*) is still used informally, e.g. by market traders, as the equivalent of half a kilogram.

Moreover, Winifred felt that Tietjen and Knittel were making her redundant. She reacted with annoyance, and then apologized again, to Knittel for example: 'it's all to do with my tremendous need to be active – and I'm always afraid – you won't leave me anything to do'. She went on: 'Be patient with me – Heinz will put me straight, never fear! – My love makes me single-minded, exclusive and inconsiderate – that's wrong, and it will change – but don't stop being fond of me – your very wicked girl.'[109]

Winifred worried constantly about Tietjen: 'They have created a new Ministry of Culture, which means that Tietjen could be appointed to Berlin at any moment. That would be a bad blow for our work here and I think too much for his health to bear.' Then she promised 'to start trying to be sensible'.[110] Matters were further complicated by the children, who eyed Tietjen jealously and rebelled when he tried to play the head of the family and interfere in their problems.

When Winifred was in Berlin, she found herself waiting for Tietjen as though she were a frustrated housewife: 'Heinz has been at work today, for instance, since 10 o'clock, and it's now 8 in the evening and he still hasn't been home for lunch.' In the daytime she was busy looking at houses for him, 'because he'd like to get out of this noisy place and into a house to himself'.[111] But then he changed his mind about the house, and she started to look for an apartment. Winifred, known to all as a feisty, self-confident lady, was behaving like the 'little woman' anxious to do everything right for the lover who strings her along, and to avoid upsetting him.

Winifred's admiration for Tietjen extended to his work as the new artistic director of the Festival. As 1932 was a closed year, he had plenty of time to prepare for his first festival, in 1933. He was planning new productions of the *Mastersingers* and parts of the *Ring*, modelled on his much-praised staging of the *Ring* in Berlin.

Emil Preetorius brought his stage-design class from the Berlin Academy of Fine Art to Bayreuth, to involve them in the new work. First of all, they inspected the existing sets, a mixture of both ancient and new scenery, with detailed representations of trees, leaves and other objects. Preetorius recorded: 'and the first thing was, as I sat there with Tietjen and Frau Wagner in the empty theatre, and the old stage-sets were brought out, well, we've got to have some air in here, the stage has got to be freed up. So out with the lot, so that the size of the stage can achieve its proper effect.' Most important of all was the lighting: 'Wagner is a matter of the light.'[112]

They worked 'as though possessed' on the new *Ring*, wrote Frida Leider later, always 'moving towards a simplification, a great monumentalizing, highlighting the main accents and cutting out all the incidentals. It had the effect of a frightening revolution, and we ourselves were astonished.'[113] Preetorius took his lead from the great reformer of stage design, Adolphe Appia, and the productions of the Kroll Opera in the 1920s. Looking back, Tietjen observed proudly: 'At any rate, to give Preetorius his due, I must say that we were the first "de-clutterers" . . . We created space; stage sets and scenery gave way to stage space.' He, Tietjen, had worked at developing the 'art of mass movement and mass control', and a psychologically individual style of direction.[114]

He also brought first-class artists from the Berlin State Opera to Bayreuth, such as Maria Müller, Käthe Heidersbach, Frida Leider, Max Lorenz, Rudolf Bockelmann, Jaro Prohaska, Herbert Janssen and, new to the role of Gurnemanz, Emanuel List: 'The people Heinz is bringing me are pearls.'[115] As far as the future was concerned, the most significant appointment was that of the lighting technician Paul Eberhardt, without whom neither Winifred's modernization nor that carried out under Wieland from 1951 would have been possible.

Tietjen took a considerable burden away from the Festival by doing everything he could in advance in Berlin, with the State Opera singers and technicians, to prepare for performances in Bayreuth. This, admittedly, turned Bayreuth into a branch of the Berlin State Opera, as critics rightly remarked. But Winifred received practically ready-made, polished shows of the highest quality, and needed far fewer people of her own for the summer: 'Well, Tietjen had his people in the palm of his hand throughout the year.'[116] Under Tietjen and Preetorius, Bayreuth emerged from its narrow provincialism and achieved world-city standards. Winifred now had a strong man at her side, and made herself subordinate to him.

In the meantime, Hitler continued to go from triumph to triumph. When Reich Chancellor Heinrich Brüning resigned on 30 May 1932, Lieselotte commented: 'We've taken another big leap forwards, and I can imagine how busy they'll be in Hitler's headquarters.'[117] The new Chancellor of the right-wing coalition government was Franz von Papen. To get Hitler's support he lifted Brüning's ban on the SA and the SS (Schutzstaffel, Guard Detachment). The fighting units of the party were now free to intervene, and intervene violently, in the campaign for the Reichstag election set for 31 July.

On 9 July 1932 the NSDAP *Gautag* (regional rally) took place in

Bayreuth, with a torchlight procession and hour-long speeches. The high point was the address by Prince August Wilhelm, who as a party member and SA leader was a welcome guest at Wahnfried. As the son of the last Kaiser, Wilhelm II, his role was to win over the monarchists and the middle classes for Hitler.

The local Nazis under Schemm made trouble at SPD meetings and terrorized SPD officials. In uniform and clearly armed, they drove up by the truckload to SPD hostelries, tried to break up meetings, and provoked brawls with Socialists and Communists. They also liked so-called revenge actions, as described by the *Fränkische Volkstribüne* (Franconian People's Tribune): 'Some Nazi is supposed to have been stabbed by somebody, and so the Nazi street-bandits "arrested" anybody they came across' – for example, three workmen whom they pushed up against a wall, yelling at them: 'You dogs, you're going to pay for it, you're going to perish.' The slogan they bawled at the top of their voices was 'Hitler takes over power on Monday!'[118]

This time Hitler's flight over Germany took him to Bayreuth, to a mass rally on the sports field of the Gymnastics Club. An SA band rallied supporters, and uniformed Nazi units paraded. The opening speech was given by Hans Krebs, a 'comrade from the endangered Sudetenland'. He complained of the 'inner turmoil of the German people . . . and the desperate mood among the Sudeten Germans languishing under Czech tyranny'. Into the middle of his speech burst the roar of engines, followed by 'a wave of loud "Heils"'. Two planes landed on the nearby airfield: 'Hitler looked natural and unassuming as he stepped out of the cabin.' There was always the same scene: small children with bouquets, SA parades, photographers and surging crowds. Hitler exchanged a few words with Hans Beer, the head of the Upper Franconian Cultural Association, a singer and a former friend of Siegfried's, and then drove through cheering crowds lining the route to the sports field.

In his speech he stressed that the Republic had had thirteen years and 'During this time they have ruined the economy and created millions of unemployed.' The *Bayreuther Tagblatt* newspaper wrote solemnly: 'And they all feel it; this simple man, this unknown corporal from the World War, has grown into a personality who has entered into immortal life in the annals of the German nation.' Hitler was admitted as a freeman of various nearby municipalities, inspected the parade of honour and drove back to the airfield. While Richard Suchenwirth from Vienna was still invoking the yearning of Austrians for the Reich, Hitler's planes were on their way to Nuremberg, where tens of thousands were waiting. The celebratory article in the *Tagblatt* closed with: 'Tomorrow is the day of destiny.'[119]

Compared with their results in the two previous Reichstag elections, the success of the NSDAP on 31 July 1932 was sensational. While the Party had polled only 2.6 per cent of the vote in 1928, it stood at 18.3 per cent in 1930; but, now, in 1932, its vote had doubled to 37.2 per cent. It was not enough, however, for a governing majority. But in Bayreuth the NSDAP, with 11,716 votes, against the SDP's 7,333, was by far the largest party.[120]

Lieselotte's view of the Papen government was: 'At the moment things look pretty rotten in politics. We don't want this big-mouth Herr von Papen, who makes himself out to be so "socially" committed, but actually has no feeling for the people at all. We won't rest until Hitler leads the people. Heil!'[121] But the constant electioneering was taking its toll of many people's enthusiasm for voting. Recent election propaganda had included leaflets produced by the Bayreuth paper, *Fränkisches Volk*, exhorting readers to boycott Jewish shops. The local group of the Central Association for German Citizens of the Jewish Faith countered by taking out advertisements: 'Fellow citizens! Do not believe the slander and calumny about Judaism that you read and hear. They are a miserable election manoeuvre to trap you into believing the slogan "It's all the fault of the Jews!"' . . . We German Jews are human beings just like you, and German like you, no better and no worse. Only domestic peace can guarantee the revival of the Fatherland.'[122]

The Nazis got a shock in the elections of 6 November 1932,* which they had hoped would give them a ruling majority at last. They managed to hold on to only 196 of the 230 Reichstag seats they had won in July. Stassen, engaged at the time on his Lohengrin drawings 'for him, our Führer, divinely ordained', reported: 'In these fateful days Frau Wagner came to Berlin . . . one always drew strength and solace from her unswerving loyalty.'[123]

On 17 November Papen resigned as Reich Chancellor. Negotiations to form a government with Hitler as Vice-Chancellor foundered, because he continued his strategy of refusing to enter government except as Chancellor.

---

*New elections were held on 6 November 1932 because of the deadlock after the outcome in July. Hitler had by far the largest number of seats in the Reichstag, and was therefore entitled to try to form a government. But President Hindenburg refused to offer him more than inclusion in a presidential cabinet. Hitler rejected the President's offer. Chancellor Papen therefore dissolved the Reichstag at its first sitting in September 1932, and called for the November election.

On 3 December 1932 General Kurt von Schleicher became Reich Chancellor, and secretly offered Hitler's party rival, Gregor Strasser, the Vice-Chancellorship. He did not refuse, and thereby asserted a bid to lead the party and deprive Hitler of power. The confusion was so great that Hitler declared gloomily to Goebbels: 'If the Party should fall apart, then I'll put an end to it all in three minutes with my revolver.'[124] The great crisis ended on 8 December with Strasser, isolated, stepping down from all his party offices. Hitler had regained secure control of the party. From then on, Schleicher was the great hate-object of the NSDAP. But he too failed to form a stable government.

Winifred spent the turn of the year and January in Berlin, working with Tietjen on artists' contracts for the Festival. 'It was there that she received Hitler's letter to 'My admired and dear Winnie!': 'For weeks I've been bogged down in hard and heavy work. Worry upon worry!' He mentioned Geli once more:

> For the past two years Christmas has been nothing to me but a festival of mourning. And I can't bring myself to be the same as before . . . I believe the time will surely come when I can show my devotion to you in deeds and not words. Unfortunately, there are always new mountains to climb. I understand now why Wagner and his destiny spoke more to me in my youth than any other great German. It is of course the burden of the eternal struggle against hatred, envy and incomprehension. The concerns are the same.

Then he touched on the Festival: 'May you be successful this summer! Perhaps fate will allow me to make some contribution, after all! Once more, thanks and most loyal greetings, happiness and blessings, Your AHWolf.'[125]

At this time fifteen-year-old Wieland, with Lieselotte's help, wrote a 'colossal' essay on the topic of 'what prevents us from hoping for Germany's revival, and what makes us still believe in it'. Lieselotte said that the second part 'was entirely about Hitler, and if the teacher is not a Nazi, then we'll finish up with a mark of 5 for it [lowest mark in the marking system in Germany].'[126]

In fact, the NSDAP showed its strength again in the election for the Lippe regional parliament on 15 January 1933, gaining 39.5 per cent of the vote. Schleicher resigned as Chancellor. The Weimar Republic was finished. It had in any case been undermined for years by the use of emergency decrees. The way was now clear for Hitler; not through a putsch, but by legal means.

CHAPTER 8

Hitler in Power

(1933)

HITLER AND THE WAGNERS CELEBRATE

On 30 January 1933 Hitler was appointed Reich Chancellor in a coalition government. Winifred was sceptical, believing that 'the same thing will probably happen to him as to others in that position, since he hasn't got an overall majority'.[1] Edwin Bechstein described to her the 'overwhelming' torchlight procession of the Nazis in Berlin, and told her: 'I hear that all the Jews have already left Berlin.'[2] On 1 February Hitler dissolved the Reichstag and set 5 March as the date for new elections.

Frida Leider learned of Hitler's 'seizure of power' while making a guest appearance in the USA, and wanted to know from Heinz Tietjen what was going to happen now in Germany. She felt she had two reasons to worry: she was the wife of a Jew and the mother of a 'half-Jewish' son. Tietjen, indulging himself making great plans for Bayreuth, allayed her fears, pointing out that his ultimate boss was not Goebbels, but Goering. Frida Leider summed up his position: 'Goering had given him the greatest licence ever allowed to a director. Correspondingly, he viewed the situation very optimistically.'[3] Tietjen aimed to maintain the same high artistic standards in Berlin as in Bayreuth. He paid high fees; and he felt safe under Goering's protection.

It was scarcely two weeks after Hitler's accession to power that Winifred had a chance to congratulate her friend personally. The new Reich Chancellor lost no time in publicly demonstrating his admiration for

Richard Wagner, and appeared as the guest of honour in the Leipzig Gewandhaus (Cloth Hall) to help commemorate the fiftieth anniversary of Wagner's death. He launched a competition (admittedly already announced in 1932) for the best idea for a Wagner monument in the Master's birthplace, Leipzig. In Leipzig, Franz Stassen's finest hour had come when he was able to shake the hand of the Reich Chancellor:

> It was a moving moment . . . But just think how the unbelievers, those un-teachable people, have gone on prophesying that it couldn't work, it was bound to collapse, the programme was utopian, unachievable, Germany's end had come. Oh, those poor prophets, what fools they've made of them-selves day after day with that besetting national sin, their addiction to carping.[4]

The thirteenth of February 1933, the fiftieth anniversary of Wagner's death, commenced in Bayreuth with a procession of town dignitaries past the grave of the Master, where they laid wreaths. Winifred hosted a reception in Villa Wahnfried, declaring it an open house for the day. Seven thousand school-children moved through the house and garden and past the Master's grave, which was decorated with magnificent wreaths sent by Hitler and by Crown Prince Rupprecht of Bavaria. Talking about the wreath contributed by the exiled ex-Kaiser Wilhelm II, Lieselotte commented: 'Poor man, he still seems to be living under the delusion that he can return to Germany some day as Kaiser.'[5]

On this day of celebration, the town of Bayreuth settled its differences with Wahnfried. Winifred, Eva Chamberlain, Daniela Thode and Blandine Gravina, as well as Arturo Toscanini, were all given the freedom of the city. The approach to the Festival Theatre was named Siegfried Wagner Avenue. To strengthen this friendship, Winifred made a donation of 1,000 marks for the poor of the town. The town approved a sum of 2,000 marks to go to the Awards Foundation and the purchase of Festival tickets.[6] But it took Toscanini six weeks to acknowledge the honour bestowed upon him.

The Berlin State Opera under Tietjen celebrated the Wagner Year by staging all of Wagner's works, beginning with his early opera *Das Liebesverbot* (Love Prohibited). Winifred was among the guests of honour. By February there was a scandal, involving a spectacular new production of *Tannhäuser* under Otto von Klemperer, directed by Jürgen Fehling. The 'non-Aryan' Klemperer was thereafter banned from conducting. The *Allgemeine Musik-*

Zeitung (General Journal of Music) called the Modernist production a 'crime against art', and, allegedly prompted by the audience, had the effrontery to demand: 'Bring us the head of the General Intendant [Tietjen] on a silver platter.'[7] As the representative of 'left' theatre culture he was now in an exposed position, and the new management of the Festival with him.

The burning of the Reichstag on 27 February, towards the end of the election campaign, offered the Nazis the pretext of an alleged Communist uprising, which they used to lash out at the KPD (German Communist Party). The KPD members of the Reichstag were arrested, and KPD newspapers were banned. Hitler posed as the saviour of the nation from subversives and Bolsheviks. He seized his opportunity, and persuaded Hindenburg to pass a 'decree for the protection of the state and the people', which suspended important basic rights. The French ambassador, André François-Poncet, an astonished observer of this scene, remarked: 'But the majority of the German people are less repelled than impressed by all this bold energy. They quiver like a horse that suddenly feels the fist and the spurs of its master.'[8]

The Reichstag elections gave the NSDAP almost 44 per cent of the vote, and an increase from 196 to 288 seats, but still no absolute majority. In Bayreuth the NSDAP polled 60 per cent of votes. To celebrate the election victory Wahnfried put out the biggest swastika flags in Bayreuth: 2.4 × 7 metres, and 'so heavy that a flag-pole bent over yesterday like a matchstick'. Now the flag-poles were cemented in, 'so that in future we can hang out our flags without restraint'.[9] Winifred was keen to spend as much time as possible in the vicinity of her successful friend, and often went to Berlin: 'I simply can't stand it – and was lucky enough to see Hitler twice – once I had a cosy lunch with him. Wonderful that he is getting his chance at last!!!!'[10] She liked his unscrupulous way of eliminating opponents by all means possible. When she had trouble again with the Awards Foundation, she joked in March 1933: 'Can't we just sanction a bit of cleansing; we've got such a refreshing example now throughout the Reich?!'[11]

Prominent Nazis from among the Wagners' circle were appointed to high office in Bavaria. The popular Franz Ritter von Epp became first of all Reich Commissar for Bavaria, with full executive powers; and then, a month later, Reichsstatthalter (Governor), signifying a sweeping reduction of the Minister-President's power. Hans Frank became Justice Minister; Hans Schemm, Education Minister.

Bayreuth held a great celebration in honour of Schemm. In his speech of thanks he lauded the Führer's 'work of liberation', sketched out the 'edifice of the National Socialist world-view' and its antecedents in the work of Wagner and Chamberlain, and promised 'to tear out root and branch the last pernicious liberal and Marxist influences in this Bavarian land'. The imperatives now were 'race, honour, resistance, personality, Christianity, religion and prayer'.[12]

Members of the opposition were being hunted down everywhere. On 7 March at the Dresden State Opera, vicious Nazis loudly barracked the director, Fritz Busch, and stopped him conducting: 'Down with Busch! – Out with traitors!' Previously so highly acclaimed, he could not grasp the rapid change of climate as the terror silenced even old friends, and he found himself isolated: 'Regarded with suspicion, pursued to the point of physical threats by hatred that extended from schoolchildren to our devoted servants, condemned to inactivity, I learned every day that I was an unpatriotic individual and a moral degenerate.' When Busch complained to Goering about these excesses, and demanded that Hitler should publicly restore his good name, the Führer declined on the grounds that he was obliged to support his party.[13]

Bruno Walter, returning in March 1933 from a guest performance in the USA to a Germany swathed in swastikas, met many people 'who thought that the cruel actions and wicked utterances of the party, even its anti-Semitism, were just the infantile ailments of an essentially healthy movement, and believed we would quickly return to decency and normality'.[14] The concert that Walter was engaged to conduct in the Leipzig Gewandhaus was banned by the police. The directors complained to the government of Saxony. Max Brockhaus, their chairman, telephoned Winifred several times to ask for her help. She immediately called Goering, who declared that as Prussian Minister-President he had no jurisdiction. The concert did not take place.[15] Dejected, Walter set off for Berlin to his next engagement, only to be informed: 'If you . . . persist with the concert, you can be sure that everything in the hall will be smashed to pulp.' When he then decided to withdraw, he was told the concert would go ahead, but under the baton of Richard Strauss.[16]

On the morning of 10 March, when the order went out to police authorities everywhere 'to take all Communist officials into protective custody immediately', nineteen Communists and eighteen Social Democrats were arrested in Bayreuth. Of the original seven SPD town councillors, only four remained. Gauleiter Schemm went round in person with his men to the editorial office of the Bayreuth SPD newspaper, to give the staff a brutal lesson in the folly of criticizing the regime from then on. The newspaper *Fränkische Volk* (Franconian People) reported that: 'Disgusting scenes ensued. It was a totally spineless bunch that had been rounded up . . . That great loud-mouth and muckraker-in-chief of the Bayreuth lefty paper, Hacke, collapsed and had to be taken off to hospital, nothing but a pathetically wailing bag of bones.' An SPD town councillor, Adam Seeser, had attempted suicide. The *Bayreuther Tagblatt* editorialized on 16 March: 'No one will shed a tear for these Social Democratic functionaries who have now fortunately disappeared. They clearly belong to that class of contemporary Germans who sustained the erstwhile democratic and parliamentary system, and are in need of a long and thorough education.'

There was no popular resistance at all to the brutal treatment of left-wingers. In Bayreuth as elsewhere, informers went eagerly to work: 'Having received a great many reports about persons not yet arrested, the police are collaborating quickly and surely with our trusty SA and SS to deal successfully with their allotted task.'[17]

Lotte Warburg, now classified as 'half-Aryan', was amazed when her physician, Albert Angerer, captain of the local tennis club, came round to make her resign her membership. She commented scornfully: 'As he was not in the SA, he was scared of being deposed as captain at the meeting that evening, and he did not want to lose the role of sports physician that he had been building up. He was terrified that I would say "sorry, I'm not quitting". But I instantly threw the whole thing back in his face with a laugh.'

Lotte Warburg also noted: 'A good many people are committing suicide; the relatives of people who have died are held as hostages, such as the sons-in-law or daughters of various Social Democrats. Jews are said to be simply disappearing from their homes.' She added: '"Aryan girls pilloried" reads a newspaper headline above a report that Aryan girls have been caught going on weekend outings with Jewish men. They were confronted by SA men, and their names appeared in the paper and will continue to be publicized in future.'[18] The Meyer-Viol-Warburg family emigrated soon afterwards.

With his sense of the symbolism of historic places, Hitler transferred the official opening of the Reichstag – since its Berlin seat had been closed by the fire – on 21 March to the Garrison Church in Potsdam, the burial place of Frederick the Great. Reich Chancellor Hitler and Reich-President Hindenburg combined in a gesture of deference to Prussian tradition. Among the guests were members of the former imperial family, with Crown

Prince Wilhelm at their head. The Bayreuth Festival choir sang. Winifred was among the guests of honour.

The great day culminated in a performance at the State Opera of *The Mastersingers of Nuremberg* under Wilhelm Furtwängler. The *Völkischer Beobachter* rejoiced: 'Anyone who witnessed how the people of Nuremberg turned in Act Three to the box where the Führer was sitting with all his staff . . . felt once again that Germany has reached the turning point. It is impossible to imagine a more fitting climax to 21 March 1933.'

Furthermore, the audience was different from previous ones. 'Lovely, tastefully dressed German women, not exotically painted females dripping with jewellery.'[19] Winifred, too, precisely embodied the stereotype of 'German' womanhood, free of make-up.

The first session of the newly elected Reichstag took place in the converted Kroll Opera House. On 24 March 1933 the 'Enabling Law', valid for four years, was passed by 441 votes, against the ninety-six SPD votes still available. The government now had the power to enact laws, and even alter the constitution, without consulting either Parliament or the Reich-President. Parliament had effectively stripped itself of power.

The SPD's resistance provoked Hitler into an angry, threatening speech: '. . . don't confuse us with the bourgeois world! . . . Gentlemen, the star of Germany is in the ascendant, and yours will wane.' The Wagners listened to the speech on the radio. Lieselotte's response was: 'His reply to the leftists was his most brilliant speech to date. Like a raging lion or a volcano erupting; everything came out, but without a single unconsidered word. Magnificent.'[20]

On 29 March 1933 Winifred wrote: 'We certainly are living through elemental times, and the Führer and his work stand before us like an incomprehensible miracle that we can only admire with gratitude. What a joy it was when we were able to hoist our flag in front of Wahnfried at last. The children throw themselves enthusiastically into the mood whenever popular rallies take place in the marketplace, or on the radio. Recently, on the evening of the 21st [the day of Potsdam], Wieland marched at the head of the Hitler Youth carrying his flag. A real grandson of Wagner. There was something quite touching about it.'[21]

One new law followed another. The Civil Service Employment Bill, for example, decreed that 'non-Aryan' and politically undesirable officials should be removed from their posts; they were replaced by Nazis. In Weimar the Wagners' friend Hans Severus Ziegler became Director of the German

National Theatre, and thereby took over a key position in the world of 'German art'. This was a symbolically charged place, fiercely fought over since 1918 by democrats and nationalists.

On 1 April 1933 Winifred and fifteen-year-old Friedelind were invited to join a large party for lunch at the Reich Chancellery. Winifred hoped to be able to talk over her concerns about Bayreuth with Hitler, especially the question of whether she would be allowed to retain the Jewish singers already firmly booked to perform there. As Friedelind describes the occasion, the great reception hall looked like a charity bazaar, the tables already laden with presents for Hitler's birthday, mostly consisting of 'embroidered or patterned materials with swastikas in every conceivable arrangement'. The guests had to wait for an hour and a half before Hitler, 'in an excellent mood', took his place at the long table in the enormous dining room, with Winifred on his right and Ilse Hess on his left. The table was weighed down with heavy silverware decorated with coats of arms, 'looking like heirlooms from imperial Germany'.

Hitler held forth in monologues, and Winifred had no opportunity to raise her problem. Over coffee the frightened guests could hear Hitler furiously berating his adjutant Julius Schaub in an adjoining room. After ten minutes the storm had abated. Winifred said to Friedelind later: 'The poor Führer. He's so sensitive, and Schaub should avoid doing anything to upset him.'[22] She had achieved nothing, and had good reason to be dejected.

On the same day, 1 April 1933, the German government called for a boycott of Jewish businesses, supposedly in retaliation for an 'international atrocity propaganda campaign' directed against Germany. Goebbels proclaimed that 'If the hate campaign abroad is ended, then the boycott will be dropped; otherwise, a struggle to the bitter end will begin here. So it's up to the German Jews to prevail upon their racial comrades throughout the world, to save their own necks.'[23]

In Bayreuth on that day, all Jewish businesses were closed, and their entrances guarded by SA sentries. To intimidate the Jews, the German newspapers published anti-Semitic propaganda. The Bayreuth businessman Simon Pfefferkorn was made to sell his house and textile business at No. 2 Maxstrasse to the National Socialist Cultural Press, which belonged to Schemm. Three weeks later Schemm also forced the 'non-Aryan' Johanna Hirschmann to sell the neighbouring house, No. 4 Maxstrasse. Those properties, in a prime town-centre location, were converted into the 'Brown House', the administrative centre of the newly created *Gau*, the Bavarian Ostmark, which extended as far as Passau.[24]

On the evening of 1 April, while Goebbels was venomously attacking 'the Jews' in a speech to 100,000 parading Hitler Youth members, Friedelind was at a performance of The Magic Flute in the State Opera, and witnessed a spontaneous public tribute to two Jewish artists: the conductor Leo Blech and the bass singer Alexander Kipnis, who sang Sorostro and was also engaged for Bayreuth. Friedelind observed: 'Mozart had given the Nazis their answer!'[25] The party's revenge was not long in coming. Once again Winifred was anxious on behalf of Tietjen, who was ultimately accountable for the evening.

In New York, precisely on 1 April 1933, prominent artists formed a solidarity committee for their threatened Jewish colleagues in Germany and appealed to Toscanini to participate; he happened to be in New York at the time. His name headed the list of signatories on a protest telegram to the German government, and he was given an ovation.

In retaliation, Goebbels banned all German radio stations from broadcasting work featuring the signatories – including Toscanini. This news was carried by the international press, unfortunately at the same time as a report that Hitler had invited Winifred to dinner in Berlin. The rumours that Toscanini was going to cancel his Bayreuth contract became more persistent. In her anxiety Winifred implored Hitler to approach the maestro personally and calm him down. After some deliberation, Hitler said he was prepared to send a personal telegram to Toscanini, and assure the maestro of his admiration for him. Friedelind recalls that 'the cost of this telegram, fifty-nine marks, made a big impression on me'.[26] It was followed on 3 April by a personal letter from Hitler, read out to Winifred in her hotel by his adjutant. Hitler expressed his pleasure at the prospect 'of soon being able to greet in Bayreuth the great maestro of our friends, the Italian nation'.

It took Toscanini four weeks to reply, in English, to 'Your Excellency', saying that Hitler knew how closely tied he felt to Bayreuth, and what great satisfaction it gave him to be able to dedicate his 'little' contribution to a genius such as Wagner, for whom his love was boundless. That was why it would be a bitter disappointment to him if any circumstances should thwart his intention of taking part in the coming Festival; he hoped that his strength, very much reduced in the last few weeks, would be equal to the task.[27] This could be read as an appeal to Hitler to change his policy towards the Jews.

Winifred sent a telegram putting pressure on Toscanini: 'Bayreuth-friendly foreigners concerned about whether Tosca coming. Seek permission to con-

firm definitely coming, starting rehearsals end June and conducting all performances of Parsifal and Mastersingers.'[28]

In the meantime Tietjen was taking soundings from Busch, banished
from Dresden, as to whether he was prepared to step in at Bayreuth if necessary. Winifred was willing to forget the resentments that had arisen in
1925. Busch said: 'An outstretched hand offered me everything I had previously wanted; and I knew I would not take it.' In his memoirs Busch
described a meeting at which Toscanini showed him Hitler's letter and
asked: 'What will Bayreuth do if I back out?' Busch replied: 'Then they will
invite me, Maestro. Tietjen, who is expecting you to cancel, has taken
steps in advance ... That is to say, I have already been invited.' And
then, savouring Toscanini's astonishment, he went on: 'Naturally, I will
refuse, just as you will.' Later he commented: 'We both remained silent,
lost in sad thought.'[29]

On 26 May 1933 Winifred sent her sister-in-law Daniela to Milan, 'not to
plead with him or talk him round, but for an explanation and a definitive
statement from him'.[30] The outcome was that Toscanini sat down on 28 May
with both his solicitor and Daniela Thode to compose his telegram of cancellation:

> Since, contrary to my hopes, there has been no change in the actions
> which have offended my feelings as an artist and a human being, I regard
> it as my duty to break the silence I have imposed upon myself over the last
> two months, and inform you that it is better for my peace of mind, as well
> as yours and that of all concerned, to cease thinking about the possibility
> of my coming to Bayreuth. With enduring feelings of friendship towards
> the house of Wagner, Arturo Toscanini.[31]

Friedelind described her mother's reaction to 'Tosca's' cancellation: 'She
was desperate; her blue eyes, usually so clear, clouded with pain, and her face
was deathly pale when she rang Hitler to tell him this disastrous news.' The
girl deduced, from the telephone conversation and the reports carried by
Hitler's adjutants between the Reich Chancellery and Winifred's hotel, that
'Hitler felt ill-treated, since he had generously allowed Mother to retain her
Jewish artists.'[32] Made vulnerable by sending first a telegram and then a
letter to Toscanini, Hitler had been humiliated by the cancellation, and
vented his anger on Winifred for having made him take this step.

But even Winifred and her faithful echo Lieselotte could understand the risk Toscanini would have been running by appearing in this inflammatory atmosphere. As Lieselotte put it:

> You can almost understand him. I can't believe he would have escaped unscathed in this young, seething Germany. Even the Führer's great and noble example would not have been enough to stop the exasperated Teutons from holding counter-demonstrations, and then what would have happened if he had chucked down his baton again? But he is and will always be irreplaceable.[33]

Coming such a short while before the beginning of rehearsals, the resignation was at first kept quiet. Tietjen rang Busch in Zurich, and he in his turn duly declined. Busch was especially disturbed by this phone call because it meant that the German authorities knew about the secret address he was staying at, with Zurich friends. His every step was being monitored, even abroad. As his wife Grete wrote: 'We were not used to the Gestapo system at the time.'[34]

After two months of soul-searching and contemplating suicide, Busch emigrated, having accepted an offer from the Teatro Colón in Buenos Aires. Hitler was still regretting his loss in 1942. He gave as the reason for Busch's emigration Gauleiter Mutschmann's intention to 'place long-standing Party members in the orchestra to inject some National Socialist spirit into it'.[35]

On 1 June 1933, all the Jewish members of the Berlin State Opera were dismissed. But exceptions were still being made: as a concession from Goering to Tietjen, Leo Blech was allowed to remain for the time being. And the Jewish bass singers Kipnis and Emanuel List stayed on too, as Hitler had promised Winifred in connection with Bayreuth.

The search for a celebrity conductor continued. The obvious solution, an invitation to Furtwängler, was ruled out by the 1931 dispute, apart from the suspicion that he and Berta Geissmar had started the campaign against Bayreuth. Furtwängler's fans had in fact protested in the spring about Toscanini's appointment to Bayreuth. In the end, Tietjen sounded out Strauss, asking Winifred to go and talk to him personally in Garmisch. 'That was difficult for me to do, because Strauss is a great man, after all . . . and was bound to feel he was just a stop-gap.' But her reception had been 'touching', and he agreed to take on *Parsifal*.[36] The last time Strauss had conducted in Bayreuth had been in 1894, at a performance of *Tannhäuser*. Apart from him, Karl Elmendorff would conduct, and Tietjen was going to hold himself in readiness to take over in the Bayreuth orchestra pit as an unseen and anonymous conductor.

Meanwhile, Toscanini was creating another sensation. He agreed to participate in the Salzburg Festival. Under the direction of the 'non-Aryan' Max Reinhardt, it had become a sanctuary for artists displaced from Germany, and soon came to be seen as the 'Jewish' counterpart of 'German' Bayreuth.

Latterly, it had become politically impossible for artists to perform at both festivals, as they had done previously. They were obliged to choose. After accepting Bayreuth, Strauss therefore had to back out of the Salzburg *Fidelio*. From then on, he was boycotted in Austria. The immediate result was that the Vienna State Opera would no longer put on his works. Some Viennese newspapers thought this no great loss: 'It was only the *Rosenkavalier* that was successful. Speaking in terms of theatre history, all of Strauss's other works are hopeless.'[37] The German contralto Sigrid Onegin, born in Stockholm to a French mother and widow of the Russian composer Yevgeny Onegin, backed out of Salzburg at short notice, and was singing a few days later in Bayreuth. Her excuse was that 'superior orders' had left her no choice, but from then on many non-German opera houses refused to employ her.[38]

German artists now needed official permission to perform abroad, and it was rarely granted. Many of them, such as Frida Leider, were forced to cancel foreign engagements. Incurring the wrath of their audiences, they were often unjustly labelled as Nazis.

THE CAMPAIGN AGAINST TIETJEN

In April 1933 a press campaign was launched against Tietjen, the most powerful representative of the 'old theatre system'. It was run from behind the scenes by the Reich Propaganda Ministry under Goebbels. His aim was simultaneously to strike a blow at his rival Goering, who as Minister-President of Prussia was Tietjen's boss. The prime mover of the campaign was State Commissar Hans Hinkel, Prussian regional head of the Fighting League for German Culture. His ambition was to cut down to size the cosmopolitan, progressive cultural life of Berlin, to fit the dimensions of Nazi Aryan-racist ideology. The baritone Wilhelm Rode, who hated Tietjen, served Hinkel as a keen informer.[39]

The campaign began with a sensational story in all the newspapers. The little-known singer Charlotte Boerner had supposedly gone missing, and the farewell letters she had left for the Fighting League for German Culture and for Goebbels pointed to suicide. As a party member, she blamed Tietjen for blocking her chances of work at the State Opera, thus forcing her into poverty. 'Please, Herr Minister, help me to hold on to my firm belief in the new Germany. Every vote was important for the great project – but the fate of every German is still important today.'

The letter she had written to Tietjen, which was also published, culminated in the accusation that on the day of Potsdam, 'the day that my Fatherland celebrated its national resurgence, I who as a German artist had so proudly and successfully upheld Germany's reputation abroad, was turned away from the State Opera like a mangy cur'. She also alleged sexual harassment on the part of Ludwig Seelig, head of a ministry department, who was a 'non-Aryan' friend of Tietjen's.[40] Three days later the singer was discovered, in an allegedly 'disturbed' state, in a hotel near Berlin, and her 'suicide' averted. Seelig had already been forced to retire on 1 March 1933. Now under attack, he succeeded with Tietjen's help in escaping to France. Another friend of Tietjen's, theatre director Arthur Illing, shot himself in April.[41]

The main charges against Tietjen were that he had 'no sympathy for artists who share our ideology' and that 'his inner nature made him politically incompatible with the *völkisch* state'. He had 'shown unusual favouritism to Jews and foreigners, but unjustly neglected German artists'. The *Magic Flute* performance on 1 April was particularly damning: it placed no fewer than nine Jews on the stage.

The extensive files contain much evidence by singers who had been overlooked, and many references to Tietjen's Jewish friends. One eager informer was Tietjen's former secretary Kosmehl. She was at that time 'in a treatment centre for alcoholism', and was in a position to reveal 'unbelievable irregularities'. Witnesses were questioned for weeks. But the files also record that Tietjen had been careful to 'spin his web in the other direction', too, and had 'gained the friendship of Frau Wagner-Bayreuth, and in this way created links with the Führer and in general with high-ranking NSDAP men'.[42]

Winifred joined in unbidden, with a forceful letter to the Prussian education minister Bernhard Rust, since 'my name has frequently been referred to publicly, and my Bayreuth collaborator Heinz Tietjen has been subjected to unprecedented attacks in the press, which has made not the slightest attempt to inform itself of the facts'. She corrected Boerner's version, and demanded as head of the Bayreuth Festival a thorough investigation of this affair, and restoration of the good name of a colleague who, with the exception of his service at the front, has devoted himself beyond reproach for thirty years to the interests of the German theatre, and without whom there would no longer be a German theatre. Ask the professionals, Herr Minister.[43]

She even managed to get this letter published by a Bayreuth newspaper, and she sent a copy to Lene Roesener with the comment: 'Today I resigned from the Fighting League for German Culture, and fired off a stiff letter . . . to Rust . . . Well – there aren't enough walls to be driven up!!!!!'[44] Boerner defended herself with a furious counter-declaration to State Commissar Hinkel.[45]

In this dangerous situation Winifred tried to get in touch with Hitler, but he did not respond. Then, for his birthday, she made him a present of a box at the Festival Theatre for twenty-one performances. She had to wait two months for his thanks. It was the period in which the episode of Toscanini's cancellation occurred. In the middle of May Lieselotte wrote:

> My mistress is going through a bad time in Berlin. The campaign against Bayreuth – which has Jewish origins (you know who I'm talking about [Geissmar]) – stops at no lies or villainy, and in their rage all of them, including those who would have liked work at Bayreuth . . . are spouting the same line. It's a real witches' Sabbath.[46]

Nothing was heard from Hitler. Without explaining exactly what had happened, Lieselotte penned whole recitations of woe to her parents:

> It's the most tragic thing that precisely now, in the 3rd Reich, Bayreuth should be under attack from all sides as never before . . . We're caught in icy isolation, out of our minds . . . All I can say is that we'd like to put the Festival Theatre on wheels and drive it to neutral territory. The Germans are behaving like berserkers, and really don't deserve this shrine.

But, she added 'it won't force us to our knees; we'd rather go down with pride and honour'.[47] Winifred put it more briefly to Lene: 'There's never been a year as shitty as this one, and yet we had the highest hopes.'[48]

Political friction between Germany and Austria further reduced visitor numbers. The German regime put effective pressure on travel to Austria with its 'thousand mark barrier': every German citizen now had to pay 1,000 marks for a visa for Austria. The Austrians retaliated on 19 June with a ban on the NSDAP and corresponding travel restrictions for Austrians wanting to visit Germany. The result was that not only the Salzburg Festival, but Bayreuth as well, faced ruin, since Austria had traditionally provided the largest contingent of foreign visitors. Winifred introduced severe economy measures, unified and reduced the fees paid, and earned herself more opprobrium in the process.

Since February there had been endless enquiries from what Lieselotte called 'rampant Nazis' who wanted to know when Hitler was coming to the Festival, 'so that they could get tickets for the same performances'. But Hitler remained silent on the subject, and the constant unanswerable questions made matters even more trying. Precisely now that Hitler had reached his goal, Winifred felt she had been left in the lurch. And yet how she had always dreamed of welcoming Wolf to the Festival as Reich Chancellor!

In this 'regrettable state of total desolation' Lieselotte suggested employing her lover Hans Frank as go-between. In a hotel room near the Anhalter Station in Berlin she had three hours in which to describe the situation to Frank: 'With me talking ten to the dozen, everything came out, including a number of private accusations that we can't quite spare the 3rd Reich from . . . There was a lot that really shook him.' Even if Frank could not help, 'somebody here ought to know what a tragic battle is going on and tell the Führer a bit about it, so that it doesn't come like a bolt from the blue when B[ayreuth] is weakened beyond endurance'. Frank had an appointment with Hitler that very evening, and promised to raise the subject.[49]

In Frank's surviving papers, there is a unique document: a summary, written by Lieselotte, of Bayreuth's problems at the beginning of June 1933, and marked 'for my personal use only, please':

Since April concentrated campaign against T.

T. finally requests an official disciplinary enquiry into his affairs. Enquiry is completed, producing nothing, but the reinstatement of reputation he demands is not forthcoming.

The beginning of the campaign: it was agreed with the government that T., who has fought hard against the Jews for years, should let the Jew (conductor) Klemperer and the director Jürgen Fehling put on a Jewish mess of a production of *Tannhäuser*. The government would then step in, prohibit the performance and make an example. Through lack of time the government did not intervene, and T. got all the blame.

Furtwängler (his Jewish secretary Geissmar) the sworn enemy of Tietjen and Frau Wagner.

Tietjen is the only artist in Germany (the world?) who can conduct and direct, the only replacement for the combination of abilities of Richard, Cosima, Siegfried Wagner, a real gift of the gods after Siegfried's death. Like Tosca, he is loyal, selfless, not vain.

Then the focus switches to 'Frau W.'s personal relationship' to the government:

Practically cut off since April.

Up until then for example G[oebbels] had been saying: 'We'll take any number of tickets. 300,000 marks is not much to pay for B'th.'

Frau W. is no longer received (by G.)

For [Hitler's] birthday she sent 220 tickets: no official acknowledgement.

Her financial position: she and her children will come out of this year's Festival ruined.[50]

The shocking passage about Klemperer and Fehling could hardly have come from Winifred, but is clearly in Tietjen's style, a risky interpretation that twists the truth; though we should bear in mind that in 1933 Tietjen's very livelihood was at stake. He had planned Fehling's *Tannhäuser* long before Hitler came to power. If the regime had wanted to, it would have been easy to send rampaging SA men into the opera house, as had happened with Walter, Busch and others. It is far more likely that, fourteen days after the 'seizure of power', Tietjen was still underestimating the danger, and was quite rightly proud of the production. But when he suddenly found himself wrong-footed, he distanced himself from his friends in a somewhat indecent way. And after 1945 he was recommending Fehling's *Tannhäuser* production as a model for young directors, especially Wieland: 'It seems to me that today's new Bayreuth could learn from it. What we were putting on the stage was revolutionary!' He considered Fehling to be 'heaven knows, a marvellous director'.[51] The 'Jewish mess' was forgotten.

To return to Frank: his intervention was successful. After two months of silence Hitler sent a birthday telegram on 23 June 1933, and expressed thanks for the Festival tickets. Lieselotte said: 'Silently, I thanked him so much for not forgetting, and I think it has eased the pain of my Mistress's heart, too.'[52] The infatuated Lieselotte could hardly contain her pride in Frank. Bayreuth was fêting him 'as the guardian angel and the only person who has a proper appreciation of the Bayreuth mission'.[53]

At least Winifred was able to celebrate with Tietjen, whose birthday was the day after hers, 'actually for 48 hours', but 'only in short bursts . . . on the evening of the 23rd Heinz and I christened the new building with crayfish and a hot stove'. The firm of Rosenthal had sent her a new table service – 'in exchange for being allowed to call a new service "Winifred"!'[54]

This was the first Festival to be run by the new team of Winifred, Tietjen and Preetorius, and the strain was considerable. During the first rehearsals there were disputes between Daniela Thode, the costume designer up to this point, and Preetorius. He declared that Daniela's costume designs were 'the most dreadful thing of all . . . they needed simplifying, given clear lines adapted to these sets'. Daniela was in tears when she saw a set-building rehearsal for the second act of the *Valkyrie*: 'For God's sake, what on earth are you doing? . . . You can't just turn it into a completely different work.' Hostile pamphlets were propagating the notion that Preetorius was a 'Jew in disguise' who had insinuated himself into Bayreuth in order to destroy Wagner.

Tietjen soothed Daniela's distress by suggesting that she should write down her criticisms on little slips of paper, and pass them on to him. All the same, Daniela left the dress rehearsal of *Siegfried* protesting loudly. And she began to produce an endless stream of little notes pointing out infringements against the Master's directions. This happened after every performance, and became so trying that Winifred finally 'made a violent scene and expressed her indignation about my notes'.[55] To calm the overheated atmosphere, Winifred made her sister-in-law director of *Parsifal*, which Lieselotte thought was a clever move. 'Frau Thode is too distracted and excited by this new project to have time to make mischief.' In any case, the stage designs for the production were already in place.[56]

Wolfgang Wagner later said that his mother had been tired of the 'endless squabbling and stubborn insistence on "tradition"', and 'with malicious irony' had given Daniela the project in order to demonstrate the miserable state of the original costumes.[57] The family had known that Winifred aimed at a new production with new costumes ever since her outburst one day: 'I'm utterly sick of these old designs.'[58] But without Hitler and financial support from him, a spectacular new production was impossible.

Colleagues and artists were already rehearsing, but Winifred did not have enough funds to pay the salaries that were due on 1 July. At Tietjen's request, on 27 June Daniela went to see Goebbels in Berlin, to ask for a subsidy in the form of a bulk purchase of tickets.[59] After an hour's discussion, Goebbels granted the money, noting in his diary: 'Visit from Frau Thode about Bayreuth. They're short of 300,000 marks. They're impossible on the Jewish question . . . What would Wagner think if he came back!'[60] Wahnfried was obviously not anti-Semitic enough for him, or at least less anti-Semitic than he thought the Master had been.

The following day, however, Hitler entered the scene. Lieselotte reported:

Wolf has recognized our problems. He called the Mistress to Berlin, she flew there, and within a quarter of an hour we had the help we needed – in plenty! It's just as we always suspected; him unsuspecting, but surrounded by people who, perhaps for all too human reasons, are not well disposed to us – cherchez la femme

'– by which she once again meant Berta Geissmar. She said that Winifred had taken the plane for Berlin at 8 a.m., and was back in Bayreuth the following night at 4.30. As ever, there had been '"perfect agreement" with Hitler, no hint of annoyance or anything coming between them. Now we have the security we need to produce artistic work.'[61]

What is more, Schemm promised to buy Festival tickets for the National Socialist Teachers' Association. The Bavarian Council of Ministers set aside 50,000 marks for the purchase of tickets, and called upon the other German Länder to do likewise. All of Bayreuth knew about the imminent financial ruin of the Festival, and its sudden rescue. Bayreuth Town Council noted with satisfaction at the end of July 1933: 'The Reich's acquisition of entrance tickets, and their distribution free of charge or at low cost to the public at large, [is] more than just a support measure in difficult times; it is a statement of faith by the new Germany in Richard Wagner, his art and his ethos.' It also helped meet the wish of the Master to make the Festival accessible to a large part of the population.[62]

For the rest of her life, Winifred never tired of emphasizing that Hitler saved the Bayreuth Festival in 1933, and asking people to understand her position: 'It would have been irresponsible to reject Hitler's offer of financial support for the Bayreuth Festival, and, as every fair-minded judge will concede, practically impossible to do so in the Third Reich.' Furthermore, Hitler had defended the Festival against the party's negative attitude to Wagner: 'Richard Wagner's music was called "baroque" and "emotional", and he was accused of having a "Middle Eastern racial soul" . . . Rosenberg even declared in his "Mythos" [des zwanzigsten Jahrhunderts, Myth of the Twentieth Century] that Tristan was not a drama of love, but of honour, and that the Ring needed re-composing.' Hitler knew about these hostile currents, and had accepted Winifred's view 'that there was a certain danger in them for the survival of the Festival. He thought the most effective way to fight them was by regularly visiting Bayreuth, by which he intended to set a long-term example.'[63]

THE NEW REICH CHANCELLOR

At extremely short notice, Hitler announced his intention to visit the Festival officially as Reich Chancellor; and not just to attend the opening, but to stay for a whole cycle, roughly a week. All the big hotels were booked, as were private lodgings. On top of the stress of dress rehearsals, Winifred now had to find accommodation for Hitler and his entourage. After much effort she managed to persuade the rich wholesale thread supplier Fritz Böhner to vacate his elegant villa on the edge of the Hofgarten at No. 4 Parkstrasse. He and his wife went to stay with relatives. The villa and all its contents, from bedlinen to silverware, were let to Hitler at the modest rate of 36 marks a day and 3 marks per bed. The house could accommodate eight people apart from him, mainly his staff guard. With great difficulty other personnel, including two maids, three aides and three chauffeurs, were found rooms in the neighbourhood.[64]

From Wahnfried Winifred sent over to Parkstrasse household equipment for the kitchen and the garden, including deck chairs and all sorts of useful things; she even hired a piano. Her truly robust constitution showed the strain of the last few weeks' excitement, and she broke down 'in bitter tears', said Lieselotte, at a tribute to Siegfried's memory; 'she's so exhausted emotionally'.[65]

Hitler's accommodation turned out to be the perfect solution. In the white house with its wide steps and well-tended garden, he could invite guests, enjoy privacy and easily visit Villa Wahnfried, just a few steps away through the Hofgarten. Sentry boxes were placed in front of the house for his SS guard. Swastika flags fluttered from the rooftop.

The Reich Chancellor's visit caused big security problems in the Festival Theatre. After two bomb threats the local Bayreuth force was reinforced by extra policemen, detectives and SA men. Before the opening performances, arrangements were made for 'exhaustive police searches of the Festival Theatre', 'in order to reveal and prevent any potential criminal attacks'. The Festival management employed its own security team. As Lieselotte said: 'We can't just rely on the fire brigade up here; if our own safety measures fail, we're lost.'[66]

As a 'precaution', at the beginning of the Festival the Bayreuth police arrested known opponents of the regime. Two days before the opening, on 19 July, the Ministry of the Interior ordered a search of Jewish organizations, businesses and houses. No incriminating material was found, and there were no arrests,[67] but the main aim was achieved: the Jews of Bayreuth, as well as the Social Democrats and other dissidents, were thoroughly intimidated.

The town basked in its pride at hosting such a distinguished visitor, and covered itself in swastika flags. The mayor proclaimed that Bayreuth had been 'recognized by the Reich and the country before the whole world as one of the greatest patrons of German art and culture', and he called upon his fellow-citizens to 'openly display your pleasure at this honour! Hoist the flags! . . . So that everyone will see that this town is proudly aware of its great cultural mission!' However, the Führer should not be so overwhelmed with demonstrations of love, gratitude and loyalty that he could not enjoy his rest.[68]

Hitler was supposed to arrive at around 4 p.m. on the day before the opening. Onlookers gathered in the Parkstrasse, but the Chancellor did not come. By ten o'clock, only Goebbels had appeared, and the disappointed crowd dispersed. Only a few were still there, standing in front of the Böhner villa, when Hitler's car drew up at 1 a.m. and he disappeared into the house.

The next day he visited the Wagners in Wahnfried. The children asked him somewhat shyly whether they must stop calling him 'du' now that he was such a highly important person. Hitler waved this aside with a laugh, and so for the children he continued to be Wolf.[69]

The opening of the jubilee Festival of 1933, the fiftieth anniversary of Richard Wagner's death, outshone all previous occasions. In a real triumphal procession, in 'proper Hitler-weather', as Lieselotte enthused, the Chancellor drove in a column of cars from the Böhner villa, past saluting policemen and dense crowds lining the pavement, up to the Festival Theatre. The

Bayreuther Tagblatt painted the picture: 'The crowd goes mad with enthusiasm. There is a constant roar of 'Heils' across the square . . . Everyone wants a glimpse of the Chancellor who has succeeded in giving the German people new faith and new hope.'[70]

A beaming Winifred, as director of the Festival, had the pleasure of welcoming her old friend for the first time at the door of honour, or 'King's Entrance': 'He kissed my hand, much to the disapproval of the SA, who found it inappropriate.' Officially, they addressed each other as 'Sie' (rather than their usual intimate 'du'): 'We were amused by it, all the play-acting.'[71] Then she followed the old Bayreuth tradition of showing respect for high dignitaries by escorting him to the royal box. The Master had shown this courtesy to Kaiser Wilhelm I in 1876, and Cosima and Siegfried to the ex-Tsar of Bulgaria. When Hitler entered the box with Winifred, the audience stood up for them, and then silently took their seats again. This, too, was customary for special guests of honour.

A disappointing replacement for Toscanini, Elmendorff conducted the new production of the *Mastersingers*, directed by Tietjen, with sets by Preetorius and costumes by Kurt Palm. In the Festival meadow scene at the end, there were 800 people on the massive stage, backed up by lighting effects of a kind never seen before in Bayreuth. The singers – Rudolf Bockelmann as Hans Sachs, Maria Müller as Eve – had been prepared by Tietjen in Berlin for months beforehand, and were first class. The sensation of the evening was Max Lorenz's Stolzing. It was the first time Lorenz had sung at Bayreuth. Winifred reported to Lene Roesener: 'a great success – wonderful atmosphere and the Führer totally enthusiastic!'[72]

During the interval the Führer went to a window to receive the tributes of his followers. The *Bayreuther Tagblatt* proudly quoted the *Leipziger Neueste Nachrichten* (Leipzig News), whose editorial referred to 'Bayreuth, the symbol of the Third Reich'.[73]

The presence of the Führer attracted other guests of honour, including Goebbels and his wife, the Bavarian Minister-President Siebert, Prince August Wilhelm of Prussia, Hjalmar Schacht, Goering, Hitler's chief press officer, Otto Dietrich and others.

For a week the small Upper Franconian town became the centre of politics. On 22 July Hitler spoke from Bayreuth on all the German radio stations, on the subject of the forthcoming church synod elections. He mentioned the Concordat that had just been agreed with the Vatican, guaranteeing Catholics freedom of belief (and banning priests from involvement in politics), and suggested a similar understanding with the Protestant church, 'but on the assumption that if possible the many Protestant churches should be replaced by a single Reich Church'.[74] The twenty-eight regional Protestant churches were expected to combine to form a united Reich Church, known as the 'German Church', under the new Reich Bishop, Ludwig Müller. It amounted more or less to 'Gleichschaltung', or bringing into line with Nazism. Even before Hitler had left town, the highly respected Bayreuth Senior Ecclesiastical Councillor and District Superintendent Karl Prieser, in office since 1921, was appealing in his main weekly service for a campaign to defend the freedom of the church.

Winifred was too loosely associated with the church to take much interest in ecclesiastical elections: 'We long-standing members of the Party were originally convinced that we all agreed about religion.' It was only in the course of 1933 that it was revealed that Hitler's 'positive Christianity' did not coincide with that of the churches.[75] Reich Bishop Müller, known as 'Reibi' for short, was not taken seriously in Wahnfried.

The tiny Bayreuth airfield was kept very busy during Hitler's stay. Aside from unscheduled planes, there was at least one daily direct flight to Berlin and back. The National Socialist Aviation Day, when war veterans as well as flying schools paraded their flags, was also held there.

In order not to miss *Siegfried*, Hitler and his pilot Hans Baur even created a flying record, whose timetable was published in all the newspapers: take-off in the Junkers 52 at 8 a.m. in Bayreuth; nine o'clock, land in Munich to welcome 450 Italian Fascist Youth members in the Residence. Eleven o'clock, take-off from Munich for Berlin for the funeral of Admiral Ludwig von Schröder, famed as 'the Lion of Flanders' in the World War. Three o'clock, take-off from Berlin for Bayreuth, where Hitler appeared shortly after five in the Festival Theatre.[76]

What the German papers did not report was that Winifred had postponed the performance at short notice from four till five o'clock, keeping nearly 2,000 people waiting for more than an hour. But it was noted in the foreign press. The English classical music producer Walter Legge stated that the constant 'displays of nationalist politics' in Bayreuth had alienated international music-lovers.[77] On the other hand, Winifred was hardly a free agent, since the party had bought a large proportion of the tickets. Considering the plaudits he was receiving from all sides, Hitler behaved modestly, for example when he distributed cards printed with the following text:

ON BEHALF OF THE CHANCELLOR

The Führer requests that you refrain from singing 'Deutschland über alles'
or 'The Horst Wessel song', and similar demonstrations, after the performances.

There is no more glorious expression of the German spirit than the
immortal works of the Master himself.

SS LIEUTENANT GENERAL BRÜCKNER, ADJUTANT OF THE FÜHRER

At breakfast in Wahnfried, according to Lieselotte, Hitler was 'overwhelmingly kind and helpful, ready to do anything for Bayreuth ... we're only just
beginning to appreciate the impression that these first few performances,
ennobled by the presence of the Führer, have made artistically upon the
whole world, and actually it has been like a decisive battle that we have
won'.[78]

The re-created *Ring of the Nibelung*, with its very unusual stage-set by
Preetorius, had a mixed reception. Hitler's response was positive, while
Goebbels, Tietjen's avowed enemy, reacted unfavourably. Although he
thought the singing in the *Valkyrie* was wonderful, 'the scenery on the other
hand was very kitschy. That's Tietjen for you. No colour sense. And striving
for effect.' Even Lorenz's much admired performance as Siegfried failed to
appeal to him: 'Lorenz as Siegfried completely wrong. It's all better in Berlin.
No heroic conception.'[79]

Goebbels ensured that the newspapers were full of praise for Hitler as the
saviour of Bayreuth, especially the *Völkischer Beobachter*:

If he, absorbed in the performance with his unique respect for the divine
in man, had not been sent to us, there would be no Bayreuth today; without him there would be chaos. Everyone should remember that, even
those who speak with foreign tongues. The Festival Theatre, that glorious
symbol of the German spirit, might have been demolished, or it might
have become a Communist parliamentary talking-shop, or something
even worse.[80]

The new Mayor of Bayreuth, Karl Schumprecht, seized his golden opportunity. In his SS uniform and chain of office, accompanied by local party
notables and the acting Gauleiter, Ludwig Ruckdeschel, he made his way to
the Parkstrasse to bestow the freedom of the town on Hitler. The minutes of

the town council read: 'The whole of Bayreuth is breathing a sigh of relief, in the liberating knowledge that the days of deliberate oppression, even humiliation of this town by an ideologically hostile national government, with its extreme party-political stance, are now over.' It had been replaced by 'the will to make amends for the injustice done to Bayreuth by the former national government'.[81]

Hitler behaved in Bayreuth like a benevolent monarch. He enjoyed professional discussions with Winifred and Strauss, made suggestions for improving the training of singers, and wanted to see good support for ensembles. The state should promote the training of leading singers, especially Wagnerian tenors.[82] He ordered the installation of a ventilating system in the constantly overheated Festival Theatre; it was indeed in operation by 1934.[83] He thanked the Böhners charmingly for the inconvenience they had put up with; he chatted with their little grandchildren and gave them oranges.[84]

On his last day Hitler was 'completely *en famille*' at lunch with them, says Winifred, and he stayed until four in the afternoon. He contemplated buying the house in the Parkstrasse, in order to have a permanent home in Bayreuth. 'He was completely his old self', and left Winifred with the promise that 'he will help financially when and where he can'. Tietjen did not put in an appearance: 'unfortunately, H.T. ducked out of it'.[85] The press were on hand when Hitler laid wreaths, decorated with ribbons in black, white and red which bore his monogram, at the graves of Richard, Cosima and Siegfried Wagner. 'It was clear that he was deeply moved as he was leaving the graveside,' reported the newspaper.[86]

The Reich Chancellery settled the bill for Hitler's ten-day stay in the Parkstrasse; six beds for ten nights @ six Reichsmarks, making 360 marks in total, a reduction even on the low rate originally agreed. Böhner passed the money on to the town treasurer for charitable purposes, since it 'had been a great privilege and pleasure' for him to place his house at the disposal of the Chancellor.[87] The town thanked him and informed the donor that the money would be used 'as the Führer would wish, to support old and needy SA comrades'.[88]

Even after Hitler had left, the scene at the once so elegant Festival was dominated by the uniforms of party members who had obtained complimentary tickets. Lotte Warburg noted in her diary that Bayreuth was 'full of brown jackets, and everywhere there are complimentary tables and complimentary beds and eating places available for the Hitler Youth currently filling the Theatre'.[89] Many an SS or SA man preferred to spend his time in drinking places, however, despite the free tickets.

During the second *Ring* cycle, Hitler's big election speech broadcast was relayed by loudspeakers in the interval between Acts II and III. The speech became quite lengthy. When it was over, furthermore, the 'brown jackets' went on to sing 'Deutschland über alles' and 'The Horst Wessel song'. The beginning of Act III was delayed by a full two hours.[90] It was enough to make even the oldest, most well-disposed Festival-goer disaffected.

The striking changes in the atmosphere of Bayreuth were recorded by Legge in the *Manchester Guardian*. To judge by the behaviour of the audience, he wrote, they seemed to think this was a 'Hitler Festival', and 'since Hitler likes Wagner's music, we're here as well'. In the past every Bayreuth shop, whatever it sold, used to display at least one portrait of Wagner, while the windows of the china shops were full of dozens of Wagner busts staring into eternity. Bookshops set out copies of Wagner's autobiography. But that year the porcelain shops were full to bursting with Hitler plaques. *Mein Kampf* had displaced *My Life*. The swastika was flown from every flagpole and from almost every window. Brown shirts were almost *de rigueur*, and when you passed the Café Tannhäuser or the Rhinegold Inn, all you heard was 'The Horst Wessel song'.[91]

Despite all the Party's efforts, the 1933 Festival closed with a loss of 180,200 marks.[92] The dilemma was obvious. Precisely then, with Bayreuth under the new leadership of Winifred, Tietjen and Preetorius undergoing a fundamental reform, matching the standards of the great international opera houses, and finally enjoying public esteem and state financial support, the music enthusiasts and Wagner-lovers were staying away, despite the unusually high artistic quality. The fact was that Hitler, the 'saviour of the Festival', was not a 'normal' Reich Chancellor, and the NSDAP was no 'normal' party. The traditional Festival audience, many of whom belonged to groups now reviled and excluded – Jews, 'half-breeds', democrats, liberals, Communists, Social Democrats, Freemasons, homosexuals – understandably shied away from rubbing shoulders with the brown-shirts.

Hitler wanted to lead 'the people' to Wagner. But with some exceptions his new audience could not be won round to a love of Wagner. They were after all mostly Party members who had been ordered to attend the Festival as 'guests of the Führer'. The result was that participants in the Bayreuth Festival, whether artists or audience, increasingly became mere accessories, allowing Hitler the Wagner connoisseur to commune with the Master.

Thomas Mann's description was brief and to the point: 'Hitler's court theatre'.

On the other hand, as soon as the Festival was over, the traditionalists deluged the Reich Chancellor with protests about the new Bayreuth and about Tietjen. The president of the Vienna Wagner Association, Winifred's old enemy Max von Millenkovich, complained about the new *Mastersingers*. The groups of maidens on the Festival meadow had been reminiscent of the dubious modern genre of the cabaret revue – a very long way from Wagner and Bayreuth; the maids had become showgirls. The Reich Chancellor, 'as high protector of German art', should end 'this perilous link with professionals who, however outstanding and distinguished, are at home only "out there", in the opera houses and the big run-of-the-mill theatres'.[93] Like other protesters, he received no reply.

Despite all his personal antipathy to Tietjen, from 1933 onwards Hitler faced down not only the rabble-rousers of the Reichskulturkammer (Reich Culture Chamber), but also the 'old Wagnerians', even though they were led by those awesome daughters of Cosima, Eva and Daniela, who were long-standing party members to boot.

Tietjen, Preetorius, Palm, Eberhardt and of course Winifred saw the modernizing of Bayreuth as a great artistic mission, the realization of which looked possible at last. Tietjen, politically under pressure, was fully aware that it was only Hitler's love of Bayreuth that allowed him to stay on and continue working. As long as he was successful and indispensable in Bayreuth, he could count on keeping his powerful position in Berlin as well. Winifred had a key role to play. As long as she remained loyal to Tietjen, and he behaved cautiously, he was fairly sure to be kept on. After all, he knew Goering would protect him. Like Preetorius, he kept his distance from the Nazis and Hitler, and did not join the Party. Even after 1945, Preetorius still maintained that 'to a certain extent the reformers had enjoyed Hitler's protection ... Any hostile criticism was snuffed out. That was that.'[94]

A WOMAN OF INFLUENCE

Since her old friend's seizure of power, Winifred had a direct line to the top. One word, one remark to the new Reich Chancellor would produce results. But she was no blind adherent of the NSDAP and was constantly battling with the Party organizations, be they Rosenberg's Fighting League for

German Culture or the Reich Culture Chamber, founded by Goebbels on 15 November 1933.

To obtain work, everybody engaged in cultural production had to be enrolled in some subsidiary of this organization. To be rejected by it, whether because you were 'non-Aryan' or 'half-breed', Social Democrat or Communist, was to be banned from practising your profession. At a stroke, art was 'Aryanized' and brought under the control of the state and the party. Goebbels made Strauss, the most famous living German composer, president of the Reichsmusikkammer (Reich Musicians' Chamber), with Furtwängler, the most famous conductor, as vice-president.

The law covered all German theatres, including of course the Bayreuth Festival. But Winifred obstinately refused to join the Reichstheaterkammer (Reich Theatre Chamber), arguing 'that I can only select my artists freely for their ability, and not in accordance with the views of some chamber'.[95] She could afford to refuse because she and everybody else knew that she was under the personal protection of Hitler. To Goebbels's great fury, she managed to assert the independence of Bayreuth from the Reich Musicians' Chamber.

Hitler told outsiders that the Bayreuth Festival 'had been from the earliest days a matter for the Master and his family, and that it should therefore continue to be run solely by the Wagner family. Ministerial interference was not appropriate there.'[96] The price to be paid for this privilege was that the Reich Culture Chamber became a rallying point for Winifred's enemies, something that was apparent as early as 1933. The 'old Wagnerian' Paul Pretzsch savagely attacked the new Bayreuth in the *Stahlhelm-Musik-Zeitung* (music magazine of the right-wing Stahlhelm movement), demanding that the management of Bayreuth be deposed and a board of trustees appointed.[97]

Winifred wrote to Lene from Berlin: 'That man doesn't know what he's started – with Furtwängler as Vice-President of the *Musikkammer*!!!!' She was afraid of a Furtwängler takeover at Bayreuth. She immediately rang Goebbels and asked him to 'retrieve Pretzsch's letter from the official correspondence and just go through it with me. We can do that in Hitler's presence tomorrow. It's very useful that I'm on the spot, so that I can put a stop to the whole business straight away.' And she was no longer 'staying modestly in the background – that's why I deliberately sat in Hitler's box during the *Valkyrie*, so that everybody could see us together. Tomorrow,' she said, 'I'm going to try to make them write a reply to Pretzsch that will finally shut his mouth.'[98]

As early as 1933 Winifred was being approached with requests for help from people who were having trouble with the Party. Initially, they were 'non-Aryans' and 'half-breeds' who were banned from membership of the NSDAP. Among Wagnerians, there were countless 'non-Aryans' who had joined the Party before 1933. One example was the Chrambach family from Dresden, who were early and enthusiastic National Socialists. Since Chrambach *père* was 'half-Jewish', and his wife, Melanie, was 'Aryan', their daughter Esther was 'a quarter-Jewess', ruled out of Party membership. On 12 July 1933, in a confident letter to the *Gau* leadership, Esther Chrambach declared that 'Now I have discovered that my 25% Jewish blood makes me a non-German, even though my father was an officer on active service and was wounded in the war, I see that in order to conform to this Party ruling I am obliged to resign herewith from the NSDAP (to which I have belonged since 1931). Heil Hitler!' She expected a reply making her an honourable exception. Instead, she promptly received a curt acknowledgement of her resignation, ending 'With a German salute!'

Her angry mother appealed for Winifred's support in having the resignation overruled. When there was no reply to Winifred's letter on her behalf, Melanie Chrambach went to the local branch leader to complain. He asked the regional office in Dresden for a definitive reply, 'to keep the woman quiet', and enquired at the same time 'whether the mother, Frau Chrambach, membership No. 632134, married to a baptized Jew, was entitled to remain in the Party'. The regional court of the NSDAP in Dresden then declared the Party membership of the 'Aryan' Melanie Chrambach null and void, 'since . . . maintaining a marriage with a non-Aryan is contrary to the aims of the Party'. She must also return her Party card immediately. Undeterred, Melanie Chrambach complained to Gauleiter Mutschmann. He declared to the *Gau* court on 31 July 1935: 'Even though Esther Chrambach asserts that she is and will always remain a National Socialist, we cannot betray our sacred principles, especially now, when we are engaged in the most intense battle with Jewry – even if it is only 25%. No other verdict is possible, if we wish to follow our true path.'[99]

As Winifred had yet another appointment with Hitler, she presented the case to him personally, and then asked Major Walter Buch, whom she knew, to reinstate Frau Chrambach's Party membership, 'since my discussion with the Führer, who met the lady in question in '25 or '26 through me, and who knows all the circumstances, established that this is the will of the Führer, or that he will take responsibility for it.'[100]

On 18 October 1935, after a tough battle lasting two years, Hitler personally wrote two identically worded letters to Melanie and Esther Chrambach, with a copy to the Supreme Court of the Party in Munich. He had 'decided on a pardon that will allow you to remain in the NSDAP, despite your lack of a pure Aryan pedigree'.[101] Esther Chrambach survived the Third Reich without any restrictions, but changed her Jewish first name to the old Germanic 'Ase'. Winifred was also successful in a similar case, involving the brother of the conductor Franz von Hoesslin; this 'quarter-Jew' was allowed to rejoin the Party.[102] The success of her interventions led her to think that Hitler's attitude to the persecution of the Jews was nothing like as strict as that of his Party officials. All too naively, she trusted Hitler's 'deeper understanding'.

But as Hitler's power grew, such moves became increasingly difficult. This was apparent in 1938, when the 'half-Jewish Major Chrambach applied to join the Bayreuth League'. Winifred asked Otto Daube

> whether it might not be possible to make an exception in this case if I put in a special word? Could I just mention that at my request the Führer got Ase Chrambach's Party card returned to her. (That's the daughter – the mother is Aryan.) Major Chrambach is a semi-invalid from the war, draws his pension – has been deployed in a leading role in organizing anti-aircraft defences, etc. I'm telling you all this to show that they've turned a blind eye to him in Dresden once before.

She would also have a word about the problem with the head of the local Dresden organization.[103] After a fruitless discussion with the authorities, Daube reported back resignedly: 'Our efforts were unsuccessful! Heil, just the same!'[104]

In 1934 Jews were forced to leave all the Wagner associations. Emma Louis, chair of the Nuremberg German Women's Richard Wagner Association, wrote of Winifred's reaction:

> She was extremely incensed about it, and said that under no circumstances could this be allowed to happen. She absolutely does not want it. She was angry about the persecution of Jews, and told me that a short time before, she had had a discussion with Hitler about this persecution, and asked him what the poor Jews had done that they should be made to suffer like this.[105]

It was as early as 1933 that anti-Nazis, too, began asking Winifred for help. In spring of that year, when Communists throughout Germany were being interned following the Reichstag fire, Lene Roesener advised a husband desperate on account of his wife's arrest that he should appeal to Winifred. The wife was the secondary-school teacher Lydia Beil from Stuttgart. The daughter of a pastor, she had strong socialist convictions, and was being held as an alleged Communist. Winifred looked into the case, and was certain an injustice had been committed. When she asked Hitler to have Frau Beil released, he refused to act. Next, she asked Ernst Röhm to intervene on Frau Beil's behalf with the Reich Governor of Württemberg, Wilhelm Murr. But Murr was away, she was told, and the letter remained unanswered. Who would risk unpleasantness just at that moment for the sake of a Communist?

Meanwhile, Frau Beil was transferred to the regional women's prison at Gotteszell. Winifred became impatient, and put in yet another request to Röhm. Lydia Beil said later: 'She moved heaven and earth to get me freed.' In fact, Frau Beil was found innocent and released. Winifred replied to her letter of thanks: 'There's no need at all to thank me for doing the most natural thing in the world. If I can prevent the Party from committing any brutal act, I will fight it passionately, and where I can help a decent person, I will do so for the sake of my conscience.'[106]

Winifred had a good deal to do. When she heard that the Party in Darmstadt had been inciting the population to denounce others, she exclaimed: 'Inviting denunciations is a scandal, and contrary to Goering's order prescribing *punishments* for denouncing a superior. The first chance I get, I'm going to lash out! ... I've been invited to a Nazi dinner. If not before, that's where I'm going to raise the matter of denunciations.'[107]

Then she complained to Hitler about the coarse tone of Julius Streicher and his paper *Der Stürmer*, as well as a number of articles in the *Völkischer Beobachter*. But Hitler replied only briefly that 'the VB is not written for me, but for those in need of instruction'.[108] However, he respected her dislike of Streicher, and never brought him to Wahnfried again. Winifred interfered in all sorts of matters, even quite trivial ones. In February 1933, for example, having seen Johann Häussler's film *Blutendes Deutschland* (Germany Bleeding), screened together with an Italian film, she found it so poor 'that I'm going to make trouble in Berlin about it – the Mussolini film was magnificent'.[109]

She successfully fought off a move to dismiss all Festival employees who belonged to the illegal SPD or KPD. Soon she was actually taking on more, in order to protect them. The mechanic and 'old SPD-member' Ludwig Goebel stated in 1947: 'After 1933 we had more SPD people on the books than National Socialists. The specialists and the older people were all SPD.' There was no attempt to influence the staff politically.[110] More and more people therefore came seeking help, including those under threat by the Gestapo for 'subverting the military', or for 'Communist intrigues', 'treason', 'espionage' or simply for being high-minded Christians, or homosexuals. And hesitantly – because the house of Wagner was well known to be anti-Semitic – the Jews came too; initially, Jewish Wagnerians.

Winifred intervened expressly as an 'old National Socialist' concerned about standards of order and decency in the Party. She was utterly convinced that by doing so she was also serving the interests of her revered Wolf, whom she believed to be unaware of his Party comrades' acts of brutality. Later she complained about how 'difficult, for the most part even impossible' it had been to wring any concessions from Hitler: 'It takes at least two years for Hitler to admit an injustice.' And she added 'that it had been a long haul even after that before he could bring himself to right any wrong'.[111]

She replied to Lene, who had asked her to help a protégé of hers: 'I will gladly try to talk to Hitler about him – if only I could get to him, what with all the Reichstag business and the new Reich law code etc.' She discovered in the end that it was more effective to mobilize lower authorities on her behalf, and wrote to Lene: 'I'll pass the letter to the Propaganda Ministry – no point in sending it to Hitler – he'll only delegate it, anyway.'[112]

Winifred exploited her many connections with authorities, officials and Party functionaries at all levels. Most were impressed by her status as a close friend of the Führer. She described her tactics in retrospect: 'I always imagined that Hitler was uninformed about the evils that were going on, and in many cases I approached subordinates in the first instance. They usually put an end to the things I was complaining about, obviously because they were afraid that otherwise I would take them directly to the Führer himself.' She had only bothered Hitler directly in a very few cases. The reason was that 'if Hitler said "no", then it was all over. That's why I always preferred to involve some intermediate authority.'[113] Only if all else failed and the case was really important would she approach Hitler personally, face to face or by telephone.[114]

What Winifred looked for were reliable go-betweens who could intercede with Hitler if necessary. She already had Hess, Röhm, Schemm and Ruckdeschel, and now, thanks to Lieselotte, she also had Hans Frank. Winifred did not mind him occasionally (it was not often) spending the night at Wahnfried, as Lieselotte said: 'the kind soul is genuinely pleased for us, for me, and said I should just make everything as cosy and nice as possible'.[115]

Hitler set 12 November 1933 as the date for new Reichstag elections. Since all political parties apart from the NSDAP had been dissolved in the meantime, the election amounted in practice to nothing but a demonstration of loyalty to Hitler and his party. A referendum to approve the *fait accompli* of Germany's withdrawal from the League of Nations would take place at the same time. Abstaining from the vote would incur reprisals.

Three days before the election the Wagner children played truant from school to travel to Berlin with Emma and Lieselotte. They were present when Hitler spoke to the Siemens workforce. He boasted about his economic achievements in the short time since he came to power: 'When I arrived, there were 6.2 million unemployed in Germany. Now there are only 3.71 million. That is no mean feat in nine months.'[116]

Even if these figures were massaged, both upwards and downwards, none the less Hitler's job creation programme, given wide coverage practically every day in the press, provided the best possible election propaganda. It gave the Germans, used to nothing but social and economic decline since 1914, the feeling that things were improving at last. As the *Bayreuther Tagblatt* put it: 'No nation in the world has a government that can boast such a successful record as ours so far.'[117] Nobody wanted to know precisely how far this success depended upon depriving excluded and persecuted groups of their rights, plundering them and driving them out.

On election day, the Wagner children spent three hours with Hitler over coffee and cakes, and celebrated the result with him.[118] The 'Führer's list' received 92 per cent of the votes. The 8 per cent of ballot papers that were spoilt represented some 3.4 million Germans. The Reichstag now had no function but to showcase the Führer's speeches. Within the space of ten months, Hitler had wiped the Weimar democracy out of existence. Germany was now a Führer State.

The French ambassador, André François-Poncet, a frequent visitor to the Festival, wrote about Hitler's first year as Chancellor: 'If you watch how he moves from theory to practice to put his doctrine into effect, it's almost riveting to see how coldly he suppresses everything that stands in his way.' The diplomat had the feeling that he was 'watching a stage being transformed with the stage curtains drawn back. Crude scene-shifters are at work . . . A whole world has replaced the old one in a few moments. You are confronted by a new stage-set with new lighting to match.'[119]

CHAPTER 9

Confusion around *Parsifal*

(1934–5)

REFORM VERSUS TRADITION

The new management of the Festival was determined to go on with its artistic modernization and to make no exception even for *Parsifal*, which enjoys a special, almost religious place of honour in Wagner's *oeuvre*. Winifred was well aware that to change any detail of its staging meant unleashing storms of protest by the orthodox Wagnerians. Since its première in 1882, the production, scenery and costumes had hardly been modified at all; for had not 'the eye of the Master' rested upon them? As early as 1933, Winifred cleverly involved Hitler in the debate, giving him a 'long lecture on re-staging *Parsifal*'. Triumphantly, she reported: 'I'm sure I've won completely, and the aunts are in disarray!!!!!'[1]

When the plan went public, Eva Chamberlain and Daniela Thode rolled out their heavy artillery. They composed a '*Parsifal* petition' addressed to the Festival management, and sent it, with a request for supporting signatures, to all Festival staff and colleagues and to prominent Wagnerians. The whole lengthy declamation ended with a call for 'the stage-consecrating festival drama *Parsifal* to be produced in future in the original stage-setting of 1882, thereby establishing the only ... memorial worthy of the Master of Bayreuth'.[2] By the end of October there were 900 signatures.

Attitudes hardened when Winifred fired Gil Gravina, engaged as a Festival flautist, for signing the *Parsifal* petition. Winifred declined to negotiate with her

sisters-in-law. They in turn spread the rumour that Winifred had a Jewish secretary; they were referring to the anti-Semite Lieselotte Schmidt![3]

Winifred dealt with the interminable protest letters sent by the Swiss
jeweller Adolf Zinsstag by enquiring:

> Logically speaking, why don't you demand . . . that we use the same gas
> lighting for which the stage sets were designed in those days? Every gen-
> eration has always had to work at reclaiming the great masters for itself, to
> keep them fresh . . . You have absolutely no right to issue any kind of ulti-
> matum on behalf of the German people and the rest of the cultural world,
> because you are only the mouthpiece of a tiny group that is dwindling in
> number . . . and whose understanding and support I have learnt to
> renounce as my work goes on.[4]

In the final analysis, Winifred had the upper hand. Since 1 October 1933,
she had had an elegant flat in Berlin, and found it easier to contact Hitler. At
the end of October he invited her for a meal. 'I showed him the *Parsifal*
appeal, and he was furious! – He wants us to answer it by putting on a new
production by next year, and I'm racking my brains trying to work out how
we can manage it. We've got to do it somehow . . . Hitler says that if necessary he'll step in and take the matter up himself. At any rate, with him I'm
nicely protected!' Admittedly, there was no money for a new production,
something Winifred had difficulty in bringing home to Hitler: 'he absolutely
must have the new production of *Parsifal* in '34, and we poor devils have no
idea how to manage it!!!'[5]

In November Hitler agreed to finance the new *Parsifal*. He had also been
thinking about a stage designer, as Winifred related in later years: 'and then
he came to me very, very humbly with a question, a request, a wish. He said,
"Can't you give Alfred Roller the production design for Parsifal?" . . .
Naturally, Tietjen was very enthusiastic about Roller, too.'[6]

Working with Gustav Mahler at the Court Opera in Vienna, Roller had
already turned his back on the traditional stage by 1900, in favour of greatly
simplified sets that achieved their effect through symbolic motifs and colours
and above all through the lighting direction. It was to Mahler and Roller's
productions at the Vienna Court Opera that Hitler owed the great Wagner
experiences of his youth.[7]

Hitler's wish was Winifred's command. She wrote her first letter to Roller,
until then not known to her personally, on 22 November 1933: 'I am very

clear that this responsibility is . . . only to be undertaken if this new production, while totally in keeping with the modern Zeitgeist and modern
technical and visual resources, also strictly and unconditionally fulfils the
prescriptions of the Master . . . that is to say, in the purest sense fulfils the
Bayreuth tradition.'[8] Roller was delighted to accept.

At the beginning of January 1934 both Mistress and secretary were despon-
dent, feeling neglected by Hitler, who had failed to respond to either letters
or telephone calls. The extent to which the very existence of the Bayreuth
Festival depended upon Hitler was more apparent than ever. Lieselotte pon-
dered: 'It's a complete mystery how we're going to fill the house this year;
there's nothing doing abroad, and we've only sold a grand total of about
2,500 tickets so far (1 performance = 1,600 tickets), and that's a pathetic
number. No mention of tax exemption and such fancy things, either. We're
already contemplating shutting up shop for the summer.' There was no further
reference to the finance promised by Hitler for the new *Parsifal*: 'No word
from the Reich, and officially the Mistress has no information about Parsifal
being protected, or the 100,000 marks,' the latter having been mentioned in
the press as the supposed amount of the subsidy.[9] Many Wagnerians refused to
buy tickets, in protest against the modernizing of Bayreuth.

After weeks of waiting Winifred was invited by Hitler to dinner on
19 January 1934, with a one-to-one discussion to follow. 'That's wonderful,'
wrote Lieselotte, 'because it has been the case in the past that she's had to go
for months without hearing anything. It put some funny ideas into her
head . . . But be that as it may: when the need was greatest – and the Mistress
was really at the end of her tether – salvation was at hand once more.'[10]

Relieved, Winifred reported that 'everything had gone surprisingly well'.
There was no question of the subsidy being made dependent on control by
the Reich Culture Chamber: 'our complete independence is guaranteed,
come what may. It's now certain that there will be a new Parsifal, and we're
going to get the money, too. The best thing of all, though, is that Hitler is
still standing by us, and will never let the Third Reich interfere.' Lieselotte
commented: 'Sometimes and from some angles, [the opposite] looked very
likely, and Frau Wagner was not prepared to make any concessions whatsoever, even if the Führer himself demanded them. But he's not doing so,
thank goodness, and everything is fine. Now we have the wind fully in our
sails and can get down to work knowing that there's going to be a Festival in
1934, even if we've only disposed of 3,000 tickets so far!!!'[11]

It was highly problematical that, in contrast to the year before, in 1934 no

Jews could be employed. It was especially difficult to find substitutes in the same class as the outstanding singers Alexander Kipnis and Emanuel List. Both emigrated to the USA, where they had brilliant careers.

Time was pressing. Tietjen postponed a first meeting with Roller because of the difficulty of finding a suitable date. When one was finally agreed in February 1934, Roller was unable to travel because civil war had broken out in Austria. The dictatorial Dollfuss regime suppressed the Social Democrat opposition and bloody street-fighting ensued. The Austrian Socialist Party was banned; nine leading Social Democrats were executed, others arrested and taken to 'holding camps'. The small, abjectly poor country was now totally at the mercy of the Austrian National Socialists, who were recruiting ever more successfully.

When Roller finally got a permit to travel for 22 February, currency restrictions dictated that he could only carry 200 schillings, or 37 marks. Visibly exhausted, the seventy-year-old arrived in Bayreuth, inspected the Festival Theatre and got Paul Eberhardt to tell him about its technical resources. He visited Daniela Thode and Eva Chamberlain, and heard about the disputes. Then the ailing man travelled on to Berlin, where a first, two-and-a-half-hour meeting with Winifred and Tietjen ended, according to Roller, with 'an encouraging agreement on all the essential points'.[12]

Hitler honoured Roller, whom he did not know personally, with an invitation to the Reich Chancellery. He opened the conversation, reports Roller, 'most charmingly', and 'laughingly confessed to having prompted my invitation to design the new *Parsifal* set'. He listed the productions by Roller that he had seen in Vienna: *Tristan, Valkyrie, Rosenkavalier, The Egyptian Helena*.[13] Roller heard for the first time the story of how, in Vienna, the eighteen-year-old Hitler had even possessed a letter of recommendation addressed to him (Roller), but had been too shy to approach the much admired professor at the Court Opera and present it to him. After three attempts, he had finally thrown the letter away.

Hitler explained why he had proposed him for *Parsifal*: 'When I went to Bayreuth I saw that many visual effects were done better in Vienna. That's why I started the move to bring you in for *Parsifal*.' Then he announced his intention of passing the law protecting *Parsifal* which Cosima had demanded in 1913 in vain: it was 'outrageous [at this point he got excited and banged his right hand down flat on the table-top] that a collection of parliamentarians thought that without any debate they had a right to disregard the last testament of the great Wagner and release [for general performance] Parsifal!

. . . But if I push this law through, then I will be depriving the German theatre of something, and I will have to justify it by ensuring that the Bayreuth Parsifal production is so perfect, including the set, that no other theatre can compete.'

'He talked very firmly and clearly,' says Roller, 'without any hesitation, full of passion, but without false pathos, and not particularly loudly at all.' When Roller said that at this early stage he could not say how much the new production would cost, Hitler shrugged this off with a 'Well, the money will just have to be found!' By the end, Roller was 'completely fascinated by the indomitable will-power radiating from his eyes', and felt that he had become 'committed by oath and duty to Bayreuth'.[14]

It was the Swiss Wagnerian Zinsstag who most persistently sought to convince Roller that Hitler had been subjected to one-sided persuasion 'by those forces and personalities who only joined Bayreuth after 1914, and then took control of it in order to pursue completely different aims'. Cosima's daughters had 'an absolute moral right' to defend themselves, 'and all of us think it was very wrong of Frau Wagner to exclude them from collaboration (and consultation) for no reason immediately after the death of Siegfried Wagner'.[15]

In this phase, when Roller was working under severe time constraints, he was diagnosed with cancer of the larynx. He needed an immediate operation, followed by radiation treatment. The sick man fought desperately to finish the stage-set sketches, which were becoming increasingly urgent. When he finally had them ready, and sent them by post to Bayreuth, Hitler's restrictive policy towards Austria* meant that they were delayed for weeks in the German customs. Because of the same problems at the border, it was not possible for Roller personally to supervise the building of large flats for the scenery in Vienna. They had to be finished in a great hurry, and the final product was unsatisfactory. There was no time to put them right.[16]

By March, when tickets had been sold for only three and a half performances, Lieselotte complained angrily about the Propaganda Ministry: 'I don't understand why they can't use the radio, it wouldn't cost anything, it just seems so obvious.'[17] But Goebbels had no intention of lending his support to a recalcitrant Bayreuth. Winifred felt that her ambition to pass the Festival on intact to Wieland one day was being jeopardized. Lieselotte offered

---

*Hitler effectively applied economic sanctions to Austria, including currency restrictions, and anything sent from Austria to Germany was delayed at customs.

encouragement: 'If the outcome of this crisis is to purify the Work and strengthen the arm of Wagner's grandson and heir, then let us gladly struggle through it and have faith in its blessings. Let us not lose hope, and remember our hope isn't built on sand; Wieland will soon hammer it into shape!' [a play on the Germanic legend of 'Wayland (Wieland) the Smith'].[18]

Winifred calculated that Hitler also regarded Wieland as her future heir, and she frequently took him with her to official events. For instance, he attended the laying of the foundation stone for the Richard Wagner monument in Leipzig. During his broadcast speech, Hitler turned specifically to Frau Wagner and vowed 'to honour the will and the wishes of the great Master, to continue to cultivate his immortal works in their eternal living beauty, so that future generations will also be enabled to enter the marvellous world of this mighty artist of sound . . .'[19] As a kind of pledge for the future, he gave the seventeen-year-old Wieland the signed manuscript of his speech.

The Vice-Chancellor, von Papen, took mother and son with him in his plane to Berlin. In honour of Wieland's first flight, they flew an extra circuit over Berlin for him.[20] The following day Winifred and Wieland had lunch with Hitler in the Reich Chancellery. According to Lieselotte's account, derived from Wieland, 'it was so nice and informal . . . Wieland immediately pinned Goering down to letting him take his photograph'.[21] Wieland received permission to sell authorized portraits of Goering; he was the only photographer apart from Heinrich Hoffmann allowed to do so. From the sale of his Führer photos alone, which were often signed, Wieland earned 30,000 marks. It hardly cost him any effort, because the Festival photographer Pieperhoff took care of print production and despatch, and paid Wieland a fixed percentage.[22] The young man, his mother wrote, was 'very proud that H. recently ordered 30 more pictures from him, and that he seems to like using them'.[23] Wieland thus had a good deal of money at his disposal, in addition to what had been paid to him regularly since Siegfried's death by the rich Wagnerian Max Wiskott.[24]

The most important result of the meeting with Hitler was a telephone call to Bayreuth from Hitler's adjutant Julius Schaub, asking 'where to deposit the promised funding'.[25]

On his birthday, Hitler favoured the Wagners with a special mark of respect. Although he was aware that Winifred was not in Bayreuth, he drove with a column of five cars past Villa Wahnfried, and was spotted by the chauffeur, Paul: 'The Führer stood in his car, drove past quite slowly, and looked and saluted in this direction.' But Lieselotte lamented: 'We've been quite sad since then. How pleased the Führer would have been if one of the children had gone out to meet him!'[26]

In the middle of May the first ticket bookings from the Party began to trickle in. The National Socialist Women's Association ordered 100 tickets. Hans Schemm made 50,000 marks available to the National Socialist Teachers' League for Festival tickets. 'In the meantime he has been firing up the Civil Servants' League and the top echelons of the SA, who will also splash out,' but 'there's still nothing from the Reich'.[27] Nobody knew whether Hitler would be coming to the Festival.

On 22 May, shortly before rehearsals began, Roller was taken to hospital once again, for a course of radiotherapy. He could neither sleep nor eat, and was becoming progressively weaker. Though extremely sick, he struggled to get to Berlin from Vienna on 26 May for discussions with Tietjen and Winifred, and then on to Bayreuth, where things had already become fairly hectic. It was not until 28 June, during the rehearsals, that the scenery arrived.

Not even half the tickets had been sold yet, although dress rehearsals were about to start. 'In our hour of need I've alerted F[rank] once more . . . he's sure to be able to help . . . not that we're facing the final disaster, because in the end there's always the Führer, but the waiting is nerve-racking.' They had no idea how they were going to pay their 'army of employees'.[28]

THE RÖHM MASSACRE

On 13 May 1934 Ernst Röhm, Chief of Staff of the SA and Reich Minister without Portfolio, held a spectacular rally in Bayreuth, bringing together 25,000 Upper Franconian SA men. To the sound of 'The Entry of the Gods' from Wagner's *Rhinegold*, and in front of a crowd of thousands of onlookers, he reviewed a march-past of his troops in the Marktplatz. The Bayreuth newspapers sang his praises as 'the Führer's steadfast paladin' and 'the Chancellor's First Soldier' who had 'created the SA, the Führer's Guard, and trained them in the spirit of military obedience that enabled the Führer to smash the power of Marxism almost without bloodshed'.[29]

Since the early twenties, Röhm had been a welcome guest at Wahnfried, and after the seizure of power he proved to be a helpful and generous friend to Winifred. On 9 June 1934, for example, Lieselotte wrote: 'Yesterday I was on the phone several times to SA headquarters in Munich. The Chief of Staff has decided to invite all the top SA leaders to the first cycle. So he needs 70 of our best seats.'[30] On 29 June she stressed that so far, 'with the exception of Goering and Röhm', none of the National Socialist leaders had ordered any tickets. 'Today the Mistress sent a very frank letter to Wolf, and I think that alone gives us new hope. I'm sure he's been left uninformed once again, although the people around him know the facts. But in a certain biased and influential quarter we're being ignored and frozen out to the point where we can't stand it much longer.' She meant Goebbels and the Reich Culture Chamber. Lieselotte was still defiant: 'If they think they can force us to our knees and then take us over, then they're mistaken, because maybe we are the only people they can't touch.'[31]

That night Hitler flew to Munich and drove on to Bad Wiessee, where the SA leadership was assembled. In the first light of dawn on 30 June he had his old comrade Röhm dragged out of bed, accused of treason, and locked up with over a hundred other SA men in Munich-Stadelheim.

In this 'Nacht der langen Messer' [night of the long knives],* members of the SA and of the left wing of the NSDAP were murdered. They included much-feared radicals such as the 'lynch-mob murderer' Edmund Heines, but also dissident clerics, journalists and two secretaries of the Vice-Chancellor, von Papen. The murderers no more hesitated to kill the former Reich Chancellor, Kurt von Schleicher, than they did Gregor Strasser, who as Hitler's party rival in 1932 had made common cause with Schleicher. The corpse of Gustav von Kahr, who in November 1923 had sent in his police force against the Hitler putschists in Munich, was later found, mutilated with pickaxes, in the Dachau marshes.[32]

Outsiders were also murdered, such as two members of the Hitler Youth, and Willi Schmid, the music critic of the Munich paper the *Münchner Neueste Nachrichten* (Munich News), who was well known in Bayreuth. The

---

*Hitler feared that Ernst Röhm's SA was challenging the army and thereby alienating it: he relied on the army to carry out his expansionary foreign policy. Furthermore, Röhm and other radicals were demanding a national socialist revolution, while Hitler was trying to take the German establishment along with him. He promised the army that it would have the exclusive right to bear arms. On 30 June 1934 he used the pretext of a suspected plot against him to massacre Röhm and hundreds of others. Hitler also took the opportunity of settling a number of other old scores against politicians who had crossed him.

murderers had confused him with a friend of Strasser's.[33] Local party notables and SS men, as well as Goering, Himmler, Heydrich, Bormann and Hess, all used the night of killing to carry out private acts of vengeance. Hans Frank, the Bavarian Minister of Justice, rushed to Stadelheim and tried to stop the executions on legal grounds. Hitler's reply to him on the telephone was: 'The legal argument for everything that is happening is the survival of the Reich!' Nineteen prisoners were then shot by the SS.[34] Röhm survived the night in prison. When General Franz von Epp begged for his friend's life to be spared, Hitler wavered for a day. Then Röhm too was shot in his cell.

Wahnfried was truly horrified by the bloodbath, above all by the death of Röhm, who was considered Hitler's best friend. The victims were depicted in the press as traitors and putschists whom the SS had forestalled with their massacre. Hitler was highly acclaimed for having employed 'an iron fist to carry out a cleansing action that had cost the blood and lives of individuals, so that the whole should live'.[35]

The international reverberations were devastating. The London *Times* talked about a medieval frenzy of killing that mocked the deep-rooted instinct of every European for justice. The *Wiener Zeitung* (Viennese Newspaper) thought that the night of bloodshed vouchsafed 'a glimpse into the inferno that Germany has become in 17 months under the swastika', and expressed the hope that the Hitler state would soon collapse.[36]

Gradually, news of other victims emerged. A few who were thought dead had in fact survived, however, such as Röhm's friend Gerhard Rossbach, who had taken refuge in the woods, and the former Freikorps commander Hermann Ehrhardt, well known in Wahnfried. Röhm's young secretary, Count Leu Du Moulin Eckart (son of Count Richard), also survived the night, but was despatched to Dachau concentration camp.

Early in July the seasoned Festival visitor Maria Sembach came to see Winifred. Her husband, Emil, an NSDAP member of the Reichstag, had been arrested while on a bathing party during the night of killing. He was shot, and his body tied up in a bundle and thrown into a reservoir.[37] Frau Sembach had investigated the circumstances of his death, and passed on to Winifred the findings of public prosecutor Brieg from Breslau. They 'incriminated circles very close to Hitler'. She begged Winifred to send the papers on to Hitler personally, so that he could be properly informed. In this case it was clear that Hitler had not issued the order for the murder.

According to Maria Sembach, Winifred agreed immediately, 'appalled by the ugly light cast by this event and others upon the sinister machinations of the Nazi movement'. However, looking back in 1947, Maria Sembach wrote that Winifred had been fobbed off with 'the declaration that a thorough investigation had been ordered, etc., while nothing was done at all, and the murderers were protected'.[38]

In October 1934 the Silesian Gauleiter Helmuth Brückner, whom Winifred had contacted, composed a memorandum that bore an undeniable resemblance to Winifred's style, and was probably based on a draft by her: 'Is it National Socialist to connect the murder of the National Socialist Reichstag Member Sembach, untruthfully and against all justice . . . with the Röhm rebellion and the list drawn up under emergency decree, and link it with the name and honour of the Führer?' Anger about murders such as that of Sembach was causing 'endless disquiet among the population, including the old guard of the NSDAP'.[39] Winifred was a member of this 'old guard'.

While Bayreuth was still recovering from the shock of the massacre, the news came on 6 July 1934 that the Propaganda Ministry, on Hitler's orders, had agreed to requisition and pay for all tickets unsold by 10 July. With this last-minute concession, Hitler once more came to the rescue of the Festival, and he did more than that. He underwrote deficits anticipated for future years.[40] A few days later he came to the Festival, staying in the Böhners' house, and spent his first evening at Wahnfried. With him was his new personal physician Karl Brandt, who was soon to do Winifred some good turns as an intermediary.

Winifred had previously warned everybody present not to mention the subject of Röhm in Hitler's presence. The atmosphere, initially tense, relaxed somewhat when Hitler himself, according to Friedelind, 'started talking with cool detachment about the "cleansing"'. This encouraged the Wagners to raise questions. 'Hitler swore that only seventy-seven people had been executed in all. It had been inevitable that one or two should be shot by mistake.' In the case of the music critic Schmid, Hitler said he had arranged for his widow and children to receive a state pension.[41]

When Winifred raised the subject of Leu Du Moulin, keeping her promise to his father (Cosima's biographer, Richard Count Du Moulin Eckart), Hitler responded dismissively: 'Don't appeal to me on behalf of that character. He's the worst of them all.' With Röhm's connivance, he had betrayed party secrets to the Social Democrats.[42] But a few weeks later Winifred's intervention proved successful, after all. Retrospectively, she commented that young Du Moulin had 'played a mysterious part in the Röhm Putsch, and I managed to save his life at the time'.[43]

Hitler displayed anger at the murder of Sembach and, using his example, must have explained to Winifred that while he publicly took responsibility for the massacre, he had not actually ordered all of the 'executions', including Sembach's murder.[44] He represented himself as a man who had suffered greatly as a result of his friend Röhm's 'treachery'. Röhm had offended against the code of loyalty, and so placed himself beyond redemption. Wolfgang Wagner recollects that Hitler compared the Röhm murders to the story of Charlemagne. By slaughtering the Saxon rebels, he had laid the foundations of France, and, as is well known, he was canonized.[45] Hitler justified his actions by invoking the principle that whatever served the German nation was right.

In the end, Winifred conquered her doubts and accepted the version circulating widely in the press, that the Röhm killings had been necessary to suppress a planned revolt against Hitler. She was eventually so convinced of Röhm's disloyalty that, Friedelind says, she pitied 'the poor Führer': 'What a terrible shock it must have been for him to find himself betrayed by his best friend.'[46]

Since the murders had largely been 'justified' by Röhm's homosexuality, a vindictive campaign against homosexuals got under way. Countless artists and Festival employees were in danger. Precisely at this moment there was the threat of a trial involving the star singer Max Lorenz, who had been informed upon and arrested. He is said by Wolfgang Wagner to have been caught backstage *in flagrante* with a young man. The trial was 'of course painful' for Winifred, 'since I was his employer, and moreover one of our repetiteurs was involved'. Hitler thought Lorenz no longer acceptable at the Festival. Winifred shot back at him: 'All right, I might as well shut Bayreuth down, then. I can't do Bayreuth without him.'[47] In 1934 Lorenz was supposed to be singing Stolzing in the *Mastersingers*, and – even more important – Siegfried in the *Ring*. After an anxious wait, the case was quashed. Not only was Lorenz free to sing at Bayreuth, but Goering even provided his Jewish wife, who was also Lorenz's agent and from whom he refused to be separated, with 'Aryan' papers, in accordance with the slogan 'I'll tell you who is a Jew or not.' (This was Winifred's phrase for such manoeuvres.[48])

At Bayreuth, Hitler showed no fear of contact with the Jewess Lotte Lorenz. A foreign Festival visitor related in Berlin how Hitler 'quite conspicuously . . . neglected the self-important Frau Winifred in favour of a mysterious blonde. She was the wife of *Kammersänger* Max Lorenz. Hitler

was laughing and chatting and slapping his thighs, enjoying himself hysteri-
cally. There was no trace of the fierce, curt and humourless behaviour he
generally displays.' Hitler was so mesmerized by the 'golden voice of Max
Lorenz' that he overlooked his 'racial offence' with his Jewish wife. The
American journalist Bella Fromm heard similar stories, leading to her comment that 'it was as though Hitler's "artistic leanings" sometimes seduced
him into unwonted forbearance'.[49]

THE 1934 FESTIVAL AND THE VIENNESE PUTSCH

Just two weeks after the Röhm massacre, Hitler's ceremonial arrival at the
Festival Theatre was perhaps even more of a triumphal procession than in
the previous year. Hitler showed special respect for *Parsifal* by appearing in
tails rather than a dinner jacket. Whether it was due to the solemn atmosphere of *Parsifal*, or a demonstration of how devastated he was by Röhm's
alleged treachery, almost every observer noted that he appeared particularly
serious: 'The Chancellor's profoundly earnest demeanour made a powerful
impression on all those who greeted him with enthusiastic shouts of "Heil!"
in front of the Festival Theatre, or, in that consecrated space dedicated to
the celebration of German art, silently raised a hand in salute.'[50] The guests
included Goebbels and his wife, the Grand Duke of Hesse and his family, the
Duke of Coburg and the President of the Reich Bank, Hjalmar Schacht.
Also listed among the prominent guests is Röhm's friend, SA Gruppenführer
(lieutenant general) Prince August Wilhelm, who had only narrowly escaped
the massacre.

At the première, Hitler sat next to Winifred. Lieselotte says that 'they
were prepared to let it all wash over them, whether [the production was] a
disgrace or a triumph – because it could easily have gone badly. The Führer
trembled in sympathy with her, for after all he was "complicit", too.'[51]

The evening was specially significant also because *Parsifal* was Strauss's
farewell performance as conductor at Bayreuth. Helge Rosvaenge, who sang
Parsifal, recalled: 'Everybody noticed how solemn he was, and that day we
sang with sorrow in our hearts. He and we gave it our all, however; and
behold, when we compared the length of the acts, we found that the times
were exactly the same, to the minute, as when Richard Wagner personally
conducted a rehearsal for the very first performance of Parsifal in 1882.'[52]
Innovative as the evening was, the tempi at least stayed true to the original

production. The Dane Rosvaenge, a specialist in Italian opera who had never sung Wagner before, enjoyed great success.

Roller's stage-sets aroused the greatest interest. He had been keen above all to create a new setting for the entry of the Knights of the Grail into the Grail Temple, a key scene which he found particularly critical. The music lasts so long that the knights in most productions have to cover the width of the stage several times, which Roller thought unsatisfactory. So he used the vast space at the Festival Theatre to the full, emphasizing the depth of the stage with columns that created perspective by diminishing in height towards the rear. They were like a forest of pillars through which, from the depths of the stage, the Knights of the Grail moved slowly forward. The scene gained new dignity and solemnity,[53] but marked most clearly the departure from Bayreuth tradition. The Grail Temple had previously always been represented as a round temple, modelled upon Siena Cathedral.

Hitler was very proud of the success of Roller, whom he had recommended; he invited him over at the end of the performance. Lieselotte said that the old gentleman 'came back from the Führer quite transfigured. The Führer is blissfully happy, and it's a weight lifted from all our hearts.' The new *Parsifal* was 'a victory against a world of enemies'.[54] At the celebration for the première Roller had the place of honour next to Hitler.

Winifred's verdict on Roller's sets was more mixed. She thought the flower garden was a failure as 'Roller imposed too many technical difficulties on our primitive stage'. But 'the temple scenes are sublimely beautiful!' In general, she held that the 1934 Festival was 'undeniably a great success; I've now got solid ground under my feet, despite everything that upsets our old ladies so much'.[55]

At a reception for the artists in Siegfried's house, Winifred took the opportunity to introduce Alice Strauss to Hitler. The Jewish daughter-in-law of Richard Strauss was staying in the house with her whole family during the Festival. Having been subjected to harassment and threats from the Party, the young woman was scared and anxious; Strauss was very worried on her behalf and that of his two half-Jewish grandsons. Hitler's handshake in front of so many witnesses was a warning to zealous party officials to beware. Alice Strauss could now point out that she knew the Führer personally.

Traditionalists wrote numerous letters protesting angrily about the new *Parsifal*. Zinsstag compared Roller's Grail Temple to an 'orgy from Hell', as well as a 'congress hall' or even 'hotel lobby', and condemned what he called the 'de-Christianizing of the most Christian of all theatrical works'.[56] In

Germany, however, since this was Hitler's own project, the reaction was positive. The *Völkischer Beobachter* struck only one jarring note: Roller's stage-sets were 'a model for all other theatres the world over', but the traditional form of the Grail Temple was preferable.[57] This meant that Goebbels, for one, did not agree with the treatment of the Temple scene.

The promised law limiting *Parsifal* performances exclusively to Bayreuth never came about. When Hitler 'actually proposed to do it', Winifred later recalled, 'I persuaded him not to, because there was no way to prohibit performances abroad, and so, depending on where they lived, Germans could travel to see them in Brussels, Paris, Zurich, Prague, Vienna, Copenhagen etc.'[58]

On 25 July there was a sudden commotion around Hitler. He informed Winifred abruptly that Goering would be arriving in an hour, and asked her to find quarters for him. Since Wahnfried was full to overflowing, Siegfried's house had to be vacated and its current residents – the young Strauss couple, Albert Knittel and Lieselotte – found alternative accommodation. 'There were heaps of clothes and stuff everywhere,' groaned Lieselotte, who made up a bed for herself in Winifred's dressing room. While the performance was in progress, Winifred rushed to the airfield to meet Goering at seven o'clock. After a long wait she heard that his plane had been diverted and she raced back to the performance. 'Hermann the Magnificent' finally arrived in Bayreuth at 3.30 in the morning, and went straight to Hitler. Something unusual was happening in the Böhners' house where Hitler was staying, but the Wagners had no idea what.[59]

Friedelind reports that unusual things had been going on during the performance of *Rhinegold*, too: 'Schaub and Brückner took it in turns to run to and fro between Hitler's box and the lobby of our box, where there was a telephone; one picked up the news over the phone, while the other hurried over to whisper it in Hitler's ear.' Friedelind says that, 'highly agitated', Hitler had told them about the murder of the Austrian Chancellor Engelbert Dollfuss that afternoon. The assassins were Austrian National Socialists, who simultaneously embarked on a putsch throughout the small country in a bid to take control. But as the outcome of the putsch was not yet clear, Hitler asked the Wagners not to discuss it, and went off to supper with them as usual in the Festival restaurant. According to Friedelind he remarked, 'I've got to stay here for an hour or so and be seen . . . otherwise people might think I had something to do with this business.' He acted as though nothing had happened, quietly getting on with his liver dumpling soup.[60]

In the background of Dollfuss's murder, Gauleiter Theo Habicht, who was press attaché at the German embassy in Vienna, had been pulling political strings. Hitler was ready to take over power in Austria, but the alliance between Dollfuss and Mussolini still held good. When Italian troops moved up to threaten the Brenner frontier,* the putsch collapsed. After seven o'clock, while *Rhinegold* was being performed in Bayreuth, the putschists pulled out. They were placed under arrest, and interned in the same 'holding camps' where the Social Democrats had been confined since 1934.

Later, after the putsch had failed, *Rhinegold* had finished and Hitler had made a public show of nonchalance in the Festival restaurant, the Böhner villa became a hive of activity. He had the unsuspecting Vice-Chancellor, Papen, a personal friend of Dollfuss, roused from his bed in Berlin at two in the morning, and, 'immensely agitated', ordered him to take over as ambassador in Vienna immediately. The incumbent of the post at that time was facing a court martial. When Papen hesitated – he had not yet got over the shock of the Röhm massacre, and after all, the two secretaries closest to him had been murdered – Hitler invited him for immediate discussions in Bayreuth, putting his aircraft at his disposal.

By the time the morning papers came out, reporting the events in Vienna, Papen had arrived in Bayreuth, and found Hitler 'in a hysterical state about the recklessness of his Party comrades in Austria for having put him in this terrible situation'. Habicht, too, had been ordered to Bayreuth, and, Papen says, 'in my presence, the bitterest reproaches were heaped upon him and he was relieved of all his responsibilities'.[61] Hitler then declared that the attempted putsch had been entirely the work of the Austrian Nazis, and went out of his way to stress the peace and harmony prevailing between Germany and Austria. On 26 July he soothed troubled minds by appointing Papen as German ambassador and special emissary to Vienna.

Toscanini conducted Verdi's *Requiem* at a memorial ceremony for Dollfuss in Vienna. But Roller in Bayreuth was told that his 23-year-old son Ulrich was among the Austrian Nazis under arrest. He was studying stage design at the Vienna Academy of Fine Art, the place where Hitler had twice failed the entrance examination. The Rollers had a country home by the Mondsee,

---

*The Brenner frontier between Italy and Austria was a thorny problem because of the German-speaking South Tyrolean minority within Italy. This was a constant pressure point until Hitler renounced German claims to South Tyrol as part of a deal with Mussolini after the annexation of Austria by Nazi Germany in 1938.

and Ulrich had taken part in the insurrection there. Extremely worried, his father hurried back earlier than planned to Vienna. He died in 1935 without ever seeing his son again.

In the meantime, Hitler had no intention of missing the *Valkyrie*, with the young Kirsten Flagstad making her debut as Sieglinde. In Lieselotte's words, 'the performances reached heights never seen before . . . Because of the radio broadcasts, enthusiastic letters have been arriving from far and wide; it has given enjoyment to the whole world.'[62] Thomas Mann's family were listening to the *Twilight of the Gods* on the radio in Zurich, while the paterfamilias preferred to leave the room: 'It revolted me. I don't want to hear anything from Germany. Nothing that comes from there is innocent; there's cultural propaganda behind all of it.'[63]

And yet Mann had not even heard Winifred's interview introducing the transmission of the *Ring*. She produced the purest pro-Hitler propaganda, mixed with typical Bayreuth emotionalism. Describing Wagner's financial problems during the first Festival in 1876, and the difficulty of starting up again in 1924, she declared that 'The people in power at the time had no sense of what was authentically German . . . [but] when I was gripped by anxiety about how to sustain the Festival in 1933, a miracle occurred – thanks to the Führer; Bayreuth under the Third Reich was accorded the place in cultural life for which it was destined, and for which Wagner longed and hoped.' Bayreuth could at last fulfil Wagner's dearest wish: 'All working people, whether workers with the head or with the hand, will be able to enjoy the wonder of Bayreuth, in accordance with the desire of the Führer, and in these hours of consecration find spiritual strength and edification, to return home proudly aware that it was German will and genius that created this hallowed place.' She concluded: 'Wagner's legacy is in good hands as long as our Führer is the patron and protector of Bayreuth.'[64]

On Festival Hill, meanwhile, they were worried that the imminent death of 86-year-old Reich-President Paul von Hindenburg might interrupt the Festival. On 31 July Hitler, Goebbels and Goering left Bayreuth with their staff for Neudeck, in Prussia, to visit the President. Lieselotte sighed: 'The poor Führer got no rest at all at this time; it was like an unlucky star.'[65]

Hindenburg died on 2 August 1934. The same day, the Reichstag passed a law to merge the offices of Reich-President and Chancellor. Hitler became Commander-in-Chief of the armed forces, who swore an oath of loyalty to him personally; a change greatly facilitated by the elimination of Röhm and the disarming of the SA as a revolutionary army. In order to 'legitimate' this law, a referendum was set for 19 August.

Goebbels organized a campaign to promote the referendum, and asked Winifred to take part in it. A three-minute propaganda message was compiled from the interview recorded in connection with the *Ring* broadcast. It was transmitted on the morning of 10 August between eleven and twelve, and repeated twice.[66] Thomas Mann heard this broadcast and wrote with disgust in his diary: 'Winifred Wagner as electioneering propagandist. "The Republic heaped hatred and mockery upon R. Wagner. Through Adolf Hitler he has been miraculously resurrected." Tremendous.'[67]

On the day before the referendum the beginning of the performance was postponed from four to five o'clock, so that, as Lieselotte said, 'audience and personnel alike could gather around the loudspeakers and listen to Hitler's speech'. She found it 'once again so passionate and inspiring that it didn't seem too long at all, and we had no trouble getting in tune with him, because the Führer and Bayreuth are one and the same, and the work of the Master and that of the Führer both spring from the same idealism and serve the same German nation'.[68]

In a newspaper interview Winifred praised Hitler for having single-handedly saved the Festival and for creating the new audience that – at government cost – now existed, 'including comrades who may be impoverished Wagner-enthusiasts, perhaps music teachers or SA men or German workers in the Kraft durch Freude [or KdF, "Strength through Joy", an organization founded to develop state-subsidized leisure activities for workers] . . . A number of music-loving SA and SS units have been sent tickets and formally invited, so that they can carry with them for ever, as a kind of consecration through art, the impressions they take away from here.'

She expressed herself rather strangely on the subject of the absence of foreigners from the Festival. Even two years before, Bayreuth had still been 'a social citadel where an international, often snobbish clientele would mingle'. Luxury cars, 'including Rolls-Royces', had queued up in front of the hotels. However, the influence of 'a certain part of the foreign press', with its 'boycott of things German', had kept foreigners away from the Festival. In the end, though, said Winifred, nobody was interested in creating in Bayreuth 'an international event where you could flirt and amuse yourself'; for that was 'all it had often amounted to'.[69]

It was true that the image of the Festival had changed since 1933. Hitler's party not only supplied the majority of Festival-goers, but also exploited the opportunity of the presence of thousands of guests and curious onlookers to show itself to advantage. Thus the *Gau* administration in 1934 organized with great pomp the unveiling of a 'monument to the movement', created by the Bayreuth architect Hans Reissinger, in front of the town hall. Four thousand five hundred political leaders of the NSDAP marched up in their brown uniforms to a 'consecration hour' ceremony, featured on the radio and in newsreels, with speeches by Gauleiter Schemm and the head of the organization, Robert Ley.

The monument, sculpted out of granite from the Fichtelgebirge mountains of Bavaria, took the form of a massive swastika laid out horizontally, from the middle of which there rose a 'bronze fist . . . strangling in its powerful grip the snakes of subversion and discord'.[70] (According to eyewitnesses the monument was outstandingly hideous, and since it was accessible and stood chest-high right in the centre of town, it made a nicely secluded *pissoir* for the Bayreuthers after dark. There was no alternative but to demolish it.)

From 1934 onwards, the KdF turned Bayreuth, even outside the Festival season, into a veritable fairground for cultural tourism run by the NSDAP. The KdF organized cheap holidays and short breaks on behalf of 'German national comrades', including mass trips to the Munich Oktoberfest and luxury tours of the Wagner sights as well as Festival visits. The organization operated at a substantial profit; for example, according to Friedelind, it dropped the price of a tour of the Festival Theatre from one mark to ten pfennigs, but collected twenty pfennigs per person from the employers who financed their workers' KdF trips. As hundreds of thousands of people were conducted through Bayreuth every year, there were tidy profits for both the KdF and the Wagners.[71] Wagnerians making the pilgrimage to the grave of the Master found their devotions disturbed by crowds of KdF trippers.

YOUTH AND ART ARE BROUGHT INTO LINE

As she was the mother of four adolescent children, the National Socialist Hitler-Jugend organization very soon loomed large in Winifred's life. With the *Gleichschaltung* (bringing into line) of youth training, traditional youth activities were suppressed, from gymnastic clubs to choirs. Having herself suffered from the iron discipline of an orphanage, Winifred had deliberately brought up her children in an anti-authoritarian atmosphere. She could not accept the mass activities of the Hitler-Jugend, especially the military drill they imposed. The remorseless way that young people were driven and made to exercise until they dropped, was against her principles. But as usual, it was not Hitler she blamed for this, but his subordinates in the Party, in this case Baldur von Schirach

The campfire romanticism and exposure to the national community in the HJ did not impress the untamed, self-confident Wagner children. They rejected both orders and discipline, loudly voiced their objections and knew that they could get away with it. The most they had to fear was being thrown out, and that was precisely what they wanted.

As early as January 1934, the conflict between the Wagner boys and the HJ reached crisis point. While exercising on the rings, fourteen-year-old Wolfgang fell two and a half metres and broke his arm. He tried to recover his medical costs from the official HJ insurance, but it transpired that the monies paid in compulsorily had been embezzled. When this was reported, nothing happened. There was even a threat to bring in the Reich Youth Leader himself to deal with Wolfgang, at which he retorted angrily, 'If you crooks are going to get him to cover for you, then he's as big a crook as you are.'[72] He is also alleged to have told an HJ leader who wanted to make him his 'adjutant', 'Oh, no, I'm not playing stooge to you.'[73] Wieland must have been almost as rebellious. On 16 August 1935, both boys were expelled from the HJ,* and received a caution about 'insulting the Reich Youth Leader: disciplinary offences'.[74] Friedelind likewise lasted only eighteen months in the BDM, Bund deutscher Mädel (League of German Girls).[75]

One witness was 'really shaken' by how far the Wagner children went in criticizing the Party and making fun of it. When she asked Wolfgang why he did not work harder (at school), he replied: 'Because I want to acquire the right leadership qualities, and the more stupid you are, the more suited to being a Nazi leader.'[76]

In January 1935 Bayreuth was made the seat of the HJ regional leadership, and of the BDM leadership of the *Gau*. The 27-year-old Baldur von Schirach proposed to celebrate this with a great festival and rally, and wanted the Festival Theatre as his venue. Winifred scotched this plan, and reported to Lene how Hitler had 'been gloriously helpful in getting me out of a fix: on 5 January Schirach made a big fuss here, and even wanted the Festival

---

*Until December 1936, the HJ was ostensibly a voluntary organization; after that date, membership became compulsory.

Theatre. I wasted no time in phoning Hitler, and he ruled it out straight away – "Thanks – that's all I wanted to hear", I said, and the local HJ bigwigs finished up with very long faces.'[77]

With her antipathy to the HJ, Winifred took special pleasure in coming to the aid of youngsters who had got on the wrong side of the youth organization. In any such case, she always supported the parents, and even told the Education Minister so: 'I can vouchsafe to you that a good many parents are bound to be against it. I am one of them – and I am prepared to tell you why, whenever you like.'[78] To her friend Lene she wrote: 'I can understand your anger at the HJ only too well, and it's certain that nothing is going to improve until all of us parents get together and make a stink! But hardly anybody has the courage. You should use the opportunity to talk to Wolf about it.'[79]

There was something else that annoyed Winifred: 'In the HJ and BDM training camps there is strong opposition to Richard Wagner and Bayreuth, and young people have the presumption to say pityingly – "Oh well, we'll just have to let the Führer have his Wagner craze."'[80] The HJ sold very few Festival tickets.

Schools too were brought into line with Nazi ideology; this applied especially to private schools and faith-based schools, such as those attended by Friedelind and Verena. In the autumn of 1934 the Abbess of Heiligengrabe Convent School, Elisabeth von Saldern, a former lady-in-waiting at the Imperial court, turned to Winifred with an urgent plea for help. She and three other members of staff had been denounced by two Nazis; one was another teacher, and the other the son of the foundation's pastor. The abbess had called the regime's Jewish boycott 'a cultural disgrace', and Schirach a 'young whippersnapper'. Furthermore, a girl at the school had failed to give the Nazi salute. The result was a surprise visit of inspection by the Gestapo, which identified a 'reactionary spirit' in the lessons, and ruled the convent teachers incapable of 'basing their institution totally on the foundations of the national transformation'. The abbess must be replaced, the teachers in question dismissed, and a full-time National Socialist head of the school appointed.[81]

The abbess's defence was that the convent school did in fact promote the National Socialist principles of 'Christian convictions, obedience and love of the nation'. She pointed out the 'numerous acts of repression' the foundation had suffered under 'Marxist governments'. The ladies of the convent had therefore greeted 30 January 1933 'joyously', and 'had destroyed the black–red–gold flag [of the Republic] in the presence of girls from aristocratic families'. Pastor Oestreich, who was behind the accusation, was a bad teacher, and it was strange 'that it is precisely children from families who have been National Socialist for years, such as young Friedelind Wagner from Bayreuth, who reject him'. It was all to no avail. The three teachers who had been denounced were dismissed, and the abbess removed from control.[82] As she was the only one who could teach them, the girls in the top class had to leave school five months before they were due to take their *Abitur* (school leaving certificate examinations).

Enraged by these events, Winifred sent a telegram to State Councillor Wilhelm Kube, president of the province of Brandenburg: 'An ambitious convent teacher and an over-zealous pastor are trying to denounce the Heiligengrabe convent school and its head-teacher, von Saldern, as reactionary, and the school as alien to the present State. A school which has been educating my daughter for three years is neither of these things. I know how to deal with informers, and request your personal intervention.'[83]

Kube then informed ministers Rust, Hess, Goering and Schirach of the matter, 'with due regard for the fact . . . that Frau Winifred Wagner is supporting the cause of the convent'. Schirach pursued his complaint in connection with the 'whippersnapper' remark. Winifred had also sent a telegram of protest to Education Minister Rust, and she now composed a long statement for the defence under the title 'Heiligengrabe – a model educational establishment in terms of the Third Reich':

> As one of the most long-standing National Socialists, it infuriates me that lying and calumny have chosen to represent this model educational establishment as reactionary and alien to the present State. My children are fortunate enough to know nothing but a National Socialist worldview. Friedelind, who is a very keen critic and observer of her surroundings, and (so far as it can be said of a child) is politically minded, has never had any cause to complain of anti-National Socialist attitudes at Heiligengrabe.

A 'practical National Socialism', she claimed, had prevailed at Heiligengrabe since its foundation almost a hundred years earlier: all proceeds were used for welfare purposes; a third of the seventy girls were orphans who paid no fees; the convent teachers had very low incomes; the uniforms worn by the pupils eliminated class distinctions, serving to promote communal values. In reply to the complaint that daughters of 'former ruling houses' were sent to the school, she asserted that this was the 'expression of a commendable desire on the part of these princely families to educate their children to be useful members of the national community in the National Socialist sense', and to break down differences of rank. After attacking Schirach, she concluded with the observation that 'Heiligengrabe fulfils a real national and social function'.[84]

In a paper circulating internally, the ministry's reaction to her interference was extremely irritable: 'With all due respect for the standing of Frau Wagner as a National Socialist, as well as artistically, it must be said that the accident of her daughter's attendance at this school cannot be allowed to have a decisive influence on the fundamental evaluation of the case.' The author of the paper refers, moreover, to Bismarck's *Gedanken und Erinnerungen* (Thoughts and Recollections), 'where he speaks of the personal influence of privileged women on political matters'.[85] The outcome of Winifred's efforts was that, while the school was put under Nazi direction, it was not closed. But she had once again made enemies of several government ministers and high-ranking officials.

Bursting with pride, the abbess wrote to Winifred in 1937 to say that the Führer had spoken to her briefly and said to her, 'most kindly' that 'yours is a fine and rewarding task'. Friedelind commented: 'Let's hope those words help her when it comes to the lesser bigwigs![86] Once again the Wagners were seeing Hitler as the epitome of kindness and justice, contrasted with a despotic party.

Gleichschaltung soon caught up with Furtwängler, too; he had made himself unpopular by his efforts to help Jewish musicians and his support for the composer Paul Hindemith, blacklisted by the Nazis. In December 1934 he was forced to resign from all his positions: head of the Berlin Philharmonic, director of the State Opera and vice-president of the Reich Musicians' Chamber. His rival Clemens Krauss was appointed to succeed him at the State Opera and the Philharmonie. Although Winifred disliked Furtwängler, she felt sorry for him, and wrote to the Roeseners: 'What do you think about Fu? Now they've really thrown the baby out with the bathwater – I think he should have been left to get on with his art, but relieved of his cultural-political posts, because he'll never be a Nazi! – Krauss has been appointed like a pig in a poke . . . But Wolf says he's his man, so that's that!'[87]

Political pressure was exerted on Furtwängler to prevent him from emigrating. Goering and Goebbels even agreed on the fact that he 'must not be allowed to go abroad'.[88] The situation became even bleaker in March of the following year when, despite the furious resistance he put up, Furtwängler's closest associate Berta Geissmar was obliged to leave Germany because of her 'non-Aryan' origins. After some discussion, Goebbels noted: 'he goes on raising objections, then gives in, and even says so publicly. Great moral victory for us. These artists are the strangest folk in the world. Not a clue about politics.' Hitler agreed, writing 'now we just have to worry about how to employ him'.[89]

Hitler then asked Winifred to put the old conflict aside, and enlist Furtwängler for the new production of *Lohengrin* planned for the Olympic year of 1936; it was a potential international sensation. Winifred wrote on the subject: 'I had a talk with him recently in Berlin, and we agreed to draw a line under the past and make a fresh start.'[90] Furtwängler told his mother he had accepted the invitation, though admittedly 'more for practical reasons than from any real passion'.[91]

Writing to Krauss, Strauss commented on this unexpected outbreak of harmony in Bayreuth: 'What do you say to Furtwängler–Tietjen? . . . What a delicious spectacle! After all that furious cursing about "Fu" as a Wagner conductor, this new "heartfelt" relationship seems rather ridiculous . . . Poor Frau Winifred! Does she know what she's doing?'[92]

In July 1935 Strauss was deposed as president of the Reich Musicians' Chamber. This resulted from the intercepting of a letter to his 'non-Aryan' friend and librettist Stefan Zweig. In vain, Strauss tried for months to get an appointment with Hitler or Goebbels, and asked in despair, 'Is there any prospect of an opera of mine ever being produced in Berlin again?'[93] Apart from his constant worry about his part-Jewish family, like Furtwängler he was forced to recognize that he had been used merely as a celebrity adornment to the Reich Musicians' Chamber.

The way was now clear for the Reich Controller of Culture, Hans Hinkel, to reorganize the Reich Culture Chamber. Mocking Strauss, he said 'that one of the greatest creative artists we have today has failed in cultural politics, in fact was bound to fail as soon as he was called upon to assert obvious racial requirements in a particular field'. Hinkel also actively resumed his campaign against Tietjen. In November 1935 he sent the old file on the Boerner case to Hitler's adjutant Fritz Wiedemann for forwarding.[94]

While Tietjen appeared on the blacklist of Goebbels, the head of the Reich Culture Chamber, Goering recognized his services with the title of 'Prussian State Councillor', and thus gave him a degree of protection from further Party attack.

FAVOURS FOR WINIFRED

Winifred felt safe under Hitler's protection, of which he provided constant reminders, as he did before Christmas 1934. 'Hitler's big plane landed here unannounced, bringing an enormous picture of the Führer, which Captain Baur had orders to deliver to me personally.' Terrified, people were 'still standing to attention out there on the airfield', expecting the Führer himself . . . 'But I must say he shows his friendship and his gratitude at every opportunity, and I'm extremely happy about that!'[95] From then on the portrait hung above Winifred's desk. Thanking him, she wrote:

> My dear, dear friend and Führer!
> I just cannot put into words the joy you have given me with your picture; I'm completely beside myself with joy and happiness and gratitude, and you will have to accept this stammering in place of a sensible letter! – You could not have given me greater pleasure than with this wonderful present, which is a masterpiece of skill and faithfulness, and bestows upon my humble home the blessing of your constant presence! –
> My endless thanks to you, giver of such inexpressible joy! –
> In true friendship, your Winnie.[96]

Hitler visited Bayreuth fairly frequently at this time, usually without warning, as Lieselotte noted: 'Wolf was here, completely alone, for a long time, very relaxed.' He had 'gone about it very cleverly, got someone to phone us and then came in a car with a Cologne number-plate, closed so that not a soul recognized him, was here from 6.30 to 12 o'clock, and all bosom friends . . . So Bayreuth still doesn't know the Führer was here and for how long.'[97] It was a time when Winifred had plenty of opportunities to tell him about her worries and wishes.

During this visit in October 1934, she brought up 'the whole question of the inheritance of the Wahnfried estate',[98] with a view to making Wieland sole heir. The Reich estate inheritance law passed the year before was actually intended to apply to farm properties, to protect them from being broken up, and from excessive debt burdens. The farm was declared indivisible, as the property of the family. It had to be passed on to a sole (naturally 'pure Aryan') inheritor, but could not be sold or mortgaged. Other relatives, especially siblings, were excluded from the settlement and male heirs were given preference over females. It was just such a law that had been advocated at the turn of the century by members of the Eden colony, including Karl Klindworth, to prevent land speculation and the impoverishment of farmers.

Extended to Wahnfried, the law would have invalidated Siegfried's will, which envisaged all four children as equal heirs. Wieland would have become sole heir, and his three siblings would have received nothing. But Hitler rejected Winifred's approach as, according to Wolfgang, 'he clearly did not want to interfere so drastically in an internationally recognized institution such as Bayreuth, or be accused of abusing the law of contract'.[99]

Hitler's visit after the state funeral of Gauleiter Schemm was much more extended. At the beginning of March 1935, Schemm's plane crashed on take-off from the Bayreuth airfield, and he died soon afterwards. The funeral on 8 March was the biggest Bayreuth had ever seen, and far more ostentatious than Richard Wagner's. When all the guests had taken their places for the funeral ceremony, Hitler arrived unexpectedly, and walked silently between the ranks of raised arms. In the name of the Führer, who was supposedly suffering from a cold, Hess delivered the main funeral oration, followed by Goebbels, Frick, Frank, Rosenberg, Himmler and many others. The ceremony concluded with the funeral march from *The Twilight of the Gods*. Hitler stood for a minute 'in a last silent farewell tribute' in front of the coffin, wordlessly shook hands with Schemm's family, and left the funeral. Because of his cold he did not stay for the actual interment.

Five minutes later, with the briefest of warnings, he arrived at Wahnfried, where only Lieselotte Schmidt and Emma Bär were present to receive him. Winifred and Wieland were obliged, as she reported, 'to race home from the ceremony, because we weren't allowed to drive there, and going by car the Führer naturally got to Wahnfried ahead of us'.[100] Lieselotte described him as 'very agitated and serious at first, walking up and down the room, where there was a warming fire alight, and we brought him a cup of peppermint tea'.[101] When Winifred finally arrived, Hitler relaxed. They ate 'completely *en famille*', as she related, 'and he told us he wasn't unwell at all – this was just a diplomatic way of showing the British they could no longer do what they liked with us – and they'd certainly got his message.'[102] The British Foreign Minister John A. Simon and Anthony Eden, the Lord Privy Seal, had announced that they were going to visit Hitler on 7 March, to convey to him British concern about German rearmament, and remind him of the conditions of the Versailles Treaty, but Hitler postponed the meeting because of his alleged cold. He was already planning the reintroduction of general conscription, and wanted to present the British with a *fait accompli*.

Important participants at the funeral gradually began to arrive at Wahnfried. After some talk about Schemm's accident, Hitler's monologues by the fireside led to discussions about building plans and models for Bayreuth, this time concerning a new congress hall. He mentioned the autobahn, too, and remarked that he had had to 'fight like a lion to ensure that it went through Bayreuth, because the experts thought it was too near the border', but he saw the autobahn as a compensation for Bayreuth's poor railway connections.

The mayor was critical of the way an autobahn flyover was going to spoil the Eremitageallee (Hermitage Avenue). Two pillars had already been put up, and now it was too late to do anything. Hitler replied, 'Why didn't you tell me? That's out of the question; there will have to be an underpass instead.' He asked, 'in vigorous, almost angry tones', to be put through to Fritz Todt, head of autobahn construction, immediately. But it was a Saturday afternoon, and it was difficult to locate Todt. The information that he was at the Leipzig Trade Fair sparked off a hunt, ultimately successful, through all the Leipzig hotels. Hitler ordered Todt to come to Bayreuth immediately to carry out the change of plan. Lieselotte was impressed: 'The way it all went so quickly was wonderful, a significant moment, after all, and you could really see what it meant for the Führer to "take action".'[103] He ordered the pillars to be blown up and an underpass constructed.

That evening Winifred found Hitler 'in terrifically high spirits, and he told us masses of interesting things, but I can only pass it all on to you in person'.[104] The company stayed together until six o'clock, 'hanging on the Führer's words'. Then he gave the signal to leave, and the visitors duly departed, including his adjutants. But, Lieselotte says, the Führer stayed on: 'It was just one wonder after another.' A vegetarian supper was quickly put together. Hitler carried on talking amidst this smaller family circle until ten at night, mostly about earlier times; 'about his first time here, and it was so intimate and touching, the things that came back to him'. During the whole time Hitler admirers stood at the entrance to Wahnfried, 'and lots and lots of them got their feet cold without ever seeing the Führer. Who would have thought it, ten hours in Wahnfried, sharing this precious, full life with him for ten hours!!!' That was how Lieselotte saw the visit.[105] Winifred must have reacted less poetically to Hitler's endless monologues; she had left hospital only a short while before, following treatment for a severe case of jaundice. She still needed time to recuperate, but was forced to keep up appearances.

From then on, the memory of Schemm was a shining beacon for the NSDAP in Bayreuth. His reputed last words were echoed in practically every speech: 'Make the Bavarian Ostmark strong for me once more!' However, the doctor who had attended him, Wolfgang Deubzer, reported that in his fear of death he had 'cried out to his Saviour'. This version was officially banned. From then on, Dr Deubzer was regarded as politically unreliable.[106]

Despite the Versailles Treaty, on 16 March general conscription was reintroduced in Germany, something Lieselotte regarded as a 'proud, liberating act of the Führer's', not actually announced by him personally, because 'for diplomatic reasons' he was at a health spa in Wiesbaden. In private, he had previously said 'quite frankly' that 'we are not exactly defenceless; we've got the most pilots, the biggest tanks, in fact everything in the best quality and size. But it's probably wiser not to tell the whole world about it.'[107]

The discussions with Simon and Eden took place in Berlin on 25 and 26 March, in a friendly atmosphere. In long monologues, Hitler evoked the bolshevist menace and demanded military parity for Germany. Paul Schmidt, translating for Hitler for the first time, was amazed: 'Even two years ago in Geneva the sky would have fallen in if German representatives had made the kind of demands that Hitler made here, as though it were the most self-evident thing in the world.'[108]

Winifred had been invited to the farewell dinner on the last evening of the talks, to partner Simon; Lieselotte maintained that this was because 'clever and linguistically able women were completely lacking' in Hitler's coterie.[109] Well prepared, Winifred eagerly adopted Hitler's goal of making a friend of Britain, and talked to Simon so intently in English that she forgot to eat. At least he had been completely open to her arguments, she said later. But Eden, whom she disparagingly called a 'disciple of Churchill', had stayed 'tight lipped'.[110] Three well-known singers sang Wagner, and Hitler was a 'charming host'.[111]

When the British guests left, at nearly eleven o'clock, Hitler ordered a tray of delicacies for Winifred and a carafe of wine, remarking, 'You worked so hard at your political mission that you hardly touched a thing. I can't have that. So please make up for lost time, and tuck in.'[112] Winifred liked to quote this as an example of Hitler's sensitivity.

On 10 April 1935 Winifred was invited to the wedding of Goering and the actress Emmy Sonnemann in Berlin Cathedral, to be followed by a reception in the Kaiserhof. She thought that 'since the Führer invited me to dinner with Simon, he [Goering] probably imagines it's "smart" to invite me!!!!! I can't think of any other explanation. It will be a dreadful affair. Anything less than 1,000 [guests] certainly won't do for him!!!!!!!!!![113] She made fun of the lavishly attired Prussian Minister President, criticizing him, 'as a Minister of the Reich', for 'requisitioning the contents of a Jewish jeweller's shop [that is, wearing so many gaudy decorations]'.[114] In the eyes of his contemporaries, Goering embodied the opposite of the simplicity of the Führer, who generally wore no decorations at all apart from his Iron Cross from the World War. In Germany, many who still remembered the resplendent uniforms worn by William II were deeply impressed by this deliberately plain style of dress.

Soon afterwards, Winifred was invited to Hitler's apartment in Munich to meet the young Englishwomen Unity and Diana Mitford; the British fascist leader Oswald Mosley; the Kaiser's daughter Duchess Viktoria Luise of Brunswick with her daughter Friederike (later to become Queen of Greece); as well as Goebbels, and Hitler's foreign policy adviser Joachim von Ribbentrop. Winifred's role was partly to act as interpreter. Hitler had only known Unity for two months, but she was a passionate admirer who had 'stalked' him for a long time, and forced herself upon his attention. During his first conversation with her (her middle name was Valkyrie), he had raised the subject of Bayreuth and invited her to the next Festival.[115] Winifred took a critical view of this over-excited girl, but had a high regard for her grandfather, Lord Bertie Redesdale, who had translated Chamberlain's works into English, and had known Siegfried well.

Winifred found it flattering to be invited on such occasions. Somewhat overtaxed, though, she wrote to Lene from Munich: 'When and how I'm going to get away from here is a big question – because when Wolf has time, he has lots of time.'[116] She showed clear symptoms of fatigue, to which her private life contributed. Her relationship with Tietjen had reached crisis point. He was still not keen on marrying, and was always stalling; he hardly ever appeared in Bayreuth any more, and when he did, he brought the afflicted Nena with him, since, as he claimed, he could not leave her by herself. He was more reserved than ever with Winifred, bad-tempered and unloving, pleading sickness. She, on the other hand, was worried, and showed her feelings like an open book.

They had agreed to spend three weeks at Winifred's holiday home on Lake Constance, but Tietjen suddenly insisted on bringing Nena with him, and she in turn brought along her brother and her dog. Winifred was overburdened, having practically no help in the house; and she was bitterly disappointed, as she confessed to her friend, 'precisely because I was looking forward to 3 weeks here alone with Heinz, and that was the plan, the harsh reality is hard to bear! . . . It's indescribably painful to see this supposedly sick woman constantly bullying him. The whole day centres on the feelings of this person, who is more changeable and spoilt than anyone I've ever met.' Tietjen 'just puts up with all this without batting an eyelid – out of sheer concern for her, he becomes completely unconcerned about others, without even noticing it; it's a tragedy and it's making me suffer badly . . . whatever you hope and long for, it's nothing but renounce, renounce – sometimes I feel very stupid for continuing to hope at all!'[117]

After this wearying summer, Winifred was guest of honour at a new production of the *Mastersingers* in the Nuremberg Opera House. Furtwängler was conducting and the sets were by the *Reichsbühnenbildner* [Reich Stage Designer] Benno von Arent, known in Wahnfried as 'Reibübi'.* While creating his designs Arent worked closely with Hitler and incorporated his suggestions. Hence his pride in presenting his work on the eve of the 1935 Party rally.

It seems that one day Hitler had presented Arent, 'by way of stimulus', as he said, with 'neatly executed sketches for stage-sets, in coloured pencil, for every act of Tristan and Isolde'; and on another occasion sketches for every single scene of the *Ring*. Speer recalled that 'He recounted with great satisfaction at lunch how he had worked on them night after night for three weeks, which I found particularly astonishing because it was a period when Hitler's diary happened to be very crowded with visitors, speeches, inspection visits, and other public events.' Hitler would have preferred to see Arent working at Bayreuth, rather than Preetorius. But Winifred was obstinate, says Speer, and 'acted as though she had not noticed Hitler's wishes'.[118]

Party members' interest in the *Mastersingers* was limited, said Friedelind: 'One of the best orchestras in Germany, with a celebrated conductor and some outstanding singers, played to a completely apathetic audience, mostly consisting of snoring Nazi high-ups, so that Hitler had to send his adjutants along the rows and order them to clap.' The ensuing 'overdone military ovation' was more painful than the preceding silence.[119] Winifred saw her

---

*Winifred's family enjoyed mildly satirizing the Nazi habit of abbreviating official titles.

attendance as a social duty: 'After Act I, Hitler commanded us to come to his box, where we sat enthroned next to him until the end.' Then she quickly left for home, for 'I had thereby performed an effective *acte de présence*'.[120]

It was at this so-called 'Party Rally for Liberty', on 15 September, that the Nuremberg race laws were proclaimed. The Reich Citizenship Law deprived all 'non-Aryan' Germans of their civil rights. The Law for the Protection of German Blood and German Honour forbade marriage or extra-marital relations between 'people of German blood' and Jews, and prescribed gaol sentences for violations, called 'racial offences'. What Chamberlain claimed were laws of nature concerning the life-threatening mixture of the 'Aryan' race with 'inferior', 'non-Aryan' races, were thus taken up politically in Germany and rigorously applied. The aim of these laws, constantly reiterated, was to make the German people strong and warlike. In Bayreuth the *Gau* authorities put up weatherproof metal signs with the inscription 'Jews not wanted here', and distributed a list of the twenty-eight remaining 'Jew shops' which Bayreuth's citizens were no longer permitted to patronize.[121]

In October there was a large-scale blackout exercise, that ran from six in the evening until 6 a.m. As Lieselotte reported it, 'in Wahnfried we were naturally more Catholic than the Pope, using packing paper a few centimetres thick (the roll weighed several hundredweight!) and about 100 drawing pins to cover all the windows . . . We have no idea what all this palaver is about; in a real emergency you'd never have time to bother with all this fuss and preparation.'[122]

THE NEW GAULEITER

After Schemm's death, Winifred wrote prophetically to Lene: 'Here we're all reeling from the impact of Schemm's death – as a son of Bayreuth and founder of the local group, he is so closely connected with everyone who lives here, that we all feel his loss quite personally. He was a great friend and patron of the Festival, and we're all worried about who his successor might be; he won't have an easy time of it, anyway, because Schemm was so popular.'[123]

And indeed the atmosphere of Bayreuth changed overnight when, in December 1935, Fritz Wächtler from Thuringia became the new gauleiter and leader of the National Socialist Teachers' League. In place of the elegant, affable Schemm, a brilliant orator, there appeared the ungainly figure of the oratorically untalented and philistine Wächtler, whose dogged adherence to the Party line soon earned him the epithet 'megalomaniac schoolteacher'.[124] He rigorously put the increasingly draconian new laws into effect, above all those aimed at Jews and the churches, and as an outsider he made enemies in the area by his wholesale meddling in the mayor's sphere of influence. Moreover, he was not prepared to recognize the privileged position of Villa Wahnfried, whereas Schemm had done so without a moment's hesitation.

The verdict of the Bayreuth doctor Wolfgang Deubzer on him was: 'He introduced a system of arbitrary power and compulsion, and it gave rise to very vigorous counter-movements, probably unparalleled in any other town.' When it came to filling posts, Wächtler 'always tried to bring in absolutely reliable Party functionaries; while the mayor's main criterion was competence to do the job'. The Bayreuth mayors would never have been able to sustain their years of bitter resistance to the Gauleiter 'so vigorously and honestly, without Frau Wagner to supply the necessary backbone'.[125] On the other hand, anyone who felt badly treated by Winifred or the mayor would now complain to the Gauleiter. This debilitating battle between the Gauleiter and his officials on one side, and the Mayor, Winifred and a large number of Bayreuthers on the other, dragged on until 1945.

For example, when work was needed on the extension to Siegfried's house, Winifred arranged as usual to hire the building firm run by Konrad Pöhner, but as he had a Jewish wife, he was no longer eligible to undertake public contracts. There was a protest from one of Pöhner's competitors, who threatened to appeal to the Gauleiter. Winifred was undeterred, retorting, 'Just let the Gauleiter's people come. She wasn't going to be told who she could do business with.' Pöhner deeply respected Winifred's attitude as 'moral and emotional support and encouragement . . . for me and my family'.[126]

What most annoyed the Gauleiter was Winifred's role as the 'guardian of the Party's morals'. Whenever charges of graft or corruption in the local party were raised, she was the one who complained to the authorities on behalf of those affected. For example, she sent Hitler a letter of complaint from Edith Müller-Eggert of Bayreuth, which she had typed herself. Frau Müller-Eggert accused the Gauleiter first of requisitioning her husband's factory because of his criticism of the party, and then of closing it down. The resulting legal wrangle went on until 1940, and exposed a good deal of corruption in the *Gau* administration, as well as the 'discrepancy between word and deed' that prevailed there. Frau Müller-Eggert later made clear that Winifred had 'regularly expressed her outrage at the leading Nazis' notions of justice and honour'.[127]

The struggle over the churches, too, was becoming heated in Bayreuth. The new Gauleiter lost no time in drawing up battle lines, assigning the Spitalskirche (Church of the Infirmary) to the Nazi-sponsored German Church and having his own son christened there. Decent clergymen were persecuted with renewed vigour. There had certainly been arrests and persecution under Schemm, but with a nostalgic aura enveloping his memory, the Bayreuthers blamed the new Gauleiter for everything.

The Wagners were not churchgoers, but they adhered to their traditional Lutheranism. Although the party hounded clerics it did not like, Winifred was confident of Hitler's own position, for after all he had written in *Mein Kampf* that 'The political leader should not interfere in his nation's religious beliefs and institutions.'[128] She liked to refer to clause 24 of the NSDAP manifesto: 'We demand freedom for all religious faiths in the state, in so far as they do not endanger its existence or offend against the principles and moral feelings of the Germanic race. The standpoint of the Party as such is a positive Christianity, not tied to a particular denomination.'

To be on the safe side, fifteen-year-old Verena asked Hitler himself, 'Wolf, are you actually still a church member?' He replied that he had never left the church. 'But weren't you thrown out?' He said nobody had thrown him out, so he was a Catholic. For a while, the girl was thinking of going over to the 'German Christians', but Hitler told her it would be better to stay with her own church.[129] The Wagners were therefore certain that the Führer had nothing to do with the persecution of the churches. The Gauleiter was to blame.

Winifred suited herself. She kept up contact with old friends, whether they were Jewish, 'Jewish-intermarried', homosexuals or priests. She made donations to the church, and bought from Jewish shops. She did not go about it quietly, either, but drew attention to herself with her usual animated presence. Her behaviour was a red rag to the local Nazis. 'Under cover of a mask of politeness, a real battle began,' she reported.[130]

Since Wächtler, too, had a direct line to Hitler, and the latter disliked conflict with his gauleiters, the outcome of this battle was uncertain. Hitler's adjutant, Fritz Wiedemann, described Hitler as 'cocking a deaf ear' when it came to his top party officials.[131] It was only during the early years of his regime, when their relationship was still untroubled, that Winifred had any success against party functionaries.

In October 1935, the Bayreuth district administration, together with the National Socialist Teachers' League, launched a campaign against the Freemasons. Bayreuth was (and is) the home of the German Grand Lodge, and thus the centre of German Freemasonry, with the most important Masonic museum. In Bayreuth the Masons belonged to the upper class, and they were mostly nationalist and politically conservative; anything but the revolutionaries and internationalists the Nazis made them out to be. In April the fine building that housed the Bayreuth lodge, standing in the Hofgarten close to Wahnfried, had been requisitioned, along with the lodge funds. The whole, very valuable, contents of the museum and the archive were carted off to Berlin, and are still missing today. The house was turned into a kindergarten run by the National Socialist welfare organization.

At the invitation of the district administration, party member Professor Hornung from Erlangen gave a public lecture in Bayreuth castigating 'Jesuitism, Pan-Judaism and Freemasonry', and accused the Masons of pursuing anti-nationalist aims hostile to the Germanic race. He claimed that during the war, there had been makeshift lodges behind the German lines 'in which Masons in the German army had consorted with their French and Belgian Masonic "brethren" '. The two-hour lecture ended with an expression of satisfaction at National Socialism 'finally having eliminated the dark spectre of Freemasonry'.

When a long newspaper article reported this talk, under the heading 'The Scourge of International Freemasonry',[132] Fritz Böhner, Hitler's landlord during the 1933 and 1934 Festivals, protested in a plain-speaking letter to the editor; he also cancelled his subscription to the paper. He declared that he had been a Mason until the self-dissolution of the lodge in April 1933, and strongly objected to the slanders contained in the article.[133]

In consequence, the editor-in-chief of the *Bayerische Ostmark* (The Bavarian Ostmark) approached Winifred to inform her that it was impossible for Hitler to stay in Böhner's house again.[134] She had no choice but to give in to pressure from the new *Gau* administration. Hitler was unable to help, because he could not publicly ignore his own injunctions by lodging in a Mason's home. Winifred was angered by all the trouble the Bayreuth Nazis made for her. She had to look for a new house for Hitler, however difficult that might be. In the end it was he himself who, during his next visit, provided the solution. As Hitler was shown around the new alterations to Siegfried's house, Winifred recalled that 'he really loved the rooms, and said to me: "You know, now I've seen this house, I'm really not so fond of the

Obersalzberg [his mountain retreat] any more." Well, knowing him pretty well, I said: "I suppose you would actually like to live here?" – "Ah," he said, "if only I could, that would be marvellous."'[135]

To ensure Hitler's security, the house needed further building work, and the garden it shared with Wahnfried had to be sealed off. Lotte Warburg recounts that

> a big wall was erected around Wahnfried, so that nothing could be seen when the Führer was visiting. This sandstone wall, which is head height, is finished by a hideous wooden gate that blocks the view. On one side, where you might still get a glimpse of the garden, a metal wall has been put up. It is extraordinary what lengths the Führer will go to in order to shut himself away and his beloved people out.[136]

The Gauleiter had no idea that Pöhner the builder, who carried out the work, was a Mason, as was the owner of the Hotel Bube in Berneck, where Hitler liked to stay overnight. The Masonic vow of secrecy paid off at such times.

During those years, Hitler was particularly friendly towards the Wagner family. After a visit from him early in April 1935, Winifred wrote to Lene: 'He was enthusiastic about the set for Lohengrin, and is going to give Wieland a car!'[137] The eighteen-year-old was taking driving lessons at the time. When he passed his test, Hitler called him personally to invite him to Munich. Jakob Werlin, a Daimler-Benz director, collected the young man from Hitler's apartment on the Prinzregentenplatz, took him to the Mercedes showroom, and handed over a silver-grey Mercedes convertible, with dark blue leather seats, fitted out 'with every possible optional extra', together with 'one or two special features ordered by the Führer' – and very expensive.

A concerned mother, Winifred had sent the sixteen-year-old Wolfgang to Munich as well, to keep Wieland company on his first drive, from Munich to Bayreuth. The lads had supper alone with Hitler. As he had to leave for Berlin around nine o'clock, the boys were even allowed to spend the night in his apartment. 'Wieland in the Führer's own bed! It's hard to imagine!' exclaimed Lieselotte. Hitler too had given some thought to Wieland's first drive in his new car; he was allowed to take the wheel himself, but Hitler's chauffeur Julius Schreck was to be at his side. As Schreck had to be back in

Munich the same evening, Hitler ordered a second car (in which Schreck's wife travelled) to follow him and bring him back.[138]

The Wagners fulfilled Hitler's need for the warmth of family intimacy. But he was the one who determined where and when he would see them, without reference to the plans and obligations of family members. In December 1935, for instance, as reported by Winifred,

> around 2 o'clock on the afternoon of the 29th, there was a call from Brückner in Munich – the Führer had to travel overnight to Berlin and wanted us to go with him! – We packed in 20 minutes – set off at 2.38, and all of us, including the two lads (who had previously been alerted) were having supper with him in Munich by half past seven. His special train left at 9.21. We sat chatting with him until 12; in Berlin he took us with him for breakfast at the Chancellery, then we had to come back for lunch – and celebrated the New Year with him entirely alone from 11 at night until 5 o'clock in the morning!!!![139]

There was a great deal of gossip in Bayreuth, and among Hitler's entourage, about the nature of the relationship between him and Winifred. Speer, who sometimes accompanied Hitler to Bayreuth and Berneck, was 'quite certain, because of numerous small but revealing signs' that Hitler was having an affair with Winifred. How else to account for Hitler's 'strangely exalted mood' whenever he returned from Bayreuth, 'with some kind of gleam in his eye – quite blissful . . . That had been more or less the consensus of everybody involved in these trips. Sometimes, when a bad mood of Hitler's went on for days, they used to say "jokingly" that it was time for the Führer to go and get his "Bayreuth treatment" again.'[140]

It was certainly true that, when Hitler was staying in Berneck, he did not usually come back from Wahnfried before dawn, and this helped feed the rumours. But as every guest at Wahnfried, as well as the staff and the children, could have attested, he did not spend the night in Winifred's bedroom, but with an intimate circle around the hearth. As Winifred said, 'however warm it was, the fire had to be lit, and he sat by the hearth and fussed around with the fire for hours. He absolutely loved that.'[141] In the Wagner family circle, the teetotaller even permitted himself the occasional small glass of Austrian schnapps.

Winifred was very proud of Hitler's devotion, but his sudden visits and invitations imposed a strain that only a robust nature like hers could bear without complaint. A particularly sensitive spot was touched by his call on 7 May 1936, when she was at long last alone once more with Tietjen in Berlin. Hitler phoned from Dresden to say: 'Since I've got your children here with me, why don't you join us?' Earlier he had sent for fifteen-year-old Verena to be brought to his hotel from her convent school, still in her uniform. 'She was first of all greeted by the Führer all by himself, and then he took her with him on his trip down the Elbe to Spandau.'[142] When Verena told him that Wieland was at the nearby Reich Labour Service camp at Grossenhain, he was roped in as well. As his work clothes were too dirty, he was quickly supplied with a new outfit, and taken by police launch to join the others on board the *Hindenburg*.

After the Elbe trip, Hitler said goodbye to his Party companions – he could not stand Gauleiter Martin Mutschmann, anyway – and had supper alone with the two young people. He joked with Verena about the over-strict headmistress of the Luise School, Baroness Löwenclau [literally 'lion-claw'], whom he called 'cat's-claw'. Using a high female voice, he did an impersonation of her sternly giving orders: 'Number 33, to the Headmistress's office!'[143]

Then he had the idea of calling Winifred over from Berlin. She left Tietjen behind, cancelled her appointments, took the night train to Dresden and had breakfast with Hitler and her children. He then decided on the spur of the moment to travel with the Wagners back to Bayreuth, and arranged for both Verena and Wieland to have a few days' leave of absence. The trip from Dresden to the Hotel Bube in Berneck took place in four cars, Wieland travelling in Hitler's own vehicle. Then there was the usual game of hide-and-seek with the Bayreuthers. Paul Eberhardt took Hitler and Winifred in Winifred's car to Wahnfried. The others followed on inconspicuously.

When they all sat down at the tea-table, Hitler had a slight mishap. A bread roll fell on 'his beautiful light-grey trousers, butter-side down, naturally', said Lieselotte

> That was a job for me, hot water handy, plus a handkerchief; so there's me, fiddling around with the Führer's trouser-leg like nobody's business, so to speak. He helped me very tactfully, and the main thing was that after it had dried there really wasn't a trace left. The nicest thing that's ever happened to me, of course . . . He was terrifically affable and calm, not talking about Party affairs at all, but relaxed, and very funny, too; a real nice uncle out of a story-book.[144]

The tea lasted a long time. It was followed by a stroll through the garden of Wahnfried, and apart from a couple of people who had been informed, 'not a soul was aware of the hidden treasure behind the walls of Wahnfried'. At 8.30 there was supper, followed by the usual hours by the fireside. Lieselotte praises at length Hitler's affection for the Wagner family: 'his glance growing ever more radiant, he looks from the children to the mother and back, and knows that if there is such a thing as a home on this earth for him, he won't find a better one than here, in Wahnfried, with these people'.

During the many hours that Hitler spent in her home, Winifred frequently took the opportunity of raising all sorts of problem cases. She declared after 1945 that she had often discussed the situation of the Jews in the Third Reich, and had 'told him my opinion openly and honestly. In response to these remarks, he explained that he intended to deal with the Jewish problem generously, and give half- and quarter-Jews the same status as Aryans.'[145] She believed these assurances, and continued to blame any faults on the local Nazis, and not on the system.

After this eventful weekend, Winifred first of all took Verena back to the convent school, went on with Wieland to the Labour Service camp at Grossenhain, and then raced back to Berlin. But all her hectic activity was at least rewarded. Wolf fulfilled a major wish of hers. Wieland was allowed to move to Kulmbach Camp near Bayreuth, and spend his weekends at home from then on. During the Festival period he was exempt from Reich Labour Service, in any case, and was often released at other times, to work on stage-set sketches with Franz Stassen.

A much-vaunted 'centre of German art', Wahnfried received many kinds of support, and not just in connection with the Festival. Above all, the money was now available to stage Siegfried's operas, which brought the family not only honour, but also royalties. Hitler took a special interest as 'Siegfried was a personal friend of mine, although politically passive! He couldn't help it; the Jews had him in a vice. Now that spell is broken, and more of his work is being staged. Those filthy Jews managed to break him! I heard the Bärenhäuter [The Idler] when I was young, and the Schmied von Marienburg [Smith of Marienburg] is said to be the best thing he did.'[146]

However, when the Königsberg Opera was about to adopt *The Smith of Marienburg* into its repertoire in 1934, the Reich Culture Chamber withheld permission. Referring to the friendship and non-aggression pact concluded in January 1934 between Hitler and Pilsudski, the Chamber warned that staging a work that was not exactly pro-Polish might cause political problems. They asked for a copy of the libretto to examine, and recommended that Siegfried's publisher, Brockhaus, should put off the production 'for special practical reasons', which was tantamount to a ban. Winifred, who saw Hitler twice soon afterwards, successfully protested. The Reich Culture Chamber lifted the ban, while advising the Königsberg Theatre 'that the director should avoid anything that might cause offence'.[147]

But even the most magnificent production ever enjoyed by any work of Siegfried's, *The Smith of Marienburg* on 6 March 1938 at the Berlin State Opera, directed by Tietjen with sets by Preetorius, failed to popularize Siegfried's music. There was only one repeat performance.

CHAPTER 10

Lohengrin and the 'Thousand-year Reich'

(1936–8)

THE FESTIVAL AND THE OLYMPIC GAMES

In 1936 Bayreuth had four jubilees to celebrate: 13 August was the sixtieth anniversary of the first Festival performance; 13 June marked fifty years since the death of Wagner's sponsor and patron King Ludwig II; on 31 July it would be fifty years since the death of Cosima's father Franz Liszt; and on 2 July a thousand years since the death of King Henry I, 'Heinrich der Vogler' (the Fowler), commemorated in Wagner's *Lohengrin*.

Hitler, too, ordered celebrations in honour of Henry I, a duke of Saxony whose settlement with Bavaria and Swabia united the Reich and secured its external borders, especially against the West Frankish Empire. He did all this at a time when the Reich was also threatened by constant incursions, by the Magyars* in particular; and he laid the foundations for the brilliant reign of his son Otto I.

Hitler's 'Third Reich' placed itself in the line of succession from the 'First Reich', which survived until 1806, down through the 'Second Reich' of Bismarck and the Hohenzollerns, from 1871 to 1918. Heinrich Himmler, Reich leader of the SS, was in charge of the festivities. In hundreds of ceremonies of dedication, Henry was celebrated simultaneously with Hitler, his

---

*Earlier name for the Hungarians.

'successor'. Himmler said of Henry that he was the first among equals – and one thousand years ago, he was a Führer.

As the artistic high point of the millennial celebrations, Hitler wanted Bayreuth to stage a new production of *Lohengrin* (no longer on the repertoire), to be conducted by Furtwängler. Bearing in mind the large number of foreigners expected to attend the Olympic Games in Berlin, and hoping to attract them to Bayreuth, Hitler proposed that the Festival should be divided into two phases. From 19 to 30 July, before the Olympics began, the first cycle would be put on, to be followed after the Games by the second cycle, from 18 to 31 August. The Reich Sports Leader, Hans von Tschammer und Osten, affirmed the link between Bayreuth and the Olympics with a telegram of homage to Winifred: 'At this historic moment, bringing together the work of Richard Wagner with the cultural background of the Olympic ideal, German sport salutes you as the bearer of a great tradition.'[1]

Tietjen's production of *Lohengrin*, with stage design by Preetorius, was (at Hitler's expense) the most luxurious ever seen. In the bridal procession, Maria Müller as Elsa was preceded by seventy pages bearing candles. The blue and white material of her wedding dress was woven in the traditional manner, on a wooden loom; the other festive costumes were decorated with heraldic motifs picked out with pearls. In Act III all the cast wore armour and carried arms, Lohengrin being clad 'from top to toe in gleaming silver'. 'The whole is a shimmering chain-mail encasing the body', made of countless small silver-plated aluminium rings which reduced the weight to 25 pounds, from what would otherwise have been 125 pounds.[2] Hitler must have contributed vastly more than the customary subsidy of 55,000 marks for a new production.

Shortly before the Festival opened, Winifred appointed another new assistant. Ulrich, the 25-year-old son of Alfred Roller, like all the other Austrian Nazis who had been held under lock and key, had been released from internment after Hitler's July agreement with Austria and was looking for work as a stage designer. The tall, attractive young man quickly became Wieland's admired friend and mentor. In the autumn he embarked on a promising career at the German Opera in Berlin, under the kindly paternalistic eye of Hitler.

In preparation for Hitler's visit to Bayreuth, many suspects were taken into preventive custody, including an ex-Communist labourer who had said, 'Hitler's OK, but all the others are swine.'[3] For reasons of security, the garden of Wahnfried had been closed off on the street side. Lieselotte Schmidt observed that 'the barrier can hardly be seen from outside, but of course there are police-men all over the place, and at the front there are two sentries [from the Leibstandarte SS, Hitler's house-guards], and nobody gets in without a pass'.[4]

Accompanied by an outsize retinue of ministers, gauleiters and generals, Hitler arrived in Bayreuth in his special train on the morning of 19 July, the opening day of the Festival. He stayed at Siegfried's house, known from then on as the 'Führer's building'. Winifred handed 'the whole house over to him . . . his majordomo or whatever you call him, his name is Kannenberg, was given an inventory, brought all his own staff, and the house was left to him, so to speak . . . Although he did insist that at least one member of the family, and more if possible, should join him for at least one meal a day.'[5] Hitler came over to Wahnfried only by special invitation, and unaccompanied.

Having the Führer as a neighbour was not just an honour for the Wagners, but also involved some inconvenience. Closed access meant considerable limits on their freedom of movement. All the activity centring on the 'Führer's building' resulted in an enormously increased amount of traffic in front of Villa Wahnfried. Crowds of Hitler-spotters massed around the garden gates to catch a glimpse of the Führer. Moreover, that year a packed special train brought 1,600 Sudeten Germans from the town of Eger, which had belonged to Czechoslovakia since 1919. They expressed their devotion to Hitler, and resorted to rhythmic chanting to ask him to annex the German-speaking regions of Czechoslovakia to the German Reich: '*Unser Führer, Ostmarksohn, komm heraus auf den Balkon*' (Führer, son of Ostmark's pride, come and speak to us outside). The press carried photographs of these Germans from non-German countries, picturesque in their folk costumes.

As a special feature of the production, Tietjen arranged for Franz Völker to sing the second part of the 'Grail legend'. It had never been heard in Bayreuth, having been dropped by Wagner from the première in Weimar for fear of over-taxing the tenor voice of Karl Beck. Völker's voice was more robust and coped well with the strain. The addition, which had not been announced in advance, made this *Lohengrin* as distinct musically as it was in other ways.

The première gave Hitler the chance to show what a connoisseur he was. As Winifred, seated next to him, never tired of relating, when Völker unexpectedly launched into the extended narrative of the Grail legend, her guest reacted immediately. At first he was startled, she said, and then merely surprised; he clutched at her hand as though to question her, and then nodded approvingly. Afterwards he said he was very pleased to get to know this version.[6]

Hitler signalled the special quality of the occasion by going up on stage

after Act II, accompanied by Winifred, Tietjen and Furtwängler, in order, as
the Bayreuth newspaper put it, 'to salute the company of artists with splendid words of gratitude, surrounded by the mighty architecture of the castle
courtyard'.[7] Such a gesture by a head of state was unprecedented in Bayreuth.
The mood was euphoric, especially when Hitler joined the artists in the
Festival restaurant after the performance.

Musically and visually, this *Lohengrin* under Furtwängler was the Bayreuth
Festival's greatest hour of glory. Broadcast worldwide, it projected an image of
the Third Reich as a sponsor of the arts – a propaganda coup for Hitler.
Among the myriad listeners abroad was Thomas Mann, whose ambivalent
reaction is recorded in his diary: 'One should not have listened, not have lent
an ear to that swindle, because basically one despised everybody taking part.'[8]

Once again, Hitler and his entourage carried on political business from
their boxes in the theatre. The day before the première of *Lohengrin*, General
Franco and his troops had begun a putsch in Morocco against the left-wing
government in Madrid. The start of the Spanish Civil War prompted hectic
activity. Generals, ministers and ambassadors arrived in Bayreuth from
Berlin. Hitler's secretary Christa Schroeder said that it was 'like being in an
army camp'.[9] The political and military staff assembled every day for discussions in the garden room of Siegfried's house. The situation was confused,
and there were no maps on which to follow the ever-changing shape of the
front from day to day. When nobody knew the precise location of Tetuán,
the capital of the Protectorate of Spanish Morocco, Hitler asked sixteen-
year-old Wolfgang to rush off and fetch his school atlas.[10] These were the
maps used to follow the struggle in Spain. But despite world events, Hitler
appeared punctually every day at the Festival Theatre. Urgent news was
brought to him in his box.

The military prospects of the Spanish putschists were at first far from
rosy. Since the navy had declined to join them, there was a lack of ships to
ferry the soldiers across from Morocco to Spain. There were hardly any
planes, either. In this tight spot, Franco asked for help from Mussolini and
Hitler, and sent negotiators to Bayreuth.

On 22 July 1936 Goebbels noted: 'Still unclear in Spain. But situation
improved in favour of the rebels.' And on 24 July: 'Nothing decided in
Spain yet. We've sent two armoured cruisers. That will make an impact.'
Alongside Mussolini, who was also supporting Franco, Hitler was presented
with the chance of shaping an alliance against the 'Bolsheviks', the
European Left.

After the *Valkyrie*, Goebbels wrote: 'Terrible, bloody fighting in Spain, but indecisive. Restrained tripartite conference in London. Germany not represented, but is the victor, all the same. Splendid Walküre ... Telling stories late into the evening. The Führer in great form.'[11] On 25 July, during *Siegfried*, Spanish officers caused a commotion when they appeared in their splendid uniforms in the Führer's box.[12] On 27 July Goebbels noted: 'We're a little bit involved in Spain ... Not visibly. Who knows if there's any point. Still no clear outcome. But the nationalists are making progress.' Later, KdF ships were requisitioned for military back-up, much to the annoyance of the organization.[13]

Even during this busy summer, Hitler invited about a hundred artists to a reception in Siegfried's house. Hitler's majordomo Kannenberg, a former Berlin publican, played the accordion and sang Berlin songs. The party went on until three in the morning. Goebbels found the evening 'very nice and entertaining. I have a word with Furtwängler and Hoesslin. The artists fool about.' Goebbels chatted to Furtwängler, and noted in his diary: 'He's learnt a lot, and he's on our side completely ... In Richard Wagner's drawing room. Very strange. Quite museum-like. But sanctified.' Goebbels had no time for the simple, clear lines of Preetorius's stage designs, and thought that the *Twilight of the Gods* was 'scenically perhaps a little primitive. But musically, under Furtwängler, quite unique ... We are all deeply in thrall to the spell of Wagner. The Führer is quite wistful. Moving leave-taking between him and Frau Wagner. Farewell, Bayreuth! ... Pacified quarrel between Frau Wagner and Eva Chamberlain.'[14] However, Winifred recalled that he had missed 'a little joke' concealed in Act II: 'among the chorus we had created look-alikes of some of the leading people of the time. For instance, we had a Goebbels, and a Goering.' But nobody noticed.[15]

Hitler was so proud of the Bayreuth *Lohengrin* that he wanted to make the new British monarch, Edward VIII, a present of an identical staging of this production, in honour of his coronation. As Edward was reputed to be a Nazi sympathizer, Hitler believed himself close to achieving his aim of an alliance with Britain. The idea was to reproduce *Lohengrin* at Covent Garden, complete with the original Bayreuth costumes and stage-sets, and performed by Bayreuth artists. When Edward heard about the offer of this enormously expensive gift, he observed curtly that 'he personally had nothing against it, as long as he didn't have to go to the damned opera himself'. So the plan collapsed. It could not have been realized in any case, in a venue as small as Covent Garden.[16]

At Hitler's behest, Tietjen then began to plan at least one guest appearance in London by the Berlin State Opera, and set about strengthening his
links with Covent Garden and its director, Thomas Beecham, who was
believed to be a friend of the King's. The new German ambassador in
London, Joachim von Ribbentrop, offered the London Philharmonic the
quid pro quo of a tour of Germany.

Beecham announced that he would be sending his 'General Secretary' to
Bayreuth for preliminary talks at the end of June. This turned out to be
none other than Furtwängler's former manager Berta Geissmar, whose Jewish
origins had forced her to emigrate the year before. From bitter experience,
she was afraid she would encounter problems in Germany, so Beecham
demanded guarantees of her safety from Ribbentrop, who duly vouchsafed
them. He had even been assured, he said, that Berta Geissmar had 'nothing
but friends in Germany', and everybody there was proud that he had a
German secretary. Geissmar commented: 'That was vintage Ribbentrop. I
was used to most things, but such a blatant and cynical lie . . . was really
going too far.'[17]

Berta Geissmar was startled when she arrived in Bayreuth on 22 July:
'What a change in that little town, which used to be so poetic in normal
times! It was scarcely recognizable. There were swastika flags fluttering
everywhere, and the whole length of the road up to Festival Hill was draped
in long blood-red swastika banners.' Some things had not changed, of course:
'Furtwängler was having a row with somebody or other, and the whole place
was buzzing with rumours. There was a great deal of anger directed at me,
too, because I had called the head of the foreign department of the Reich
Music Chamber an idiot.'[18]

Then she learned that Winifred planned a breakfast meeting with Hitler
and Beecham and that she, Geissmar, was obviously cordially invited. But
Beecham declined the invitation by telegram. Highly disconcerted, Winifred
responded with: 'But this won't do. The Führer is expecting Sir Thomas, and
is looking forward to sharing a box with him!' Ribbentrop's agent thought
'something's definitely happened; very likely the Italians are behind the
whole affair!'[19] It was said that Mussolini was opposed to a German–English
rapprochement. Be that as it may, the fact is that the same 'full-blood Jewess'
Geissmar who had been thrown out of Germany found herself enjoying the
Festival from the front row of the Wagner family box, and being courted as
a guest of honour.

Another date was proposed for Hitler's meeting with Sir Thomas. But

Beecham was unmoved; he made no mention at all of Hitler's invitation, and said he would prefer to come to Bayreuth for the second *Ring* cycle, because he would have more peace to work. He knew that Hitler would have left by then. All the agitation about Beecham's refusal revealed to Berta Geissmar 'the Nazis' incredible naivety about British politics. They seriously thought they could draw conclusions about the general situation from the stance of one man, simply because he was reputed to belong to the King's inner circle.'[20]

That year, Hitler took Unity and Diana Mitford with him to Bayreuth, and they hardly left his side. Goebbels had given the two ladies £10,000 to support the British fascists and their leader Oswald Mosley, who had previously received £20,000, but had actually been looking for £100,000.[21] Hitler and Ribbentrop overestimated the significance of the British fascists, just as they overestimated the influence of Beecham on the King, and that of the Mitford sisters on the British conservatives and the aristocracy. But Goebbels's comment was 'who knows if it'll do any good'.

After the first cycle of the Festival, Friedelind, Verena and most of the Bayreuth artists happily made use of complimentary tickets, donated by Hitler, for the Olympiad in Berlin. At the opening ceremony on 1 August, the Bayreuth Festival choir sang Richard Strauss's Olympic anthem and Handel's 'Hallelujah Chorus'.

Winifred was otherwise engaged. The thorough cleaning of Siegfried's house, recently vacated by Hitler, had to be completed before the next set of guests arrived. Living next door, the Wagners had gained many insights into Hitler's household. For instance, majordomo Kannenberg had complained how difficult it was to cook for his master, since he was afraid of being poisoned. 'You can't believe how careful we have to be. When my wife prepares his meals, nobody's allowed to go within ten metres of the cooking pots . . . As if anyone would want to eat that tasteless stuff.'[22] Even when Hitler was a guest at Wahnfried, one of his body-guards would keep watch 'to make sure', says Lieselotte, 'that we don't put poison in his food!!!!'[23]

The Berlin of the 1936 Olympics presented a façade of openness and internationalism. Every luxury was available. Even harassment of the Jews was not much in evidence during this period. Hitler was able to offer his international guests a perfectly organized Olympiad. The programme included a stylish celebration, with a gala reception at the Berlin State Opera.

On 4 August the Wagner girls were the only females present among high-ranking company at lunch in the Reich Chancellery. Hitler discoursed about Mussolini, the Abyssinian war and the varying qualities of soldiers. For him, the best soldiers in the world were the Germans, the British and the Poles. Friedelind says he had nothing but scorn for the military quality of the Italians, and called them 'milksops'.[24]

During this week of the Olympics, Winifred was worried about Lieselotte Schmidt, who had been unwell for some time: 'Lieselotte seems to have become utterly bewildered by her relationship with Fr[ank] and she's got . . . a nervous stomach that won't hold anything down, so she's deteriorating badly.'[25] And then, to cap it all, Lieselotte was involved in a serious car accident. She was taken to hospital in Bamberg with cuts to her face, a shattered jaw and torn lips. She was ill for months. On the subject of Frank, Friedelind tells us that: 'He never divorced his wife as he had promised to do, but went on patriotically having another child every year, while consoling Lieselotte with mere hopes.'[26]

On 18 August Hitler visited Bayreuth for one night, accompanied by Himmler, to see *Lohengrin* once more. Once he had left, Beecham appeared. Sitting in the Wagners' box next to Winifred during *Parsifal*, he spent the first interval with her and Tietjen, and the next with Furtwängler, discussing guest performances. He wanted Preetorius to design the sets for Covent Garden's *Flying Dutchman*.

After the Festival the Wagners met Hitler in Nuremberg, at a performance of the *Mastersingers* on the evening before the party rally, and stayed with him until three in the morning. During his big speech on the following day he eloquently evoked the Bolshevik menace, citing the example of the Spanish Civil War. 'An international Jewish revolutionary control centre' was pursuing 'from Moscow the revolutionizing of this continent'. By conjuring up a hostile left-wing conspiracy, he justified his costly re-armament programme and the extension of military service, and called upon the Germans to economize.[27] While her children watched the night-time torch-light parade, Winifred drove back to Bayreuth. 'I'm not one for such mass affairs with all those pushing crowds, and at the moment I'm leading a restful life here!'[28]

Beecham's German tour with the London Philharmonic took place in November, and included a concert in the Berlin Philharmonie Concert Hall, in the presence of Hitler and practically the whole government. Goebbels compared Beecham to Furtwängler, and said the difference was like that between Kannenberg and Beniamino Gigli*: 'And embarrassing, because you had to clap out of politeness.' And the press had its orders: no damning reviews.[29] Winifred attended Beecham's Munich concert, as well as the 'monster reception'[30] given by Rudolf Hess for Sir Thomas.

All efforts to gain the favour of Edward VIII soon became redundant, however. On 10 December the King was forced to abdicate because of his proposed marriage to the divorced American Wallis Simpson. His pro-Hitler sympathies were a contributory factor.

In Wahnfried that autumn there were serious family conflicts. Friedelind, the most talented of Wagner's grandchildren, was now eighteen, and wanted to go into the arts and the theatre. She was interested in directing; from an early age she had felt an affinity for artists. Her aunts, knowing their wishes coincided with Siegfried's, had made the girl their favourite. A close friend reported that 'the two old ladies simply thought that Friedelind – as the most "genuine" child of Wagner – should take over the direction of the Festival!!!'[31] Tietjen, too, supported Friedelind, encouraging her hopes and allegedly telling her 'You're the only one suitable to inherit Bayreuth!'[32]

Nineteen-year-old Wieland, meanwhile, remained undecided and uncertain. It was true that, under Stassen's tutelage, he had designed the sets for a few of Siegfried's operas, such as the production of *The Idler* in Lübeck; and in 1936 he had restored the traditional Grail Temple to the stage. But he did not possess any great musicality. His passions were painting and photography. All the same, he saw himself as the sole heir, and agreed with his mother that Friedelind must not be allowed to participate in the running of the Festival. Some letters from Tietjen to Friedelind fell into the hands of the archivist Otto Strobel, as a result of which he was able to assert that the big family row of November 1936 was caused by the refusal of 'Frau W. and Wieland to contemplate the idea of Friedelind helping to manage the Festival before Wieland was ready to do so!!!'[33]

As ever, Winifred took the side of her eldest child. The quarrel was aggravated by Winifred's jealousy of her daughter, who for some time had been deeply attached to Tietjen, and had even given up a trip to Rome in order to be with him. 'When all's said and done – even if she is my daughter – he's thrown me out, so to speak – and sends for Mausi, for whom he says he has time, though he hasn't got time for me.'[34]

*Gigli (1890–1957) was the most famous operatic tenor of his day. Kannenberg was Hitler's accordion-playing majordomo.

This jealousy becomes understandable if you read Tietjen's letters to Friedelind from the period, where he addressed her (in English) as 'Charming girl'. He showed little loyalty to Winifred, and played the mother off against the daughter. In November 1936, for example: 'Your mother has only made a short visit during this whole time, and as you've often enough seen for yourself, things ended in a row.' He had noticed that 'all your clothes and things have disappeared from my flat. Whether you will find them back in Bayreuth, or whether they're being stored somewhere else in Berlin, I don't know. (Of course, you haven't heard this officially.)' There had once again been 'very unpleasant and bitter arguments', Tietjen told Friedelind, 'about the know-all utterances of the heir [Wieland], which I'm afraid your mother regards as already part of his artistic oeuvre; and you know that Wolf thinks he's a genius, too'.[35]

After a serious discussion with Winifred, Tietjen then suddenly dashed all the eighteen-year-old's hopes of a future role in Bayreuth, writing: 'I think you have lost all chance of participating in the Work.' He suggested she look for a job, as the only way out of 'your irreparable relationship with your mother', and told her to 'Above all break out of Wahnfried.' Then he advised the animal-loving Friedelind to find work breeding domestic animals: 'When it comes to work in the countryside, one might even make use of Teddy – Hermann Goering, that is.'[36]

Tietjen also touched on another sore point. Friedelind had fallen in love with Max Lorenz and insisted she wanted to marry him, thinking she could manage to 'make a proper man' (as Winifred later put it[37]) out of the singer, who took no interest in women. Tietjen told the girl frankly to forget miracles; Lorenz would never be parted from his Jewish wife and manager. Regarding Friedelind's hope 'that some tightening of the law would produce changes' that might impose a divorce, he assured her 'Instead of him divorcing her, "she" would drag him abroad.'[38] The letter put an end to Friedelind's admiration for Tietjen. Winifred once more solved the problem by sending her daughter away from Bayreuth, this time to a very expensive institution in England: 'Every month in England is a relief for all of us,' said Winifred.[39]

The highly intelligent Tietjen, an astute power-politician, knew that he could not afford to dispense with Winifred entirely, because he needed her and Bayreuth as a safety-net in case of further attacks on him by the party. And he was fully aware that she in turn needed him, since he had the entire organization of the Festival in his hands. Winifred wanted more. Tietjen was the great love of her life. But he had many affairs with much younger women, and from 1936 onwards a steady relationship with the woman who later became his wife. Lieselott Michaelis, prima ballerina at the Berlin State Opera, was twenty-five at the time.[40] Winifred suspected none of this. Meanwhile, she frequently sat in his Berlin flat looking after the mentally confused Nena, 'to give Heinz a chance to get out, do his work, and think about other things'.[41]

In mid-December, after the family quarrel, Wolfgang played truant from school and Wieland from his labour camp, citing 'an urgent mission to the Führer'. They drove to Berlin, enjoyed some nice days there, and telephoned Hitler, who immediately invited them in for a few hours' chat. He also gave them his Christmas presents for the family: two gold watches for the lads, two gold bracelets for the girls and for Winifred what she called 'a charming letter'[42] and a portrait photo of himself with the dedication: 'Frau Winnie Wagner for Christmas 1936, with unfailing devotion and heartfelt admiration Af Hitler.'[43]

VICTIMIZATION AND TERROR

Around New Year 1937 Gauleiter Wächtler pushed the struggle for power to an open confrontation with the citizens of Bayreuth. Against the wishes of the mayor and the hospital, he appointed two of his Party friends from outside to the two well-paid top posts at the Municipal Hospital, ignoring the claims of the popular long-serving doctors, Wolfgang Deubzer and Hermann Körber. The population, whose discontent had already been provoked by the arrest of highly regarded churchmen, directed its anger at the Party and its dubious practices with regard to appointments. Lieselotte wrote in January 1937: 'It's pretty bad that there are complaints about irregularities everywhere, whether it's the church, academic life, the law, the schools – and unfortunately it's often more than malicious griping; it's a genuine, responsible concern' on the part of the Bayreuthers. But she does not blame Hitler; on the contrary: 'What the Führer has to put up with and deal with!'[44]

By agreement with Winifred, the mayor made this a test case, 'to confront Gauleiter Wächtler once and for all with the question of who has a say in the administration of town affairs'.[45] In a secret meeting of the town council on 2 March, the tried and trusted doctors were offered the two posts: Deubzer that of head of a department, and Körber, director of the hospital. In order to safeguard the town council's decision by securing Hitler's agreement,

Winifred went to Berlin for two days in March, met Hitler and succeeded in her mission. Despite threats from the Gauleiter, the two doctors took up their appointments on 1 April. By 13 April they had been arrested, but after pressure from an enraged population they returned to their posts, now under surveillance by the 'brown sisters', nurses of the Nationalsozialistische Volkswohlfahrt (NSV – National Socialist People's Welfare organization), who assiduously collected incriminating evidence.

In February 1938 the two doctors were ambushed, and again placed under arrest by Wächtler. Deubzer was even dragged away from the operating theatre. Lieselotte Schmidt reported: 'There are new doctors in the hospital, appointed from outside. There is an enormous amount of anger in the town.'[46] Under Party pressure, nineteen council members were forced to resign, as did the mayor, Otto Schmidt. Since the Gauleiter did not even permit him to deliver his farewell address, Winifred sent the text to people in high office in the Party.[47] In the hospital, all nurses from the Protestant order were dismissed. The 'brown sisters' of the NSV took over the care regime completely. Rumours about the state of affairs in Bayreuth created ripples in medical circles throughout Germany.

Winifred was bombarded with requests, especially from Deubzer's wife, to seek redress from Hitler, and she took the matter energetically in hand. Deubzer was released in May. Körber became seriously ill, but was repeatedly interrogated and remained under arrest. Winifred felt all the more obliged to intervene because Wächtler had used her name to justify himself and said that both Frau Wagner and Mayor Schmidt had agreed to the arrest of the two doctors. She protested against this in a long letter to Himmler, head of the Gestapo: the Gauleiter had 'misused her name'. She knew there were irregularities at the hospital, but believed 'that the overworked doctors were in no way responsible' for them; the fault lay with the matron of the NSV. The Munich Gestapo had simply ignored the defence: 'The report culminates in the charge that the accused doctors were enemies of the people and the State.' The inspector who had conducted the enquiry had 'received his instructions daily from the Gauleiter'.

The whole affair, Winifred thought, was in reality a battle for power in Bayreuth. She was on the side of the mayor and the doctors, 'and I think I can safely assert that the bitterness among the Bayreuth population has taken on really threatening proportions as a result of the fact that the Gauleiter has had himself confirmed as acting mayor of the town'. Finally, she appealed to Himmler: 'We Bayreuthers are loyal National Socialists and staunch supporters of the Reich, but the way the affair of the Bayreuth hospital doctors has been handled is making us doubt our belief that the Third Reich will not tolerate perversions of justice.' Then she requested a neutral commission of enquiry.[48]

On the same day she wrote an official letter to Hitler: 'Mein Führer! . . . it is the opinion of most of the Bayreuth population that the situation has become truly intolerable, and all are hoping for personal intervention on your part – I have been deputed to express this urgent request in the name of almost all Bayreuthers. With grateful devotion, your Winifred Wagner.'[49]

When Hitler next visited Bayreuth, Winifred explained the situation to him, 'talking herself hoarse'. But Hitler simply listened to her, and then at the end put his head in his hands, groaning, 'the trouble these schoolteachers make for me!' That was all he did.[50]

On 20 September Winifred gave evidence on behalf of Körber in a disciplinary hearing, although according to Körber, Wächtler had warned her against 'doing anything for a traitor like me, because I belonged to a group that were plotting to assassinate Hitler in February'. There was not a grain of truth in this. All the other intended witnesses had been intimidated by Wächtler.[51] Körber was not released until December. The sufferings of the two doctors continued for more than four years, until 1941.

Deubzer said later, 'Frau Wagner was always pointing out the abuses, the indefensible attitude of Fritz Wächtler, and the damage being done to the Party by that drunken jack-in-office.' But she never got anywhere with Hitler. She 'ground away at him again and again', but he 'wrapped himself in an icy silence'.[52]

Winifred's well-known direct line to Hitler meant that many desperate people tried to enlist her support. The offspring of Richard Wagner's Jewish friends were a case in point. In 1937 there was an appeal from the 71-year-old writer Elsa Bernstein-Porges, daughter of the musical-stage writer, Heinrich Porges; she was the librettist of Humperdinck's opera *Königskinder* (Children of the King). Elsa and her younger sister Gabriele were about to be evicted from their Munich apartment, where they had run a literary and musical salon for decades. Winifred's intercession with the Bavarian Minister President[53] succeeded in postponing the eviction for a few years.

There followed a request for help from Elsa Bernstein's daughter, the 43-year-old violinist Eva Hauptmann, who had met her husband, the son of Gerhart Hauptmann, in Bayreuth. Being 'racially full-blood Jewish', she was excluded from the Reich Music Chamber, and had not been able to work or give concerts since 1935. Winifred advised her to write to the Führer's private office, and gave her some concrete advice:

> The first thing to stress is your high percentage of Aryan blood, because as far as I can recall, you are blonde, light-skinned etc. Enclose a photo – there is a directive which very often makes appearance decisive in cases like yours. Then I would scrape together all the Aryan ancestors you can find – but not neglecting to present the services of your grandfather [Porges] to Wagner in the right light.

She added: 'I know what I'm telling you all sounds terribly stupid, but I'd like you to know that I really want to help you.'[54] But all her efforts were in vain.

She suffered a similar setback trying to help the young 'half-Jewess' Susi Ottenheimer gain acceptance by the Reich Culture Chamber in order to work as a singer.[55] The only assistance Winifred could give her was to employ her – illegally – as a flower girl in Parsifal. She gave work to other racially persecuted people, such as Frida Leider's 'half-Jewish' son Hans Deman, with a job in the Festival office from 1 November 1937,[56] or the 'mixed race' Bayreuther Wolfgang Beyer, who became a motor-cycle messenger.[57]

Sometimes the response was different, as with the plea from Lydia Beil, via Lene Roesener, on behalf of persecuted friends: 'I can't help poor Liddie this time! One of the teachers has rejected the Third Reich, and she has openly said so often enough.' About a second case, obviously Jewish, she replied, 'Freudenberger can't teach publicly, but he can carry on with his private lessons – so he won't be entirely lost to humanity!'[58] There must have been many more such cases, all with the same negative result. The Nuremberg Laws against the Jews were unambiguous, and they were strictly applied, especially if the Reich Culture Chamber was involved. Winifred's constant appeals to 'give mercy precedence over the law' fell on deaf ears.

On 1 July 1937 Pastor Martin Niemöller, the leading light of the Bekennende Kirch (Confessing Church – an oppositional Protestant church), was arrested for subversive activities. A submarine captain in the World War, former admirer of Hitler, and opponent of the Weimar Republic and the Left, Niemöller had gone into opposition only when the 'Deutsche Christen' (the officially installed, pro-Nazi Protestant church) were established. So many people flooded in to hear his sermons in his church at Dahlem, Berlin, that even Goebbels started to worry. 'Crack down on him now until he can't even hear or see any more . . . No room for sentimentality; the safety of the people and the State come before everything else.'[59] Winifred's childhood friend Hans Joachim Lange, who had served with Niemöller in the navy, asked her to approach Hitler. 'By using my personal influence with the Führer, I tried to get him released, but it became impossible when Niemöller, conditionally allowed to preach again, persisted with the same message.'[60] When she took the first opportunity she could to enquire about the fate of Niemöller's wife and children, she received the reply: 'They are being looked after.'[61] Looking back, probably to explain her failure to achieve very much for church people, Winifred held that Hitler simply did not want to hear anything about church matters, and said that every question about the church caused him sleepless nights.[62]

Homosexuals, too, were now subjected to more extreme persecution. Gustav Gründgens, the highly respected intendant of the Berlin Theatre, was suddenly under vicious attack by the Goebbels press, which caused a crisis in the Prussian state theatres. Winifred reported:

> It's a terrible shame about him, blown out of the water by Goebbels like that. He's queer – and the National Socialist press has been ordered to ruin his name. They managed to reduce him to despair with their criticism of the way he played Hamlet. The *Völkischer Beobachter* for instance wrote that his Hamlet was soft and sweet – i.e. he was being himself! – He's too highly strung to cope with that kind of nastiness. Goebbels is doing his utmost to make life miserable for Teddy [Goering], in order to take over the theatres himself eventually.[63]

Goebbels continued to try to turn Hitler against Gründgens, and wrote with great self-satisfaction in his diary that the Führer thought 'that Gründgens would have to go completely ... But these queers are all as hysterical as women.'[64]

In the summer Goebbels turned his attention to Bayreuth artists. He had 'sat up late in Wahnfried with the Wagners and the Führer. Chatted about Section 175 [of the German statute book, concerning homosexuals]. Führer completely implacable on the subject. No mercy. Quite rightly. We must cleanse the theatres of it, too. And thoroughly.' In the Eule public house, he named a name: '*Kammersänger* Janssen involved in Section 175. Postponed for the time being. But Bayreuth is in big trouble. We've got to take the vacuum cleaner to it. I talk to Frau Wagner about this. She is very upset over it. But she knows things can't go on as they are.'[65] Herbert Janssen, who sang

Amfortas, escaped soon afterwards to America, where he was welcomed with open arms by the Metropolitan Opera.

Other cases were less difficult for Winifred to resolve. In spring 1938 friends of hers in Eisenach made her aware that the local regional leader had ordered the large cross on top of the Wartburg (the fortress where Luther translated the New Testament), an important symbol for every Lutheran, to be replaced by a swastika – and this during Holy Week. Arguing that this was 'an anti-Christian act', she protested to the Thuringian government. The cross was reinstated soon after Easter. Then she passed on complaints by the citizens of Eisenach about having their religious services constantly disturbed by Party parades; here, too, she was successful.[66]

It was a motley collection of supplicants who sought Winifred's intercession with Hitler. The tuberculosis expert Dr Walter 'wants me to help him coordinate the battle [against TB]'.[67] There was a man 'who claims to be able to turn sea-water into petrol'.[68] A woman came all the way from Vienna to promote the inventions of a certain Viktor Schauberger.[69] Winifred was soon referring to him as *Schlauberger* (crafty customer), and he gave her a lot of trouble. He asked her to present Hitler with his blueprints for a disc-shaped aeroplane, a kind of flying saucer, 'and I passed them on to Hitler as requested!' When there were speculations in 1975 that Hitler had escaped to a stronghold in the Antarctic using a UFO built at the South Pole, and was still living there, Winifred recalled Schauberger's designs, which may have been the legendary 'secret weapon of the Third Reich'.[70]

She gladly offered practical tips to those people who wanted her to pass on written communications to the Führer. 'However, as a lay person I cannot follow what you are saying – I'm only telling you this because it's possible that if you want to address the Führer, you might put it more briefly, plainly and clearly.'[71]

THE 1937 FESTIVAL

Although it had been announced that Furtwängler was to conduct, ticket sales were still so poor that Tietjen paid a visit to the Propaganda Ministry. Ticket sales were 'extremely good', he maintained, but pointed out that

the Führer sets great store by the partial selection of audiences for Festival performances . . . In the Führer's words, the people who should be invited to

Bayreuth were above all the musical directors and intendants of German opera houses, students at music colleges, military and Labour Service bandmasters, and musically trained members of the HJ if sufficiently mature.

What he was asking for, therefore, was a better-informed type of audience. Frau Wagner would be happy to put 3,000 out of the total of 8,000 tickets available at the disposal of the Propaganda Ministry, at a cost of 90,000 marks.[72]

Goebbels's ministry prevaricated. It was not only the large sum they had to consider, they also mentioned all the work involved in distributing the complimentary tickets, and negotiating with the Reich railways over special trains and cut-price fares. The Propaganda Ministry pointed out other ministries who might buy tickets. Goebbels's diary recorded: 'Many tickets still unsold in Bayreuth. It's difficult working with Frau Wagner.'[73] All the same, Lieselotte said that the National Socialist Teachers' League took up 60,000 marks worth of tickets, and the KdF paid 15,000 marks for theirs.[74]

From the beginning of 1937 the 'Travel, Rambling and Holidays' department of the KdF was run by a lawyer, a very capable organizer. The forty-year-old Bodo Lafferentz, with his striking good looks and excellent manners, had joined the NSDAP only in 1933. In addition to his leading position in the KdF, he was also one of the founders of the Society to Facilitate the German People's Car (Volkswagen). Winifred got on with him very well and valued his organizational skills, which lifted some of the burden from her.

Even before rehearsals began, a quarrel with Furtwängler loomed. Winifred despaired: 'It's all vanity and insecurity with him – perhaps the big explosion will come this year – under no circumstances am I going to have him back here in '39 . . . I'll get Wolf to see reason.'[75] Lieselotte regretted that 'the Mistress and Tietjen are often really depressed about Fu and how powerless we basically are – we can't afford to start a row, because the Führer thinks highly of him, despite everything, and stands up for him. He [Furtwängler] wouldn't have such a nerve otherwise.' Many of the artists were angry, too, 'but, as I say, nobody dares to rebel, because they'd be risking their necks'.[76]

Gertrud Strobel states that the Gestapo had set up a permanent observation-post close to Winifred's office: 'Gestapo officials with a card-index of all the Festival artists: no white cards, just pink, yellow or red ones, with all their remarks etc. recorded on them.'[77] Preetorius too had a fight on his hands:

'somebody' had decided that 'the shields in *Twilight of the Gods* should all have swastikas on them. And I refused point-blank, even though I was reminded, quite rightly, that the swastika was an ancient Germanic symbol. I replied that we didn't have to use that one specifically; there were many others, and I preferred to use the others.'[78]

Friedelind wrote to her aunts, who had ostentatiously taken themselves off to the Salzburg Festival – even though it was perceived as 'Jewish' and they were anti-Semites in the old Bayreuth tradition – that they would be seeing Toscanini's *Mastersingers* 'secure among the Jewish masses'.[79] Winifred suspected that Daniela 'had been deputed by Toscanini to approach all the good German singers and make them desert Bayreuth in favour of Salzburg'.[80]

Shortly before Hitler's arrival, extra detectives and security police from outside were drafted in, and as the internal report of the mayor recorded: 'In addition, on 23.7 three trainloads of anti-aircraft artillery arrived, and the batteries took up positions around the town.'[81]

Hitler's mania for secrecy about his movements increased from year to year. He never had a police car escorting him, only an inconspicuous SS vehicle; he always varied his routes and modes of transport, and kept his schedule strictly secret. Hans Severus Ziegler provided details about Hitler's frequent journeys between Weimar and Bayreuth. It was 'almost impossible' to follow a direct route. 'One village would alert another, one town warn the next, and the Mercedes cars simply could not get through.' Ziegler would steer Hitler out of town on back roads, and then stop on a country road to call Bayreuth and announce his imminent arrival.[82] He usually arrived after dark.

The Festival opened on 23 July 1937 with *Parsifal* under Furtwängler. The stage-sets were no longer the work of Roller, but of twenty-year-old Wieland, provoking Goebbels to comment: 'Musically superb, Furtwängler splendid, even if heavily criticized by the Wagners . . . But the staging is somewhat deficient. By Wieland Wagner. Very dilettante. The projections especially somewhat embarrassing.' Two days later, after a conversation with the Reich Stage Designer, he returned to the topic: 'Arent is dissatisfied with *Parsifal* as well. Too dilettante. Little Wagner is still too young. This can't be allowed to be a family preserve.'[83] However, according to Lieselotte, Wieland 'had reason to be satisfied . . . with what the Führer said to him about it'.[84] And it was Hitler's opinion that counted.

It was not only Goebbels who thought that the young man was not up to the task. A friend of the family, Gertrud Beckel, who watched the *Parsifal* première from the family box, recalled: 'Wieland sat behind me. In Act III I heard some light snoring; Wieland had nodded off. At first I let him go on sleeping. But when the snoring got heavier, I woke him up. At the end of the act he said to me: "With senile music like that it's not surprising if you fall asleep."'[85]

The Nazi press naturally praised Wagner's heir. When a tiny publication called *Markenartikel* (Brand Goods) took the liberty of being critical of him, Wieland protested to Goebbels and demanded a ban on the journal. Even for Goebbels, that was going too far: 'We can't ban the publication *Markenartikel*. Little Wagner is being a bit oversensitive. And anyway, it was two months ago now.'[86] It was clear that, having elbowed Friedelind aside, the young man was strenuously manoeuvring for power, something both Tietjen and Preetorius saw as arrogant, but also as a threat to 'the new Bayreuth'. Preetorius said with hindsight, 'I can see today that I should have left Bayreuth much earlier; at the point where they gave Parsifal to Wieland.'[87]

Nor was there much agreement over Furtwängler's leadership. While Goebbels worshipped him, Tietjen still thought that Fu took too much of the limelight, and above all that he conducted so wilfully that the music was at odds with the dramatic direction. This 'prima donna of the rostrum', this 'perfumer of Richard Wagner' did not fit into Bayreuth, said Tietjen. 'For 10 years I tried to teach him what faithfulness to the work means, and what came out of it was hypnotic for the audience, but a loss for R[ichard] W[agner] – and it wore us out!'[88]

Hermann Goering was a rare visitor to Bayreuth, and Hitler chose to use *Parsifal* to try to put him off his passion for hunting, one of Goering's posts being that of Reich Game Warden. At the point in Act I where the young and innocent Parsifal shoots the sacred swan and Gurnemanz makes him aware of his misdeed, Hitler leant over to Goering, sitting next to him, and said, 'Do you still want to hunt innocent animals?'[89] It seems that Goering's only reply was a wry smile.

Goering stayed in Siegfried's house with Hitler. The topic of the hour was fine art. At great expense, Hitler had arranged for an exhibition of those living German artists who corresponded to his *völkisch* ideal, to be held in the new House of German Art in Munich. A counter-exhibition opened the following day, likewise in Munich, designed to have a repulsive impact. The exhibits consisted of 'degenerate' and 'Jewish' works removed from German galleries, and were displayed in a deliberately chaotic and heartless way. The result was unexpected. There was a veritable stampede towards 'Degenerate Art', whereas 'German Art' attracted far fewer visitors. Goebbels was forced to concede that 'the "Degenerate Art" exhibition is an enormous success and a heavy blow. The *Führer* is supporting me stoutly against all attacks.'[90]

Connoisseurs of art, some of them prominent National Socialists, were appalled at the denigration of first-rate artists. After all, Education Minister Bernhard Rust owned canvases by the banned painter Hans von Marées and Foreign Minister Ribbentrop had commissioned Otto Dix to paint his children's portraits.[91] The widow of the architect Paul Troost, considered 'fantastically intelligent' by Winifred, persuaded Hitler to remove a few names from the list of 'degenerate artists'.[92] When even Hess was calling on Goebbels in Bayreuth to extend protection to a 'degenerate' painter, the latter grumbled, 'If I take everybody out of the exhibition that someone wants protected, I might as well just shut down.' He had given an order that all art galleries should be 'cleansed'. After three months he got the 'all clear' signal.[93]

Wolfgang says that, questioned by Wieland, Hitler replied that 'after a period of self-discovery, this kind of art would be shown again in Germany; it hadn't been destroyed, but preserved by being sold abroad. The proceeds had been used to buy important Old Masters, which would enrich German galleries.'[94]

On 28 July special trains once again arrived from Eger, bearing Sudeten Germans in their folk costumes. The desire of the Sudeten Germans to be united with Germany, publicized with great clamour by the German press, served on the one hand to heighten the political pressure on Czechoslovakia, and on the other to stoke up anti-Czech feeling among the German population, and prepare them for the crisis to come.

The *Gau* administration organized a ceremony of dedication for 720 Hitler Youth, so-called 'Ostmarkfahrer' (Ostmark Explorers), camped on the nearby German–Czech border. Gauleiter Wächtler called upon them to be 'warriors against the East'. 'The frontier with Bohemia was created entirely by the Versailles Treaty. It has divided Germans from Germans, and handed millions of them over to a state that knows only how to oppress them.'[95]

The Bayreuth cinema was showing the new film *Von Königsberg bis Berchtesgaden* (From Königsberg to Berchtesgaden), a journey along the

'German eastern frontier'. 'From the Baltic beaches via Königsberg, Tannenberg, Marienburg, Elbing, the old city of Danzig . . . to all those towns displaced from the interior of the former Reich to the furthest frontiers by the arbitrary decisions of the Versailles Treaty.'[96] In the parliament of the Free City of Danzig, the Nazis were already in the majority, and were putting intense pressure on Poland.

On 29 July 1937 Hitler gave his reception for the Bayreuth artists. Carl Schlottmann, a Knight of the Grail in *Parsifal*, supplies a long eyewitness account. From eight o'clock onwards Winifred received guests at the entrance to Villa Wahnfried, and directed them on to Siegfried's house, where Tietjen presented them to Hitler. Each was greeted with a handshake. There was a cold buffet: 'Punch, beer and orangeade were the drinks on offer. In their black trousers with white stripes and their short white jackets, SS men acted as waiters.' Then the whole party went out into the garden, where 'red and green Bengal lights' were fired off, lanterns decorated the grounds and Kannenberg struck up dance music on his accordion.

There Hitler, surrounded by artists, delivered a one-and-a-half hour monologue. As Schlottmann puts it, 'he does not speak; it's more that something speaks through him'. Hitler thought in 'centuries, not in years . . . hence his saying that history is not made in 2, 4 or 8 years, and that kind of time-span is only a preparation for it'.

Back in the house, with sixteen-year-old Verena seated on the arm of his chair, Hitler continued his monologue. When somebody talked about their awe at being in the presence of the Führer, 'he laughs and says, "I can't imagine anyone being afraid of me."' Then there was another recital, with one eye on Ulrich Roller, of the story of the timid young Hitler in Vienna. Invited to say a few words next day from the rostrum to the orchestra, Hitler declined with thanks, 'since he did not want to be thought vain; and where such men did their work – here he glanced at Furtwängler, in conversation nearby – was no place for him'.

As usual when he was in a good mood, Hitler waxed sentimental and started reminiscing about his days as a youngster in Linz. His revered history teacher, Leopold Poetsch, was wheeled out again, and then Hitler's favourite anecdote. He recounted how as a boy he had precisely calculated that 'if you go off and play a forbidden game you get beaten. The game lasts 8 hours, the beating 2 or at most 3 minutes. So I opted for the beating.' He did not forget to mention reading Karl May (Wild West adventure stories) under the desk.

When someone asked him about events in Russia, he replied, 'Monstrous things are happening there – it's like the age of Genghis Khan.' He compared Stalin's show trials with medieval witch hunts, 'where one innocent person pulls another down with him, and so on until it becomes monstrous. The confessions are as though [Reich War Minister Werner von] Blomberg, for example, were to declare that in building up the armed forces the only thing he had in mind was to deliver the army into the hands of the French – completely idiotic.'

Hitler regretted not having enough time to go to the opera. He did not like arriving late, either, but 'I'm sure the door-keepers would still let me in, just as they let in police chiefs and the like, for fear of ending up in "Oranienburg" ' – that is to say, in Sachsenhausen concentration camp. 'At this point, the Führer laughs.' Then he described how hard it had been for him to give up coffee. It went on like this until two in the morning. He did not get around to any discussions with the artists. And finally, Schlottmann says, 'he kissed the ladies' hands with a gallantry lost to our age'.[97]

Hitler wanted to see the latest models for new developments in Bayreuth, as he always did during Festival visits. He had designated Bayreuth – like Nuremberg, Munich, Linz and other towns that had special meaning for him – as an 'improvement area', and allocated considerable funding to the project. 'We debated until late into the night . . .' recorded Goebbels. 'Führer explains his plans for Bayreuth: hotel and theatre. But the money. His civil list is too small. The Finance Ministry treats him like Mr Nobody. I would-n't put up with it. Prussian King got 36 million.'[98]

The local architect Hans Reissinger, responsible for the House of German Education and the swastika-monument that had already been demolished, had been commissioned to build an enormous sports complex for the NSDAP Sports Training Camp, with a stadium and swimming pool. He now presented Hitler with construction plans for three more large-scale projects: a new town theatre, a massive luxury hotel and a *Gau* centre – to include a *Gau* forum, with an avenue for parades and a hall for meetings – which would be situated to the west of the Hofgarten. These mammoth projects alone would require a whole section of the town to be demolished, which is why the architect had long been known in Bayreuth not as Reissinger, but 'Abreissinger' (*abreissen* = to tear down).

What Speer called Hitler's 'absolutely manic passion for building opera houses' did not stop short of Bayreuth.[99] When he found out that there were 8,000 inhabitants in Bayreuth in 1750, he calculated that 'the opera house at that time had 500 seats, so now, with six times the population, you could well argue that you need a theatre that can hold as many as 3,000'. He chose the largest of the proposals presented to him, and urged Wieland to 'get to work on population policy [that is, go and procreate] so as to increase the number of inhabitants'. To the objection that it would be difficult to fill all the seats, Hitler replied that demand increased with supply, and pointed to the example of the autobahns, which were not under-used.[100]

Hitler was not keen to pull down the old Festival Theatre, but he was enthusiastic about putting up a giant new building. It would be officially opened in 1941, when Wieland took over as head of the Festival. Winifred was sceptical, but for the moment she went along with Hitler's wishes: 'I didn't argue with him because I knew him very well, and knew that initially you had to play along so that you weren't immediately at loggerheads, and didn't finish up with the exact opposite of what you wanted.' Hitler envisaged performances taking place in both houses, with the Festival Theatre using the old stage-settings, and the new designs in the new theatre. This all seemed 'somewhat laborious' to Winifred. But at Hitler's request she toured the area looking for suitable sites to build on. 'I travelled . . . along the higher ground to the west, and the site I suggested was on one of these rises, with a lovely view of the surrounding country. He agreed, and was very enthusiastic.' This time it was the architect Emil Mewes who won the contract. He was already working on plans for the Volkswagen works in Wolfsburg.

Winifred sat down with Mewes and told him 'that I was actually very much against building a new Festival Theatre, but would approve if there were plans to expand and improve the existing house, and add on the outbuildings we needed'. Mewes then made a model, 'more or less putting the old Festival Theatre under what I always thought of as a cheese-dish. That is to say, preserving the old house with its acoustic and everything, but reconstructing it and covering it in.'[101]

Hitler was so excited about his building projects, particularly what was under construction on the vast Party rally grounds in Nuremberg, that on 15 August 1937 he suddenly invited all Festival personnel to come and see the Nuremberg building work – the very next day (16 August), in fact, when there was no performance. Everything had to be organized at a breakneck pace once again, said Lieselotte:

> Overnight the railway people got together carriages from Berlin and Leipzig to make up the special train. We had to alert the whole personnel

together with their support staff, and we did manage to assemble some 800 'boys and girls', from conductors and soloists down to the lowest stage-hand and cleaning lady. It really was a wonderful folk community.

They set off after midday. Winifred, Tietjen, the children and guests of Wahnfried all went along. In Nuremberg thirty buses stood ready to take the party on a two-hour tour of the grounds at Luitpoldhain.

Hitler invited his guests for a snack at the elegant Deutscher Hof Hotel at six o'clock, and asked Winifred and a few soloists to join him at his table. There was a short musical interlude featuring the Nuremberg ballet. Then Hitler mingled with the people in the hotel hall, and, if Lieselotte is to be believed, 'was practically torn apart' out of sheer enthusiasm as he approached the company, and again when he left them. On the way home, it had to be said, there were a number of 'casualties', as many were overcome by the strong wine. 'But still, it was a great experience, and never were so many beaming and blissful faces seen together in one place.'

The Wagner children were allowed to stay overnight in Nuremberg, and persuaded Wolf to return to the Festival. So it was that at one o'clock on 17 August Winifred was suddenly informed that Hitler was due to arrive in Bayreuth at 2.30. 'It was a matter of whisking Schuster-Woldan instantly out of the Führer's room, where he was camping,' said Lieselotte, 'sorting out another room each for Brückner and Krause as well, and then conjuring up accommodation from somewhere for a staff of 19. The other house guests – the Roeseners, the Knittels and Overhoff – could stay in the new building; when the Führer turns up unexpectedly, he doesn't want any fuss made, and just fits into the enlarged family circle.'[102]

On this occasion Hitler brought along Alfred Rosenberg, known to be unmusical, and announced to Winifred that he was going to show him *The Twilight of the Gods* and convert him to Wagner. When she asked Hitler after the first act whether he wanted to talk to Rosenberg yet, he asked her to wait until after the second, until 'Rosenberg has been really impressed'.[103] Still full of pride, Winifred later wrote that in the end Rosenberg revised his opinion of Wagner: 'Rosenberg presented me at that time with a "mountain of roses" [*Rosenberg* = rose mountain], which I took to be a token of his appreciation of the return of the ring [to the Rhine Maidens].'[104]

The Wagners met up with Hitler again at the Nuremberg party rally, Winifred told Lene: '4 times we spent the evening with the Führer . . . mind you, we always had to stay up with him till 4 in the morning – you know how it is . . .'[105] And Hitler had yet another request. The Japanese Prince Chichibu, a brother of the Emperor Hirohito, was visiting Germany, and Hitler had invited him to Bayreuth for three days. A special relationship with Japan had been declared; like Germany and Italy, the country was pursuing a nationalist and expansionary policy. Seeking to assert its hegemony in Asia, Japan invaded China in 1937 and was advancing rapidly and ruthlessly.

Winifred knew very little about the political situation, but was faced with enormous problems of organization. She rushed back to Bayreuth, cleared out her house for Hitler's party, had every available room made ready, and engaged extra servants and kitchen staff. She could not accommodate all the guests anticipated, so she took over the nearby Rosvaenge villa as well.

When the guests arrived, the atmosphere was friendly and pleasant, but troubled by language difficulties. The most tiring aspect was that the lady of the house had to entertain the Prince and his retinue from breakfast until midnight, although the Prince spoke not a single word of German and only broken English, while Winifred knew no Japanese. The Wagner children enjoyed the exotic visitors' stay, and being spoiled and praised by them. Later, they told funny stories about them, although almost all arose out of their ignorance of Japanese customs.

Afterwards Winifred totted up the numbers:

In the small house there were the Prince, the ambassador, the valet (Japanese) and a German servant, as well as the German detective. In Wahnfried there were: the secretary of the Legation, a major (Japanese) and Count Strachwitz from the Foreign Office. In the Rosvaenges' house I placed the Japanese General Oshima and a Japanese captain (naval attaché) as well as two German gentlemen from the overseas office. So there were 7 Japanese to 6 Germans – of those, 11 had their meals with me – 2 with the staff.

Two extra waiters were needed.[106]

After three days the guests and their hostess hurried to Nuremberg to attend the closing congress and tattoo of the Party rally. When it was all over, from one until five in the morning Winifred and Verena were 'all alone with the Führer. He touchingly maintains that this was the nicest possible way for him to round things off!!!' Prince Chichibu 'gave Hitler an enthusiastic description of my hospitality . . . Wolf is so grateful that he

wants Nickel [Verena] and me to come to his reception for Mussolini on 25
September, and to be in Berlin on the 29th or 30th for the closing parade of
the visit.'[107]

Hitler was in excellent spirits. Looking back in 1942, he was still relish-
ing the two high points of his calendar in the peacetime years from 1933 to
1939: the Bayreuth Festival and the Nuremberg Party Rally: 'The day after
the end of the Festival, and the Tuesday at the end of Nuremberg, were as sad
for me as taking down the decorations on the Christmas tree.'[108]

THE ANSCHLUSS (ANNEXATION)

At the end of September 1937 Winifred was present at the grand closing
dinner of Mussolini's state visit, and heard Hitler's toast: 'At a time when the
world is full of tension and restless confusion, in which dangerous elements
are attempting to attack and destroy the ancient culture of Europe, Italy and
Germany have come together in sincere friendship to engage in a shared
political task.'[109] This could be taken to refer to the Spanish Civil War.
But, dropping his old Austrian allies whom he had supported in 1934, the
Duce had also given Hitler *carte blanche* for his march into Austria.

After Mussolini's departure Winifred and Verena spent the evening with
Hitler listening to radio messages reporting 'the various points Mussolini had
reached in his journey to the border . . . What a sigh of relief went up from
all of us when he crossed the frontier at 3.33 in the morning. Everybody
stood up and clinked glasses; a ton weight of responsibility was lifted from
the Führer's shoulders. He is very pleased with the way the whole visit
went.'[110]

In October the conflict with Furtwängler entered its decisive phase. The
conductor looked to Goebbels for protection: 'Furtwängler told me all about
the row between him and Frau Wagner and Tietjen. Frau Wagner has been
very badly advised. Tietjen is not a conductor but an organizer, and at best a
toady. Without Furtwängler, the whole Bayreuth affair amounts to just one
family and its clique.'[111]

It was true that Tietjen was the driving force behind Winifred. He was not
satisfied simply to be artistic director and to direct productions; he was very
ambitious to conduct and to figure as the guardian of the Bayreuth tradition.
Furtwängler, on the other hand, wanted to be more than a conductor; he
claimed a voice in all artistic decisions. Furthermore, both were fighting

proxy wars: Tietjen on behalf of Goering, Furtwängler for Goebbels. In this conflict Winifred, with her access to Hitler, was an important lever for Tietjen.

After a long struggle, Hitler settled the feud in favour of Winifred and against his favourite conductor, Furtwängler. On 3 November Goebbels noted that Hitler 'has decided to drop Furtwängler from Bayreuth, after all. I express every possible reservation to him. This will be a heavy loss for Bayreuth. Tietjen is a crafty schemer.' And, referring to Winifred, 'Well, pity poor Bayreuth, when women rule!'[112]

Furtwängler did not give up, particularly when he heard that Tietjen was proposing to conduct the *Ring* in Bayreuth in 1938. In an abrasive letter to Winifred, with copies to Hitler, Goering and Goebbels, he wrote:

> You seriously think a first-class, leading musician is not necessary at Bayreuth. You know so little about the vital role played in Wagner's *Gesamtkunstwerk* [total work of art] by the musical aspect, and therefore by the conductor; you are hardly aware how endangered the position of Bayreuth is in the world today, and how essential it is to appoint only the best, if Bayreuth is even to have the right to exist in the future.

And then a punch below the belt: 'You are relying on the power of the authoritarian state. Precisely because Bayreuth has that power at its disposal, your behaviour should be doubly responsible.'[113]

Goebbels wrote in his diary: 'Furtwängler has written a rude letter to Frau Wagner. Now she'll go off the deep end. But he's not entirely wrong.' And a week later: 'Winifred Wagner has fired off a really fierce letter at Furtwängler. He won't enjoy that much, either.'[114] Winifred sent a copy of her letter to Hitler, and told Lene, 'The Führer wrote to me after he got my letter, and said it was all right – Fu wouldn't get anywhere with him!!!'[115] And Wolfgang put it bluntly: 'Mama's finally got rid of Furtwängler . . . The Führer naturally gave his approval – in the end, that's what matters.'[116]

In the winter of 1937–8, Wieland fell seriously ill. He had contracted inflammation of the lungs, with a possible embolism. Winifred was to spend weeks at her son's bedside in the private hospital run by Dr Helmut Treuter and his wife, who were friends of the family. During that time her heart went out to a three-year-old girl, Betty Steinlein, who was physically underdeveloped, suffered from severe disabilities, had 'bad blood' (as Winifred called it) and a serious skin complaint. She came from a family of poor smallholders who could not afford the time for intensive nursing and no longer wanted the child. The private hospital could not keep Betty permanently because, in Winifred's words, she was 'a great drain on the resources of the clinic – and hardly ever got out into the fresh air'.[117] According to Dr Treuter, her only chance of recovery was to be moved to a place where she could enjoy constant nursing and a vitamin-rich diet.

Unhesitatingly, Winifred took the child back with her to Wahnfried, to try to restore her to health with the help of a visiting nurse and of Emma Bär. This turned out to be a laborious task. One can only surmise why Winifred invested so much emotion in the child. It might have been an expression of gratitude to the Treuters, but could also have been to do with the kind of illness she had. For Betty had 'a bad head – which is always completely bandaged up'. Clearly, the symptoms resembled the psoriasis that Winifred still suffered from occasionally. Perhaps she identified the sick child with her former self, the orphan with the bleeding, flaky skin who had been ejected from the orphanage. At that time the old Klindworth couple had lovingly taken her in, thus paving the way to Wahnfried. Perhaps, too, it was some kind of bargaining with fate: Winifred was afraid for Wieland's life, and wanted to do something to earn his survival. At any rate, she was quite infatuated with Betty. She wrote to Lene that the child was 'extremely gifted – funny and jolly . . . She's getting only fruit and vegetables until we have overcome the vitamin deficiency.'[118]

The doctor consulted, Dr Deubzer, described Betty's condition: 'She was covered all over with suppurating skin eruptions . . . I've seen many a revolting and repellent sight, but seldom have I seen a human being who looked as wretched as this child.' Winifred had nursed her 'personally – her own mother could not have shown greater dedication'.[119]

Winifred was thrilled to see any sign of improvement, however short-lived. Betty's hair was growing again, and she continued to develop 'perfectly and amusingly – but she has definitely become more refined under Emma's influence!!!'[120] Pampered and spoilt, she stayed in Wahnfried for six years, which she regarded as the best time of her life.[121] Wieland recovered, although his lungs were permanently weakened.

In the spring of 1938 politics was once more the focus of interest. On 11 March Lieselotte wrote that Bayreuth was in a state of alert: 'A number of reservists have been called up, even older men who served in the war. Ammunition and machine-gun supplies have been sent off, too, whether to the border or wherever, nobody knows. Probably it's just some kind of dress

Karl and Henriette
Klindworth with
Winifred Williams.
(Nationalarchiv der
Richard-Wagner-
Stiftung, Bayreuth)

The 'hall' at Wahnfried and Richard Wagner's library. (Nationalarchiv der Richard-Wagner-Stiftung, Bayreuth)

The Wagners around the time of Hitler's first visit. From left to right: Wolfgang, Siegfried, Verena, Winifred, Wieland and Friedelind. (Author's collection)

Julius Streicher in front of the Town Hall inciting the Munich crowd to nationalist revolution. (Author's collection)

From left to right: Wolfgang, Verena, Wieland and Friedelind.
The Wagner children are dressed in cut-down replicas, made
by Daniela, of the original *Ring* costumes. (Nationalarchiv der
Richard-Wagner-Stiftung, Bayreuth)

Lieselotte Schmidt with Wieland and Verena doing their homework.
(Nationalarchiv der Richard-Wagner-Stiftung, Bayreuth)

BAYREUTHER BÜHNENFESTSPIELE 1931

Winifred, the Bayreuth Festival Theatre and three conductors of the 1931 Festival.
(Author's collection)

Heinz Tietjen as a family man. Left to right: Wieland, Winifred, Verena, Tietjen (rear), Wolfgang and Friedelind. (Nationalarchiv der Richard-Wagner-Stiftung, Bayreuth)

'Wolf and Winnie'. The first public appearance of the Reich Chancellor with the Head of the Festival, 1933.
(Author's collection)

A stylized stage-set by Emil Preetorius for the *Valkyrie*. (Author's collection)

A cosy social occasion in Siegfried's house. Roller is on the left, Goebbels on the right, talking to Maria Müller. (Author's collection)

Verena with Goering and Gauleiter Wächtler at Wahnfried. (Author's collection)

Winifred seated beneath the Führer's gaze. (Author's collection)

Hitler on stage congratulating the cast of *Lohengrin*: Heinz Tietjen and Wilhelm Furtwängler to the left of Hitler. (Author's collection)

Hitler holding forth at
the artists' reception.
(Author's collection)

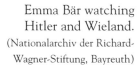

Emma Bär watching
Hitler and Wieland.
(Nationalarchiv der Richard-
Wagner-Stiftung, Bayreuth)

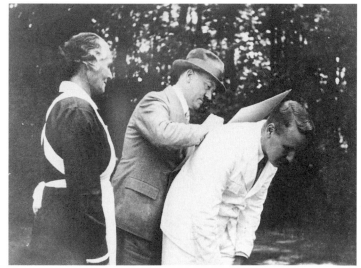

A child-friendly
Hitler during the
interval on
Festival Hill.
(Author's collection)

'The Führer's Guests' being conducted to the Festival Theatre. (The banner reads: 'The city of Richard Wagner welcomes guests of the Führer!') (Nationalarchiv der Richard-Wagner-Stiftung, Bayreuth)

Mother and son in the 1950s. (Nationalarchiv der Richard-Wagner-Stiftung, Bayreuth)

'Omi' (Granny) with her grandson, Wieland's son, Wolf Siegfried. (Author's collection)

rehearsal . . . All the horses have been requisitioned, as well.' When there was a plan to locate a transport depot in the Festival Theatre, Winifred protested about the fire risk. In Bayreuth nobody had any idea what was happening. People were talking about troops moving towards the frontier. They meant the Czech frontier.[122]

The following day, all became clear: Hitler's troops had marched into Austria, and received a joyful welcome. The German–Austrian border had been abolished. Lieselotte, 'half deafened from constant listening to the radio', was overjoyed by 'the Führer's extraordinary, unique action, and how lucky we are to live through this'. After Potsdam day, this was 'the Führer's second victory parade, and this time he must be all the more moved, because it is his own homeland that he has now led to freedom . . . The telegram to Mussolini was wonderful; it said it all. The Duce's attitude is fabulous, too.'[123] As agreed with Hitler in September 1937, this time Mussolini did not come to the aid of his old ally Austria.

The entry of German troops into Austria in March 1938 forced many newly endangered people to take flight from Nazism: Jews, Social Democrats, gipsies, Communists, monarchists, democrats and homosexuals. Many, such as Bruno Walter, who had fled to Austria in 1933, were obliged to resume their flight. The Austrian Jews living in Germany were now German Jews, no longer protected by their status as foreigners. This applied, for instance, to Frida Leider's husband, the Austrian Rudolf Deman.

Hitler came to Bayreuth only a week after his triumph in Vienna, to Winifred's great satisfaction: 'I had him here completely to myself from 2 till 6, completely relaxed – it was really lovely – because with me he can touch on the quite private personal things that went very deep with him in Braunau and Linz – I know both towns – and his experiences there in his earliest years!!! I was so pleased about his liveliness and how good he looked. The result of enjoying success, no doubt!' He saw nobody in Bayreuth apart from her. Gauleiter Wächtler 'was apparently livid with fury!!!!'[124]

Lieselotte reported on this visit to her parents: 'The Mistress heard about all sorts of details, of course; the way everything happened with lightning speed and it came as a surprise even to the Führer. By the way, did you know that a short while ago, around 18–19 March, we were just about to march into Lithuania, if that business hadn't been sorted out at the last minute; everybody in East Prussia was mobilized.'[125] The dispute concerned the German-speaking Memel region, separated from Germany under the terms of the Versailles Treaty.

To 'legitimize' his march into Austria, Hitler ordered a plebiscite to be held on 10 April 1938 throughout what was now 'Greater Germany'. The day before the plebiscite, rallies took place in every town. Hitler's speech was relayed from Vienna, and torchlight processions were held. Villa Wahnfried was illuminated for the occasion. Lieselotte described how 'the wall was framed by a garland of fir branches and lights, glittering with the snow on it. You couldn't help thinking of Christmas, it looked like something out of a fairy-tale . . . It's hard to believe there's a single person left in Germany who will not say "yes".'[126]

The plebiscite provided Hitler with the predicted confirmation. In former Austria, the 'yes' vote was as high as 99.73, with an almost 100 per cent turn-out. By 1 April, the first trainload of anti-Nazi Austrians was leaving for Dachau concentration camp.

CHAPTER 11

Towards War

(1938–9)

SECRET FUNDS AND ARCHIVES

The Wagner family was uniquely privileged in the Hitler period. In 1937 and 1938 Winifred obtained all the foreign currency she needed to take her grown-up children to Italy on sight-seeing holidays that lasted for weeks. Friedelind was sent to an expensive school in England; paying her fees involved a monthly application for currency, which was always granted. For the Festival season, there was a generous special allocation of foreign luxury goods. Even the Revenue Office was considerate, or so Winifred assumed, since 'we got off lightly in our tax assessment. It looks as though somebody higher up has given a hint that the Festival should not be treated like a stocking factory.' Albert Knittel was 'naturally very pleased' about it.[1]

It was only after Siegfried's death that the Festival began to present businesslike accounts. For decades, little distinction had been made between Festival funds and private money. The substantial donations received were not clearly earmarked for any particular purpose, and it was the same with legacies. A large legacy must have been received in July 1932, passed on by Margarethe Strauss, an official of the Awards Foundation and Winifred's friend. Winifred wrote to her: 'I never have doubts – I leave them to Knittel, the painstaking business manager. But it took my breath away to discover that there is still a soul left today seriously prepared to make out a will in favour of completely idealistic causes! We two understand each other . . . so let us not say another word about it.'[2] Further information is lacking, but Winifred's choice of words points to legal difficulties, probably to do with foreign funds. This letter was a chance find, and there must be more sources of the same kind not accessible at the moment.

In 1930 Winifred began to put a conspicuous amount of money 'into material assets'.[3] She extended both the Festival Theatre and Siegfried's house, and laid out a tennis court in the garden of Wahnfried. She paid 40,000 marks for the holiday cottage on Lake Constance, with a lakeside plot of 14,000 square metres, and commissioned extensive new building work.[4] In 1935 she bought a weekend house in the Fichtelgebirge mountains, an 'utterly idyllic spot' in Oberwarmensteinach, twenty-three kilometres from Bayreuth. Surrounded by woods, 'not visible from the road', it had been built in 1930, and was equipped with a swimming pool. Here again, large-scale building work was put in train. Her sisters-in-law were embittered by this ostentatious show of affluence, Winifred having discontinued all allowances to them in 1932. There was 'a glaring discrepancy', said Daniela, 'between one set of my mother's offspring that lives in wealth and luxury, and the other . . . in poverty'.[5]

What is certain is that with Winifred's consent, Knittel was running a separate account under the name of the long-since liquidated Tannhäuser Fund, and by clever investing had increased the capital to the tidy sum of about 800,000 marks. The money to buy the house on Lake Constance was officially raised with a loan from this account. In 1937 Winifred was looking for a pair of semi-detached houses to buy for herself and Tietjen in Berlin: 'Albert always likes to invest money from the Tannhäuser Fund in property, so it naturally occurred to me that the Tannhäuser Fund could buy us a pair of houses – which in Berlin would be a good invest-ment, and at most we would only have to pay the interest!!!!'[6] The plan foundered on Tietjen's reluctance to consolidate his relationship with Winifred.

It is not clear whether Winifred knew that Tietjen, too, was availing himself of the Tannhäuser Fund. At any rate, in 1935 he asked Knittel for a loan of 10,000 marks in order to pay off his debt to Goering. Knittel would understand, he said, that he, Tietjen, was now keen to repay 'this man above all, who shows blind faith in me, and gives me daily evidence of his trust'. He requested the loan from Knittel for two years, repayable with interest.[7] It is not known whether he ever paid it back.

What is certain, however, is that after 1930 Winifred deposited at least

some of the money in Switzerland; and that after 1933, when Hitler introduced tight currency controls, she did not transfer it back to Germany. She
says that many years later, in 1969, Udo Proksch, the husband of a family
member, attempted to 'blackmail the Wagners with what he claimed to
know about the illicit transfer of Festival funds to Switzerland!! – It's beyond
me how the fellow can possibly know that old Knittel advised me to deposit
capital in Switzerland between '30 and '33!' Proksch even claimed 'to know
the account number, which I don't know myself'.[8]

In April 1938, when the scandal of the Bayreuth doctors and the row with
Gauleiter Wächtler were at their height, customs investigation officers
brought criminal charges against Wahnfried for illegal transfer of currency
abroad. An informer was probably at work.

Albert Knittel, the rich Karlsruhe publisher, had in no way enriched himself while managing the Wagners' finances. He had acted solely in Winifred's
interest and with her consent, and he had done so in an honorary capacity.[9]
Now the old gentleman faced the possibility of a scandalous court case, a
prison sentence and the ruin of his livelihood; Winifred faced the probabil-
ity of highly embarrassing criminal proceedings. Totally distraught, and
fearing to lose Hitler's friendship, she turned for help to Hans Frank, who was
now a Minister without Portfolio in Berlin. She wanted him to see Tietjen
and discuss the matter. She hoped, as she wrote to Lene, that Tietjen 'will be
a much better advocate than I can be, since I'm partly implicated – if only we
can save the old Master of Heiligenberg [a country estate owned by Knittel]
from disaster!'[10]

Once again, said Winifred, Frank 'acted superbly, issuing an order that
first of all everything to do with hearings etc. was to be moved away from
Bayreuth, and then that they must take place in private'. This averted disaster. As far as Knittel was concerned, Frank could not help at that time, 'but
later, when everything has been settled, Section 51 can be brought into
play', that is, exemption on grounds of diminished responsibility.[11]

It was agreed that, with his own consent, Knittel should be declared the
sole guilty party and placed under arrest for a while, to spare Wahnfried and
the head of the house, Winifred, from charges. Relieved, she wrote to Lene:
'All in all, things seem to be working out well for me . . . I'll be glad when it's
all over.'[12] But it was not quite all over. In May Winifred was put through five
hours of interrogation by the Karlsruhe public prosecutor's office. The Swiss
money was confiscated and repatriated, 'in accordance with the currency regulations of the 3rd Reich', as Winifred wrote.[13] Moreover, the worst

consequence of the affair was that access to all Wahnfried funds was legally blocked for the duration of the investigation.[14] Hitler granted special dispensation so that at least enough money was released for the Festival to continue.

When Friedelind returned to Bayreuth from England in June 1938, she found her mother totally altered. 'Her face, usually so lively, so full of colour, was grey, her eyes were almost black and had a hunted look, and her hair, her lovely, glossy hair was lifeless, with a few grey streaks.' It was not from her mother but from Emma that Friedelind discovered that Knittel had been arrested for misappropriation of funds and currency smuggling.[15]

Finally, the doctor appointed by the court confirmed the expert opinion of Winifred's friend Professor Wolfgang Veil that the old gentleman was only partly responsible for his actions, and consigned him to a mental hospital for eleven months. Winifred's comment to Lene was that 'this means there will be no hearings or further interrogations – and I hope there will be no need for Wolf to learn about the matter, either'. This solution was very important for Knittel's family, 'because otherwise the sons would have lost their officer's commissions . . . etc.'.[16] All this was kept confidential, even from the Wagner children. The case never reached the courts.

Even in those difficult times, in the spring of 1938 Wieland and Wolfgang obtained enough currency to spend several weeks travelling through Italy down to Sicily in Wieland's new Mercedes. The two brothers, while very different, complemented and understood each other well. Winifred observed that 'Wolfi looks after Wieland like a nanny, because even the military haven't managed to cure his absent-mindedness.'[17]

At the time, Hitler was in Rome returning Mussolini's visit. Grand parades demonstrated the unity between the two leaders, but Mussolini could not be persuaded to enter into a formal alliance.

After his return, Hitler came to Bayreuth. A letter from Winifred told her sons what he said about Italy. 'He was bored by the Quirinal, and could not express enough scorn at the whole court ceremonial, in Naples as well as Rome.' Hitler talked about Mussolini 'with the highest regard' and 'greatly regretted that you did not get in touch. You could have called on him in the Quirinal!!!!' But she immediately added: 'Perhaps not – with your experience of etiquette!!!!'[18]

The currency affair did not prevent Hitler, on the anniversary of Richard Wagner's birthday, 22 May 1938, from following up an idea of Winifred's and giving instructions for the creation of a Richard Wagner Research Centre. The state agreed to cover half the yearly costs, around 10,000 marks; the other 50 per cent were to be met by the town of Bayreuth.[19] It would be headed by the Wahnfried archivist, Otto Strobel.

Hitler's fascination with Wagner's letters, writings and scores meant that it was a relatively simple task for Winifred to persuade him to set up this research institute. His interest was particularly in evidence in 1935, when he procured and studied pre-publication copies of the correspondence between Wagner and King Ludwig II. Winifred relates how 'I mobilized a policeman (!) to take the copies of the Wagner–King Ludwig letters safely to Munich – where our Gauleiter was not to be deprived of handing them over to the Führer in person.'[20]

Among the aims of the research centre, as formulated by Winifred, were 'to defend' Wagner's person and work 'against all tendentious attacks'; 'to clarify Wagner's pure Aryan descent'; to produce a critical edition of the collected works; and to prepare a new biography of the Master.[21] Winifred had ultimate responsibility for everything written about Wagner, and barred party officials from interfering. The research centre was intended to defend and promulgate Wahnfried's strict articles of faith, and ward off all attempts to research the subject of Wagner's putative Jewish father. She was thereby following Cosima's intentions, and knew that Hitler had an equal interest in suppressing this sensitive topic.

However, Winifred's main motive for founding the centre may have been to acquire a power-base for use against her sisters-in-law, with whom she had been waging a bitter war for many years over the contents of the Wagner archives. Important documents were constantly disappearing from the collection and reappearing in the hands of Eva Chamberlain or Daniela Thode. After Cosima's death, Eva had taken away papers by the basketful.

In 1932 Winifred was surprised when Eva suddenly 'made her a present' of Cosima's letters to Siegfried. 'It's a complete puzzle to me how she came by them – naturally, she destroyed some, without authorization!!!'[22] This meant that, in keeping with Bayreuth tradition, after careful sifting some letters had been weeded out. Anything compromising had been got rid of, while any containing potential ammunition against Winifred had been retained. Winifred, who used similar methods, and was very interested in any material incriminating her sisters-in-law, was beside herself with vexation. During the *Parsifal* crisis in 1934, even the correspondence between Richard and Cosima disappeared, a core holding of the archive. When Winifred notified the police, Eva declared that she had burnt the letters on Siegfried's instructions. Winifred could not bring herself to believe it.

In 1935 Eva, deeply hurt at the time, had presented the town of Bayreuth with her greatest treasure, the twenty-one volumes of Cosima's diary, with the proviso that it should remain sealed in a safe until thirty years after her (Eva's) death. Apart from her and Daniela, nobody had ever glimpsed the contents, not even Siegfried. Winifred never ceased to claim this important document for the Wahnfried archive, as part of her children's and descendants' legacy.

The sisters-in-law collected written eyewitness accounts concerning the family quarrels of the last few years. Eva wrote to the leading actress Anna Bahr-Mildenburg in Vienna, for instance (and to many others), asking her to write down 'in typescript' everything she had experienced in Bayreuth. Eva proposed to place the document in the Wagner memorial collection of Helena Wallem 'for safekeeping'. 'It is part of an extensive written record that Daniela and I have already deposited there. These testimonies may prove useful in the distant future.'[23]

Adolf von Gross, the Wagners' former finance manager, whose dealings with Siegfried and Winifred had left him deeply disillusioned, also embellished the town archive with documents about the Wagner family, including critical ones from the twenties. He specified that these sources should be available for researchers to use 'in case anything was later said against him!' There was still a dispute in 1946 over the Gross papers between the town of Bayreuth and the Wagner family, 'who wanted to arrange for the papers in question to disappear'.[24]

Helena Wallem, champion of the aunts and guardian of important documents and manuscripts in the town collection, was the sworn enemy of the Wahnfried archivist Strobel, whose wife Gertrud complained that Wallem 'had not compiled any catalogue of original manuscripts; nobody knew what was in her secret closet!'[25] But the closets at Wahnfried were just as secret. The war of the archives continued for decades.

The archive in Wahnfried had hardly ever been opened to independent scholars. Nearly all of those who asked for access were turned away on the (unjustified) grounds that 'The Wahnfried archive has been so thoroughly researched that it is highly unlikely you will find anything new. In any case, it is no longer accessible.' Instead, enquirers were directed to Wallem's Wagner Museum, where neither the library nor the archive were usable, or to the Wagner Museum in Eisenach, or libraries in Berlin, Munich and Leipzig, as though equally valuable Wagner autographs were to be found there.[26]

The new, publicly subsidized research centre continued this tradition of obstruction, but it did at least manage to complete the five volumes of correspondence between Ludwig II and Wagner, which was edited by Strobel, jointly published by Winifred and the Wittelsbach Equalization Fund, and printed by Knittel's publishing house in Karlsruhe. The contract gave two thirds of the proceeds to the Wagner family, and a third to the Wittelsbachs (former ruling house of Bavaria).[27] The 'aunts' protested against the publication, of course.

The research centre was concerned solely with the Master, not with Cosima or Siegfried. Their papers had already been very thoroughly combed through by Winifred and excellently organized. She was the only one with the keys to the so-called Siegfried cabinet, and nobody ever saw inside it, not even her children.[28]

FRANZ VON HOESSLIN AND THE 1938 FESTIVAL

Ever since 1933, the Director General of Music in Breslau, Franz von Hoesslin, who had been conducting in Bayreuth since Siegfried's time, had been in trouble with Goebbels and the Breslau *Gau* administration. He was 'one quarter Jewish', and steadfastly refused to divorce his Jewish wife, the alto singer Erna Liebenthal. Besides, he was a devout Catholic who made absolutely no attempt to disguise his opinion of the NSDAP. He was subjected to considerable harassment in Breslau, as illustrated by one first-hand account: 'It was quite often the case that at a quarter to 8, when the concert was due to begin, Hoesslin had no idea whether or not he was going to be allowed to take the rostrum. So he rang Bayreuth, and Frau Wagner rang Berlin, and then shortly after 8 o'clock he was allowed to start conducting. That happened more than once.'[29]

In June 1936, however, he was dismissed, and banned from performing. Not a single German theatre would give the outlawed Hoesslin an engagement, with the exception of Bayreuth. Immediately after his appointment was announced, Winifred received an unpleasant letter from Hitler's right-hand man, Martin Bormann. According to information from the party in Breslau, Hoesslin

> was married to a full-blood Jewess, and consequently relieved of his post in Breslau when his contract came to an end. He is considered to be totally

unreliable politically. Among other things, it has been asserted that he owed his post in Breslau entirely to support from the Social Democrats and the Centre Party. During guest performances abroad he had appeared together with his wife. I would be neglecting my duty if I failed to tell you about the climate of opinion around him. Heil Hitler! Your obedient servant, Bormann.[30]

This was a clear demand that she should drop Hoesslin.

Winifred fought back, and managed to get Hitler to meet Hoesslin. The outcome was that he was allowed to continue conducting in Bayreuth, on condition that his wife did not return to Germany, nor perform abroad. The terms were harsh, because she and her daughter depended on her income as a singer.

Winifred's reply to Bormann consisted of four densely covered pages, where she dealt with 'the hostile climate once again being created in certain local Party quarters'. It was time to 'make known the attitude of the Führer with regard to the question of employing Herr von Hoesslin, and finally put a stop to this ruthless harassment'. Then she described Hoesslin's private situation in detail. He had four Aryan children from his first marriage to support; his Aryan first wife had been unfaithful to him while he was away at the front.

His Jewish second wife, Erna, 'had been a good mother to his children, and a loyal partner'. She had often given him the option of divorcing her, and 'went quietly and without protest into exile with her daughter'. Hoesslin was one of 'the most competent German conductors' (although Furtwängler thought otherwise), and 'everywhere emphatically committed to the cause of German art. If no German intendant was prepared to employ him, then I see that as cowardice on the part of the intendants, grovelling to "local Party quarters".'

She closed with the confident assertion that she had taken up Hoesslin's cause in this way in order not 'to rob this man of his faith in the power and effect of the Führer's word'. Despite having Jewish wives, many Aryans were being tacitly employed 'in really prominent positions in German artistic life . . . God knows it feels strange to be playing the advocate for this one case. I am doing it . . . in the belief that the Party is also capable of decent and humane decisions'. Could Bormann please inform her whether 'she must conform to the "climate of opinion" in local Party quarters, despite the Führer's decision?'[31]

The pressure on Winifred was intensified. The SS Security Service, monitoring the mood of the Bayreuth population, but also acting as the Gauleiter's mouthpiece, reported at the time: 'The participation of artists related to Jews at the Bayreuth Festival attracted comment.'[32] The reference was to Hoesslin, Frida Leider and Max Lorenz in particular.

The fact remains that Hoesslin continued to conduct in Bayreuth in 1938, 1940 and 1941. But he faced continuous hostility. Worn out, he finally emigrated to Switzerland to join his wife. Retrospectively, Winifred commented: 'I had hoped that my example would encourage the German theatres to give Hoesslin work. Nobody lifted a finger for him, so he had to go abroad to earn a living for himself and his large family.'[33]

At Hitler's request, the Festival now became an annual event, in contrast to the usual pattern of a year's interval after two festival years. Hitler's reason was that he did not know 'how he would get through a summer without a Festival. The Festival was simply his only recreation.' Additionally, he pointed out economic advantages for the town, and 'the continuity of the technical and administrative apparatus'.[34]

Winifred had no choice but to comply with this flattering request, and basically she agreed with it, in any case.

> Our decision looks splendid . . . seen from the outside, of course, but in reality it's our financial crisis that has forced us into it. The cost to us of a non-Festival year cannot be recuperated within two Festival years – the ongoing repairs to the theatre, the taxes, the retained staff salaries and pensions, amount to some 240,000 marks – which we always have to carry forward as a deficit into a Festival year. Even if we don't make a profit in 1938, at least these sums will be covered – or productively spent.[35]

After the exceptional intermezzo of the Olympic year, when large numbers of foreigners included Bayreuth in their itinerary, in international terms the Festival was now practically isolated. Adolf Zinsstag in Zurich felt that 'You can't have normal dealings with the Germans any more; everything is coloured by the consciousness of "Greater Germany". It's better to limit correspondence to what is strictly necessary. I don't feel that's any great loss.'[36]

Once more, advance ticket sales were poor. Once more the Party came to the rescue. The KdF took over two complete performances (6 and 7 August),[37] and bought 3,000 tickets altogether. However, these were not intended for 'special guests of the Führer', that is, as complimentary tickets, but were put on sale by the KdF, in a package that included three performances, travel, meals and overnight accommodation for 65 marks, a considerable saving, and quite affordable for middle-class Wagner aficionados.

When yet another mayor resigned in Bayreuth, Winifred made Hitler promise to ensure 'that we get a new mayor within a month',[38] and one who would not be dependent on the Gauleiter. Hitler was as good as his word. In July 1938 the new mayor, Fritz Kempfler from Fürth, took up office. The first visit he made in Bayreuth was to the 'Mistress of Bayreuth' in Wahnfried, as he wrote, because the Festival season was approaching, and he was responsible for security and 'Führer protection'. The two took to each other. Kempfler later called Winifred 'the most remarkable lady I've met in a long lifetime'. He valued her natural dignity, her energy and industry, her charm and her helpfulness. It was not worth making an enemy of her, because 'she could also be a ruthless opponent, as Gauleiter Wächtler in particular had discovered'.[39] Winifred now possessed a reliable ally against the Gauleiter.

Family life in Wahnfried at that time was under a cloud because of worries about Lieselotte. She had come back from the clinic just before the Festival, completely changed, with 'the mentality of a retarded child', in Friedelind's words. Her condition, no doubt the result of too many powerful drugs over a period of years, made her unable to follow any conversation; she would 'giggle and babble nonsensically'.[40] The young woman died of a septic liver at the end of August 1938. With her died a historically important, if effusive, source of information about the daily life of Villa Wahnfried.

Police preparations for the arrival of Hitler had been going on for months. People who lived in the houses along the approach roads were registered by the police, and under orders 'to report every change concerning tenants, subtenants and guests. They were checked out in their turn.' During the check on Wahnfried, it transpired that Tietjen, who was registered there, had a so-called 'Yellow Card', denoting a security risk, because he had allegedly once belonged to the Social Democratic Party.[41]

Once again, to reinforce 'security measures within the framework of Führer protection', on this occasion there appeared about 'a hundred police officers from outside the area, but under their own separate command', and unknown even to the mayor. Wearing evening dress, they kept the audience under surveillance during performances, especially those in the boxes, and during the intervals they mingled with the visitors.[42] Once more, about

1,500 Sudeten Germans travelled to Bayreuth on a group passport, and were under careful observation, for fear that Czech 'chauvinists' might have infiltrated their ranks. No. 1 Company of the house-guard, Leibstandarte SS, arrived the day before Hitler did.

Hitler came by special train on 23 July. Kempfler reported that while still at the station, and before getting into his car, he had turned to the chief of police and said: 'Rattenhuber, I'm in great danger here – the Czech border is so near, and the tense atmosphere between Czechoslovakia and us could positively provoke an assassination attempt; so just be aware of your responsibility!' The 'Führer's car convoy' was preceded as ever by a local police vehicle, which indicated with a flag the approach of the Führer. 'From that moment onwards no cars are allowed on to the road from side streets, and the windows and doors of houses lining the route must be kept shut.'[43]

As usual, immediately upon arriving Hitler called on Winifred, strolling with her around the garden of Wahnfried. To her great relief, he was as friendly as ever, and made no mention of the Knittel affair. 'Knows about the A.K. business from the files – but he doesn't want it to be raised . . . so there wasn't a word about it.'[44] However, there must have been some discussion of Winifred's difficulties with Wächtler. The very next morning he visited the Gauleiter in the hospital, to which he had retreated, and 'tore him off a strip, so loudly that everybody could hear', as a nursing assistant later reported.[45]

The Festival opened on 24 July 1938 with *Tristan and Isolde* conducted by Karl Elmendorff, with Frida Leider and Max Lorenz in the title roles. Three other important Nazi figures were present besides Hitler: Speer, Bormann and Frank. *Parsifal*, under Hoesslin's baton, saw the Bayreuth debut of the French singer Germaine Lubin as Kundry; she was a tall, blonde beauty with a penchant for everything German. Goebbels thought *Parsifal* a flop, despite the lovely Kundry: 'One mishap after another. The moving scenery doesn't work, the sacred lance falls down. Wolff's singing as Parsifal is absolutely hopeless. It's really embarrassing. The Führer is very annoyed. But Bayreuth is only a matter for women and children now. It's got to be reformed. They blather on about the Master, and let his work be spoilt.'[46]

While the Sudeten Germans were cheering Hitler on with their 'Heim ins Reich' [Return to the Reich] slogans, the newspapers were full of reports of the most serious acts of violence committed by Czechs against the German minority. Via his ambassador, Hitler informed the British government about these 'atrocities', and asked it to restrain the Czech government. He assured Britain that Germany wanted a peaceful solution. The news from Czechoslovakia was received with indignant comment among the small circle present in the 'Führer's building'. Hitler listened to this and then, according to Franz Stassen, 'suddenly, with a loud laugh, declared that he himself was the instigator of all the violence'.[47]

The new mayor, Kempfler, took careful notes of all his encounters with Hitler, including Sunday lunch in Siegfried's house. Sitting between Winifred and Verena, Hitler described the Reichstag fire,* and then went on to talk at length about the 'West Wall', known in Britain as the 'Siegfried Line': 'I couldn't sleep until I had ordered the building of defences which have already made it impossible for the enemy to launch a surprise attack on us from the west. I want the German people to enjoy a good night's sleep again, too.' The Minister for Church Affairs, Hanns Kerrl, ventured the flattering remark: 'My Führer, as long as you live, the German people will always sleep well.'[48] Hitler had a large room in Siegfried's house closed off, 'because they were building the model of the West Wall there. But it was a very long time before I found out about it', Winifred said later.[49]

Kempfler was also present at Hitler's reception for the artists. First of all Hitler went from table to table, chatting, carrying a glass of the weak beer (2 per cent) he had specially brewed for him. 'Obviously in a good mood', he had chatted with Kempfler, too, and with the acting Gauleiter, Ludwig Ruckdeschel, complaining about the discomfort of wearing tails and how they made him sweat. When a few ladies talked about having given up smoking, he lectured them on this, a favourite topic of his: 'The Indians have had plenty of revenge for the fire-water we took them, by sending us back nicotine over the Atlantic. It's a really dangerous poison – one drop is enough to kill a dog. It's only because people take it in unbelievably small doses that its effect is not fatal.' Then there was some chat about beards. Hitler predicted that 'the fashion for beards will never come back. It has dis-

---

*On 30 January 1933 Hitler was finally appointed Chancellor, and demanded new elections in March. On 27 February, just a few days before polling day, the Reichstag was set alight. The culprit was identified as the mentally unstable Dutch Communist Marinus van der Lubbe, but in recent years strong evidence has emerged to indicate that the Nazis themselves were accomplices in the act of arson. They then claimed that the fire signalled an imminent Communist uprising, and persuaded Hindenburg to sign a pre-emptive 'emergency decree' that stayed in force for the next twelve years.

appeared since the World War because of gasmasks – and ultimately today every man must be prepared to wear a gasmask again.'[50]

Hitler sought to gain the favour of the lovely Germaine Lubin, and sent Friedelind over to bring her to his table. At the end of their conversation, he said to her: 'Frau *Kammersängerin*, you are a seductress.' However, she found him very shy. The next day he sent her red roses and a photo of himself with the inscription, 'To Frau Germaine Lubin, with sincere admiration and appreciation'. Tietjen also sent her flowers, and gave her a heartfelt kiss in her dressing room. She found him 'madly charming'.[51]

On 30 July 1938 Hitler missed *Siegfried*, travelling instead to Breslau for the German Gymnastics and Sports Festival. Unity Mitford fully earned her nickname of 'Mitfahrt' (hitch-hiker) again by taking up his invitation to travel with him. In Breslau Sudeten Germans once more resorted to chanting en masse to beg him to 'liberate' them. The initiative was organized by Reich Sports Leader Hans von Tschammer und Osten and the German gymnastic clubs in Czechoslovakia. Simultaneously, a choral festival was taking place, again with Sudeten German choirs in folk costume.

Hitler's last Bayreuth evening, after *Twilight of the Gods* on 1 August 1938, was devoted to the Wagner family. This time it was Wieland who was the focus of celebrations: he had just joined the NSDAP, with the membership number 6,078,301.[52] In the meantime, he had decided on the next step in his training, as Winifred wrote: 'He wants to be a painter – still involved in music, but not as a profession. So now he's going to art college – probably Munich – with music as a sideline.' Even if it would be a long time before he could contribute to Bayreuth, 'at least he would have the inner satisfaction of his painting studies'.[53] He declined to take a regular course of study, choosing instead to be privately taught by Ferdinand Staeger, whose art fulfilled Hitler's aesthetic ideal. His mother set him up in a studio in Munich.

It turned into a rather long evening. Friedelind recalled: 'the guests tried to suppress their yawns; Frau Goebbels took a few illicit puffs on her cigarette, hidden under the table. To stay awake, we started up a "table concert", with mother gobbling like a turkey, Germaine Lubin giving a masterly performance as a cooing pigeon, and me doing my best duck noise. In the end, even that got boring, and Hitler was the only one still talking.' At two in the morning Hitler released his guests and sent his adjutants to bed. But he asked the Wagners, including the four children, to stay on for a 'cosy' session together. He went on with his monologue until nearly six in the morning.[54]

On 2 August 1938 Hitler, Goebbels and a large entourage flew off to

Berlin, but they forgot Unity Mitford, who was ill. Winifred was concerned about the solitary young woman, who was taken to Dr Treuter's private clinic suffering from serious mental problems and inflammation of the lungs. Unity wrote to her parents about Winifred: 'She's such a nice motherly person.'[55]

Shortly afterwards the telephone woke the Wagners with a start at four in the morning. It was Hitler's personal physician, Theodor Morell, asking whether Unity was in Bayreuth. He came a few times from Berlin, at Hitler's expense, especially to give the young woman a course of injections. He made himself very unpopular with the Wagners, particularly when they heard from Treuter that, in Winifred's words, 'Morell had taken a syringe wrapped in grubby cotton-wool from his trouser pocket and injected Unity with it!' Later, the story in the family was that Verena had said to Hitler in disgust: 'I simply don't understand how you can stand having that pig as your doctor.' Winifred corrected this: '"Letting him touch you" is what she actually said.'[56] Hitler never brought Morell with him to Bayreuth again after that. His other doctor, Karl Brandt, well-liked by the family, came instead. Then Unity's worried mother arrived from England, and finally her father, Lord Redesdale. He expressed his gratitude to Winifred, went to Munich with his daughter to reimburse Hitler's expenses, and took her back to England.

Towards the middle of the Festival the fifty-year-old Frida Leider, who sang the demanding roles of Brünnhilde and Isolde, suffered a crisis affecting both her nerves and her voice. When Winifred gave her a few days' leave, necessitating the re-casting of Isolde, Tietjen exploded, and vented his anger first on Winifred, then on Frida Leider's husband, Rudolf Deman. This blazing row with an erstwhile friend ended with Tietjen, 'white-hot with rage', as he later wrote, 'showing Deman the door and throwing him out'.[57]

'With an enormous effort', Frida Leider completed the last *Tristan* performances, but not well enough for Tietjen. She suffered a nervous and physical breakdown, and was bedridden for months. She never performed again at Bayreuth.[58] Her 'non-Aryan' husband soon took refuge in Switzerland, but could not get a work permit there, and lived in near-penury. The couple were parted for eight years.

During these turbulent days twenty-year-old Friedelind was at Frida's side, and witnessed her breakdown and the quarrel with Tietjen. The latter complained later 'that from the moment I threw Deman out, Mausi never said another word to me, avoided me with a tight-lipped expression, and cut me dead, right up until the moment she escaped to Switzerland. With one blow, Deman had torn her away from me.'[59] Friedelind saw it differently.

A MURDEROUS NIGHT

The crisis centring on the Sudeten Germans in Czechoslovakia was moving towards its dénouement. Friedelind, who was in Paris, reported to her aunts on 14 September:

> The political situation is getting worse, from hour to hour, you might say . . .
> I don't feel very happy about sitting in a foreign country in these circum-
> stances. Yesterday there were another 7 murders in Czechoslovakia –
> Sudeten Germans and Czechs. Everything depends on the Führer now!
> King Henry's words come back to me: 'Lord, let me be wise'.[60]

Daniela wrote, 'in a terribly serious state of mind', to her friend Zinsstag in Zurich on 28 September: 'But believe me; in this hour of extreme peril, the whole of Germany stands behind its Führer, the martyr to a just cause. Thousands of refugees are pouring through our town, there is inexpressible misery and despair all around us, and we are practising with gasmasks etc.'[61]

Before the meeting that same day between Hitler, Mussolini, Daladier and Chamberlain in Munich, Winifred wrote to Lene: 'We are sitting here still fervently hoping that the four statesmen can somehow find a way to reach peaceful agreement! I'm assuming that Wolf is ready to make overtures, and that he wants to get Mussolini to cover our backs . . . Nobody thinks it's the real thing! Let's hope they're right!'[62]

The early morning news on 30 September reported the 'Munich Agreement', concluded overnight. Britain had given Hitler a free hand in the German-speaking areas of Czechoslovakia, in return for a guarantee that he would make no more territorial demands. Hitler had once more success-fully invoked the right of self-determination of nations, and agreed to a plebiscite. In a joint declaration, Hitler and Neville Chamberlain assured each other of their peaceful intentions: 'We regard the . . . agreement, and the Anglo-German Naval Agreement [of 1935], as symbolic of the desire of our two peoples never to go to war with each other again.' They also resolved in future 'to continue our efforts to remove possible sources of difference and thus to contribute to assure the peace of Europe'.[63] Nevile Henderson, the

British ambassador in Berlin, later asserted that neither Britain nor France was ready for war at the time.[64]

Winifred characterized the day in her own inimitable style as one on which 'the miracle occurred, and Wolf gave us the gift of peace instead of the apparently inevitable war'.[65] She felt confirmed in her conviction that Hitler did not want war with Britain, whatever happened. On 1 October 1938 German troops marched into the Sudetenland and were received as liberators by the German population. Friedelind wrote to Eva Chamberlain from Paris: 'You can be really proud of your namesake.' (In fact, Neville and Houston Stewart Chamberlain were cousins.) In Paris the atmosphere was 'naturally cheerful and relieved . . . The general mood is "long may it continue – may Russia be locked out – and may cooperation and mutual understanding among the Four prevail!"'[66]

The aims of the Pan-Germans had been achieved. In accordance with the much deployed slogan, 'Ein Volk, ein Reich, ein Führer', 'Greater Germany' had been created, including the Saar and the Rhineland, Austria and the Sudetenland, but not South Tyrol. Hitler could regard himself as having completed Bismarck's work of unification, and at the same time be celebrated as a peace-making hero.

Soon afterwards, the Pan-German League was dissolved, and the Alldeutsche Blätter was banned. Only the old leader of the movement, Heinrich Class, persisted in his version of Pan-Germany, and made himself a figure of fun with his cult of antique Germania. Once more, Hitler had shouldered aside an old patron and companion of earlier days in his journey.

On 9 November 1938 Gauleiter Wächtler and his deputy, Reckdeschel, went to Munich for the commemoration of the fifteenth anniversary of the 'March on the Felderrnhalle'. The other Bayreuth party functionaries celebrated the day in the Siebert Hall (now the Bayreuth Stadthalle), and went home at 10 p.m. At 10.30 the Gau office received a call from the Gauleiter in Munich informing them that the Secretary to the German embassy in Paris, Ernst vom Rath, had been assassinated by a Jew. In response, 'spontaneous demonstrations' were already taking place against Jews. Wächtler gave orders for similar 'demonstrations' to be organized outside the synagogue in Bayreuth. Party members should take part only in civilian clothes. The impression of a 'spontaneous outbreak of popular anger' was to be created, and that was the headline of the following day's Bayreuther Tagblatt.

At 10.45 Chief of Police Kesselring rang Mayor Kempfler to tell him that the synagogue in nearby Bamberg was on fire and that the one in Bayreuth was also threatened. He had already sent out the police and the fire brigade to protect it, and needed the Mayor's approval.[67] The excuse he gave for these safety precautions was that a fire in the synagogue would inevitably spread to the adjacent baroque opera house, the town's most precious architectural gem.

This protective action represented a considerable risk both for the Mayor and the police chief. There were just two factors that made it possible at all: one was that Gauleiter Wächtler was away from Bayreuth; the other, that Winifred declared her readiness to secure Hitler's backing for the move that very night. Like Kempfler, she was convinced that individual Party members must be to blame for these acts of violence: 'I could not possibly accept that such acts had been approved by the government, which means ultimately by Hitler.' Kempfler justified his decision on the grounds that Hitler had dealt incisively with anti-Jewish violence in Franconia in 1933 and 1935, and at that time had even imposed restraint upon his close friend Julius Streicher.[68] Meanwhile, the frightened Jewish congregation rushed to the synagogue to rescue precious and devotional objects, from prayer scrolls to founding charters.

The Bayreuth synagogue was one of the few in Germany to be spared from destruction by arson. But the police could not prevent gangs of SA thugs, mobilized by the regional Party authorities and dressed in civilian clothes as instructed, from rampaging through it for an hour, smashing up the interior, pulling down the galleries and throwing the wreckage out on to the street. When the electric lighting failed, the men went on rampaging by the light of pocket torches, until the whole place was completely ransacked.

After that, the 'demolition groups' set about the four remaining Jewish shops, smashing in their fronts, wrecking the displays and plundering the tills, although Goebbels, who initiated the action, had forbidden all looting. Then the 'arrest groups', armed with lists of names supplied by the local party, went to work. They dragged about sixty of the 120 Jews still living in Bayreuth out of their beds, maltreated them and placed them under arrest. Twenty-three Jewish men were taken off to gaol. When Fritz Ruthenberg, bleeding after being beaten up, called his physician Dr Hering, the latter hurried round to help, but was menaced and driven off the premises. 'German' doctors were not allowed to treat Jews. Hering was penalized by exclusion from the SA.[69]

The police had little chance of asserting themselves against the bully-boys scattered throughout the town, so by agreement with the chief of police the Mayor had all those arrested taken to the Rotmain Hall and placed under police protection. Most were released around noon the following day. By about four o'clock calm had been restored to Bayreuth. On 11 November a 'strict order' went out to the public 'to refrain from all further demonstrations and actions against the Jews, of any kind whatsoever'.[70] Nobody knew that a struggle for power was taking place in Berlin between Goebbels and Goering – won on this occasion by Goering.

The demolished shops were made secure by the police, and permanently closed; makeshift repairs were carried out on damaged homes. The population carted away the smashed-up woodwork of the synagogue to use for fuel. It is true that Police Chief Kesselring made his officers log the damage, and in every single case laid charges with the Gestapo – but to no effect. On the contrary, Jewish shopkeepers were forced to surrender to the government their insurance claims for repairs following the pogrom and pay for all the damage themselves. In addition, one billion marks was demanded from the German Jews, to 'atone' for the death of vom Rath.

The Bayreuth Jews were now 'aware of the extreme hopelessness of their situation', as the leader of the Jewish community later put it.[71] Hitler confirmed to Winifred that this was precisely the point of the exercise. When she complained to him about the horrors of the pogrom night, he replied, 'Well, something like that had to happen, to finally get the Jews out of Germany.'[72] He was less open with the Wagner children, denying any involvement in the pogrom, according to Wolfgang. He claimed that it had been 'an independent action by Goebbels, which had taken him by surprise'.[73]

Jews lost more and more of their rights. From 12 November 1938 they were no longer allowed in theatres, cinemas or concerts. From 15 November Jewish children were excluded from 'German' schools. From 3 December Jews had to hand in their driving licences and car documents, and deposit all their shares and securities with a particular bank. The Bayreuth synagogue, which was almost unscathed from the outside but whose interior was in ruins, was compulsorily purchased by the state of Bavaria for 2,000 marks. On 7 December the *Bayerische Ostmark* reported with satisfaction that there were no Jewish shops left in Bayreuth.[74]

For many Jews the so-called 'Reich Crystal Night' was the final spur needed to drive them out of Germany. Fear dominated the lives of those who remained. Richard Strauss, greatly concerned for his Jewish daughter-in-law, appealed to Tietjen to put in a word with Hitler and Goering on her behalf, because 'we are seriously worried about the fate of my wonderful daughter-in-law (she was introduced to the Führer at Wahnfried, and you too . . . know her pretty well, and what a genuine, splendid person she is)'. It was only thanks to chance and the intervention of Gauleiter Adolf Wagner that she had escaped a 'terrible fate' in Garmisch, 'but she suffered so much from her humiliation that she has come down with a serious attack of bilious fever'. Her passport had been confiscated, as well as her hunting and driving licences. 'She's not even allowed to go to the theatre to see her father-in-law's operas.' She had spent two weeks confined to her home in 'protective custody', and could not buy basic necessities, because she did not yet 'dare to venture into any shops in Garmisch! . . . Please help, my dear friend.' In a subsequent letter he begged for the 'restoration of the most natural human rights'.[75]

On 21 February 1939 Jews were required to hand over all jewellery and precious metals, even down to cutlery. Further confiscation of property meant that by the end of the year, all the Bayreuth Jews had lost their homes and land.[76] Finance offices took over the administration of the assets that had been frozen – until there were none left. On 30 April Jewish tenants lost the protection of the law, and could be evicted from their homes at any time. Visas were now unobtainable, which ruled out escape from the country, and in any case by this time there was hardly any money left to pay the Reich emigration tax. More and more Jews chose suicide as the only way out.

The famous mathematician Professor Alfred Pringsheim, Thomas Mann's father-in-law, was also under threat. His magnificent house in the Arcisstrasse in Munich, once a meeting point for artists and intellectuals, had already been pulled down in 1933, to make way for Hitler's new Führer buildings. All the same, for a long time Pringsheim, a German nationalist and a Wagnerian, refused to leave Germany. Mann wrote in his diary in July 1939 that 'thanks to the influence of W[inifred] Wagner . . . the old people are doing better than most – relatively speaking'.[77] Soon afterwards Pringsheim, nearly eighty-nine, and his wife, Hedwig, succeeded in getting to Switzerland. They 'clearly owed their exit visa, a fairly unusual act of decency for the Nazis, entirely to Winifred's intercession with Hitler on their behalf', wrote their grandson Klaus H. Pringsheim.[78] The Pringsheims' famous majolica collection was auctioned in London in 1939 to swell Nazi coffers, the sum realized no doubt representing the price of their permission to leave Germany. When Pringsheim died two years later, his widow burnt the letters of Richard Wagner, which had been her husband's most treasured possession.

WAR CLOSES IN

On 14 March 1939, under German pressure, Slovakia seceded from Czechoslovakia, and declared its independence under Jozef Tiso. Contrary to Hitler's promise in the Munich Agreement, German troops marched into the 'rump Czech Republic'. Following Austria, yet another European state ceased to exist, becoming the 'Protectorate of Bohemia and Moravia'.

One of the German soldiers involved was nineteen-year-old Wolfgang Wagner. There was no fighting, and Wieland joked to Ulrich Roller: 'Wolf took part in "Czechia" and repressed the population there. He put on five pounds in this war from eating whipped cream.'[79] The specific highlighting of cream indicates how rare luxury goods had become for Germans by this time and how rich this subjugated country seemed to them, boasting not only cream but also gold, industries and cultural goods of all kinds, now appropriated to finance Hitler's armaments.

The German newsreels as usual showed only beaming faces, not the despair and fear of the Czechs. This was no German country, after all; nobody had pleaded for *Anschluss*. There was no longer any question of the much-trumpeted right to national self-determination. Hitler had crossed the Rubicon here, meeting with no resistance from the Great Powers, apart from a few diplomatic protests. He appeared like a sovereign ruler in the castle of the kings of Bohemia in Prague, recounting later that 'looking down from the Hradčany [Castle]', he had felt deeply 'that with this unprecedented tough and difficult political solution, avoiding all bloodshed, he had "preserved the lives of tens of thousands of German mothers' sons"'.[80]

On 23 March the Germans also marched into the German-speaking Memel region, which had belonged to East Prussia until 1919. The Poles saw the 're-incorporating' of the Memel lands as a threat, and responded with a partial mobilization of troops in the Polish Corridor*. On 31 March Britain and France issued guarantees of the security of the Polish state, which made little impression on Hitler.

In the triumphant mood of the hour, the celebration of Hitler's fiftieth

---

*A strip of German territory, between 20 and 70 miles wide, granted to Poland in the Versailles Treaty, 1919. It gave Poland a Baltic Sea outlet. Germans had the right of free access to East Prussia, which was separated from the rest of Germany by the Corridor. It was a constant cause of tension between Poland and Germany, and it was this issue that gave Hitler the pretext for invading Poland in September 1939.

birthday on 20 April 1939 became a truly euphoric festival. According to Kempfler, Hitler now enjoyed 'a victorious aura comparable in the modern era only to those of Napoleon or Bismarck'.[81] Gifts poured in from all over the world. The Japanese government sent an ancient suit of Samurai armour, the Duce a collection of Piranesi engravings, the Arabs a replica of the 'Sword of Islam', and the firm of Märklin their latest model railway.[82] The town of Bayreuth granted funds to build an estate, called 'The Adolf Hitler Appreciation Foundation', for retired Festival personnel. The war intervened before it could be built.

By far the most valuable present came from German industry: a boxed set of Wagner's original scores, presented by the composer to his patron King Ludwig II of Bavaria in thanks for his most generous support. These manuscripts had been acquired by the Wittelsbach Equalization Fund after the end of the monarchy in 1918, and it had now sold them for the very high price of 800,000 Reichsmarks.[83] In detail, the collection consisted of the original scores of the *Feen* (Fairies) in three volumes; *Liebesverbot* (Love Prohibited), two volumes; and *Rienzi*, four volumes; an orchestral sketch for *The Flying Dutchman*; the original fair copies of scores for *Rhinegold* and *The Valkyrie*; the original fair copy of the orchestral sketch of Act III of *Siegfried*; and a copy of the orchestral sketch for *Twilight of the Gods*, made by Hans Richter and several copyists.[84]

Albert Speer described Hitler's reaction: 'He was particularly excited about the orchestral sketch for *Twilight of the Gods*, which he showed to those present, sheet by sheet, with well-informed comments.'[85] For Winifred, though, this gift was more a source of anxiety. At the next opportunity she asked Hitler to deposit the scores in the archive at Wahnfried. But he wanted to keep them near him, because, as he said, to be close to the manuscripts of Richard Wagner meant a great deal to him. In the fullness of time he would hand them over to the archive.[86]

In practically every issue, the *Völkischer Beobachter* praised the superb equipment of the German army, the superiority of the Luftwaffe and the Siegfried Line as 'the most modern defence system in the world'. The outpourings of hatred against Poland became ever more virulent. No newspaper reader could be in doubt about who was to be Hitler's next victim.

On 10 June the Vienna State Opera performed Richard Strauss's opera *Friedenstag* (Day of Peace) in honour of his seventy-fifth birthday. It is set in 1648, in the last days of the Thirty Years War, and climaxes in an apotheosis of peace, where friend and foe stretch out a conciliatory hand to each other. Hitler appeared unannounced at this performance, to cast his eye over the stage and costume designs of his protégé Ulrich Roller. He used the occasion to project himself as a 'Prince of Peace'.

The supporting programme for the 1939 Festival, organized by the *Gau* administration, was characterized by contradictory messages about war and peace. On 22 July the 42nd Infantry Regiment, stationed in Bayreuth, pitched its 'Peace Camp' on the heights at Hollfeld. On the other hand, on 24 July the National Socialist Teachers' League, with much propagandizing, opened an exhibition with the title 'Forwards! 1914–18: Fighters and Comrades in the World War'. It featured pictures of the front, glorifying the deeds and sufferings of German soldiers in the war.

Any reading of newspapers was calculated to raise the level of anxiety. Under the heading 'Important Developments of the Day', there were reports of air-raid precaution exercises in Berlin and its environs, and – by way of reassurance – it was stressed that every one of the 100,000 dwellings in Berlin had an air-raid warden and a fire watch at the ready. Preparations for a possible air raid had been made 'down to the last detail'.[87]

After his visit to Memel, Hitler arrived in Bayreuth on the evening of 24 July. For the opening on 25 July he appeared, not in his usual tails, but in Party uniform, which caused some surprise and a feeling that something out of the ordinary might be in the offing. For the first time, the fanfares from the balcony of the Festival Theatre, summoning the guests to the performance, were sounded by the Führer's faithful SS bodyguard unit, recently christened 'Leibstandarte-SS Adolf Hitler'.

The *Völkischer Beobachter*, its front page featuring Winifred welcoming Hitler to Bayreuth, carried a headline proclaiming a new horror story from Poland: 'Ethnic Germans Sent to Central Poland for Forced Labour'.

That year the Festival opened with *The Flying Dutchman*. It had last been in the programme on 2 August 1914, when it had been cancelled because of the outbreak of war. Emil Preetorius said in retrospect: 'And then the whole of Bayreuth had a premonition that another world war was about to break out.'[88]

The star conductor of this Festival was Victor De Sabata, Toscanini's successor as head of La Scala, Milan. Hitler had seen him in action in 1937 in a Berlin guest appearance conducting Verdi's *Aida*, and he had probably suggested De Sabata for Bayreuth, especially as engaging him would be a mark of German–Italian friendship. The *Bayerische Ostmark* commented: 'Although De Sabata lays no particular stress on it, we feel in this commitment the spiritual and therefore racial affinity between two great nations and their peoples.'[89]

At the invitation of the Leaders of Women in the Reich, a guest at the Festival was the Japanese woman, Yayoi Yoshioka.* The Bayreuth press published articles paying tribute to Japan, which through shrewd policies 'had made itself master of the whole eastern part of the Chinese empire, with its almost inexhaustible supply of raw materials. Not from a lust for conquest, but from shortage of territory . . . to feed its population, increasing yearly by a million.'[90]

The Goebbels couple provided the stuff of gossip. Magda Goebbels was tired of her husband's endless affairs, and wanted a divorce in order to be able to marry Karl Hanke, Secretary of State at the Propaganda Ministry. However, Hitler would not give his permission and required them to appear together in public. In Bayreuth, for the sake of the press and to put on a show of marital harmony, Frau Goebbels was obliged to sit between Hitler and Winifred in the middle box for *Tristan and Isolde*. Speer saw her during the interval, 'a broken woman, sobbing helplessly in the corner of a reception room, while Hitler and Goebbels greeted the crowd from the window and did their best to ignore this painful scene'.[91] Winifred did her bit by giving the couple a double room, 'so that at least in Bayreuth they have to sleep together'.[92]

Germaine Lubin sang Isolde in place of Frida Leider. Hitler was once again so thrilled with her that in the interval he asked her to choose any gift she wanted. She declined the offer. 'No, never, nothing for myself,' she replied loudly in the crowded refreshment room, 'but – give all of us peace!'[93]

The heightened level of activity around the sealed-off Siegfried House told the Wagners just how tense the political atmosphere was. Military men, ministers and aides came and went until late into the night; maps were being pored over in the Garden Room. The younger members of the family pricked up their ears. When Verena picked up the mysterious word 'Lysagora', Wieland reached for the encyclopaedia and located a place in Poland. The Wagner family became more uneasy than ever. Wolfgang, given a few weeks' leave from military service to be at the Festival, was due to return to his unit soon. And it was stationed on the Polish border.[94]

---

*The founder of the Tokyo Women's Medical College; born in Shizuoka in 1900, she devoted her life to women's medical education.

The headlines on 31 July, intended to be reassuring, made clear how serious the situation was: 'New World Record for German Bombers – 2,000 km at 501 km.p.h. – More Proud Proof of Luftwaffe's Prowess'. Winifred's anxieties were increased by the American Wagnerian Lady Mabel Dunn, a friend of Eleanor Roosevelt's, who concluded from her knowledge of the American economy that Germany's chances of winning a war were slim if America came to the aid of Britain, which she was sure would be the case. She had written to tell Hitler this several times, said Lady Dunn, but never received a reply.[95]

Hitler attended performances every day, driving through the cheering crowds lining his route and acting as though nothing mattered to him but Wagner. He patted infants affably, was photographed 'and appeared extremely jovial', as Kempfler reported.[96] He listened with obvious pleasure to Verena's story from Italy; she had been in Rome to learn Italian, and from the window of her language school she had watched the *bersaglieri* during a military parade. The riflemen had repeatedly doubled back all the way round the Victor Emmanuel Monument at their traditional trotting pace, and then rejoined the parade. Genially, Hitler remarked that this was a wonderful observation. Really, only female military attachés ought to be deployed, he said.[97]

But when Verena told him she wanted to study medicine, Hitler did not approve. He warned the delicate eighteen-year-old that she would develop 'male characteristics' if she did so. He asked, 'Do you want to become like Klara Zetkin [the famous Communist Party Member of Parliament during the Weimar Republic]?' Then he once again showed off his talent as a mimic, calling out parliamentary exclamations in Verena's very high, rather squeaky voice, 'Hear, hear!' and the like, making his listeners laugh.[98] With a sure touch, he conveyed a sense of security and calm.

On 30 July, during the interval of *The Valkyrie*, Hitler bestowed upon the director of the Festival the Cross of Honour for Mothers of Numerous Progeny in bronze, the appropriate recognition for raising four 'genetically sound' children 'of German blood'.

In Bayreuth there was also diplomatic activity to try to achieve an understanding between Germany and Britain. Hitler's press chief, Otto Dietrich, had invited over the British newspaper publisher Lord Kemsley, to negotiate an exchange of articles between German and British newspapers. Dietrich arranged an hour-long meeting between Kemsley and Hitler in Siegfried's villa. When Kemsley expressed his concerns about European peace, Hitler replied coldly that it all depended on Britain.[99] Goebbels laid on a luxurious lunch in Bayreuth for the British press mogul Lord Rothermere.

On 29 July the pro-German British ambassador, Sir Nevile Henderson, arrived as a guest of the Festival, with the self-prescribed aim of making personal contact with Hitler and establishing a consensus between Britain and Germany. Winifred, Tietjen and Kempfler were only too happy to support this initiative. But Hitler chose precisely this moment to interrupt his stay, and flew off with Ribbentrop to Saarbrücken to observe troop manoeuvres demonstrating the 'invincibility' of the Siegfried Line. To stop Henderson from leaving and keep him occupied until Hitler's return, Winifred and Kempfler organized a leisure programme for him, including trout fishing in Berneck. Henderson stayed on, convinced as he was 'that the prevention of war was my mission'.[100]

On 30 July, after Hitler's return and before a performance of *The Valkyrie*, Stassen witnessed a scene which unfolded before him. (It has to be said, however, that his account of it was not recorded until 1946, when he appeared as a defence witness for Tietjen at a de-nazification hearing, and unwarrantably enhanced Tietjen's role in the story.) In the early afternoon before the performance, Tietjen had said in Henderson's presence, 'This is the great opportunity to secure peace', appealing to Winifred to go to Hitler in Siegfried's house, and ask him to agree to meet the ambassador. 'Frau Wagner did go over, but came back saying that Hitler had rejected her proposal abruptly. Tietjen, very agitated, pleaded with Frau Wagner to try once more straight away, which she did, despite her brusque reception. But she came back very depressed from Hitler, who, she said, had turned her away even more abruptly than the first time.' Then Winifred had dared to make a third attempt. Would Hitler at least agree to let the ambassador sit next to him in his box that evening,[101] which, in Winifred's words, 'would be welcomed by the whole world as a gesture of friendship'? But Hitler declined because 'at a time like this he must not compromise himself'.[102]

The scenario was similar to that of the year before, when Czechoslovakia was the target, but this time Hitler was not going to expose himself to any new British peacemaking efforts. He refused to receive Henderson. All the ambassador achieved was to see Hitler at a distance in the opera house, hear a 'marvellous performance' of *The Valkyrie* and make the acquaintance of Winifred, for whom he had a high regard.[103]

Hitler's press chief, Dietrich, wrote that 'Hardly anybody in Germany thought it possible that Hitler could fail to master this situation, after he had so often proved his political skill and gained so much trust. Nobody believed he would let it go as far as a war with Britain.'[104] Winifred, too, went on believing in Hitler's oft-avowed love of peace.

The newspapers saw a chance to link the *Siegfried* production with praise of Hitler, 'who forged anew the broken sword of his people, and gave them back their honour and their belief in their own strength and their own worth', to quote the *Bayreuther Tagblatt*. 'The glorious figure of Siegfried . . . was marvellously brought to life by Max Lorenz . . . What a contrast between the glowing, clean-limbed splendour of this Siegfried, and the crumpled, dwarfish figure of the evil, stupid, covetous Mime!' Siegfried and Mime symbolized 'the two conflicting worlds, the bright world of free heroism, and the sinister realm of selfish, cowardly evil'.[105]

Hitler did finally show signs of nervousness – during the *Twilight of the Gods*, when the horse that had played Grane for years died after the first act. Hitler had been present in 1925 when the stage steed kicked out, injuring the Siegfried of the day, breaking a stagehand's ankle and, to top it all, ruining Brünnhilde's leap into the flames.[106] Afraid that an inexperienced substitute mount might jump into the orchestra pit, Hitler wanted the opera to continue horseless. Tietjen, however, thought Grane absolutely indispensable, and put a new, hastily located horse on the stage. Kempfler says that Hitler was clearly uneasy: 'Everybody involved, especially him, was glad when Grane plunged into the flames with Brünnhilde.'[107]

Unusually, after the *Twilight of the Gods*, at about eleven o'clock on the evening of 2 August, Hitler took part in a political event, although he had always attended the Festival in a purely private capacity. The military tattoo for the 'Day of the German Forces' commemorated the twenty-fifth anniversary of the outbreak of the World War, and was performed by the Bayreuth Infantry Regiment.

At the artists' reception in Wahnfried, as everywhere, there was much talk about the possibility of war, especially when the news filtered through that petrol stations were being allowed to sell only up to five litres. Hitler urged calm: the storage tanks were just being converted to take synthetic fuel, and 'it would all be over in a few weeks'. Kempfler says that, in front of a large circle of guests, the singer Marta Fuchs asked Hitler in her Swabian dialect, 'Is that right, my Führer, you ain't goin' to make war?' To which Hitler replied with a smile, 'You can believe me, Frau Fuchs, there will be no war.' 'For my part,' says Kempfler, 'I did believe him, and went around telling . . . everyone I knew that I had it from Hitler personally, there wasn't going to be a war.'[108]

In Wahnfried on his last day at Bayreuth, 3 August 1939, Hitler met up with the friend of his youth, August Kubizek, whom he had invited to the Festival. Kubizek was a trained musician, and had introduced the young Hitler to Wagner during his days in Linz. In 1908 the two young men had shared a gloomy, bug-ridden back room in Vienna.[109] In April 1938, in Linz after the *Anschluss*, they had seen each other again for the first time in nearly thirty years. The 'Führer of the Greater German Reich', as he now was, made a life-long dream come true for the Wagner enthusiast by inviting him to Bayreuth. Kubizek had once dreamed of a great career in music and had worked hard to finish his studies, but he had been thrown off course when badly injured in the war. He was living in modest circumstances, working for a local authority in Upper Austria. Married to a violinist, he had three musical sons.

Hitler's adjutant Julius Schaub led the shy, slight man into the hall at Wahnfried,

> where there were a good many people I knew from Linz, or from pictures in magazines. There was Frau Wagner in lively conversation with Reich Minister Rudolf Hess. SS General Wilhelm Brückner was talking to Herr von Neurath and some army generals. Altogether, there were quite a few military people in the room, and it struck me in a flash that the situation was very tense, especially with regard to Poland, and that there was talk of a military solution. I felt very out of place in this high-tension atmosphere.[110]

Schaub guided him to Hitler, in another room, and shut the door behind him.

'With a beaming smile,' says Kubizek, 'he comes towards me. Nothing about him betrays the terrible responsibility resting on his shoulders . . . He reflects the happy atmosphere radiated by Bayreuth . . . This affectionate welcome in such a hallowed place moved me so deeply that I could hardly speak.' Hitler did not address him with the old familiar 'du', or as 'Gustl', but as 'Herr Kubizek'. The latter called him 'my Führer'. They talked about the Festival, and about the Wagner performances of their youth in Linz and Vienna. Hitler spoke about his desire to make Wagner's work 'accessible to as many sections of the German people as possible', adding that that year he had invited to Bayreuth 'six thousand people . . . who would otherwise never have had the chance to visit the Festival'. And, he added, 'now I've got you here as a witness, Kubizek – the only one who was there when, as a poor, unknown young man, I was developing these ideas for the first time'.

Finally, Kubizek laid a whole pack of Hitler photos ('I thought of the people at home, and pulled myself together') in front of Hitler for signing. Putting on his glasses, he did so, while Kubizek hastened to dry the ink neatly with a blotter.

Then Hitler took his old friend to Wagner's grave, a gesture romantically embellished by Kubizek: 'He took my hand in his. I felt how moved he was.' Kubizek seemed 'to feel the wings of eternity beating'. Hitler went on to show him around Villa Wahnfried, with Wieland opening up the individual rooms for them, and jokily presented Kubizek to Winifred: 'This is Herr Kubizek. He's a member of your League of German Women. Isn't that nice!' (Kubizek was wearing the badge of the Linz branch of the Richard Wagner League of German Women, and had been deputed to represent this organization in Bayreuth.)

Hitler at this point once again recited the all-too-familiar story of how he had seen *Rienzi* for the first time with Kubizek in Linz. He now assigned to the experience of thirty years earlier a special place in history: 'It was at that moment that it all began.' Rienzi sings, 'But if you choose me as the protector/ of the people's given rights, /then you may look back upon your forebears,/ and see me as the people's tribune!' To which the assembled people reply, 'Rienzi, hail to you, tribune of the people . . .'

The wealth of meaning Hitler gave to the short phrase 'It began at that moment!' shows how much he felt the need, precisely here in Wahnfried, to testify that Wagner had pointed the way for him to his political vocation. This testimony in the presence of the witness, Kubizek, in the house of the Master, and before Winifred, the head of the family, was a kind of self-consecration preceding a momentous event. It resembled his first visit to Wagner's grave before the putsch attempt of 1923. Now, in 1939, Hitler knew that he would soon be leading 'his people' into a war.

The opera *Rienzi*, an early work not adopted by Wagner for the Festival repertoire, always had a special significance for Hitler. The lively overture was played as the prelude to the Nuremberg rally. Just the year before, in Bayreuth, Robert Ley had tried to persuade Hitler to substitute a modern composition for the *Rienzi* overture: 'The National Socialist world-view should be expressed in music, too.' Neither Hitler nor Winifred was convinced. Ley would not give in, however, so on a performance-free day they drove to an empty Luitpold Hall in Nuremberg to evaluate, for two hours, Ley's suggested replacements, played by a symphony orchestra. After a long silence Hitler just said briefly, 'Yesterday I expressed a wish to hear the *Rienzi* overture played on this occasion, too.'

It was Ley's turn to hear the story about *Rienzi* in Linz:

You know, Ley, it's not accidental that the Party Rally always opens with the overture from Rienzi. It's not just a musical question. By invoking the splendours of the Imperial past, this son of a small inn-keeper succeeds, at 24 years of age, in persuading the Roman people to drive out the corrupt Senate. It was while listening as a young man to this divinely blessed music in the theatre in Linz that the inspiration came to me that I was likewise destined to unite the German Reich and make it great.[111]

Hitler asked Winifred to send Bayreuth tickets to Kubizek every year from then on, specifically for the performances that he himself would be attending. 'I'd like to have you here with me always,' he told Kubizek, who was moved to tears, as he waved him off from the gate of Wahnfried.

Audiences began to thin out towards the end of the Festival because of the persistent rumours of impending war. Germaine Lubin left for Paris, cancelling her last appearance. Winifred had great difficulty in finding a stand-in for the final performance of *Tristan*. Gauleiter Wächtler helped to fill the empty rows by inviting to Bayreuth all the *Gau* officials of the National Socialist Teachers' League. That was still not enough, so Bodo Lafferentz bought tickets for the KdF.

The organization invited a hundred Italian workers, on holiday from Cremona, to come to *The Flying Dutchman*. The only comment they made in interviews was that they were not used to sitting still for so long.[112] Thirty-one teachers from Bulgaria, a country allied to Germany, were the lucky recipients of tickets for *Parsifal*; they were taking part in a ten-day German–Bulgarian gathering in Bayreuth.

Torn between hope and fear, on 24 August Winifred said goodbye to Wolfgang, who had to return to barracks immediately after the Festival. His company was then sent to Rosenberg in Upper Silesia, close to the Polish border.

FRIEDELIND'S CONVERSION

During this period, when it was feared that the frontiers might be closed at any time, Friedelind, Daniela and Eva were not in Bayreuth, but at the Lucerne Festival, which had become the political and musical counterweight to Bayreuth now that Salzburg had been 'brought into line' by the Nazis. In Winifred's view, Toscanini, Rachmaninov, Vladimir Horowitz, Pablo Casals and Bronislaw Huberman made the Lucerne Festival weeks into 'anti-German cultural events, fostering . . . Jews and émigrés'.[113]

While her aunts made their way with all possible haste back to Bayreuth, Friedelind stayed in Switzerland. In the two years she had by then spent abroad, she had undergone a fundamental transformation. Arriving in England in 1936, the eighteen-year-old Hitler enthusiast complained that as a 'good German' she was not having an easy time of it among the 'very closed-minded islanders', and had tried to win them over to Hitler: 'It's quite good to tell people the truth about Hitler and the new Germany – although it's difficult to clear all that hate propaganda out of their minds.'[114]

As a daughter of the house of Wagner, she still had all the Bayreuth prejudices. After attending an Albert Hall concert starring the black baritone Paul Robeson, she remarked, 'perhaps I'm too over-sensitive [sic] – but it cost me a great effort to see out the afternoon and keep looking at the stage; no race is as repugnant to me as the Negroes. And what's more, there was a half-breed Negro piano accompanist . . . I couldn't even bring myself to applaud, lovely as so much of it was!' Her verdict on the Jews also reflected family attitudes, but she thought that 'the Jewish element' did not really draw attention to itself in London, 'I mean in the theatre – though elsewhere, only too obviously! . . . There's no doubt that there are plenty around, but they don't have a chance to make themselves unbearable with modern kitsch, as they do everywhere else in the world.'[115]

But then, after a rehearsal of Beethoven's Ninth in Lucerne under Toscanini, she enthused: 'sacred art: it's the only bridge, and international in the most ideal sense! And so, through all these days, we really were an Island of the Blessed – it didn't bother me any more whether anyone was Jewish or whatever – it is in unity that you find yourself – when you share a great, the greatest experience!' Under Toscanini, even the 'most dreadful Negro music became something magnificent!'[116]

In London as in Switzerland, Friedelind heard about the sufferings of exiled artists, and what they had gone through in Germany. For all her blunt exterior, she was sensitive, with a highly developed sense of fair play. She took up the cause of the persecuted and the exiled, who gave her generous backing in England. She lived for a while with Berta Geissmar, and helped her with correspondence at Covent Garden. Winifred found this astonishing: 'What a funny child! She won't do it for Bayreuth or her mother, but she works voluntarily for this Jewess!!!'[117]

In Toscanini's circles Friedelind met many Jews, including his son-in-law, the pianist Horowitz, whom she greatly admired. She developed a great liking for Lady Cholmondeley. Related to the Rothschilds, and a devotee of Toscanini, she maintained an artistic salon in London, and aided many exiles, Friedelind included.

Those few top German artists, such as Frida Leider, who were sent by Goebbels to make guest appearances abroad, made a very unhappy impression. Friedelind reported that

Frida looked ill, her radiant vitality was dimmed. I asked her not to go back to Germany, to save herself while she still could, but she just shrugged her shoulders, and replied that her mother and everything she had built up in a lifetime were in Germany, her house, all the money she had saved up. She was not a young singer any more, no longer young enough to make a new start without a penny.[118]

German artists abroad had financial problems, in any case, because the Propaganda Ministry not only cancelled all contracts, but also withheld the better part of all fees.

From 1939 onwards Friedelind, now living in Tribschen near Lucerne, avoided all contact with Wahnfried, and wrote only to her aunts. At a loss, Winifred lamented to her sister-in-law Daniela: 'And I, her mother (!) don't even know her address.'[119] The girl did nothing about Winifred's birthday in June, and did not attend the rehearsals or the Festival. In great agitation, while the Festival was still in progress and the rumours of war were mounting, Winifred sent eighteen-year-old Verena to Switzerland with a mission to persuade her sister to come home at once. She did not want Verena to travel alone, so she consented to her being accompanied by her friend, the twenty-year-old Bayreuth medical student Philipp Hausser. In their haste, no one was deterred by the fact that the blond, good-looking Hausser was a so-called 'half-breed of the second degree'.

The two sisters had always been very close to each other, and they spent two days together in the idyllic setting of Tribschen on Lake Lucerne. Friedelind declared that she was not mad enough to go back to a country where her friends lived in fear and were being arrested. She told her mother via Verena that she should quickly get as much money out of Germany as possible for safe-keeping abroad, and that applied especially to the Wagner family's valuables, above all the autographs. When Verena enquired anxiously how Friedelind would manage to live abroad when Wahnfried could no longer send her any money, Friedelind replied simply that she had friends. Besides, she could give talks. The family was not to worry about her. She proudly invoked Richard Wagner as her model of a political fugitive; it was to Zurich that he had once come, a wanted man. When they parted, she gave her sister a watch, vainly expressing the hope that Verena would join her.

With her mission unaccomplished, her thoughts depressed, Verena returned to Bayreuth – and then had to leave for Berlin, to report to Hitler personally in the Reich Chancellery. It seems that Hitler listened to the girl for a long time in silence, a situation that had never occurred before.[120]

On 20 August Friedelind sent her mother from Tribschen, by registered post, a long letter full of recriminations, especially about her relationship with Tietjen. Winifred was hurt because instead of 'parental home' her daughter constantly referred to her 'paternal home'; and she refused to meet her mother. Winifred replied that Friedelind had false friends, as Max Lorenz had told her, 'and I must try to get you back home again'.[121]

On 23 August, to universal surprise, Ribbentrop concluded the Russo–German friendship and non-aggression pact. On 25 August Great Britain signed an agreement to support Poland. The hate campaign of the Goebbels press against the Poles became ever more vicious. On 26 August, for example, the headline read: 'Terrible Mass Murder near Bielitz and Lodz: Price Placed on German Heads'. Bayreuth prepared itself to receive some 10,000 refugees.

Christian Ebersberger, an intimate of the Wagner family, recalled that 'While the fanfares were sounding for the last time for *Parsifal*, the heavy tanks were already rolling along the autobahn. The Bayreuth colleagues said their farewells in a mood of the deepest gloom; would they ever see each other again?'[122]

Until 30 August, Ambassador Henderson in Berlin fought to achieve a peaceful solution. On 1 September war began with the German attack on Poland, and in a Reichstag speech Hitler blamed the Polish government:

'Now, since 5.45 this morning, we have been returning fire! And from now on, bomb will be repaid with bomb! If you fight with poison, we will fight you with poison gas.' On the same day Danzig's 'restoration' to 'Greater Germany' was proclaimed. The German population was not told that German troops, far from 'returning fire', had invaded Poland. Listening to foreign radio stations was forbidden on pain of severe punishment. Foreign newspapers were confiscated at the frontier.

The *Neue Zürcher Zeitung* (New Zurich Newspaper) recorded that the German population 'shows not a trace of war fever . . . by contrast, there is an admittedly vague, and scarcely credible, hope that Britain might still opt for non-intervention'.[123] This hope, shared by Winifred, was in vain. The patience of Britain and France was exhausted. Fulfilling their treaty with Poland, on 3 September they both declared war on the German Reich. This came as a shock to the Germans, and also to Hitler.

She, too, was surprised by the outbreak of war, asserted Winifred, 'like everybody else who had built their faith in Hitler upon the love of peace that he constantly proclaimed . . . His great reconstruction programme of social renewal for the good of the wider population, as well as his promotion of art and the theatre and his long-term cultural building project, were for me always a broadly based proof of his peaceful intentions.'[124] She was still saying in 1975, 'every one of us regretted the outbreak of war. Including every National Socialist. I do not believe that we were all fanatical war-mongers . . . no reasonable person could help seeing that, with our enemies' superior numbers, surrounding Germany . . . that this small country was not viable in the long run, that there was bound to be a disaster.'[125] Friedelind must have picked up a similar impression from her mother, because she wrote in September 1939 to the conductor Erich Kleiber, who had fled to Buenos Aires, that people in Germany were expecting 'a revolution', and that Winifred was 'no longer so enthusiastically pro-Adolf'.[126]

Kempfler identified 'a deep depression everywhere' as the 'mood of the population and of the soldiers'. Those who had been through the First World War were particularly shaken: 'Food rationing and clothing coupons were no novelty for us, but we also remembered how long the hunger and deprivation had lasted.'[127]

Wolfgang, nineteen, was in Poland with the army. Eighteen-year-old Verena volunteered as a nurse with the Red Cross. Cosima's Italian grandson Count Gilberto Gravina joined the German side, as he had in the First World War, whereupon his English wife 'made off', with their three sons, 'because she did not want to be married to somebody who was fighting against her mother country'.[128] Twenty-five-year-old Unity Mitford, despairing, put a bullet in her head in the English Garden (Park) in Munich. She survived, badly injured, and was taken back to England. Twenty-two-year-old Wieland went on living his life as usual, concentrating on his painting. According to Winifred, he belonged, 'with 24 other young men, to the select group whom Adolf Hitler wished at all costs to preserve from a hero's death, and hence personally exempted from conscription'.[129] Hitler had deputed Winifred to draw up this list of the 'divinely blessed', following his own suggestions. Aside from Wieland, it included the tenor Peter Anders, the composer Gottfried Müller and the stage designer Ulrich Roller.[130]

The outbreak of war prevented Germans who were abroad from returning; Friedelind, in Switzerland, was one; another was Lotte Bechstein, who happened to be with the firm's London branch at the time. As an enemy alien, she was deported with many other fellow-countrymen to a detention camp on the Isle of Man, and stayed in captivity for five years, until Hitler repatriated some British prisoners of war in return for her release in 1944.[131]

In Germany, drastic tax rises were imposed as a 'sacrifice' for the financing of the war effort, and there was a good deal of requisitioning, of cars for example. Public transport became limited. Meat and coffee rations were reduced. People with purely ornamental gardens had to dig them up to grow fruit and vegetables, since there was no longer any place for 'selfish hobbies', that is, cultivating flowers. From then on, all aspects of life were dominated by the war.

CHAPTER 12

Wartime Festivals

(1940–42)

The first news from Wolfgang on the Polish front came on 3 September 1939 from Czestochowa, reporting a rapid advance. Winifred gave his army post office number to friends, asking them to send parcels and letters.[1]

On 15 September Wolfgang was badly wounded. Winifred wrote: 'He was out on patrol with 8 others. They came under attack, he was wounded, and 3 of them were taken prisoner. After two days a Polish officer ordered that the wounded and the POWs should be left behind, so as not to hold up their own retreat. So he has had a tough time – but his bad luck turned out to be lucky for him, too.'[2] A bullet had gone through his hand, splintering the bone and damaging an artery. He also had a flesh wound in the thigh, from which he had lost much blood. He was taken by air to Breslau and from there to the military hospital at Liegnitz. He and another soldier were 'the very first wounded of the war, and as a result attracted special attention'. When his wounds became infected, he was transferred to the Charité hospital in Berlin.[3] There he was operated on by the most famous surgeon in Germany, Ferdinand Sauerbruch. Winifred stayed in Berlin for a while to be near her son, and organized people to visit him as he got better. Hitler appeared twice at Wolfgang's bedside.

Winifred showed no sign of weakness in her letters to Friedelind. In

Wolfgang's company '4 Iron Crosses had been awarded. 6 men have been killed so far.'[4] Friedelind sent a 'packet of luxury chocolates' from Switzerland, but did not answer her mother's letter. Undeterred, Winifred continued to keep her daughter up to date: Wolfgang's wound was suppurating badly; he was feverish and needed blood transfusions. Hitler had sent his doctor, Karl Brandt, to the hospital to provide constant information about Wolfgang's condition.[5]

Winifred appealed once more to Friedelind to show solidarity in wartime: 'I am extremely sorry that in this difficult hour of destiny you can see fit to place yourself outside the family and outside the national community.' She stressed that 'whatever has happened in the past is insignificant compared to what we have to put up with now, and this really is the time for you to be with your family and at your mother's side'.[6] That was not the right tone to take with Friedelind. Living abroad, she had access to quite different information about the war, and knew perfectly well that it was purely a war of aggression. Much later, Winifred summarized Friedelind's view at that time: 'You will see where your Hitler is taking you – into the abyss, to your ruin.' Almost eighty by then, Winifred noted that 'unfortunately, she was right about that, too'.[7]

On 27 September, after a desperate but hopeless defence, Warsaw fell. In accordance with the secret Soviet–German agreement, the USSR had already marched into eastern Poland. There was no longer a Polish state. Following his 'lightning victory', Hitler made a 'peace offer' to the western powers, which was much talked up in all the German papers. He emphasized once more that the German Reich had now achieved all its aims, and required the allies to recognize his act of pillage. However, they declined to do so. On 12 October Hans Frank became governor general of all the Polish territories not incorporated into the German Reich, the so-called 'Gouvernement Général', ultimately containing 12 million people dispossessed of their rights. He was accountable directly to Hitler, and had his seat in the old citadel of the Polish kings, the Vavel. The hunting down of Polish Jews began.

It took Friedelind until Christmas 1939 finally to send a letter. Her mother answered at length, requesting her, out of consideration for her siblings, 'at least to cultivate these blood-ties somewhat more, and more lovingly, than in the past year'. She went on: 'Everything is fantastically well organized. We're familiar with the rationing system from the [First] World War, and then we've got the 100-points clothing card, to ensure fair shares for all. So everybody is satisfied because he can be absolutely sure of getting promptly what is due to him.'[8]

Shortly before, she had asked an affluent woman friend not only for Christmas supplies of liqueur and French cognac, but above all for paper handkerchiefs, sanitary towels and cotton-wool.[9] Under these circumstances, Hitler's 1939 Christmas present, a kilo of real coffee, was a rare treat.[10] The gift came from a consignment of forty sacks of coffee sent by the Imam of the Yemen to the Führer, whom he admired; it was distributed by Hitler to his closest friends.

When Friedelind announced that she would like to emigrate to America, Winifred begged her to come back to Bayreuth, 'because of course . . . once you're over there, it's going to be extremely difficult for you to get home again, if you come back at all'. Would she not want to say goodbye to her aunts? For 'at their age it's uncertain how many years they've got left'. Furthermore, 'Whoever it was that told you that great nonsense about being locked up in an insane asylum if you come home, belongs in one himself.' She would do everything she could to get a visa for Switzerland, in spite of the closed border, 'so that I can come and see you once more before you leave'.[11] Wieland wrote to his sister in January 1940 that he had to accept that she did not want to 'find her way home': 'the influence of your Jewish "friends" is no doubt too powerful to allow you to get your ideas straight.'[12]

Her aunts, too, implored Friedelind to return, and asked for help from Adolf Zinsstag in Basel, but he replied only that this was 'completely point-less' as 'Friedelind has a will of iron when it comes to deciding her own fate and future. We should respect her for the courage she has shown in rebelling against everything that made her turn her back on the Third Reich.' She was in good hands in Tribschen, and had become 'so attached to our Swiss dem-ocratic way of life that it is impossible for her ever again to accept the dictatorial control of ideas and conscience back home'.[13]

To obtain her travel permit, Winifred had to see Himmler personally, at Gestapo headquarters in Berlin. Himmler remarked that he had read all the letters from Friedelind to her aunts, as well as to her mother; in other words, they had been intercepted. It was imperative that the girl should return to Germany: 'If she won't do so voluntarily, then we'll have to help her.'[14] Winifred knew full well how effectively the Gestapo could operate, even on neutral soil.

She booked two rooms in a top Zurich hotel, the Baur au Lac, and asked her daughter to meet her there on 9 February.[15] Their two days together cul-minated in a tempestuous row, following Winifred's ever more insistent attempts to persuade her daughter to come home. Himmler's threats were brought to bear; Friedelind must stop her public 'prattle against Hitler' because 'if you don't consent, then you'll be dragged away by force and held in a safe place'. And then, according to Friedelind, her mother said, 'And if you won't listen, the order will go out for you to be exterminated and eradi-cated at the first opportunity.'[16] Those were Himmler's words, and they had to be taken extremely seriously.

All Winifred's fear for her daughter came out in her fury. Friedelind simply would not see that she was in mortal danger, and was endangering the family besides. Even as her train pulled out, she was still pleading with her daugh-ter, 'with her voice breaking': 'Come home, Mausi! Please come. I need you!'[17] Winifred had to go straight to Berlin to report to Himmler.

However, it appears to be quite untrue that the encounter ended in con-flict, as Friedelind wrote in her book, since a letter to her mother of 29 February 1940 thanked Winifred 'for taking the trouble to travel all that way. But it was worth it, wasn't it?' She had not yet made up her mind ('who knows how things will be in a few weeks' time!'), and she promised, 'I won't do anything rash! And of course I'm just as concerned to stay in touch with you at home.' She ended the letter with the greeting: 'All good wishes and love to you all. Heartfelt thanks for everything, love, your Mausi.'[18]

On 18 March the President of the City of Lucerne informed the two aunts that 'Fräulein Friedelind' had left Lucerne on 1 March. 'Destination, America. There's nothing we can do except wish her well with all our hearts, and be patient.' Meanwhile, in fact, Friedelind was not in the USA, but in London.[19] Before setting off, she had sent a parcel to Bayreuth containing chocolate and salami.[20]

On 27 March Winifred urgently asked the Lucerne City President for 'information about the whereabouts of my daughter. Rumours have reached me that she has gone away.' Surely Friedelind had left a forwarding address, or had de-registered with the police? 'You will understand that in these trou-bled times it is disturbing for me not to know where my child is, how she got there etc.'[21]

The uncertainty ended at the beginning of May. At Hitler's request, Martin Bormann informed Winifred that Friedelind had been interned as an enemy alien on the Isle of Man, and had been making some very unpleasant revelations to the press. Bormann said, 'Friedelind must not come back to Germany; otherwise I will be obliged to take her before the People's Court.'[22]

Just how dangerous this affair was (it was kept secret in Germany) is shown by Goebbels's diary; for example, the entry for 4 May 1940: 'That fat little Wagner girl has been putting her revelations about the Führer in writing in London. The little wretch! This could get a bit embarrassing.' On 5 May he wrote: 'The Führer has been telling Wieland Wagner about his nice little sister. It's a serious scandal, what that stupid girl has been up to.' And on 10 May:

> The fat Wagner girl has published her first report against the Führer in the London press; a dirty business. Obviously trying to incite Italy against us. The Führer's views on Mussolini, calculated to put the Duce in a rage. An English propagandist has been collaborating with her. This fat wretch has committed out-and-out treason. She's been extremely badly brought up. Revolting!

Friedelind had relayed a crude version of Hitler's casual remarks about Mussolini, made at lunch in the Reich Chancellery on 4 August 1936. She had also embellished them, and made fun of the Führer personally. Alongside the 'virile' Mussolini, Hitler had seemed like 'an old maid'. On his return visit to Italy, Hitler had behaved awkwardly, like 'a badly brought-up infant', and Mussolini had had to 'play nursemaid to him'. And, Friedelind claimed, 'his own people were "fed up to the back teeth" with Hitler'.[23]

She also passed on a story supposedly told by Hitler around the fireside at Wahnfried. He had delayed the execution of a sex murderer until he could be lured into revealing the chemical formula for a deadly poison that left no trace. The prisoner had carried out the uncomplicated production process four times; the Gestapo had tried out the poison first on animals, then on terminally ill patients, and finally on healthy convicts. Autopsies had indeed shown no trace of the poison. The story shocked the Wagner children.[24] British propaganda made use of this tale, and a degree of scepticism is therefore in order. Verena has no recollection of any such anecdote.

Wahnfried reacted to Friedelind's article with consternation and fear of the consequences. Winifred was well aware that the usual way of silencing family members abroad was to arrest their relatives in Germany: 'If we had been anybody but the Wagner family, we would have gone straight to a concentration camp. There's no doubt about it.'[25]

Goebbels says that Hitler was 'shaken by the base behaviour of Friedelind Wagner. He held her aunts responsible . . . A traitor.'[26] Winifred's enemies in the Party had been handed a powerful weapon. Brandt reported that

> it was inevitable that Frau Wagner was to an extent implicated in the attitude to Hitler of her daughter Friedelind, living abroad. Martin Bormann made no secret of the fact that the Wagner girl's attitude was only possible because of the children's liberal upbringing in Wahnfried. It almost goes without saying that there were also sharply critical references to Frau Wagner's family ties in England.[27]

When Winifred was invited to a discussion with Himmler in his private apartment in Berlin, she used the imminence of the Festival as an excuse to avoid the interview, and sent Verena instead. Her hope was that the 'SS Reich Führer' could not be so severe with the girl. Himmler received Verena informally, even joking with her, and reminding her how in 1928 she had hauled him around in a hand-cart for 10 pfennigs, in the garden at Wahnfried. Then, producing newspaper cuttings, he read out quotations from Friedelind, including the sentence, 'That swine Himmler should be strung up from the nearest lamp-post.'

In that tricky moment, said Verena later, the only thing she could think of was to make light of it. At any rate, she said casually, 'Reich Führer, that would be a crazy sight!' Himmler was not much inclined to appreciate the joke, and pointed out forcefully that Friedelind would be arrested as a traitor the moment she stepped on to German soil. Verena assured him that Friedelind would certainly not be returning to Germany until the war was over.[28] The fear of further remarks by Friedelind overshadowed life in Wahnfried from then on. Winifred later held that this affair was the reason for 'the worsening of relations between Hitler and the Wagner household'.[29]

Because of her important contribution to the war effort, Friedelind was released from internment camp in Britain and, with special permission from Churchill, allowed to travel to Buenos Aires in March 1941. There, Toscanini arranged a visa for her to enter the USA. Lotte Bechstein and Ernst Hanfstaengl maintained that the internees left behind on the Isle of Man regarded Friedelind as a traitor.

An unpleasant sequel to Verena's trip to Switzerland with Philipp Hausser shortly before the war was another thing that weighed heavily upon the Wagner family. The young man had literary ambitions and had written a novella quoting barbed remarks by Friedelind about Hitler. Moreover, he had depicted a romantic love-story, including a bedroom scene that was described in full and featured a girl recognizable as Verena. The novella was not intended for publication, but a copy reached the hands of Gauleiter Wächtler by a tortuous route. He passed it on to Hitler, who, Gertrud Strobel claimed, 'read it attentively!'[30]

A Gestapo man came over from Nuremburg to search the idyllic house of the Schwabacher–Hausser family and confiscate the original typescript of the novella. This was all the more menacing for the family because Hausser's father was already on trial in a special court in Bamberg for making negative remarks about the Party. And worst of all, Hausser's 75-year-old Jewish grandfather, Edmund Schwabacher, was still living in the house with his 'Aryan' wife, no longer daring to go out since the pogrom night. He was utterly terrified by this visit from the Gestapo.[31]

Winifred received a peremptory letter from Bormann ordering her not to let her daughter have any further contact with the 'quarter-Jew' Hausser. It was not possible 'for Villa Wahnfried to maintain close and friendly relations with non-Aryan families and persons'. The whole business became danger-ous when Julius Streicher threatened to publish revelations about 'racial scandal in the house of Wagner' in Der Stürmer.[32] But Verena swore that she had not had intimate relations with Hausser. This time, Winifred had to solicit Hitler's help in a cause closer to home, that of her daughter. Instead of replying to Bormann, she wrote to Hitler. She read out this letter to Hausser, who reports: 'She said to Hitler that he ought to know her well enough to be aware that she was not one to change her friends as she might change her coat, simply because of a change of government, and she rejected any attempt to tell her who to mix with in her private life.' The Stürmer arti-cle did not appear.

Winifred had been acting on Philipp Hausser's behalf for years. His origins had created great problems for him in his medical studies, and later with obtaining a licence to practise. Through Hitler's doctor, Brandt, Winifred was able to help. Hausser was only a 'quarter-Jew'. A 'half-Jew' would not have had his opportunities, and for 'full Jews', the chances of surviving in Hitler's Reich once the war began were practically nil. Winifred could not help in such cases, though she did show solidarity. For example, when the Schwabachers' GP of many years' standing refused to treat them any longer after 1933, Winifred ostentatiously visited the old couple, as their grandson attested: 'She went very publicly to visit my grandfather, a full Jew.'[33]

Edmund Schwabacher took his own life in 1941, so as 'not to stand in the way of the family any longer'.[34]

THE FIRST WARTIME FESTIVAL

'While the war lasts, Bayreuth will stay dark – if it should all be over by April, then we can go ahead – later than that, and it can't be done!', wrote Winifred to Otto Daube in December 1939.[35] Bayreuth calculated that it would be a short war. Rumours were circulating to the effect that 'the Führer had replied, to an enquiry from Frau Wagner, that preparations for the next Festival could begin, since the war would end in the course of this year [1940]'.[36]

But when Heinz Tietjen enquired of her in January 1940 whether the Festival would be going ahead, Winifred replied,

> I'm afraid I've got to say there is no chance. We have no regulation air-raid shelters, and knowing the house as you do, you will be aware that building shelters on such an exposed site would hardly afford protection for the personnel and the public . . . besides that, there are problems with the food-rationing system, limited travel and transport facilities, the ban on all private car travel etc. etc. It would also be extremely difficult to get hold of the necessary raw materials for the stage-sets, costumes, laundry, cleaning the theatre etc.

The decision to close down the Festival Theatre was a hard one for her to take. She asked Tietjen to 'go on supporting her as a loyal adviser during this interregnum' [sic]. But 'until the resumption of the Festival after a (hopefully) victorious war', she would have to ask him to act 'in an honorary capacity'.[37] The Wagners adjusted to the idea of a free year, and planned their summer accordingly. No artists were engaged.

On 7 April 1940 Hitler's sudden decision to hold a Festival after all, caused panic and hectic activity. He had in mind the miserable state of Bayreuth between 1914 and 1918 and not only guaranteed adequate funding, but also complete artistic freedom. The Salzburg Festival likewise continued throughout the war.

Winifred protested that she lacked the necessary six months' preparation time, and that anyway almost all artists and technical crew had been called up. Hitler countered all her objections, as Winifred reported: 'the quality would be guaranteed by the fact that most artists were classified unsuitable for military service, anyway; the other staff Bayreuth needed could be similarly classified for the rehearsal and performance period'.[38] Another problem was that there would be no audiences, because even servicemen's wives were indispensable: 'Women have taken the place of men everywhere . . . particularly on the land, but elsewhere, too, they have taken over men's jobs and are keeping businesses going. I told him I could not expect an audience. "Yes, yes," he said, "I can't address an empty Reichstag, either." So he took the point.'[39]

Hitler soon came up with the solution. The National Socialist KdF ('Strength through Joy') organization, through its Department of Travel and Rambling, that is, Bodo Lafferentz, would supply audiences, especially from the ranks of the wounded with their nursing attendants, and the munitions workers. Everyone who had rendered good service would be rewarded with free travel, accommodation, meals and opera tickets. It would represent a kind of recognition, 'the thanks of the Führer and the country in general'.[40] After all, Wagner's music was 'spiritually uplifting . . . in a way that only pure art can be'.[41]

However, in view of the shortness of preparation time, Hitler allowed the programme to be shortened. Besides *The Ring of the Nibelung*, he wanted to see *The Flying Dutchman* put on, because the idea for this sea-faring opera had come to Wagner during a violent storm off the coast of Norway. There was a connection here with the course of the war, because on 9 April 1940, without declaring war, German troops had invaded Denmark and Norway by sea. While Denmark surrendered the next day, Norway fought on tenaciously, but had to capitulate by 10 June.

Singers, orchestral players, technicians, craftsmen and stagehands were assembled from all points of the compass. Winifred groaned that 'Getting people released for the Festival is creating enormous difficulties, and takes an age,'[42] but they were all keen to take part. It meant at least three months away from the military, as well as being able to practise their profession. The two old friends, Karl Elmendorff and Franz von Hoesslin, were signed up as conductors. Hitler did not veto the latter.

The Festival was totally dependent on Hitler and the Party, but the 'Strength through Joy' solution held great advantages for Winifred. She was free of the laborious business of selling tickets, advertising and creating press publicity. The KdF would organize the flow of visitors from start to finish, from distributing tickets to arrivals, accommodation, catering and leisure activities. Moreover, the house of Wagner was assured a good income for relatively little effort. The KdF took all the tickets *en bloc*, and in return covered the total costs of the Festival: fees, lighting, costumes, cleaning, copying and so on. Winifred added to these costs her profit margin of 5 per cent, which yielded somewhere between 30,000 and 50,000 marks a year;[43] about the same as Tietjen earned, or a star singer such as Max Lorenz. It is not surprising that, behind his back, Winifred was soon calling Lafferentz her *'Dukatenscheisser'* (milch-cow, cash machine).[44] Secondary earnings from, for example, cloakroom charges and guided tours brought in roughly another 18,000 marks.[45] Additionally, there were royalties from gramophone records, and the then frequent radio broadcasts (*c.* 15,000 marks), plus interest returns of about 24,000 marks – a truly comfortable state of affairs that Richard, Cosima or Siegfried Wagner could not have imagined in their wildest dreams.

By agreement between the KdF and the high command of the armed services, about 75 per cent of the visitors would be drawn from the forces and the rest from the munitions industry. They would be expected to show, said Winifred, 'receptivity and a particular interest in the works of Richard Wagner. Those recovering from wounds, from the ordinary private up to the General; medical staff from the Red Cross nurse up to the Chief Medical Director; male and female employees in the munitions industry throughout Germany' – they were all welcome to apply for an invitation to Bayreuth.[46]

On 10 May 1940 the offensive against France was launched, with an even more rapid advance than in 1914, and the breaching of the Maginot Line*. Constant special radio bulletins announced that Germany had marched into the neutral states of Holland, Belgium and Luxembourg.

Hopes of a peace with Britain were doomed to disappointment. In May Neville Chamberlain, the champion of appeasement, was forced to give way to Winston Churchill. In his first speech as Prime Minister on 13 May 1940 Churchill called upon the British to fight back against Hitler's 'monstrous tyranny'. 'I have nothing to offer but blood, toil, tears and sweat . . . [Our

---

*A line of powerful fortifications built by the French between 1929 and 1940, named after André Maginot, Minister of War from 1928–1932, and stretching from Switzerland to the Ardennes. It was supposedly impregnable, but in May 1940 Hitler simply ignored it and outflanked it by attacking France through the allegedly 'impenetrable' densely wooded Ardennes Massif in neutral Belgium.

policy is] to wage war, by sea, land and air, with all our might and with all the strength that God can give us.' The aim was 'victory. Victory at all costs, victory in spite of all terror.' He succeeded in bringing the other parties into line behind this policy.

On 10 June 1940 Italy entered the war alongside Germany. That day Wolfgang wrote to Roller: 'In Bayreuth everything is going at full pelt . . . but all this seems so unimportant and trivial at such a great time. However, the Führer wanted a Festival, and you just have to assume that there is some specific point to it.'[47] On 14 June the Germans entered Paris. Refugees from the defeated countries wandered through Europe, above all Jews from France, Norway, Denmark, Belgium, Holland, Poland, Austria and Czechoslovakia. Gertrud Strobel noted a remark by a soldier returning from Denmark, 'They've got bread and butter rationing there as well now; the population hates Germany. He doesn't think the war will be over soon, because America will join in!'[48]

At the beginning of rehearsals on 30 June, Tietjen's address to his colleagues cited Hitler's words,

> Either we will still be at war in July, when we begin [the Festival] . . . in which case this Bayreuth Festival will be a convincing demonstration to the entire world, an expression of the inner strength of a Germany able to display the achievements of German culture in the midst of the confusion of war, and in the most hallowed place we know. Or the war will be over, in which case the Bayreuth Festival will light a torch to introduce a new, unprecedented era of art, emanating from Germany and spreading out over the world.[49]

Naturally, Bayreuth hoped that 1940 would see a magnificent 'victory and peace Festival'. On 1 July Strobel mentioned 'Belgian prisoners digging air-raid trenches behind the Festival Theatre who can already say "Heil Hitler!"' Bayreuth cheered on the war heroes: there were 'dreadful crowds in the town' during the reception for a successful U-boat crew.[50]

At the beginning of July British planes flew over Bayreuth for the first time, accompanied by an air-raid warning. Mayor Kempfler was puzzled by the British interest in the small town, until he discovered from Winifred that Hitler's Pullman railway coach had been stationed nearby, and she had met him there for discussions. Kempfler believed that 'obviously it was him the bombers were after'. He observed that 'Churchill has a superb espionage service at his disposal!' Winifred's hopes of peace were strengthened by her nocturnal meeting with Hitler, as Kempfler reported. Evidently Hitler had told Winifred that negotiations with Britain were far more advanced than the public realized. Hitler had promised her verbatim: 'This year your front stalls will be filled with emperors, kings and all the powerful men of this earth.' Admittedly, Winifred thought that 'this remark of the Führer's . . . was rather vainglorious'.[51]

For the first time since 1933, Hitler was not present for the opening of the Festival. Winifred stayed in contact with him by telephone, and hoped that he might come over to Bayreuth for an evening. Almost 20,000 workers and servicemen were brought in on special trains, to be greeted at the station by a brass band and a reception by the organizers. They were each given a booklet of coupons for accommodation, the performance, talks, guided tours, food, cigarettes, sweets, fat, biscuits and a glass of wine.

The opening wore a rather different aspect on this occasion. Uniforms dominated the scene: the grey of the army, the blue of the navy, the light blue of the airmen. Scattered throughout were the nurses in their white caps, and the female munitions workers. Many of the servicemen hobbled on crutches, wore head-bandages or had lost limbs. Winifred later described an audience consisting of 'the seriously wounded, holders of the Knight's Cross or Iron Cross, all brave men and officers who had distinguished them-selves . . . so many cripples came along, accompanied by nurses, without whom they could not move at all'.[52] From then on, Hitler's words were often quoted in Bayreuth: 'I want us to have the most beautiful, the best culture. I want German art to be there, not just for the upper ten thousand as in Britain, but for the benefit of the whole people.'[53]

These 'guests of the Führer' came in tight-knit groups and always travelled together, as was customary with the KdF. They were invariably given a talk on the day before the performance, which in most cases was the first opera they had seen, to get them 'acclimatized' to its subject-matter. They were also told when it was permissible to clap.

Siegfried above all was pressed into the service of propaganda. 'A new Siegfried sword has been forged. From the broken pieces of our fathers' weapons it has been fashioned by "the man who knew no fear". Siegfried-Germany stands now, in the full might of arms, and trusts to its strength alone.' The evil dragon had not yet been utterly destroyed, but when the redemption motif swelled up after Siegfried's death, then one could under-stand Wagner's prophecy: 'From the self-sacrifice of our dead heroes, from our willingness to sacrifice ourselves, will arise out of the ruins of a declining age a new and better world order.'[54]

For the music-lovers in the audience, visiting the Festival was a moving experience, which many fondly recalled for the rest of their lives. However, many young people had accepted the invitation to Bayreuth in the expectation of a few restful, carefree days in beautiful surroundings and then had found themselves being lectured at from dawn to dusk on Wagner and his works, and obliged to spend half the day sitting on the hard seats of the Festival Theatre, with practically no opportunity to enjoy the warm summer. They joined the ranks of those who swore they never wanted to attend a Wagner performance again.

In his Reichstag speech of 19 July, having completed his 'lightning war' against France, Hitler offered Churchill, Germany's most powerful opponent, the chance to negotiate. He demanded nothing less than British recognition of German hegemony on the European continent. If Britain declined this offer, he threatened that the war could end only with 'the total destruction of one side or the other'. 'I regret the victims it will claim.' The assembled Festival guests listened to this speech over loudspeakers in the crowded Festival restaurant after *Rhinegold*, and Gertrud Strobel wrote that day: 'everybody applauds!'[55]

The British government fiercely rejected Hitler's brazen proposal. Taken in by Goebbels's propaganda, however, most Germans blamed the British, and especially Churchill, for the continuation of the war.

There was great surprise in Bayreuth when Hitler appeared for the *Twilight of the Gods*. He got Wolfgang to pick him up from Berneck, where he had stayed overnight. Gertrud Strobel observed him and Winifred strolling in the garden of Wahnfried, 'with her talking in a very agitated manner, and him saying nothing, until he's called away by an adjutant'.[56] Aside from the business of Friedelind, then still current, that conversation must have centred on the replacement of Gauleiter Wächtler, for which Winifred so fervently hoped. Dr Deubzer stated that Hitler proposed Baldur von Schirach as the new gauleiter; he had just lost his post as Reich Youth Leader. Knowing Winifred's antipathy to Schirach, Deubzer went on: 'But since he didn't seem to be the right personality for the Bavarian Ostmark either, she withdrew her request.'[57] Schirach became gauleiter and Reich governor in Vienna.

Before the performance, Hitler took tea with the family. He talked enthusiastically about his short visit to Paris. Winifred brought the conversation around to Germaine Lubin. Her son, in the French army, had been reported missing. At Lubin's request she had already made enquiries and located the young Frenchman in a German POW camp. She urged Hitler to take a pro-tective interest in him – which he did, evidently, because October found Winifred writing to the singer: 'Thank God the Führer kept his promise . . . and released your poor son.' That letter was delivered by a friend of Winifred's youth, Hans Joachim Lange, then a lieutenant commander sta-tioned in occupied Paris. She had warmly recommended him to Mme Lubin. 'You can entrust anything to him, letters for me or whatever.'[58]

In response to a question from Winifred about whether they should build an air-raid shelter, Hitler replied, 'that would be crazy. The war is taking place hundreds of kilometres away from Bayreuth. He was always very opti-mistic.'[59] Asked about future prospects, he rose to rhetorical heights: 'I can hear the wings of the victory goddess beating'; to which Winifred replied, as brash as she was admiring: 'And you're going to catch the blighter as usual!'[60]

Hitler had brought a present from Paris, which he claimed to have bought in a gallery, a Lenbach portrait from the Thodes' villa on Lake Garda, which had been confiscated with its entire contents by the Italians in 1918.[61] Daniela, then nearly eighty, was dying, so Winifred hung the picture in the music room of the 'Führer building'. Daniela died on 28 July 1940, and was buried with full Party honours as a prominent recipient of the Party Badge in Gold, as was Eva Chamberlain when she died in 1942.

At that time, in the occupied part of France, German archivists and his-torians under Rosenberg's direction were combing through archives and museums and looting musical items on a grand scale, including the manu-scripts of German composers. Wagner's letters and autographs were particularly sought after. Hitler must have possessed a large Wagner collec-tion, which is still missing to this day. He sent Winifred a Wagner letter for Christmas 1940.[62]

Hitler's route to Festival Hill was strewn with blossom by the Bayreuthers who had hastily gathered, and by 'guests of the Führer'. He was in field-grey; Verena wore her nurse's uniform. Mayor Kempfler and acting Gauleiter Rückdeschel, as well as the KdF leaders Ley and Lafferentz, all appeared in SS uniform. One man was not in uniform – August Kubizek, who met Hitler during the interval. Hitler went up to him 'beaming with pleasure', accord-ing to Verena's first-hand account. The Wagners tactfully withdrew. Kubizek was nothing like as enthusiastic as the crowds outside, with their untiring chanting of 'Führer, listen to our plea, come outside and let us see!' Kubizek was worried about his three sons, all on active service. Hitler was so thoughtful on this occasion that he almost seemed to want to 'justify himself' to his old friend. Hitler said to him, 'This war is going to put us back years in our reconstruction work. It's a shame. I didn't become Chancellor of the Greater German Reich in order to go to war.' Conscious of his old friend's fifty-two years, he went on, 'I've still got an enormous amount left to do. Who else can do it? And yet I've got to see my best years wasted by the war. It's a shame. We're getting older, Kubizek. How many years left?' Then they chatted about old times.[63]

Immediately after the performance, Hitler left Bayreuth in his armoured train. Winifred did not suspect that she would never see her friend Wolf again. And Hitler did not suspect that this was to be his last visit to Bayreuth.

AIR-RAIDS AND HESS'S FLIGHT TO SCOTLAND

Neither the British nor the Germans spared civilian targets in the air war. One of the many bombing raids on London destroyed Berta Geissmar's apartment on 24 September 1940, along with all the family possessions she had brought out of Germany with so much effort in 1935.[64]

Bayreuth was overflowing with incomers. After air-raids on Hamburg, the authorities evacuated children from the city to Bavaria, and thus to Bayreuth. Ursel Gossmann, daughter of the Wagner-sponsor Heinrich Bales, fled to Bayreuth from Cologne with her three infants, and was given accommodation in Winifred's week-end cottage in Oberwarmensteinach.

Even after the war began, Winifred continued her efforts on behalf of the persecuted. She enjoyed some success, as in the case of the wife of the Leipzig music critic Eugen Schmitz. Hanna Schmitz had become involved in a political conflict with Gauleiter Martin Muschmann and Hitler's half-sister Angela Raubal, then Frau Hammitzsch. When Frau Schmitz was arrested by the Gestapo, Winifred intervened 'personally and very forcefully', as Hanna Schmitz said later, 'engaging implacably with the Party, the Gestapo and the Reich Protector himself'. She managed to bring about a proper trial, which ended with Frau Schmitz's acquittal in 1940. As Hanna Schmitz said, 'by interceding for me, Frau Wagner . . . drew down upon herself the embittered wrath of Mutschmann and his clique'.[65] Once again it was a case of Party corruption in high places.

Winifred also took an interest in Siegfried's friends. In 1939 she managed to get the singer Hans Beer released from the punishment battalion in Buchenwald concentration camp. For Beer, 'it amounted to the same thing as pulling me back from the brink of death itself'.[66] When an old family friend, Albert Jordan of Eisenach, was about to be ruined by an accusation under Section 175, Winifred gave evidence on his behalf, and he was released.[67] She told Lene about a cry for help from her old school-friend Ruth Langhoff, 'whose husband had been taken out of Veil's clinic to the gaol in Erfurt. I did at least manage to get him transferred to the Erfurt hospital. The things that go on! Apparently he made defeatist remarks.'[68]

The easiest way to help out in this deteriorating climate was with everyday things, such as food and clothing. The food supply in Bayreuth degenerated quickly. In the autumn the newspapers made much of the rich pickings of mushrooms and berries to be had in the woods. Civil servants were given two weeks 'recreational leave . . . to help bring in the harvest' because nearly all farm-workers were on active service.

The fuel shortage induced a great deal of panic about the onset of winter. Even by spring 1940, Gertrud Strobel had noted in her diary: 'The rabble up in arms about coal (worse than 1918!).' There were threats against Wächtler: 'He'd better give up his 50 hundredweight [of coal]!' Unperturbed, the Gauleiter went on enjoying a seasonal 'meatfest' in the Fantaisie Palace with his Party cronies.[69]

Daily reports of victories served constantly to raise the spirits of the *Volk*. On 1 September a radio link broadcast brought reports from the occupied territories: 'German soldiers keep watch from the North Cape to Biscay'.

As usual, the Wagner family got its information direct from Hitler personally. He gave contradictory answers to the question of when peace could be expected. Meeting Tietjen and Wolfgang in November 1940 to discuss the next Festival, he maintained that 'he was 90% certain that the war would end next summer, but even he obviously could not account for the other 10%'. At the end of December 1940, however, he asked Verena not to begin her medical studies yet, and to stay on as a Red Cross nurse until October 1941, 'because "when it starts, things will get really bad!"'[70]

In January 1941 a stray aeroplane dropped three bombs on the outskirts of Bayreuth. Gertrud Strobel experienced a 'terrible feeling of vulnerability and helplessness in the shelter'.[71] Winifred suffered from bad panic attacks at the sound of an air-raid warning, with severe bowel-control problems and a frenzied compulsion to scramble into the cellar. She confessed to Lene that she was 'an instinctive coward . . . and simply a terrible liability for every-body whenever the alarm goes off'.[72]

During the night of 9 to 10 April 1941, the German State Opera on Unter den Linden in Berlin was burnt to the ground by incendiary bombs. Goebbels wrote: 'A tragic loss. The University and the State Library badly hit too. We'll tell the world openly about this under the heading "attack on Berlin cultural quarter". Especially to counteract the atrocity stories about Belgrade . . . Tietjen is completely shattered . . . Britain will pay dearly for this.'[73] The destruction of the State Opera was a heavy blow for Bayreuth, because that was where the sets and costumes for all Festival productions were created.

Hitler issued orders for the State Opera to be rebuilt immediately, with no expense spared. While the house was out of action, Goebbels exploited the opportunity to send the State Opera Company on propaganda visits abroad, under the rising star conductor Herbert von Karajan. The programme for guest tours always included at least one Wagner opera. As a representative of the house of Wagner, Winifred travelled with the company; in March 1941 on a German–Italian friendship visit to Rome, for example. At Hitler's behest, the Teatro Reale mounted *The Mastersingers* with the original Bayreuth cast and staging. In April Winifred and Tietjen took the Bayreuth *Valkyrie* to Budapest.

Special bulletins announced victory after victory. By April, German troops were in Belgrade, and were marching into Athens. 'The swastika flies over the Acropolis.'[74] Crete was conquered in May 1941. Rommel's North African campaign filled pages of newsprint.

Relations with the USSR remained good so far, and a production of *The Valkyrie* was planned for Moscow in early summer 1941. Winifred was invited by the Soviet government, and proposed to Kempfler: 'Mr Mayor, we'll both go, and travel in your car and with your chauffeur!' But when Kempfler enquired with the Foreign Office in April about the necessary travel for-malities, a sobering message came back. At that particular moment a trip to Russia was not desirable.[75] Early rumours of a Soviet–German rift were denied. Gertrud Strobel noted in her diary on 30 April 1941 that 'the ten-sion with Russia is said to have eased: troops already embarked for the east were brought back to the west on the Führer's birthday'.[76]

In May and June Winifred accompanied the Berlin State Opera on a Goebbels-organized tour of defeated France – a massive undertaking, with 250 people involved. The high points were the celebrations in Meudon

near Paris, the place where Richard Wagner first stayed in France; a concert
in the Palais Chaillot; and four evenings in the Grand Opéra, with two performances each of Mozart's *Abduction from the Seraglio* and Wagner's *Tristan
and Isolde* in productions by Tietjen and Preetorius. Isolde was sung by
Germaine Lubin, who had shown herself to be very pro-German in occupied
Paris and enjoyed excellent contacts with the German military, especially
with Winifred's old friend Lange. 'Lange fell in love at first sight with this
beautiful woman,' wrote Winifred, 'and had a wonderful "romance" with her
throughout the war, supported by Speidel, Reichenau etc. etc. – who were all
as taken with her as Lange and USA!!!!'[77] (In the jargon of unreconstructed
Nazis after 1945, 'USA' stood for 'Unser seliger Adolf', our blessed Adolf.)

Germaine Lubin had enjoyed yet another favour from Hitler shortly
before. When her Jewish repetiteur was arrested, she had refused to take part
in a charity concert organized by the Germans in Paris. The prisoner was
released, and she was free to sing in *Tristan*.[78] She was pleased to meet up
again with Winifred, Tietjen and many other Bayreuth people, and to take
the stage once more with Max Lorenz.

In Paris Winifred visited the Invalides, a place that Hitler particularly
revered. At the foot of Napoleon's sarcophagus there now stood the coffin of
his son by the Hapsburg Marie Louise. The Duke of Reichstadt, also known
as Napoleon II or King of Rome, had died young. To the fury of the
Viennese, Hitler had the coffin removed from the Capuchin Crypt (the
tomb of the Hapsburgs) in the Austrian capital and transferred to Paris as a
symbolic historical gift to the French nation.[79]

Back in Bayreuth, Winifred proudly handed a batch of reviews to the
reporter from the *Bayerische Ostmark*. 'They show the enthusiastic reception
of contemporary German opera in France.'[80] From the time of these visits
onwards, she greatly admired the conductor Karajan, and never ceased to do
so. But Hitler would not satisfy her ambition to enlist Karajan for Bayreuth.

On 10 May 1941, exactly a year after Churchill became premier, Hitler's
deputy and friend Rudolf Hess took off on his bizarre flight to Scotland. He
was privy to the secret plans for a German invasion of the USSR, and he
claimed that his flight was a peace mission intended to strengthen the opposition in Britain, bring about the fall of Churchill and broker a peace treaty
between Germany and the British. Hess was convinced that Germany could
not win a war against Great Britain, especially not the imminent war on two
fronts.

Hess felt he had the backing of the many Germans who longed for peace with Britain. He was still confirming that Winifred was among their number when he wrote to his wife from prison in 1949:

> Perhaps she [Winifred] remembers that, at one time in Berlin, probably autumn 1940, she was very concerned, and asked me whether it was still our intention to avoid all-out war against Britain, and not to ruin the Empire – whether the policy was still one of détente? I reassured her that it was, and I thought, if only you knew that I'm preparing to make a little 'contribution' along those lines myself!

He was sure that 'if it had been necessary and possible for her to throw her weight behind my plan to fly to Britain, she would have done so'.[81]

The mission was a failure. Hess parachuted out over Scotland, and was arrested and interrogated. Politicians refused to talk to him. Hitler immediately distanced himself from Hess, declared him insane and dismissed him from office. Goebbels noted: 'The Führer is utterly shattered. What a sight for the world to see: the Führer's second-in-command is deranged. Horrifying and unimaginable.'[82] The office of Führer's deputy was abolished and a Party chancellery created under Martin Bormann. Because of his constant proximity to Hitler, Bormann now became the most influential man in Germany.

Winifred took an intense interest in the news about Hess's flight. Asked about it by her friend Änne Klönne, she wrote out 'the whole episode from the Valkyrie for her by way of explanation – the scene between Wotan and the Valkyrie!'[83] The quotation comes from Act II, where Wotan, the Father of the Gods, is limited in his freedom of action by many ties, and cannot do what he would really like. He says as much to his favourite daughter Brünnhilde, who assures him: 'tell me / what it is you want: / who am I / if I am not your will?'

Winifred asserted on 14 May 1941 that 'there is no question of betrayal on Hess's part – his loyalty to the Führer is beyond dispute . . . In the Führer's own words', Hess 'knew Hitler's thoughts better than anyone else'. That, she said, 'was why he had made him his deputy!' She said of Hitler, 'We all know, of course, that the Führer did not want a war against Britain, and did everything in his power to avoid it.' He had said at Wahnfried that 'it was absolute madness for the white race to indulge in mutual destruction, ruining the prestige of the white race itself in the rest of the world! . . . How bitter it must have been for him to be forced to accept that Britain was the main enemy and order her subjugation by all possible means!' Hess was a very sick man. 'His dearest wish will be to render one last great service to the Führer, whatever the cost – even if it costs him his life!' He had really believed, 'idealist and fantasist' as he was, that with this unusual step he could succeed 'in bringing his English friends to see reason – and through them wider circles – and thus bring about the fall of the British government'. He did not consider what his action might lead to. But she closes her long letter optimistically: this failed move would have no influence 'on the future of Germany, on the final victory'.[84]

By this time, Winifred's personal contacts with Hitler were very limited. She had practically no further access to inside information. Her interpretation of the Hess affair relied upon her instincts, her intimate knowledge of both Hitler and Hess and her basic sympathy for any attempt to make peace with Britain.

It was disastrous for Winifred's rescue efforts that Bormann replaced Hess. This soon became clear in the case of a private Protestant girls' school in Weiblingen near Heidelberg. Engaged in a desperate struggle to maintain the independence of her school, the headmistress, Elisabeth von Thadden, had turned to Winifred for assistance. She appealed to Hess, and the petition was duly handed on to Bormann, who rejected it.[85] The school was 'brought into line', and the unrepentant Elisabeth von Thadden was arrested, found guilty of 'subverting the war effort' and executed on 8 September 1944 in Plötzensee prison in Berlin.

Since it was Bormann who decided what information Hitler received and who was allowed access to him, Winifred had to find a different way to get to him; either through personal messengers, the adjutants, Schaub and Brückner, or via Hitler's doctor, Brandt. The latter said that Bormann's attitude to Winifred was very negative: 'Martin Bormann talked about Frau Wagner in the most disparaging terms, repeatedly declaring that in her heart of hearts Frau Winifred Wagner was no National Socialist, but was just adhering to the old Wagner line, which, as is commonly the case in artistic circles, was apolitical, with internationalist tendencies.'[86] Martin Bormann, whose informants were everywhere, was from then on invariably known in the Wagner household as 'that pig Bormann'. His brother Albert, on the other hand, who was at loggerheads with him, was always 'the nice Bormann'. He was a frequent visitor to the Festival, and stayed in touch with Winifred privately after 1945.[87]

In view of these problems, there was one piece of news that was disturbing for Wahnfried. In the summer of 1941 Bormann of all people, having spent hardly any time in Bayreuth, bought the magnificent Rosvaenge Villa in the Parsifalstrasse on Green Hill. The price for the 6,500 square metre property, with an adjoining plot of 19,000 square metres, was 165,000 marks.[88] Bormann also had houses in Munich and on the Obersalzberg, and he never occupied the Bayreuth villa, possibly due to the war, or because he had simply been acting as a front man for Hitler. It is certainly true that Hitler said to Schirach that 'he loved Bayreuth so much that he liked to imagine spending the evening of his life in that highly cultured little town, permeated by the spirit of Richard Wagner'.[89] But he said something similar about his home town, Linz.

WAR ON ALL FRONTS

During the Festival rehearsals, on 22 June 1941, came the startling news of the German invasion of the USSR. Winifred's reaction was bemused and uncomprehending. She had thought the victorious end of the war close at hand, and now it was being dangerously extended. Most Germans were similarly confused. In 1939 enormous efforts had been made to win them over to the new 'German–Soviet friendship', following the Hitler–Stalin pact. With the speed of events, libraries and offices that had pulped anti-Soviet books and leaflets in 1939 now lacked propaganda material to use against the new military opponent.[90]

The German population listened with bated breath to success stories about their troops' advances in the east. On 29 June, for example, Gertrud Strobel sat by her radio from seven o'clock in the morning, and could hardly get on with her cooking as twelve special announcements broke in. 'We're completely stunned by these colossal triumphs!' The following day there was a news flash about the capture of Lemberg (Lvov). On 1 July she heard that 'yesterday 280 Russian planes were shot down!' And then: 'We are already in bed when Frau Kittel calls about another news flash – Riga has fallen!'[91]

To help people follow the advance, the papers provided geography lessons: Dnieper, Kiev, Pripyat Marshes, Lake Peipus, Vitebsk, Leningrad. There were descriptions of street life in Moscow: 'the people, for the most part in dirty clothes, have something of the earth, an earthy smell about them', that is to say, they are uncultivated. Only a few months before, reports on Russian art had projected a very different image to the Germans.

There was good news from North Africa, too: German bombing of the British base at Alexandria had caused a mass exodus of the population. There were reports of a German air-raid on Port Said, and a push through the desert. In contrast to 1916, there was going to be a successful break-through to the Suez Canal. This time, after all, it was no longer necessary 'for each piece of artillery to be dragged over the sand by 24 buffaloes'. The German army was 'the best equipped in the world', and fully motorized. There were constant claims that 'the war criminal Churchill' was visibly frightened.[92]

Attending the wartime Bayreuth Festival in 1941, Goebbels noted: 'This little residence-town of the Margraves* presents a picture of perfect peace and a really restorative idyll. The war is not much in evidence here. If you come from Berlin and all the tensions of a city of millions, the calm of this place settles on your restless soul like a balm.'[93]

While the programme was the same as in 1940, the practical problems of carrying it out became ever more onerous. Performances had to end when the blackout began, at the times published in the papers. In the first week of the Festival, for instance, there was a total blackout between 21.12 and 5.32 hours. Performances had to begin shortly after noon, in order for large num-bers of people to make their way down from the hill and get to their accommodation in town before the onset of complete darkness.

A request from Winifred to Hitler for a special allocation of petrol pro-duced no reaction at first. Two weeks later it was Mayor Kempfler, and not Winifred, who received a call from Führer headquarters. On behalf of Hitler, a general asked Kempfler to convey to her that there could be no question of an extra petrol ration. 'You wouldn't believe the problems we're having to battle with here; the roads are terrible, practically just mud and sand, so that we need far greater supplies of fuel than we thought.'[94] It all sounded rather different from the triumphant radio bulletins.

That year the Festival reached listeners abroad by short-wave transmis-sion. Together with the singer Margery Booth, Winifred was responsible for the presentation in English. The Russian-language presenter was the

---

*Margrave (German 'Markgraf') was the hereditary title of some princes of the Holy Roman Empire. The Margraves of Brandenburg–Bayreuth had their seat (Residenz) in Bayreuth, in the New Palace.

Wotan singer, Jaro Prohaska, who had learnt Russian as a POW in the First World War.[95]

Tietjen had successfully pushed for higher fees this time – including his own. Gertrud Strobel remarked that 'The top artists are now getting 3,000 marks per appearance! The Führer will have to increase the subsidy by a good deal.' Tietjen's total honorarium for the 1941 Festival – as organizer, director and conductor of the *Ring* – amounted to 30,000 marks. In his hatred of Tietjen, Wieland found this outrageous. 'The villain, the villain! He's lucky we let him conduct the *Rhinegold* here at all.'[96]

Despite all the reports of success, the hoped-for lightning victory in the east did not materialize. By October 1941, after seeing a newsreel, Gertrud Strobel was struck by 'shots of the Führer looking very old and worn-out', and 'Goebbels, who looks like a ghost with a death's head'.[97] German cities were increasingly defenceless against night-time bombing. Contrary to all expectations, the war in the east stretched on into the winter of 1941–2. Women – including Winifred – knitted socks, scarves and ear-muffs for the soldiers. Jews were made to hand over all their winter clothing: furs, coats, boots and socks.

In hushed tones, information was passed on from soldiers back in Bayreuth convalescing. One soldier returning to the front after his leave could no longer find his company; it had been wiped out. An auxiliary nurse told of terrible conditions in a field hospital in the east. Gertrud Strobel noted on 1 December 1941 what a soldier told her about the eastern front:

> shooting of all Jews (including women and children); Russian POWs and population starving to death; the deadening effect on the men; low morale because of leave being stopped, and the terrible winter. Nothing to smoke, no alcohol, no cake, nothing; just tinned food. The nearest army post office is 200 km away! They won't even have a Christmas tree, because there's no forest for miles (Charkov area).[98]

A returning soldier reported on a camp for Russian POWs: 'the prisoners are starving or eating each other; officers etc. who are convinced communists are shot!' The son of the architect Hans Reissinger had died of a lung wound in Russia. He had always written 'very desperate letters . . . especially about being completely cut off from home'. In January 1942 the landlady of the Anker Hotel in Bayreuth complained that she had neither beer nor wine to serve, 'although there are 5,000 soldiers in town, en route to Russia'. Soon afterwards, 'a frostbite train from Russia arrives here',[99] that is, transport bringing back wounded men with severe frostbite.

Among the many who died on the eastern front was Hitler's protégé Ulrich Roller. Immediately after the *Anschluss*, he had returned to his home city, Vienna. With his political connections, he became stage designer and head of the costume department at the Vienna State Opera. After the successful production of *Friedenstag* (Day of Peace) in 1939, he worked with Richard Strauss on the sets for Strauss's opera *Daphne*. A self-confident young man, he seems to have quarrelled with the administration of the opera house, where the directors were constantly changing. The files point to a kind of minor war being waged.

He was then called up, with effect from 1 November 1940. The Vienna State Opera made no attempt to retain him. But according to Hitler's instructions he could not be sent to the front, and was on Winifred's list of artists not liable for war service. So he was deployed elsewhere; as an SS man of the Death's Head Standard.* The two years he had spent interned in Austria for political activities were a sufficient qualification, and he was 'posted to the SS guard in Oranienburg';[100] specifically, to the homosexuals' section of the Sachsenhausen concentration camp. Confronted with the reality of the concentration camps, the young artist, who had believed in Hitler and admired him, suffered an existential crisis. He begged and pleaded with Winifred to remove him from her list. He wanted a transfer to the front – he could not tell her why. The Roller family later interpreted this step as a clear decision to commit suicide.[101]

In better times Winifred would have rung Hitler and talked the matter over with him, but he was in his headquarters in East Prussia, constantly shadowed by Bormann and therefore inaccessible to her. At Roller's urgent insistence, she finally removed him from the list. On 28 December 1941, the thirty-year-old was killed on the outskirts of the village of Stollpomka, near Kaluga, on the Moscow front. Hitler was horrified by Roller's death, and utterly incensed by Winifred's handling of the case. She later maintained that this was the only grave falling-out between them: 'He was really angry.'[102]

When Hitler learned about the history of problems at the Vienna State Opera, Schirach too bore the brunt of fury from on high as he had ultimate

---

*A regiment of the SS, supplying concentration-camp guards.

responsibility for cultural matters in Vienna. 'Some Russian idiot shooting down a man like that! Look how many we have classified exempt from service; what difference does it make if five or six hundred talented people are let off! You can't replace a man like that. Why didn't Schirach report it to me? ... I would have withdrawn him and got him posted elsewhere.'[103] Goebbels's diary noted that the Führer had 'a high regard for Alfred Roller, and would have preferred to see his son classified exempt from the military. Our ministry actually applied for that, but unfortunately the State Opera handled it rather laxly, and now we've lost one of our most capable stage designers.'[104]

Winifred wrote to Roller's mother, Mileva, an enthusiastically pro-Hitler Serbian, whom she did not know personally: 'The news has just reached me, though I cannot grasp it yet, that your dear son Uli has died a hero's death for his fatherland and for his beloved Führer. I bow my head in silent respect for what you, his mother, must be going through . . . For us it is like losing a dear member of the family.' Bayreuth was in mourning 'for the loss of such an extraordinarily gifted artist – whom Wieland had selected to be his eventual collaborator . . . Now his young life has been fulfilled, and he died as he lived: believing in the Führer and the National Socialist idea; believing in the great fatherland of the future. He was faithful unto death, and set a shining example for us all.'[105]

In the summers at Bayreuth, Wieland had formed a close attachment to Roller, six years his senior. He was always asking him for artistic advice and sending him designs for evaluation with the note, 'you'll have to tell me in the summer how to do it better'. Usually so brusque, on this occasion he struck a personal note in his letter of condolence to Frau Roller: 'I was very attached to him, as you know, and had great hopes for our collaboration in Bayreuth.' Ulrich was to have worked together with Wieland for the first time at the 1942 Festival, and provided the costumes for the new *Tannhäuser*. 'My thoughts were often with him in Russia – he was the only one I wrote to regularly.'[106]

On 7 December 1941 the Japanese attacked the American base at Pearl Harbor in Hawaii. Both states had allies who were drawn into the war, which now spanned the entire globe. On 11 December Hitler declared war on the USA; 'shoulder to shoulder with Japan'. He also gave the figures for the war in the east: the Germans had taken 3.8 million prisoners, and destroyed or captured 17,322 Soviet planes and 21,391 tanks. On the German side so far, since June, there were 62,314 dead, 571,767 wounded and 33,334 missing.[107]

That month Winifred received what the Strobel diary called a 'charming report from Dr Brandt', describing a visit to Hitler's 'Wolf's Lair' headquarters in East Prussia. 'The Führer sat for hours in his bunker with his cat on his lap, feeding it titbits! When approached by soldiers, he asked every one of them in detail about his health, his family etc.; he has a lot of time on his hands at the moment!'[108] He also had time to reflect on the favours he had bestowed on Bayreuth: 'And now, with a war on, I've been able to achieve what Wagner wanted, to provide free access to the Festival for audiences selected from among the ordinary people, soldiers and peasants! The ten days in Bayreuth every year were always my favourite time, and I'm looking forward to our first trip back there again!'[109]

Albert Speer, the new armaments minister, who often saw Hitler in Wolf's Lair, recorded: 'Time and again, Hitler ranked having to forgo the whole world of the theatre foremost among the deprivations the war had imposed on him.' Whenever Goebbels visited him, Hitler's 'first question to him concerned the well-being of his favourite singers. He was keen to hear tales of gossip, and the destruction of an opera house pained him more than the bombing of a whole residential district.'[110] His attitude to Winifred was friendly, 'But after all, Frau Wagner did bring Bayreuth together with National Socialism – that is her great historical contribution.'[111]

Marlene von Exner, Hitler's dietary adviser in Wolf's Lair, when asked whether he listened to much music there, replied that he never played any Wagner, but nearly always Franz Lehár's *Merry Widow*, in various recordings and excerpts,[112] such as 'I'm off to Chez Maxime', 'Being male, we may fail, but we try', or 'Love unspoken, strings are playing, / Hear them saying, "love me true" '. Clearly, Hitler was trying to ward off the great emotions he associated with Wagner's music.

WIELAND'S REVOLT AGAINST TIETJEN

Wieland decided in 1940, after much indecision, to take up his Bayreuth inheritance, and turn his private painting studies into a sideline. To help him with his preparations for the task, he decided to appoint as his mentor the 38-year-old Kurt Overhoff, Director General of Music in Heidelberg, who had already been working with him for months, since being given refuge by Winifred as a house-guest when he was suffering from a serious nervous disorder. On 1 September 1940 he resigned from his Heidelberg post and became Wieland's private tutor, on the same financial terms as he had enjoyed in Heidelberg. Overhoff thought his main job, initially, was to take Wieland, who had 'no particular musical talent', through Wagner's scores with the aim of developing dramatic direction out of the spirit of the music; this would enable Wieland to bring his visual gifts to bear.[113] However, Wieland was soon groaning that 'he had gone off the tracks a bit by having to go so deeply into music'.[114]

Tietjen had set out a comprehensive study plan, envisaging four or five years' training for the Wagner grandchildren. The idea was to have them ready to take over the direction of the Festival by 1944–5, with a new production of *Tannhäuser* in the planned new Festival Theatre.[115] Wolfgang, whose crippled hand had ruled out a career as a conductor, was taken on at the Berlin State Opera as an assistant stage manager, where Tietjen introduced him to practical theatre work from the bottom up.

Overhoff found himself 'drawn into a turbulent atmosphere of intrigue . . . such as I had never known before, constantly stirred up by the mutual hatred between Wieland Wagner and Tietjen'. He had to fight on two fronts at once: on the one hand, to represent Wieland's legitimate rights *vis-à-vis* Tietjen; and on the other, to free the young man 'from his false traditionalist ideas'. Wieland was in the habit of attacking Tietjen 'for the slightest violation of fixed tradition', and he rigidly rejected any kind of modernization. Strobel gives Overhoff's verdict on his pupil after eight months as

very highly talented, but completely at odds with himself; antipathy to his grandfather ('if grandpa hadn't existed, my father would have been a famous man!') . . . total lack of respect for everything great, idolizing of the Führer (placed above Richard Wagner!), complete indecision and vacillation about his own future (painter today, musician tomorrow etc.), no stamina to see things through, fits of temper (smashing new china etc.), and boundless hatred of Tietjen![116]

Even Gertrud Strobel, who actively supported Wieland, criticized the unruly young man: 'And Wieland still has no idea of his duty, the greatness of his grandfather, etc. It's hopeless.'[117]

In his permanent war against Tietjen, Wieland recruited Herr and Frau Strobel to note down even the slightest deviation from the score whenever Tietjen was conducting. The Strobels complained in 1941, for example, that Max Lorenz's singing of Siegfried was 'beneath criticism', and furthermore he had got the text wrong. Instead of singing 'Sterben die Menschenmütter an ihren Söhnen?' ('Do the mothers of mankind die of their sons?'), he had sung 'Sterben die Menschensöhne an ihren Müttern?' ('Do the sons of mankind die of their mothers?'). Irritated, Gertrud Strobel turned to Dr Deubzer, sitting near her, to ask whether this was 'medically possible; and he said, "Not medically, but – looking far ahead – in terms of racist politics, yes!"'[118]

After the commemorative concert for the anniversary of Siegfried's death on 4 August 1941, Wieland's long-pent-up wrath against Tietjen finally exploded. He accused him of having engineered Overhoff's sudden call-up to the military. Tietjen's aim was to obstruct his, Wieland's, development, which was coming on all too well. Overhoff says that 'Wieland was obsessed with the notion that Tietjen was deliberately holding him back intellectually.' According to Wieland, Tietjen wanted to 'eliminate him, the rightful heir, so that he could remain in sole charge on Festival Hill'.[119]

To air their difficulties, a meeting of the two opponents, Wieland and Tietjen, was arranged for 5 August in Wahnfried. They each brought a witness along – August Roesener and Overhoff. They had only reached the garden of Wahnfried when a loud argument broke out, observed by the neighbour, Gertrud Strobel. While the men shouted at each other, Winifred stood by helpless, 'crying the whole time'.[120] She was accused by each fighting cock of taking the side of the other. Overhoff wrote disapprovingly that in this quarrel she had stuck to Tietjen 'in her own blind way'.[121] Tietjen, on the other hand, accused her of dependence on her favourite Wieland. Overhoff was soon ruled ineligible for military service and returned to his pupil.

Tietjen had meanwhile discovered that an 'order' had been issued (and this could only mean an order from Hitler) that preliminary work should begin on a new *Tannhäuser* under Wieland. But Preetorius already had a complete and finished production of *Tannhäuser* available that had cost tens of thousands of marks to create. And, as the technical director Paul Ehrhardt angrily objected, 'the necessary materials had been extremely difficult to come by'. Wieland was clearly using political pressure to impede the staging of Preetorius's far too modern production. Tietjen was not prepared to put up with this, and threatened to resign immediately from the directorship of the Festival. Thereupon, the 'lads' countered with: 'then they would have to get the Führer to persuade Heinz [Tietjen] to stay on!!!

It obviously wouldn't work without him!'[122] They had neither a ready-made production, nor artists and technicians prepared to work with them.

For Wieland it was purely a question of power. His tone to Tietjen, who was always concerned to preserve polite forms of exchange, became so aggressive that Tietjen suggested, for the sake of 'peaceful cooperation', that they should communicate only in writing from then on. The whole of Bayreuth knew about the power struggle on Festival Hill, because Wieland complained about Tietjen to everybody he met, as he did to Gertrud Beckel, a family friend: 'I'm so furious with Tietjen that I'd like to slap him around the ears with a wet towel.'[123]

Winifred said of her older son in later years that 'He stood on the stage, constantly slating everything Preetorius did, everything that Tietjen did, slating everything. Good Lord, of course I was very angry about it.'[124] On the other hand, being a loving mother, she wanted to mediate on behalf of the two 'lads'. After the Festival, she wrote a long letter to Tietjen, and asked him to have patience with their youth. Wieland felt 'that everything had been done and was being done to hold him back from his mission'. He thought that, particularly after his work on Roller's *Parsifal*, 'he had at least acquired the right to compete with Preetorius – naturally with the proviso that if Preetorius delivered a better design, then it would be adopted'. She referred to the fact that the Führer had released Wieland from military service 'in view of his later mission'. But 'now it was really embarrassing for Wieland that, as things stood, he didn't have even a modest sample to show the Führer of his contribution to the Work at Bayreuth, so that the Führer would have every right to doubt Wieland's ability to lead Bayreuth in the future'. Wolfgang, too, would like to take on more responsibility for the Festival.

She thought that 'wanting to make a more positive contribution was entirely justified'. The 'unbearable tensions' of that summer, 'which had betrayed the boys into using the wrong means', had come about mainly because Tietjen had not taken any time over the young people. She knew 'that it is your wish, too, that the lads should eventually take over in Bayreuth. So in the meantime it must also be your wish to be able to bring them on, lead them in that direction and instruct them.'[125]

Tietjen's reply to 'the youth of Wahnfried' came on 21 August 1941 in the form of a seven-page letter, which showed that gossip had contributed much to the catalogue of Wieland's sins. It appeared that Tietjen's daughter Elsa had heard that Wieland had called Tietjen's conducting 'terrible rubbish'.

The personnel director, Kirchner, had told people in the inn that Wieland 'would take over the running of Bayreuth', and said that 'All the outsiders who have come in over the last ten years will first have to get out' – a remark aimed at Tietjen and Preetorius, but also at Winifred herself.[126] Wagner's grandchildren were not yet ready for a leading role, said Tietjen. This letter reached Wieland on the day he was married in Nussdorf to his former teenage girlfriend Gertrud Reissinger.

Grimly, Wieland continued his fight against Tietjen, and in a letter to Overhoff asked the latter to supply him with evidence of Tietjen's conducting mistakes, because he had to justify the term 'rubbish'. He also wanted details of Tietjen's alleged 'remarks about "extravagant living in Wahnfried" etc. etc. . . . as much as possible'. And 'since I shall be held responsible if Tietjen resigns, you must help me . . . to put together as much unchallengeable material as possible'. This was all to do with the possibility of a confrontation between Wieland and Tietjen in the presence of Hitler. Wieland said to Overhoff, 'So next week there will be a discussion in Berlin.' It had to be said that Wolfgang feared that 'Heinz knew a good deal that could embarrass us . . . Heavy guns will be used.'[127]

Among the evidence for the prosecution assembled by Wieland against Tietjen, there was the 1939 story contributed by the Strobels concerning Grane, the horse that died. Tietjen had failed to follow the Führer's orders at the time, and was therefore unacceptable.[128]

At the end of September, well armed, Wieland went to see Hitler in Berlin. The Führer had his own way of settling this complicated dispute. He received Wieland via a private entrance, while Tietjen, General Intendant of the Prussian State Theatres, was kept waiting in the Reich Chancellery, and was not admitted to the presence. Thus Hitler avoided a confrontation with the self-confident Tietjen, superior to him in intelligence and debating power. He talked for a long time to Wieland, and listened to all his charges against Tietjen, but he must also have calmed the young man down and offered the prospect of future consolations.

Tietjen felt thoroughly humiliated, waiting outside a closed door, with no idea what was going on. When he finally asked whether he could possibly be allowed in to see Hitler, the sentries informed him that the Führer had already left the building.[129] The singer Barbara Kemp later reported that Wieland's alliance with Hitler and Goebbels had left Tietjen exposed to a 'war of destruction'.[130]

Wieland tried to win the artists over to his side as well. If they were uncooperative, he became abusive. Singers such as 'Bockelmann, who is said to have behaved disgustingly, and Prohaska should clear off'. He confided to Gertrud Strobel: 'Basically, I am confident about taking over the Festival now. But the artists wouldn't have any respect for me!' Strobel wrote: 'And now he wants to go to the Führer and describe the whole situation here in Bayreuth and explain that the so-called "armistice" had only been declared out of consideration for him, the Führer, and the continuation of the Festival in wartime!'[131]

The background to the power struggle between Wieland and Tietjen was the power struggle in cultural politics between Goebbels and Goering. Goering was standing firmly behind Tietjen, while Goebbels was trying with the help of the Wagner children to collect enough material on Tietjen to eliminate him, take command of the Prussian State Theatres, and depose Goering as head of the theatre world in Prussia*. While Winifred was still in favour with Hitler, Goebbels had no chance. But now that her star was waning, Hitler's protégé Wieland, out of hatred for Tietjen, placed himself under the patronage of Goebbels, consciously exploiting this rivalry for his own ends.

Friedelind's voice was then suddenly heard, too, in an American broadcast on the fifty-ninth anniversary of Wagner's death, 14 February 1942. Speaking from the Metropolitan Opera in New York, she touched on fundamental questions. Opera houses throughout the world were boycotting Wagner's works because of their contamination by Hitler. Meanwhile, in New York an international ensemble, including many emigrant Bayreuthers, were singing *Tannhäuser* in German. The broadcast was introduced by an interview held by the émigré journalist Erika Mann [daughter of Thomas], with Wagner's granddaughter Friedelind, who told the world, 'Although our country is at war with Germany, we are celebrating this great German. We are not fighting the spirit of Goethe, Beethoven or Wagner, but Hitler's vicious ideology and lust for conquest.'

She specifically addressed her German-speaking listeners in the USA, the émigrés. The question she had put to herself when deciding whether or not to leave Germany because of Hitler was: 'How would my grandfather Richard Wagner have acted in my position? Would he have stayed? Would

---

*Prussia was by then merely a geographical area. In 1934 the Nazi regime abolished the autonomy of all the German states, but the name continued to be used to indicate a territorial unit.

he have placed himself at the disposal of the Nazis?' The answer she gave herself was unambiguous: 'No doubt about it. Richard Wagner, who loved liberty and justice even more than he loved music, would not have been able to breathe in Hitler's Germany . . . Never would he have made common cause with the destroyer of all liberty and justice in Germany.'

Hitler had made Wagner his

> personal and state composer, and he wants the world to believe that if Richard Wagner were alive today he would write music in honour of him, the Führer. My grandfather is dead and cannot defend himself against this abuse. But I, his granddaughter, speak in his spirit and with his convictions when I tell you that "Senta's pure love", as well as *Lohengrin* and *Parsifal*, arise out of landscapes where no Nazi jackboot ever trod.

Hitler's abuse of power would be followed by a twilight of the gods. Hitler the blasphemer had also blasphemed against Richard Wagner, by making him his favourite. 'That is why I left Germany.'[132]

On 20 February 1942 Winifred received a letter from a high-ranking SS officer and official of the Propaganda Ministry. On the occasion of a Wagner anniversary, it said, over the US channel WGEA, somebody purporting to be his granddaughter, Friedelind Wagner, had broadcast a 'crudely anti-German speech'. He wanted Winifred to inform him whether this was an impostor or the real granddaughter of Wagner, which was 'hardly likely'. These things 'had to be counteracted where necessary'. He went on to supply a full transcript of the broadcast. Winifred must have reacted with great alarm, because she received a careful and reassuring letter back from Berlin in reply. He was sorry, he said, 'unwittingly . . . to have touched a raw nerve. A young girl, especially one from such a highly gifted artistic family, is bound to be particularly sensitive and easily influenced. It does not mean she is bad through and through.' It was 'naturally' a pity that a real granddaughter of Wagner was involved, but 'the public in Germany knows nothing about this, and never will'. Expressing the hope 'that your daughter will return home after the war, if she can be brought back under German influence', the Goebbels official signed off with a 'Heil Hitler and best wishes'.[133] Verena attempted to defend her sister to Goebbels, according to the latter, by 'trying to explain, if not excuse, Friedelind's nasty behaviour; but she was knocking at the wrong door with me'.[134]

WARTIME FESTIVAL, 1942

Winifred reported that at the beginning of 1942, when she wrote to ask Hitler whether there should be a Festival in the summer, 'he immediately replied "yes" . . . That means I can retain my most important people on the Hill, and I can start putting in my claims for what I need (perhaps the only place in the whole Reich that can!).' There was no programme as yet. The inclusion of *Tristan* depended on 'whether Lubin can bring herself to sing in Bayreuth while the war is still on'. Wieland needed another year for his preliminary studies in Eisenach (that is, in the Wartburg) for *Tannhäuser*.[135] What is more, Ulrich Roller was gone, and Wieland had been counting very much on his help and advice.

On 12 February Winifred wrote to Hitler: 'Most respected, dear friend and Führer. It fills us with pride and gratitude to know that on your orders the Festival Theatre is permitted to open its doors again, and we hope once more that we can do our duty in our way!' She made suggestions about the programme, and asked him to decide. Her main concern was to avoid putting on the complete *Ring* again, because visitors could in any case attend only one of the evenings, 'and to make the long journey from Styria, say, and then only see the *Rhinegold*, would be hard'. *Tristan* could be mounted again, but Act III, with the long monologues of the sick and dying Tristan 'might be too much for some badly wounded onlookers to bear'. Her suggestion was that 'A work like the Mastersingers would suit our present audiences best.'[136]

The tone of Winifred's letter is noticeably more deferential than before. It reflects not only the total dependence of the Festival upon Hitler personally, but also the changed relationship between Hitler and Winifred. She had not met him in person since August 1940. During this period, however, he had given frequent and extensive audiences to Wieland, as well as Verena and Wolfgang. With diminishing personal contact, Winifred's influence was also waning. But she could still pin her hopes on better times.

The regime, not excepting Goebbels himself, once more showed great generosity to Bayreuth. When a cinema company wanted to make a big film on Richard Wagner, Winifred suggested that it should appear in two parts. Goebbels's response was: 'I think that is right in this case, for Richard Wagner is one of our greatest cultural treasures, and presenting him artistically in the right light through film is one of the chief tasks of the developing music film in Germany.'[137]

Once again, Tietjen raised the rates of pay. From 391,000 marks the year before, the wage bill went up to 622,000 marks in 1942. He countered the objections of the tax adviser by saying that 'Bayreuth doesn't have to worry about these costs; they would simply apply to Berlin to have them reimbursed.'[138]

Hitler decided on a new production of the *Mastersingers*, for which Wieland was to do the stage designs. When Tietjen, as director, planned for 500 fewer people to appear in the Festival meadow scene, given the difficulty of procuring enough extras in the third year of the war, an irate Wieland asked the Strobels to look through the notes on the first production to see whether Tietjen's directive ran counter to the intentions of the Master. Wieland's letters of complaint to Tietjen, Preetorius and Winifred were mostly composed by the lawyer Fritz Meyer. The 'big gun' he wheeled up to threaten them with was: 'I just won't do the Mastersinger designs at all, then!'[139] Confident of victory, he announced he would go to Hitler and let him arbitrate. This caused Winifred great uneasiness, especially as she had not heard from Hitler. She was really worried that Wieland might actually persuade Hitler to dismiss Tietjen, or that Tietjen might feel sufficiently worn down to decide to resign. Wieland had said to Strobel 'that the big row with Tietjen was bound to come to a head eventually, and then he'd be finished in Berlin as well as Bayreuth; he [Wieland] would make sure of that!'[140]

In March, Wieland saw Hitler in Berlin and 'poured his heart out', says Gertrud Strobel. Hitler's decision was unexpected: 'The Führer doesn't want new productions in wartime; he would like to be there himself for any new *Mastersingers*! There should be one complete performance of the *Ring*, and in addition a couple of performances each of *Twilight of the Gods* and the *Dutchman*.' To compensate for the cancelled new production, he agreed 'for the first time to the appointment of extra staff, so that you could think of 1942 as a "reconstruction Festival"'.[141]

The next time Wieland saw Hitler, in April, the conversation turned to *Parsifal*. This 'Sacred Music Drama' was rejected by the ideologues of the NSDAP because it hardly fitted the cliché of the strong Germanic hero and warrior. As Winifred put it, 'the National Socialists thought they had to reject Parsifal as "ideologically unacceptable"'.[142] Neither Rosenberg, nor Himmler, nor Goebbels was willing to see *Parsifal* staged. Goebbels' verdict was: 'too pious for me. And too emotional. Not the thing for an old heathen . . . I prefer it when the old gods quarrel and trick each other. That is Life. Nature. Struggle.' He thought that 'the staging of *Parsifal* ought to be modernized. If we don't give up this mystical Christian style, we won't be able to keep *Parsifal* in the modern repertoire in the long run.'[143]

Wieland recounted that Hitler, who had 'gone completely grey!', had confessed to him that he would love to see *Parsifal* again. When Wieland mentioned Verena's suggestion, in the light of Rosenberg's opposition, that 'for the Third Reich, only Act II should be put on', that is, the 'heathen', secular act with Klingsor's magic garden and the flower maidens, Hitler 'roared with laughter'.[144] At any rate, he was thinking about 'creating a single, uniform staging of Parsifal to be used anywhere in Germany'. He was looking 'for an interpretation of Parsifal suitable for our time, while Himmler is trying to force through a ban on the work!!!' If that happened, said Wieland, then he [Wieland] would demand that Bach's entire *œuvre* should also be prohibited; and as he told the Strobels, 'If anything happens to the Führer, then we've had it anyway!'[145]

At another meeting, Hitler apparently commissioned Wieland 'to design a timeless Grail Temple! He wants to see Parsifal performed against the will of his own Party, as it were!!!! Now and for the next 20 years certain precautions would be necessary, but later the work would appear timeless, like the Matthew Passion!'[146]

On the question of when the war would end, Hitler made a number of different predictions to Wieland. In April 1942 he thought 'there wouldn't be a peacetime Festival the next year, but definitely the one after that!' In June he said that 'the Russian business would be over' before the year was out. In any case, Hitler told Wieland, the construction of the new Festival Theatre 'should begin immediately after the war ends . . . so there shouldn't be any Festival straight away! The new building should be finished within a year!'[147]

The extent of Winifred's exclusion is clear from Hitler's invitation to Verena and Wolfgang, two days after Wieland's. It was for lunch on 10 June 1942 in the Osteria Bavaria in Munich, together with Gerdy Troost. On that occasion Hitler emphasized that he regarded Wieland and Wolfgang as heirs to Bayreuth; Wieland for the musical side, and Wolfgang for the technical.[148]

The artists arrived in Bayreuth at the end of June. Gertrud Strobel noted 'how wretched many of them looked, and what the Cologne people have to say about their ruined city (the Bremen people haven't even been able to get here yet because of the air-raids!).' She also heard about Lidice*: 'Up until the arrest of Heydrich's murderers it seems that they've been shooting 20–30 people a day in the Protectorate, mainly intellectuals (the women going to concentration camps, the children to approved schools), and the little town where they found a radio transmitter has been razed to the ground, all the men shot, the women taken to camps etc.'[149]

These private stories contrast with the news flashes on the radio. 'The enemy forces penned in on the Volkhov have been destroyed!' Mersa Matruh had been taken. 'Sebastopol has been captured! . . . The German and Romanian anthems are being played.'[150]

Due to paper shortages, the weekend edition of the *Bayerische Ostmark* was only eight pages long. Food was by then in short supply even in the hotels and inns. The artists envied the 'guests of the Führer' their extra rations, 'and so', said Winifred, 'we made the concession of giving them one coupon-free meal a day up in the Festival Restaurant'.[151] Asked what she wanted for her birthday, Winifred replied 'coffee, tea, or nappies'.[152] On 12 June 1942 Iris was born, the first child of Wieland and Gertrud, and Winifred's first grandchild.

On 8 July the special trains carrying 'guests of the Führer' pulled into Bayreuth, to be welcomed by Winifred; Reich Leader of the KdF Lafferentz; Gauleiter Wächtler; Mayor Kempfler; and a band playing. The following day the Festival opened with the *Twilight of the Gods*. As highlighted by the newspapers, apart from front-line German troops, among the guests were 'members of all the European voluntary brigades fighting shoulder to shoulder on the eastern front with German soldiers against the common Bolshevik foe'; Croats, Belgians, French and others. Tickets for the second *Ring* cycle were issued only to wounded men from the eastern front.[153] Winifred welcomed the Japanese ambassador, Hiroshi Oshima, and his wife. He had accompanied Prince Chichibu on his visit to Bayreuth in 1937.

In the compulsory introductory lecture, a representative of the Gauleiter explained once more that the Festival expressed 'especially during wartime,

---

*Located in the north west of the Czech Republic. In 1942 the SS man Reinhard Heydrich, Protector of Czechoslovakia since 1941, was assassinated by Czech partisans flown in from England. German reprisals included razing the village of Lidice to the ground, shooting the 173 male inhabitants, and deporting the women to concentration camps.

the unbroken cultural life-spirit of the German people'. Explaining the con-tent of Wagner's work, the lecturer pointed out 'that Wagner had always dreamed of "the Greater German Reich", and in his works had repeatedly expressed his belief in the Reich'. Inevitably, he quoted King Henry from *Lohengrin*: '. . . with savage threats the foe takes up his arms./ Now is the time to save the honour of the Reich;/ whether to East or West, let all beware!/ In every German land, draw up the fighting hosts,/ No one then will scorn the German Reich!'[154]

Lafferentz described the Bayreuth Festival of 1942, with its 35,000 'guests of the Führer', as 'the crowning glory of KdF efforts for the troops during the war'. Many had had a long journey to get to Bayreuth, for the area the KdF was responsible for – corresponding to Hitler's conquests – stretched from the North Cape to the Sahara, from the Atlantic to the depths of Russia; a sur-face area ten times the size of the German Reich. Then he talked about 'the profound connections between war and culture', describing war as the real father of every culture. For above all, they were fighting 'the fight for the preservation of our culture'.[155]

Between Lafferentz, a married man, and Verena, half his age, a great love developed in that period. The powerful KdF functionary was soon to play a big part in the war of the Bayreuth succession, supporting Wieland at Verena's side. This became apparent by July 1942. The 'non-Aryan' Lotte Warburg, who had fled with her family to Holland, received a surprise visit from a representative of 'Strength through Joy'. Robert Ley was interested in the Warburg estate near Bayreuth, Grunau, and wanted to buy it. The mar-ried couple, the Meyer-Viol-Warburgs, were invited to Paris for discussions. The necessary visas had been taken care of.

In Paris it was not Ley who turned up to negotiate, but Lafferentz; accord-ing to Lotte Warburg,

a very good-looking gentleman, with whom the conversation went very amicably. He said that they [the KdF] wanted Grunau as a residence for Frau Wagner, as they were keen that she should have a solid base in the Bayreuth district. They proposed to build a house for her up on the hill and use our house, currently uninhabitable because of the damp, only as a guest house. I said we had lived there for twelve years, and had all been in good health. To which he replied, 'You were lucky, then.' In short, like a good businessman he ran down everything as much as he could.

When they showed no inclination to sell, Lafferentz made his message plainer: 'They had already "been obliged to" requisition a number of prop-erties where necessary for the common good and the economy.' Besides, the KdF naturally did not want to 'give Frau Wagner anything that would just cost her money rather than bring in income'. And she 'absolutely must have some woodland attached . . . The woods were now state-owned, but Goering would no doubt be reasonable.'[156]

The sale never took place. Winifred doggedly refused to accept such a gift. She saw that the aim of the move was to evict her from Villa Wahnfried, and had no intention of being pushed out. The 'Wielands' had their second child by then, and did not want to live anywhere but in Wahnfried, but they did not want his mother around. In the end Winifred decided, for the sake of keeping the peace in the family, to divide Wahnfried immediately after the Festival into two separate dwellings for herself and Wieland, with guest-rooms for the other children. This meant expensive and prolonged rebuilding in the very large but impractical old house, with workmen and materials in short supply.

It was not quite as easy as he had imagined for 25-year-old Wieland to dis-place his 45-year-old, robust and energetic mother as head of the Festival. Amidst war and destruction, highly privileged and freed from military serv-ice and every kind of alternative duty, he fought to achieve his one great aim, his 'seizure of power' in Bayreuth. In August 1942 he made a new assault, announcing that he was going to persuade the Führer to intervene. Strobel commented: 'Wieland must have a chance to tell the Führer everything, to get everything sorted out once and for all.'[157]

In the eleven-page draft of a letter, Wieland first of all went on the attack against Preetorius, but without naming names. It had been a scandal to con-front the Führer with meretricious Cubist and Expressionist constructs on the Bayreuth stage in 1934.[158] These were common terms for 'degenerate art', which was banned in the Third Reich. Wieland himself as a painter belonged to the approved 'German artists', whose portrait in oils of his father Siegfried had even been selected by Hitler for the German Art Exhibition of 1940.

Wieland's attack on Preetorius was also an act of open rebellion against his mother and Tietjen. He could afford to be as bold as this only because he was certain of protection in the highest places. More and more he made his mother feel that the blood of the Master flowed in his veins, while she was an outsider, a Wagner merely by marriage. The balance of power in Wahnfried had shifted with Wieland's closeness to Hitler, even if Winifred was still the Mistress as far as the public were concerned.

Wieland took an ever greater part in the running of things. Gertrud Strobel said that, in the name of the Research Centre, he even tried to give instructions to the radio company about their broadcasts: 'He wants to suggest to Goebbels and Ley that special recordings of Wagner's works should be made for the radio, with Furtwängler and Krauss as the only conductors; and that other recordings should be banned from the air waves.'[159] That would have meant eliminating performances under Carl Muck or Karajan. Recordings by Toscanini, Fritz Busch, Otto Klemperer, Erich Kleiber, Bruno Walter and others had been prohibited since 1933.

Wieland then demanded to be given not only Preetorius's job as stage designer for Bayreuth, but also Tietjen's as director. On 29 October 1942 Overhoff was in a position to report to the Strobels 'that "high places" are now in possession of all the facts about Tietjen, and that Wieland is going to Berlin himself tomorrow to complete the presentation . . . Wieland has changed completely: relaxed, lively, and happy!'[160] In Berlin Wieland met not only Hitler but Goebbels. The reaction of the latter was cautious, however, especially since all this came amidst the reports of disaster on the eastern front, and his diary entry for 24 November 1942 reads: '. . . I don't much want to get drawn into these family affairs. Bayreuth has always been a gossip and rumour factory, anyway, and mud will just stick to anyone who touches all that dirt.'[161]

A fortnight later, though, on 8 December, Wieland's latest approach was rewarded with an assurance from Goebbels that he could count on his 'active support' against Tietjen. Wieland, he said, had 'matured a good deal in the last few years, and made an exceptionally solid and reliable impression'.[162] Wieland intended, as he told the Strobels, 'to stay away from Bayreuth during the Festival next year, to make the dividing line perfectly clear to the outside world!'[163]

Precisely at this time, in December 1942, Preetorius was charged by a 'Dr Gk', of the Goebbels-run Reich Music Chamber, with being 'philo-Semitic'. The accuser was Herbert Gerigk, the powerful head of the Music Directorate in Rosenberg's DBFU, Dienststelle des Beautragten des Führers für die Überwachung der gesamten geistigen und weltanschaulichen Schulung und Erziehung der NSDAP ('Office of the Führer's Commissioner for the supervision of the entire intellectual and ideological training and education of the NSDAP', or OFCS) and co-editor of the infamous *Encyclopaedia of Jews in*

Music, a reference volume about Jewish musicians and composers, whose works could no longer be performed in Germany. Gerigk was a notorious and much feared Jew-baiter.

Preetorius's mail was inspected, and his house was searched. The search did indeed produce some friendly correspondence with Jews in Holland. Preetorius was forbidden to work, and declared an 'enemy of the State' by Gauleiter Paul Giesler of Munich. His experience of what he later described as 'the sorcery of terror' in his interrogations by the Gestapo stayed with him for the rest of his life. 'All the terrible things I've been through, with vaults crashing down, cellars reduced to rubble and people dying in agony – none of that compares with interrogation by the Gestapo . . . being so completely helpless, so defenceless against those horrible people is so paralysing that I suddenly understood how in such a situation you could give in and start "confessing".'[164]

In this life-and-death situation, someone must have intervened on behalf of Preetorius, and everything points to Goering, via Tietjen. The fact is that when Bormann put this 'occurrence' to Hitler at the beginning of January 1943, and asked for instructions about what to do with this 'enemy of the State', Hitler played it down and decided 'that Preetorius could go on working unhindered, despite his attitude'. On being asked 'how the Party press should deal with Preetorius', the Munich chancellery of the Party said it had nothing to say about the matter, 'except that a certain reserve seemed to be in order, without appearing to insult Preetorius by suppressing his name'.[165] The worst had been avoided, and at least Preetorius had his freedom again. For the rest of his life he was tormented by the question of who had denounced him to the Gestapo. His hatred and scorn for Wieland, whom he suspected, endured for years. It was to be ten years before Preetorius entered the Festival Theatre again.

Tietjen, however, retained his posts both in Berlin and in Bayreuth, and he could hardly have done so unless it was Hitler's specific wish. Despite his affection for the oldest grandchild of the Master, Hitler was obviously wary of taking his beloved Bayreuth away from the proven and artistically successful control of Tietjen, and putting it in the hands of the (by then 26-year-old) inexperienced novice Wieland, thereby jeopardizing its very existence. In return, he was prepared to overlook Tietjen's political unreliability.

CHAPTER 13

The Long Ending

(1943–5)

DEPORTATIONS

The war was being fought not only against enemy states, but expressly and especially against 'international Jewry', including 'the enemy within', German Jewry. Lacking information, surrounded by an indifferent population, the Jews were trapped. Emigration was practically impossible. The frontiers were closed. On 21 November 1941, they lost their German citizenship. What was left of their assets was confiscated by the state. A special penal dispensation was introduced for Poles and Jews that permitted instant verdicts, up to and including the death sentence, without the right of appeal.[1] The Jews were outside the law.

Of the original Jewish population of 260, there were only about seventy still living in Bayreuth in 1941 (estimates differ). On 27 November 1941 forty-six of them were sent on a three-day journey, first to a reception camp and then to Kaiserwald concentration camp in Riga.[2] On 16 January 1942 eleven Bayreuth Jews aged over sixty, including the once highly respected Justice Berthold Klein and his wife, were taken to the 'White Dove' old-age home in Bamberg, and were charged a five-figure sum for the privilege. What the Bayreuthers did not know was that in September 1942 they would be taken from there to Theresienstadt, and thence to Lithuania or Auschwitz. None survived.[3]

The remaining seven Bayreuth Jews lived under terrible conditions; one family even in the unheated mortuary of the Jewish cemetery. Two of them committed suicide, and four died. The last, Justin Steinhäuser, a front-line soldier in the First World War, in which he lost an arm and was awarded the Iron Cross, was taken in November 1944 to a work camp in Thuringia, and from there to the Flossenbürg concentration camp. He survived.

Winifred received many pleas for help at that time. As she reported after 1945, 75 per cent of her daily post consisted of such appeals, 'and there was not a single case that I did not deal with. I never addressed Hitler directly, since I knew that such letters never reached his hands, and so could never achieve anything.'[4] Not having met Hitler since the summer of 1940, she had only limited channels open to her.

There were more and more strangers among the supplicants, mostly friends and relatives of people she had helped before. Among the thirty or so letters she received daily, 'at least twenty were from people I didn't know at all, who wanted something or other from me'.[5] By then, it usually involved sheer survival, especially where Jews were concerned.

Helping out on just a single occasion was sufficient only when it was a matter of assistance to emigrate, as with the Pringsheims. Otherwise, most of Winifred's protégés needed help more than once, and this became increasingly difficult. With the successful experience of 1936 behind her, the blind Elsa Bernstein turned to Winifred again in autumn 1941 with a request for help in obtaining US visas for herself and her sister Gabriele Porges. Winifred managed to get a visa for the 75-year-old Elsa, but not for her 73-year-old sister. Elsa Bernstein was not prepared to leave without her sister; she gave up the expensive visa, and stayed.[6]

To fend off their impending deportation, in June 1942 the sisters, who were staunch Protestants and German nationalists, begged Winifred to arrange for their 'Aryanization', that is, their official conversion into 'Aryans', as she had succeeded in doing in 1935 in the Chrambach case. Aryanization was a long and arduous process, and by 1942 had little prospect of success, especially not for two old ladies who could hardly be thought useful to the Nazis. None the less, Winifred immediately wrote off to the Reich Minister of Justice asking him to cast a favourable eye over the two ladies' applications to be Aryanized. The letter was unsuccessful. In June 1942 the sisters were taken to the Theresienstadt concentration camp, where Gabriele Porges died a month later from an intestinal infection.

It took prolonged efforts on Winifred's part to have Elsa Bernstein transferred in November 1942 to the 'important persons' camp' within Theresienstadt. It held fewer than a hundred people – academics, artists, high-ranking politi-cians and aristocrats. The blind old lady was cared for, permitted to write and to receive parcels, had her own bed, was better fed and was safe from deportation. The survival rate in this VIP camp was 85 per cent. By contrast, ghetto inmates had only a 14 per cent chance of survival, those deported to the east only 4 per cent, and, actuarially speaking, people of Elsa Bernstein's age had no prospect of surviving at all.[7] During one of the dreaded sudden 'registrations', Elsa Bernstein found out that the name of Winifred Wagner carried weight in Theresienstadt. Asked by two officials, 'Can you name any Aryan contacts?', she mentioned Winifred, as well as Elsa Bruckmann, and was left in peace.[8] Elsa Bernstein survived. She was liberated in 1945 at the age of seventy-nine, and was later to provide written evidence in Winifred's defence.[9]

Such privilege was highly exceptional. How exceptional is shown up by contrast with the fate of Kurt Singer, the conductor, and founder of the Jewish Cultural League. Although he was able to produce a letter from Furtwängler, his application to be classified as a VIP was turned down. He died at fifty-nine in the 'ordinary' Theresienstadt concentration camp.[10]

Rescuing the former Darmstadt musical director Paul Ottenheimer took place in two stages. The singer Susi Ottenheimer appeared in Wahnfried in May 1943 looking for help. Her Jewish father had been taken away by the Gestapo and was threatened with deportation. Winifred promised to do 'everything in her power'. Ottenheimer was indeed suddenly freed, after four weeks in Gestapo hands: 'I was still saying "where are you taking me?"', but they said I was free, I could go home. There I found out who I had to thank for getting me out . . . But it's the most wonderful thing that could ever happen to anyone, coming to my aid like that.'[11]

Ottenheimer, by then seventy-two, was nevertheless back on the depor-tation list by early 1945, and his daughter cycled the 200 kilometres to Wahnfried to enlist Winifred's help once more. While she was away, her father was 'collected' and taken to Theresienstadt. Winifred kept the exhausted and desperate young woman with her for two days in Wahnfried while she considered what to do. It was impossible to get Ottenheimer released from the concentration camp. But it took Winifred only three days to have him transferred to the VIP camp, where he survived the last few months of the Third Reich.[12]

Verena said later that many concentration camp commandants were keen to do favours for the Mistress of Bayreuth, simply because they feared she might lodge a complaint with Hitler. That may have been true of the following case. The 'non-Aryan' doctor Klaus Rauh from Gera was denounced because of critical remarks about the 'Men of the Third Reich', and arrested by the Gestapo in 1943 for 'publicly subverting the war effort'. He became very ill in prison, and Winifred managed to secure his transfer to hospital. Three weeks later, when he was taken to Sachsenhausen concentration camp, she arranged with the camp commandant that he should not be mistreated. His situation as a prisoner was therefore 'not a comfortable one, certainly, but at least it did not lead to the scaffold'. Rauh claims that because of him Winifred had 'serious conflicts with Himmler'.[13]

After 1945 the mother of the Augsburg Jew Hans Winternitz described his sufferings. For twelve years he had been 'unimaginably persecuted and tormented'.

> Three times the 'Jew wagon' stood outside our door ready to take him to forced labour or to Poland to be gassed. The first time, his superior managed to hold on to him. The second time, he took poison, but was revived. The third time he escaped to Berlin, where he lived underground like a hunted animal for two years without a name, without anywhere to live, and without a ration card. Five minutes before Berlin fell he was putting out fires, in the service of others, when he was killed by a hand grenade.

In these years of 'extreme persecution and anguish', Winifred had been a 'motherly friend' to him. 'She took him, the outlawed Jew, into her house as a guest, gave him lodgings, sheltered him with true charity, and tried to use her connections in high places to intervene in his tragic fate.'[14] She did in fact succeed in placing Winternitz in a job for a time with a businessman friend of hers called Schickedanz.[15]

Alice Ripper, the 'non-Aryan' Hungarian pianist, a pupil of Liszt's, went underground in Vienna and was able to survive with Winifred's assistance, which would have been impossible but for Winifred's contact with Baldur von Schirach, who was Gauleiter at the time.[16] There were probably other cases, but success was rare in these years, and depended on such accidents as whether Winifred happened to come across a decent human being, or somebody who thought she still had influence with Hitler. When the crisis was at its height, and the deportation of Jews was in full operation, there was very little Winifred could do to help. After 1945 she had to admit that, though she had saved many people, 'in many more cases, my efforts to influence the people in charge were in vain'.[17]

The ignorance of many Germans even as late as wartime about the true nature of the concentration camps is attested by the example of Richard Strauss. In 1942 his family were concerned for Paula Neumann, Alice Strauss's Jewish grandmother. When they heard that the old lady had been deported to Theresienstadt, described in the newspapers as a 'model camp', Strauss decided to act. Driving from Dresden to Vienna, he got his chauffeur to make a detour to Theresienstadt. He announced himself at the entrance: 'I am Richard Strauss, and I have come to take Frau Neumann away.' The sentries were baffled. When he insisted, they went off to fetch a superior officer. Strauss had a long wait before the answer came back: 'No access for anybody.'[18] Paula Neumann was deported to the east in 1943, and her life ended there.

Deportations were carried out without warning. There was rarely time to launch a rescue bid, especially as wartime conditions made postal and telephone communications difficult. The authorities pointed time and again to their legal obligations. To contravene them, from the Nuremberg Laws to the subsequent 'Jewish laws', was to incur punishment.

In January 1941 Winifred received a pleading letter from a doctor, Melanie Adler, not known to her personally, who was the daughter of the Viennese music historian Guido Adler. The 'full Jew' Adler, eighty-five years old and terminally ill, had written a biography of Wagner; he was an opponent of the orthodox Wagnerism of the 'Cosimans'. He was still living in his villa in Vienna, but was about to be moved to a Viennese 'Jewish camp'. Winifred held out little hope: 'I have tried to take steps to prevent your elderly father from being moved, but I don't know whether an exception can be made to the law in this case. I will let you know the answer.'[19] Adler died a month later, but had at least been able to stay in his own home. The story in Vienna was that he had been protected during those weeks by his ex-student and successor at the university, the Mozart biographer Erich Schenk.

After her father's death, his 'full-blood Jewish' daughter and sole heiress was under threat. Her inheritance, aside from the villa, included a valuable library, a world-famous collection of music autographs, and Adler's correspondence with the foremost composers and musicians of the day, such as his old friend Gustav Mahler.[20] Melanie Adler was not allowed to assume her inheritance; nor, on the other hand, did she have the visa or the money she needed to emigrate. Threatened with deportation, she was concerned above all with how the collection and the library were to be preserved for posterity. Since she could no longer take care of it herself, she asked Winifred to appeal to the relevant authorities to make sure the library remained intact. The matter went on for months.

In October 1941 there was another letter from Melanie Adler. 'It's true that I'm still in my home. But since the latest events I don't know how long that will last, and what will become of me, since I have heard nothing about the results of your kind intervention on my behalf. With my greatest respect and gratitude, my dear lady.'[21] Frau Adler suggested sending the library to Wahnfried to ensure its safety. As she optimistically wrote to the Munich music historian Rudolf von Ficker at the end of 1941, Winifred had 'taken the matter of custodianship energetically in hand, so that there was every prospect of a positive outcome'.[22] Who it was that Winifred was negotiating with in Vienna is not known. No further letters to her from Melanie Adler are extant.

In May 1942, when Ficker was looking for Frau Adler in Vienna, he observed that the Adler library 'was being deposited and piled up, together with all the personal documents and accessories', at the Music Institute of the University of Vienna. Asking Schenk about Adler's daughter, Ficker received the reply that her behaviour had been 'bloody stupid' – she had protested about the Gestapo confiscating the library. She had meanwhile escaped, but the Gestapo would soon find her, and then it would be 'on your way, to Poland!'[23] Sure enough, Melanie Adler, having gone underground just before Christmas 1941, was betrayed, and deported to Minsk on 20 May 1942. There is no trace of her from that point onwards.[24]

Another remarkable story was told by Winifred, without mentioning any date, to the American officers in 1946. Elisabeth Graf from Darmstadt had asked her to help her 'to get in touch with her daughter, living in Auschwitz. I approached the Reich Organization for Jews in Berlin and got a severe mauling from Himmler.' This 'mauling' was passed on to her by Police Commissioner Benno Martin and Mayor Fritz Kempfler.[25] Nothing more is known.

Winifred's relations with Hitler were now limited to telephone calls about the Festival, many letters from her, a few brief replies from him, and a food parcel once a year, at Christmas, which as Winifred said was 'identical in content to those sent to all the leading artists in Germany at Christmas'.[26]

After 1945 she stated that 'As soon as positive discussion became impossible because of conflicting views, Hitler never came to see me again, and I did not try to see him.'[27] The reasons she listed for this estrangement were her support for the British ambassador in trying to prevent the war in 1939, Friedelind's anti-Hitler campaign in exile, and finally, the events that led to Ulrich Roller's death. In addition, she cited troublemaking by powerful enemies such as Goebbels, Bormann, Wächtler and others; and not least, Wieland's increasing influence over Hitler.

The main reason no doubt was in fact Winifred's efforts on behalf of endangered Jews. Hitler's reaction can be gauged by the experience of Henriette von Schirach in the Berghof in 1943. She had known Hitler since she was a child, but when she tried to bring the fate of the Dutch Jews to his attention, he shouted angrily at her, and refused all further contact with her.[28] Flight Captain Hans Baur once asked Hitler, who was by then becoming increasingly isolated, why he kept his old friends at a distance. Hitler replied that he could no longer maintain these contacts, because 'If I accept an invitation to visit someone, the lady of the house is bound to come and ask me for something. As a guest, it's hard to reject a request. But if I don't inwardly agree with her request, I can't reconcile fulfilling it with my conscience.'[29]

In the meantime, even those in Hitler's circle who were well used to helping her were tiring of Winifred's interference. The Party had become very nervous of her because her letters always spelt complications, annoyance and effort for them. Handing over a letter to Dr Brandt in Berlin, the Bayreuth mayor, Kempfler, commented, 'It's about a Jew again.' When Kempfler explained that it was a 'half-Jew' this time, Brandt replied dryly, 'Well, things are starting to improve, then.' Winifred's reaction on being told of this remark was typically self-confident: 'They'll just have to start getting used to it; I'm surprised it's taking them so long.'[30] Even to her friend Kempfler she did not want to admit how ineffectual she was.

The help that Winifred gave to so many Jews was spontaneous, unquestioning, full of human sympathy, and not at all calculating. There is no doubt that she knew what was going on in the east. And yet, in the old Bayreuth manner, she went on using anti-Semitic propaganda phrases, even though the misery of the Jews confronted her daily. Writing to her friend Lene, for example, who had entrusted further needy cases to her:

> I wrote straight away to Rauter about Wijsenbeek – but this stricter measure against *all* Jews has to be seen as a reprisal for the terror attacks [Allied air-raids], because it's international Jewry that's behind them, after all –

individuals have got to pay for it – but I don't believe W. will be killed unless he's done something particularly bad, and that doesn't seem to be the case.[31]

Shortly before the end of the war she did actually manage to get this young Dutch Jew, Louis Wijsenbeek, released from Gestapo custody and returned to The Hague.[32]

STALINGRAD

While the Goebbels press went on reporting successes in the east in the winter of 1942–3, Winifred was well informed about the disastrous military situation. Her informant was Kempfler, who in turn got his information from a telephonist on the eastern front. For days on end it had seemed 'as though the front was collapsing completely. But then by some miracle, contact between the [German] armies was just about restored, and the Russian troops were held off for the time being.' For the first time, such news made Kempfler consider that this war might not be winnable. But he had faith 'in Hitler's skill as a statesman – amply demonstrated in the years 1933–39 – and therefore in a more or less acceptable political solution'; in other words, a negotiated peace.[33] Winifred shared his optimism.

On 22 January 1943, after hearing nothing but constant triumphant reports, almost all Germans were utterly surprised by the sudden news ('the most serious army bulletin since the war began', in Otto Strobel's words) of 'retreat in the eastern Caucasus; Russian penetration from the west of the Stalingrad defences; pulling back of the front by "several kilometres"; retreat in Africa as far as Tripoli!!! We are completely stunned.' On 3 February came the news of the end of the 6th Army at Stalingrad. 'Goebbels has given orders that all theatres, cinemas etc. will stay closed until Saturday, and all events are cancelled.' Gertrud Strobel noted that 'the radio is only broadcasting Beethoven etc. – all of a sudden!'[34]

The regime tried to lighten the depressed mood by announcing bigger bread and meat rations, which according to the situation report of the SS Security Service 'initially served substantially to push all political and military reports (for example, Stalingrad) into the background'.[35] The quantity and quality of foodstuffs deteriorated again soon afterwards. Indefinable substitute products, chestnuts for example, were mixed in with bread dough, leading to stomach pains and diarrhoea among a population which was already debilitated.

There were new reports every day about those killed or missing. But even on 22 February, when the scale of the defeat at Stalingrad was public knowledge, Winifred remained loyal to the state – that is, not 'defeatist' – and tried to reassure herself and her friend Lene, 'despite the terribly dangerous military situation'. 'I am assuming we will make it,' she wrote, 'for one thing because we must, and for another, because we've got the Führer.'[36] Later, however, she confessed that 'after Stalingrad, I no longer believed in the Final Victory'.[37]

Increasingly, bombers flew over Bayreuth to carry out heavy raids on Nuremberg; associated with the Nazi Party rallies, the town had a powerful symbolic significance for the Allies. Winifred described to Lene how

> you could see the flashes from the barrels of the ack-ack guns every time they fired . . . we saw two planes coming down after being hit, too – what I'm going to do is to place myself on look-out duty on the balcony. Emma will sit in Wolfi's bedroom, and at a signal from me she can grab Betty immediately and take her down to the cellar, while I make a dash for Iris – but so far I've just let the children go on sleeping, and they haven't noticed a thing.

Wieland's six-month-old daughter Iris was too delicate to be constantly woken up, so Winifred took the risk of 'waiting for the first shot'. You simply had to get used to it, despite your overstrained nerves.[38] Meanwhile, Winifred served as an air-raid warden, using gasmasks, on air-raid training exercises.

Whole pages of the newspapers were filling up with the names of those killed on active service, as well as of air-raid victims. Masses of refugees poured out of the big cities into areas like Upper Franconia, looking for shelter, and with terrible tales to tell. Amidst all this, Winifred wrote very obsequiously to Hitler on 8 March 1943, asking for his decision about the Festival programme: 'My most respected, dear friend and Führer! . . . I would be most grateful if you could let me have your final decision on this matter.' She ended with the sentence: 'All my thoughts and dearest wishes are with you in your colossal undertaking! In everlasting gratitude and admiration, your faithful and devoted Winifred.'[39]

On 21 March, 'Heroes Commemoration Day', Hitler read out a speech over the radio – far too quickly, thought Strobel. It was also hard to understand and lacking in content, 'no way to honour heroes, really; the whole thing was quite strange. It left us quite bewildered.'[40] Rumours that Hitler was seriously ill proliferated. He was certainly no longer projecting the spellbinding power for which he had always been famous.

Fewer and fewer Germans believed in a great victory, but anyone who voiced these doubts risked being denounced and arrested for 'defeatism'. That is what befell the 31-year-old Bayreuth policeman Willi Wagner. He was arrested and sentenced to death by a court martial. The verdict was already final and absolute, but had not yet been confirmed by Berlin, when his wife, then twenty-six, implored Winifred to help, although she did not know her personally. Winifred read the relevant papers, and found that the arguments put forward in the trial did not hold water. She decided to go for an appeal, but first of all suggested a petition for clemency, which she composed herself and had conveyed to Berlin by an intermediary. Betty Wagner went to see the relevant General in Berlin, mentioned Winifred's name, was admitted and allowed to present her case. The result was a second trial in May 1943, where all the witnesses were recalled. The death sentence was commuted to 'front-line probation'. Willi Wagner survived.[41]

Meanwhile, Wieland, still exempt from the military, was causing further turbulence. He felt he had reached the point in his training under Kurt Overhoff where he needed practical theatre experience. He wanted to produce the entire *Ring*, complete with direction, sets and costumes. 'So he demanded forcefully that I should be given a theatre for this purpose, where I could introduce him to the practical side,' says Overhoff.[42]

When his wish was not immediately fulfilled, Wieland suspected machinations on Tietjen's part. Verena came to her brother's aid, and raised the subject over tea with Magda Goebbels in Berlin. The latter suggested that she should stay for dinner and ask Goebbels himself about the matter. In his capacity now as supreme director of all theatres in Germany, he ordered Overhoff's appointment as 'chief musical director' at the Altenburg Theatre in Thuringia.[43] Help was also forthcoming from the Wagnerian Hans Severus Ziegler, the most powerful cultural official in Thuringia.[44] Goebbels awarded the small theatre a special state subsidy of 120,000 marks for Wieland's *Ring* production.[45] Overhoff took up his post in Altenburg in April 1943. Wieland and Gertrud shared accommodation with him, while little Iris stayed with Winifred. Wieland treated the Altenburg Theatre as his private property. In order to test the lighting at his leisure, he closed the theatre for a week, without prior warning, before the première of the *Twilight of the Gods*.[46]

In Wahnfried, meanwhile, preparations were going ahead for the wedding of Wolfgang and Ellen Drexel, a dancer from the Berlin State Opera. Winifred went to Berlin for a few days in February 1943 to buy furniture and household goods for the young couple's home. This was a tall order in the fourth year of the war. Finding no suitable furniture there, she followed a tip and enquired at the Central Bureau for the Settlement of Jewish Affairs in Prague. It was selling off, at reasonable prices, furniture and other goods from former Jewish properties. And sure enough, Winifred was soon driving to Prague with Kempfler in his large car, the back seats having been removed. Whether or not she really came back only with a child's bath and one or two other small items, as she was later to claim during the de-nazification hearings, remains to be established.

Wolfgang and Ellen were married on 11 April 1943 in Bayreuth. Wolfgang sang his mother's praises to the Roeseners for having organized everything down to the last detail, including everything they needed for their new household, 'because she's a real virtuoso at that kind of thing!!' The registrar and mayor's speeches were 'personal and nice', as Wolfgang wrote, 'so that we didn't feel the lack of a clergyman, and weren't annoyed by stupid National Socialist clichés, either'.[47] This was a fairly dangerous thing to write, given that the mail was not secure.

A few weeks later the young couple presented themselves to pay their respects to Hitler in the Reich Chancellery, and Winifred proudly reported to Lene: 'He received them alone for a whole hour.'[48] She herself had not seen Hitler for almost three years.

BOMBS OVER BAYREUTH

After Preetorius's enforced departure, the Festival could no longer use his stage-sets, and thus faced a dilemma. The only non-Preetorius production was Wieland's 1937 *Parsifal*, not a suitable work for wartime audiences. The very expensive *Flying Dutchman* production of 1939, as well as the entire *Ring*, had to remain in storage. The only available stage designer was 26-year-old Wieland – exactly the situation he had been aiming at all along.

For reasons of economy, in agreement with Hitler a decision was reached to present only one work, the most popular. Producing *The Mastersingers* also served to commemorate its première seventy-five years earlier. When Wieland once again began to make difficulties, as he had the year before, demanding that Tietjen should now resign, Winifred remained unmoved: 'If Wieland refuses to do his [Tietjen's] *Mastersingers*, like last year, then we'll just have to look for another stage designer and proceed as normal with him.'[49] Only after protracted wrangling did the young man consent to get down to work. Gertrud Strobel summed it up: 'He had to do the designs for this year's *Mastersingers*, or else face a complete break with his mother! He has been told that he's the reason why the *Dutchman* can't be put on here! The whole of the *Ring* is being packed away, too.' She reported that the situation at Wahnfried was 'appalling!'[50]

Hitler successfully put pressure on Furtwängler to conduct at Bayreuth. Sixteen performances were planned, with a day's break between each, in order to facilitate the arrival of the guests, who were now only staying one night in Bayreuth. Winifred told Lene, 'It makes everything more difficult to carry out – but if that's what the Führer wants, then that's how it has to be.'[51]

There was a shortage of material for making costumes, but Tietjen helped out with a loan of the costumes made for the grand reopening of the Berlin State Opera the previous year. Wieland suspected a further Tietjen plot, but in the end, said Winifred, 'Wieland condescended to design stage-sets for Bayreuth.'[52] Tietjen was going to be directing as usual, so the arch-enemies were compelled to work together, whether they liked it or not.

Great difficulties arose because Armaments Minister Speer would not release the necessary staff: waiters, chefs, hairdressers and other tradespeople. He told Winifred to further limit the personnel, 'to the absolute minimum necessary'.[53] The town of Bayreuth allocated a few forced labourers to the Festival for the summer months. Forty work-service conscripts were employed as waitresses in the Festival restaurant, and a few volunteers appeared from the National Socialist Women's League. There were, after all, some 1,500 people to be catered for every day.

The labour-intensive household at Wahnfried also had help from forced labour. The seventeen-year-old Ukrainian girl Anna Turkot, from Stepkovka near Uman,[54] was a pretty, delicate, round-faced girl, according to Verena. She lived with the two other housemaids in the gardeners' house, ate the same food as them, had regular days off and quickly learned German. She told them about her home. She was the only child of Catholic parents, and, as Winifred said, had been 'forcibly removed'.[55] Rumours were circulating in Bayreuth about how forced labour was 'recruited'. For example, the building contractor Konrad Pöhner, who had a few construction teams working in Russia, talked about 'the terrible impression made on him by the enforced transportation of Russian women workers to Germany: the way they were herded together with rubber truncheons, the loud wailing of their relatives etc.!'[56]

After all the turmoil, musically speaking the Mastersingers produced first-rate performances. Furtwängler conducted the first series with Maria Müller as Eva, Max Lorenz as Stolzing, and Jaro Prohaska as Sachs. In the second series, under Hermann Abendroth, the younger generation of singers had a chance to shine: Paul Schöffler as Sachs, Erich Kunz as Beckmesser and Hilde Scheppan as Eva.

Furtwängler's interpretation had an almost chamber-music quality. As he explained in an interview, 'It would be wrong to present Wagner in an emotional style. As we encounter him in his works, he is human, plain and even functional. This is the main characteristic that contradicts a partly misunderstood tradition.'[57] Clearly, these words gainsay both the Gauleiter's speeches and Wieland's stage designs in the old Bayreuth style of 'German art': highly representational, with an excessive amount of Nuremberg half-timbering, just the way Wolf and the Reich Stage Designer Benno von Arent liked. The Festival meadow scene, crowned by the award of the German Master's and Artist's prize, was dominated by an outsize flag with the old Imperial Eagle as a national emblem. Unwilling to reduce the size of the cast on the Festival meadow, Wieland had fallen back on Party organizations. With regard to the amateur performers (naturally in costume), the programme stated that 'In addition to the chorus, also appearing on the Festival meadow are members of the Hitler Youth and German Girls League, and men of the SS Viking Standard.' Wieland's 1943 and 1944 Mastersingers therefore had by far the most political and regime-friendly stage designs of the Winifred–Tietjen era.

The only jarring note was provided by the costumes borrowed from Berlin. Gertrud Strobel noted with relish the negative comment by a man from the Munich theatre on the costume worn by Kothner (the baker): 'He looks like a fifth fart by Preetorius!' By contrast, she praised 'Wieland's sound ideas for directing the Festival meadow scene'.[58] Once again, at Wieland's request she sat through performances noting 'the changes in intonation introduced by Herr Tietjen'. Her critical pencil was sharpened ready for the radio broadcast of the Mastersingers, too: 'I'm playing the "Marker" (noting

wilful deviations by Tietjen!).' (The Marker is the judge in the song competition in the *Mastersingers*.)[59]

In the souvenir book *Richard Wagner and his 'Mastersingers'*, handed out to
every 'guest of the Führer', Winifred's introductory words of welcome read
like a compilation of the purest party jargon. The *Mastersingers*, she said,
showed

> in the most impressive form gifted German Man in his will to create,
> stemming from his *völkisch* heritage . . . which is endowing our soldiers, in
> the present struggle between the European cultural world and the destruc-
> tive spirit of the plutocratic-Bolshevist world conspiracy, with invincible
> fighting strength and a fanatical belief in the victory of our arms.[60]

The SS Security Service, monitoring the public mood on behalf of the
Gauleiter, reported great annoyance among Bayreuthers. They 'often
could not understand' why the Festival was going ahead at all in 1943, and
felt that

> it was hardly appropriate in total warfare to impose this mass transporta-
> tion of about 30,000 people on a railway system that was already
> overstretched. Was it acceptable that the majority of these national com-
> rades were being taken out of some armaments factory for at least 5 days?
> In other parts of the Reich, national comrades' property and lives were
> being destroyed by bombing, while a 'state entertainment' was being laid
> on in Bayreuth.

Resentment was caused by the fact that both Festival visitors and artists
enjoyed, in contrast to the locals, what was said to be 'almost a peace-time
level of catering'. A soldier who could not get a drink complained, 'You come
back from the front line and then have to watch these artists drinking all the
wine at home.'

To the landlords and -ladies of Bayreuth, the one-night-only Festival visitors were nothing but a plague. Their rates per night were kept very low, and
they had to change the bedlinen for each of the sixteen nights of performances. Not only had bedclothes been rationed for some time, they were also
expensive, and difficult to wash in the absence of soap powder.

There were further complaints that the tenor Lorenz, well known to be a
'175-er' (homosexual), was still working for the Festival and (worse still) that

his Jewish wife had 'unlimited access to the Festival premises, and enjoyed the same privileges in the Restaurant as everybody else'. This had 'incited a real outcry among all the Festival participants who know about it, and was regarded in National Socialist circles as provocative'.[61]

Winifred gave a long interview to a film team on 10 July 1943, dealing with the history of the Bayreuth Festival and the Wagner family. The film was made as part of an official project, a 'film archive of personalities', not meant for public screening. On completion, the reels were packed in lead capsules and placed in the archive, to preserve for later generations a record of the leading personalities of the 1940s. Nervously twisting her fingers, Winifred sat at her desk, on which stood a framed picture of the younger Hitler. The 46-year-old talked freely and made a youthful impression; her voice was high, she was a little awkward – an attractive woman still, though, despite the severe pinned-up hairstyle and the lack of make-up.

Self-confidently, and with a disarming naturalness, she described her position as head of the Festival. She had no ambitions towards artistic activity, unlike her mother-in-law, Cosima, who had worked as a director. What she, Winifred, wanted to do was 'to remove all obstacles from the path' of the artistic director, Herr Tietjen, and his staff (especially organizational obstacles), so that they could devote themselves entirely to art. She mentions Hitler and the year 1923: 'we were lucky enough to have him here with us in the house'. She told the story of her visit to Munich at the time of the putsch, its failure and the years that followed: 'We were among those who went on steadfastly believing in the Führer, and we stood by him through thick and thin . . . Both gracious and generous, nobody knew better than the Führer himself how to express gratitude.'

When the new Festival team of Winifred and Tietjen had taken over in 1933, Hitler as Reich Chancellor had supported them 'with his whole devotion and love for Richard Wagner and Bayreuth', and made a point of visiting and promoting the Festival, previously shunned by Berlin politicians. She acclaimed the wartime Festivals, which were actually Hitler's idea. 'Thank God, the Führer was ready to sustain us in every way, and immediately ordered that the Festival should go on, despite the war.' She went into some detail on the question of the succession. She felt that as head of the Festival she was 'only an intermediary' between her husband and her two sons, for she believed it was desirable to place the leadership 'in male hands'. Then she went on to spell out in detail the qualities of Wieland and Wolfgang, taking care to give equal attention to both.[62] She also mentioned the appropriate division of authority, with artistic control going to Wieland, and practical responsibility to Wolfgang.

During the Festival, on 25 July 1943, came news of the fall of Mussolini. One soldier, Georg Marischka, a patient in the field hospital at the time, recorded how at six in the morning a beaming nurse 'shook me awake and told me the news, which I thought was a joke at first'. From the corridor he could hear 'sounds of laughter and cheering. Deadly enemies hugged each other, convinced it would soon be all over now!' Everyone was sure the war would end soon, 'because for a long time we'd been listening eagerly to reports on the radio from England about the Sicily landings, the fall of Palermo – we'd even laid bets'.[63] Nobody believed the official announcement that Mussolini had resigned on health grounds. Hopes of peace soon evaporated when Italy surrendered on 8 September, and went over to the Allies a month later.

Nervousness was heightened in Bayreuth over the Festival period particularly by what evacuees from Hamburg had to report. More than 30,000 people were killed in a few days there, in mass raids using incendiary bombs. The unease was intensified by the news that a British plane had been shot down near Bayreuth: the pilot had bailed out. While the hunt for him was on, the public were warned to be on the alert. On the Hill there were informers everywhere, and there were numerous arrests for 'defeatist' remarks. The 21-year-old soldier Marischka was among 'the Führer's guests'. After what he thought was a wonderful performance of the *Mastersingers*, he had made some rather too bold comments to a pretty girl; he was arrested for sedition, deposited in the Bayreuth gaol, and finally sentenced to death. However, he survived, although not before he had accumulated a rich experience of prison life.[64]

In the midst of this fearful time of heavy raids on German cities, Otto Strobel and Wieland persuaded Winifred to write to Himmler. She requested him, as Reich Führer of the SS, 'to issue a ban on all publications about Richard Wagner not arising in consultation with the Research Centre'.[65] Yet again, somebody had speculated about Wagner's origins without consulting the research centre.

Himmler brought the Reich Chancellery into it, and the Chancellery passed the matter on to the Minister of Justice. He had some reservations, pointing out that he had no jurisdiction over foreign publications; and handed the question on to Propaganda Minister Goebbels and Education Minister Rust, neither of them exactly well disposed to the strong-minded head of the Festival. Both then posed as defenders of academic freedom. Goebbels thought it was 'quite out of the question . . . to put all writings about a great German under the supervision of an archivist'. Otherwise the Goethe Society and others could justifiably claim the same rights. 'All censorship carried out by officials jeopardizes the free development of cultural life.' Furthermore he, Goebbels, was determined 'as soon as possible after the war to relax the restrictions on German cultural life' made necessary by the war.[66]

Rust, too, thought that giving Bayreuth a 'dominating monopoly' was 'highly questionable'. Anyway, at present, in the middle of a war, there was 'no endless stream of writings on Wagner'. This plan 'had to be opposed by all possible means, to avoid causing serious misunderstandings among the public'.[67]

Hans Heinrich Lammers was responsible for the Research Centre, and his answer to Himmler's recommendation to put the matter to the Führer was that it was not necessary, 'unless the SS Reich Führer feared that Frau Wagner might find some pretext to approach the Führer directly and obtain his agreement'.[68] Both men knew that there was nothing to fear in this respect, and so they could afford to leave things as they stood.

At that time the Wagner family was increasing from year to year. Preparations were in hand for Verena's marriage to Bodo Lafferentz. The Wielands were expecting their second child. In view of this, Wieland and Gertrud demanded that Betty, now ten, should leave the house. As Winifred says, 'they didn't want their children to grow up with Betty'. And in any case, Betty's parents wanted their child back; they would be able to put her to work quite soon.[69] Wahnfried had been Betty's home for six years, and she was deeply unhappy at the prospect of leaving.

Wieland and Gertrud's second child was born in December 1943, and the names he was given, Wolf Siegfried, were rich in associations. Winifred called him 'little Wolf'.[70]

For his new household, Lafferentz rented a palatial villa with five bathrooms, next door to Himmler in Dahlem, a select suburb of Berlin. Winifred went to Berlin in November 1943 to furnish the villa. This turned out to be very difficult, because 'the whole house is in the Baroque style, from top to bottom. All the walls are divided up the way they are in Schloss Brühl or Sanssouci, with appropriate colours – her bedroom is blue and white – Bodo's is green and gold – and so on, throughout the whole house.' The landlady, Countess Dohna, had put all her valuable furniture in store for safe-keeping, so now Winifred had to try to acquire 'either some grand antique pieces, or unpolished period-style furniture' that could be painted. However, the following day she did take the time to have breakfast with Tietjen in the Hotel Adlon, and was pleased when he praised Wolfgang's work. But, 'being shit-scared of air-raids', she then left Berlin, in an experimental gas-fuelled car that Lafferentz had procured from the Volkswagen works.[71]

Back in Bayreuth, she discovered that Lafferentz had not yet filed his suit for divorce from his first wife 'and those two innocents had already been talking about 2 December as their wedding day!'[72] In the case of such important people, the authorities were capable of working fast, and the divorce was already absolute by 14 December 1943. On 26 December 1943 the civil marriage took place in the hall at Wahnfried, with Wieland and Wolfgang as witnesses. In their haste, the couple had not been able to get all the necessary papers together, so they needed two guarantors to testify that everything was in order, including their ancestry and 'racial health'. The two guarantors were listed in absentia as 'The Führer, Adolf Hitler' and 'The SS Reich Führer, Reich Minister Heinrich Himmler'.[73]

For Winifred, the celebratory mood was not to last long. At 6.30 on the morning of 27 December, while the wedding guests were still sleeping, she received a visit from Herbert Schulz, a farmer who was also a convicted prisoner, and had been granted a few days' leave from gaol. He had supplied pigs to the National Socialist Welfare Organization (Nationalsozialistische Volkswohlfahrt), and had been sentenced to four and a half years in prison for misappropriating six pigs. He could prove that the NSV had diverted the animals for use in their own Berlin canteen, but he could not get a hearing. Winifred examined his evidence, and then wrote a series of letters to the Justice Minister, the NSV and the governor of the prison in Zwickau. Although Schulz received a sentence of fifty-one days' imprisonment for approaching Winifred without authorization, none the less he was released from gaol by 1 July 1944. A re-trial was not permitted, 'to avoid damaging the reputation of the NSDAP, and above all to avoid stirring up any more trouble', so he could not be acquitted, and therefore could not get his business back. After further bouts with the authorities and with party officials, by January 1945 Winifred had succeeded in having the farmer completely reinstated.[74]

On Christmas Eve 1943 Winifred invited the Bayreuth Pastor Urhan to Wahnfried with his confirmation class to sing the old Christmas carols, because, as she told him, she could not stand the Party songs. Then she asked the pastor to read the traditional Christmas gospel passages, and gave a generous donation to the church. Looking back, the pastor commented: 'I very much admired Frau Wagner's courage, because she must have been aware that calling in a pastor and singing carols to celebrate Christmas at Wahnfried was bound to cause astonishment and offence in the highest echelons of the Party.'[75]

The Christmas and wedding celebrations had served only to exacerbate Wieland's bad temper, to the extent that Winifred poured out her woes to her friend Lene: 'his children get on his nerves – the telephone gets on his nerves – That man hasn't got a clue what we're having to put up with!!!! – Today he was so annoyed that his work wasn't going right that he pushed over a table in the playroom and smashed a standard lamp to bits.' And she added: 'Poor Emma is just as worn out and shattered as I am.'[76]

By then the Luftwaffe were increasingly powerless against mass Allied bombing. In the shelter of the Hotel Bristol, fifty people lost their lives in an air-raid, including some generals and a few mayors, as well as the oldest son of Winifred's friend, the Dortmund steel magnate Klönne. Winifred was worried about Wolfgang in Berlin, and sought permission for him to use the 'Führer bunker'. Hitler granted her request, but Wolfgang politely declined the offer, preferring an ordinary shelter where he could be with his friends. Verena's hope of being allowed to use Himmler's private bunker next door came to nothing when the Himmler villa suffered a direct hit.

In May 1944 Verena was 'colossally lucky', as Winifred reported to her friends, when 'a high-explosive bomb fell 5 metres from the house, between the house and the garage – it brought down an internal wall, and everything was covered in 40cm of masonry dust – all the doors, windows, wall-units, light-fittings smashed – 85 per cent of the crockery, the food stores, except for eggs – all gone'.[77]

Most of the great opera houses – Frankfurt, Cologne, Hamburg, Mannheim, Karlsruhe – had been bombed out, so that Winifred fought with more determination than ever to preserve the still-intact Festival Theatre. With the backing of Mayor Kempfler, she fended off every attempt at a military takeover that would have provided a target for the enemy. The Luftwaffe wanted to use the Festival Theatre as a camp, and put an air-raid observation post on the roof. The struggle 'was not always easy, considering how requisition-happy the forces were'.[78]

Increasing numbers of refugees and evacuees sought accommodation, food and clothing in the little town. Food supplies were practically exhausted; there were hardly any medicines; and by then there was no petrol and no fuel for heating. In January 1944 Wahnfried had its telephone number withdrawn, and Winifred grumbled to Lene: 'It's only concerns that are decisive for the war-effort that are getting phone numbers, not just those that are important for it – when they said that to me, I told them straight that they wouldn't *let* me decide the war – otherwise, I'd be glad to do so!!!!' Once again, an exception was made for the Wagners, and they were given a number.[79]

Amidst all this commotion, Winifred still had the energy to protest vehemently when the town, planning to commemorate the anniversary of Wagner's death, wanted to include the 'Wesendonck Lieder' in the programme.

> In a town which owes its cultural significance not only to the Master, in the first instance, but also very much to his spouse Cosima, the Wagner family thinks it is tactless to publicly commemorate Richard Wagner's connection with Mathilde Wesendonck. The whole world knows about the prominent role played by that lady in his life and work – she can be remembered on 361 other days of the year, but not on 13.11. – or on 22.5. – or 25.12, or 1.4' (the dates of Richard and Cosima Wagner's birthdays and death).[80]

The Master's love for Mathilde Wesendonck had always been a taboo subject with Cosima.

German and Romanian troops evacuated the Crimea on 12 May 1944 as the Red Army marched in. On 4 June, the Allies entered Rome, a powerful symbolic moment for them. News of the Allies' Normandy landings reached Wahnfried during a belated celebration of Siegfried's seventy-fifth birthday, on 6 June. Like many other Germans, Kempfler still believed in the 'Final Victory'; he welcomed the invasion, and was convinced of the 'invincibility of the defences' in the Atlantic Wall, and that the 'forces that had landed would be thrown back into the sea'.[81] That would have enabled the longed-for peace talks to take place. Later he admitted that he too had been 'a victim of propaganda'.

The well-equipped, strongly motivated and fresh Allied troops fought on for weeks, and suffered heavy casualties. The weakness of the German army was then exposed. The Allies embarked on the reconquest of France.

Despite the situation, Hitler stuck to his order that the Festival should take place again in 1944. This time, shrapnel-protection trenches had to be dug all round the Festival Theatre, a measure that Kempfler considered 'would have proved totally useless in practice for the 2,500 people on the Hill'.[82] The heaviest navvying work was done by Flemish prisoners of war.

Following further clashes with Wieland over the Festival programme and his demand for exclusive control, a compromise was reached: in 1944, once more, only the *Mastersingers* would be presented, with twelve performances. The singers, musicians and technicians, released from the military, were only too pleased to be there. Furtwängler conducted on two evenings, mainly because of the radio broadcasts, and Hermann Abendroth took over the rest. No new production was planned until 1945, and then it would be one which, in Winifred's words, 'Wieland would do completely independently (sets and directing). Outwardly, Heinz would preserve his authority – but privately Wieland could work completely independently of him – and that arrangement could go on for a couple of years, until Wieland really has acquired the necessary authority.'[83]

The 1944 Festival gave Winifred a welcome pretext to send for the French violinist and forced labourer Rolland Trolley de Prévaux, a descendant of Franz Liszt, to join the orchestra, thus getting him released from imprisonment. On Hitler's birthday on 20 April 1944 he had failed to hang a swastika flag out of his window, and was committed to prison in Dresden as 'politically suspect'. 'I was left there for months in terrible uncertainty about my fate, because they said I was going to be sent to a concentration camp as a political criminal.' Winifred explained that 'Actually, Prévaux could not have played in the orchestra, because he had no chance to practise the violin while he was a prisoner – but we honoured his contract financially, to help him out – he was completely penniless.'[84]

The local Party officials were asserting themselves more than before. The leadership of the *Kreis* (region) protested, for example, when the Bayreuth military chaplain presided over the religious marriage ceremony at Wahnfried of Winifred's godchild, Ingeborg Becker, daughter of her friend Lies. The Becker family, having been bombed out, had been living with the Wagners since 1943. Winifred defended herself on paper, and there followed a discussion with the head of the *Kreis* and Gauleiter Wächtler on the church under National Socialism. The minutes record that 'Frau Wagner's position was that the Führer rejected a reform of the German people, and that Section 24 of the Party manifesto committed the Party to base itself on positive Christianity.'

The head of the *Kreis*, on the other hand, wanted to convince Winifred 'that the crowning achievement of the National Socialist revolution, and the ultimate sense of the present war, lay in replacing the 2,000-year-old doctrines of Christianity with the new National Socialist world-view'. He referred to Rosenberg, 'whose arguments with the churches are well enough known'.[85] No agreement was reached.

Meanwhile, the 'Führer's guests' were arriving, an event described by Otto Daube as follows: 'While special trains were pulling in to one platform of the main Bayreuth station, bringing Festival visitors to be greeted by a band, at another platform more trains were arriving bearing refugees from the nights of bombing in the big cities, with their pillars of fire and their desolate wastes of rubble.'[86]

During the second interval of the *Mastersingers* on 20 July, there were rumours of an attempt on Hitler's life. A tense period of waiting followed, with speculation about what might have taken place in the Wolf's Lair in East Prussia. At one a.m. that night Hitler himself, in a broadcast address, offered some clarification. He had survived, with minor wounds. 'I take it to be a confirmation of the mission for which I have been chosen by providence, to pursue my life's goal as I have always done.'

Four conspirators, including Count Claus Stauffenberg, had already been shot. The hunt for their accomplices was going on. Every day brought news of fresh arrests, including those of accomplices' relatives, and of executions.

Winifred's view of the resistance movement was unambiguous, and did not differ from that of very many Germans. She condemned the conspirators of 20 July as 'traitors', and not only traitors to Hitler, but also to the German people, because they were siding with the enemy while the country was at war, and hastening the demise of Germany. Winifred maintained this opinion even after 1945. Writing to Gerdy Troost after having met the son of Count Stauffenberg at a dinner, the eighty-year-old referred to him as 'the son of the traitor'.[87]

On 25 July the headline in the *Bayreuther Kurier* (Bayreuth Courier) was 'Bitter Fighting on all Fronts'. Goebbels once again appealed for 'total war', a second mobilization which 'not least must be a mobilization of minds, the transformation of our thinking from the bourgeois to the warlike'. That also meant a limit on cultural events, 'so that the forces and the armaments industry are not deprived of resources'. He went on: 'I will use my authority . . . to make sure that anyone who possibly can, does important war work.' All exemptions from military service were cancelled. All men between sixteen and sixty were called up to serve in the *Volkssturm* (Home

Guard) – even Wolfgang, despite his crippled hand. All the artists in the Berlin State Opera company, from the singers to the *corps de ballet*, were liable for munitions work.

The Festival was allowed to run its course according to plan. The last performance of the *Mastersingers* was given on 9 August, the last opera performance ever to take place in the Third Reich. Kempfler was present, and recalls that 'when Hans Sachs delivered his speech, "If the Holy Roman Empire should crumble into dust, then holy German art would still be ours", it sent shivers down my spine, because I knew that in a few months we would be standing among the ruins of the Reich'.[88]

Paris was liberated on 25 August 1944, and the tricolour flew over the Eiffel Tower. The German occupying forces had already fled. The hunting down of collaborators began. French women who had had affairs with Germans were arrested. One of them was the soprano Germaine Lubin. Her love for the German officer Hans Joachim Lange was well known, as were her social contacts with the top German military. It counted as powerful evidence against her that Hitler had her son released from a German prisoner of war camp in 1940; not to speak of her appearance with the Berlin State Opera during its propaganda guest performance in 1941 in the Paris Grand Opéra. Undaunted, she protested to her interrogators that 'German music is the most beautiful in the world, and German musicians and artists are my friends. And our whole circle never concerned itself with politics.'[89]

Germaine Lubin, wrote Winifred, was 'in prison for ten months – was banned from performing for 5 years, and was excluded from central Paris for that whole time! She behaved extremely well.'[90] Winifred later blamed herself: 'I can't help thinking that everything that happened to her after the war was my fault. I introduced her to Hitler. I sent Hans Joachim Lange to her . . . It's terrible how you castigate yourself. But who could have predicted it? Everybody came to Bayreuth, everybody, including Hitler.'[91]

Brussels was liberated on 3 September. But the Warsaw uprising against the German occupation was crushed after two months, on 2 October.

WIELAND AND THE BAYREUTH SATELLITE CONCENTRATION CAMP

Even when the demands of 'total war' led to the cancelling of all exemptions from military service, 27-year-old Wieland remained one of the very few healthy young German men to enjoy immunity. He was not even made to perform the alternative service in the armaments industry that was compulsory for all artists. But just in case he was called up after all, his powerful brother-in-law Lafferentz was keeping essential war work open for him in Bayreuth.

Through marrying into the Wagner family and organizing the yearly wartime festivals, Lafferentz had acquired a second focus in his life, after Berlin. He and his brother-in-law Wieland were good friends, and he helped Wieland whenever he could. He had represented the latter's interests in the matter of the Warburg estate. He made every effort to secure the contract to build the new Festival Theatre for the architect Hans Reissinger, Gertrud's uncle, and to keep Emil Mewes out.[92] And he helped Wieland's parents-in-law, who had been bombed out in Munich and returned to Bayreuth without a penny. For Adolf Reissinger, a retired secondary-school teacher and Party member from the earliest days, he created the post of director of a research institute especially founded for him, with the sonorous title of 'Bavarian Shale Oil Company, Bayreuth'. This one-man institute was tasked with developing the process of obtaining oil from bituminous shale, an enterprise that had no difficulty in acquiring funding at a time when the Third Reich was in desperate need of raw materials. It is not known whether any useful research ever resulted.[93]

Lafferentz ran another institute in Bayreuth, employing about forty Ukrainian chemists from Kiev who had escaped from the Soviet Union, and were working on the storing of energy in accumulators; they lived in makeshift barracks on the edge of town. The inventive, powerful Lafferentz, holder of multiple offices, had a talent for thinking up attractive ideas to alleviate the disastrous shortfall of raw materials and energy. For instance, there was a shortage of rubber, at the VW works as elsewhere, and he planned a biological solution by cultivating plantations of the rubber-plant *Kosagis*, which was found in Russia. The intention had been to set up this large-scale project in cooperation with Heinrich Himmler, who was in overall charge of concentration camps, at Rajsko, a satellite camp of Auschwitz. However, because of the turn taken by the war, this proved impossible to carry out.[94] Another institute founded by Lafferentz was on Lake Constance, and dealt with wind-powered energy.

On 17 January 1944 Lafferentz – who as an SS Obersturmbannführer (lieutenant-colonel) had just been awarded the Death's Head Ring of the SS for 'loyalty to the Führer'[95] – paid a courtesy visit with Verena to Goebbels, and 'told him a great many interesting things', according to Goebbels. 'In particular, he was able to pass on the word among ordinary people about the work we're doing on our secret weapon, something I find extremely interesting. It shows you how much hope the German people are investing in our retaliation ['V1' = *Vergeltungswaffe 1*, or 'Revenge Weapon Mark I']. I hope it can be fulfilled, to some extent at least.'[96]

Lafferentz's fertile mind had no difficulty in coming up with an arresting idea for furthering the development of the 'wonder weapon'. The main drawback with the V1 and V2 rockets was their lack of accuracy, and so he founded a top-secret Institute for Physics Research in Bayreuth to work on the problem. It was supposed to develop the 'Ikonoskop', a 'sighted bomb', to improve the accuracy of rockets launched from planes or submarines; something akin to the later cruise missiles, in other words. Like the others, this new institute was supported and financed by the Berlin Research and Utilization Company, which was under the aegis of the VW concern, and headed by Lafferentz. The scientific director was Dr Werner Rambauske of the Askania Works, which needed these precision components. On 22 May 1944 the Askania Works signed a planning application to build barracks for SS guards, and to construct works premises of 1,700 square metres on the site of the New Cotton Mills, on the outskirts of Bayreuth. Responsibility for building supplies was borne by the Reich Minister of Aviation and Supreme Commander of the Luftwaffe, Goering.[97]

As skilled workers were in very short supply, the 'institute' was run as a satellite concentration camp. The obvious main camp for Bayreuth was nearby Flossenbürg, which already had about a hundred outcamps, including – since 1943 – one with workshops producing the Messerschmitt 109 fighter plane. The specialist workers needed for the new institute, from electricians to precision engineers, technicians and physicists, were collected together from various concentration camps, and transferred to Bayreuth via Flossenbürg, which derived income from 'loaning out' such workers. As with every concentration camp, the SS were to run and supervise the site. The fourteen or so guards were mostly older SS men unfit for active service. If necessary, civilian experts could be recruited for some specialist tasks. According to statements by surviving prisoners, the civilians were 'only too happy not to be sent to the eastern front'.[98]

The plan for the complex envisaged 400 prisoners,[99] but it reached only a fifth of that number. The main building was the former thread factory, now lying idle for want of raw materials. Placed alongside a large camp for some

2,000 forced labourers working for Siemens, the 'institute' was inconspicuous. For the local population it was almost impossible to distinguish the inmates, who did not wear uniforms, from the forced labourers, especially as the entire area of the camp was surrounded by barbed wire, and civilians were among those who went in and out of the 'institute'.

The first thirty-three technically skilled prisoners to be selected came from Neuengamme concentration camp, were transferred to Flossenbürg, and brought from there to Bayreuth with five other prisoners on 13 June 1944. Thus began the work of the Bayreuth camp.[100] On that day a V1 flying bomb missed its intended target, Tower Bridge in London, by thirty kilometres. This was concealed from the public, but underlined the point about the need for rapid improvement.

Returning from Altenburg in August when all the German theatres were closed down, Wieland avoided his call-up to the *Volkssturm* by taking up the post of civilian acting governor of the Bayreuth satellite camp. To this day it is not known what his job description was, or what he actually did. Lafferentz later told Geoffrey Skelton, Wieland's biographer, that his brother-in-law spent his time at the 'institute' building model stage-sets and working on a new lighting system. He had been assisted by prisoners.[101] He certainly had his own office there, and could easily have called upon inmates, such as electricians, to help him. According to Wolfgang, Wieland's role at the 'institute' 'was of course just a kind of protective front in this "total war" situation'.[102]

Conditions for prisoners in the 'institute' were much more bearable than in the standard concentration camps, such as Flossenbürg. And it may be true that the highly qualified workers felt more secure there than they did where they had come from. After 1945, ex-inmate Hans Imhof described his stay in Bayreuth as 'the best part of my whole time in concentration camp'. At the de-nazification hearings he attested to Lafferentz's correct behaviour and humane attitude.[103]

A gallows was installed at Bayreuth, as in all other concentration camps, but we now know it was never used for executions. There was some abuse, however, in the form of kicks and beatings when the work was going too slowly. Inmates charged with worse offences were sent to Flossenbürg for 'sentencing'; sick people were also sent to the main camp. Hunger was the worst thing. The inmates got very little food, for the most part just potatoes and cabbage, as a former prisoner stated. The SS guards once shot a superannuated guard-dog, added the ex-prisoner: 'Our Czech cook made dog soup, which was practically inedible.'[104]

Wieland is mentioned only once in the report of the former inmate Imhof, acting as a witness in Lafferentz's defence. After two prisoners had escaped on 2 November 1944, the others feared reprisals from the SS. They asked Wieland to call in Lafferentz, who forcefully pointed out to the SS the 'institute's' crucially important war work.[105] This indicates that Wieland was a kind of deputy for Lafferentz, who was often away. The crisis ended with the SS guards being reposted by way of punishment.[106]

Wieland enjoyed considerable privilege in the satellite concentration camp. 'Because of his elevated position', he did not have to adhere to strict hours; he arrived late in the morning and left early in the afternoon. Winifred took him to task for this in December 1944, because she thought he was identifying too little with soldiers and munitions workers. However, Lafferentz defended him, and 'gave her a really awful piece of his mind about it'. Wieland was disappointed that his mother made no attempt to have him released from his work, perhaps by an appeal to Hitler: 'she would rather do the opposite!'[107]

Wieland's wife Gertrud claimed to know nothing about her husband's work, according to her biographer. 'But she saw him becoming ever grimmer, more embittered and more reserved. He did go so far as to reveal that he came into contact with concentration camp inmates in his work.' The result had been the beginnings of 'deep doubts' for him, 'fundamental doubts about the National Socialist regime, the justification for war, and the chance of a good outcome'. His belief in the 'Final Victory' had become untenable.[108] At the age of twenty-seven, therefore, Wieland had begun to grasp some of the reality of the Third Reich, and in response his thoughts turned to the supreme father-figure, Hitler. He must come to Wieland's rescue.

Overhoff supported his pupil and, Strobel said, made all sorts of 'impossible suggestions: the Führer should send Wieland and his family to safety in Switzerland, together with Richard Strauss, so that they would survive – even in the case of defeat!!!' Overhoff, in his 'naivety', even thought that 'Stalin as an opponent of the Jews would protect Bayreuth'. Otto Strobel reproached him for 'putting ideas about Switzerland etc.' into Wieland's head.[109] But Wagner's grandson was by then firmly convinced that the way to save his life was by leaving the country, on Hitler's orders.

A Russian prisoner succeeded in escaping from the 'institute' on 21 December 1944, and eighteen inmates, including eleven Russians, were taken to Flossenbürg. One of them, a Pole, was executed there on 4 January 1945. In March a Russian prisoner developed TB. He too was taken to

Flossenbürg, where he died soon after. Altogether, eleven of the eighty-five prisoners working in the 'institute' failed to survive the war.[110]

Wieland was employed at the 'institute' until April 1945. For the rest of his life, he made no mention of what he had seen or done there. Its SS guards were put on trial in 1947 and 1951, but acquitted for lack of evidence.

The first time the Bayreuthers heard about the camp was in 1989, thanks to the work of a grammar-school student, Karin Osiander. However, she did not yet know about the involvement of Lafferentz and Wieland. When the journalist Peter Engelbrecht took up the subject, tracing survivors and supplying details, the still intact workshop of the concentration camp was abruptly torn down. A memorial stone in a car park, placed there after pressure from the press, is the only visible reminder of the Bayreuth satellite camp.

PANIC SPREADS

A serious quarrel broke out in the Führer's headquarters in October 1944 between his personal physicians. Karl Brandt, who was popular in Bayreuth, openly opposed Theodor Morell, accusing him of trying to poison Hitler with strychnine injections. Although Hitler had a horror of poisoning, he reacted unexpectedly to these accusations: he retained Morell, but replaced Brandt with another doctor.[111]

This was a heavy blow for Winifred and all those she wanted to help, because for years Brandt had been providing reliable, if not enthusiastic, mediation – bypassing Bormann – in securing aid for her protégés and herself from an increasingly remote Hitler. Now this last link with Hitler was broken. Winifred told Lydia Beil, who was still sending supplicants to her, that the Führer was kept in ignorance much of the time: 'Bormann has built a wall around him. Hardly any of my letters have been getting through to him for ages.'[112]

She was afraid for Hitler's mental state and for his life. She believed Brandt's assertion that Morell was systematically poisoning Hitler. This hypothesis left her with the comforting conviction that in his normal state of health her beloved Führer would never have led the Germans into such a catastrophe. The injections were to blame for everything, as she was still writing in 1970: 'We are gradually recognizing what opposition forces were leading him [Hitler] and us to destruction.' She talks about Morell 'being employed by enemies to administer medicines that negatively influenced his mind'.[113]

In the months after 20 July 1944, when rumours of Hitler's death abounded in Germany, Winifred was among the prominent people called upon to make a public 'declaration of loyalty' to Adolf Hitler. On 16 October she wrote two pages in her stiff Party style, referring to the first time she had pledged her support for him, after the failed putsch of 1923, and adding

> Today, after nearly twenty years of the most passionate struggle for the German soul, after undreamt of successes and the deepest human disappointments – the Führer still stands before us, his example and his flawless personality a beacon to us, as they have always been . . . his stature has grown ever more heroic, he is our Leader through the darkness towards the light . . . from our faithful hearts we swear that in our love and devotion, our belief in his divine mission, we are unchanged, and always will be.[114]

The strain of those weeks, combined with the constant clashes with Wieland and Gertrud, undermined Winifred's normally robust health. In October she was taken to hospital with a temperature of 40° centigrade, suffering from inflammation of the lungs. As there were no antibiotics and no other effective medicines available, she was given belladonna to reduce the fever, but (as Gertrud Strobel suggested) 'probably the wrong dosage, so that she went into a frenzied fit, and then could not stop vomiting etc.'[115] Even her illness did not weaken Winifred's faithfulness to her principles. When she was released from the clinic for a few hours and returned to Wahnfried for the first time after some weeks, she learned about Wieland's plan to persuade Hitler to let him leave the country, and was 'fuming with rage!!!', said Gertrud Strobel.[116]

In the meantime, Wieland had sent letters to Hitler and Goebbels in Berlin via trusted intermediaries. In addition, Gertrud was supposed to 'ask Schaub whether it would be possible for Wieland to visit the Führer'.[117] The tension of waiting for an answer was ended when Hitler phoned on 2 December with birthday greetings for Verena. When he learned that not only the Lafferentz couple, but also Wieland and Gertrud were in Berlin, he invited the four of them to lunch. 'Little Bormann' – that is, Albert – would phone to tell them the precise time. The Wagners were astonished that the lunch was arranged for two in the morning on 7 December, and that it would be held 'upstairs' in the Reich Chancellery, not down in the bunker.

The young people were seeing Wolf for the first time since 20 July, and were shocked by this visibly aged, apathetic man, desperately trying to keep his shaking arm still with the other hand. They observed his adjutant, Otto Günsche, putting a cushion behind his back to ease his seated posture. His valet stayed in the background, ready to step in if necessary. Martin Bormann looked in occasionally.

Hitler did his best to make this nocturnal 'lunch' for five appear as normal as possible. As usual, they talked about old times. He reminded Verena of the summer of 1936, when he had taken her out of boarding school and the grip of the stern 'Cat's Claws', for a boat-trip on the Elbe. He also mentioned a train journey to Berlin in the company of Winifred.

According to Gertrud Strobel, who made a note of what Wieland told her, Hitler talked about the injuries he had sustained on 20 July. He had severe bruising on his left arm, his left hand was shaking, he had serious burns on his back, concussion, 'both eardrums burst by the terrible bang (he still can't hear any high notes!), and a haematoma above his larynx, so that he had to have an operation on his vocal cords. That was the reason for the six weeks' bed-rest, which had enabled him to recover from the concussion.' Hitler looked 'strangely like Frederick the Great!', said Wieland. 'He had not become greyer, but his eyes had become even bigger, the lower part of his face protruding towards his nose, and his figure very bent. He still can't sit properly because of the burns.' So the injuries were more serious than the public had been told.

Hitler approved of the start that Wieland had made in Altenburg. But 'when Wieland told him what he was doing at the moment, he didn't listen'.[118] He did not want to know about the 'institute', either. It was impossible for Wieland to raise the question of leaving the country.

As far as the war was concerned, Hitler was confident that it would soon take a turn towards the 'Final Victory'.[119] Verena was telling him with horror about the bombing of Heilbronn the day before, when Bormann started frantically signalling from behind Hitler's back for her to stop. Verena carried on talking. Hitler listened intently, and then said sharply to Bormann, 'Why don't I know about this?' It was a great surprise to the young people that the mighty Wolf had obviously not been kept fully informed about the hopeless military situation and the scale of the destruction.

Hitler said Bayreuth must put every effort into preparing for the first 'peacetime Festival', in 1945. It had to be something special. Lafferentz reported that he had already laid in supplies of expensive materials for costumes and sets in Bayreuth.

Wieland told his mother that, although Hitler certainly seemed ill, 'all you can say, is that if it was possible for him to be even more trusting, even nicer etc. than before, then that is how he was'.[120] Even after Hitler's death, Wieland's wife, Gertrud, was still marvelling at 'the F's soft voice, talking with Wieland about nothing but artistic matters. The laborious way he got up and down! His charming, comradely manner towards his servants! . . . His cute young Alsatian dog, its chin always resting on his lap as he fed it biscuits! . . . All deeply moving and strange!'[121]

Around noon, Hitler asked Wieland to take a stroll with him so that they could have a detailed discussion about the 1945 Festival, under Wieland's direction.[122] Winifred was angry that Wieland had stolen a march with Hitler, and Gertrud Strobel said that 'Frau Wagner immediately assumed that the visit to Hitler was pre-arranged, and maintained that Wieland had put these ideas about the Festival into Hitler's head! There must have been terrible scenes!!!' Wieland had said that he would never speak to his mother again.[123]

However, Winifred also heard from Tietjen on 17 December 1944: 'You will be astonished to know that when the Führer asks me whether, artistically and technically speaking, we can put on a Festival in 1945, I am able to answer "yes" without a second thought. No new special orders from the Führer are needed.' There were even sufficient sets and costumes available in case a new production was wanted. 'However, in my view at the moment that would be morally indefensible.' For the *Mastersingers*, the Berlin costumes could be brought in 'from our salt mines in Thuringia'. There was clearly no question in Tietjen's mind of a 'peacetime' or 'victory' Festival initiating a takeover by 'the lads', or of a lavish new production of *The Valkyrie* by Wieland.[124]

Wieland saw himself being robbed of his inheritance, and wrote his mother a long letter, dated 22 December 1944, which he showed to the Strobels. He stressed that Hitler had ordered a Festival in 1945 with the *Mastersingers* and a new *Valkyrie*. Strobel reported that in the letter Wieland was 'adamant that he and Wolfgang, whom he has won over to his side after a bit of "backbone stiffening", must run the next Festival'. He faced his mother with the need to decide: she would have to choose between him and Tietjen. 'After losing one child, you would be losing me, too.' He did not intend to hand the letter over until after the holidays. In the meantime,

Wolfgang was supposed to be persuading Tietjen to 'step down voluntarily!!!' Moreover, 'Wieland went to Furtwängler and secured his participation in advance!'[125]

Everyday life in Germany had by then become extremely difficult, with daily worries about the availability of food, medicine, fuel for heating and gas for cooking; all this in overcrowded dwellings with air-raid warnings practically every day. Even a generous hostess such as Winifred had to confess to guests invited for the evening that she had nothing to offer them. When Gertrud Strobel returned hungry to her ice-cold home, she wrote in her diary: 'Desperate, we eat the last two apples.'[126]

In January 1945 a transport of concentration camp prisoners passed through Bayreuth on its way to a camp in the west. They were Jewish women. After 1945 Winifred testified on Kempfler's behalf that, although it was strictly forbidden, he had provided some food for these half-starved prisoners.[127]

On 5 January Wieland gave his mother his seven-page letter, in which he insistently referred to Hitler. The Führer wanted him, Wieland, to direct the Festival in 1945. They had already discussed questions of organization. Next came the accusations: out of concern for Tietjen, his mother had ignored the wishes of her sons. She obviously found it unbearable to think of passing on responsibility for artistic matters to Wieland; in fact, she even thought it was her mission to protect the Work of Bayreuth from him. She remained loyal to Tietjen, even though the latter was deceiving her. 'It is bitter for us to see how this loyalty outweighs your duty to stand by us and help us.' What was more, his mother had declined to take an interest in his stage designing – 'in contrast to the Führer, who talked to me at length about my work in Altenburg, and appreciates my work'. He, Wieland, was never going to work under Tietjen, 'who had been trying for years to split the family'.

He reassured his mother that she could remain titular head of the Festival, but only if her sons become artistic directors. Such a good opportunity to make the changeover would never come again. After the war it would be much more difficult to prevent the press from writing critically about Bayreuth. In the name of her children, he called upon his mother finally to break with Tietjen.[128]

Wieland's problem was that Hitler had not given any clear orders at all for him to take over the directorship of the Festival. Knowing her son and his tendency to exaggerate, Winifred did not take the letter seriously. Her written reply was very brief, saying she would think everything over and 'then tell him . . . whether *she* (!) could put on a Festival! Signed, "Your most loyal Mama".' Tietjen, too, ignored Wieland's aggressive tone. Gertrud Strobel wrote: 'Wieland is beside himself. He's now thinking of going straight to Tietjen and getting him to resign. The Führer, whom he had told all about Tietjen years ago, would surely not intervene; he was too much of a "cavalier" for that.'[129]

Wolfgang, in Berlin, was (not only geographically) at one remove from the intrigues of Bayreuth, but was drawn into the conflict whenever Wieland needed him. By nature realistic and level-headed, trained in diplomacy in Berlin by his boss, Tietjen, he tried to rein in the ambitions of his irascible brother. It would be 'the most inept move' for Wieland to take over the 'dubious' Festival precisely at this moment, because 'we're going to lose the war anyway. And where will you be then? Just wait!'[130] But that was exactly what Wieland refused to do. With the solicitor Fritz Meyer, he was constantly looking for a suitable interpretation of Siegfried's will that would cut his siblings out of the succession.[131] He kept his brother on his side by reminding him that 'only the Festival could save him, because otherwise he would be called up again on 15 March'.[132]

Although she could not even bear to think about a Festival in 1945, in the end Winifred took a positive line, writing to Overhoff that 'selfishly, the Festival was the only way she could see of keeping Wolfgang out of the army for a while'. It was 'doubtful' whether Wieland's new *Valkyrie* was feasible, 'when the army and the *Volkssturm* need every last vestige of cloth for uniforms, and countless hundreds of thousands of people have been bombed out'.[133]

On the other hand, she was also engaged in an argument with Tietjen, in this case about the unreasonably high cost of the wartime festivals, which he had now raised to more than 700,000 marks. With her auditor, Wilhelm Hieber, she set about reducing it 'to what was previously the normal level'.[134] This meant that she was also prepared to take a cut in her own income. Tietjen, by contrast, was clearly concerned to make as much money as possible while he could, for the Strength through Joy organization under Lafferentz and Ley always paid up willingly, on Hitler's orders.

In January 1945 Gauleiter Wächtler suddenly appeared in Wahnfried and told Winifred that her doctor, Dr Treuter, had been suspended on 15 January from his post as medical director of the Winifred Wagner

Hospital. He could expect to be tried by the People's Court for defeatist utterances. A death sentence was likely. Treuter's 'crime' consisted of the remarks: 'How can I help it if Adolf wants to fight a war!' and 'The whole thing's finished; we're not doing the "Heil Hitler" salute, we're clenching our fists [to contain our anger]'.[135] Winifred was involved in the case to the extent that, after Kempfler, Treuter was her closest confidant in Bayreuth, and was regarded with suspicion by the younger Wagners. Wieland, mean-while, had become friendly with Winifred's enemy Wächtler, who was understandably very pleased about this. 'He likes Wieland a lot, and takes a great interest in him,' said Strobel.[136]

Verena eavesdropped on Winifred's discussion with Wächtler, and reported it to Wieland, who told Gertrud Strobel. The note in the latter's diary is thus not 100 per cent reliable, but it does serve to bring out the poisonous atmosphere in the family. Winifred had asked the Gauleiter, 'Don't you think Wieland may have gone to see the Führer in Berlin about Treuter, to blacken his name or get him eliminated?' Wächtler replied that he would not have thought so.[137]

Winifred's suspicion of Wieland was misplaced. It emerged later that it was Treuter's fellow-doctor Albert Angerer who, jealous of his more successful colleague, had encouraged the 'Brown Sisters', that is, the Nazi nurses, to denounce him. The latter were furious in their turn because the director openly preferred the deaconesses as nurses. They accused Treuter of treating too generously the French prisoners of war who worked in the hospital. At Christmas he even invited them in for wine and fruit-loaf, and had given a speech in French. Another charge was that Treuter was all too collegial in his manner towards the Ukrainian female medical students deployed as auxiliary nurses.[138]

Winifred was not yet aware of these details. Highly agitated, she asked Brandt to put the case to Hitler and save Treuter. She begged Kempfler to intervene on Treuter's behalf, and approached Hitler, and probably Himmler, by letter to persuade them to have the case dropped.[139] However, Hitler's reply came through Bormann, and it insisted that the trial should go ahead. What is more, Hitler took the unusual step of personally signing the order to prosecute, and thereby practically instructing the court to pass the death sentence.[140] Kempfler commented: 'It was a frightening example of his hardened attitude, even towards his best and oldest friends.'[141]

Now that Winifred was completely out of favour with Hitler, she knew that she was a danger to those she had been protecting for years. At that time, for example, Konrad Pöhner, the building contractor with the 'half-Jewish' wife, came home 'quite horrified' and said 'in a completely toneless voice', 'Even she can't do anything any more.'[142] Winifred was so distraught that her children thought her no longer accountable for her actions, and wanted her placed 'under supervision'.[143] There was no doubt about it; this strong, courageous woman was frightened. Her daughter-in-law Gertrud described coolly how she sat in the drawing room, 'her stomach churning with fear', turning the radio dial to catch the news, 'while above her there was the idol, still inviolate, in his high, polished boots, in the pose of a great commander; the life-size portrait of the "Führer"'.[144]

In the end it was Mayor Kempfler who saved Dr Treuter from the gallows, by an appeal to SS Obergruppenführer Martin and to the prosecutor, Oswald Rothaug, who was decisive in this case. Kempfler convinced both of them that Treuter was the victim of the most spiteful denunciation and 'plotting'. Rothaug stated in 1947 that the Treuter case was very uncommon, 'since there was an order to prosecute signed by Hitler'. But the malicious denunciations were so obvious that 'no court in the world' would have convicted the doctor.[145] At any rate, it was precisely the prosecutor himself who requested that the accused be acquitted for lack of evidence, and because 'the witnesses were not totally credible'. The doctor regained his freedom and was able to return to practice.

Winifred celebrated the acquittal of her friend in March 1945 as her own personal triumph. Gertrud Strobel passed on Wieland's complaint that 'he can't talk to his mother at the moment; she's too busy celebrating Dr Treuter's acquittal!!!'[146] In all her letters, Winifred was now talking about peace, as she did to the Graz Wagnerite Fred Fritsch: 'I believe we're all longing for peace – there's so much that one would like to help to rebuild, isn't there?'[147]

Wieland was very busy meanwhile trying to achieve a few things with Hitler's help before the final collapse, in accordance with a maxim of his, reported by Gertrud Strobel: 'If we are living in a lawless time, at least we should get some advantage out of it!'[148] On 9 January he asked Hitler to give orders for Cosima's diaries to be reclaimed from their then rightful owner, the town of Bayreuth, and deposited in the Wahnfried archive. 'He wants to discuss everything else with him [Hitler] personally.'[149]

At Wieland's insistence, and after much hesitation, Winifred also sent a letter to Himmler, asking him to 'have the diaries requisitioned for Wahnfried by the Gestapo'.[150] But despite his friendship with Winifred, Kempfler had no intention of handing the documents over under duress. He pre-empted their seizure by depositing the sealed packet in a Bavarian government strongroom in Munich. There it was that Cosima's diaries survived the war.

In January 1945, Wieland had a further request. He wanted Hitler to fund the Research Centre to produce a new complete edition of all of Wagner's scores, piano excerpts and libretti.[151] Such a critical edition would have been a mammoth undertaking, requiring years of work by a team of researchers and huge resources. The request showed Wieland's concern, in view of Hitler's deteriorating health, to gain as much advantage as possible for Bayreuth while he still could.

On 3 February the luxuriously rebuilt Berlin State Opera House was once again destroyed by bombing. There were constant air-raid warnings in Bayreuth. But as Kempfler wrote: 'Although enemy planes often flew in their hundreds over the town . . . there was never any bombing in Bayreuth. The wildest rumours were circulating to explain this: it was said that American Wagnerites had exerted an influence; Friedelind Wagner had prevailed upon Roosevelt to spare the town of Richard Wagner.'[152] According to Strobel's diary, Hitler said to Wieland: 'I can't give Bayreuth any special protection, but I will say that if it is still standing by February, it will be all right after that!'[153]

On 24 March the Vienna State Opera went up in flames. Wieland's stage designs for the *Ring of the Nibelung* planned for Vienna were incinerated in the office of the director, Karl Böhm. In Berlin, Preetorius's and Tietjen's homes were burnt to the ground, with the loss of many papers relevant to the history of the Wagner family.

In view of the danger of bombing, Winifred was working flat out to transfer precious items from the Wagner archive, as well as important paintings, to the basement of the Winifred Wagner Hospital, behind Festival Hill. She stored Wagner's valuable reference library in Count Giech's mansion in Wiesenfeld in Franconia, but records that

> I would obviously have liked to move all the historic furniture. When I was on the point of doing so, however, the head of the local Gestapo came and said: 'Frau Wagner, I must warn you, this won't do! It's defeatism! When the Bayreuthers see you moving things out, they'll immediately say, "Aha, she's been tipped off by somebody high up."'

All objections were in vain. 'Sad to say, a lot of things were lost because of that; for example, Richard Wagner's desk, where there was still an old timetable, his spectacles and his writing case with blotting paper which still had his imprints upon it.'[154]

During the night of 13–14 February Dresden, its population swollen by an influx of 500,000 refugees, was practically destroyed by the fire-storm that followed British and American bombing. The Opera House, built by Richard Wagner's friend Gottfried Semper, was also lost in the flames. The number of dead has never been established.

The destruction of Dresden was such a shock for Winifred that she called a family conference. It would be irresponsible of her to allow the whole family to go on staying together in one place, she said. She proposed that Gertrud and Verena, who were both pregnant, should go to Lake Constance with their three infants and their maids. Her sons, who could not be spared from the *Volkssturm* and the 'institute' respectively, would stay in Bayreuth, along with Wolfgang's heavily pregnant wife Ellen.

Wolfgang drove the women and children, accompanied by Lafferentz, safely to Nussdorf in a car propelled by a wood-burner, which kept on breaking down and having to be repaired. In their luggage they had the score of *Tristan and Isolde*, and the correspondence between Wagner and Liszt. These archival items were to be hidden in Nussdorf, as a precautionary measure.[155]

Both Wahnfried and Siegfried's house were overcrowded. Apart from the extended Wagner family, various people who had been bombed out had been living there since 1943. Winifred lists 'Lies Becker and daughter; Ernst Günther Jordan with his shrew [of a wife]; and Dr and Frau Vering'. They all had to be fed. More refugees arrived daily, among them Ellen's mother and brother, bombed out of their home in Wiesbaden, as well as acquaintances both close and distant. 'Who's that on the doorstep this time?' was the reception Otto Strobel got from Winifred on 16 February. She explained that the previous evening the family of Gauleiter Karl Hanke from Breslau (all eight of them) had turned up asking for a night's accommodation. Wieland was forced to give up his bed for them.[156] For some time, the air-raid shelter in the basement had been far too small.

After Verena, Gertrud and the three children had moved out, Winifred accommodated some new guests, selected from the refugee camp. Baron von Seherr-Thoss with his wife and daughter, from Schadewalde in Silesia, had lost everything they owned. 'Although we ourselves had never belonged to the Party or any of its organizations', Winifred had 'in the most generous, warm-hearted, and hospitable way provided us with bed and

board for more than 9 months, without even the slightest monetary rec-
ompense from us.' This was the Baron's way of thanking Winifred after the
war, when Winifred had to give an account of herself to the de-nazification
hearings.[157]

Meanwhile, Wieland went on trying to reach Hitler by telephone, and
increased his contacts with Gauleiter Wächtler, hoping to use him as a
way of gaining Hitler's attention. But, said Gertrud Strobel, 'the evil genius
Bormann' always blocked the way. There was no reply to further letters from
Wieland.[158] Wieland now demanded that his mother should telephone
Hitler to preserve him from the threat of call-up to the *Volkssturm*.
However, Winifred was loath to do so. Hitler had failed to respond to many
requests from her in recent times, and was never available by phone. She
had not seen him for nearly five years. She rejected Wieland's request,
arguing that she could not ask Hitler for help 'when everyone else had to let
their sons go'.[159]

At the end of February Wieland got Otto Strobel to hand over to him the
piano excerpts from *Parsifal* from the archive, and went off to Lake
Constance with Lafferentz, who had 'some negotiations to carry out in
Switzerland'. Gertrud Strobel watched the two of them leave. 'Frau Wagner
looked so upset!'[160] What Winifred surely suspected, but did not know, was
that both families were preparing their escape to Switzerland – with the
help of the research institute near Radolfzell on Lake Constance, of which
Lafferentz was the director. A research boat belonging to the institute was
being prepared to take them across the lake to the Swiss side.[161] Winifred
was extremely worried. The penalty for attempting to flee abroad was death.
When Wieland finally reappeared in Bayreuth, he did not say a word, and
neither did Lafferentz.

In Berlin, bombs destroyed the People's Court. About 400 political prisoners reached Bayreuth after a 'hellish eleven-day journey' from Berlin, and
were handed over to the crowded Bayreuth prison. One of them described
his arrival in Bayreuth: 'In this early springtime, a community blossoms all
around that has not yet felt the fist of war. Glittering window-panes, clean
pavements . . . The citizens of Bayreuth carry their heads self-righteously
high, as though ruin could never rain down on them here; they even look
quite pro-Hitler still.'[162]

The Russians were advancing in the east. One concentration camp after
another was abandoned. Inmates not fit to work were shot, or taken to
extermination camps, where the unthinkable machinery of murder ground

on incessantly. Those capable of working were force-marched westwards by the SS, to arrive at the Flossenbürg concentration camp, among others. Fifteen thousand people were crammed into a space designed to hold 5,000 at most.

Appeals for Winifred's help continued to come in, like the one in mid-March from the Hamburg writer Lisa de Boor. Her daughter, the young doctor Ursula de Boor, had been held since December 1943 for anti-Nazi remarks, and transferred in March 1945 from Cottbus to prison in Bayreuth.[163] She was threatened with a trial in the People's Court. Winifred acted at once; she went to the prison and succeeded in getting access to the young woman in her cell. Ursula de Boor later described the encounter to her family. She was thirty at the time, very undernourished, and apathetic after such a long time in gaol. Suddenly this tall, imposing woman had turned up, a complete stranger who introduced herself as Winifred Wagner, saying she wanted to talk to her. The conversation was very halting. When Frau Wagner enquired if she could do anything for her, she asked for food. But Winifred replied that, unfortunately, she did not even have enough for herself. This was very largely true; but although Winifred had lost 50 pounds by then, she still looked well fed compared with the half-starved young woman. However, she did her best to comfort Ursula, reassuring her that the end must come soon and she would be released. The whole scene seemed to the young woman as unreal as a mirage.[164] All the same, Winifred immediately made contact with the de Boors's Hamburg solicitor, Willhöft, to find some way of securing Ursula's release.[165] In the meantime, the Americans were getting closer. Ursula de Boor never did have to face trial.

The streets of Bayreuth were jammed with decrepit military vehicles in retreat. 'The troops seem tired, worn out and completely listless,' said Kempfler.[166] Amidst all the confusion of people wandering about, Hitler's majordomo, Arthur Kannenberg, was greatly concerned for the Reich Chancellery wine store. With great effort he had managed to get the precious bottles out of Berlin to safety in Dresden, and was on his way to Upper Bavaria. Near Bayreuth, however, his trucks had been requisitioned to carry munitions.

Their cargo had been unloaded, leaving Kannenberg sitting by the roadside – as Hitler's pilot, Hans Baur, told the story – and needing to find somewhere to store his wine provisionally. It is fairly certain that he would have appealed to Winifred for help, as he knew her well. Once Kannenberg had seen to it that his bottles were in safe hands, he returned to Berlin to ask

for more trucks. But the teetotaller Hitler thoroughly approved of the requisition: 'this is not the time for rescuing wine'. In the end, Bormann
organized two wood-fuelled cars, which Kannenberg took back to Bayreuth,
and then on to Upper Bavaria. Neither he nor the wine were ever seen in
Berlin again.[167]

BAYREUTH BOMBED

By 24 March 1945 American tanks were already in Aschaffenburg, 200
kilometres from Bayreuth as the crow flies. By 27 March they had taken
Coburg, and Bamberg fell shortly afterwards.

Despite Hitler's orders to defend Bayreuth to the last man, Mayor
Kempfler was determined to hand the town over to the Americans without
a fight, to avoid destruction and casualties. Winifred fully backed his plan.
But the Americans took their time, advancing very cautiously. The fear in
Bayreuth of becoming a last-minute victim of air-raids and incendiary bombs
grew more intense by the hour.

On 29 March the local and *Gau* authorities gave orders for tank traps to
be set up on the approach roads to Bayreuth for the defence of the town. To
carry out the work of excavation the *Volkssturm* was mobilized, including
many officials and key local-authority workers, so that vital services such as
gas, electricity and water supplies, as well as the slaughterhouse and even the
hospitals, were put out of action. What is more, in the course of all this hasty
digging, cables and gas and water pipes in the town centre were damaged. It
was clear to all concerned that the tank traps were no real obstacle to a well-
equipped army. The chaos grew ever greater.

Then a 'battle commander' turned up in Bayreuth, armed with unlimited authority, and considering blowing up houses and confiscating
buildings in exposed positions to turn them into small forts. When
Kempfler urged Winifred to get Hitler to change the order, she wearily
brushed the idea aside. 'From my long years of acquaintance with the circumstances and the character of the leading personalities, the prospects of
success are nil; the more likely result would be a stiffening of the original
resolve.'[168]

Kempfler felt 'like a passenger on an express train whose driver has gone
mad and is racing towards disaster. I can't go forward to the engine and stop
the train. All I can do is stay in my carriage and do what I can to alleviate

the effects of the crash. I can only tell the other passengers how to behave and how to protect themselves.' By contrast, at Easter 1945 Gauleiter Wächtler was still calling for a fight 'to the last breath'. 'Every farm a stronghold, every factory a fortress, every house a bulwark. The Lord will bless our arms, Heil to our Führer! Heil to our German Fatherland!'[169]

On 30 March Winifred recommended an acquaintance, who was bewailing her fate as a refugee, to have faith in the wisdom of the Führer. 'Let us hope things will take a turn for the better . . . I am still convinced that the Führer has an ace up his sleeve that none of us even suspects!'[170] She was worried about Wolfgang: 'This morning at 8 Wolfgang had to go off to barracks with the Volkssturm, supposedly for a week! – I hope he comes out again!'[171] Wieland went on working at the 'institute'.

The defence of Bayreuth was to be concentrated mainly upon the nearby village of Hollfeld. There was a secret meeting in the house of the local parish priest there during the night of 2–3 April, attended by the Bamberg suffragan bishop, SS General Benno Martin and Kempfler. They discussed how the Upper Franconian towns, including Bayreuth, could be surrendered without combat. Both Winifred and the Bayreuth chief of police were privy to these plans. The coded sentence to announce the approach of the Americans was 'You can put the kettle on for tea.'[172]

At noon on 5 April, the first bombs fell on Bayreuth, destroying the area around the station and, in a second attack, whole rows of houses in the town. Beneath the bombed-out cotton mill alone, 100 people lay buried, mostly young foreign workers. Seven firemen were burnt to death in their fire engines. Because of the lack of technical equipment and shortage of helpers, only a few people were rescued alive from the ruins. In the hospital the doctors, under Dr Deubzer, operated at ten operating tables simultaneously, without anaesthetics.

Then came the event which, according to the official US bomber report, resulted in 'Approximately 25 craters in a wooded park.'[173] The reference was to Villa Wahnfried and the Hofgarten. Gertrud Strobel recorded in her diary how she emerged distraught from the cellar: 'But there's daylight, and a draft of air: the cellar window on the right is broken; there is the opening to the house next door, but the house has disappeared!' Her neighbour's wife was buried under the rubble. 'We could hear her groaning, but we couldn't help.'

'Completely stunned' and 'covered with a centimetre of mortar-dust', the survivors made their way up to Villa Wahnfried. At the garden gate Strobel met the chorus member Friedrich Theiss, and both were overcome by emotion. 'Sobbing, I rush with Theiss towards the house, which stands before us like a place of death and horror! The bomb fell diagonally into the side of the house facing the garden, half of the "hall" has vanished, the "playroom" has collapsed completely, and the roof is hanging down low.'

They shouted in case there were survivors, but feared the worst, knowing that the Wagners usually took shelter in the cellar of Wahnfried. It had been completely destroyed. Nobody could have left it alive. But after a while Winifred emerged from the cellar of Siegfried's house, also known as 'the Führer building', stepped over the debris, gave Gertrud Strobel her hand and, looking at the ruins of Wahnfried, said quite calmly, 'Well, that seems to be it, then.' Wolfgang's heavily pregnant wife, Ellen, was also completely unharmed, as were Emma Bär and the various evacuee and refugee lodgers. Looking back, Winifred recollects: 'All sorts of things could easily have happened to us, too. A wall collapsed in the cellar . . . We pulled our old Emma out of the way just in time.'[174]

There were 150 fires to be put out in the grounds of Wahnfried. But the façade remained intact, and the Master's inscription above the entrance was still clearly visible: 'Hier wo mein Wähnen Frieden fand – / Wahnfried / sei dieses Haus von mir benannt' (Here where my imaginings found peace, let Wahnfried be the name I call this house). The grave of the Master lay undisturbed, as did those of the dogs and parrots.

The two sons of the house had not been at home during the air-raid. Wolfgang was at a training-ground outside the town, practising the use of anti-tank weapons with his crippled hand. Wieland was with Lafferentz at the 'institute'. The three men hurried straight to Wahnfried. Gertrud Strobel noted of Wieland: 'Although outwardly calm, he seems completely confused.' In front of a neighbour's house 'I noticed him watching dispassionately but with intense interest as a woman collapsed in tears.'[175] On that day even the gates of the satellite concentration camp were opened, so that the inmates could defuse unexploded bombs under SS guard.

On the same day Wolfgang began trying to shore up the shattered roof of Wahnfried, and searching the ruins for undamaged items. Winifred, however, together with her daughter-in-law Ellen, Emma Bär, the Seherr-Thoss family and the Ukrainian Anna Turkot, left the bombed town on 6 April and sought refuge in her weekend house in the Fichtelgebirge mountains. It was very crowded there, because the timber chalet was already accommodating a billeted family with seven children and Ursel Gossmann with three children. Winifred's most urgent worry was about Ursel, who had suffered a still-birth after learning that her husband had gone missing in Russia. As Winifred had previously told her, 'I feel just as responsible for you as I do for my own children.'[176] Wolfgang also laboriously transported the boxes of archive materials, stored in the hospital basement, to the Fichtelgebirge, since further air-raids on the town were expected.

Lafferentz and Wieland set off for Berlin on the night of 6 April in a wood-fuelled car, to persuade Hitler to hand over the Wagner scores he had been given for his fiftieth birthday. They succeeded in getting through, and with much difficulty reached Alfred Bormann on the telephone. After making enquiries with Hitler, Bormann reported that there was no need to worry, as the documents were in the safest possible place, which was interpreted in Bayreuth to mean a safe in the bunker of Hitler's private chancellery in the Voss-Strasse. This district was overrun by the Russian army at the end of April. It is not clear whether the scores remained in Berlin, or were transported with other valuables by air to Salzburg to be stored in the deep tunnels under the Berghof. The Berghof was destroyed by bombing on 20 April, followed by an orgy of looting. To this day, the precious manuscripts have never been traced.

Without having spoken to Hitler, Wieland and Lafferentz set off on the difficult journey home. The autobahn to Munich was blocked by American troops, so they made their way to Bayreuth via country roads. When they arrived there on 8 April, more bombs were falling. Without bothering any further about the 'institute', the two men drove off to join their wives on Lake Constance. Once more, they took Wagner autographs with them from the archive. They implored Winifred, too, to get away, but, wrote Wolfgang, 'she categorically rejected this request'. She was staying on, and was prepared to face whatever was to come, and 'to protect from harm the work and heritage of Wagner entrusted to her by Richard Wagner's son'.[177]

In Bayreuth the dead were being brought in. Due to the lack of coffins, the corpses had to be stacked next to each other in the mortuary without protection; and in the mild spring weather they quickly decomposed. The mass funerals on 8 April, taking place in two cemeteries, were interrupted by air-raid warnings, dive-bomber attacks and another massive incendiary-bomb raid. In the almost complete absence of firemen, fire engines and water, there was no way to fight the flames. While the injured, the bombed-out and the starving stood around helplessly in the streets, the *Gau* officials were busy composing reports for higher authorities. Kempfler captured the mood: 'The Gauleiter and the Party are being cursed out loud, and expressions like villain, rogue, scoundrel and over-fed swine are used fearlessly.'[178]

When Kempfler was summoned to the Gauleiter, he took with him a revolver with the safety-catch off, 'determined to shoot Wächtler if he made any move to have me arrested'. But all the Gauleiter did was to ask politely for ration cards for his family, whom he intended to send away. 'He himself was going to stay in the town, barricade himself in to the House of German Education with his loyal Party comrades, and die there fighting to the last bullet.'[179]

On 9 April prominent members of the German resistance were executed in Flossenbürg concentration camp, among them the theologian Dietrich Bonhoeffer, Admiral Wilhelm Canaris and Major-General Hans Oster.

The 11th of April 1945 was, according to Kempfler, the 'most terrible day in the history of Bayreuth'. It saw a large-scale air-raid with direct hits on the post office, the old town hall in the Palais Raitzenstein, the nearby Layritz house with its beautiful rococo façade and the House of German Education. There were no long-distance telephone connections, no electricity supply and no lighting, even in the overcrowded hospital. Now that the printing works had been destroyed as well, there were no more newspapers. Thirty-five per cent of Bayreuth lay in ruins. The prison received a direct hit. Many prisoners, including a number of Czechs and Poles, died helplessly in their cells. Others, such as Ursula de Boor, were able to escape into the woods to await the Americans.

After ten months of existence, the Bayreuth concentration camp, having suffered bomb damage, was disbanded. Sixty-one inmates were forced to take part in an 'evacuation march' to Flossenbürg, where they arrived on 14 April. On this march of eighty kilometres, a 39-year-old Italian died after kicks and rifle-butt blows from the SS guards, and was interred by the wayside. One Pole managed to escape.[180]

On the morning of 12 April, when Hitler was issuing renewed threats to execute anybody who surrendered, Gauleiter Wächtler left the ruined town with his high-ranking Party functionaries and several lorries full of food, spirits and cigarettes. Mayor Kempfler could now prepare unhindered for the peaceful surrender of the town, in order to save whatever was left of it.

At this point the former acting Gauleiter Ruckdeschel returned to Bayreuth, and at last saw his chance to eliminate his deadly enemy Wächtler once and for all. Despite the difficulties, he managed to convey the news of

Wächtler's flight to Hitler. Hitler responded with one of his last commands. 'An example was to be made' of Gauleiter Wächtler. The *Gau* headquarters were now in the Bavarian Forest, 140 kilometres from Bayreuth. It was there that an SS man carried out the death sentence on Wächtler. Ruckdeschel had finally achieved his heart's desire by becoming Gauleiter. Unfortunately, however, there was no *Gau*, and there was hardly a Party any more; soon there would be no Führer, either. But the diehards had still not given up hope.

The Americans arrived at last on 14 April. The Bayreuthers hung out tablecloths, sheets, shirts and rags, to show their peaceful intentions. The balcony of the Festival Theatre likewise sported a white flag. Kempfler negotiated successfully with the Americans, and worked with them for four days to achieve an orderly hand-over of the town. Then he was taken to an internment camp, where he waited two years to be de-nazified. The Bayreuthers destroyed their party badges and pictures of Hitler. In Winifred's absence, her friend Lisa Becker, still living in the 'Führer building', cut the big Hitler portrait behind Winifred's desk out of its frame and burned it. Winifred later very much regretted this.[181]

Amazingly, the Americans knew where to look, and in the bombed and abandoned satellite concentration camp they seized important documents relating to weapons development. They soon took up contact with the scientific director Rambauske, whom they did not intern, but took to the USA within the framework of 'Operation Paperclip' on account of his specialized expertise in guided weapons systems. There he continued with his work, now for the benefit of the US Air Force.[182]

The gates of the Bayreuth prisons opened. Thanksgiving services were held. The utterly exhausted Ursula de Boor set off for home on foot, and later told her children how wonderful this long, solitary journey through the spring had been. It was not until the end of May that she reached her goal, Marburg.[183]

With the war already over in Bayreuth, on 14 April the small village of Warmensteinach in the Fichtelgebirge came under artillery fire. Wolfgang's wife, Ellen, went into labour. With an alarm on, nobody dared venture out on to the streets, including the midwife. 'So I looked after both the child and the new mother there,' says Winifred, 'but everything went well, so if necessary I could earn my living as a midwife!!!!'[184] Later, she never tired of telling the dramatic story of Eva's birth: 'born under artillery fire – the roar of the squadrons passing overhead, the dive-bombers right near us etc. etc. –

I rushed off into the woods with the baby, scarcely 24 hours old then, while Ellen was taken on a ladder covered with mattresses down into the so-called cellar, in case the flimsy wooden house should collapse!!! – Well, there'll be plenty of tales to tell about it to your children and grandchildren for years to come!'[185]

Without encountering resistance, the Americans moved into Warmensteinach on 19 April. In the meantime, Bayreuthers and liberated prisoners had taken advantage of the absence of the 'boss', Winifred, to loot the ruins of Wahnfried, as well as the 'Führer building' and the Festival Theatre. Rage against the Nazis vented itself everywhere. 'For 8 days,' wrote Winifred,

> the amount of looting here defied description – from the new building e.g. they stole all the linen, the silver, the pillows, eiderdowns etc. – all the clothes we had in the air-raid shelter etc. etc. – they even rummaged through the ruins of Wahnfried and took bits away. All my Festival Theatre equipment, all the machinery, tools, typewriters and calculators etc. disappeared – every single door smashed in, every cupboard forced open.[186]

It is not known if Hitler ever received Winifred's last birthday letter, written for 20 April 1945. On that day the convent at Heiligengrabe was destroyed, and its Mother Superior, Fräulein von Auerswald, was shot as the Russians moved in.[187] On the same day Flossenbürg concentration camp was vacated. The inmates were forced by the guards to march south, while the 1,500 of their number too weak to move were liberated by the Americans on 23 April.

The 'battle for Berlin' began on 20 April. The Bechstein villa was burnt to the ground, and with it the family's extensive archive containing important Hitler correspondence, as well as that of the Klindworth and Wagner families, and numerous photographs.

In Nussdorf, on the night of 21 April, Wieland and Lafferentz attempted to put into effect their long-planned escape to Switzerland. With their pregnant wives and three infants they drove in a large Volkswagen car procured by Lafferentz to Überlingen, and boarded a well-prepared boat, with a friend at the helm, in which they intended to cross Lake Constance to Switzerland. They had the Wagner manuscripts with them to provide initial funds.

In the middle of the lake they were stopped by the Swiss police, and claimed that the Wille family was prepared to take them in, although in reality they had no contact with the Willes.[188] What they did not know was that the Willes had had political difficulties in Switzerland because of their pro-German sympathies, and that it did more harm than good for the would-be escapees to mention them. They were sent straight back to the German side of the lake; a very ignominious experience, according to Verena. They found the car and were able to return undetected to their house, which gave 'the fisherman's wife and the evacuees a shock, because they had looted the whole house in the meantime!'[189]

Ellen Beerli, custodian of the Richard Wagner Museum in Tribschen near Lucerne, told Friedelind about the escape bid and the Swiss denial of entry: 'You won't hold it against our authorities when you learn that their reason was the [Wagners'] close and intimate connection with "Uncle Adolf". Everything has to be paid for in the end: previously, Switzerland and its people were despised and avoided by all good Nazis – among whom your loved ones must be counted – and voilà the result.'[190]

On 27 April Hitler's homeland, Austria, broke away from Germany and declared its independence. On 9 May, following an unconditional surrender, the war in Europe was over at last. There was no question of a 'stab-in-the-back' myth arising, as it did in 1918, for, as Winifred said, '1945 was an absolute surrender. There was no other option whatsoever.'[191]

CHAPTER 14

De-nazification

(1945–9)

NAZIS ON TRIAL

As the population learned about the atrocities committed in the concentration camps, and more and more information emerged about the utterly unimaginable crimes perpetrated in their name, and by their compatriots, Germans were in turn shocked, ashamed and angry about these murders, but also afraid that vengeance would be exacted.

The whole world felt a disgust and horror that was directed not just at the Nazis, but at all Germans. The Allies hunted down the culprits. Hitler, Goebbels, Bormann and Himmler had already committed suicide. Ley, the head of the Deutsche Arbeitsfront (German Work Service) and of Strength through Joy, followed their example, as did many others. A few had escaped abroad using aliases, above all to South America. Hess was brought back from Britain to face trial in Germany. Goering, Frank, Ribbentrop, Speer, Brandt and many others had been arrested and were in Nuremberg awaiting trial.

All Party members were deposed from office – from mayors to teachers and bureaucrats. Many, if not all, of Winifred's friends were interned in Allied camps. They included Fritz Kempfler, Edwin Bechstein, Hans Joachim Lange, Franz Stassen, Hans Severus Ziegler, Franz von Epp (who died in the camp in 1946), the friend of Hitler's youth, August Kubizek from Linz, Wieland's father-in-law Adolf Reissinger, the Hohenzollern Prince August

Wilhelm, Paul Eberhardt, the technical director of the Festival, and the Wahnfried archivist Otto Strobel. Without a doubt, the head of the Bayreuth Festival would have been interned, too, if she had not been a woman. For sound reasons, Wieland, a party member, did not return to Bayreuth but stayed at Lake Constance in the French Zone. Wolfgang, who had never joined the Party, was assigned to rubble-clearing duties.

The Americans requisitioned the Festival Theatre, the ruins of Wahnfried and the undamaged Siegfried house with all its contents. The refugees quartered there, including the Becker family, were forced to leave. The local commander of the American troops moved into Siegfried's house, the former 'Führer building'. A thorough search was made of Winifred's abandoned study. American soldiers played hit songs and jazz – once so denigrated by Siegfried – on the 'sacred' grand pianos of Wagner and Liszt.

Winifred wrote about the Festival Theatre, which had survived the war almost intact: 'most of the damage was done by coloured American troops, who unthinkingly . . . stormed the building, looting the wardrobe and all the lighting installations . . . all the expensive apparatus, the lenses etc., they shot them all to pieces with their revolvers, and a pile of debris, that is to say a pile of broken glass, lay on the stage'.[1] It was a great joke for the men to dress up as Lohengrin or Wotan out of the theatre's stores. There was much lamentation about the 'desecration' of the Wagner family's hallowed heirlooms. Gertrud Strobel was horrified that 'the Yanks made a hat stand' out of a venerable limewood head of Christ, under which all the Wagner children had been baptized, and that 'they stole the family christening vessel!'[2]

The Wagners' assets were confiscated, to be administered by a trust. Two hundred marks were doled out monthly to Winifred, far too little to cover her subsistence costs. She had to pay 50 marks rent for her own house in the Fichtelgebirge, and 19 marks 32 pfennigs in pension insurance for Emma, who would not accept any pay. That left 70 marks for frugal housekeeping, and 60 marks for everything else.[3] When the Festival funds, too, were frozen, there was no money to pay Christian Ebersborger (previously 350 marks per month) or the handyman, Paul Düreth. Both went on working without pay.[4]

Richard Wagner, Hitler's favourite composer, was boycotted by radio stations and opera houses throughout the world, and the Bayreuth singers were condemned as Nazis. Kurt Overhoff was dismissed from the Altenburg Theatre on 26 May 1945 on the grounds that

Your close involvement with the Wagner family, now such an obstacle to your artistic activity, counts against you in two respects. First, in your post here you were directly responsible to Hitler. Second, in this post you have associated yourself with the most decadent German music . . . Hitler and Wagner are a single entity, on which history long ago pronounced its verdict. That is why you must forgo your association with us.[5]

At the end of June the Americans gathered together the former forced labourers in their zone for repatriation to their own countries. This would also include Anna Turkot. Winifred liked the girl very much, and she was full of misgivings. Rumours were circulating that, in the case of pro-German and German-speaking forced labourers, the Soviets were not sending them back to their homes, but deporting them to labour camps as collaborators. Anna spoke very good German, and had formed a close bond with the Wagner family.

In her anxiety, Winifred begged the girl to stay with her, if necessary going into hiding, initially in the Fichtelgebirge. However, Anna wanted to return to the Ukraine to see her parents again, although she promised to come back later to live in Germany. Extremely concerned, Winifred said goodbye, and at noon by the church in Oberwarmensteinach watched her climbing into the lorry provided to transport foreign workers. Winifred found out that she had been taken to a camp in the Fichtelgebirge. 'When we tried to get some information about her later, however, she wasn't there any more, and we never did discover whether or not she reached her home.'[6] Not a word was ever heard from Anna Turkot again. An official missing person's search produced no results, and to this day it still has not.

Many refugees and evacuees remained in Bayreuth for the time being, not knowing where else to go. But many more were now being added to their number. Long, wretched columns of Sudeten Germans poured over the border every day from nearby Czechoslovakia, making their way through Bayreuth. They had been driven out by the Czechs in retaliation for Hitler's policies.

After a long odyssey, the soprano Maria Müller also arrived, completely penniless. As she originally came from Czechoslovakia, she had at first been repatriated there. Then the Czechs sent her back to Germany, because she had collaborated with the Germans and had sung in Bayreuth. All her luggage, including some valuable jewellery, had been stolen. Once celebrated, and according to Tietjen 'the greatest that we had', the singer came seeking refuge in Bayreuth. She was destitute, suffering from severe gout, prohibited from working, altogether 'a picture of misery'.[7] Her husband was missing, and she never saw him again.

It was difficult to cope with everyday life. There were no trains, post or telephones. Contaminated water supplies and fractured sewers spread typhus and diphtheria throughout the town, and these diseases swept through the starving population in their overcrowded dwellings. It was a long time since there had been any medicines.

But the first makeshift cinemas were opening among the ruins. In the war years, cheerful UFA films had raised German spirits. But in the newsreels the Germans were now being confronted with the horrors the Allies had encountered when they liberated the concentration camps: the mountains of corpses, the vacant and apathetic eyes of the emaciated survivors in their prison garb. Only now, in these moving pictures, did the horror that they had so often repressed become visible to the population.

Gradually, but increasingly as the months went by, former Bayreuthers returned to their home town: soldiers and other conscripts, freed political prisoners, POWs, disabled men discharged from the military hospitals, and evacuees. Justin Steinhäuser, the first of seven Jews who came back to live in Bayreuth, was released from Flossenbürg.[8] It emerged that sixty-six of the original Bayreuth Jewish population of 260 had perished in the concentration camps of Theresienstadt, Riga or Auschwitz.

Americans were constantly turning up around Winifred's timber chalet in the Fichtelgebirge, 'spying', as she said. 'They were naïve enough to come looking for Hitler at my place; they had some really crazy ideas about me.'[9] In June 1945, two young reporters in American uniforms appeared, asking for an interview for the US army newspaper *Stars and Stripes*. They were the German émigrés Klaus Mann, eldest son of Thomas Mann, and Curt Riess. They had been on the move for weeks, following the advancing front. Having witnessed the collapse of the regime in many German cities, they met no one throughout the length and breadth of the country who admitted to having been a Nazi. 'All Germans insist that they "knew nothing about it" (as far as the gas chambers are concerned); they all say that they were "against it from the start", against Hitler, that is to say . . . It transpired that there had never been any Nazis in Germany . . .! Suddenly they all discover their democratic past and, if at all possible, their "non-Aryan" granny.'

Winifred was markedly different from other Germans. As an English-woman by birth, she insisted on speaking English to the 'alleged Americans'.

Thereupon, Riess 'just sat there and never said a word'. Mann, too, was embarrassed to find that the 'Nazi' spoke better English than him, an American. Winifred's later comment was: 'I was so maddened by those people – Germans suddenly turning up in American uniform . . . It just isn't on, I really can't understand it.' Having got out of Germany, the least they could do was keep their mouths shut, she thought.[10]

Their questions about Hitler received clear answers. 'Were we friends? Indeed we were!' said Winifred, continuing (in English), 'Certainly! And how!' Klaus Mann said, 'She even seemed to be proud of it! She sat there facing me, head held high, blonde and voluptuous, a Valkyrie of imposing dimensions and imposing insolence.' 'He [Hitler] was so attractive,' she said. 'I don't know much about politics, but quite a lot about men. Hitler was charming. A real Austrian, you know! Warm-hearted and engaging! And his sense of humour was just wonderful.'

'One way of describing him,' commented Mann, adding, 'But still, it was refreshing to meet the shamelessly honest daughter-in-law of the German genius.'[11] Only one person in Germany had the 'courage or the (undeniably impressive) impudence' to stand up for Hitler. It was a source of pride for Winifred later that Klaus Mann had called her declaration of allegiance to Hitler 'shamelessly honest'.[12]

Winifred asked the two journalists if they knew anything about Friedelind, and they told her that her daughter was living in New York, working for the radio and the newspapers. The 27-year old was much in demand as a speaker on the Third Reich, Hitler and the Germans, as she wrote to Ellen Beerli: 'funnily enough, my political lectures are the most popular; it seems I am one of the few people who know what they're talking about where Germany is concerned. Most people get it all out of books.'[13]

The interview in the *Stars and Stripes* made Winifred famous, and infamous, as a unique case of an unshakeable Hitler supporter. It brought more reporters to the isolated house in the Fichtelgebirge. No, she repeated obligingly, she had never slept with Hitler. No, she had never seen Eva Braun*. Yes, Hitler had always been a good friend of the house of Wagner; she, Winifred, admired him and was grateful to him. Yes, he had been misled by

---

*Eva Braun (1912–45) was the woman Hitler married in his bunker on 29 April 1945, the day before they both committed suicide as the Russians approached. Hitler kept her and their relationship strictly out of the public realm, and few Germans even knew of her existence.

the people around him, and pushed into making bad decisions – it was clearly Bormann she had in mind. Yes, she had occasionally criticized him for political errors, which had infuriated him. She maintained that in the end he usually conceded that she had been right. (This was obviously not accurate.)[14]

An astonished Ellen Beerli wrote to Friedelind: 'I know your mother told an American colonel that she never listened to foreign radio stations, so she had no idea what was going on. Was she really so dutiful? I know these are difficult times for your mother to live through, and how hard it must be to hear what sort of legacy her "god", or rather idol, and his gang have saddled the German people with.'[15]

Friedelind was incensed: 'My stupid mother is still giving interviews expressing her admiration for Hitler; you can't imagine anything more idiotic!!!! Is it possible to live so UTTERLY apart from world events that you see and hear nothing at all????'[16] And she criticized her mother in one of her first letters to Wieland: 'I'm always reading interviews she's given to the press over here. Much as I admire her honesty – I've got to say, she's so stupid and short-sighted! Why is she putting the future of Bayreuth at risk, and the future of you three and your families?????!!! Can't you talk to her and make her see that silence is the best policy at the moment?'[17]

When interrogated by the US Counter Intelligence Corps (CIC), as she frequently was, Winifred continued to maintain that her relationship with Hitler had been purely personal, and had absolutely nothing to do with politics. 'If I had political ambitions, can you explain why I didn't hold even the most minor Party office, and had the courage to fight for my own personal freedoms?'[18]

During 1945 Winifred composed a long letter of self-defence in English to give to Colonel Fiori, for his information and for the record, before he went on leave back to America. It leaves no room for doubt about her sense of a 'mission' as head of the Festival. Since 1876 it had been 'the only aim and the only ambition of the family to stage [Wagner's] everlasting works . . . in a perfect way'; that is, faithfully, in accordance with the Master's intentions, 'a task, which I undertook as a holy mission fate seems to have charged me with'. After her, Winifred's, death, her children would have to carry on this duty. She emphasized that the Festival Theatre and Villa Wahnfried were the property of the Wagner family, and that no Nazi money was ever put into the building or equipping of those two buildings. She expanded upon the 'thorny path' leading from the Master's money worries, into the First World War and the inflation period, and up to the present 'most serious crisis', which was 'due to the fact, that I myself was a friend of Hitler's and as such a member of the party'.

She strenuously denied Fiori's insinuation that she treated her artists badly. For the artists, Bayreuth had been a shrine of great art and an 'oasis in this world of terror and sorrow'. To the charge 'that I myself have unduly [sic] enriched myself', she responded briefly by pointing to her income tax declarations, and asserting that if Richard Wagner had been an American, she as his daughter-in-law would be a (dollar) millionaire by now. But as things were, in Germany the Wagner family 'has not even brought it to a shabby million of German Reichsmark!' She accused the town of Bayreuth of not providing storage space for the Wagners' valuable historic objects and collections, 'doing nothing to prevent all the Wagner-souvenirs, the traditional furniture etc. etc. to go to pieces'. Wagners' grandchildren did not have 'the most modest home' in Bayreuth. She asked Fiori to excuse the bitterness of a widow, mother of four and grandmother of six.

Winifred pulled out all the stops, and eventually her energetic manner and command of English made her an important interlocutor for the Americans. Her relationship with Fiori and his wife became so amicable that she managed to involve the American authorities in the search for the lost scores; 'but their investigations produced no results, either'.[19]

Winifred faced a sterner test with Fiori's colleague John H. Lichtblau. After one interrogation, his minutes recorded that, in political terms, Winifred was 'one of the earliest and staunchest supporters of Adolf Hitler'. It appeared from newspaper reports that her husband 'had already been making very pro-Nazi remarks in New York during his guest tour in 1924'. Apart from Hitler, Winifred was well acquainted with Hess, Bormann and Goebbels. Asked if she had had an 'intimate relationship' with Hitler, she replied, 'that's all just empty newspaper prattle . . . The only feelings she had for Hitler were finer ones; admiration and friendship.' And, very proudly, she added, 'Recent events have not diminished these feelings.'

Faced with the accusation that her correspondence did little to reflect the help she had supposedly given to those in need, but a good deal to reveal her connections with highly placed Nazis, she declared forcefully that it was not only high-ranking German politicians she had known, but also British ones such as Nevile Henderson, Anthony Eden and John A. Simon. Then she brought out her usual stories about Bormann being 'the driving force behind the throne of the Third Reich'. She had noted on various occasions that, whenever Bormann disagreed with Hitler, the latter always gave in to Bormann in the end, and let him have his way. She then mentioned Hitler's promise to do all he could to reach an understanding with Britain, adding the anecdote about Henderson in 1939. She also expounded her theory about Rudolf Hess's flight to Scotland.[20]

The CIC's chief interest was centred on the Hitler letters, but Winifred convinced Lichtblau that all she had received from Hitler were insignificant items such as Christmas and birthday greetings. Once she had copied them out for herself, she handed them over to him. Every year at Christmas and on her birthday, Hitler had sent her handwritten good wishes, and after 1933 these felicitations had arrived on a white card headed with the insignia of the Reich and the name Adolf Hitler in gold. That was an honour which, according to Hitler's secretary Christa Schroeder, apart from Winifred was afforded only to the wives of Goebbels, Goering and Ley.[21]

Winifred was adamant that she possessed no other letters from Hitler. After an interrogation on 14 September 1946, Lichtblau duly minuted that Hitler's letters to Winifred had all been 'of a purely personal nature, concerning only such things as Christmas and birthday greetings'.[22] This delicate matter was thereby pushed to one side. Retrospectively, however, Winifred wrote: 'One CIC man, Mr Lichtblau, told me at that time, in 1945, that I had to hand over all the letters to him – which of course I didn't – I just gave him a few, of which I've still got copies, and I kept the rest.'[23] She carefully preserved and treasured for the rest of her life the many important and substantial letters that Hitler wrote to her and Siegfried. To this day they are lodged with an undisclosed granddaughter of hers.

Winifred was thus able to express unconcern in 1960, when a US journalist proposed to publish Hitler's letters to her:

In any case, those letters are in no way detrimental to me or to Hitler – and I find it pretty stupid that he wants to publish them now, when attitudes are absolutely ANTI! – It seems there are letters from Himmler among them, too – they could only have got them from the files at Wahnfried – and they can't put me in a negative light, either! Whenever I approached Himmler, it was only to try to help somebody![24]

Moreover, if there were papers missing, Winifred had a good explanation ready: the losses were the Americans' own fault. Searching the various offices in 1945, they had 'muddled up all the papers, throwing them around, tearing some of them up, and leaving some exposed to the effects of wind and weather, so that it is practically impossible to reconstruct earlier events'.[25]

Even among those Americans who were investigating her connections with Hitler, Winifred was constantly coming across helpful people. For example, on New Year's Eve an American called Baerwald came to see her, an émigré and oboist employed as a mail censor, 'who had found out my whole story from my letters, and wanted to help me'. He 'dependably sent weekly parcels containing nice things', but he also 'served as a useful go-between' in terms of providing information and press articles.[26] Gertrud said that Baerwald 'brought whole big boxes full of groceries for Frau W.!'[27]

ÉMIGRÉS AND NON-ÉMIGRÉS

In the autumn of 1945, the émigré Thomas Mann triggered a heated discussion with his article 'Why I will not be going back to Germany', which was published in America. Mann said, 'It was not permissible, it was impossible, to create "culture" in Germany while all those things that we know about were going on around you. It would have meant glossing over depravity, adorning criminality.' Then, without naming him, he mentions his friend Emil Preetorius: 'It is possible to think of more honourable occupations than stage-designing for Hitler's Bayreuth – strangely, though, there seems to be no sensitivity to this . . . creating cultural propaganda for the Third Reich through clever lectures – I am not saying it was disgraceful; I am only saying that I do not understand it, and that I shrink from re-encountering certain people.'[28]

Preetorius was deeply hurt. He had never been a Hitler supporter; he had never renounced his Jewish friends, or his art, which the Nazis pronounced 'degenerate'. But he had stayed in Germany, keeping his distance from the regime, and concentrated on his work and his small, reliable circle of people. He had been hounded out of Bayreuth, and put through painful Gestapo interrogations; but he had survived.

His answer to Thomas Mann's charges took the form of a defence of Richard Wagner. He did not believe it was right 'to boycott Wagner as a kind of Nazi, and his music and philosophy as promoting Nazism'. This would be 'to fail to recognize Wagner's passionate anti-war convictions, his exalted belief in the wonder-working power of art, of his art, that of a new mythology, commanding a magic that would close the unfortunate chasms between power and spirit, the individual and the community, and would redeem all mankind'.[29]

As far as his work in Bayreuth was concerned, he pleaded for understanding. 'It wasn't Hitler's Bayreuth, but Wagner's Bayreuth I worked for; the imperative to fulfil the testament of a great man informed by noble intentions.' He asked Mann whether it was not understandable that he 'did not abandon this Work in 1933 . . . I was caught up in my work, under its spell. And, after all, my stage designs created a new model, not only for Germany, but for the rest of the world, which continued to flock to Bayreuth until 1938.'

He mentioned

the harassment and pressures to which I was increasingly subject, despite Bayreuth and all my external celebrity: the intercepting of my mail; house searches; interdictions; and finally, in 1943, following the discovery of my extensive, friendly correspondence with Jews in Holland, the declaration by the Gauleiter and the Gestapo that I was an enemy of the State – I was suspect from the beginning, and placed in an exposed position, so to speak, because of my unambiguous loyalty to the Jews, which I maintained; maintained until the very end.

He had received no honours in the Third Reich, and joined no party organizations. 'But none of it was simple or without danger, especially in my precarious position.' When Mann talked 'in an almost dismissive tone about terror', then he, Preetorius, could only say, 'My dear friend, you have no idea about the sorcery of terror.'

Yet on a number of counts, he agreed with Thomas Mann. 'No German today has the right to complain, even if he has lost what is most precious, suffered the most terrible things, and become utterly destitute. Among many questionable German postures, self-pity is the most pathetic.'[30] Mann drew back from any further discussion with the sentence: 'We outside and you inside – we both have a somewhat pathological sensitivity when it comes to this Third Reich. Enough!'[31]

Such discussions were being conducted at every level after 1945, and polarized the nation in the most unfortunate way. On the one hand, there were the 'bad' Germans who had stayed in Germany, and, on the other, the 'good' Germans who had gone into exile on account of Hitler. But, said Preetorius, there had been a third way, that of 'inner emigration' – a term that many used as an excuse, but which was justified in many cases.

Furtwängler's defence when confronted by hate-filled demonstrations abroad was 'my love for my homeland and my people'. He had been convinced that 'he had a vocation here, to alleviate injustice . . . Abroad, you can only protest. Anybody can do that.' He went on:

> It was impossible for anyone who was not here in Germany at the time to form an opinion about how things were. Thomas Mann really thought it was wrong to play Beethoven in Himmler's Germany. Could he not imagine that it was precisely those Germans who had to live under Himmler's terror who had more need than anybody of Beethoven and his message of freedom and love for mankind?[32]

In the Wagner family it was the émigré Friedelind who raised the temperature. By September 1945 she had renewed her contact with Europe, writing first to Ellen Beerli in Lucerne. She was doing 'brilliantly'. 'Of course, I've met up with so many old friends here; in my hotel alone we've got half the orchestra staying . . . how lucky to be here and not in Europe!' She asked Ellen Beerli for news, 'because the last five years just represent a big hole where my family is concerned'. She asked about her siblings, especially about Verena. She did not mention her mother at all.[33] Meanwhile, Winifred was trying to get in touch with her distant daughter, having received some information from Klaus Mann, as well as from the American Elizabeth Watts, who appeared in the Festival Theatre in the role of 'a funny old woman' in the play *Ten Little Nigger Boys*.[34]

The Festival Theatre was put to use entertaining the troops, or, in Winifred's word's 'unimaginably desecrated' by the variety shows and revues that were included in the programme:

> I'm fighting as sustained a campaign as I can to restore the dignity of the house – but it's very difficult at the moment, because people have the most fantastic impression about my position in the Third Reich, and I haven't yet succeeded in clearing up all the stupid rumours. But I haven't given up hope that one day the truth will win out, and that we will recover our heritage and go on using it for the benefit of mankind.[35]

Since there was as yet no international postal service, Winifred entrusted her first letter to Friedelind to an American chorus-singer, who appeared in *Die Fledermaus* with a forces' theatre group, and was due to return to New York.

Over five densely typed pages, she reported the most important family events of the last five years, and gave news about friends and acquaintances: who had been bombed out, gone missing in Russia, been wounded, killed in action, arrested, or had fled, disappeared or emigrated. She described the bombing in Bayreuth and the destruction of Wahnfried, but also mentioned that *Die Fledermaus* was being put on in the Festival Theatre, and that the Festival restaurant was baking '12 to 15,000 doughnuts a day' for the US troops. And Friedelind's dog Tobi was still alive; with his 'lady', Banja, 'he has just brought 12 offspring into the world'.[36] There was no reply.

In September 1945 Wieland, knowing that without the help of the émigré Friedelind there was not much hope of a future for the Festival, appealed to the sister whom he had once forced out of Bayreuth. Not having an address for her, he sent the letter to Toscanini. He described the situation to her: 'From this bald account of the facts you will see – reading between the lines! – that you have a mission – the existence of the Festival is in danger.' He wanted her to ask Toscanini 'for help and support', and he closed his letter with the appeal: 'Only you can save our heritage now!'[37]

In a separate letter he implored Toscanini: 'You, honoured Maestro, with your impeccable artistic and human credentials in the international sphere, are the only one who can rescue the testament and the heritage of Richard Wagner from extinction . . . After the years of chaotic horror and cultural emptiness', the third generation of the house of Wagner was ready to continue the mission of Bayreuth. 'Having been subjected since 1939 to the harsh rules of a senseless war, and ordered to provide only for audiences consisting of wounded men and workers . . . must "Bayreuth", after the victory of the United Nations, continue to be nothing more than a forces' theatre, and so be finally condemned to silence?' He begs the Maestro to come to Europe with Friedelind, and 'take up the cause of this unprotected shrine'. He, Wieland, 'full of devout trust, was placing the future of Bayreuth' in the hands of Toscanini.[38]

After weeks of silence, Friedelind's answer to her brother was self-confident. 'Everybody here naturally wants to save the Work; and 8 years ago, when I left you, I knew as well as I do now what my mission would one day be. I know that I am the only one who can ensure the continued life of the Festival, although we must be aware that it will probably take years. The Maestro will always be at my side as friend and adviser.' To clarify the conditions of ownership, she asked for a copy of her father's will, and commented, 'You will all understand that nobody will lift a finger for the future of the Festival as long as Mama is at the head of it. But I am hoping that the idea of the Festival is sacred enough to her to prevent her standing in the way of its resurrection.'

His sister had little patience with Wieland's complaints about the desecration of the Festival Theatre. 'War is war, and God knows "Strength through Joy" was no great adornment, either – and in any case, the genuine Festival and Wagnerian shrine must be completely re-launched, so to speak – and the last twelve years will be buried and forgotten!' It was good that the house was in use, she said, 'better than abandoning it to the elements, as in '14 to '24'.[39]

In the meantime and after much deliberation, Oskar Meyer, the new mayor, had reached a decision. The Festival was important to the town, and should be reopened. It should be led once more by a member of the Wagner family. There was one thing that was not acceptable to him, however: that the old management of the Festival, heavily tainted by Hitlerism, should simply continue as though nothing had happened. Meyer not only thought Winifred herself ineligible, but also her trio of children who had remained in Germany. There had to be a new beginning, under the direction of a decent democrat from the house of Wagner, who had left Germany in 1939 – Friedelind, in other words.

In spring 1946 Meyer made an initial contact with Friedelind, communicating to 'the very gracious and respected Miss', 'the desire of your home town that . . . you should inherit the artistic legacy of your grandfather and continue it'.[40] Wieland saw all his hopes being dashed, and wrote gloomily to Overhoff: 'It seems that Bayreuth is going to continue to be a women's affair. I have no illusions about my sister's plans . . . But I'm not going to give up, any more than I did in my struggle with the Berlin system,'[41] that is, Tietjen. The Wagners were angered when, in a commemorative speech in honour of the seventieth anniversary of the Festival, Meyer asserted that the last twenty years of the Festival's history must be 'struck out and expunged'. The family, he said, had abused its responsibility.[42] Furthermore, he demanded 'that Frau Wagner should be totally dispossessed and sentenced to 5 years in a labour camp'.[43]

The much-courted Friedelind remained silent. On 9 July 1946 the Mayor made a new appeal to her:

Along with all the friends of Wagner in Bayreuth, may I cherish the hope that you are aware of the significance of the great responsibility history has placed upon you, for we are firmly convinced that the administration of the Bayreuth legacy would be in the safest possible hands with you, and that your position regarding National Socialism is the most secure guarantee that the intellectual and artistic aberration and estrangement suffered by the Bayreuth tradition under Winifred Wagner will remain an episode we have put behind us.

Knowing about Friedelind's strong bond with her father, he proposed that her team of collaborators should consist of politically blameless persons 'from the time of your father'. 'But I do not want to make any decisions before I have received your response.'[44]

Friedelind declined this worthy offer, and thus improved Wieland's prospects considerably. What factors led her to renounce her claim is not clear, but lack of self-confidence surely was not among them, for she was very well aware that in her exile years she had learnt a good deal, far more than her siblings who had stayed at home. Aside from her command of languages, her excellent knowledge of music put her far ahead of Wieland, and through her substitute father and mentor, Toscanini, she could call upon a network of international contacts with singers and musicians.

It was an enticing thought for many Wagnerites that Toscanini, together with Friedelind and a select band of international artists, might revive the Bayreuth Festival. It was an especially attractive proposition for all those to whom the narrow nationalist spirit of Bayreuth had been anathema ever since Cosima's time. But on the other hand, Friedelind knew that her siblings had young families, and were very badly off. So she procrastinated over her decision, and when asked later why she turned down the offer, she replied (in English): 'You can't kick a man when he is down.'[45] At a time when her family were in a bad way, she could not bring herself to deliver the unkindest cut of all by taking the Festival away from them. Despite all the difficulties, she had a highly developed sense of family loyalty, demonstrated by the many parcels she sent to her brothers and sister via Ellen Beerli, despite her own deprivations.

It may be that nervousness about going home and about conflicts with her family played its part, but the main reason was that she was applying for US citizenship, which was granted on 9 June 1947. She felt very closely bound to her new country, and especially to New York. In her very first letter to Wieland, she had made clear where she thought the true Bayreuth now lay – among the émigrés:

I believe that at present New York is the 'most Bayreuthian' city in the world; not a day goes by when I don't run into 'old' Bayreuthians, whether singers or visitors to the Festival, and in fact the city is full of émigré inhabitants of the town itself. And the old feeling of closeness to and through the Work is unchanged – as powerful as ever, so that anyone who was there belongs to a large family. That's why I have never felt like a stranger; I was 'at home' here from the moment I arrived.[46]

Winifred was furious about the overtures being made to the 28-year old.

They want to make my daughter the heir, because she is the only one who is 'worthy', despite all the conditions of the [Siegfried's] will, and contrary to criteria of merit. I just can't understand the way values have been twisted – by putting herself at the service of the British government in 1940, this child is supposed to have shown courage, good sense etc. . . . well, we had a different upbringing, and that behaviour in wartime went by a different name![47]

For Winifred, emigration was a betrayal of the Fatherland, a dishonourable act, and a deadly offence against the much-invoked creed of 'loyalty'.

Once the combat troops had been withdrawn, Siegfried's house was turned into an American Officers' Club complete with bar ('Special Service'). The Americans did not feel particularly obliged to take care of the premises, because according to Winifred they never grasped 'that the house is my private property, but insisted until the very end that it belonged to Adolf Hitler'.[48]

The Wagners' battle with the trustees – initially American, then locally appointed by the town – lasted for some four years. The family stood by helplessly as the trust used up the money needed for the reopening of the Festival, and rode roughshod over Richard Wagner's intentions with expensive rebuilding projects. For instance, the theatre was converted for all-year-round use with the installation of a heating system, and the orchestra pit, the famous 'mysterious abyss', was completely covered over by a new apron stage. When the trust then submitted a high estimate for the rebuilding of Villa Wahnfried, Winifred protested: 'The question is, when everything else has been taken away from us, whether we should put money into a house we are not likely ever to live in again – because we think we're worth a bit more than just being put on view like monkeys in a cage for the price of an entrance ticket.'[49]

For a while Wieland hoped that with Friedelind's help he might be able to get to the USA. There were rumours that the Metropolitan Opera had him in mind as director and stage designer for a production of the *Ring of the Nibelung* ('for 100,000 dollars!'), but these turned out to be unfounded. Friedelind's influence in New York was wildly overestimated by her family.

Their nervousness about Friedelind's demands ('the high-explosive bomb in the USA', as Winifred put it) was fostered by her plan to take *Tristan and Isolde* on tour. 'What we've got to do first and foremost is defend ourselves against Friedelind's claims; she has already announced quite officially in her prospectus for *Tristan* that with this tour she plans to "conquer Bayreuth from the outside".'[50] When the tour failed to come off, there was relief both in Bayreuth and on Lake Constance. Friedelind 'is making no progress', wrote Winifred. 'There's not enough money for her *Tristan* tour, and nobody's interested in her lectures any more. There were 50 people in New York in a hall that held 2,000!'[51] 'Mausi's' situation was 'a hard lesson, but quite a good one, teaching her to stop imagining she could just conquer wherever she went. And every setback she suffers over there will benefit her relationship to her brothers later on.'[52]

THE DE-NAZIFICATION TRIAL

On 5 March 1946 the American Military Government proclaimed its 'Law for Liberation', a law for the emancipation or political cleansing of Germany from National Socialism and militarism. Repeated in the other three zones of occupation, it affected altogether more than 13 million former members of the NSDAP, who could now expect to be tried in a *Spruchkammer*, or de-nazification court.

Every German had to fill out a lengthy questionnaire which would determine whether a trial was necessary or not. All Germans would fall into one of five categories: (I) major offenders, (II) offenders (activists), (III) lesser offenders, (IV) followers and (V) non-offenders. The law was directed at members of a party that had been legal at the time that they voted for it (in a universal, fair and secret ballot, at any rate up till 1933), and that came to power legally. The procedure was juridically questionable, contravening the principle of '*nulla poena sine lege*' ('no punishment

without a law'). The de-nazification courts were clearly political, not judi-
cial arrangements.

Category I, the major offenders, who automatically faced trial, included
all Party Members with a Party number below 100,000, such as Ebersberger,
Emma Bär, Stassen and Winifred. Maximum sentences for them could
extend to loss of assets and ten years in a labour camp. Winifred knew 'that
as an early member of the Party I am a category I major offender and can
expect to face charges. – At least that way I will have a chance to defend
myself, and I'm hoping it will be an opportunity to clear up all the myths surrounding my relationship with Hitler.' Like all Germans, she groaned that
'With all these questionnaires, you can't concentrate on any work!'[53] There
were 131 questions, with severe penalties both for not answering them and
for giving false answers.

The courts consisted of lay people. The prosecution was led by proven
anti-Nazis and victims of the Nazis, mostly Social Democrats and
Communists. Only the chair was supposed to have had a legal training, if
possible.

The Wagners could breathe a sigh of relief about one aspect of the law:
Verena had been born after the cut-off date, 1 January 1919, and so did not
need to fear de-nazification. Wolfgang had never joined the Party, so apart
from Winifred it was only Wieland who came under the new law. He had
been a Nazi Party member since 1938; was well known to be a favourite of
Hitler's; had held political office in Bayreuth; and above all, had a leading
position in the satellite concentration camp. Wisely, he kept out of the
clutches of the Bayreuth *Spruchkammer* by staying in the French Zone, on
Lake Constance.

He wrote to Overhoff on 6 May that he had 'significant reservations
about going back to the other zone until the Bayreuth business has been settled and I have a guarantee that I won't be made into a "case" '. Neither did
he want to play the part of 'a scapegoat, or a representative of his mother,
because she is hardly likely to get a [Bayreuth] programme up and running
again in the future'. Above all, he did not want to risk internment. 'All it
takes is for some dear friend from Bayreuth or the Office of the Stirrer-in-
Chief, the House of Hirth (Preetorius!!), to get a denunciation going – and
then it doesn't matter whether you've actually been up to anything or not.'[54]
By 'Office of the Stirrer-in-Chief' he meant the group around the former
Munich journal *Jugend* (Youth) and its publisher, Georg Hirth. It had been
a focal point for the Munich Modernists, who had a variety of personal and

artistic connections abroad and earned the epithet 'degenerate art'. One of the most prominent members of the group was Preetorius, Wieland's victim, and now an enemy to be feared.

Wieland stayed at Lake Constance not only because there was less chance of being confronted by incriminating witnesses there, but also because de-nazification measures in the French Zone were less stringent. In contrast to the Americans, who prescribed due process for all Party members across the board, the French concentrated on investigating the more prominent Nazis, while setting up for the others committees of inquiry which exercised restraint, and only ordered trials for the more important cases. Wieland was left in peace.

Meanwhile, Winifred was protesting her innocence to many Wagnerians. 'My great offence was to believe in Hitler – we've all been punished more than enough for that; we didn't need any de-nazification courts.'[55] She asked her friends to refute the charges against her. 'So far, all people know about me is the myths; they don't know that I always spoke out against injustice and cruelty everywhere, usually with success.' She thought that 'If Gründgens and Furtwängler can be back in business, it should be possible for me too, once I'm allowed to defend myself and successfully manage to do so.'[56]

She fought back vigorously against accusations concerning the 'wartime festivals'. 'What happened in the years 1940 to 1944 was never an abuse – however much that is trumpeted abroad in the press and on the radio by the present trustees!' There had never been any interference with artistic free-dom, 'it was only the audience that was "organized" for us, because it was impossible to sell tickets in the normal way, with the restrictions on travel etc.'. The Wagner family would be fully capable of 'gradually reconstructing the Festival, as long as the capital we intend to use for the purpose is not expropriated for "reparations payments"'. The funds in question consisted of 750,000 marks in the Festival account.[57]

Small animosities created bitterness, as when the town of Bayreuth demanded (precisely on Winifred's birthday) that she should take over the upkeep of the graves of the Chamberlains and Daniela Thode; all three were Freemen of the town. 'They appropriated our priceless legacy – they had no qualms about doing that – but they can't and won't afford the 30 marks a year!'[58] And of course she was infuriated by the sight of Mayor Meyer riding around Bayreuth in her requisitioned car, when all she had was a bicycle on which to haul heavy rucksacks through the town.

In those times of hardship, Winifred showed resourcefulness and skill at living off the land. 'As a "destitute person" I've received a licence to gather firewood, and now I'm allowed to collect wood in the forest with my back-pannier like any old crone searching for roots – and I work hard at it!'[59] In her foraging trips she often covered seventy kilometres a day on her bicycle. One day her route took her to the small farm run by Betty's parents. Her former foster-child later described the scene: 'A lady in an old, flower-patterned dress cycled into our yard, dressed just like one of the refugee women at that time. We hardly recognized her. We gave her bread, meat and eggs, whatever we had. And she thanked us with tears in her eyes.' Betty went on: 'To think of her as she was, with her elegant hairdo and everything, and then for her to come cycling into our yard, because she was in such a bad way . . . That wasn't fair. It really hurt me to see it.'[60] Winifred reported to Friedelind that Betty's skin had deteriorated again. 'I go and visit her from time to time, and whenever I do, she puts on her little dress from Paris that [Germaine] Lubin gave her!'[61]

During the period of de-nazification, no family members were allowed to enter Wahnfried. 'The occupation authorities confiscated everything from me, in accordance with Section 52; it says on the forms "ardent Nazi admirer". And now the Germans are following suit and confiscating every-thing . . . Even the pictures, the library, and the archive come under the trustees' administration.' There was no right of appeal.[62]

Winifred did not renounce her right to run the Festival, and in reply to enquiries from Wagnerians she wrote: 'Whatever the verdict of the *Spruchkammer*, there will be no valid grounds for removing me from the leadership of the Festival, and I will never give up the struggle for my rights and my duty until I know the legacy is safe in the hands of the only rightful inheritors.'[63]

It proved difficult to find a defence counsel, because the majority of lawyers first had to be 'de-browned' themselves, including Fritz Meyer, the family's solicitor. In this emergency, Winifred turned in June 1946 to an old friend of her husband's, the music critic and writer Erich Ebermeyer, who was also a lawyer, and 'had many links with Bayreuth and with our family, and above all is familiar with creative people of every hue'.[64] Ebermeyer accepted the defence brief, and was surprised at 'the keenness of the Jews etc. whom Frau Wagner had helped, to supply evidence in her defence'.[65]

And indeed, at Easter 1946, just after the international postal service had been restored, Winifred received an unsolicited letter of gratitude from the Hungarian pianist Alice Ripper in Vienna, who with her help had survived the Hitler period by going underground. 'Now that I can breathe freely again', she wanted to express her 'sincere and heartfelt thanks': 'without your efforts I would certainly have been destroyed, like the many millions who had no guardian angel by their side'.[66]

Knowing that it was not only her own fate that depended on the verdict, but the future of the Festival and the whole Wagner family, Winifred concentrated very hard on preparing her defence. She put together a 64-page memorandum on her relationship with Hitler and the Third Reich, with numerous documents about her initiatives to help the persecuted. Copies in German and English were sent to Wagnerians throughout the world. As paper was scarce and postage expensive, Winifred asked others who were interested to borrow a copy of the memorandum from acquaintances, 'and if you have influential connections, whether friend or foe, please pass it on. It is a sober account of the facts!'[67]

Naturally, the CIC officer Fiori received a copy immediately. Gertrud Strobel reported: 'Colonel Fiori visited her with his wife. She gave him her defence document, and by yesterday afternoon he had already come back, obviously very impressed, to tell her that nothing could happen to her. When she saw him today in his car, he even whipped his cap off to her!'[68] Friedelind, too, was sent the memorandum, along with the information from Winifred that 'if I am dispossessed by the court', at any rate her part of the legacy would be safe, 'since you are a recognized anti-fascist'. Only her own, Winifred's, private property could be confiscated, which was to say the houses in Nussdorf and Oberwarmensteinach, and about 100,000 marks in cash assets. If she were to be sent to a labour camp, Friedelind would be kept informed by her brothers. Once more, she asserted that she had harmed no one. But one just had to accept 'that through a completely new application of the law, one had got into a situation one wouldn't have thought possible – being made answerable for something that was not against the law when it was carried out'. She was referring to her membership of the NSDAP.

She complained about being short of money, having only about one mark per person per day at her disposal. Recently an acquaintance of hers had given her a sheet of stamps because she couldn't afford to send letters any more. 'I'm learning what "an eye for an eye and a tooth for a tooth" means – although I never deprived anyone of an "eye" or a "tooth". But I hope I can go on holding out with dignity.'[69]

In the memorandum, too, she is self-confident. 'At 33 I took up the task of continuing the Work on the Green Hill. I believe I have carried it out in the last 15 years in a way that does honour to Siegfried, Cosima and Richard Wagner.' She had last seen Hitler in 1940, after the *Twilight of the Gods*. 'He never again invited me to come and see him, and for my own part I never tried to visit him again.'[70]

She strenuously denied the charge of self-enrichment. The family not only had to mount the Festival, but were also responsible for the upkeep of all the buildings on the Hill, 'the maintenance of Wahnfried and its heritage, the archive etc.'. Furthermore, she had a public, representative function. 'It is self-evident that we earn our keep through the work of our hands, and surely this work can be allowed to support the next generation of Wagners? – What else should we live on?'

On a key point of the charges against her, the Jewish question, Winifred stressed that she had 'not changed her position from 1923 to the present. I maintained contact with my Jewish friends, and as far as I could I helped Jews who were total strangers to me. My written submissions to every possible authority eventually led to all sorts of friction and difficulties . . . My efforts on behalf of Jews continued in the war, right up to the last months of the Third Reich.'

Central to all hearings after 1945 was the question of how much was known about the extermination programme, and her answer was evasive:

> If you ask me what Germans knew at that time about conditions in the concentration camps, you must realize that under dictatorship there was a complete absence of press freedom, and we were only told certain things; moreover, if the inmates of concentration camps were released they had to swear not to reveal anything, and their fear ensured that they complied. You depended on rumours, which were completely contradictory, depending on which political direction they came from.[71]

Against her better knowledge, she wrote of having known about only three concentration camps: Oranienburg, Dachau and Belsen-Buchenwald.[72] In the same memorandum, however, she included documents showing her interventions in Theresienstadt, and mentioned her protégés' fear of Auschwitz. This discrepancy could perhaps be explained by the fact that not only Wolfgang, but also the lawyer, participated in the writing of the memorandum, and amended the text when it came to this awkward subject.

Winifred's engagement on behalf of those persecuted and deprived of rights by the Nazis was attested in the memorandum by fifty-four credible and often moving letters of thanks. 'As I could not change the policy in general, I did everything I could to help these unfortunate people. I tried to achieve release for every concentration camp inmate for whom my help was requested, without inquiring into reasons.'[73]

Winifred soon had plenty of opportunity to get to know the practice of de-nazification; at first in the case of Emma Bär, and then of her doctor and friend, Helmut Treuter. The atmosphere was full of hatred. Treuter's close links with the house of Wagner counted against him, especially after the statement of his old rival and party comrade Albert Angerer, who appeared as the chief witness for the prosecution. Treuter had 'wormed his way into Wahnfried . . . and displaced me'; he had used his position as Winifred's 'personal physician' for self-promotion. She had 'held her protective hand over him on every occasion'.[74] A further accusation was that Treuter had exerted great influence over Gauleiter Fritz Wächtler and had even visited a sauna with him – which he hotly denied. Above all, Angerer maintained that Treuter's acquittal by the People's Court in 1945 would not have been possible without good party connections.

The verdict and sentence were harsh: group I categorization, that is, as a 'major offender'; confiscation of assets; disbarment from practice; and five years labour camp. Treuter lodged an appeal, but was taken straight from the hearing to Sankt Georgen prison in Bayreuth. His large practice was confiscated and handed over to a victim of the regime.[75] His wife, Ella, also lost her practice and her married home; 'in error', as it transpired years later. Winifred was shocked by the process and the hateful tone of the hearings, and could only fear the worst for herself.

Before his appeal hearing in November 1946, Dr Treuter was released from gaol. At that time, a number of credible witnesses for the defence came forward; he was reclassified as a 'follower', and set free. Whereupon the president of the District Medical Association of Bayreuth objected, threatening to bring in the prosecutor general, and warning that the acquittal would lead many prominent democrats to resign from office. The case went to appeal again, this time in Nuremberg. 'So it becomes an endless circular process,' Winifred complained, 'a new artificial rift between German people – and how are we supposed to achieve peace?'[76] After much nerve-racking to-ing and fro-ing from one trial to another, it took until November 1949 for Treuter to be fully reinstated and allowed to go back to work.

It became very clear in the Treuter case that it was not the witnesses for the defence who mattered (and there were plenty of them, especially Jews, Ukrainian auxiliary nurses and forced labourers). It was the prosecution witnesses who counted. This was where old scores could all too easily be settled, and a single significant witness was enough to secure a conviction. Treuter's trials were a continuation of the disputes that had led to his prosecution in the People's Court in 1945. One witness who gave evidence both before and after 1945 said he was astonished that Treuter was now being labelled 500 per cent Nazi, whereas before 1945 he had been regarded as an equally pernicious Communist.[77]

The few returning 'racially persecuted' people were mostly loath to appear as witnesses for the prosecution, for fear of jeopardizing their newly established lives. So, for example, Lotte Meyer-Viol, née Warburg, refused to testify that in 1933 Angerer, her former doctor, had forced her to resign from the tennis club of which he was president. After all that had happened, she was not inclined to press charges 'over something so trivial'. The doctor's 'attitude was pathetic', she said, but 'that was all'. At the time, she had 'dropped him as her GP', and anyway she had left Bayreuth shortly afterwards. Her refusal is all the more understandable in the light of the consequences of the incriminating evidence given by Paula Schwabacher in the case of Angerer himself. From 1933 onwards he had refused point-blank to go on treating the Jewish and half-Jewish members of the Schwabacher family. Angerer's defending counsel submitted a medical report stating that the witness was not of sound mind.[78]

While the public mood and the newspapers were predominantly spiteful, as in Winifred's case, to compound matters many of the potential witnesses for the defence preferred to keep silent, to avoid getting themselves into difficulty, especially when their own de-nazification process was not yet complete. It is all the more astonishing, therefore, that so many witnesses were willing to testify on Winifred's behalf.

The verdicts of the Nuremberg War Crimes Trials were announced on 1 October 1946, and the death sentences carried out on 16 October. Special editions of the newspapers included pictures of those hanged, some of whom Winifred knew well: Hans Frank, Joachim von Ribbentrop, Alfred Rosenberg, Wilhelm Frick and Julius Streicher. Hermann Goering had evaded execution by taking poison. Martin Bormann, condemned to death, had disappeared but – although this was not yet known – was already dead. Albert Speer and Baldur von Schirach got off with twenty-year prison sentences. Rudolf Hess received a life sentence.

Winifred, deeply sceptical about the law, and worried about her hearings in the *Spruchkammer*, hoped 'that I will bear what awaits me with dignity, and that in one or two decades I will see the return of normal concepts of legality'.[79]

CUCKOOS IN THE NEST

As Friedelind showed no sign of taking up the invitation to head the Festival, Mayor Meyer, in the name of the Americans, turned to another Wagner grandchild who had emigrated. Franz W. Beidler was the son of Isolde, the daughter disowned by Cosima. Beidler had been banished by his grandmother Cosima in 1925, when he married a Jewess. He emigrated with his wife to Zurich in 1933.

He accepted an invitation to come to Bayreuth, especially as he had a personal motive for visiting. For his planned critical biography of his grandmother, he was hoping to consult his mother's letters and Cosima's diaries in the Bayreuth collections. The Americans granted him permission to travel as well as the right of access to the Wahnfried archives. Wolfgang made thorough preparations for the visit of his unwelcome relative. Otto Strobel, the archivist, was still interned, but his wife, Gertrud, helped to read through and select the papers: 'Wolfi read the Isolde letters that were *not* going to be handed over to Dr Beidler.'[80]

When Beidler arrived armed with his right of access, Wolfgang made it clear in the presence of the Mayor that, while his cousin could of course see the archive, most documents were still stored elsewhere and could not be consulted. Regarding those that were 'still accessible', you couldn't 'just have everybody coming . . . and picking out whatever they liked . . . Somebody had to take control, and from a family point of view, at the moment he was that person.' As far as Cosima's diaries were concerned, he regretfully pointed out the facts of Eva's will and the strongroom in Munich, at which point Beidler joined in the family's indignation at Aunt Eva's treatment of historically important archival items. Wolfgang went on to detail how much material had been destroyed or lost because of the Americans. The only catalogue, an old one, had been lost in the looting.[81] In short, there was hardly anything available that would be of use to Beidler.

Neither the Mayor nor the American officers had any idea where any particular archive items were, and had to rely entirely on Wolfgang. Beidler

could look only at whatever his cousin had selected for him. For five weeks
he struggled to make progress. Although Wolfgang and Gertrud Strobel
were friendly to their guest from Zurich, they made sure he knew he was
there only by courtesy of the occupying power. He was an intruder, but more
than anything else he was a threat to the property and the future of the
Wagner family. Even the émigré Friedelind was against her cousin, and made
some good suggestions, as is evident from Winifred's remark in a letter to her
daughter. As to Beidler, 'that's a brilliant idea of yours for giving him the
knock-out blow!' So far, however, 'he has almost completely failed to get a
look at anything, so he is hardly in danger of infringing copyright'.[82]

Gertrud Strobel said that he avoided contact with Winifred altogether,
because 'his friends in Switzerland might disapprove! He says that he personally is very sorry, since he has nothing at all against her; but he hopes she
will understand his position.'[83]

An important weapon in the family's armoury was Siegfried's will, making
Winifred the immediate heir, and her four children her successors. In order
to install Isolde's son in Bayreuth, it would be necessary to confiscate the
Festival Theatre, Villa Wahnfried, the Wagner archive and all the Wagners'
assets; this was scarcely possible in law. But the family could not prevent
Beidler and the trustees from negotiating over the future of the Festival, and
quickly coming up with a plan. It entailed a formal request to him on
20 December 1946 from the Americans and the town of Bayreuth to offer
Thomas Mann the chair of a proposed Festival Foundation. As Beidler wrote
to the mayor, Mann was 'today the leading representative throughout the
world of that other Germany which we all, despite painful evidence to the
contrary, believe to be the true one'. With Mann at its head, 'Bayreuth
would be announcing to the world that it has radically and decisively broken
with its offensive past, and is willing to reconnect with the true Wagnerian
tradition.'[84] Beidler reserved the post of general secretary for himself.

Beidler wrote to his highly esteemed friend Mann in California from 'this
particularly desecrated place which, although degraded to the status of a Nazi
cult site, is still basically so dear to us all'. He was proud to appear here
'entirely as a representative of our American friends, both military and civilian'. For 'as expected, this feels like enemy territory, and without the
occupation forces, people with our convictions would be dead within
24 hours. The poison has bitten so deep, that after such a short time it could
hardly be otherwise.' He found 'really quite repulsive' the 'two-faced dishonesty' of many people, with whom he none the less had to collaborate,

'simply because there is no one else available'. 'The ruins of the German towns,' he said, 'were only a reflection of the moral ruin before which we stand.' He presented his idea for a Festival 'that would finally do some justice to the work and the ideas of Wagner', and asked Mann 'to accept the Honorary Presidency to which you alone are entitled'.[85]

Thomas Mann replied that he had 'studied the documents thoroughly, with the sort of excitement that these things, these plans, possibilities, prospects plunge one into'. But he was 'so heavily engaged in the final battle with my novel [Dr Faustus]', that he did not have sufficient concentration left for this enterprise, although for him 'of course it was something like the fantastic fulfilment of a youthful dream and love of mine'. He wondered whether it was honourable 'to take up any public office in Germany, even that of a cultural figurehead, which could only be held under the protection of foreign bayonets'.[86] But his answer was not quite conclusive. Beidler's plan was thus left up in the air, and became ever more unrealistic as time went on.

Winifred wrote to August Roesener: 'Isolde's son has gone again after staying about five weeks, but not without leaving a cuckoo's egg behind, in the form of a proposal to the Allied Control Council. Our business is to be expropriated without compensation, and an international Foundation Committee formed, chaired by Thomas Mann, and containing nothing but Jews.' She thought that was over-egging the pudding, however.[87] And indeed, on 20 June 1947, Beidler wrote to the civic authority of Bayreuth withdrawing from the Festival plan, as the time was not yet ripe for it.

Friedelind's book The Heritage of Fire appeared in the USA in May 1945. The text comprised a variety of articles written for the print and radio media, but it had been extensively revised for the US market by her co-author, the journalist Page Cooper. Consisting as it did of first-hand accounts of the private life of Hitler, the book was a great success. Winifred heard rumours about the volume, which was coming out at a very awkward moment for her, but she had no opportunity of obtaining a copy.

On 7 April 1946 she wrote again to her taciturn daughter, reporting on her impending trial: 'It's being said that the main accusation against me will be drawn from your book.' She asked Friedelind to send her a copy urgently, 'so that I can work through it and be correspondingly informed'.[88] Instead of a reply, Winifred discovered that her first two letters, of September and October 1945, had been published in an American music journal. So

Friedelind had received them, but merely turned them straight into cash. Once again, there was no reply.

In May 1946, for a fourth time, Winifred begged her daughter to answer. 'Perhaps you will get this letter just at Whitsun or on Daddy's birthday – then we'll know we're both thinking of each other.' She described the disastrous food-supply situation in detail.[89] Friedelind maintained her silence, but sent food parcels to her nephews and nieces via Ellen Beerli.

Friedelind's book appeared in autumn 1946 in Holland, and finally in German translation in Switzerland. Winifred got hold of a copy at last, from an American, at the beginning of November 1946.[90] In January and February 1947, the magazine *Auslese* (Selection) published a few chapters in successive issues. The German press quoted some of the more titillating passages at length.

Winifred, working flat out on her defence, complained about the 'campaign of lies in the press', especially at the beginning of March 1947 when the *Bayerischer Rundfunk* (Bavarian Radio Station) broadcast a reading of 'the worst chapter of the whole book'. It dealt with the last meeting between mother and daughter, in Zurich in 1940, and Winifred's alleged words to Friedelind (already quoted here) warning her that if she did not end her propaganda war against Hitler she would be 'destroyed and exterminated'. Winifred was able to prove that this meeting did not represent the final breach with Friedelind by referring to her, Friedelind's, letters: 'one of 14.1.40, and one of 29.2.40 (my visit to Switzerland took place between these two dates)'.[91] In the malicious reports in the German press Winifred saw a plan 'to get mother and daughter to wipe each other out – and it's easy to see what that would lead to!'[92], that is to say, the expropriation of the Festival.

Although investigations in connection with her court hearings were supposed to have been concluded by 1 March 1947, Winifred was interrogated again on 3 March, leaving her with the impression 'that the interrogations so far still aren't enough to stage the show trial the press have promised the public. They pulled out all the stops, from Gestapo-type questioning, to nasty threats, to normal conversation.' The main accusations were 'that I made Hitler "socially acceptable" – and I had received special rations (true, during the Festival period)'.[93]

And once more Winifred begged her daughter in New York to get in touch. 'On 3 and 15 March I was subjected to more interrogations – Your book plays a big part in this – but as I can point out many mistakes in it by quoting your own letters, I'm hoping it won't be as significant as expected.' She said that Friedelind ought to be glad she was not living in Germany.[94]

In order to demonstrate the book's lack of credibility, Winifred turned to other people with a 'history' in the Nazi period; Gerdy Troost (Hitler's artistic adviser) and Richard Strauss, for example, who had also been unjustly incriminated by Friedelind. In particular, Winifred made herself into an advocate for Tietjen, asking her daughter: 'I know you don't have much time for Tietjen any more – but perhaps you have enough human feeling for him to find a way of fulfilling his request?' After all, what was at stake was whether or not he was allowed to work again. Tietjen had been able to prove that 'he had rendered great service to the resistance movement', but, on the other hand, there was this sentence in Friedelind's book: 'H.T. has a new occupation; interrogating British spies.' 'That is a mistake on your part,' wrote Winifred, 'you must have mixed him up with Teddie (Goering) – because I remember telling you that time in Zurich about Teddie personally interrogating British pilots who had been shot down (not spies!).' Tietjen 'had nobody in the whole of Germany who can disprove this – but also nobody who can prove it either, because actually he didn't do it. You're the only one who can help! . . . He hasn't got a penny left to live on; he has a serious heart condition; and he really must get permission to work . . . just in order to avoid coming to a miserable end.' She knew her daughter would not want to inflict life-long damage on anyone. In writing the book, she could have had 'no conception of the possible consequences', but 'you've certainly made trouble for a few people; can't you find it in your heart to help H.T.?'[95]

Friedelind had also incriminated Germaine Lubin, her generous hostess in Paris. She asserted that Tietjen had hired Lubin for Bayreuth in 1938 'for political reasons'. He had remarked that her voice was 'not quite up to Bayreuth standards', adding 'but Germaine is a very beautiful woman!'[96] The implication was that she had been engaged for Hitler's sake, and it contributed to the harshness of Lubin's sentence. It was to be five years altogether before she regained her freedom, in May 1949.

Winifred did not receive her first letter from Friedelind until May 1947, after seven years of silence. It mainly concerned questions of financial assets. Winifred replied that the children's inheritance was not jeopardized: 'They say vengeance will not be taken against relatives. So your prospects are not bad.' But she pointed out that Wahnfried lay in ruins, that it had to be rebuilt as soon as possible and that there were hardly any disposable funds available. 'On the one hand, I'm always afraid of being a burden to you all –

but I haven't even got a rope to hang myself with, and besides, my courage as well as my curiosity about how we're going to get out of this mess keep me alive, even if I get sent to labour camp for a few years – "off to a quiet place", as one elder of the church so tactfully put it to me!'[97]

In mid-May Preetorius, now the highly respected Vice-President of the Bavarian Academy of Fine Art in Munich, declined to make a statement to the *Spruchkammer*, writing to Winifred: 'No, I don't want to come.' For one thing, he had already told everything he knew. But, above all,

> I don't want to meet your children again, none of whom treated me very well; Wieland in particular was positively hostile, treacherous, even contemptuous. And it's here, in respect of your children, that I'm afraid I may be forced to testify in a way that is not helpful to you. The incredible arrogance of your children – especially Wieland, who exploited his connections with Hitler and Bormann to get away with absolutely everything – that arrogance, lack of respect, and unwillingness to recognize anyone else's achievements, or give them their due at all – I'm so bitter about it, that I can't be sure I won't violently erupt and create an atmosphere not at all favourable for you.

He had never received many thanks for his contribution to Bayreuth , 'but what I did get was hostility and disparagement from your children. – No, my dear Frau Wagner, for all my friendship towards you, please understand – I cannot come!'[98]

Tietjen agreed to give evidence on Winifred's behalf, but soon began to have doubts, and wrote to a confidante: 'Omi' (Granny), by which he meant Winifred, 'writes with extraordinary optimism. By contrast, I'm very pessimistic about her, because it's all going to come down to the time before 1933, and none of us knows anything about that.'[99]

THE FIRST DE-NAZIFICATION PROCEEDINGS

The written case for the prosecution was presented on 14 May 1947, and as had been feared, most of the charges originated from Friedelind's book. Precisely at that moment, when it was vital to rebut the accusations quickly and efficiently, Winifred's defence lawyer Ebermeyer was arrested for false questionnaire declarations. After his release he went on sick leave until

27 May, and then calmly went off to a film conference in Berlin without giving Winifred's trial a further thought.[100]

In this crisis, on 25 May 1947, Winifred turned to her old lawyer, Fritz Meyer, who had by then been 'de-nazified'. The lists of witnesses were supposed to be submitted by 11 June. 'In my case it is much more than the fate of an individual that is at stake, and I've got to construct an extremely tight defence . . . with your support I'd have much more confidence going into the dock! – You know the assessors, the chairman, the prosecutor, the witnesses for the prosecution etc. etc.' Everything had been prepared. Now it was a matter of establishing the 'general lines of the defence case'.[101]

The meagre list of witnesses for the prosecution, and especially the content and nature of the accusations, quickly indicated to Winifred that the court had no incriminating material about her relating to the 1920s, above all none of the early letters to and from Hitler. But as the Treuter case had shown, the utmost care would have to be taken even with the few, very unconvincing witnesses the prosecution was able to produce.

Concerning the two prosecutors, Winifred commented: 'one was a factory worker from Bayreuth, and the other was an itinerant preacher from Silesia. So neither of them in my view had the slightest notion what it was all about. But that was generally the case everywhere.' Winifred knew the workman. 'I employed him as a building labourer; he worked on this house [Siegfried's house].' He had 'distributed illegal leaflets from Switzerland, and landed up in gaol. Construction workers were very hard to come by in those days, and I tried to get him released, and succeeded in doing so. That wasn't mentioned, of course.' She had noticed 'that the man was a bit embarrassed about me'.[102]

Robert Aign, the former parish priest designated to chair the court, stepped down on health grounds shortly before the case was due to begin. As his daughter later said, he hated his involvement in the *Spruchkammer*.[103] It may be that he felt especially uncomfortable dealing with Winifred. For his brother Walter, a year younger than him, had been close to Siegfried for years. There was a danger that, in the over-heated atmosphere of the courtroom, old stories would be revived, and that was not in the interest either of the Aign family or the Wagners.

There had still been no statement of any kind from Friedelind, who had received a copy of the prosecution case some time before. The only news of her was the rumour that she was off to Hollywood to become a film director. Winifred's response was brief and exasperated: 'The main thing is that she shouldn't come back here disturbing the peace of the family!'[104] On 3 June 1947 she wrote to her daughter:

> I'm expecting a labour-camp sentence in the first instance, and that means . . . I'll be taken straight from the courtroom to St Georgen prison, from where you get allocated to a camp. It makes no difference even if you submit an appeal; you still get packed off straight away. What a sight for the good citizens of Bayreuth, by the way, your grandfather's daughter-in-law being led through the streets escorted by two armed policemen.

She appealed to her daughter not to abandon family solidarity, 'because only by standing together can we hope to achieve our aims'.[105]

It was not until 18 June 1947, practically at the last minute, that Friedelind sent a telegram to the mayor, which arrived in Bayreuth on 20 June:

> after consultations with appropriate advisers washington and new york I request postponement of winifred wagner trial until I arrive Bayreuth stop as legal representative of the wagner legacy and american citizen I must insist on giving evidence.[106]

Winifred saw this as a good sign and 'a turn for the better' in the trial; she expected Friedelind to arrive within a week.[107] But the prosecutor declined the opportunity to question Friedelind; neither was her book accepted as admissible evidence. So she stayed in America, but she showed her good will by announcing a transatlantic call for Winifred's fiftieth birthday; it would be at three o'clock on 23 June. The news caused a great stir. For Winifred, not yet de-nazified, had no telephone, and could take the call only in the international telephone call room in the Grand Hotel, Nuremberg. The eighty-kilometre journey to Nuremberg took a stressful fifteen hours. But as Winifred later wrote to Friedelind: 'even if it had taken me ten or a hundred times longer, I want you to know what a great thrill it was for me that day'.[108]

For a long while it was not certain where the trial would take place. 'Yesterday I heard via Wolfgang, who always keeps his ears open,' wrote Winifred to a friend, 'that my hearing will apparently take place in Munich. One wag commented that in that case they would have to lay on a special train from Bayreuth to Munich to take all the curious spectators!'[109] To

Winifred's intense disappointment, Tietjen produced a medical certificate shortly before the proceedings began, excusing him from giving evidence. His own de-nazification was taking a long time, and he wanted to avoid risks.

The court hearings started on 25 June in Bayreuth, and lasted four days, with morning and afternoon sessions. The new chairman, Otto Säger, according to Wolfgang 'a rather senile former senior civil servant',[110] had practically no time to prepare. The large courtroom was completely full, and there were many reporters, as well as a newsreel team. Entrance tickets had been distributed with a view to maintaining a balance: supporters and opponents were present in roughly equal numbers in the public gallery.

Excellently prepared, Winifred appeared in the court at nine o'clock, a tall, upright lady dressed in a dark outfit. Wolfgang was the only one of her children present. The first day was given over to the prosecution, which was not in a strong position. In contrast to the fifty-four written testimonies for the defence – and another thirty witnesses who had come to give evidence in person – there were only a few prosecution witnesses, and they were unreliable. The Bavarian Education and Culture Ministry had therefore sent a professor from Munich to reinforce the attack. His long report was immediately rejected by the defence, because three quarters of it consisted of accusations taken from Friedelind's book.

During the hearing, the defendant was first asked whether she had joined the NSDAP as early as 1920 or 1921, as Friedelind asserted in her book. Winifred could prove that she had not joined the Party until 1926, adding that she had never given it more than her 1 mark 80 pfennigs subscription, and had never held office in the Party. Then the questioning moved on to the years 1923 and 1924, with both the prosecution and the chair revealing large gaps in their historical knowledge. Quotations were produced from two books of the Hitler period to prove that Winifred 'had believed Hitler to be the coming man even in 1923', which she in no way denied.

Following a newspaper article and some CIC minutes, the long report from Munich was read out, and refuted in detail. The prosecution then tried to represent Winifred's rescue activities as favours done for Party comrades, for example the Hoesslin couple; Franz von Hoesslin was accused of 'conducting in a brown shirt'. An expert came to the aid of the prosecution, asserting that to go on conducting at the Festival until 1941 could only mean that Hoesslin was a National Socialist. He accused him of spinelessness, and pointed out that Hoesslin's brother had been a Nazi.

Hoesslin was well known in Bayreuth, and everyone was aware how hard things had been for him, and how fiercely Winifred had fought on his behalf. The ignorance of the Munich expert, the prosecutor and the chair were embarrassing. The defence emphatically refuted these false accusations by producing an eyewitness, as well as three detailed statements made under oath. Many spectators were angry at the unfairness of condemning a dead man (Hoesslin and his Jewish wife had been killed the year before in a plane crash).

Then there were long discussions of Hitler's love of Wagner's music; about whether Hitler had any comprehension of music at all (which the expert denied); and finally about Richard Wagner's anti-Semitism. None of this had any bearing on Winifred's personal guilt or innocence; it was pure mood-music.

Then came the witnesses for the prosecution. The Bayreuth newspaper editor Georg Spitzer, then eighty years old, produced a copy of a letter bearing some 1,000 signatures, one of which was Winifred's. It was Chamberlain's letter of 1 December 1923 to Hitler in Landsberg gaol.[111] The second witness was the former head of the Bayreuth Trade and Food Supply Office, an NSDAP member from 1933 to 1943, who had been dismissed by Mayor Kempfler for corruption, and who now stepped forward in the guise of a political victim. He stated that in June 1943 two crates of eggs had been delivered to Wahnfried, and he also mentioned supplies of fruit and vegetables. Moreover, Kempfler and Winifred had once driven together to Prague with the back seats removed from their car, and the CIC had asked the witness 'whether Frau Wagner was known to have gone in and out of Gestapo headquarters in Prague'.[112]

As far as the eggs and vegetables were concerned, Winifred replied, naturally she had received special rations, as well as cigarettes and wine, during the Festival period, for house-guests and for the Festival restaurant. She strenuously denied the accusation concerning the Gestapo, but confirmed that she had been in Prague with Kempfler, and that she had brought back presents from there for her grandchildren: 'a baby bath, a pram, spoons etc.'.

The most serious charge came from the witness Grete Zimmermann, who accused Winifred of failing to rescue from the concentration camp the Bayreuth Socialist Oswald Merz, the Wagners' chief local opponent. But she did also mention that 'Herr Merz really hated Frau Wagner'. Winifred's defence was that:

Herr Merz's family appealed to me in a letter in February or March 1945, not before. I was always expecting a call on behalf of Herr Merz. The letter arrived at the very last moment. I was forced to write at the time that it was completely hopeless, as there were no longer any post or telephone connections . . . It was just shortly before the end. I always preferred to tell people the truth about how things stood, rather than build up false hopes.[113]

A fellow-inmate in Dachau said that Merz had told him, 'Frau Wagner won't do anything for me. That woman can't stand Reds.' He also said, 'Frau Wagner accepts some people, and turns others away.'[114] The crucial question of whether Winifred had been asked for help before 1945 could not be answered. Merz died in 1946.

The accusation shows what strange notions many people had about Winifred's influence; as though all it took to get someone out of a concentration camp forthwith was a simple call to Hitler. It also became apparent how insulated life in Villa Wahnfried was from the life of the 'ordinary people' in Bayreuth. Social Democrats had never been welcomed there, and knew next to nothing about life behind its walls.

The following day it was the turn of the defence. First, Körber and Deubzer gave an account of Winifred's role in the scandal of the Bayreuth doctors. Körber began his evidence by expressing 'the satisfaction I feel at being able to appear on behalf of Frau Wagner . . . in the same building and in the same courtroom where she spoke out for me on 20.9.1938, when I was facing criminal proceedings. Frau Wagner did me and Dr Deubzer a tremendous service in the most miserable period of my life . . . It is to her above all that I owe my rescue.'[115] His long statement was constantly and rudely interrupted by the prosecutor, the 'Silesian itinerant preacher'. 'We don't want to hear all your personal tales of woe; just give us Frau Wagner's defence.'

KÖRBER: I've given you Frau Wagner's defence. But what you and all the other *Spruchkammer* courts have got to learn is that there were people in those difficult times in Germany who helped others, and Frau Wagner was one of them.

PROSECUTOR: What is clear to me is that Frau Wagner is one of the guiltiest people; she helped to breed and nourish the Party.

KÖRBER: All the same, Frau Wagner stood up for me. I won't take back a word.

On the subject of the doctors' acquittal after four years in custody, the prosecutor contended: 'So you were acquitted because the judges did their duty.'

KÖRBER: But there were judges at the time who did not do their duty . . . and everybody who stood up for me was taking a risk.

PROSECUTOR: It ended in an acquittal because there was no other way that trial could have gone.

KÖRBER: There certainly were other ways it could have gone.[116]

And so it went on.

After Philipp Hausser, who spoke on behalf of the Schwabacher family, the next witness to appear was Justus Michel from Fulda, a 47-year-old member of the Franciscan Order. He stated that he had not met Frau Wagner 'until the day before yesterday', as they had previously only corresponded with each other. The chairman, said Winifred, 'cruelly allowed' the invalid to stand (he had lost a leg in the war), as he did with others. 'But I brought chairs for them while they testified.'[117]

Father Justus, as Prior of the Hadamar Monastery in Hesse, had been arrested by the Gestapo, like many other clerics, for alleged indecency against pupils. The monastery was taken over and in 1940 – although this was not mentioned in the trial – turned into a 'euthanasia institute' where thousands of sick people were murdered. Having spent fifty-one months in the concentration camp, Father Justus was unexpectedly released from Dachau, after his family had followed the advice of a Mother Superior of his Order and appealed to Winifred for help. From December 1942 onwards, Winifred had been active for seven months on his behalf. After writing in vain to Reich Governor Epp and to Goering, she composed an appeal to Himmler, and kept 'plugging away, so that the appeal was not forgotten'. Father Justus produced the relevant documents in evidence, and expressed the most sincere gratitude.

He vigorously rejected objections from the prosecutor to the effect that Winifred Wagner 'had acted from selfish motives. What did she stand to gain from me, an unknown monk? . . . Does everyone have to lose their head to prove that his actions are selfless and dangerous? It's not the man who drowns while rescuing somebody who gets the medal, but the one who successfully achieves a dangerous rescue.' Finally, he expressed his wish 'from a grateful heart that this selfless, helpful deed may contribute to her complete exoneration'.

This was followed by spontaneous applause from the spectators, and the chairman had the courtroom cleared. 'We're not having any of these Nazi methods here: it looks as though all the entrance tickets have gone to National Socialists.'[118] This accusation caused massive indignation. After consultations, the court came to the conclusion that the applause 'had nothing at all to do with Nazism . . . but was a spontaneous reaction to the words of an excellent orator, delivered in a very priestly fashion'.[119] The public were allowed back to hear the following exchange:

PROSECUTOR (to Father Justus): Are you claiming that you were only released because of Frau Wagner's intervention?

FATHER JUSTUS: Certainly!

PROSECUTOR: Weren't there hundreds of thousands of people in the same situation in the concentration camps who were just as innocent as you? What happened to the other 99,999 not lucky enough to have Frau Wagner on their side?

FATHER JUSTUS: I can't comment on that.

PROSECUTOR: Do you believe that a non-National Socialist, somebody who had no influence in the Party, could have achieved such a thing?

FATHER JUSTUS: No!

PROSECUTOR : Do you know that Himmler was the most brutal and callous of those around Hitler?

And, after several more questions along the same lines, 'Do you know that the National Socialist tyranny was only possible after the putsch of 1923 because highly placed, international celebrities like Frau Wagner personally supported Hitler?'

FATHER JUSTUS: I don't know that.[120]

The monk's place was taken by a deposed former SPD town councillor, employed by Winifred as a first-aid attendant during festivals. After him came the musical director Paul Ottenheimer, who described what he had suffered. 'I am proud and happy to be able to repeat these words of gratitude here, in this forum.'[121]

While the sixty-year-old anthroposophist Lydia Beil was making her long statement, a buzz ran round the courtroom at the arrival of a new spectator: the author Karl Würzburger. Having fled to Switzerland in 1936, he was visiting his home town for a few days, and took an interest in the hearings. Although Winifred had been of service to him, too (she had successfully called Schemm's bully-boy squads to order in the summer of 1934 when they had beaten up 'the Jew' Würzburger[122]), his attitude to her was sceptical: 'How would Frau W.W. be placed now if Hitler had won his war? I can just see what kind of celebratory Festival would have been held in Bayreuth then!'[123] For Würzburger, even Lydia Beil's emotional thanks to Winifred were 'somewhat unappealing'.

But when the prosecutor started to rant at the witness (Lydia Beil) 'in the crudest possible manner' (as Würzburger put it), attempting to destroy her credibility with unfounded insinuations, Würzburger was dismayed, observing that 'the public and above all the court itself were bound to be losing faith in both the integrity and the intelligence of the prosecutor. I was deeply upset by it. Is this the proper justice to dispense in a *Spruchkammer*? And in a trial, moreover, that might well command the interest of a global public?'

There was a further confrontation when the prosecutor kept on rudely interrupting the witness. When she began, 'I see these things from a different point of view', the prosecutor broke in with, 'Your different point of view is of no interest to us here.' The defence lawyer then remonstrated: 'We are all here to establish the truth and see justice done. I cannot see why an old lady should be attacked and shouted at in this way. I protest.'[124]

The statements recounting individual histories piled up, showing the variety of strategies Winifred had employed in her rescue efforts. As the day came to an end, the defence lawyer observed that he could have produced eighty witnesses, instead of the thirty who had actually appeared; and he read out further written depositions to be added to the files.

Würzburger was also there to see Winifred face up to cross-examination. 'Frau W. stood very calmly, and carried herself really well in court,' although he felt that she was perhaps 'a touch over-confident, a little superior', and she 'clearly did not fear the verdict, however it might turn out . . . Undeniably, that lent her dignity, at any rate.' The impression she created was one of 'provocative frankness'.

The prosecutor involved her in a discussion of the Party's programme, and then of Hitler's proclaimed 'positive Christianity'. Had it not occurred to her that the latter blatantly contradicted the teachings of the apostles John and Paul? The long and pointless discussion that followed was, according to Würzburger, 'pure blasphemy'. And anyway, 'nobody in the courtroom was inclined to be critical of people's predilection for the Führer-idea, where they had already previously been fully indoctrinated with the Master-idea'.[125]

The prosecutor was not impressed by the wealth of defence material, observing: 'What she wants us to accept as her defence actually incriminates her, because it betokens her close connections with Hitler, which protected the defendant in every respect.' Her charitable acts did not count in the defendant's favour, 'because these actions did not arise out of anti-National Socialist sentiments, and do not imply a rejection of National Socialism'.[126] He classified Winifred as belonging to Group I (major offenders), and asked for a sentence of six years' labour camp and confiscation of all assets.

In his emotional, but effective, summing-up of the case for the defence, Meyer presented Winifred's relationship to Hitler as a non-political, purely personal one, originating in a time before Hitler became powerful. Concerning the sheer number of defence witnesses, he drew attention to the name you occasionally heard people calling Winifred, 'the Madonna of the Nazis', a blasphemous variation on the term invented by Franz Stassen, 'Winihilf des 3. Reiches' (literally 'Winihelp of the Third Reich', a play on 'Mariahilf', suggesting intercessions by the Mother of God).[127] 'What we are dealing with here is not a trivial matter, but the life of a person, a family and a great work.'

The verdict was announced on 2 July 1947. Winifred was classified as group II (offender or activist). The 'penance' prescribed was 450 days of community service, 60 per cent of assets to be confiscated, and so on. The proceedings were brought to an end with the words: 'This court has refrained from passing a labour-camp sentence because the defendant has committed no acts of violence; because she did not behave in any way brutally or reprehensibly; and finally, because she displayed a generous spirit and great humanity.'[128]

After the verdict was announced, the prosecutor lodged an appeal; 'his face distorted with rage', by Gertrud Strobel's account. 'There were cries of "bravo", but outside there were protests, too: "I thought the lady was even going to get a reward!" – "They cart the small fry away, but take the big villains home by car! It's disgraceful!".'[129] The defence also lodged an appeal. However, Winifred was not arrested in the courtroom, nor did she have to sweep Station Square in Bayreuth or the street in Warmensteinach, as tourists are often told to this day.

Content with the outcome, Winifred wrote to Friedelind: 'I held out well, and calmly look forward to further developments. The attitude of the local press is perhaps the nastiest thing, but you have to expect that, because even the public prosecutor stressed in his summing-up that I have been judged according to a political law, and that I owe my punishment to my political attitude – so he was forced to admit that in human terms and as the custodian of the Festival I was not guilty of anything dishonourable.' Wolfgang was behaving 'incredibly well'.[130]

Würzburger summed up his impressions: 'If I became afraid for Germany at any time during my 12-day visit, then it was during the court hearings.' Winifred, so young at the time, 'had [fallen] prey to the magnetism of a man who had lured many more people than her into his power, and who was indeed consciously used by politicians and the military for their own ends. To treat membership of the Party as a punishable crime, however, offends against my sense of honour.' He continued: 'I suspect that W.W. remained loyal to Hitler because, like millions of others, she was foolish enough to fall for the dangerous myth that he did not know what was being done in his name. This punishable stupidity, or at least turning a blind eye, is surely all that is left of the case against her. In my view, Frau W. is being made to pay a very high price for it.' Because of the political, not juridical, basis of the court, the accusation against her had become 'an iniquitous campaign against a hate-figure'.[131]

The harsh sentence brought Winifred a good deal of sympathy. Father Justus sent her his witness's allowance of 140 marks, some cigarettes and some chocolate. 'Other people sent her lots of things like that, too!' noted Gertrud Strobel.[132] Friedelind reported that the Bayreuth singers in New York 'all feel closely involved, and are extremely furious'. The singer Herbert Janssen and his wife had sent off 'a 22-pound parcel to Mama'.[133] Winifred found that 'my friend's' loyalty is exemplary, and hardly a day passes without somebody coming to see me – out of concern for Bayreuth, people are even coming from England!'[134]

For example, Mrs Gilpatrick, the German-born wife of an officer in the occupation forces, offered her services to Winifred. She was soon being called by her nickname, 'Stinky', as she frequently drove Winifred from the Fichtelgebirge to Bayreuth and back, saving Winifred the half-hour trek to the station, the train ticket, the labour of lugging a rucksack around and a good deal of time. Stinky had no trouble obtaining currency, and often visited her children in a Swiss boarding-school, so she was soon conveying useful items back and forth between Lake Constance and Bayreuth, and later, when the borders between the zones were relaxed somewhat, she did the same for Winifred's grandchildren. She was joined by the American Captain Doyle, a loyal helper over a number of years, whose praises Winifred was still singing in 1953. 'The affection such Yankees showed was really touching.'[135] There were also secret gifts of money, something with which Winifred's neighbour Philipp Hausser was able to help by providing an address; 'a helpful friend with a completely clean record, to whom things can be sent without attracting attention'.[136] She wrote to Alice Strauss: 'I'm still living like a lily of the field – on nothing at all, so to speak, except for the support of my dear friends!'[137]

Tietjen, forced to write begging letters for money to buy coal, wood and potatoes, was full of resentment when he heard from a member of the chorus 'that the holy family is eating well and being inundated with "care-parcels" from sympathizers'.[138]

Shortly after Winifred's hearings, Hitler's personal physician, Karl Brandt, once a familiar visitor to Wahnfried and conveyor of Winifred's letters to Hitler, was sentenced to death in the Nuremberg medical trials. He was one of the two doctors to whom Hitler had given responsibility for carrying out the euthanasia programme, the systematic murder of the mentally ill and the disabled. After 1942 he was directly accountable to Hitler as the Commissioner General for Health and Hygiene, and also responsible for coordinating human experiments in the concentration camps. At the instigation of Bormann, in March 1945 he was arrested for defeatism, and in April 1945 condemned to death. He expected to be acquitted at Nuremberg, but he was once more sentenced to death, this time for his involvement in human experiments. He was hanged in June 1948 in Landsberg. From his cell in Nuremberg he made a written statement in Winifred's favour.[139] She had known Brandt only as a helpful and well-educated man, and she was horrified by the sentence: 'What a nice, decent fellow he was, and what a price he's got to pay now for the things he was made to represent.'[140]

More and more she regarded her old friends as victims of the occupying powers and the German authorities. The *Spruchkammer* hearings confirmed her sense that justice was not the issue, but rather vengeance against people with differing political ideas. She was now helping the needy relatives of those executed or interned, listening to their concerns, and gradually but consistently moving towards opposition to the new democracy.

The tendency was reinforced by her daily experience of seeing how nearly all the Germans who had once cheered so enthusiastically for Hitler were now acting as though they had been against him all along. Surrounded by lying on all sides, Winifred felt honour-bound to assert the courage of her convictions by proclaiming loyalty to her friend Hitler, even after his death, although she usually added that the 'Führer' knew nothing about the crimes being committed in his name, thanks to Morell's injections and Bormann's deviousness.

TIMES CHANGE

Illegally (without a permit), in November 1947 Wieland returned to Bayreuth for the first time. Winifred was thrilled to see him again, and full of 'the joy of the run-up to Christmas: he was here for all of three weeks, and it was great to be able to have a proper talk with the lad, and make plans for the future, although of course it's out of our hands! We are just outlaws in chains!' Full of maternal pride, she praised her eldest child: 'Wieland is working terribly hard – some painting, some directing work (no application for it at the moment, of course) and stage-designing – and his mind is always actively mulling these things over. He's matured a good deal, and I'm proud and pleased about the way he's developed, the gifts and abilities which he's shown a lot of diligence and stamina in developing, and still is.'[141] She must have written something similar to Tietjen, for the latter complained that 'the Heir' was now ruling in Bayreuth, 'and Granny – is once more all melting motherly devotion; unfortunately, Wolfi is also under his spell, and from abroad Mausi completes the farce'.[142]

Two and a half years had elapsed since mother and son had last met. Wieland was now thirty, the father of four children. In Nussdorf, he painted pictures that he often exchanged for food or other necessities, he cultivated his garden and he played with his children. His daughter Nike later called these years on Lake Constance 'idyllic . . . with no sense of the responsibilities to come', even if times were hard.[143] The claim that he 'read Freud, Jung and Adler, discovered Klee and Picasso, and studied Greek theatre as well as modern science' was described in retrospect by his wife Gertrud as a 'mystification' and a 'myth' that he spun around himself later.[144] But there is no doubt that hard work at this time enabled him to discover his own independent artistic direction.

How he dealt with National Socialism and his own close connection with Hitler is not clear, since he kept silent about it for the rest of his life. Like so many of his contemporaries, Wieland invented a new past for himself, which bore no relation to reality. Writing to a woman friend in 1946, he claimed that 'I always kept my distance from the Party and its Wagner-hating, philistine, leading figures . . . because the dogged representatives of the Will to Power were worlds apart from me, the grandson of Richard Wagner. You know that for me, as for my parents, the Jewish question and anti-Semitism simply did not exist.'[145] He left no doubt about his wish to inherit Bayreuth as soon as possible, and for the time being he threw himself intensively, even obsessively, into his work on *Parsifal*.

Returning to Bayreuth, he was full of suspicion, fearing (according to Gertrud Strobel) 'that Frau W. is conspiring with Mausi against the sons!!! . . . Wolf the "legacy hunter" . . . Frau W. and Mausi "the two females". His hope: verdict from the *Spruchkammer* putting Frau W. out of action! . . . A terrible temperament!' He conducted a fight against his mother, brother and sisters; insisted on the rights of primogeniture of which his father had deprived him; conferred with Meyer, the lawyer; and was determined to run the Festival alone, with the 'females' excluded and his brother in a subordinate role.[146]

Winifred was not in a position to sign over her rights of inheritance to the children, however much they wanted it, because no property was permitted to change hands after the cut-off date of 14 April 1945. So she hit upon the idea of 'solving the problem by marrying, because that would lead to the same result!'[147] According to Siegfried's will, she would forfeit the inheritance if she married again. Tietjen, however, had married his young girlfriend of several years standing, Lieselott Michaelis, in February 1946, eliciting Wieland's comment: 'The cunning gentleman is distancing himself and creating an excuse . . . The rats are leaving the sinking ship . . . Mama wrote diplomatically, but very bitterly, that he was using the opportunity of the hard times she's going through, to ditch her – just typical.'[148]

Gertrud Strobel claimed to know that 'she would prefer to marry an old Englishman, and has already issued instructions to find one for her, so that she can go to England!!!'[149] But these plans came to nothing. To make it easier for her children to inherit, 'if that's possible without marrying or dying', Winifred tried to acquire British nationality, especially as she thought that as an Englishwoman she might get off more lightly in the appeal hearings, and would at last be able to travel again more easily.[150] Preetorius wrote to Tietjen: 'Frau W. wants to become English again and withdraw from everything; with her lovely brood, that's the best thing she could do.'[151]

Having no family documents, and not even knowing the dates of her parents' births and deaths, she wrote to English vicars and relatives. In the end, she discovered the address of her half-sister Maude, the child of her father's first marriage, and wrote the unknown woman a long letter. She introduced herself as '"little" sister Winnie', and asked her for information about the birthplace of the father they shared. Writing about her children and grandchildren, and the destruction of Villa Wahnfried, she also mentioned that she had been a member of the Nazi Party, 'as everybody was, who had anything to do with public life'. Her assets had been seized, and if it were not that 'a few . . . kind friends are helping us to clothe and feed the babies – on rations solely we would all starve to death'.[152] This very heavy hint prompted a few charitable parcels from England.

When Maude informed her of the existence of two half-brothers, one in South Africa, the other in Canada, Winifred was pleased, writing back straight away: 'My children are such a mixture: on our side English or Welsh, Danish, and further back German, and on hubby's [Siegfried's] side not only German, but French, Swiss and Hungarian – "an international bunch", the Nazis used to call us Wagners, until they found out that their Führer was a Wagnerian!' She added that 'my own daughter Friedelind is now an American!'[153]

Winifred's willingness to renounce the directorship of the Festival improved her chances in the appeal hearings. 'I now have the impression that nobody is thinking any longer of expropriation etc.! So time has turned out to be on our side, and our patience and perseverance have paid off!'[154] In March 1948 she was pleased to report:

> Wonders never cease. The Bavarian Education and Culture Ministry, in the form of a Secretary of State, received Wieland and Wolfgang on 13 February, and they seem to be prepared to let my sons take up their mission, as long as I disappear from the scene immediately. I am of course quite happy to make this sacrifice to the continuation of the Work, and have absolute confidence that they have now acquired the necessary maturity and knowledge.[155]

On 8 May 1948, with no end in sight to their de-nazification process, the Americans called a halt. No one could afford to keep hundreds of thousands waiting in camps for a verdict, or deprive the country of highly qualified workers for years to come. The remaining trials were dealt with quickly and leniently. As a result, many serious cases, long postponed because of the need to assemble numerous witnesses, were settled very favourably for the defendants, which led to further injustices.

Then at last many of Winifred's acquaintances were set free. The *Spruchkammer* classified Fritz Kempfler as a lesser offender, recognizing his services to the Jews, and his role in saving the town at the end of the war.[156] Hitler's architect in Bayreuth, Hans Reissinger, was classed as a 'follower' and fined 1,000 marks. His brother, Wieland's father-in-law, who had once worked on *Der Stürmer*, was categorized as a 'follower', as was the archivist Otto Strobel, now urgently needed in Wahnfried.[157] The prosecutor even told Paul Eberhardt, the Festival's technical director, that the wartime Festivals had been a pure oasis, while, as Winifred recalled with astonishment, 'to me, the same official called them a "brown circus". Paul has now spent 2½ years behind barbed wire, and refugees have taken over his home in the meantime.' He had no idea where to go.[158]

The prospects for Winifred's appeal hearing were encouraging in the light of these verdicts, especially as expressions of gratitude had continued to arrive. Mother and sons were already working on draft contracts, drawing up conditions that would secure the sons' roles as directors of the Festival in the future. There was no mention of the daughters. Wieland's wife, Gertrud, was already claiming the title of 'the Mistress of Wahnfried', which enraged Wolfgang. This was a case of 'handing out chickens before they're hatched', and 'the concept of "Mistress" sums up the whole idiotic business, because it clearly expresses the impossibility of reasonable co-existence!!'[159]

In May 1948 came the political turning-point in Bayreuth. The new mayor was the Social Democrat Hans Rollwagen, who had made a strong point in his election campaign of supporting a speedy restoration of the Festival under the command of the Wagner family. He was confident in his dealings with the Americans. He put the finances in order, instituted administrative reform and forced the pace of reconstruction. 'We have now got permission to rebuild Wahnfried, but no allocation of building materials as yet!', wrote Winifred.[160]

Negotiations over the introduction of a new common currency in all four zones collapsed because of increasing East–West friction. The currency reform that took place on 21 June 1948 was confined to the three Western zones. The old Reichsmark was replaced by the 'Deutsche Mark' in a ratio of 10:1. The Soviet Zone followed suit with its own currency on 23 June, cementing the division between East and West Germany. In the West, things

improved rapidly. The three western zonal frontiers disappeared, which particularly facilitated travel. Reconstruction began.

In August 1948 the new mayor sent a representative to Oberwarmensteinach, to invite Winifred to talks, 'as the town is now inclined to draw a
line under the past (by which they mean the last three years), and make up
for past mistakes as far as possible . . . I've always maintained they would turn
up one day asking us to come back – well, it seems to have happened', wrote
Winifred.[161]

Writing to Otto Daube that October, Winifred rejoiced. 'Clay – the governor in Bavaria – and the local governor have already announced their
interest in seeing Bayreuth restored soon – the new mayor has recorded his
decent attitude to the family – so we can actually begin – if only we had the
missing million!!!!!!'[162] When the specialists in the Bavarian government
expressed a preference for Tietjen as future director of the Festival, Winifred
responded: 'For Wieland's sake I'd bravely say "no" – even if I'm just repeat-
ing what he says himself; but I want to stay out of it, and let the boys look
after themselves.'[163]

The *Fränkische Presse* (Franconian Press) reported in November 1948
that 'there were unlikely to be any sensations' in Winifred's appeal proceedings. Winifred had every right to be self-confident, as she wrote to Lene:
'Because they won't give me less than III [lesser offender], and that's been
established for some time, as a matter of prestige. So why all this fuss and
bother? The chairman is supposed to have said that as far as he's concerned
I could be a "follower" . . . well, one way or the other, it's a different wind
that's blowing, and if we could get access to our assets, we could try to get
things straight again.'

When Wieland returned with his family to Bayreuth, however, Winifred
was worried. 'He's so easily put out, always thinking I still want to be
involved, which would not suit him. At the same time, more and more
people here and abroad are saying my experience is indispensable, etc.'[164]
Overhoff, too, had moved to Bayreuth with his wife, working very intensively without pay as Wieland's mentor and artistic adviser.

Winifred's appeal was heard on 1 December 1948 in the Bayreuth court
building. No witnesses were called. In her defence, Meyer presented more
witness statements, this time with an emphasis on Winifred's efforts on
behalf of Christians. The atmosphere was business-like, with none of the vit-
riol of the first trial. The auditor Wilhelm Hieber read out a lengthy report
on the finances of the wartime Festivals. It established that, apart from

Hitler's 550,000 marks of special funding for new productions, the Festivals had cost the following amounts, paid for by the German Labour Front: 1940, 1,000,000 Reichsmarks; 1941, 1,190,000 RM; 1942, 1,300,000 RM; 1944, 1,300,000 RM.[165] Winifred's fee had been 5 per cent of this total.

Her sons and daughters-in-law accompanied Winifred to court on 8 December to learn the verdict. She was classified as a 'lesser offender', and had to pay 6,000 marks to the reparations fund. During a probation period of two and a half years she would not be allowed (in addition to other restrictions) to run, supervise, control or acquire any enterprise. Her assets remained frozen for the duration of the probation period.

The panel of judges, in its very carefully argued twenty-page justification for the sentence, evaluated Winifred's speech in the Lieb Restaurant in Bayreuth in 1923 as 'significant support' for Hitler, 'substantially serving to uphold the movement in Bayreuth and thereby to uphold tyranny'. The $100 dollar cheque for Ludendorff in 1923 was also interpreted as support, 'in view of the great publicity the matter attracted at the time'. But although Winifred had 'thrown the weight of one of the greatest names in cultural history into the scales in Hitler's favour', her influence should not be overestimated, 'since many Wagnerians were Hitlerites from the outset'. In those circles 'it was unlikely that many had thrown in their lot with Hitler because of Winifred Wagner'. The charge of illegally profiting from the wartime Festivals was not justified, since services had been rendered in return for the income. It was not Winifred's fault that 'great ignorance and confusion prevailed in the finances and management' of 'Strength through Joy'; that the organization had spent far too much on the Festivals, in other words.

The court accepted as a mitigating factor Winifred's youth in the 1920s, 'especially as the environment of Wahnfried, heavily influenced by the *völkisch* thinking of Chamberlain, powerfully encouraged receptiveness to Hitler's ideology'. Winifred's many kind deeds were recognized by the court as acts of 'pure humanity', in the case of the doctors in Jena and the Jewish front-line combatants,[166] but also as 'anti-Nazi' and a rejection of racist ideology.

It was obvious, however, that Winifred, as one of the 'important and influential personalities of the Hitler period', could not simply resume her place in the public eye. Her willingness to step down from the directorship of the Festival was acknowledged, and there was some prospect of a curtailing of the trusteeship and the period of probation. (Both came to an end within a year, in fact.) Alluding to Winifred's 'long series of rescue actions', the court's summing-up of the verdict concluded with a quotation from *Parsifal*: 'Only the spear that made the wound can heal it.'[167]

Winifred sent Friedelind newspaper cuttings about the proceedings.

> Thank God Wieland was present at court this time, so that he did not need to fear that we could have done everything differently and better – which is easy to imagine when you are far away. – He was also pretty impressed by my composure, because he gave me a kiss afterwards, without a word – and coming from Wieland, that means a lot! . . . The mood in this provincial corner has completely swung round in my/our favour. So everything falls back into place, given enough time . . . The attitude of the Yanks has been so touching throughout the hearings – and when I went with Stinky to the American officers' club, they all congratulated me and said we could make amends by buying the coffee!!!![168]

On 1 January 1949 Winifred regained her British citizenship, while retaining her German nationality. How times had changed – and how keen the town of Bayreuth was to get its Festival back – became apparent two days later. Quietly, without witnesses, without any court proceedings, in the absence of the 'defendant', and with a factual statement, 31-year-old Wieland was cleared of political charges, despite his Nazi past. He was declared a 'follower', and suffered no restrictions whatsoever.[169] His failure to mention in his questionnaire declaration his activities in the satellite concentration camp did not endanger him, since all enquiries had ceased. Tietjen wrote to Preetorius: 'so the Heir seizes the Work for himself, and the Bavarian government falls for this most odious of Hitler favourites'.[170]

Many years later Winifred stated frankly that Wieland had been treated very favourably. 'Wieland too could easily have been made to defend himself in court. For example, he was Head of Culture for the *Gau* here in Bayreuth, and what have you.' He was spared a year's military service, and all active service. 'Dear God, you've got to say he benefited unfairly . . . He was never charged by the *Spruchkammer* . . . It's a very good thing for Bayreuth that Wieland got off so lightly . . . but basically it's beyond comprehension . . . To spell it out quite clearly, I took everything on my own back . . . I was the scapegoat . . . And by doing so I cleared the two boys, so to speak.'[171] Lafferentz was released from internment camp in mid-1949, classified as a 'follower' and with a smaller reparations fine to pay than Winifred, who thought this unfair in the light of her son-in-law's high rank in the SS and all his party functions.[172] Like many Germans caught up in the early 'de-browning' proceedings, Winifred felt she had been dealt with unjustly. But all talk about the past was soon displaced by the shared enterprise of recon-struction.

Winifred reported triumphantly to Friedelind that when the *Bayreuther Zeitung* (Bayreuth Newspaper) complained to the military governor about Winifred's invitation to a charity ball in aid of German orphans, the gover-nor replied 'evenly' that

> they had nothing at all against me, and that tolerance was part of democ-racy!!!!! – The American chaplain came out strongly for me too, spreading the truth everywhere and tackling prejudice. Now he's beaming, because his judgement about my position has been vindicated. – Small-minded people just can't grasp that one could be somebody in one's own right, and didn't just become something because of the Nazis – and therefore that one is still somebody in one's own right.[173]

She looked to the future with confidence: 'It can't be denied that we all went through a lot of tough times, and God knows what's ahead of us. – The out-come of my appeal is not exactly wonderful – but at least no stain has been left upon Bayreuth or me . . . Basically, both the state and the town want to see a Festival taking place in 1950, and they want my sons to carry it out – but we're not going to be rushed.'[174]

CHAPTER 15

Superannuation

(1949–73)

THE INHERITORS TAKE OVER

'I hereby solemnly swear to relinquish all participation in the organization, management and direction of the Bayreuth Festival. In accordance with my long-standing intentions, I propose to entrust the above responsibilities to my sons Wieland and Wolfgang, and transfer to them the corresponding authority to act.'[1] That was the text of Winifred's abdication as director of the Festival, dated Oberwarmensteinach, 21 January 1949. She commented bitterly:

> The 'victory' has been dearly bought; the Festival is only able to continue because I have declared that I won't take any further part in running it – but, as ever, the main thing is that it will stay in the hands of the family, and that my sons are in a position to replace me completely . . . What I've got to do now is adjust to a world which has taken away all my rights – or rather, all the duties I've become so fond of.[2]

A solicitor helped to draw up a contract between mother and sons. 'It's very hard,' wrote Winifred, 'to create a settlement for myself while also doing justice to my two daughters as co-heirs. The whole palaver would be unnecessary if only everything could have been left as it was; then I could be in charge as before, with my sons as my right and left hands.'[3]

Legally speaking, nothing could be done to alter the succession laid down in Siegfried's will of 1929 giving all four children equal inheritance. In practice, though, mother and sons ignored the rights of the daughters, arranging everything among themselves. The daughters protested. Verena wrote to her mother: 'I've been feeling for a long time what Friedelind has been forced to write to you all so bitterly: that nobody takes any notice of us, and no one thinks for a moment that we not only love Bayreuth, but have rights there which you ought to be defending.' She, Verena, was no longer prepared 'to go along with the usual family practice of passing over awkward and uncomfortable things in silence'.[4]

Many discussions took place, all fruitless. Winifred confided to Lene: 'If only I could find some way to disabuse Verena of the delusion that my arrangements have "disinherited" her – there is simply no money to be made out of the Festival for the time being, and who can say that the boys haven't actually been disadvantaged by their mission!'[5]

In April 1949 the Bavarian Asset Management and Reparations Office returned the Festival Theatre to its rightful owner, Winifred Wagner. She put it at her sons' disposal, and they in turn paid her rent, to provide her with an income. Another move, on 25 May, was to give them control over the various Festival accounts.[6] In June Winifred outlined to Ilse Hess how she envisaged her future. She was going to 'stay right in the background – but since the boys will be using my property and my money to stage the Festival, they are accountable to me, of course, and nothing is going to happen without my agreement'. Obviously, she did not intend to interfere in artistic matters. Yet in the same letter she mentions having recommended a member of the Hess family to Wieland for the role of Parsifal.[7]

While Wolfgang bought a house on Festival Hill, in May 1949 Wieland put a building loan of 12,000 DM to use in constructing a simple family house, to a design by Hans Reissinger, within the ruined area of Villa Wahnfried. In doing so, he pulled down some undamaged parts of the villa, losing precious plasterwork, painted walls and flooring that could have been restored. Winifred was indignant: 'Wieland was more destructive than the bombs. He even smashed up the old furniture . . . out of sheer anger at his grandfather's superiority . . . Yes, he was radical, he wanted nothing to do with the past; he always said that for him it was only the future that mattered. He wasn't an easy customer to deal with, Wieland.'[8] In her fury, she forgot that in her great clearing-out exercise at Wahnfried in 1932, when she was tired of living in a museum, she too had ruined a good deal of historical material.

In the new concrete building, clashing ostentatiously with the old part of the house, a new generation of Wagners was growing up who, as Winifred complained, 'were not being brought up in the family tradition. They don't know the anniversary dates, when their famous great-grandfather was born etc.' On one occasion when her grandchildren were with her, there was something by Liszt on the radio. She told them to 'be quiet, they're playing music by your great-great-grandfather. "By who?" "Well, by Liszt." The children responded with: "You mean to say we're related to him, too?"'[9] Traditions of any kind were anathema to the new master of Wahnfried; even the valuable old family portraits. Winifred recalled that 'one day, in a fit of rage, he tore all the pictures down from the walls, saying "I just can't stand the sight of the family any more", and packed them off to the lumber room'.[10]

Very few outside observers thought the Wagner sons capable of running the Festival, least of all Emil Preetorius, who continued to curse 'the arsehole of Bayreuth' [Wieland]: 'But what is grotesque is that there is no longer any stigma attached to being a Nazi, anti-Semite etc.; in fact, the contrary is almost the case – being anti-Nazi makes you suspect. It's all an idiotic farce.'[11] The émigré Fritz Busch was just as sceptical: 'Bayreuth is such a big concept, and so important culturally, that inexperienced children brought up with Nazi ideology should not be trusted to restore it.' Busch aspired to direct the Festival himself, together with Tietjen as artistic director, and a Jewish conductor, 'so as to drive away the stale smell of Nazism from Festival Hill!'[12]

Against all the expectations of the sceptics, in September 1949 Wolfgang set out a detailed financial plan, with estimated costs of around 670,000 DM, for a Festival in 1950.[13] At the same time, thanks to an initiative by the former Freikorps leader Gerhard Rossbach, a 'Society of Friends of Bayreuth' was established, with the aim of providing as much money as possible for the Festival. Rossbach persuaded industrialists and CEOs to make a commitment to Bayreuth. Winifred's old friend, the Dortmund steel magnate Moritz Klönne, became president of the Friends.

At the Klönnes' place in Dortmund, Winifred met Fritz Thyssen's widow and other potential donors, and later reported proudly to Lene Roesener that she had negotiated 'with a new sponsor for Bayreuth, the richest man in Westphalia, and got him to agree to a meeting with Wolfgang . . . The boys were so pleased that they paid my return fare!'[14] She was back in demand. 'I have to go into Bayreuth a lot nowadays, because the present city fathers want to make up for the sins of their predecessors, so they invite me to official functions, and I don't want to be petty-minded and repay evil with evil; I put on a friendly face for the sake of my sons, because we must restore the good old relationship between Wahnfried and the town.'[15]

For a while Konrad Pöhner took on the office of mayor and cultural adviser, explicitly in order to work with the Wagners to re-establish the Festival in Bayreuth.[16] His uncle Karl Würzburger, back from his Swiss exile, became head of the Bayreuth Culture Department with the same aim in mind. There was a successful appeal to the townsfolk to make accommodation available for Festival visitors.

While Wieland concentrated entirely on his new productions, in consultation with Kurt Overhoff and Hans Knappertsbusch, who was living in Bayreuth, Wolfgang was covering the length and breadth of West Germany on his motorcycle and conducting tough negotiations with sponsors, ministries and officials about financing the Festival. Würzburger used his contacts with broadcasting institutions to attract generous funding from them and arrange favourable contracts for future broadcasts.

Following their enforced idleness in the de-nazification period, Bayreuth and the rest of Germany plunged into a veritable frenzy of work and reconstruction. Former victims and former Nazis all worked together within the great national consensus: to look forward and forget the past as though it had never happened. When the Bavarian Minister of Education and Culture alluded to Bayreuth's Nazi past, the émigré Karl Würzburger replied, 'Herr Minister, I don't think we should forget the swastika flags that flew over Munich.'[17]

It was apparent to the city fathers that, as a small provincial town, Bayreuth owed its international significance entirely to the Festival. Würzburger said, 'We are the hospitable home of this world-wide Work. That is a good deal, but it's also more or less all we are.'[18]

By Whitsun 1950, in the Festival Theatre where the first general meeting of the Society of Friends was held, Klönne was able to declare that an advance of DM 400,000 was available. Thereupon, Wolfgang announced that the Festival would reopen on 29 July 1951. Winifred wrote to Ilse Hess: 'At any rate, the boys are sailing full steam ahead towards a Festival in 1951, and want to start in grand style with the Ring and Parsifal as well as the Mastersingers.' However, Wilhelm Furtwängler would not commit himself until the 1952 season. As Winifred said, 'if I know him, he wants to keep a low profile at first, and wait and see how the business goes under its youthful management'.[19] But he did agree to conduct the opening concert.

The sons declined to make any public statements about the Hitler period, and bound their mother to strict silence. Above all, she was prohibited from giving any interviews. But as the enquiries continued to come in, with Wieland and Wolfgang constantly having to fight them off, she said frankly, 'I'm extremely sorry to be such a bother to you because of my past – but . . . if my stance had been any different after 1933, the consequence would probably have been no Festival for you to inherit.'[20] This was a reminder to her sons that Hitler had rescued the bankrupt Festival in 1933, and very largely financed it thereafter until 1944. But the subject of Hitler was no longer mentioned in Bayreuth.

Winifred had to force herself not to interfere, but she was full of regrets. 'I am not at all "embittered" – as the journalists like to say – but I have been cut out and pushed into the corner – that was my punishment.'[21] During a break in rehearsals for The Valkyrie on 11 July 1951, she wrote to her friend Lene urgently asking her to come to Bayreuth. 'This is a difficult time for me, but it's even harder to bear when you're alone! It's the first time I've been so completely isolated . . . You sit in the auditorium – and try to accept the situation and struggle to be positive, but many things go too deep and hurt too much!' She added that '99% of the artists are strangers to me – no Fidi – no Heinz – it breaks my heart!!' There was endless friction on the Hill, including that between Wieland and Paul Eberhardt: 'Rows – crash – finished – over – that's what young people are like – no emotional resources.'[22]

Just like old times, though, was the conflict around Furtwängler. When Fu spotted his young rival Herbert von Karajan (whom he called 'the K man') in the auditorium at one of his rehearsals, he flew into a rage, and Karajan left the theatre in silence.[23] Furtwängler conducted the opening concert of the Festival on 29 July, with Beethoven's Ninth. The concert went out over the radio, evoking a deep emotional response.

Once more, leaflets were distributed on the Hill, and the audience requested to refrain from political 'discussions and debates', with the well-known quotation from the Master: 'Here we serve art.' Whereas in 1925 Siegfried had requested abstention from demonstrations of German nationalism and anti-Semitism, the object now was to ban all mention of the Wagner family's involvement in the Third Reich. (No one remembered that Hitler had likewise ordered notices to be distributed asking the audience not to sing the 'Horst Wessel Song'.) The three Western high commissioners were in attendance, including, representing France, a figure well known in pre-war Bayreuth, the former ambassador André François-Poncet.

The new era was launched in spectacular fashion on 30 July with Wieland's production of *Parsifal*, anticipated by Winifred with motherly pride.

> He's not just doing the stage-sets, but the whole production, and since he's the questing type, of a mystical and spiritual disposition, a lot that is good as well as problematical is bound to come out of it. – He has immersed himself as intensively as possible in the content of the work – he's read all the previous writings on the Parsifal theme that he could get hold of – studied religious and philosophical questions – contacted the Church and the clerics etc. etc. . . . He's definitely got the 'eye' – and I think the 'heart' will reveal itself in due course![24]

At first, Winifred was not irritated by the sparse décor and costumes. 'At that time,' she wrote, 'I didn't take it seriously. I assumed . . . well, we haven't got anything; it's just an economy measure. Simply because there was nothing. I thought it was a sort of transitional phase.' She was amazed to discover that 'it's supposed to be the new style, so to speak'.[25]

Knappertsbusch was the conductor. The 63-year-old was highly disconcerted by the design, thinking at first that the reason the stage was so empty was that Wieland simply had not had enough time to finish it. The stage 'disc' that soon became Wieland's hallmark was known to Knappertsbusch as 'the hot-plate'.[26] When he said he must have the traditional floating dove in the final scene, Wieland suspended it so high up that the conductor could see it, but not the audience.

The stage was a *tabula rasa*: empty and quite dark. There was no temple, and neither were there any meadows, forest, swan or dove. There were only diminutive-looking, solitary people on the stage, revealing their feelings and concerns through music. The grandson was rebelling against Wagner, the Wagnerians, his grandmother, father and mother. There was nothing that represented a link with the past. Sweeping the stage clean of a tradition that had become suspect corresponded to the mind-set of the so-called 'Zero Hour' generation at the end of the war. Wieland had precisely captured the *Zeitgeist*.

After Wieland's (rather less provoking) *Ring of the Nibelung*, nerves were calmed by a traditional *Mastersingers of Nuremberg*. The production was

Rudolf Hartmann's, with stage-sets by Gertrud's uncle, Hitler's architect Reissinger. The costumes were on free loan from the Nuremberg City Opera. This production, in traditional costume, of the politically most tainted Wagner opera was no doubt a gesture towards the taste of sponsors. Furthermore, since Wieland otherwise took charge of all the productions and sets in this relaunch year, delegating the *Mastersingers* can be understood as a way of avoiding comparisons with his own *Mastersingers* of 1943–44. To have Karajan conducting was a guarantee of musical quality. The young Elisabeth Schwarzkopf sang Eva. The press was enormously receptive. Bayreuth as an artistic centre was back in the public eye.

Preetorius did not attend the 1951 Festival, and took a jaundiced view of it. It was 'crafty of Wieland to disguise his paucity of ideas as a designer by minimizing all the visual aspects, thereby at the same time eliciting howls of acclaim from the Abstractionist crowd'.[27] Connoisseurs such as Tietjen and himself agreed that Wieland was drawing on the directing concepts of the Kroll Opera in the 1920s under Otto Klemperer and Jürgen Fehling, and taking them to extremes.

Initially, Winifred hoped her son would take a more moderate turn. On the contrary, however, Wieland was encouraged by the reviews he received, becoming more provocative from year to year, and thus making himself one of the earliest German representatives of modern 'director's theatre'.

Almost daily, Winifred was confronted by the indignation of the orthodox Wagnerites. The main objection was that the director was not serving the work, but arrogantly interfering with it and changing its nature. The director, Wagner's own grandson, was conducting a battle with Wagner's work on the stage, and falsifying it. There was a demand for 'faithfulness to the work'. At first, Winifred made an effort to soothe tempers.

> It's understandable that youth wants to go its own way, and equally understandable that not everybody will follow. A generation that experienced daily the loss of the values that we held to be indispensable, learned through bitter experience to distinguish what is essential from what is inessential, and that emerged with tragic clarity and great forcefulness from Wieland's creative work. This kind of production only brought out the inner content of the work more profoundly and movingly.[28]

Winifred was torn between pride in her successful son, and outrage at his disrespectful treatment of the Master's works. Preetorius, driven by curiosity in spite of himself, was back in Bayreuth for the 1952 Festival, and wrote to Tietjen: 'Frau W.W., whom I had not seen for ten years, threw herself upon my neck on the Hill, in tears, and exclaiming loudly "what do you think of all this nonsense here!"'[29]

On the other hand, she rallied behind Wieland: 'The "anti" clique won't get any further than they did in my day!'[30] And she certainly made sure that she savoured Wieland's successes abroad. In 1955, for example, she wrote: 'My son Wieland makes sure I get around the world a bit – I go to all his productions outside Bayreuth, and very much enjoy his achievements. In November it was Fidelio in Frankfurt, then Tristan in Brussels, in February we're off with the Stuttgart Fidelio to Paris, and in March to Barcelona with Parsifal, Tristan and the Valkyrie.'[31] Wolfgang as a director was overshadowed by his brother, but his mother always took special care to sing his praises, as in 1953, when she referred to one of his productions as a 'restrained Tietjen performance'.[32]

Unwaveringly, despite all their conflicts, Winifred maintained her connection with Tietjen, enjoyed good relations with his wife, and never missed a chance to meet up with him. In 1953 she took advantage of a special offer of a bus trip to Berlin for DM 27, and Tietjen conducted a performance of *Twilight of the Gods* 'especially for me'. 'I'm looking forward to it very much – though seeing the city again for the first time since '43 will be strangely sad!'[33]

In 1954 Tietjen expressed an interest in Wieland's work, attended the Festival, and said to Winifred after Wieland's *Tannhäuser* production: 'You'll be disappointed – I'm not as disappointed by Tannhäuser as I expected to be.' Winifred also reported that 'he praised Wieland for his boldness and determination! It seems that directors think his ideas are fantastically good – and that's wonderful.'[34] Tietjen's hostility was transformed into recognition of Wieland's artistic achievement, and in 1958 he invited him to put on a new *Lohengrin* production in Hamburg, where he had been intendant since 1956. Winifred went up for the première, and reported to a friend that she had seen 'Wieland's quite poor and almost boring "Lohengrin" – though it was conducted by Tietjen in a very youthful and lively manner'.[35]

In return, Tietjen conducted three performances of *Lohengrin* at the 1959 Festival. Winifred found them 'a refreshing pleasure for my "Bayreuth" ears – musically, it was exactly as it should be, and the singers and the orchestra all went along with it enthusiastically . . . We had some good days and hours in honour of the past.'[36] Together with Tietjen's wife, of course, the two of them were soon jointly celebrating their birthdays, on 23 and 24 July.

FRIEDELIND PAYS A VISIT

The family were still uneasily awaiting their reunion with Friedelind. According to Winifred, 'she doesn't get in touch often, and when she does it's usually unpleasant or uncomfortable for the family'.[37] In the meantime, a new scandal broke in 1951: Baroness Gerta von Einem, the mother of Friedelind's former friend the composer Gottfried von Einem, demanded the return of the jewellery she had entrusted to Friedelind in Switzerland in 1939. In view of the uncertainty of the times, the idea was that Friedelind should take it (illegally) to the USA. But when hard pressed, Friedelind had pawned the jewellery, and had not had enough money to redeem it. Now there were arguments over the value of the jewellery, and demands for payment.

The Wagners made not the least effort to help Friedelind out of her difficulty; on the contrary, there was every indication that the scandal and the subsequent embarrassing court action in Bayreuth suited the family quite well, as it compromised Friedelind and put her out of the running for the directorship of the Festival. In this difficult situation, it was only Verena who stood by her and proposed a simple solution to her mother, as reported by Winifred: 'Suddenly I'm being told it's my duty to rescue Mausi!!!!! And since I've done nothing for her since '39, I've piled up so many obligations to her that I ought not to mind paying for Baroness Einem's missing jewellery!!!!'[38] The matter dragged on for years, and at the end both the von Einem family and Friedelind were left resenting their treatment at the hands of the Wagners.[39]

With conditions so unfavourable for Friedelind's first visit to Bayreuth for fifteen years, the family were surprised when she actually arrived there for the 1953 Festival. Winifred's impression was that

> She has changed very much for the better – she's much slimmer, and although her blonde hair seemed strange to me at first, it suits her well. She's adopted Lubin's upward glance, and is going for the charming look in place of her former tomboyish one. We all got the impression that she had come with good intentions, and the whole family gave her a nice welcome, thank goodness.

Friedelind was much taken with her nephews and nieces.[40]

Wieland's daughter Daphne, seven years old at the time, still remembered her adored American aunt decades later: 'First of all, she looked terrific – like Marilyn Monroe – with her hair dyed platinum blonde, quite thin, dressed in a chic American style, something you never saw in our small-town post-war Bayreuth – a fantastic woman. And she was always particularly open and kind to us children.'[41]

Winifred was delighted that Friedelind was 'very impressed by the boys' work, and thank goodness there was no bone of contention between them'. After so many years, Winifred enjoyed gathering her whole family around her, including her grandchildren. Many people were surprised that mother and daughter were on such good terms, considering all that had taken place since 1938. But Winifred remained cautious:

> We have skilfully navigated our way round all the rocks – nobody breathed a word about her book, and we all just started from where we are now and came to terms with it. Because everybody was concerned to clear the air, we managed to do so, and thank goodness it now looks as though we can start relating to each other in a natural and relaxed way.[42]

After the Festival, mother and daughter drove in Winifred's small car to Lake Constance to see Verena, and then on to Switzerland. At the Lucerne Festival they went to concerts conducted by Furtwängler and Guido Cantelli. An attempt to visit Toscanini in Pallanza came to nothing. 'He simply wouldn't see us,' said Winifred.[43]

Friedelind was talking once again about taking *Tristan and Isolde* on a countrywide tour of America, which Winifred thought was too ambitious, given her daughter's lack of organizing experience. 'Will her whole tour idea collapse? I wouldn't be surprised, because she hasn't succeeded in a single enterprise so far . . .'[44] 'We all feel that she's not on firm ground over there, and not everybody is well disposed to her here in Germany! However, she has become a US citizen of her own free will and will have to live with the consequences.'[45]

Friedelind spent Christmas 1953 in Wahnfried. 'She's still a problem for us all,' declared Winifred, because she would have liked to work with her brothers in the Festival Theatre, but lacked the training to do so. 'And then, she's become so American: night and day she harps on about publicity, publicity. But we hate press intrusion. We get enough of it during the Festivals, and we're glad of every week of private life.'[46]

From 1959 onwards, Friedelind regularly attended the Festivals, organizing master classes for musicians and singers from abroad, as Winifred told Lene, 'with talks about stage design, directing, lighting etc. etc. She's already set up a foundation for the purpose over there, and she's going to create a registered company here . . . The boys let her get on with it – I'm sceptical about the business – because I can't imagine such talks attracting many people . . . The Yanks are less demanding than we are!'[47] Friedelind signed up members of the Festival company 'to give classes in every aspect of opera production, from costume design to wig-making, make-up, repetiteur work, singing etc. She was happy with that, and it brought her back to Bayreuth every year'.[48] Winifred thought that the master classes in 1959 had been 'nicely successful for her, and she might as well go on channelling her energies like this'.[49] What Friedelind continued to face in Bayreuth is shown, however, by the dismissive name given to her master classes in the family's private language: 'Kleistermassen' (a spoonerism for Meisterklassen = masterclasses, where *Kleister* = 'paste', and *Massen* = 'masses').[50]

Relations between mother and daughter remained unstable, but there were certainly periods of affection and mutual support. Whenever her mother, usually so strong, showed signs of weakness, as for instance when she was ill, Friedelind was at her side. They were united in their love for Siegfried, whose ninetieth birthday fell in June 1959. From that distance in time, Winifred took a very rosy view of her marriage: 'It's true Siegfried-weather today, with the sun shining, birds celebrating, and flowers blooming luxuriantly – and my thoughts drift back to those 15 years of untroubled happiness at the side of that exceptional person – full of gratitude and full of love!'[51] Proudly, and accompanied by her daughter, she travelled to performances of Siegfried's works, pleased that 'it will probably produce a few marks in royalties for me'.[52]

The brothers kept a wary eye open in case the unwelcome Friedelind should try to interfere in the Festival; they denied her any authority, although she contributed some important input. In 1958, for example, she recommended a young singer to Wieland: 'She has a really sensationally beautiful and flourishing mezzo-soprano voice. She is black, but I hope nobody will object to that nowadays. It actually seems to be quite an attraction.'[53] The singer was Grace Bumbry. Wieland cast her in 1961 as Venus in *Tannhäuser*, as a black sex symbol for the white man, much to the displeasure of his mother, who found 'the black Venus completely unnecessary'.[54]

WALLS GO UP IN GERMANY AND WAHNFRIED

Despite the division of Germany and the Cold War, Winifred transcended all political and ideological boundaries to keep in touch with her friends on the other side of the Iron Curtain. In 1949 she went on a three-week visit to the Eastern Zone. 'I simply had to see all sorts of old friends.' She went to Weimar, Eisenach, Halberstadt and Leipzig – 'and it felt like being in Russia! Horrible!'[55] For as long as she could, she invited the poor and needy to the Fichtelgebirge. 'In addition, I've always got a sort of miniature sanatorium going here for totally exhausted people arriving from the Eastern Zone and in need of rest and care. Actually, one guest seems constantly to take the place of the last.'[56]

At the end of February 1952 she accepted an official invitation from the GDR, permitting her to visit some of the places she was keen to go to, such as Leipzig, Dresden and Zwickau. Surprisingly, it never occurred to her that her trip might cause political complications, though hardly anyone from the Federal Republic visited the Eastern Zone in those years. She was simply going to visit old friends, especially the music critic Eugen Schmitz in Leipzig, and his son, who was musical director in Zwickau. And she also visited the places associated with the Master, such as the small museum in Graupa near Dresden, installed in the house where in 1846 Wagner had written the first sketches for *Lohengrin*. She later sent an appreciative letter of thanks for the guided tour.[57]

The GDR newspapers were astonished and proud to note this high-profile visit from the West, and published Winifred's letter of thanks, as well as a very long letter to Max Burghardt, the General Intendant of the Leipzig City Theatres. In it she praised the excellent ensemble playing of the Gewandhaus orchestra, and added the offensive (in Cold War terms) sentence: 'To my especial satisfaction, I was able to establish that the art of Richard Wagner is still cultivated in the GDR.' She went on to say: 'It is a comfort to know in our present strife-torn world that art ignores frontiers, and in the finest sense connects peoples, countries and continents.'[58]

The text of this letter was published in West Germany, and caused uproar. Winifred was lending herself to Communist propaganda, and was 'as impressed by Grotewohl* as she had been by Hitler'.[59] She failed to

---

*Otto Grotewohl (1894–1964) was the first minister–president of the GDR, from 1949, and stayed in high office there until his retirement in 1960.

understand what the fuss was about, insisting that she could not be forbidden to visit friends, or send a polite letter to thank her hosts. Once again she was in the headlines for her supposed inclination towards authoritarian regimes, and once again she did what she thought right.

In 1958 she informally offered seats in the family box to two visitors from East Berlin who did not have Festival tickets. One of them was the acting Minister of Culture of the GDR, Hans Pischner. There was a political scandal in 1963, that is to say two years after the building of the Berlin Wall, when Pischner – now Intendant of the State Opera – appeared in Bayreuth with two companions to honour the eightieth anniversary of Wagner's death. Both Wolfgang Wagner and the mayor of Bayreuth declined to meet the delegation. 'On the contrary,' said Winifred, 'I was asked to inform them that there would be no joint ceremony at the graveside, and that they were to come an hour later!' Winifred's temper 'reached boiling point', and she invited the officially unwelcome guests to supper in Siegfried's house.

The following morning she accompanied the three Wagnerians to their wreath-laying ceremony, 'chiefly because I noticed that a whole lot of detectives were designated to escort us on this walk! – There were also lots of press photographers standing around the grave.'[60] The reception afterwards in Winifred's home was also attended by Friedelind, who, like her mother, always sided with those under attack. Finally, Wolfgang put in an appearance, to sound out his GDR colleagues as to 'whether artists could be obtained from the East', as Winifred put it.

The next morning, when Winifred discovered that 'the ribbon had been removed from the Eastern Zone wreath, no doubt because it had GDR written on it', she protested to the mayor. The day after that, she saw that 'the missing bit of the ribbon had been carefully fixed on again with paperclips. People are always talking about re-unification, but treating everybody who comes across to us as our worst enemy, who can't be trusted an inch!'[61]

Later, she accepted an invitation to Romania, and was proud to be chauffeur-driven to Bucharest. 'We had free access to the castles, museums, churches etc. – and in Bucharest we were received by the Minister of Culture . . . who gave a banquet for us – an honour I've never been shown by any German minister!'[62] She reported to Fritz Kempfler 'that a Culture Minister in a Communist country laid on a banquet in my honour; in Bucharest the orchestra played the overture to the Mastersingers for me; I received invitations from archbishops etc. etc.'[63]

Once more, she saw her stance as completely apolitical, particularly as there could be no doubt about her rejection of Communism. But she even went so far as to side with the opposition in football. 'Personally, I was pleased to see our arrogant players losing to the GDR!!!!'[64]

Wieland consistently maintained his policy of not allowing a word to be said about his past or about Hitler. He assured journalists, as well as his children, that he had been on the 'right side' – and that he had always opposed his Nazi mother. He gladly contributed to the myth-making of friendly journalists, demonstrating his anti-Nazi credentials by attacking his mother and a dumbfounded Emil Preetorius, who wrote: 'Apparently, Wieland attacked me in a Franconian newspaper for being a former "leading Nazi" . . . If it's really true, then all I can say is: difficile est non scribere satiram.'[65]

There was only one person prepared to challenge the image of the 'anti-Nazi' Wieland. His teacher and mentor Kurt Overhoff accused him of power-lust and dishonesty, because he 'had put the story about that his mother had repressed his personality by imposing her Nazism on him . . . a myth that turned the historical truth on its head, but was faithfully believed by the public, and became firmly entrenched'.[66] 'For Wieland at that time,' he went on, 'there was only one idol and one model – Adolf Hitler, his beloved Uncle Wolf – and if anyone dared to offer the slightest criticism of his idol, he broke off the discussion and threatened to "report" the speaker – that is the absolute truth.'[67] Wieland exploited Overhoff's psychological problems to represent him as a fool and a liar, and dismiss him.

Condemned as a Nazi, Winifred was always furious about the false conception Wieland's children had formed of the Nazi period and their father's role in it. Occasionally, 'in a humorous way', she attempted to put the record straight, especially when the children thought 'that I was the only one in the family who valued A.H. and enjoyed his friendship'. When the subject of the *Spruchkammer* came up, 'I let them know that it was only because their father happened to be in the French Zone at the time that he was not prohibited from running the Festival, too, for profiting from Nazism!'[68] But the children believed what their father told them. Granny had been a Nazi, but Daddy? – never.[69]

The family quarrels grew steadily worse. Forced to work together every day, in private the two brothers were hostile to each other. Wieland's children were not allowed to play with Wolfgang's. The artists and other personnel, and even the journalists, were split into two rival camps. Whenever Winifred tried to mediate, she was attacked from both sides. At this time she was inclined to support Wolfgang, because she thought Wieland treated him unjustly. 'Well, you see,' she said, 'that's what Wieland is like. He's talented, without a doubt, but he can't be bothered with orga-nizational matters . . . Wolfgang has to carry the whole burden of organizing, especially fund-raising.' That was why he rarely mounted any productions of his own. But Winifred declared, 'I prefer his style; it's sounder.'[70]

Wieland became increasingly angry with his mother. His biographer wrote: 'It is said that after telephone conversations between mother and son, an official from the telephone company often had to deliver a new phone to him, because he had smashed the cradle of the old one.'[71]

In the winter of 1955–6 the 58-year-old Winifred fell ill. Following heavy bleeding, Dr Treuter diagnosed cancer of the uterus. Hospital treatment in Erlangen included radiation and radium therapy, which led to bladder burns. Outpatient treatment, lasting months, could not be undertaken from the remote village in the Fichtelgebirge, especially as Winifred could no longer tolerate the cold.

Hence her decision to move into Siegfried's house, which had been stand-ing empty since the Americans left it in 1954. Her sons could hardly object to the move, although, as Winifred wrote: 'Wieland does not seem to be exactly delighted by my decision, because the first thing he did was to build a wall almost 4 metres high between Wahnfried and the new building! Round at the back, on the park side – it looks horrible, and it's robbed me of my view, and all the evening sun.'[72]

All the same, she was pleased to be in Siegfried's house, which she con-tinued openly to call 'the Führer building'. Using old furniture, she fitted herself out with what she called 'a very severe dining-room in the Führer's style'.[73] The little extension to the front of the house, where Hitler's body-guards used to stay, she continued to call 'the SS dining-room'. And when she once again decided on a clear-out, she kept only the furniture 'that USA used to have in his quarters here. – It gives me a special secret pleasure! HIS desk, HIS armchair etc. etc.'[74] 'USA' was the acronym for '*Unser seliger Adolf*' (Our blessed Adolf). Contrary to expectations, she overcame her seri-ous illness.

The conflict between the next-door neighbours, Wieland and Gertrud against Winifred, became fiercer, exacerbated by gossip. Winifred confided to Lene that 'according to Heinz Tietjen, Wieland is supposed to have said that he will never set foot in my house! I have no idea why! But he's certainly never been here!!!!!! – Can anyone ever understand their own children?'[75]

Her relationship with her sons had deteriorated so much that Winifred's mind was turning to ways of retaliating, should the situation become unbearable for her. 'As acting director of the Festival, I'm entitled to cancel the contract with my sons from one year to the next – but they won't let things go that far!'[76]

In abundant angry letters to friends and acquaintances, she recorded her annoyance with Wieland's productions. Apart from his arbitrary way with a score, she was incensed by his provocative introduction of a sexual revolution on to the stage. Writing about his *Flying Dutchman* of 1959, she described how 'the second act takes place in a concrete bunker without doors or windows – the whole chorus has been given udders (you can't call them breasts) drooping down to their thighs – Why? – Wieland believes that all of R.W.'s works arose out of a repressed erotic complex . . . and these preposterous and unaesthetic breasts are supposed to express the erotic!' What is more, Wieland had cut the redemption motif out of the overture and the ending. 'I'm beside myself about Wieland's re-interpretation of the *Dutchman* – beside myself about the MAIN MOTIF being dropped.'[77]

The *Tannhäuser* ballet of 1954, choreographed by her daughter-in-law Gertrud, 'beggared all description', in Winifred's words.[78] The dancers performed in couples wearing flesh-coloured leotards; that is, as good as naked. The sensuous, veiled eroticism of earlier times gave way to a uniform, cold sexuality. These theatrical sensations at Bayreuth attracted newspaper attention, and increased Wieland's celebrity.

Winifred knew how to provoke maximum irritation in her sons: by giving interviews. She made great use of this device, not hesitating to drop subtle hints about Wieland's politics. In 1959, for example, she said, 'Because Germanic myths are no longer popular these days, Wieland tries to turn them into Greek mythology; his Wotan is more like a Zeus. But that is a violation.' The woman interviewer: 'But that is surely a matter of conviction for him?' Winifred: 'Not conviction; it's a concession to the times we live in!'[79] She repeated this statement in many variants. 'If the Third Reich had not collapsed, it seems to me that Wieland would never have hit upon his style.'[80]

For their part, her sons knew what hurt their mother most: not being able to see her grandchildren, all of whom she had helped to bring up. When thus deprived, she got acquaintances to tell her how they were doing, and imagined all sorts of horrors. Somebody had observed Eva at school, for example, 'standing in front of her music teacher in floods of tears! I'm sure she hasn't got a mother at home to help her or comfort her when something goes wrong at school! – Things like that always get to me!'[81]

Winifred sought and found consolation with old friends, such as the Mitford family and the former British fascist leader Oswald Mosley. 'I enjoy friendly relations with him and his family, naturally linked to the big questions of England–Germany–Europe. Mosley is definitely one of the more perceptive Englishmen, and he has put down new roots since he and his wife were interned during the war.'[82] She read Mosley's autobiography 'with breathless excitement', and found it full of 'the wisdom of age'.[83]

While the Mitfords began coming to the Festival again quite early on, Oswald and Diana Mosley did not appear there until 1969, staying 'completely incognito' at the Fantaisie Palace: 'Chancellor Erhard banned him from visiting Germany for five years. Kiesinger raised the ban, and two days later they were here!!' 'Gradually,' said Winifred, 'I'm becoming accepted again. It's only Germany that is wary of me!'[84]

She continued to be very interested in British politics, but detested Winston Churchill as much as ever: 'Well – old man Churchill – my view is that he's getting back into power too late to save Britain from being sold out!'[85] After a visit to Germany by Charles de Gaulle, she wrote to Gerdy Troost that she was 'just as captivated by his personality as you are – and didn't the reaction of our good Germans show how much they yearn for a FÜHRER?' She thought, 'with the way things have developed', that Hitler too, 'reasonable as he was, would have welcomed this Franco-German friendship'.[86]

The old network still functioned smoothly, and Winifred's Bayreuth 'Führer building' became a favourite rendezvous. Those who gathered there included Ilse Hess, Emmy and Edda Goering, Gerdy Troost, Hitler's former adjutants such as Nikolaus von Below, Hitler's pilot Hans Baur, former secretaries and valets, and of course Lotte Bechstein. The old crowd of loyalists lent each other mutual support; and many of them were in need of assistance. The widows and fatherless children of the once-powerful Nazi leaders were dispossessed, publicly ostracized and dependent upon donations, like Ilse Hess, who ran a small boarding house. They all knew that Winifred would make them welcome and that they would get help from her, as well as the latest information about others of their kind. Above all, when they were with her they could do what they did not dare to do even among their own children: talk openly about old times, which for all of them were the best times of their lives. And they could express their enthusiasm for the Führer to their heart's content.

Hans Severus Ziegler, once the powerful Intendant of Weimar, now penniless and solitary, finally decided to move to Bayreuth. Winifred took care of the old man, who liked to play the part of the sensitive poet, favouring perfumes and cosmetics. Every year she organized a birthday celebration for him, accompanied by a collection on his behalf. It was this occasion that prompted Wolfgang to call Winifred 'the mother hen of all gays'; Ziegler was no isolated case. She wrote that 'I must say I admire myself for the way I've stood by all of Siegfried's old friends.'[87]

The former UFA* director Karl Ritter, who had settled in Argentina, visited Winifred regularly on his trips to Europe. She met Karl Kaufmann, the former gauleiter, 'whose health is really bad – and who told me a lot about his recent imprisonment and his belief that it was all a matter of trying to find out about his and his friends' connections with the Arabs'.[88] In 1960 she was proud to meet SS General Wolf. 'At the end of the war he handed over the German army intact in Italy – surrendering independently – which made him quite famous, for having saved the lives of thousands.'[89] Karl Wolff was Heinrich Himmler's personal adjutant from 1933 to 1943, and enjoyed the reputation of being 'the SS general with the clean hands'. He appeared at Nuremberg as a witness for the prosecution. However, in 1962 he was arrested for his involvement in the deportation of Jews, and the shooting of Jews and partisans. Although sentenced to fifteen years' imprisonment, he was released by 1971.[90]

The former Nazi notables were very well informed about each other. In 1963, on the death of Hitler's majordomo, Arthur Kannenberg, who had enlivened many an evening at Wahnfried with his accordion, Winifred commented: 'With him we're losing yet another little bit of ourselves.'[91] And it made Winifred 'really sad' to hear from Ilse Hess about the sudden death of Hitler's half-sister Angela Hammitzsch (formerly Raubal), for, as Winifred said, 'she was a part of him, after all'.[92] What Ilse Hess particularly regretted was that Geli Raubal's mother, who used to be Hitler's housekeeper at the Berghof, had not been able to write the memoirs she planned, and urged Winifred: 'you should think about it, too! . . . We women should speak out,

---

*Universum Film AG was formed in Babelsberg near Berlin in 1917, and closed down in 1945, to be succeeded by the East German DEFA Film Company on this same site.

for once! Perhaps it is a rather indirect way forward . . . we ourselves are not at all that important, but it does offer a route that is open to us right now.'[93] Writing one's memoirs was also a welcome source of income. Interest in the stories told by Hitler's valets, secretaries, and the widows and children who survived the chief players around Hitler has never flagged.

The former Nazis eagerly read all the relevant books as they came out, either recommending or criticizing them. Winifred liked Ilse Hess's memoirs. 'God grant that the book should find a great number of readers, and that it helps them to revise their opinion – not only about you two personally, but about our movement in general!' She had as high a regard for Hess as ever. 'That flight to Scotland was really something, damn it! And because he wanted peace, he's now stuck in Spandau! This world is truly bedevilled!!!!'[94]

She was fond of giving August Kubizek's book *Adolf Hitler, Friend of My Youth* as a present. Since 1939, when Kubizek first attended the Festival as Hitler's guest, she had 'maintained the Führer's tradition',[95] inviting him to the 1951 Festival as her personal guest. For her, Kubizek was above all the man who had brought Wagner's work to life for the young Hitler in Linz.

Discussing the 1961 English edition of the notes* taken down by Bormann at Hitler's 'dictation', she wrote to Gerdy Troost: 'Hitler thinks over what false moves he has made, and comes to the conclusion that, out of consideration for Mussolini, he began the Russian campaign 2 weeks too late!' In addition, he thought that 'he had dealt with France far too leniently, when he should have been more ruthless . . . Of course, he's throwing the baby out with the bathwater when he expresses his utter distrust of all generals, all aristocrats etc.! – But after the treachery and lack of understanding he encountered, it is humanly very understandable.'[96]

She was more sceptical about memoirs whose authors tried to distance themselves from Hitler. She read the book by Paul Schmidt, Hitler's chief interpreter, with interest, but was disappointed 'that he wasn't one of us. I always imagined he was. But of course it may be that his description of the Stresemann period [Weimar Republic in the 1920s] etc. is designed to keep

---

*Martin Bormann's alleged notes on Hitler's final bunker conversations in February 1945 were published in English, with an introduction by Hugh Trevor-Roper, in 1961 as *The Testament of Adolf Hitler*. They were published in German in 1981 as *Hitlers Politisches Testament. Die Bormann Diktate*.

open the possibility of re-entering his old profession, and when it comes to making a living, people can be forgiven many things.'[97]

She was 'utterly enraged' by Albert Speer's memoirs when they came out in 1969: 'as an old National Socialist, he's succeeded in delivering the death-blow to the whole movement!!!! – No enemy of Hitler's could have written anything worse.'[98] The impression Speer made, she felt, was arrogant and humble by turns. And in particular, 'he definitely presents a false picture of USA – and that annoys me. He always represents him as a despot who is basically petty-bourgeois, completely overlooking his genius or, if you like, his daemonic quality.'[99]

At seventy, Winifred went on 'a few helicopter trips' with Hitler's pilot Hanna Reitsch, 'over the Rhine, the Lahn, the Moselle and the Eifel'.[100] She reported to her friends what she had heard from Hanna Reitsch about 'the last days in the Reich Chancellery bunker', when Reitsch still hoped to fly Hitler out of Berlin. Naturally, Eva Braun was also discussed. Hanna 'thinks that USA married out of a kind of absent-mindedness'. But Winifred believed 'that he got married as an act of chivalry . . . USA was no longer of this world – he had that look of the beyond about him.'[101]

The former prominent Nazis read the same magazines, such as the *Klüter Blätter* (Klüter Journal), for instance. If a solicitor was called for, Winifred liked to recommend Friedrich Grimm, 'who was himself locked up for years by the French, and now acts so manfully on behalf of old Nazis'.[102] She passed on information about work to unemployed comrades, and always knew a way out of every difficulty. Her house was an exchange centre for all kinds of goods. For example, she offered a friend of hers, who owned a hotel in Bad Kissingen, a large painted porcelain platter, made in Berlin around 1800, for DM 260. 'I know the provenance of the plate, and I know that selling it is a matter of life or death, so to speak, and I've promised to do everything I can to help sell it.'[103]

She asked Will Vesper, the nationalist author, to advise a man who thought he was a creative writer: 'A terrible idea – that's what you'll think – but you've been on this earth long enough to know that sometimes one has to just hold one's peace and let everything flow over one – and that's what I'm begging you to do! – You'll be helping a sick but courageous man to move on.'[104]

Winifred was free with her advice to journalists and writers dealing with the Hitler period. For instance, in 1950 she was approached by Rudolf Diels. He was a relation of Goering's, and according to Winifred 'the founder of the

Gestapo and head of local government in Cologne and Hanover at the time. – He was condemned to death twice, once under Hitler and once under the Allies, and now he's supposed to be writing a serious philosophical-psychological book about Hitler.'[105] She also gave an interview to the revisionist British historian David Irving, drawing his attention to the rich resources of Lieselotte Schmidt's letters, and even handing them over for him to look through.[106]

She liked to demonstrate her expertise where Hitler was concerned. Although she had nothing to say about him as a 'historical phenomenon', she did claim 'to know much more about Hitler the HUMAN BEING than most others'. She liberally meted out her judgements, praising – for example – Hans Grimm's book *Warum, Woher, Aber Wohin?* (Why, Whence, but Whither?): 'I hope you won't take it amiss if I suggest that the leitmotif of your work is "Deutschland erwache" [Germany awake] (extended of course to "Europe awake" or "White Man awake"). – May all responsible bearers of "Aryan" blood heed, understand, and take to heart this most serious of admonitions – before it's too late!'

She was very pleased to recognize in Grimm's book quotations from Chamberlain, 'who is also among the "banned writers" '. She was particularly impressed by the way Grimm 'had done justice to the aspirations of the deceased Hitler'. If she, Winifred, had not got to know Hitler as early as 1923, it would have taken her, too, a long time to understand him, 'because for us members of the "old bourgeoisie" what they called "the Party" contained too much that was confused, false and unacceptable'. Then she deployed one of her favourite sentences once again: 'If Hitler's actions ever became unintelligible to me, then "the devout faith of friendship" came into play! He once said to me: "You should always be able to be proud of your friend", and often when he was heavily criticized he looked at me sadly and said: "Can't you all just wait?"'[107]

We may presume that this was roughly how the conversation went whenever Hitler's old friends got together. In the summer they congregated in the garden. Their talk, their laughter, above all Winifred's loud voice drifted over to Wieland, despite the high wall. He could not bear his mother's proximity, not to speak of her entourage – whom he knew well from earlier days, and never wanted to see again.

Some old comrades went so far in expressing their enthusiasm for the Führer that their books were classified as 'National Socialist restorationism', and prohibited, like Ziegler's book *Adolf Hitler, aus dem Erleben dargestellt*

(Adolf Hitler as I Knew Him). That did not prevent Winifred from enthusiastically presenting copies of the book to her friends.

Wieland was so angry with Ziegler, who had once helped him during his appointment in Altenburg, that he sent him a very unpleasant letter. He could not understand, he wrote,

> why you thought it opportune to dwell once more on the subject of Adolf Hitler and Wahnfried. Since 1945 the Festival management and the town of Bayreuth have made every effort to consign to oblivion a topic that is lethal for the Bayreuth Festival. After Auschwitz there can be no further discussion of Adolf Hitler. You have done a terrible disservice to my mother, the Bayreuth Festival, and the town of Bayreuth.[108]

THE DEATH OF WIELAND

As a director, Wieland was much sought after and well respected throughout Europe. He worked hard, made a lot of money and led a full private life, which he did not conceal from his wife. The cooperation between him and Gertrud, who worked as a choreographer in the early years, had declined. In the 'Land of the Economic Miracle' she lived a life of luxury, with expensive clothes, many holiday trips and long sessions with her favourite psychiatrists. A house was acquired in Keitum on the island of Sylt, and greatly expanded. The children had never learnt saving ways. So the debts piled up.

In 1960, at about the time of these financial crises, the twenty-year-old Anja Silja, a former child prodigy with a powerful, very high voice, made her debut in Bayreuth as Senta in *The Flying Dutchman*. Silja represented the new type of female Wagner singer: young, blonde, slim, tall, pert and anything but solemn. Her fruitful artistic partnership with Wieland developed into a great love. Anja Silja's similarity to the young Winifred was astonishing, from her Berlin speech to her 'free and easy' manner. Whereas Siegfried called his young wife's voice a 'soprano trumpet', Wieland's word for Anja's penetrating voice was 'child's trumpet'.

Although Winifred never had much liking for her daughter-in-law Gertrud, she did not approve of Wieland's relationship with Anja Silja, and as usual where her sons' women friends were concerned, she was quick to use the word 'whore'. But she was prepared to recognize Anja's artistic quality, in the role of Venus in *Tannhäuser*, for example. 'Even my jealousy has to concede that she was in fantastic voice, and at last Venus sounded like she did when Siegfried cast Jost-Arden in the role in '30.'[109] This was a very great compliment indeed. Wieland said that despite his mother's 'in some ways dynastic outlook', she thought that Silja 'had an unerring instinct for immediately putting into effect Wieland's concept of theatrical realization', while Winifred maintained that Gertrud 'had never understood her husband artistically'.[110]

But Winifred could not accept the idea that her son might marry Anja Silja and thereby make her the Mistress of Wahnfried. 'That would be a disaster. Just imagine this uneducated, gangling etc. creature effectively taking over my position here, my former position.'[111] By 1963 Gertrud was set on obtaining a divorce, and after much painful wavering she filed her petition in 1964.[112]

In early 1962 Winifred observed with concern that 'Wahnfried has been closed down completely and the children all sent to boarding school.'[113] In the school holidays, with their parents absent, the children led a wild life in Wahnfried, as described by Nike Wagner: 'the lack of family leadership led to chaos (financial included), to which the Wahnfried youngsters responded, initially at least, with the time-honoured strategy of looking for a good time'. When her grandchildren raided Winifred's wine cellar 'for their first alcoholic excesses', and Winifred reprimanded them, Wolf Siegfried replied: 'My father does what he feels like, so why shouldn't I?' Nike writes: 'Wahnfried now became known among the pupils of the local grammar schools for the wildness of the teenagers' parties, where precocious drunkenness and promiscuity were routine – to the horror of Emma, the faithful family nanny.'[114]

Wieland decided to turn the original score of *Tristan*, which was still held at Nussdorf, into the ready cash he needed. It had the status of a national cultural asset, and there was a ban on exporting it. However, without consulting Winifred (but with the collusion of Verena) Wieland took the manuscript to Barcelona, where he hoped to get a better price and conduct the business more discreetly. When Winifred heard about it, she reacted like the true Keeper of the Grail, utterly consumed with rage. The great shock of realizing that her own son threatened the loss of the *Tristan* score made her think about depriving the family of its right of access to the Master's inheritance. It was 'first and foremost' the *Tristan* affair, she said later, 'that made her come up with the idea of a foundation!'[115]

Meanwhile, Wieland was thinking of selling the entire Wagner archive, and was consulting the English music agent Walter Legge for the purpose.

Legge later reported that to try to get the best possible price, Wieland had been on the look-out for wealthy US foundations. He was very loath to let the manuscripts 'lie around in some German library. He detested post-war Germany no less than Hitler Germany.'[116] There was only one obstacle: Winifred was the legal owner of the archive, knew its contents intimately and was not to be deceived about it. The reason for her mistrust was that she knew Wieland's aversion to Richard Wagner only too well. 'Basically, Wieland hates his grandfather and deliberately publishes everything that expresses negative views about him.'[117] She also refused Wolfgang when he too 'pleaded with her to smuggle documents from the archive out of the country'. As she told a friend, her children lived in permanent fear of 'starving to death unless they could sell some manuscripts'.[118] Wieland, meanwhile, took out a loan of DM 40,000 from the Society of Friends of Bayreuth.[119]

In 1965 there erupted a scandal that was reported in all the newspapers. Wieland's 22-year-old son Wolf Siegfried ('Wummi'), always short of money, had written off a friend's car, and resorted to purloining a small picture from the lumber room at Wahnfried and placing it with a Munich auction house. The painting was a portrait of Liszt, an original by Ingres, dedicated to Cosima's mother, Countess Marie d'Agoult. Winifred had been looking for the picture for some time, and then saw it offered in an auction catalogue at DM 25,000. She found out who had put it up for sale, and acted in a way that one would not have expected of her as a grandmother. She refused to shrug off the whole affair as a prank, demanded the return of her property and threatened to report the incident to the police. She knew no half-measures when it came to the family heritage.

Wieland became protective about his son, while Wolfgang tried to keep the scandal out of the public eye. But attempts to withdraw the picture discreetly from the auction were unsuccessful. The family were forced to bid for it themselves. The price rose to more than DM 100,000, and the auctioneers' fees were DM 36,000. When Winifred demanded this sum from Wieland on behalf of his son ('because sooner or later he's got to learn his lesson about the results of his "upbringing", and realize I intend to go on being tough!'), he refused, suggesting the money should come out of Festival funds, and went on the attack against his mother. But she steadfastly asserted the principle that 'these family documents must never be sold'. She herself had 'acted accordingly, even in times of the greatest need', and expected the same from her heirs.[120] However, at least Wieland was prepared to hand over the rest of the – by now rather battered – pictures from the lumber room for proper safe-keeping and restoration.

Wieland attempted to cover his debts by organizing a Japanese tour for the Festival; a renowned Swiss agency was engaged to do the preparatory work. He was working too hard, and was unable to resolve his personal problems, torn as he was between his love for Anja and for the children. His tired and run-down condition became apparent in an attack of 'flu in the spring of 1966, while he was working on Alban Berg's *Wozzeck* in Frankfurt under Pierre Boulez, with Anja Silja as Marie. He spent Easter with Anja in Munich, went with her to see a production of *Salome* in Rome, and then joined his family on Sylt, where quarrelling broke out again; then it was back to Bayreuth for Festival rehearsals. He was forced to break off a rehearsal because of an attack of 'nausea', and was taken to the hospital in Kulmbach, where he continued to work with the singers on their roles.[121] At the beginning of July he attended an outpatient clinic in Munich. He stayed with Anja, but concealed his true condition from her, encouraging her to go on with her appearances in Bayreuth, altogether twenty-one evenings within the month. As often as she could, she commuted between Bayreuth and Munich.

On 7 July Winifred wrote despondently to Gerdy Troost: 'A family council has made it clear to me that I should not visit Wieland in Munich, to avoid upsetting him.' The new prognosis did not sound too threatening; the tumour on his heart was benign, and could be treated without operating.[122]

Wieland concealed his weakness, went on working with his secretary in Anja's flat, sent the Festival singers detailed written notes, and on 14 July 1966 dictated a three-page letter to his Swiss agent about the proposed visit to Japan. It asked whether it would be possible to 'mortgage' the DM 40,000 proceeds of the tour and receive the money in advance; 'even without a heart, I would still fly to Japan, dead or alive'. The thought of moving to the Ticino, with the agent's help, alleviated 'my sick-bed existence'.[123]

After the Festival, Wieland and Anja went on holiday together to the Baltic. Whilst there, he began spitting blood, but made light of it. She then had to go to Vienna for rehearsals, while he returned to Munich. There, in her flat, while she was away, he was visited not only by his children, Wolfgang, and the Lafferentzes, but also by Winifred.[124] It was the last time she would see her son.

Just two days before the death of the 49-year-old, the doctors informed his family that his condition was hopeless. He himself never discovered that he was suffering from inoperable cancer of the lung. Twenty-six-year-old Anja remained in ignorance. On 15 October 1966 Winifred wrote to Gerdy Troost that Wieland was 'back in the clinic, in an extremely serious condition'. His breathing was restricted. 'The doctors have called for Wolfgang – an ominous sign.' She was not allowed to go to Munich, and was waiting for news. 'All I can do is sit at home, waiting and fretting.'[125] Gertrud, returning from a long holiday in Greece and claiming her rights as a spouse, did not wait for permission but made a surprise appearance at Wieland's bedside. Anja had a première at the Vienna State Opera, and kept in constant contact with the sick man by telephone.

Wieland Wagner died on 17 October 1966. Anja Silja, who rushed to Munich by taxi from Vienna after the première, arrived too late. His widow, Gertrud, had command of the field.

Even when Wieland's body was conveyed to Wahnfried and laid out there, Winifred was not allowed near her dead son. 'Wieland's children claimed the coffin and the silence for themselves alone,' writes Nike Wagner. 'Mother Winifred's rage was to no avail; she was kept out.' She was only allowed to attend the public memorial ceremony in the Festival Theatre. Nike later thought that the 'unfortunate ambivalence of Wieland's feelings for Winifred' was internalized by his children, and 'the mother/grandmother is perceived as a "Monster"'.[126] Wieland's widow and children were pitiless in their hatred for Winifred, who was distraught at the turn of events. She was all the more grateful for the solicitude shown her by Friedelind, Wolfgang and Verena. 'They were all full of consideration and love.'[127]

Wieland was scarcely in his grave before the most undignified family rows broke out. Gertrud demanded the right to succeed her husband as director of the Festival. Even 23-year-old Wolf Siegfried registered his claims. Wolfgang referred to the contract between himself and Wieland, according to which a surviving brother would be in sole charge of the Festival, but would be obliged to pay the deceased brother's widow a pension, in this case two thirds of Wieland's Festival salary. That was not enough for Gertrud.

Then there was a dispute over the right of residence in Wahnfried, which was mostly unoccupied, but which Wolfgang regarded as a kind of 'tied cottage' that went with the job of director. The family were united against the outsider Gertrud, and Winifred voiced their feelings: 'Gertrud is simply not going to get the chance to pose as the representative of the family – which she is not entitled to be!'[128] The dynastic principle that had served Wieland so well, safeguarded now by a few additional contracts, came to the aid of his brother Wolfgang. A new ruler brought a new court with him. Nike says that 'at any rate, Wieland's children disappeared from the "cloudy heights" of Valhalla as suddenly as if a stage trap had opened and swallowed them up'.[129] As far as Winifred was concerned, Wolfgang was now the sole guarantor of the Festival's continued existence.

Usually such an enthusiastic correspondent, during this painful time Winifred failed to respond to any enquiries. It was not until 23 November that, still in a state of confusion, she got in touch with Gerdy Troost: 'I am so out of my mind . . . I seem to have lost all sense of time.' She was suffering from a 'horrible mental turmoil that is affecting my stomach and bowels'. She went on to report that Gertrud and her children would communicate with her, Winifred, only via solicitors.[130]

When the town of Bayreuth proposed to celebrate her seventieth birthday in June 1967, Winifred declined. 'I can't bear the idea of being fêted and knowing that Wieland is no longer among the living.'[131] Once again she turned to Tietjen for comfort. For the last time, they celebrated their birthdays together. When Tietjen died a few months later at the age of eighty-six, she was forlorn. 'In him I am losing a truly intimate friend and helper, and I'm still quite dazed at this loss!'[132]

THE LONG HAUL TO A PUBLIC FOUNDATION

There were financial problems in every branch of the Wagner family. Bodo Lafferentz's firm faced bankruptcy. Winifred had already sold her house in Oberwarmensteinach for DM 100,000 and given the proceeds to Lafferentz. In June 1966 she had made the house in Nussdorf over to Verena, so that 'as Wolfgang rather gloomily pointed out to me, I'm now worse off by two houses!'[133] Winifred had passed on all her properties to one or other of her children, at a time when Friedelind, and Wieland's heirs, were in urgent need of money, too. When Lafferentz voiced expectations of a post in Bayreuth, both Winifred and Wolfgang dug their heels in. She told Ilse Ernst 'it's impossible to give Lafferentz a Festival job – after all, in contrast to me he had really responsible posts during the Third Reich – and I was just completely eclipsed – it's simply not on for the head of the KdF and director of Volkswagen to work here while I pretend not to mind!' Moreover, there was no job available with the Festival that would pay well enough for a 69-year-old father with five children to support.[134] As she could no longer draw upon investment interest, as she used to, Winifred too found herself in trouble financially. From then on she was obliged to live on the DM 1,250 that Wolfgang paid her monthly in rent for the Festival Theatre.

It became increasingly obvious to her that the Festival could not go on being run as a family enterprise. The Festival Theatre, nearly a century old, needed renovating and extending. In any case, public subsidies had been needed regularly since 1950, as the family could not meet the costs of upkeep. With all the family squabbling, always carried out in full view of the public, the funding bodies (above all the town of Bayreuth, the Federal Government and the *Land** of Bavaria) pressed for a lasting solution, as did the ever more significant – as donors – Society of Friends of Bayreuth.

On the anniversary of Richard Wagner's death, 13 February 1967, Winifred drew up a three-page codicil to her will. 'Legal, personal and financial difficulties within the Wagner family induce me to consider and put forward my deliberations about the future of the Festival and the family assets of which I am presently the custodian. My intentions and my convictions tend to the view that everything possible should be done at all costs to preserve the values of Bayreuth, so important in cultural history'; for instance, in the form of a foundation that would include the Festival Theatre. At the same time, the economic interests of Wagner's descendants should be secured.

'I do not consider it appropriate,' continued the codicil, 'that from time to time individual valuable archive items should be sold off conjointly to meet the financial exigencies of a particular member of the family.' If it were not possible during her lifetime to establish the kind of foundation she envisaged, 'I request that it should be regarded as my last will that all existing legal and conceptual conditions should be utilized in order eventually to create such an entity.'[135]

After careful preparations, and together with her old mediator Konrad Pöhner (then Finance Minister of Bavaria as well as Chairman of the Board of Trustees of the Society of Friends of Bayreuth) and the solicitor Fritz Meyer, Winifred summoned a family council for 6 January 1968. 'The foundation should be a purely Bavarian affair – to rebuild Wahnfried, take care of the archive and rent the Festival Theatre out to the current director – and

*Germany is organized into 16 federal 'states', called '*Bundesländer*', the largest of which is the '*Land*' of Bavaria.

since the family will always be in the majority, they are guaranteed the right
to appoint the director. Wolfgang has life-long tenure in any case – and a
successor can surely be found from among the younger generation.'[136]

The sum mentioned in the proposed settlement with the descendants
was five or six million marks; about a million each for Winifred and the four
families of her children. The settlement was also intended at last to right the
wrongs done to her underprivileged daughters. Even in the run-up to the
conference there was a tense atmosphere, because Wieland's widow, Gertrud,
was still insisting on becoming her husband's successor – as was Friedelind,
who had just presented her first production, *Lohengrin*, in Bielefeld, to a
rather malicious critical reception.

It was a surprise when a new and previously completely unknown member
of the family appeared. Daphne's* new husband, Udo Proksch, whose stage
name was Serge Kirchhofer, was a star of the left-wing scene in Vienna, and
had a penchant for women with famous names. He tried unsuccessfully to
increase his share of the family money by blackmailing the Wagners over the
old currency-smuggling offence of 1937.[137]

The meeting got increasingly out of hand. The grandchildren demanded
more money, hurling accusations at Wolfgang as director of the Festival, and
declaring him incompetent. And then, according to newspaper accounts
claiming to be based on reliable sources, Wolfgang called his sister Friedelind
a 'useless bitch', and spat out at his sister-in-law Gertrud: 'Why should I take
somebody back into the business who paralysed my brother during his lifetime?' Friedelind is reported to have said: 'Winifred is the evil spirit of this
family. There will be no peace while she's alive!' In the end, Wolfgang
threatened to resign with immediate effect as Festival director. He'd had
enough, he said.[138]

Pöhner called for common sense. 'Family disunity is endangering the
Festival. You must all be blind to go on like this.' Friedelind threw in a furious remark, and mounted a vicious personal attack on Pöhner, whereupon
the meeting broke up in disarray. Winifred's comment on her daughter was:
'Her bad behaviour in every respect makes it *impossible* for her to go to
Bayreuth. It will be a tough battle, but she's the one who is making it
impossible.'[139]

---

*Daphne (b. 1946), sister of Nike, was Wieland and Gertrud Wagner's fourth and
last child.

Immediately after the publication of an article, for which Friedelind had acted as informant, in the illustrated magazine *Quick*, a courier delivered a registered letter from her brother Wolfgang. He asked her harshly 'not to set foot in the Festival Theatre again until further notice'.[140] All of this strengthened Winifred's resolve to take Wagner's heritage out of the hands of his descendants.

During the years of conflict over the foundation, there was a change in the political climate of the Federal Republic. The generation of 1968 rebelled against their parents, demanding to know what they did in the Nazi period, and pressing for confessions of guilt. The war-time generation had kept silent for more than twenty years, not willing to admit their part in events, either out of reluctance to confess their mistakes, or from shame. Now an element of defiance was added, because the older generation thought younger people were not prepared to try to understand them, but only to condemn. The divisions that ran through many German families were particularly marked in the case of the Wagners. Winifred, Wolfgang and Verena were under attack, although a taboo still surrounded Wieland's past, as well as his status as a revolutionary and friend of the Left, a reputation still intact two years after his death. His children attacked only their grandmother Winifred.

The polarization of society was expressed in the new-found strength of extremist views, whether on the left with the APO (Ausserparlamentarische Opposition, the Extra-Parliamentary Opposition), or on the far right with the NPD (Nationalde mokratische Partei Deutschlands, National Democratic Party), founded in 1964. The latter paid court to Winifred, hoping she might act as their standard-bearer. She did not appear averse to doing so: 'I hope the NPD will fulfil our hopes and expectations. I've been kept fully informed, and invited to the launching ceremony in Hanover.'[141] But publicly, out of consideration for her family and for the Festival, she kept her distance.

The 1966 elections to the Bavarian *Landtag* or regional government showed that Bayreuth was still fertile soil for nationalism. The NPD polled 13.6 per cent of the vote in the town. Adolf Thadden, the leader of the NPD, attended a performance of *Siegfried* at the Festival in 1968, and during the intervals he was much photographed with the former fighter pilot Hans-Ulrich Rudel. The Bayreuth Festival was threatening once again to turn into a centre for right-wingers, following in Hitler's footsteps.

The NPD organized a special party rally in Bayreuth for February 1969.

The NPD press spokesman was quoted as saying: 'For this kind of event you do not venture into unknown territory; you go to a place where you have plenty of friends.'[142] As was previously the case in Nuremberg, in Bayreuth the NPD was deliberately linking up with old National Socialist traditions. It had no trouble hiring the municipal hall.

As the day of the rally drew near, however, protests to the town council began to build up. The SPD and the unions threatened action. The publicity officer of the Bayreuth Festival spoke out: 'For more than 20 years, every effort has been made to rid Bayreuth of the odium of its obnoxious Nazi past. These far-right provocateurs will undo all the good work of regeneration.'[143]

Winifred, on the other hand, defended her friends, especially Ziegler, a prominent local member of the new party: 'And once again they're mounting a vicious attack on our poor harmless Dr Ziegler! . . . Yesterday Wolfgang offered me a thousand marks to leave town while the conference is on.'[144] Winifred did in fact depart for Salzburg before the date of the planned party gathering.

Meanwhile, the Left were threatening to break up the NPD gathering by force. All the West German newspapers were keenly involved in the conflict. Opponents of the rally planned a massive demonstration for the day before it was due to begin, so that riots seemed inevitable. The clash of Left and Right was avoided at the last minute when the legal authorities found that the NPD were late in paying the hire fee for the hall. The contract was declared null and void, and the NPD meeting did not take place in Bayreuth.

Winifred's political attitude visibly hardened, in a renewal of her old hatred of the Left. To the like-minded Gerdy Troost, she complained about 'the radio and newspaper coverage of the 9th of November – on the one hand the glorification of the 1918 November Revolution, and on the other the hymns of hate against our 9 November – it's enough to drive you to despair!'[145] She was referring to Hitler's putsch of 1923.

At the Federal level, it looked increasingly probable that Willy Brandt would be the next Chancellor, to Winifred's disgust. 'Willi Brandt as Chancellor?????? – Ugh, revolting – that traitor Herbert Frahm!!' (Herbert Frahm was Brandt's real name.)[146] Winifred trots out all the classic hate objects, sounding off against the 'foreign domination' of Germany by the Common Market, as well as 'the whole "guest-worker economy", which costs us such a crazy amount of money – they've all got 14 to 20 children receiving child benefits etc. etc. – there's bound to be an explosion soon'.[147]

She disapproved of Wieland's daughters studying. 'My granddaughters all have big ideas – they all want to study, none of them want to learn about housekeeping, let alone do any!'[148] Although not beset by any self-doubts when she was in the public eye as director of the Festival, she now opined that 'philosophizing women are an abomination to me; it just doesn't suit women. I can see you must have women in politics, but a woman loses something from being in a public position'.[149]

The more time that had elapsed since Hitler's death, the more Winifred thought about him. To please her, Gertrud Strobel (now entirely in Winifred's camp) put a single rose on her Mistress's desk every 20 April, the Führer's birthday.[150]

After the bloody attack by Palestinians on Israeli athletes at the Munich Olympic Games, when four of the perpetrators were shot, Winifred wrote to Gerdy Troost: 'We've often tried to imagine how USA [Adolf] would have dealt with the killers . . . As it is, they did only half the job – all 8 of them should have been shot – not just four.'[151] And in response to the exploits of the cosmonauts, she thought not only of the 'possibility of a new home for mankind', but also that 'perhaps A.H. did some preparatory work for a future in space!' She felt a 'longing for those who have gone before us', especially for Siegfried, but also 'I'm always dreaming of A.H. . . . and waking up completely happy, and then I always have a good day to follow! And he always appears in his former undiminished greatness,'[152] that is, in his pre-war incarnation.

Even the celebration of Siegfried's 100th birthday in June 1969 was overshadowed by political controversy. Winifred had planned to present his friends with an edition of his letters to Cosima and his sisters, but reading through the letters once more with a critical eye, she had second thoughts. The letters 'provide some extremely rich biographical material – but they're so full of anti-Semitic remarks that there can be no question of publishing them, however valuable they are as a reflection of cultural events at the time'.[153]

Instead, she commissioned a biography of her husband, choosing as the author the 82-year-old Wagnerian traditionalist Zdenko von Kraft, who shared her political views, and had known Siegfried. The source material she made available to Kraft, never seen by any other author before or since, included Siegfried's letters to the Viennese music critic Ludwig Karpath. Winifred had asked Countess Marietta Coudenhove, who helped with the purchase of the letters in 1936, whether any of the contents were compromising. The countess replied that there were only 'a number of sharp remarks about the antagonism of the Jews', which in view of the anti-Semitic regime in power at the time could hardly be regarded as defamatory.[154] Obviously, Kraft could not publish these quotations, any more than he could quote from Siegfried's unpublished opera text, which, said Winifred, he 'once wrote in a fit of rage against Jewish profiteers – entitled "The Crook is called Jephunes", it would have placed Siegfried beyond the pale socially for good and all'.[155]

The biography was intended to present Siegfried as Winifred wanted him to be seen: as a great, brilliant, humorous artist, and an irreproachable husband and father. Siegfried's admiration for Hitler and his anti-Semitism are passed over in silence, but, as Kraft puts it, 'it is undeniable that Siegfried Wagner is very consciously German; he said so himself more than once. The fact that he wrote German operas drawing upon German folk-tales suggests a *völkisch* outlook.'[156]

Such outdated sentiments expressed in the style of a deferential account of life at court were intolerable in 1969, even without the anti-Semitism. Particularly unacceptable was the appendix dealing with the period from 1931 to 1944, that is, Winifred's era. Not only did she make sure she came in for praise, but she offered Kraft the chance to provide a flowery description of Hitler's services to Bayreuth. Once again, exactly as Winifred would have it, Hitler is depicted as the victim of the NSDAP. With his commitment to Bayreuth he had fought 'against the philistinism of his own Party and its narrow-minded propagandists'. The Party had moved into Bayreuth 'with dictatorial arrogance' and 'turned its political outlook into an ideological world-view'. So, for both Kraft and Winifred, there was no doubt: 'in those early days Hitler was isolated in the field of his artistic convictions'.[157]

When the book appeared, with a foreword by Winifred, Friedelind responded angrily with the oft-quoted remark: 'He was trying to make my father into an old Nazi!' The doting love of a daughter had led her to fashion her own image of Siegfried: that of a cosmopolitan, an apolitical artist who was drawn into politics against his will by his wife, and who actually hated Hitler. She would not accept the reality of Siegfried's letters, only hinted at by Kraft in any case. Wolfgang for his part was worried about the reputation of the Festival, and banned Kraft from giving his intended memorial address for Siegfried.

Winifred could not understand what all the fuss was about; after all, 'the poor chap' had only 'truthfully reproduced some "disreputable" remarks of

Siegfried's about National Socialism', which Wolfgang 'regarded as insensitive and tactless, and as a danger to the family and the Festival . . . Wolfgang is so nervous,' she continued, 'when people are offered any opportunity to demonstrate our "brown" past that he throws out the baby with the bathwater.'[158] 'To put it in plain language, he's afraid that everybody is talking about our "brown" ideas again, and that they want to set the mob on to "Bayreuth" once more!' To dissociate himself publicly from the archivist Gertrud Strobel, who was a friend of Kraft's, Wolfgang even had the archive closed down during the Festival period.[159]

The family feud succeeded in overshadowing Winifred's seventy-fifth birthday too, especially because of a telegram sent by Wieland's three daughters with a message that her granddaughter Nike later interpreted as an 'undisguised wish for her to die'[160]: 'Dragons have always got old – rarely has one (so it is said) survived its Siegfried – congratulations on doing so from the daughters of your son Wieland – Iris, Nike, Daphne, far removed from Wahnfried and Bayreuth, as you wished.' Winifred copied out the text for Gerdy Troost, and confessed that she was very hurt by its offensiveness. She could not possibly reply to it, she said.[161]

After some years, negotiations over the foundation entered their final stage. Winifred thought that 'the setting up of the Richard Wagner Foundation may be my last and, as I hope, my most important contribution to the preservation of Richard Wagner's legacy'.[162] Winifred was hoping for peace in the family, once the heirs finally had enough money, and she was noticeably tired. 'I am the donkey upon whose back the disputes are fought out.'[163]

Every family meeting to discuss the conditions of the foundation ended in an orgy of quarrelling over money. Winifred made every effort to explain that, while the Festival Theatre and Wahnfried certainly represented material assets, they brought in no income, though they cost a great deal. The only really valuable possession was the archive, but that could not be sold abroad. Even after they had been paid their share of the money, the family would have a voice on the board that was to be formed. Furthermore (ran her appeal to her heirs), the price that might be obtained depended on the goodwill of the buyers, and public squabbling would not make them well disposed.

Early in 1973 Winifred was taken to hospital suffering from heart problems, a lung embolism and phlebitis. It took her three months to recover. But then she won through over the negotiations. On 27 April 1973 the transfer document was finally signed. The mayor had positioned the tables where the signing took place under the portraits of Richard and Cosima Wagner, 'as though they were giving their blessing to the occasion'.

In accordance with the terms of the contract, 75-year-old Winifred, as the proprietor, handed over the whole complex of Villa Wahnfried, the Festival Theatre and the archive to the town of Bayreuth, which in turn transferred everything to the new foundation. The town leadership confirmed its intention of rebuilding Wahnfried, and creating a Wagner museum there, together with the 'National Archive of the Richard Wagner Foundation, Bayreuth'. Winifred was granted the right of life-long residence in Siegfried's house, and as a token of gratitude for her 'magnanimity' in preparing the way for the foundation, she was presented with an enormous bouquet. She shared out the money – DM 12.4 million – equally among her heirs, and proudly declared: 'Through making this gift I have saved the heirs 800,000 marks in tax!'[164]

All members of the family were thus taken care of financially, and the legacy of the Master was protected. For a while Winifred was more careful about consorting publicly with prominent Nazis, and in 1973 she stayed away from Emmy Goering's funeral, out of fear 'that the press might abuse me – and particularly with regard to my official position within the Foundation'.[165] She was relieved 'to have come by some money, really for the first time since 1945[166] . . . And after the Foundation comes into effect, I regard myself as a "free woman", released from all obligations – except for those towards the family – and so I'm going to use my few remaining years to do as much travelling as I can.'[167]

CHAPTER 16

At the End, a Film

(1974–80)

SYBERBERG AND GOTTFRIED

Winifred was getting on for eighty. She had ordered her affairs, and now she wanted to enjoy her remaining years. She continued to be active, dispensing hospitality, driving in her VW to visit Wagner Societies and see friends, and writing more letters than ever. 'I'm continuing with my daily round like "a living relic", and I'm just glad I still can!'[1]

Bayreuth was preparing for the centenary celebrations of the Festival in 1976. For the occasion, Wahnfried was being reconstructed, restored and turned into a museum. In the spring of 1974 the municipal gardens department began a programme of felling trees, cutting back the old hedges and pulling down the greenhouse in the Wahnfried garden. In order to escape from the din of building work, Winifred had rented a small flat in Munich together with her student granddaughter, Amélie Lafferentz. But when the work began on 1 September 1974, she stayed in Bayreuth to keep an eye on things, while complaining that 'this whole business of rebuilding Wahnfried is terrible for me – the noise of the builders' machines every day, and the indescribable mess . . . to take away all the building rubble, the excavator goes direct from the front garden into the kitchen and the old utilities room'. But nevertheless, she meant to stay on in Bayreuth, because the architect 'keeps asking me questions almost every day about the authentic rebuilding of Wahnfried'.[2] So she was present at the pulling down of the family home

Wieland had built into the ruins of the bombed villa, as well as the demolition of the four metre wall put up by Wieland to screen him from his mother.

Also, for the publication of the first volume of Cosima's diaries, planned to coincide with the jubilee, she took pleasure in helping the editors identify people from Cosima's circle. But she was much more reticent when journalists working on articles about the jubilee tried to consult her, especially concerning the Hitler period.

In mid-March 1975 Wolfgang's son Gottfried, twenty-eight at the time, came to see her. To her great delight, he had been paying her frequent visits of late, and even taking her on outings and to the opera. On this occasion he told her, as Winifred reports it, 'that the film the BBC were going to make for 1976 was only going to feature me speaking for about 3–4 minutes at most, and he did not think that would do justice to my contribution to Bayreuth. He was friendly with the film-maker Syberberg, who was extremely keen to make a documentary about me. After a lot of discussion, I agreed to do it, as long as Gottfried could assure me that S. was trustworthy – that he would not include anything that I did not want published etc.'[3]

The Festival was supposed to be the subject of the film. She was not told that Syberberg's real interest lay in interviewing a 'Nazi' for the Hitler film he was planning to make. As he said, 'she knew nothing as yet about my research for a Hitler film'.[4] As he saw it, his self-imposed mission was to 'coax evidence out of a contemporary of Hitler's, fairly, but inexorably . . . It was a matter of procuring a document, in any way I could.'[5] It had been difficult enough locating a 'Nazi' willing to talk. Syberberg was especially pleased to have found a woman to fulfil this role, because, as he said, 'I, at any rate, saw the whole thing as a contribution, in my own style, to the somewhat embarrassing idea of the "Year of the Woman".'[6]

Winifred entered into the project only in the hope of giving her nephew a career advantage. According to Gottfried, who at the time was staying at his 'Granny's' with his wife, Beatrice, before filming began Winifred sought advice from Leni Riefenstahl: 'I must give Leni a call!'[7] A preliminary chat with Syberberg went well. He asked about a number of people who were close to Hitler, adjutants and servants; what were they doing now, how were they getting on, and so forth. Winifred responded fully and frankly.

Filming began at ten on the morning of 10 April, in the Garden Room with its large window. On this first occasion Winifred tended to be 'rather reserved and dismissive', but, given the presence of her grandson, not at all suspicious. At most she was 'sceptical about the degree of interest she had been assured there was among the public'. Syberberg thought that 'her reserve was not a matter of conceit, but more to do with order and discipline, now tinged with something else, something like curiosity'.[8]

Syberberg did not want 'much scene-setting; no lamps, no rearranging, I wanted it to look the way it always did, pleasant and familiar'. To create the mood of an intimate conversation, he placed the sound engineer behind a screen, or in the next room. However, Gottfried stayed close at hand. Syberberg says that he operated a small tape recorder. It was left running even during the breaks in filming, and was meant to form the basis of a book the two of them intended to publish jointly.[9] Filming lasted five days. A family atmosphere prevailed. At mealtimes, everybody usually sat down together. Winifred was clearly not aware of the scale of the undertaking: 'I had made no notes or preparation for what I said – it was just a conversation between Syberberg and me.'[10]

Syberberg wrote later that 'on closer observation, the woman was very tricky and not quite naïve enough for such a venture. A sinister remark about Jews, meant as a joke and accompanied by a ringing laugh, chilled me to the bone, and is going to stay buried as an ineradicable and painful poison in my diary's memory; but it hung about the room as an unhappy fear of a possible repetition to camera.'[11]

Work then commenced on her life-story. She began on a rather stiff and formal note with her childhood in England, her account of which, says Syberberg, was 'diffidently put forward like a government statement'. To Gottfried's annoyance, the film-maker, who seemed unprepared, took a passive stance. 'From the beginning, she was in charge . . . Syberberg behaved towards her like an adoring, flirtatious sixth-former.'[12] But that was all part of his strategy.

Winifred went on to talk in detail about her time in Bayreuth in the years after 1914: about Cosima, Siegfried, the aunts, the children, the staff, Hitler's first visit to Wahnfried in 1923, and the Festival from 1924 onwards. She produced family photos, and obviously felt relaxed, talking as though entertaining some pleasant guests to coffee. By day three, when they moved on to Syberberg's real subject, that is, Hitler, she was at her ease and enjoying her role.

Syberberg produced all sorts of rumours in order to provoke her into a spirited denial, as for example when he asked whether it was true that Hitler wanted to design his own stage-sets for the Venusberg (*Tannhäuser*) in Bayreuth. Winifred replied: 'Not at all. He never even saw Tannhäuser here.'[13] The only occasions when the opera was put on in Bayreuth were in 1930–31, when Hitler did not attend the Festival. Syberberg went on to observe: 'You were known as the First Lady (*Hohe Dame*).' Winifred shot back: 'Never. That was Emmy Goering. Never me! I was never called first lady. Not at all. No, no.' He even confronted her with made-up quotations attributed to Tietjen, which she rejected without hesitation. When Syberberg suggested that the title *Mein Kampf* had been influenced by Wagner's book *Mein Leben*, she replied, 'Well, that's pretty far-fetched.' Irritated by all these gossipy stories, she finally remarked: 'My sons once suggested I should sell off all my carpets, saying they had all been bitten by Hitler. I could earn a fortune!'

The film shows Winifred's face noticeably lighting up when she begins to talk about Hitler as a person and a friend: how he had stood up for her against the aunts over *Parsifal* in 1934, how much he loved Richard Wagner, how much the children loved Hitler and so on. Her body-language alone made clear that this was a woman who loved the man Hitler, and was now transforming the past in her memory; just as, after some decades, a widow will remember only the good things about her husband and forget the rest. Winifred had taken a liking to Syberberg, and she trusted him.

In answer to the question why the Wagner family had accepted Hitler so readily, she said that 'there was a powerful German nationalist consciousness in our family. My husband was absolutely nationalistic; he suffered dreadfully under the defeat of 1918, and was always looking for contact with people ready to work for the restoration of Germany.' Why was Hitler such a popular Chancellor in 1933? 'Well, for heaven's sake, it was just that we were all thankful that here was someone who started, who attempted, to bring back order, put things straight etc., you see? And he succeeded, he had massive successes. And the people were simply grateful for that, enthusiastic.' And of course Hitler 'got unemployment under control . . . The years from '33 to '39 were very fruitful years for Germany, after all. And foreign countries recognized Hitler in every respect, which meant recognizing National Socialism too.' This was precisely the standard discourse of the old Nazis, and as such not at all sensational. However, she neglected the precaution taken by everyone else giving such interviews from 1945 onwards: that of distancing oneself from Hitler and the Third Reich, if only for opportunistic reasons.

A question that often arose, as to whether 'the Final Solution of the Jewish problem was not completely consonant with the spirit of Richard Wagner', was answered calmly: 'That's nonsense . . . At most, what Wagner had in mind was to put an end to the intellectual influence of the Jews; that is to say, with respect to German political life. But he never had in mind the physical extermination of the Jews. Absolutely not.' She pointed to Wagner's Jewish friends. 'Personally, he had nothing at all against individuals. It's exactly the same with me . . . What one objected to was the Jewish influence on cultural life . . . I mean, in those days [she meant the 1920s] there were Jews everywhere, in every important position, so to speak, playing a big part in politics, in the life of the theatre . . . That has nothing to do with individuals.' Wagner's essay 'Jewishness in Music' was 'just a modest little piece of work, compared to his other, colossal achievements'.

With regard to the history of persecution in the Hitler period, at first she tried to play it down, declaring – though she knew better – that 'in the thirties I never heard anything about . . . people being maltreated or people being locked up'. But then she remembered, after all, that she had been obliged to intervene on behalf of 'Jewish-related people', and homosexuals such as Max Lorenz.

It would have been easy for her to describe (and exploit for sympathy) her many arduous attempts to help Hitler's victims, or her petty battles with the *Gau* authorities, or with Rosenberg or Bormann. She did nothing of the sort. What she did instead was unique in post-war history. Rather than defend herself, the Festival or her position between 1933 and 1945, she defended Hitler, attributing the real guilt to 'the Party', above all to Bormann, Himmler and Streicher.

Asked whether she had doubts about Hitler after 1939, at first she denied having any. But then she turned to the war.

Oh God, I mean, nobody in the thirties had any idea where it might all be going, and I feel that, especially if the war hadn't broken out and if everything had sort of gradually quietened down, then I'm convinced that in a certain sense people would generally have been able to accept National Socialism. I mean, because of the war, of course, the whole movement and the aims of the movement somehow descended into the abyss, I freely admit that.

If it had not been for the war, perhaps 'a purer form of National Socialism' would have prevailed.

Concerning Nazi crimes, especially the mass extermination of the Jews, she did at least declare that 'I admit that everything that happened in the second half of the war is completely unacceptable. And I do reject it.' But she refused to relinquish her memories of the good side of Hitler's personality.

For her, the beginning of the war was the decisive turning point, criminality included. After 1939, 'of course a lot of people finished up in concentration camps, and I got a massive number of petitions. And if I thought they were credible at all and worthy of help, I always passed them on.' She did not add that she never met Hitler again after 1940, and that her only contact with him was by letter and through rare telephone calls. She even maintained that 'Hitler never turned down any requests from me. It did get difficult when Himmler intervened and maintained that such and such a case could not possibly be released. But I wasn't too shy about asking Himmler who had the final say, him or Adolf Hitler. In that way, I always managed to make people do what Hitler had agreed to, even Himmler, though he was often reluctant.' While this account was historically far from accurate, it corresponded to Winifred's remarks to her friends in private. In the previous thirty years she had constructed her own version of the past, and firmly believed it, especially since she had recited it countless times to her intimate circle.

Her concept of history was therefore diametrically opposed to that of the average German after 1945. Most former Nazis, including her son Wieland, reshaped their past to represent themselves as anti-Nazi before 1945. But Winifred, against her own best interests, claimed a longer and deeper friendship with Hitler than was actually the case. Her anger towards the much-despised turncoats of 1945 drove her into this strange oppositional stance, which she sustained for the rest of her life.

This stark and unusual example also serves to demonstrate the difficulties surrounding first-hand historical evidence. At seventy-eight, Winifred was mentally very alert, but her horizons had plainly shrunk in comparison with earlier times, especially with regard to personal relationships. Siegfried, dead for forty-five years, was the perfect husband; while Hitler, who had died thirty years before, was the kindest, most reliable of friends. She wallowed in the memory of her glory days in the thirties, when she was the 'Mistress of Bayreuth', and her friend 'Wolf' was the much-acclaimed 'Führer' of a reinvigorated Germany: the days of 'Wolf and Winnie'. Long since relegated, she cherished these recollections of her finest hour like a priceless treasure which it did her good to think about. Certain memories tended to be set in concrete as time passed, and assumed the character of self-quotations. In the end, she came to believe in her memories; and many of the less pleasant ones, especially her failures and disappointments, had long since been forgotten.

Her dilemma becomes apparent in the film with the question of when she last saw Hitler. She racked her brains, got tangled up with her dates, came up with 20 July, and then hesitantly suggested she last met Hitler in 1944. Syberberg proposed leaving this as an open question to be settled later; but he did not return to it. This serious mistake persisted in the film, therefore, and earned Winifred some harsh recriminations for having lied when she stated previously (to universal disbelief) that her last personal encounter with Hitler had been in 1940 – the literal truth. The fact was that she saw him last in Bayreuth in the summer of 1940, when he made a brief visit to attend the *Twilight of the Gods* after his lightning victory over France.

What she clearly did not want to confess to herself or the public was the great pain and humiliation caused her by Hitler's failure to invite her to see him, or to visit her, after 1940, while frequently meeting up with the children, particularly Wieland. Her obvious confusion also indicated that she was not in the habit of mentioning this fact during her usual reminiscing sessions with her friends; effectively, she had suppressed it. Otherwise, she would not have had to spend so long vainly casting around for an answer, but would have had it off pat, like all her other stories.

Syberberg was not well enough informed to notice the great gulf between the historical reality and the way it was being nostalgically recalled. The combative Winifred of her best days, the thirties, had little in common with the old woman bemoaning the loss of her beloved Hitler.

While the camera was running, Winifred stayed alert, and several times demanded it should be switched off when there were awkward matters to explain. When Syberberg asked her what topics she would prefer, for private reasons, not to be mentioned in this interview, she responded: 'Basically, from Wolfgang's point of view, it's undesirable for these things to be brought up again.' State subsidies were at stake. There were people 'who would always say, well, you know, those old Nazis in Bayreuth'. She, Winifred, 'did not want to contribute, for God's sake' to ruining the public mood about Bayreuth.

With the intensity of the work, and the friendly contact every day, the atmosphere became so familiar that Winifred sometimes did not even bother to have the camera stopped while she quickly indicated what passages she did not want to appear in the film. 'Well, that's a story I simply can't tell. We called each other "du" [familiar form of address]. That's . . . something I can't say in public. It's impossible. I mean, I called him Wolf, he called me Winnie . . . and the children all used "du" to him as well. They called him Wolf.' She trusted Syberberg to respect her wishes. None the less, he included this clip in his film.

When she was struggling with Toscanini's cancellation in 1933, and Syberberg was putting forward some vague speculations, she asked him to stop filming. 'If there's nobody else listening, I'll tell you the real reasons. Is that thing turned off, the sound?' Syberberg replied, 'Yes, yes, must be, it won't run with the camera off.' But the tape recorder was still on, and captured her saying that Toscanini had been worked on by 'the Jews in New York . . . You know all of New York musical life takes place in Jewish circles . . . Toscanini was dependent on them.' When Syberberg asked her, 'Why didn't you want to say so on camera?', Winifred came back with: 'Because I don't know for sure.' After some more argument, she explained: 'As I said, I'm 78 now, and I want a bit of peace and quiet. I don't relish being put through the mill again by all the Jewish newspapers . . . being called a thorough Nazi once more . . . There's no need to overdo it.' This passage was not included in the film. But it does show Winifred's great fear of getting into the clutches of the press.

During the breaks that occurred every ten minutes while the reels were being changed, Winifred immediately switched from her official interview tone into a relaxed conversational mode. When the camera was not rolling, she dropped her guard, and went on chatting quite naturally; an informative grandmother telling her grandson about everyday life in the Hitler period. But the tape recorder picked up everything; in addition to the 'off the record' conversation, it even recorded a discussion with the undertaker who suddenly arrived with the bill for Emma Bär's funeral.

The result was a mixture of 'official' and private statements, later a cause of friction, but now no longer significant. For there is no doubt that what Winifred said corresponded to her genuine opinions, which she was used to expressing (to her intimates, for example) quite proudly and openly. To take Syberberg's question about her present attitude to Hitler as an example; her reply was: 'I will never deny my friendship with him, I can't do it . . . maybe people won't understand this, but I'm capable of completely separating the Hitler I know from everything he is blamed for today.' Syberberg questioned whether that was possible, but she asserted:

Yes, yes, that's just what I can do! I mean, I regret everything else, I most profoundly regret it. I do regret it. But it makes no difference to my personal relationship to him. The part of him that I know, shall we say, I value as highly today as I ever did. And the Hitler that everybody utterly condemns does not exist in my mind, because that is not how I know him. You see, everything about my relationship to him rests absolutely on a personal basis.

When Syberberg enquired whether there were not 'repulsive things about Hitler, too', Winifred insisted:

I never saw anything repulsive about him. That's what is so remarkable. He had this Austrian . . . tactful manner and warm heart . . . after all, I knew him from '23 to '45; that's 22 years. I was never disappointed in all those 22 years. I mean, apart from things that were going on in the outside world. But that did not affect me. For me he was simply the Hitler who came here as a Wagner fan and a friend of the family.

She said she was 'basically a madly loyal person, everybody who knows me will tell you that. If I form an attachment to somebody, I maintain it through thick and thin . . . then I stand by that person, I don't stand by his misdeeds, but what I say is they just don't alter my relationship to him. I can separate the two things completely.'

Syberberg pressed on, asking whether, now that she knew so much more, she did not regard Hitler 'as a curse for Germany, as well as for the house of Wagner'. 'I will always remember him with gratitude,' she replied, 'for the way he literally smoothed my path here in Bayreuth, so to speak, and . . . helped me in every way.' He was not 'basically' the source of everything negative; 'it was Streicher in Nuremberg who was the main driving force. And he was completely obnoxious. We were all united in rejecting him.' After further discussion, Syberberg asked, 'So you would exempt Hitler?' With a spirited laugh, and only half joking, she replied, 'I would exempt Hitler altogether from the whole company.'

Even to camera, Winifred was proud to present herself as 'the only Nazi in Germany', just as she had when Klaus Mann interviewed her in 1945. And for the time being, unaware of the tape recorder, she trusted Syberberg as she did Gottfried, writing almost as an afterthought to Gerdy Troost when the filming was over:

Thanks to Gottfried . . . Syberberg was here making a film; he pestered me mercilessly, asking me all sorts of indiscreet questions, which I found really difficult to answer on the spur of the moment. – Altogether I was talking for about 450 minutes, while being filmed all the time. Of course, the whole thing will be shortened to just an hour, but even then I can't imagine the audience will want to put up with the same face for so long, and they'll probably stop watching, maybe even stop listening. And this is what they call a documentary film!

Syberberg was a 'pleasant, educated person'.[14]

Two months later she was disillusioned with Syberberg, 'because he really took me for a ride!!!!' She had now placed the whole business in Wolfgang's hands, 'because the film must not be allowed to do him any harm!'[15]

Wolfgang saw the film uncut on 17 June 1975 in Munich, and gave his approval. Syberberg took his few objections into account. The great dispute that arose later was due to the question of whether and how far Syberberg had added unapproved footage to the film by the time of its première, a question that is now beyond resolution. The première took place relatively unobtrusively a month later, during a Syberberg retrospective in Paris. Of the roughly 100 viewers, only thirty stayed to the end. Among them were Wieland's daughter Nike, and Gottfried. The latter had completely fallen out with Syberberg in Paris.

At the start of the 1975 Bayreuth Festival, a long article appeared in *Die Zeit*. Under the headline 'The Nice Uncle of Bayreuth', it provoked a public outrage. 'Friend of the family and nice uncle,' it read, 'hand-kissing and liver-dumplings: horror personified as petty-bourgeois in an idyllic retreat; everyday fascism as unbelievably limited mentality and ignorance; history, the incriminating past, seen thirty years later as a serene, happily recollected reduction of the most terrible things to a cheery anecdote and puffed-up banality.'[16]

Other newspapers rushed to follow suit. Winifred and the Festival management received many angry letters. The comments Syberberg made in an interview were lost in the torrent of public anger over 'that Nazi woman'. He asserted that Winifred was no isolated case, but that she merely represented 'the not unintelligent fellow-travellers who existed in their millions, who never harmed anybody, but for some reason fell intellectual prey to the Nazi movement. She even helped people, I gather, but she doesn't talk about that.'[17]

The fierce criticism threw Wolfgang Wagner into a panic, and Winifred lamented that 'the "brown shadow" that, as Wolfgang said, my sons wanted to banish from the Festival Theatre, has been evoked once more!'[18] At a press conference, the head of the Festival distanced himself from the film, declaring that his mother 'had delivered her last Festival 31 years ago, and completely retired from the management of the Festival after 1949'. She had 'nothing to do' with New Bayreuth. Moreover, 'since 1951 politics has been dispelled from the Festival Theatre'. He publicly banned his mother from setting foot in the Festival Theatre. This really ensured that all the papers were full of the new scandal in Bayreuth. Hardly anybody had seen the film, however, including Winifred. Being banned from the Festival Theatre was a heavy blow for her, since she had issued invitations to a good number of her friends that year as usual.

She no longer had a good word to say for Syberberg.

> Everything in the film that departed from its subject [the history of the Festival] consisted of comments I made in private conversations with S. while the reels were being changed, and not intended for the public. – But without my knowledge, the villain left the tape recorder running meanwhile, and had no compunction about making these parts available to the public, too.[19]

Central to the controversy was the most famous section, towards the end of the film, an off-camera conversation with superimposed pictures of the interior of Siegfried's house. According to the recording notes, the voices are those of Gottfried and Winifred, with her explaining to him that if he committed a murder, she would still be his grandmother. 'Maybe you don't understand it, but that's just how it is.' And then came the notorious sentence: 'If Hitler were to walk in through that door now, for instance, I'd be as happy and glad to see and have him here as ever, and that whole dark side of him, I know it exists, but it doesn't exist for me because I don't know that part of him. You see, the only thing that exists for me in a relationship with somebody is my personal experience.'

Incidentally, Albert Speer, who had also once loved and admired Hitler, was asked the same (by now very well-known) question a year later in an NBC interview. What would he do if Hitler walked in through the door? He replied, 'Here? Today? In Heidelberg? [In English] I would call the police.'[20]

Winifred's disillusionment with Syberberg was matched only by her anger at her own naivety. Once again she had fallen for the flattery of a polite, good-looking man. She commented despondently: 'I thought he was a gentleman!'[21] And added: 'Through my gullibility he has got what he wanted, that is to say statements for his Hitler film (which I knew nothing about) that he could never have got anywhere else!'[22]

Under the impact of a daily barrage of abuse Winifred aged visibly, and her attitudes hardened yet further. When the press attacks became too much for her, she took tranquillizers. She confessed to Gerdy Troost that she also had another way of calming herself. 'I think about USA [Adolf], and how it's for his sake after all that I've taken this suffering upon myself.'[23]

Strangely enough, after the film was first shown in Germany, on 15 November 1975 in Düsseldorf, things quietened down. Certainly, there were heated public debates and conflicting reactions. But after all the negative press, many were surprised that the much demonized 'Nazi woman' turned out to be a not-completely-unlikeable old lady, and definitely not the monster they had been led to expect. Winifred impressed many people as an independent-minded, courageous, unaffected woman, dealing resolutely with stupid questions, speaking her mind, and not (in contrast to most people interviewed about the Nazi period) posing as a member of the resistance. For the younger audience she was an irritating phenomenon from another world: a self-confident old woman openly declaring her affection for a man the whole world regarded as the devil incarnate. She aroused unusually mixed feelings in the audience, from astonishment to revolt.

Not a few young people recognized their own grandmothers in Winifred, and began to ask them questions. The emotions, fears and problems, the ordinariness, stupidities and susceptibilities of an entire generation were manifest in this one woman. To her surprise, Winifred now began to receive numerous appreciative letters from young people who were careful to indicate their political distance from her, but admired her openness. This gave her new heart. 'Altogether, among all the post I've had concerning that notorious film, there have been just four abusive letters! – And I don't give a damn what the press thinks.'[24]

Winifred's sudden fame as an eyewitness extended as far as America, from where she began to receive almost daily phone-calls with questions about Hitler. She would not give information over the telephone, but asked for enquiries to be put in writing. Her answers amounted to genuine expert opinions.

After every new press condemnation, Winifred received more appreciative letters. She expressed her thanks for support in the face of 'the most outrageous attacks I'm being subjected to'. She had been used to personal attacks ever since she first bore the name of Wagner. There followed a typical Siegfried-style expression of sentiment from the old days: 'Where has re-education by our enemies got us Germans? – EVERYTHING that is German and true is betrayed and maligned!'[25] She thought Germany was in a worse state than in the 1920s. 'It's an outrageous scandal the way the mainstream press drags the genius of Wagner through the mire, pours gall and poison upon it, and sullies the names of his descendants with lies! A real witch-hunt has begun!'[26]

The storm of approval and disapproval of 'the old Nazi woman' obscured the film's other sensational revelation: the clear reference to Wieland's 'brown past'. 'Hitler lived until '45, and Wieland did not renounce him until '45. So, in his lifetime, he did not do what Friedelind did.'[27] The press failed to pursue the favourite of the Left. This remained a taboo subject.

The more successful the film was, the more it irritated Winifred, who was obviously in need of a rest: 'Now they're showing the Syberberg film in Holland and England!!!!! – It's sickening.'[28] When a Dutch illustrated magazine splashed an attack on her across its pages, she commented: 'I never thought that at 80 I would gain a new title: "Winifred Wagner la dernière grande Cocotte" [the last of the great cocottes, i.e. fashionable prostitutes].'[29] To Friedelind, she wrote: 'My wretched film is now showing in England, and the BBC recently broadcast a one-and-a-half hour version – that swine Syberberg must be making a fortune out of it, and I never got a penny! (probably my own stupidity!)'[30]

PRESERVING THE HERITAGE

In the spring of 1976, the jubilee year, Winifred was 'really deeply affected' by big 'unexpected trouble – whereas the scribblings of the newspaper hacks don't bother me'.[31] Wolfgang was thinking of a divorce, in order to marry his assistant and secretary, Gudrun Mack, twenty-five years younger than himself. The crisis went on for months.

To take her mind off all the vexation, Winifred visited Friedelind in her new house in Yorkshire for a fortnight. Mother and daughter, one British, the other American, set off by car to trace their ancestry. They drove to

Wales and visited Brecon Cathedral, with its wonderful chancel. Winifred
speculated: 'Perhaps my father sang here as a boy!!!! . . . The Welsh are so
gifted artistically! – They are Celts, after all, not untalented Anglo-
Saxons!'[32] Their sightseeing took in Stonehenge and Stratford. 'I was
inspired all over again by the English landscape, completely unspoilt, not
overdeveloped!' With motherly pride, she reported that Friedelind wanted
to open 'a kind of art centre' in her house: 'she's starting her masterclasses
up again, teaching every branch of musical theatre, and she's taken up
sculpture and painting for the purpose! She's constructing the appropriate
studios in the grounds!'[33] However, elsewhere she commented with satisfaction: 'It's a good thing, because it will keep her busy and stop her from
meddling in our affairs!!!!'[34]

In Wolfgang's marital crisis Winifred reacted like Fricka, the protector of
marriage (in *The Valkyrie*), and took the part of her daughter-in-law Ellen.
After the separation, Winifred offered the distraught Ellen shelter in
Siegfried's house. Eva, Wolfgang's daughter and until then his mainstay in
running the Festival, was instantly dropped, to be replaced by Wolfgang's
new wife-to-be.

The day before Ellen was due to move into Siegfried's house, while dress
rehearsals were going on in the Festival Theatre, Winifred asked her daughter Verena to drive over to Bayreuth immediately. The two women cleared
out Winifred's personal, highly organized archive cabinet. It contained all
the documents left by Siegfried, in piles tied up with tape, arranged according to years and the names of correspondents. There were also Winifred's
private papers: letters from Siegfried, Klindworth, Walpole, Toscanini,
Tietjen and her grandchildren, as well as the carefully guarded Hitler letters
and correspondence with other prominent Nazis. Verena loaded them all
into the car, and on Winifred's instructions drove them to the safety of
Amélie's flat in Munich.

Amélie Lafferentz, thirty-one years old, was closer to Winifred than her
other grandchildren. She had studied history, was a trained archivist and was
about to marry a Munich lawyer. For Winifred this was the perfect solution
(with legal protection thrown in) to the question of, on the one hand, how
to carefully conserve the papers, of whose historical significance she was well
aware, and, on the other hand, how to preserve them from the public and
from the grasp of her needy and sensation-seeking relatives. To this day, the
documents languish in Munich, beyond the reach of all research.[35]

Winifred's well-planned move meant that the papers, a latent source of information about the family's political involvements and scandals – especially their relationship with Hitler – were successfully deposited in a secure and, for the time being, secret location. Her action showed Winifred maintaining the traditions of the Wagner family, and especially of Cosima, when it came to archival material.

At that time, it was Gottfried who gave her most concern. He was spending a lot of time in Siegfried's house with his mother, Ellen, rejected by Wolfgang, and taking a conspicuous interest in any papers to do with the Nazi period. Thanks to the business of the film, Winifred's relations with her grandson were severely strained. She felt he had let her down, and that he was spying on her. Malicious gossip served to exacerbate the dispute.[36]

In the meantime, right on cue for the jubilee Festival, the first volume of Cosima's diaries appeared. It covered the years 1869 to 1877, the period of the Franco-Prussian War and the foundation of the Second Reich, with its exuberant nationalism. The book gave an insight into Cosima and Richard's world-view, as well as their anti-Semitism. It was more apparent than ever that Winifred's political outlook incorporated the spirit, or evil genius, of the house of Wagner; or, as her granddaughter Nike put it: 'Her mother-in-law Cosima was cheering her on from the grave.'[37]

Even in the jubilee year of 1976 Wolfgang would not let the former head of the Festival set foot in the Festival Theatre. It was in vain that Winifred raged: 'you can't twist the whole history of the Festival the way my successors are trying to do – and it wouldn't take much for them to make me out to be insane'.[38] The worst day for her was 24 July, when the Richard Wagner Museum and National Archive were opened in the restored Villa Wahnfried. Nobody had worked harder than Winifred over the decades to preserve the scores and the writings of the Master; no one had given so many exhibits to the museum collection. Now she was excluded, as though she did not exist.

Connoisseurs of the scene at Bayreuth noticed the former Mistress of Bayreuth standing motionless, a large, dark figure, behind the curtains of Siegfried's house, watching the comings and goings of the Festival guests outside Villa Wahnfried.[39] This was her house, now shining with a new lustre, the house she had entered in 1915 as an eighteen-year-old girl, and which she had left when it was bombed on 6 April 1945. Now its expense had become unsustainable for the family and for the Festival, which would be opened that evening with 'the Ring of the century', conducted by Pierre Boulez, directed by Patrice Chéreau.

Everyone was quoting the dictum of the composer Boulez, 'blow up all the opera houses',[40] as well as that of 31-year-old stage director Chéreau: 'I wanted to pull Wagner down from the rostrum.' Winifred commented on the dress rehearsals: 'The stage-sets and costumes for the *Ring* are impossibly bizarre as far as I'm concerned – but this kind of parody, blasphemy, desecration of the temple is obviously what people want today – I'm never going to understand it!'[41]

The 'spoiling of the Ring' was now Winifred's favourite topic; and with the obstinacy of age, she refused to drop it. She suspected a left-wing plot, 'a group of agents run by East Germany' who had latterly entered Wolfgang's milieu, and 'whose mission it is to undermine what is almost the last bastion of German art and culture'. She was seeing agents from the East and 'Left-Radicalinskys' (the term is her own invention) everywhere, and even held them responsible for Wolfgang's divorce.[42] Her mind was haunted by the old fears of the twenties, of the threat to 'German art' from bolshevism, the Left and the Jews. 'Absolutely everywhere you sense the influence of the radical subversives.'[43]

Wolfgang's fear, that in a politically heated climate his mother's presence at the première might provoke protests among the audience, was not entirely baseless. But his mother was cherishing radical notions, too. 'It would be lovely if all those taking part in the Ring were to refuse to participate!' She also voiced fears: 'I hope the seats of the people who leave aren't taken by the Left-Radicalinskys, who will laud this Ring to the skies!!!! – What we need are protests even during the acts – interrupting the performance! That seems to me the only way to be rid of this Ring!'[44]

The *Rhinegold* became a scandal without any assistance from Winifred. In the first scene there were neither a Rhine nor Rhinemaidens; instead, there were prostitutes strolling along the top of a dam wall. A part of the audience felt provoked into reacting with indignation and loud booing. For the first time in the history of the Festival, people blew whistles. Another section of the audience applauded. Genuine rows broke out.

Disgusted Wagnerians took their sorrows to Winifred, and she had the satisfaction of seeing an 'Action Group for the Works of Richard Wagner' being formed in protest at Chéreau's *Ring*. 'The Action Group is trying to rescue Wagner from the distortions of modern directors.'[45] Elsewhere, she wrote: 'ALL my friends left before the Ring! . . . The tendency to make Wagner look ridiculous and to see the whole Ring as proof that "property is theft" is gaining strength all the time – it makes you weep!'[46]

THE LAST YEARS

Winifred's complaints about the alleged decline of the Festival filled her last years. None the less, once she was allowed back into the Festival Theatre, from 1977 onwards, she never missed a performance. She explained to a young admirer of hers: 'You've seen how many visitors come to me and pour their hearts out over the loss of "Bayreuth" – on their behalf I need to know exactly what's going on up there . . . I certainly don't attend for pleasure, for heaven's sake!'[47]

In the angry and provocative mood of her last years, Winifred expressed herself especially positively about Hitler. No visitor could miss the picture of Hitler with the inscription 'From Wolf to Winnie' that stood beside Siegfried's picture on her desk. Her grandson Gottfried spotted a framed photo of Wieland on her bedside cabinet; admittedly an old one of him in Wehrmacht uniform, the way she preferred to see her oldest child.[48]

For years she avidly followed the conspiracy theories of a doctor who claimed to be able to prove that Hitler's personal physician, Theodor Morell, collaborated with the Russians.

> Dr Röhrs assumes that Bormann used Morell as an intermediary during the war – for example, Morell ran a broadcasting station in Vinnitsa [Ukraine] – which could only have been for the purpose of passing news on to the Russians! – And Morell couldn't have made all his crooked millions during the war without Bormann's connivance – new factories were built all over the place for his useless products (insect powder etc. – vitamins) – which only Bormann could authorize. – The Russians were instantly informed about discussions in Hitler's headquarters.

At the end of the war the Americans had discovered a line of communication between Bormann and the Russians in Prague; 'one fine day' the evidence would be published and 'the most outrageous things will see the light of day!'[49]

Röhr's book appeared in 1966 with a small publisher, and led years later to a court case. Morell's widow defended her husband against the charges made by Röhr, and won her case. Later research shows the theory that Morell poisoned Hitler to be untenable.[50] Winifred was unmoved: 'I still maintain that Morell's overdose injections had a devastating effect on Hitler's health.'[51]

In September 1977 she was happy to accept an invitation from the Richard Wagner Society in Linz. Once again she was following in Hitler's footsteps. She was taken up to the Freinberg; looked down from Castle Hill towards Urfahr, where Hitler lived during his youth; then, in the most glorious weather, she went up the Pöstlingberg with the Linz Wagnerians.[52]

She often travelled to Düsseldorf to sit for the sculptor Arno Breker, who was making a bust of her to add to his series of heads of Franz Liszt and Richard and Cosima Wagner. 'He says he finds my rune-covered face attractive!' The result was 'really monumental – I scare myself!'[53] The shock was mainly due to the realism of the bust: 'such an old woman!' was her comment when it was finished. She would have preferred to be portrayed as her younger self, like Cosima.[54]

The network of old Nazis gave her support and opened the door to all sorts of activities. When Gerdy Troost was hard up and looking for a buyer for a bust of Hitler, she asked Winifred to help her, and she in turn asked Lotte Pfeiffer-Bechstein. The latter wondered 'whether the bust might be offered to Amin, the President of Uganda, who wants to erect a Hitler monument in Kampala. Although he's black, he's a passionate admirer of Hitler, and it seems to me you shouldn't have any inhibitions about selling to a Negro when you are not blessed with worldly goods! It won't cost anything to try.'[55]

Winifred received visits from foreign Nazis, too, such as the young American Matt Koehl, who came with a recommendation from Ziegler. He referred to himself as the head of the World Union of National Socialists, and he was the editor of the magazine *The National Socialist*. She invited her guest to *Siegfried*, and thought that 'as Head of the World Union of National Socialists (if the title was genuine) Koehl should really sit in the same place in the family box which was once reserved for the Leader himself on his numerous visits to the Festival Theatre'.[56]

Furthermore, Winifred read everything relating to Hitler; such as, for example, an account by a concentration camp inmate from Buchenwald. On this subject, she wrote to Gerdy Troost: 'The result of reading it is that I dream at night that people are taking a belated revenge against us, and that I'm in a concentration camp wearing prison uniform – and constantly thinking how I can bear this situation with dignity and try to comfort fellow-sufferers – Who can help *me* to do so? The thought of our Führer, of course!'[57]

She shocked many Festival artists. The American singer James King remembered the 'frightening old lady' bombarding the artists 'with gossip about the old days' at her tea-time receptions. 'She really stunned us by sounding off ecstatically about what a valuable friend Adolf Hitler was, how he loved to play with the dogs, liked raking the ashes in the hearth, and in general was "always so nice" to everybody in the household.'[58]

Winifred's last years were characterized by a provocative absence of political self-consciousness. Her reputation was in any case already damaged beyond repair. She was not prepared to climb down, so she went on to the offensive instead. Under the circumstances, it is no surprise that her eleven grown-up grandchildren had difficulty in making their peace with her. Her relationship with Wieland's children, in particular, had further deteriorated as a result of the film. They had known their grandmother only as infants, when she had helped to bring them up. Winifred's remarks about Wieland reinforced their conviction that 'Granny' was their beloved father's enemy.

In the end, however, Winifred did achieve reconciliation with Wolfgang. When she discovered that he was directing *Tristan and Isolde* at La Scala in Milan, she was full of maternal pride, and turned for help to her young friend Hermann Ernst. She would love to drive to Milan, she said, but was 'less keen to go alone. If you're driving down, can I join you???' She did not know the date of the première, 'because she had no communication at all with Wolfgang'. 'On the one hand,' she said, 'I'd love to do it, but on the other I'm very nervous!' She was delighted when Ernst agreed to take her, remembering the little hotel near La Scala where she had stayed with Siegfried in 1930. 'I'd like to remain completely incognito and anonymous in Milan – please don't tell anyone I'm going.'[59] After the première, she summed up: 'I wanted to find out whether he'd started to adopt the left-wing trend in his directing, like that damned Chéreau did here with his Ring – but no, he was following his grandfather's instructions, thank goodness.'[60]

Winifred was much relieved when her daughter-in-law Ellen moved out of Siegfried's house in September 1978, to return to her home town of Wiesbaden. Winifred's granddaughter Eva wrote gratefully to 'my dear Granny': 'Spending those two years with you was the saving of my mother. Thanks to your help and your personality (you probably had us in mind as well) you gave her back the courage to go on living. For the rest of her life she will remain someone with a broken heart, and that is hard to bear, and sad.'[61]

The way was clear for a reconciliation with Wolfgang and his new family. The great attraction for Winifred was her twelfth grandchild, Katharina, born in 1978. 'Now that Ellen is out of the house, I can spend time with Wolfgang and his young new wife free of tension and embarrassment.'[62] She was pleased to be able to take the child for one afternoon a week.

It was at that time that Winifred had two surprise visitors: her former foster-child Betty, now Frau Weiss, with her daughter. They rang the bell and were surprised that 'Aunt Winnie' did not have a maid, as in the old days, but opened the door in person. The pair were warmly received. However, Winifred scarcely recognized the little Betty she knew in this healthy, capable woman in her mid-forties, a widow with six children. Betty felt a great need to express her thanks to Winifred, for 'I owe my whole education, my whole life to her'. In Wahnfried she had been brought up to be an independent and active person, and with Winifred's example had overcome many blows of fate in her life.

She was disappointed with the reconstruction of Villa Wahnfried and the museum, explaining to her daughter that 'there's no comparison with the old days!' Previously there was ornate plasterwork on the walls and ceilings, and silk wall-coverings. She reminisced fondly about the dining room with the oval table seating a dozen, where she too had once sat, for coffee and cakes with Hitler. The china was decorated in green and gold, perfectly matching the décor of the room.[63] She could not say often enough that the six years in Wahnfried had been the best time of her life.

In April 1979 the *Deutsche Nationalzeitung* (German Nationalist Newspaper) called for a demonstration against the government's proposal to rescind the statute of limitation for Nazi crimes, and appealed to Winifred for support. The editor published her letter in his newspaper:

Dear Dr Frey,
In my 82nd year, I find it difficult to comment on the political chaos of our times. However, if it would be useful to have my 'good wishes', this is all I want to say:

'I hope the demonstration in Fürstenfeldbruck for "Limitation in Germany" will successfully convey the message that the repeal of the statute of limitation only serves the interests of our enemies, who continue to do their utmost to inflame the world-wide hatred of Germany, and whose thirst for revenge and implacability leads them to undermine any attempt at a settlement.'

With best wishes from a sympathizer, Your Winifred Wagner.[64]

In May 1979 Winifred drove her VW to Wiesbaden for a concert performance of Siegfried's *Sonnenflammen* in the State Theatre there. She was seated in the 'Kaiser's box', in the midst of Wilhelminian splendour, and was, as one observer wrote, 'an imposing figurehead, even without any kind of official function – and in an unspoken way, she still has something of the "Mistress" about her, conscious of her role as the last representative of the powerful, tragic and tangled Wagner dynasty'.[65]

At the Siegburg Music Festival in September 1979 in honour of the 125th anniversary of Engelbert Humperdinck's birth, she appeared so self-confident, 'going around talking like a Nazi',[66] that young musicians encountering her for the first time were shocked. It was the same old views over and over again. There was no doubt about it: Winifred was failing, both physically and intellectually.

In October 1979 she was the guest of honour at a rally in Bayreuth, of about 240 former Hitler Youth and *Bund deutscher Mädel* leaders, lasting several days and disguised as a holiday trip. Many were 'acquaintances or even friends from "back then"; all now between 60 and 70 – but impeccable in their attitudes and convictions'.[67]

She no longer bothered to hide her anti-Semitism, not sparing even Yehudi Menuhin, who was awarded the Peace Prize of the German Book Trade: 'despite all his achievements, I regret that the prize has been given to a Jew, because it's just more grovelling to that race on the part of this generation – have we got to go on forever bowing and scraping – haven't we got any pride?'[68] This was Siegfried's language once more, based on the writings of the Master: the Jews were seen as a threat to German culture.

At Christmas 1979 the 82-year-old, weary and worn out, went down to join her widowed daughter Verena in her old summer-house on Lake Constance. She was still ailing as a result of her earlier cancer treatment; she was becoming increasingly weak, and after the holidays she was taken to the hospital in Überlingen. Friedelind came over to see her mother once more. In these last weeks Winifred talked for the first time, to her great-granddaughter Wendy, about the hardships of her orphanage years in England. She was calm and tired; glad that she was going to die surrounded by Verena and her children, and not alone in Bayreuth.

Winifred Wagner died on 5 March 1980 in Überlingen. She was taken to Bayreuth, and laid out in an open coffin in Wahnfried. Many people took their leave of her there, including a number who had cause to thank her for her energetic and often life-saving help during the Nazi period. She lies next to Siegfried and Wieland in the cemetery at Bayreuth. She had survived her two predecessors as head of the Festival, Cosima and Siegfried, by fifty years, and her successor, Wieland, by fourteen years.

The Englishwoman Winifred entered the service of Richard Wagner when she joined the Klindworth household. She absorbed all the teachings of the Master passed on to her by Cosima and Siegfried. Despite everything, she accomplished her oft-cited 'mission' to sustain the Festival through the hard times following Siegfried's death, and to bring it up to date artistically. She was neither a heroine nor a criminal, but one of the great mass of trusting, misguided people who succumbed to the great seducer Hitler. It was in keeping with the spirit of Wahnfried that as a young woman she should have regarded the passionate Wagnerian as the 'Saviour of Germany' as well as the 'Saviour of Bayreuth'.

From her twenty-sixth year onwards she was proud of her friendship with this man, and at his side in the 1930s she experienced the glittering high points of her life. 'Punishable stupidity' was the mild verdict of the returning exile Karl Würzburger on her continuing gratitude after 1945 to her dead friend Wolf, whose crimes were plain for the whole world to see. The 'loyalty unto death' of the Nibelungs was one of those much-invoked chief virtues that Winifred had learnt in the house of the Master, Richard Wagner.

NOTES

KEY TO ABBREVIATIONS

AdK	Archiv der Akademie der Künste Berlin	Archive of the Academy of Arts, Berlin
AH	Adolf Hitler	
BA	Bundesarchiv	Federal Archive
BBl	*Bayreuther Blätter*	Bayreuth Journal
BDC	Berlin Document Center	
BOm	*Bayerische Ostmark*	Bavarian Ostmark
BStA	Bayerische Hauptstaats-Archiv München	Central Bavarian State Archive, Munich
BTb	*Bayreuther Tagblatt*	Bayreuth Daily Newspaper
CV	Centralverein der deutschen Staatsbürger jüdischen Glaubens	Central Association of German Citizens of Jewish Faith
CW	Cosima Wagner	
DFA	Deutsches Filmarchiv	German Film Archive
DRWG	Deutsche Richard Wagner Gesellschaft Bayreuth	Bayreuth Richard Wagner Society
ECh	Eva Chamberlain	
FVT	*Fränkische Volkstribüne*	Franconian People's Tribune
FW	Friedelind Wagner	
Goebbels Diary	Quotations from Elke Fröhlich (ed.), *Die Tagebücher von Joseph Goebbels*, Teil 1 (*Sämtliche Fragmente 1924–1941* [Part 1, Collected Fragments 1924–1941]) and Teil II (*Diktate 1941–1945* [Part 2, From Dictation 1941–1945]), Munich 1987 and 1993	
GSt	Gertrud Strobel, Tagebuch (RWA)	Gertrud Strobel, Diary (RWA)
HBM	*Halbmonatsberichte*	Fortnightly Reports

HR	Helena Roesener	
HT	Heinz Tietjen	
IfZ	Institut für Zeitgeschichte München	Munich Institute of Contemporary History
KK	Karl Klindworth	
LoC	Library of Congress, Washington	
LS	Lieselotte Schmidt, letters to her parents (RWA)	
MK	Adolf Hitler, *Mein Kampf*, edition in 1 vol., Munich 1940	
Mslg.	Musiksammlung	Music Collection
NbK	*Nordbayerischer Kurier*	North Bavarian Courier
n.d.	not dated	
NTh	Neill Thornborrow	
OfZ	*Oberfränkische Zeitung*	Upper Franconian Newspaper
PA	Private archive	
RKK	Reichskulturkammer	Reich Culture Chamber
RW	Richard Wagner	
RWA	Richard Wagner National Archive, Bayreuth	
RWV	Richard Wagner Verband	Richard Wagner Association
SKA	Spruchkammerakten	*Spruchkammer* files
STB	Stadtbibliothek	City Library
STLB	Stadt- und Landesbibliothek	Library of the City and *Land*
STUB	Stadt- und Universitäts- bibliothek	City and University Library
SW	Siegfried Wagner	
UB	Universitätsbibliothek	University Library
VB	*Völkischer Beobachter*	Nationalist Observer
VW and VL	Verena Wagner-Lafferentz	
WieW	Wieland Wagner	
WoW	Wolfgang Wagner	
WW	Winifred Wagner	
WW Memorandum	Winifred Wagner, Memorandum for the *Spruchkammer*, 1946, with original appendices (WoW's private archive)	
WW film	Transcript of tapes recorded while filming *Winifred Wagner*, by Hans-Jürgen Syberberg, 1975 (WoW's private archive)	
ZB	Zentralbibliothek	Central Library

1. AN ORPHAN FROM SUSSEX (1897–1915)

1   WW memorandum, 1.
2   RWA, KK to Eva Wagner, 21.4.1907.
3   WW memorandum
4   WW film, 1.
5   WW to HR, 8.4.1925.
6   WW, interview for the *Berliner Illustrierte Nachtausgabe*, 11.2.1933.
7   RWA, KK to Eva Wagner, 27.9.1908.
8   RWA, KK to CW, 19.12.1909.
9   WW film, 4.
10 RWA, KK to CW, 8.9.1907.
11 RWA, KK to Eva Chamberlain, 9.6.1913.
12 Ibid., 19.9.1901.
13 Heinrich Class, *Das Kaiserbuch*, Berlin, 1935, 41f.
14 RWA, KK to Eva Wagner, 21.4.1907.
15 RWA, KK to CW, 24.12.1913.
16 Ibid.
17 WoW, WW to Frau Stubaum, 14.2.1979.
18 *Cosima Wagner/Richard Strauss Briefwechsel*, ed. by Franz Trenner, Tutzing 1978, 280f., undated article in *Der Turm*, Berlin, 16.10.1911.
19 Markus Kiesel, *Studien zur Instrumentalmusik Siegfried Wagners*, Frankfurt a. M., 1994. 85f., SW, 'Wie mein Strauss Interview zustande kam', in BRb, 21.10.1911.
20 SW, *Erinnerungen*, Stuttgart, 1923, 150.
21 *Die Fackel*, 5.10.1912.
22 Claude Debussy, *Monsieur Croche*, Stuttgart, 1974, 99.
23 *Richard Strauss/Clemens Krauss, Briefwechsel*, ed. by Günter Brosche, Tutzing, 1997, 456, 24.3.1942.
24 RWA, Franz Stassen, 'Erinnerungen', typescript, 1938, 78.
25 RWA, KK to CW, 29.10.1911.
26 RWA, Franz Stassen, *Erinnerungen an Siegfried Wagner* (Memories of Siegfried Wagner), n.d. (1924), 34f.
27 Zdenko von Kraft, *Der Sohn. Siegfried Wagners Leben und Umwelt*, Graz, 1969, 179.
28 BStB mss., Gravina papers, both letters dated 14.11.1909.
29 Franz Wilhelm Beidler, *Cosima Wagner-Liszt*, ed. by Dieter Borchmeyer, Bilefeld, 1999, 378.
30 Kraft (see note 27), 225.
31 Maximilian Harden, 'Tutte le Corde. Siegfried und Isolde', in *Die Zukunft*, 27.6.1914.
32 RWA, KK to Eva Chamberlain, 25.5.1914.
33 RWA, KK to CW, 27.6.1914.
34 WW to Helena Boy, 22.5.1914.
35 WW film, 5.
36 RWA, Geoffrey Skelton, WW interview, BBC, 1969, 5.
37 WW to Helena Boy, 22.5.1914.
38 WW, interview (see note 6).
39 WW memorandum, 4.

40   RWA, KK to CW, 22.7.1914.
41   SW (see note 20), 144f.
42   WW film, 7.
43   Letter of a former school-friend to WW, 23.7.1977.
44   Quoted in Kraft (see note 27), 190.
45   CW to Hohenlohe, 1.1.1915, in *Briefwechsel zwischen Cosima Wagner und Fürst Ernst zu Hohenlohe-Langenburg*, Stuttgart, 1937.
46   Otto Daube, 'Siegfried Wagner im Landestheater', in *Altenburger Theater- und Konzert-Nachrichten*, 14.6.1925, 2.
47   WW to Helena Boy, 28.10.1914.
48   RWA, KK to CW, n.d.
49   Stassen (see note 26).
50   RWA, KK to CW, 23.5.1915.
51   Stassen (see note 26), 35.
52   Ibid., 38.
53   Kraft (see note 27), 192f.
54   DRWG, Curt von Westerhagen, 'Erinnerungen an Winifred Wagner'.
55   Skelton (see note 36), 6.
56   Stassen (see note 24), 81f.
57   WW to Rüdiger Pohl, 1.3.1978.
58   Skelton (see note 36), 6.
59   WW to SW, 5.7.1915, Kraft (see note 27), 200f.
60   SW to CW, n.d., Kraft (see note 27), 203.
61   RWA, KK to SW, 8.7.1915.
62   Kraft (see note 27), 201.
63   WW to Helena Boy, 6.7.1915.
64   Communication from Gertrud Rosvaenge, based on WW's reminiscences.
65   RWA, KK to SW, 10.8.1915.
66   Ibid., 5.8.1915.
67   CW to Hohenlohe (see note 45), 343, August 1915.
68   Stassen (see note 24), 82.
69   Stassen (see note 26), 38.
70   RWA, KK to CW, 20.9.1915.
71   RWA, KK to SW, 19.9.1915.
72   RWA, KK to Engelbert Humperdinck, 17.10.1915.
73   WW to Helena Boy, 2.10.1915.
74   Eva Humperdinck, *Engelbert Humperdinck in seinen persönlichen Beziehungen zu Richard, Cosima, Siegfried Wagner*, III, Koblenz, 1999, 299, CW to Humperdinck, 29.12.1915.

2. THE NEWLY-WEDS (1915–22)

1   WW film, 7.
2   Ibid., 15.
3   Ibid., 15f.
4   Ibid., 14.
5   Lies to Helena Boy, with a copy of a letter from WW, undated (1915).

6 RWA, WW to Anna Kekulé von Stradonitz, 30.10.1915.
7 RWA, Geoffrey Skelton, interview with WW, BBC 1969, 17.
8 Ibid., 9.
9 WW to Helena Boy, 2.11.1915.
10 Ibid., 18.10.1915.
11 WW film, 18f. and 16.
12 Ibid., 162.
13 Berlin BA, Schweninger papers, ECh to Ernst Schweninger, 28.1.1916.
14 Ibid., 6.10.1916.
15 WW to Helena Boy, 2.11.1915.
16 Source as in note 13, 24.1.1916.
17 Comment by Gertrud Rossvaenge, July 1999.
18 WW to Helena Boy, 18.10.1915.
19 RWA, WW to Kekulé von Stradonitz, 27.12.1915, handwritten copy.
20 Houston Stewart Chamberlain, *Die Grundlagen des 19. Jahrhunderts*, Munich, 1899, I, 278f.
21 WW to Helena Boy, 24.3.1917.
22 Lies to Boy (see note 5).
23 WW to Helena Boy, 27.9.1914.
24 Houston Stewart Chamberlain, *Briefe* (Letters) *1882–1924*, Munich, 1928, II, 250f, William II to Chamberlain, 15.1.1917.
25 RWA, Franz Stassen, *Erinnerungen an Siegfried Wagner*, n.d. (1942), 36.
26 Houston Stewart Chamberlain, *Arische Weltanschauung*, Preface to the 3rd edition, Munich, 1915, and 40.
27 Houston Stewart Chamberlain, *Zuversicht*, Munich, 1916, 11.
28 WW to Helena Boy, 17.2.1920.
29 WW film, 10.
30 Berlin BA, Schweninger papers, WW to Schweninger, 2.10.1916.
31 Vienna StLB ms., undated; from 1917 onwards, all letters from Siegfried to Millenkovich are in Winifred's handwriting.
32 Lies to Boy (see note 5).
33 WW to Helena Boy, 22.8.1916.
34 Berlin BA, Schweninger papers, WW to Schweninger, 9.10.1916.
35 Correspondence between Cosima Wagner and Prince Ernst zu Hohenlohe-Llangenburg, Stuttgart, 1937, 358, 22.12.1916.
36 Statement by Verena Lafferentz, July 2000.
37 WW to Helena Boy, 13.1.1917.
38 Stassen (see note 25), 38f., SW to Stassen, 13.1.1917.
39 Zdenko von Kraft, *Der Sohn, Siegfried Wagners Leben und Umwelt*, Graz, 1969, 214.
40 Stassen (see note 25), 39f.
41 Ibid., 39.
42 WW to Helena Boy, 17.12.1917.
43 Ibid., 24.3.1917.
44 Berlin BA, Schweninger papers, WW to Schweninger, 14.8.1917.
45 GSt, 16.8.1947.
46 Basel UB, WW to Adolf Zinsstag, 7.10 and 14.11.1917.
47 Stassen (see note 25), 40.

48 WW to Helena Boy, 15.7.1917.
49 CW (see note 35), 371, Maundy Thursday 1918.
50 Stassen (see note 25), 42.
51 WW to Helena Boy, 17.10.1918.
52 Stassen (see note 25), 86f.
53 Kraft (see note 39), 221.
54 WW to Helena Boy, 17.11.1918.
55 Ibid.
56 B. Zinner, 'Revolution in Bayreuth?', in: *Archiv für Geschichte von Oberfranken*, 53, 1973, 371ff.
57 Stassen (see note 25), 44.
58 Ibid., 49.
59 Berlin BA, Schweninger papers, WW to Schweninger, 30.11.1918.
60 Wiener Library London, SW to the Rabbi of Bayreuth, 12.6.1924, copy: quoting SW to Frau Professor Bie in Berlin, 1919.
61 CW (see note 35), 368, 14.2.1918.
62 RWA, Josef Stolzing-Cerny, *Erinnerungen an SW*, 4.8.1935, newspaper cutting.
63 WW to Helena Boy, 26.6.1919.
64 Zinner (see note 56), 303 and 403.
65 Eva Humperdinck, *Engelbert Humperdinck in seinen persönliche Beziehungen zu Richard, Cosima, Siegfried Wagner*, III, Koblenz, 1999, 326, SW to Humperdinck, 24.1.1919.
66 Cosima Wagner, *Das zweite Leben*, ed. by Dietrich Mack, Munich and Zurich, 1980, CW to Hohenlohe, 27.2.1919.
67 Rainer Trübsbach, *Geschichte der Stadt Bayreuth*, Bayreuth, 1993, 260, proclamation of 19.4.1919.
68 WW to Helena Boy, 26.6.1919.
69 FVT, 9.10.1919.
70 WW to Helena Boy, 2.10.(1919).
71 Sylvia Habermann, 'Die jüdische Gemeinde in Bayreuth vor 1900', in *Reichskristallnacht*, Bayreuth, 1988, 22.
72 WW to Helena Boy, 7.6.1920.
73 CW, *Die Tagebücher*, ed. by Martin Gregor-Dellin and Dietrich Mack, Munich and Zurich, 1976, 11.10.1879.
74 WW to Helena Boy, 6.5.1923.
75 Ibid., n.d. (about 1920).
76 CW (see note 66), 747f., 11.9.1919.
77 WW to Helena Boy, 1.4.1920.
78 WW memorandum, 7f.
79 WW to Helena Boy, 17.8.1919.
80 Uwe Lohalm, *Völkischer Radikalismus*, Hamburg, 1970, 217.
81 Martin Sabrow, *Märtyrer der Republik*, exhibition catalogue of the German Historical Museum Berlin, 226.
82 WW to Helena Boy, 2.10.1923.
83 Kraft (see note 39), 229.
84 Berlin BA, WW to Schweninger, 8.1.1919.
85 Ibid., CW to Schweninger, 3.2.1919.
86 Ibid., WW to Schweninger, 7.2.1919.

87   Kraft (see note 39), 225.
88   Statement by Verena Lafferentz.
89   All quoted from Kraft (see note 39), 230.
90   Stassen (see note 25), 47.
92   Ibid., 46.
93   WW film, 8.
94   Kraft (see note 39), 230.
95   RWA, WW to Adolf von Gross, n.d.
96   GSt, reporting Winifred's anecdotes, 15.2.1945.
97   WW to Helena Boy, 6.5.1922.
98   Kraft (see note 39), 229.
99   To Karpath, ibid., 227f.
100 German Bayreuth Festival Foundation, appeal for subscription to sponsorship
     certificates.
101 Albert von Puttkamer, 'The German Bayreuth Festival Foundation', in
     Festspielführer, 1924, 32.
102 DRWG, Otto Daube, 'Begegnungen eines Neunzigjährigen', typescript, 359f.;
     SW's letter to Püringer is preserved only in an undated handwritten copy, with
     the unconfirmed date 1921.
103 Bbl 1924, 98.
104 WW to Helena Boy, 25.3.1923.
105 BStA, SKA, WW, statement by Kirchhoff, 30.6.1937.
106 FW, *Nacht über Bayreuth*, Cologne, 3rd edition, 1997, 11.
107 OfZ, 14.8.1923.
108 WW to Helena Boy, 31.10.1923.
109 RWA, SW to Rosa Eidam, 9.6.1923, complete original handwritten copy.
110 Markus Kiesel, *Studien zur Instrumentalmusik Siegfried Wagners*, Frankfurt a. M.,
     1994, 124.
111 Bbl 1909, 248, SW, address to Festival orchestra and chorus.
112 Stassen (see note 25), 50.
113 Munich Monacensia, Krüger diary, 15.8, 24.9. and 10.10.1923.
114 Josef Müller-Marein/Hannes Reinhardt, *Das musikalische Selbsporträt*, Hamburg,
     1963, 149ff.
115 *Der Weg einer deutschen Künstlerin. Erinnerungen an Emmy Krüger*, Munich,
     1940, 63f.
116 WW to Helena Boy, 20.10.1923.
117 Rupert Hart-Davies, *Hugh Walpole*, London, undated, 233.
118 WW to Helena Boy, 20.10.1923.
119 WW to ECh and Blandine Gravina, 30.8.1923, personal handwritten copy to
     Helena Boy.

3. HITLER IN BAYREUTH (1923–4)

1   Sylvia Habermann, 'Die jüdische Gemeinde in Bayreuth vor 1900', in
    '*Reichskristallnacht*', Bayreuth, 1988, 22.
2   WW memorandum, 8.
3   D. Eckart, 'Parsifal', in *Handbuch für Festspielbesucher*, Bayreuth, 1911, 1–16.

4   BStB, *d* Hanfstaengl papers Kt. 25
5   Ibid.
6   WW to Helena Boy, 6.12.1923.
7   Georg Franz-Willing, *Krisenjahr der Hitlerbewegung 1923*, Preuss, Oldendorf, 1975, 204.
8   Brigitte Hamann, *Hitlers Wien*, Munich, 1996, 337–436.
9   Alexis Schwarzenbach, Bocken guestbook.
10 Wille to Tirpitz, 18.12.1922, cit. by Raffael Scheck, 'Swiss Funding for the Early Nazi Movement', in *Journal of Modern History*, Vol. 71, Chicago, 1999, 793ff.
11 Alexis Schwarzenbach, Zurich.
12 AH, *Monologe im Führerhauptquartier 1941–1944*, ed. by Werner Jochmann, Hamburg, 1980, 327.
13 Communication from Jürg Wille, July 2001.
14 BStB ms., Hanfstaengl papers Kt. 25, handwritten notes of a telephone conversation with Gansser in Zurich.
15 Ibid., notepad sheet, 1922.
16 CW to Hohenlohe, 2–4.7.1923, in *CW, Die Tagebücher*, ed. by Martin Gregor-Dellin and Dietrich Mack, Munich and Zurich, 1976, 750f.
17 OfZ, 18.9.1923.
18 Ibid., 26.9.1923.
19 Ibid., 28.9.1923.
20 Ibid., 1.10.1923.
21 FVT, 1.10.1923.
22 OfZ, 1.10.1923; subsequent quotations from the same source.
23 Ibid.
24 Benedikt Lochmüller, *Hans Schemm*, Munich, 1935, II, 54f.
25 FVT, 1. and 2.10.1923.
26 Published in OfZ, 24.11.1923.
27 Winfried Schüler, *Der Bayreuther Kreis von seiner Entstehung bis zum Ausgang der wilhelminischen Ära*, Münster, 1971, 126f., Stolzing-Cerny to ECh, 17.10.1923.
28 BOm, 25./26.7.1936.
29 WW to Hermann Ernst, 2.11.1971.
30 *Fränkische Presse*, 2.12.1948, WW to the de-nazification court.
31 Hans Severus Ziegler, *Adolf Hitler aus dem Erleben dargestellt*, Göttingen, 1964, 157.
32 WW to Ernst, 2.11.1971.
33 WW film, 80.
34 AH (see note 12), 24./25.1.1942.
35 Schüler (see note 27), 85, conversation with WW, 21.6.1961.
36 WW film, 81f.
37 Ibid., 164f.
38 Alexander Spring, 'Siegfried Wagner. Zur 70. Wiederkehr seines Geburtstages', in *Bayreuther Festspielführer 1939*, 22.
39 RWA, Franz Stassen, *Erinnerungen an Siegfried Wagner*, n.d. (1942), 53 and 50.
40 VB, 3.10.1923, in Franz-Willing (see note 7), 168.
41 Ernst Hanfstaengl, *Zwischen Weissem und Braunem Haus*, Munich, 1970, 77f.
42 WW to Helena Boy, 26.10.1923.
43 Berlin BA, DFA, 'Archiv der Persönlichkeiten', Winifred Wagner, 10.7.1943.

44 WW to Gerdy Troost, 11.11.1973.
45 RWA, SW, *Glück*.
46 Markus Kiesel, *Studien zur Instrumentalmusik Siegfried Wagners*, Frankfurt a. M., 1994, 149.
47 RWA, SW to Rosa Eidam, Christmas 1923.
48 WW to Helena Boy, 20.10.1923.
49 WW memorandum, 9.
50 Ibid., 9.
51 WW to Gerdy Troost, 11.11.1973.
52 Ernst Deuerlein, *Der Aufstieg der NSDAP in Augenzeugenberichten*, Munich, 1974, 200.
53 WW memorandum, 9.
54 Munich BHSA, SKA 1947, hearing of WW.
55 RWA, SW to Rosa Eidam, Christmas 1923.
56 WW film, 123.
57 Munich BSTa, SKA, transcript of 1947, 8.
58 Lochmüller (see note 24), 64, who also supplies names.
59 Ibid., 66.
60 WW to Helena Boy, 6.12.1923.
61 WW memorandum, 9f.
62 Munich BHSA, SKA, 147, transcript of hearings, 9.
63 WW to Gerdy Troost, 11.11.73.
64 WW to Helena Boy, 6.12.1923.
65 Ibid.
66 Btb, 12.11.1923, 1.
67 Munich BHSA, SKA, Spitzer hearings, 22.11.1946.
68 WW to Rudolf Hess, 25.4.1928.
69 FVT, 12.11.1923.
70 Quoted in various sources, e.g. VB, 28.7.1938.
71 BOm, 5.8.1937, on Christian Ebersberger, '40 years in the service of Wahnfried'.
72 Ibid., 4.1.1936: 'The loyalty of a great house'.
73 RWA, SW to Rosa Eidam, Christmas 1923.
74 Statement by Verena Lafferentz.
75 RWA, SW to Rosa Eidam, Christmas 1923.
76 *Das Tagebuch* (Diary), Berlin, 1924, 1000.
77 Brigitte Hamann, *Hitlers Wien*, Munich, 1996, 344f.
78 Max von Millenkovich-Morold, *Vom Abend zum Morgen*, Leipzig, 1940, 299, 316.
79 OfZ, 24.11.1923.
80 Ibid., 18.12.1923.
81 Lochmüller (see note 24), II, 71 and 79.
82 Copy enclosed by WW in letter to Helena Boy, 6.12.1923. Draft version in RWA, Chamberlain Papers, with the signatures of Houston and Eva Chamberlain.
83 WW to AH, Wahnfried, 1.12.1923, reproduced in much reduced facsimile in John Toland, *Adolf Hitler*, Bergisch Gladbach, 1977.
84 WW to Helena Boy, 6.12.1923.

85 Hanfstaengl (see note 41), 156f.
86 *Der Hitler-Putsch. Bayerische Dokumente zum 8./9. November 1923*, ed. by Ernst Deuerlein, Stuttgart, 1962, 561.
87 Rudolf Hess, *Briefe, 1908–1933*, ed. by Wolf Rüdiger Hess, Munich, 1987, 353, Hess to Ilse Pröhl, 14.10.1924.
88 BStB mss., Bruckmann papers, Elsa Bruckmann, 'Meine erste Fahrt zum Führer im Mai 1924', typescript.
89 Toland (see note 83), I, 253.
90 WW film, 66.
91 WW memorandum.
92 PA, leaflet, 'Urteil des grossen Denkers H. St. Chamberlain über Adolf Hitler'.
93 RWA, SW to Rosa Eidam, Christmas 1923.
94 WW to Helena Boy, 1.1.1924.

4. AMERICAN JOURNEY (1924)

1 WW to Helena Boy, 23.11.1922.
2 SW, *Erinnerungen*, Stuttgart, 1923, 135f.
3 RWA, SW to Antonie Speyer, 12.7.1923.
4 WW to Helena Boy, 6.7.1923.
5 Zdenko von Kraft, *Der Sohn. Siegfried Wagners Leben und Umwelt*, Graz, 1969, 236.
6 Contract located at LoC, Performing Arts, Urchs Papers.
7 RWA, WW to Rosa Eidam, Christmas 1923.
8 Kraft (see note 5), 236.
9 Basel UB, WW to Zinsstag, 30.8.1923.
10 WW to Helena Boy, 20.10.1923.
11 Kraft (see note 5), 236.
12 RWA, SW, ms. about the American journey, 1925.
13 NTh, Baltimore concert programme, 3.2.1924.
14 WW memorandum, 11.
15 WW to Helena Boy, 1.4.1924.
16 WoW.
17 Kraft (see note 5), 238f.
18 Ibid., 240.
19 Kurt G. W. Lüdecke, *I Knew Hitler*, London, 1938, facsimile of letter from AH, Landsberg, 4.12.1924.
20 Ibid., 182.
21 Advertising leaflet of the Hammer publishing house for the 27th impression, 9.9.1926.
22 For example, in the VB, 9.9.1926.
23 Ernst Hanfstaengl, *Zwischen Weissem und Braunem Haus*, Munich, 1970, 46.
24 Rudolf Hess to Henry Ford, 18.8.1922.
25 E.g. the VB of 2.4.1927, front page: 'A murderous Jewish attack on Henry Ford!'
26 Rudolf Hess, *Briefe, 1908–1933*, ed. by Wolf Rüdiger Hess, Munich, 1987, 305, Hess to his later wife, 19.9.1923.

27 James and Suzanne Pool, *Hitlers Wegbereiter zur Macht*, Berne and Munich, 1979, 114.
28 RWA, SW: radio interview preceding a Leipzig concert, 1925.
29 WW, interview of October 1977, cit. Pool (see note 27), 114.
30 WoW, *Lebens-Akte*, Munich, 1994, 422f., augmented by oral communication of January 2000.
31 WW, interview 1977, cit. Pool (see note 27), 114.
32 Ibid., 115.
33 Lüdecke (see note 19), 183f.
34 Ibid., 201.
35 WW to HR, 28.10.1927.
36 Hadassa Ben-Ittô, '*Die Protokolle der Weisen von Zion*'. *Anatomie einer Fälschung*, Berlin, 1998, 92f.
37 Henry Ford, *Der internationale Jude*, ed. by Theodor Fritsch, many editions.
38 David L. Lewis, *The Public Image of Henry Ford*, Detroit, 1976, 151.
39 Michael Karbaum, *Studien zur Geschichte der Bayreuther Festspiele (1876–1976)*, Regensburg, 1976, 72, Wiskott to Knittel, 15.10.1929.
40 Munich BSA, SKA minutes, 62, statement of Paul Ottenheimer.
41 Joseph Chapiro, 'Zum "höheren Zwecke der Kunst". Für Bayreuth, gegen Siegfried Wagner', in *Berliner Tagblatt*, 29.3.1925.
42 London Wiener Library, SW to the Rabbi of Bayreuth, 12.6.1924, copy.
43 WW to Anny Noetzli, New York, 12.2.1924.
44 RWA, SW, ms. text of a radio talk in Leipzig, 1925.
45 Kraft (see note 5), 241f.
46 Ibid., 243.
47 LoC, Urchs to SW, New York, 20.1.1925.
48 London Wiener Library, SW to the Rabbi of Bayreuth, 12.6.1924.
49 Kraft (see note 5), 245.
50 Ibid., 246.
51 RWA, Geoffrey Skelton, WW interview, BBC, 1969, 32.
52 Kraft (see note 5), 247.
53 RWA, Franz Stassen, *Erinnerungen an Siegfried Wagner*, n.d. (1942), 50.
54 SW to Karpath, 26.5.1924, in Kraft (see note 5), 247.
55 Some details of the American journey may never be established, since in 1945 'during the bombing my American address book together with all my letters to Papa etc.' were lost (WW to FW, 1.5.1948).

5. THE FESTIVAL UNDER THE SWASTIKA (1924–7)

1 WW to Helena Boy, 18.4.1924.
2 *Hans Schemm spricht. Seine Reden und sein Werk*, ed. by Gertrud Kahl-Furthmann, Bayreuth, 1935.
3 BTb, 26.4.1924.
4 RWA, WW to SW, Wahnfried, 26.4.1924, from a fragmentary copy.
5 RWA, Chamberlain to AH, written by ECh, draft, 30.4.1924.
6 BTb, 7.5.1924.
7 WoW, AH to SW, Landsberg, 5.5.1924, copy.

8   AH, *Monologe im Führerhauptquartier 1941–1944*, ed. by Werner Jochmann, Hamburg, 1980, 24./25.1.1942, 224f.
9   WW to Helena Boy, 16.5.1924.
10 London Wiener Library, SW to the Rabbi of Bayreuth, 12.6.1924, copy.
11 Ibid., Rabbi of Bayreuth to SW, 26.6.1924.
12 *Offizieller Bayreuther Festspielführer1924*, 239f. and 214.
13 Ibid., 287f., 298, 290 and elsewhere.
14 August Püringer, 'Richard Wagner and Bismarck', ibid., 175ff.
15 Berlin, BA, DFA, 'Archiv der Persönlichkeiten', Winifred Wagner.
16 GSt, 14.6.(?) 1944.
17 AH (see note 8), 19./20.2.1942, 285.
18 Mannheim, Reger Archive, Busch papers, Busch to SW, 22.5.1924.
19 Erich Ebermayer, *Magisches Bayreuth*, Stuttgart, 1951, 167.
20 Bayreuth STA, WW to Margarethe Strauss, 22.11.1927.
21 DRWG, Otto Daube, *Begegnungen eines Neunzigjährigen*, typescript, 253.
22 Bayreuth STA, WW to Margarethe Strauss, 11.11.1923.
23 Zdenko von Kraft, *Der Sohn. Siegfried Wagners. Leben und Umwelt*, Graz, 1969, 249.
24 WW to Helena Boy, 14.9.1924.
25 RWA, Geoffrey Skelton, interview with WW, BBC, 1969, 28.
26 WW film, 36.
27 Fritz Busch, *Aus dem Leben eines Musikers*, Zurich, 1949, 163.
28 Ibid., 162.
29 Mannheim Reger Archive, Carl Muck to Fritz Busch, Hamburg, 27.11.1923.
30 Ibid., SW to Busch, 24.5.1924.
31 Ibid., July 1924.
32 Busch (see note 27), 158.
33 Munich Monacensia, Krüger diary, 29.6.1924.
34 Karl Holl, *Frankfurter Zeitung*, 3.8.1924, cit. Susanna Grossmann-Vendey, *Bayreuth in der deutschen Presse*, Regensburg 1988, 184 and 183.
35 Kurt Singer, in *Vorwärts*, 17.8.1924, cit. by Grossmann-Vendrey, ibid., 180.
36 Mannheim Reger Archive.
37 WW film, 18.
38 WW to Helena Boy, 14.9.1924.
39 Ibid., 8.4.1925.
40 Sylvia Habermann, 'Die jüdische Gemeinde in Bayreuth vor 1900', in 'Reichskristallnacht', Bayreuth, 1988, 24.
41 Cit. Hans Rudolf Vaget (ed.), *Im Schatten Wagners*, Frankfurt a. M., 1999, 69.
42 *CV-Zeitung*, 13.3.1925, SW to Bruno Weil, 25.2.1925.
43 BStA, SKA, statement by WW, 94.
44 WW film, 106.
45 BStB ms., Bruckmann papers, Elsa Bruckmann, 'Zwei Episoden', typescript.
46 WW to Helena Boy, 3.1.1924 (in error: should read '1925').
47 BStA, SKA, transcript, 89.
48 WW to Helena Boy, 6.1.1924 (should read '1925').
49 FW, *Nacht über Bayreuth*, Cologne, 3rd edition 1997, 52.
50 Communication from Daphne Wagner, July 2001.
51 Ernst Hanfstaengl, *Zwischen Weissem und Braunem Haus*, Munich, 1970, 52f.
52 Daube (see note 21), 356.

53 Joseph Chapiro in *Berliner Tagblatt*, 29.3.1925.
54 WW to AH, 17.4.1925, copy in IfZ, from Besançon, Musée de la Résistance, with thanks to Klaus Lankheit.
55 *CV-Zeitung*, 19.6.1925.
56 Rupert Hart-Davis, *Hugh Walpole*, London, 1952, 263.
57 Communication from Rudolf Pfeiffer-Bechstein, December 1998.
58 AH (see note 8) 28.2./1.3.1942, 307; the photographs were destroyed in a fire in the Bechstein Villa in 1945.
59 Ibid., 3./4.2.1942, 259; Bayreuth STA, Register of Visitors, 1925.
60 GSt, 17.9.1946.
61 AH (see note 8), 28.2./1.3.1942, 308.
62 Munich Monacensia, Emmy Krüger, *Meine Erlebnisse im 'Tausendjährigen Reich' Hitlers*, typescript, 4.
63 Hart-Davis (see note 56), 263f.
64 WW to HR, 15.8.1926.
65 Ibid., 17.2.1927.
66 WW film, 59f.
67 WW memorandum, 12.
68 Hans Rudolf Vaget, in 'Thomas Mann und Bayreuth', *Thomas-Mann-Jahrbuch*, vol. 9, 1996, 125.
69 Gustav Stresemann, *Vermächtnis*, Berlin, 1933, III, 513f., 8.8.1928, to Carl Baumgärtel, living in Bayreuth; with thanks to Jonathan R. C. Wright, Oxford.
70 Communication from Rudolf Pfeiffer-Bechstein.
71 WW to Hermann Ernst, 2.11.1971.
72 WW to HR, 16.12.1926.
73 WW fim, 73.
74 Daube (see note 21), 359.
75 Ibid., 302, WW to Daube, 22.1.1926.
76 Ibid., 185, 15.2.1926.
77 GSt, 16.8.1947.
78 AH (see note 8), 315, 10./ 11.3.1942.
79 RW, SW to Anna von Kekulé, 1.10.1925, incomplete copy.
80 WW film, 72f.
81 Ibid.
82 LS, 10.6.1931.
83 WW film, 73.
84 WW memorandum, 12.
85 Berlin BDC, WW's party card.
86 WW memorandum, 12.
87 WW to HR, 11.3.1926.
88 Otto Gritschneder, *Bewährungsfrist für den Terroristen Adolf Hitler*, Munich, 1990, 130ff.
89 WW to HR, 19.4.1926.
90 Ibid., 22.11.1926.
91 Ibid., 27.2.1926.
92 Goebbels diary, 8.5.1926.
93 RWA, SW, ms. of a radio talk, 1925.
94 Otto Daube, *Die Wagner-Bewegung der Gegenwart*, in OfZ, 17.9.1927.

95 Kraft (see note 23), 264f.
96 Volker Mauersberger, *Hitler in Weimar*, Berlin, 1999, 224.
97 Goebbels diary, 6.7.1926.
98 Mauersberger (see note 96), 227.
99 Paul Pretzsch/Otto Daube, *Deutsche Festspiele in Weimar*, Bayreuth, 1926, 5 and 120.
100 WW to HR, 28.7.1926.
101 Ibid.
102 Harry Graf Kessler, *Tagebücher*, Frankfurt a. M., 1996, 578 and 722f.
103 RWA, SW to Hermann Neupert, 10.9.1929.
104 Daube (see note 21), 59.
105 BStB ms., SW to Evelyn Faltis, 29.1.1927.
106 WW to HR, 16.12.1926, and communication from Bales's daughter Ursel Gossmann.
107 Communication from Alexis Schwarzenbach.
108 WW to HR, 5.9.1926.
109 OfZ, 7.9.1926.
110 FVT, 4. and 7.9.1926.
111 WW to HR, 5.9.1926.
112 Goebbels diary, 8.9.1926.
113 WW to HR, 24.1.1928.
114 RWA, Franz Stassen, 'Erinnerungen', typescript, 1938, 97.
115 WW to HR, 24.5.1928.
116 Ebermeyer (see note 19), 171.

6. THE OLDER GENERATION GIVES WAY (1927–30)

1 Rudolf Hess, *Briefe, 1908–1933*, ed. by Wolf Rüdiger Hess, Munich, 1987, 372f., Rudolf Hess to his parents, 11.1.1927.
2 Goebbels diary, 8.5.1926.
3 VB, 9.9.1926.
4 SW to Franz Stassen, in Zdenko von Kraft, *Der Sohn. Siegfried Wagners Leben und Umwelt*, Graz, 1969, 268.
5 FVT, 12.1.1927.
6 Monthly newsletter of the Bayreuth League of German Youth, February 1927, 2.
7 BStB ms., SW to Evelyn Faltis, no place or date given.
8 LoC, SW to Ernest Urchs, 8.6.1926.
9 Ibid., 29.8.1926.
10 Ibid., Schuler and Beutter to Urchs, 12.5.1927.
11 WW to HR, 24.2.1927.
12 DRWG, Otto Daube, 'Begegnungen eines Neunzigjährigen', typescript, WW to Daube, 22.9.1926.
13 WW to HR, 24.2.1927.
14 Ibid., 28.7.1926.
15 AH, *Monologe im Führerhauptquartier 1941–1944*, ed. by Werner Jochmann, Hamburg, 1980, 28.2./1.3.1942, 308.
16 WW to HR, 7.7.1927.

17 Munich Monacensia, Krüger diary, 26.9.1927.
18 WW to HR, 19.5.1927.
19 Ibid.
20 The film was premièred on 2.9.1929 in Leipzig under the title *Wahnfried*. Both the original film and copies were confiscated by the Americans in 1945, according to Daube, and have since disappeared.
21 AH, MK, 103f.; on Ellenbogen, see Brigitte Hamann, *Hitlers Wien*, Munich, 1996, 252ff.
22 WW to HR, 24.2.1927.
23 Ibid., 27.3.1927.
24 Ibid., 18.10.1927.
25 Ibid., 20.11.1927.
26 Ibid., 12.3.1928.
27 Ibid., 20.12.1927.
28 Michael Karbaum, *Studien zur Geschichte der Bayreuther Festspiele (1876–1976)*, Regensburg, 1976, XI, 5, AH to WW, 30.12.1927.
29 WW to HR, 23.4.1928.
30 *Tages-Post*, Linz, 27.4.1928.
31 WW to Rudolf Hess, 25.4.1928.
32 WW to HR, 12.3.1928.
33 AH, MK, 1.
34 WW to HR, 8.6.1928.
35 Ibid., 7.12.1928.
36 *Hitlers Zweites Buch*, ed. by the Institut für Zeitgeschichte, Stuttgart, 1961.
37 WW to HR, 24.6.1928.
38 Goebbels diary, 28.5.1928, WW to HR, 30.5.1928.
39 WW to HR, 17.2.1927.
40 BStB ms., WW to Elsa Bruckmann, 15.10.1928.
41 Ibid., 15.12.1928.
42 WW to HR, 3.3.1931.
43 Krüger (see note 17), 13.4.1931.
44 BTb, 13.4.1929.
45 Bayreuth STA, HMB, 15.3. and 1.5.1929.
46 Gerhard Rossbach, *Mein Weg durch die Zeit*, Weissburg/Lahn, 1950, 102ff.
47 WW to Gerdy Troost, 18.2.1963.
48 Daube (see note 12), 261.
49 WoW, *Lebens-Akte*, Munich, 1994, 58.
50 Lotte Warburg, *Eine vollkommene Närrin durch meine ewigen Gefühle*, Bayreuth, 1989, 28.1.1928.
51 Erika Heck, Bayreuth, July 1998.
52 LS, 22.7.1929.
53 Frida Leider, *Das war mein Teil*, Berlin, 1981, 102.
54 WW to HR, 24.1.1928.
55 RWA, SW to Gustav Manz, 19.3.1929.
56 GSt, 23.11.1946.
57 Auction 35, autograph dealers Zisskau and Kistner, May 2000, no. 439.
58 Warburg (see note 50), 28.1.1928.
59 Text of the will in WoW (see note 49), 442ff.

60   Reader's letter from Gertrud Wagner, FAZ, 15.4.1980.
61   BStB mss., SW to Evelyn Faltis, 4.4.1929.
62   RWA, Franz Stassen, *Erinnerungen an Siegfried Wagner*, n.d. (1942), 47.
63   RWA, SW, diary.
64   Harvey Sachs, *Toscanini*, Munich/Zurich, 1980, 285.
65   WoW, Heinz Tietjen to WW, 8.11.1930.
66   Bayreuth STA, WW to Margarethe Strauss, 22.9.1929.
67   Bayreuth *Festspielführer 1927*, 256.
68   LS, 27.10.1933.
69   *Hitler aus nächster Nähe*, ed. by Henry A. Turner, Kiel 2nd edition, 1987, 16.
70   Ibid., 19.
71   LS, 4.8.1929.
72   FVT, 6.8.1929.
73   WW to Gerdy Troost, 30.9.1973.
74   WW to Albert Knittel, 12.4.1930.
75   Bayreuth STA, WW to Margarethe Strauss, 21.8.1929.
76   Ibid., 22.9.1929.
77   SW to Ludwig Karpath, clearly 1926, in Kraft (see note 4), 269.
78   FW, *Nacht über Bayreuth*, Cologne, 3rd edition, 1997, 54.
79   WW to HR, 7.7.1927.
80   Bayreuth STA, HMB, 15.5.1929.
81   Kraft (see note 4), 283.
82   Ibid., 286.
83   Ibid., 290.
84   GSt, 15.11.1947.
85   Bayreuth STA, HMB, 15.8.1930.
86   Ibid., 1.7.1930.
87   WoW, WW, Note to the Festival Theatre, n.d. (1930).
88   LS, 26.6.1930.
89   Ibid., 28.6.1930.
90   'Hugo Rüdel zum Gedächtnis', in *Bayreuther Festspielkalender 1936*, 61, 26.6.1930.
91   LS, 26.6.1930.
92   BStB, SW to Faltis., n.d., no place of publication, 23.5.1930.
93   RWA, Geoffrey Skelton, WW interview, BBC, 1969, 30.
94   WoW, Christian Ebersberger, *Drei Generationen im Hause Wahnfried*, 10f.
95   FW (see note 78), 85.
96   Bayreuth STA, HMB, 31.7.1930.
97   FW (see note 78), 83.
98   Fritz Busch, *Aus dem Leben eines Musikers*, Zurich, 1949, 159.
99   GSt, 24.11.1947.
100 Cit. by Kraft (see note 4), 290; official case-history report by Hermann Koerber.
101 FW (see note 78), 83.
102 WW memorandum, 13.
103 Ebersberger (see note 94), 17f.
104 Krüger (see note 17), 8.8.1930.
105 FW (see note 78), 86f.
106 SW, *Erinnerungen*, Stuttgart, 1923, 133f.

7. WINIFRED, THE NEW BOSS OF BAYREUTH (1930–33)

1   Erich Ebermayer, *Magisches Bayreuth*, Stuttgart, 1951; compare Thomas Mann, *Tagebücher*, ed. by Peter de Mendelssohn, Frankfurt a. M., 1978, 27.8.1934.
2   Bayreuth STA, HMB, 15.8.1934.
3   Ibid.
4   Benedikt Lochmüller, *Hans Schemm*, Bayreuth, 1935, II, 228.
5   Bayreuth STA, HMB, 31.1.1931.
6   WoW, WW to HT, 12.8.1930.
7   Munich BTA, SKA, minutes, 81, statement by auditor Wilhelm Hieber.
8   WoW, Carl Muck to WW, 1.9.1930.
9   BStB mss., WW to Evelyn Faltis, 17.9.1930.
10 WoW, HT to WW, 6.9.1930. In November 1930 the Theatre Association rejected the application for honorary royalties.
11 Ibid., 30.10.1930.
12 Ibid., 8.11.1930.
13 Ibid., 14.11.1930.
14 WW to HR, 15.11.1930.
15 LS, 31.1.1931.
16 WoW, HT to WW, 28.11.1930.
17 Berta Geissmar, *Taktstock und Schaftstiefel*, Cologne, 1996, 91.
18 WoW, WW to HT, 21.12.1930.
19 Ibid., 21.1.1931.
20 Ibid.
21 Ibid., 24.1.1931.
22 WoW, HT to WW, 24.1.1931.
23 WoW, WW to HT, 18.2.1931.
24 WW to HR, 21.4.1931.
25 Coburg StA, SKA.
26 WW to HR, 21.4.1931.
27 LS, 19.3.1931.
28 WoW, Alfred Rosenberg to WW, 24.4.1931.
29 RWA, WW to Rosenberg, 29.4.1931.
30 WoW, HT to WW, 4.3.1931.
31 Ibid., WW to HT, 6.3.1931.
32 Ibid., HT to WW, 10.3.1931.
33 WW to HR, 2.2.1931.
34 WoW, HT to WW, 25.4.1931.
35 Geissmar (see note 17), 92.
36 LS, 17.4.1931.
37 Ibid.
38 WoW, WW to Paul Pretzsch, 14.12.1931.
39 Munich Monacensia, Krüger diary, 31.12.1930.
40 WW to HR, 26.2.1931.
41 LS, 8.5.1931.
42 Ibid., 17.4.1931.
43 Geissmar (see note 17), 95f.

44 WW to Albert Osthoff, 12.5.1933, draft.
45 Geissmar (see note 17), 95.
46 Wilhelm Furtwängler, *Briefe*, ed. by Frank Thiess, Wiesbaden, 1965, 74.
47 Bayreuth STA, HMB, 1.8.1931.
48 NTh, FW to Irving Kolodin, 5.12.1955.
49 LS, 16.8.1931.
50 Bayreuth STA, HMB, 1. and 15.8.1931.
51 LS, 23.7.1931.
52 WoW, WW to Pretzsch, 14.12.1931.
53 Geissmar (see note 17).
54 WoW, WW to Pretzsch, 14.12.1931.
55 PA, Daniela Thode, 'Toscaninis Eintritt und Austritt in Bayreuth'.
56 Bayreuth STA, HMB, 1.8.1931.
57 *Textil-Einzelhandel-Zeitung*, 26.7.1931.
58 *Hamburger Nachrichten*, 13.10.1931.
59 *Volkstribüne*, 16.10.1931, WoW, copy of the eight o'clock evening supplement, n.d. (1931).
60 WoW, HT to Daniela Thode, 27.10.1931.
61 *Hamburger Nachrichten*, 17.10.1931.
62 OfZ, 29.10.1931.
63 WoW, WW to Pretzsch, 14.12.1931.
64 LS, 4.2.1931.
65 HR to WW, 9.10.1931, ms. copy.
66 WW to HR, 12.10.1931.
67 Ibid., 16.7.1932.
68 LS, 2.9.1932.
69 WW to HR, 4.1932.
70 LS, 7.6.1931.
71 Ibid., 13.11.1931.
72 Ibid., 7.3.1932.
73 Ibid., 14.1.1932.
74 WoW, AH to WW, 30.12.1931, hand-copied by WW for CIC, 1945.
75 Statement by Verena Lafferentz, 28.11.2000.
76 RWA, Franz Stassen, 'Erinnerungen', typescript, 1938, 101.
77 LS, 14.1.1932.
78 Ibid., 22.1.1932.
79 Ibid., 26.1.1932.
80 Ibid., 2. and 16.2.1932.
81 Bayreuth STA, HMB, 1.9.1931.
82 LS, 2.3.1932.
83 VB, 6.4.1932.
84 Communication from Wolfgang Wagner, December 2000.
85 WW to HR, April 1932.
86 LS, 15.4.1932.
87 Ibid., 25.4.1932.
88 Rainer Trübsbach, *Geschichte der Stadt Bayreuth*, Bayreuth, 1993, 287.
89 The whole episode can be found in LS, 3.5.1932.
90 Goebbels diary, 3.5.1932.

91   Fred K. Prieberg, *Kraftprobe*, Wiesbaden, 1986, 52, Ottmar Weber to Albert Osthoff, 7.1.1933.
92   WW to HR, 21. and 28.5.1932.
93   Ibid., 4.7.1932.
94   WoW, WW 1.1.1932, to HT for information.
95   Official proclamation, 30.1.1936, copy held by Nike Wagner.
96   Previously cited in Oliver Rathkolb, *Führertreu und gottbegnadet*, Vienna, 1991, 85f.
97   AdK, statement on oath by WW on behalf of HT, 4.4.1947.
98   WW to HR, 15.11.1930.
99   WW to Albert Knittel, 1.2.1932.
100   Lucerne STA, minutes of a meeting of the RWM Commission, 22.2.1933 and 3.12.1937.
101   LS, 2.12.1931.
102   WoW, Christian Ebersberger, 'Drei Generationen im Hause Wahnfried', typescript, 26.
103   LS, 4.11.1932.
104   WW to Knittel, 16.4.1932.
105   Ibid., 1.2.1932.
106   Ibid., 16.4.1932.
107   WW to HR, 28.5.1932 and 15.10.1932.
108   LS, 13.6.1932.
109   WW to Knittel, 4.10.1932 and 16.7.1932.
110   Ibid., 21.7.1932.
111   Ibid., Berlin, 5.9.1932.
112   AdK, N. HT, interview with Preetorius, Bayerischer Rundfunk, n.d.
113   Frida Leider, *Das war mein Teil*, Berlin, 1981, 160.
114   DRWG, radio interview with HT, NDR, 1.7.1970.
115   WW to HR, 16.7.1932.
116   Lucerne RWM, WW to Olly Rothenfelder, 17.4.1941.
117   LS, 31.5.1932.
118   FVT, 1.8.1932.
119   BTb, 1.8.1932.
120   FVT, 1.8.1932.
121   NTh, LS to FW, 18. and 26.9.1932.
122   Sylvia Habermann, 'Die Jüdische Gemeinde in Bayreuth', in *Reichskristallnacht*, Bayreuth, 1988, 25.
123   Stassen (see note 76), 106.
124   Goebbels diary, 8.12.1932.
125   WW memorandum, AH to WW, 8.1.1933, copied out by WW in 1945 for the CIC.
126   LS, 27.1.1933.

8. HITLER IN POWER (1933)

1   WoW, '*Lebens-Akte*', Munich, 1994, 46f.
2   Quoted by LS, 31.1.1933.
3   Frida Leider, *Das war mein Teil*, Berlin, 1981, 159.

4 RWA, Franz Stassen, 'Erinnerungen', typescript, 1938, 107.
5 LS, 16.2.1933.
6 Bayreuth StA, Albert Preu to WW, 14.2.1933.
7 Fred K. Prieberg, *Kraftprobe*, Wiesbaden, 1986, 137.
8 André François-Poncet, *Als Botschafter im 'Dritten Reich'*, Berlin, 1980, 104.
9 LS, 17.3.1933.
10 Bayreuth STA, WW to Margarethe Strauss, 20.3.1933.
11 Ibid., 29.3.1933.
12 BTb, 25.3.1933.
13 Fritz Busch, *Aus dem Leben eines Musikers*, Zurich, 1949, 202 and 210.
14 Bruno Walter, *Thema und Variationen*, Frankfurt a.M., 1963, 387.
15 BStA, SKA, Brockhaus to the de-nazification court.
16 Walter (see note 14), 389f.
17 History Workshop, Bayreuth, *Umgeguckt und hinterfragt*, Bayreuth, 1992, 21 and 22.
18 Lotte Warburg, *Eine vollkommene Närrin durch meine ewigen Gefühle*, Bayreuth, 1989, 31.12. and 3.8.1933.
19 VB, 23.3.1933.
20 LS, 24.3.1933.
21 Bayreuth STA, WW to Strauss, 29.3.1933.
22 FW, *Nacht über Bayreuth*, Cologne, 3rd edition, 1997, 126–9.
23 Goebbels diary, 31.3.1933.
24 Helmut Paulus, 'Die "Reichskristallnacht"', in the Archiv für Geschichte von Oberfranken, 1998, 435.
25 FW (see note 22), 130.
26 Ibid., 132.
27 RWA, Arturo Toscanini to AH, New York, 29.4.1933.
28 Mannheim, Reger Archive, Busch papers, Fritz Busch to his wife, 23.5.1933.
29 Busch (see note 13), 207 and 213.
30 LS, 2.6.1933.
31 Daniela Thode, 'Toscaninis Eintritt und Austritt in Bayreuth', manuscript, 9.
32 FW (see note 22), 131.
33 LS, 2.6.1933.
34 Grete Busch, *Fritz Busch*, Frankfurt a. M., 1970, 74.
35 AH, *Monologe im Führerhauptquartier 1941–1944*, ed. by Werner Jochmann, Hamburg, 1980, 19./20.2.1942, 285.
36 WW film, 42.
37 *Wiener Sonn- und Montagszeitung*, 30.7.1934.
38 Fritz Petzold (ed.), *Sigrid Onégin*, Magdeburg, 1939, 177f.
39 For example, Berlin BA, RKK, Rode to Hinkel, 25.4.1933.
40 All newspapers, 25.4.1933.
41 Berlin BA, RKK, Rode to Hinkel, 25.4.1933.
42 Ibid., Tietjen; especially summary of 26.5.1933.
43 OfZ, 28.4.1933, 'Was ist, Herr Tietjen?', WW letter to Rust, 28.4.1933.
44 WW to HR, 28.4.1933.
45 WoW, handwritten copy of Boerner to Hinkel, 6.5.1933.
46 LS, 19.5.1933.
47 Ibid., 26.5.1933.

48 WW to HR, 4.6.1933.
49 LS, 2.6.1933.
50 Koblenz BA, Frank papers, NL 1110, n.d.
51 DRWG, radio interview with HT, 1.7.1970.
52 LS, 23.6.1933.
53 Ibid., 30.6.1933.
54 WW to HR, 25.6.1933. AdK, Tietjen papers, statement by Preetorius on Bayerischer Rundfunk radio broadcast, transcript, n.d. (after 1945).
55 RWA, Daniela Thode, *Bayreuth seit 1930*, 5 and 11.
56 LS, 18.9.1932.
57 WoW (see note 1), 68.
58 RWA, ECh to a friend, 19.4.1936.
59 Thode (see note 55), 9.
60 Goebbels diary, 27.6.1933.
61 LS, 30.6.1933.
62 Bayreuth STA, HMB, 31.7.1933.
63 WW memorandum, 23f.
64 RWA, letter of the Transport Office to Fritz Böhner, 17.7.1933.
65 LS, 14.7.1933.
66 Ibid., 6.7.1933.
67 Bayreuth STA, HMB, 31.7.1933.
68 BTb, 20.7.1933, 1.
69 Statement by Wolfgang Wagner.
70 BTb, 22.7.1933.
71 WW film, 129 and 65.
72 WW to HR, 22.7.1933.
73 BTb, 22.7.1933.
74 AH, 22.7.1933, in Max Domarus, *Hitler, Reden und Proklamationen 1932–1945*, Wiesbaden, 1973, 291.
75 BStA, SKA, minutes, 93.
76 OfZ, 27.7.1933.
77 Walter Legge/Elisabeth Schwarzkopf, *Gehörtes, Ungehörtes*, Munich, 1982, 22.
78 LS, 26.7.1933.
79 Goebbels diary, 26. and 27.7.1933.
80 VB, 25.7.1933.
81 Bayreuth STA, HMB of the Town Council, 31.7.1933.
82 Hans Severus Ziegler, *Hitler aus dem Erleben dargestellt*, Göttingen, 1964, 167f.
83 LS reports on the construction work on 23.2.1934.
84 Kindly communicated by Christel Burkert, née Böhner, who was six at the time, while her sister Eva was ten.
85 WW to HR, 30.7.1933.
86 *Fränkisches Volk*, 31.7.1933.
87 Bayreuth STA, Fritz Böhner to the Tourist Information Office, 2.8.1933.
88 Ibid., with thanks to Walter Bartl.
89 Warburg (see note 18), 174, 3.8.1933.
90 Thode (see note 55), 9.
91 Legge/Schwarzkopf (see note 77).

92 BStA, SKA, minutes, 82, statement by Wilhelm Hieber.
93 Berlin BA, R55/1173, 7.12.1933.
94 Preetorius (see note 54).
95 WW memorandum, 24.
96 Ziegler (see note 82), 159.
97 *Stahlhelm-Musik-Zeitung*, 7.10.1933.
98 WW to HR, 5.12.1933.
99 All in BDC Chrambach.
100 BDC, WW to Walter Buch, 30.8.1935.
101 Ibid., acknowledged by the *Gau* office in Saxony, 18.11.1935.
102 BStA, SKA, interrogation, 20.
103 DRWG, Otto Daube, *Begegnungen eines Neunzigjährigen*, typescript, WW to Daube, 9.11.1938.
104 Ibid., 13.11.1938.
105 BStA, SKA, minutes, statement by Emma Louis.
106 Ibid., interrogation of Lydia Beil.
107 WW to HR, 24.3.1933.
108 WW to Gerdy Troost, 17.1.1934.
109 WW to HR, 24.2.1933.
110 BStA, minutes, 77, statement by Ludwig Goebel.
111 Ibid., declaration under oath by Hilde Walther, 1.9.1946.
112 WW to HR, 12.12.1933 and 25.4.1934.
113 *Fränkische Presse*, 2.12.1948.
114 WW memorandum, 42.
115 LS, 3.11.1933.
116 AH, speech, 10.11.1933, in Domarus (see note 74), 330.
117 BTb, 20.7.1933.
118 WW to HR, 21.11.1933.
119 François-Poncet (see note 8), 142f.

9. CONFUSION AROUND *PARSIFAL* (1934–5)

1 WW to HR, 30.7.1933.
2 Michael Karbaum, *Studien zur Geschichte der Bayreuther Festspiele 1876–1976*, Regensburg, 1976, II, 95.
3 LS, 12.1.1934.
4 Basel UB, WW to Adolf Zinsstag, 16.3.1935.
5 WW to HR, 23.10. and 21.11.1933.
6 WW film, 45.
7 Brigitte Hamann, *Hitlers Wien*, Munich/Zurich, 1996, 59ff.
8 WW to Alfred Roller, Berlin, 22.11.1933.
9 LS, 12.1.1934.
10 Ibid., 19.1.1934.
11 Ibid.
12 Berlin BA, Alfred Roller, 'Bericht über die Reise nach Bayreuth und Berlin im Febr. 1934', ms.

13   Hamann (see note 7), 87.
14   Roller (see note 12).
15   Roller, Zinsstag to Roller, April 1934.
16   WW to Ludwig Karpath, in Zdenko von Kraft, *Der Sohn. Siegfried Wagners Leben und Umwelt*, Graz, 1969, 318.
17   LS, 2.3.1934.
18   Ibid.
19   Frankfurt, Deutsches Rundfunkarchiv, 6.3.1934.
20   LS, 9.3.1934.
21   Ibid.
22   WW film, 107.
23   WW to HR, 9.1.1934.
24   Renate W. Schostack, *Hinter Wahnfrieds Mauern*, Hamburg, 1998, 257.
25   LS, 9.3.1934.
26   Ibid., 20.4.1934.
27   Ibid., 14.5. and 9.6.1934.
28   Ibid., 22.6.1934.
29   FV, 12. and 14.5.1934.
30   LS, 9.6.1934.
31   Ibid., 29.6.1934.
32   Heinz Höhne, *Mordsache Röhm*, Hamburg, 1984, 271.
33   Ibid.
34   Hans Frank, *Im Angesicht des Galgens*, Munich, 1953, 149ff.
35   VB, 1.7.1934.
36   *Wiener Zeitung*, 2.7.1934.
37   Höhne (see note 32), 284.
38   BSt, SKA, Maria Sembach, 23.4.1947. She claims that Winifred contacted Hitler's adjutant (Wilhelm) Brückner, whereas it was actually Gauleiter Helmuth Brückner she addressed.
39   Höhne (see note 32), 299.
40   WW, interview with the *Leipziger Tageszeitung*, 20.7.1934.
41   FW, *Nacht über Bayreuth*, Cologne, 3rd edition, 1997, 157f.
42   Ibid., 158f.
43   WW to Gerdy Troost, 1.10.1969.
44   Höhne (see note 32), 293.
45   Communication from Wolfgang Wagner.
46   FW (see note 41), 157.
47   WW film, 76f.
48   WW to Walter Hermann, 1.5.1976.
49   Bella Fromm, *Als Hitler mir die Hand küsste*, Hamburg, 1993, 274f.
50   Paul Bülow in the *Fränkisches Volk*, 24.7.1934.
51   LS, 23.7.1934.
52   Helge Rosvaenge, *Lache Bajazzo*, Munich, n.d. (1953), 47.
53   Communication from Alfred Roller's son Dietrich Roller, March 1998.
54   LS, 23.7.1934.
55   Kraft (see note 16), 319, WW to Karpath, n.d.
56   RWA, 'Das Schicksal der Bayreuther Festspiele', Zinsstag to WW, 18.4.1935.
57   VB, 24.7.1934.

58 WW to Hermann Ernst, 2.1.1971.
59 LS, 27.7.1940.
60 FW (see note 41), 159f.
61 Franz von Papen, *Der Wahrheit eine Gasse*, Munich, 1952, 381.
62 LS, 10.8.1934.
63 Thomas Mann, *Tagebücher*, ed. by Peter de Mendelssohn, Frankfurt a.M., 1978, 9.8.1934.
64 Frankfurt Deutsches Rundfunkarchiv, WW, interview with a broadcast of the *Ring*, 10.8.1934.
65 LS, 1.8.1934.
66 LS, 9.8.1934.
67 Mann (see note 63), 21.8.1934.
68 LS, 17.8.1934.
69 *Leipziger Tageszeitung*, 20.7.1934, interview with WW.
70 Bayreuth STA, HMB, 4.8.1934.
71 NTh, FW, 'The Inside Story of how Hitler raised a Billion Marks for his War', typescript.
72 WoW, *Lebens-Akte*, Munich, 1994, 80.
73 Schostack (see note 24), 125.
74 Berlin BA, BDC.
75 WW memorandum, 30.
76 BStA, SKA, statement by Lydia Beil, 84.
77 WW to HR, 25.12.1934.
78 Stiftsarchiv Heiligengrabe, 'Chronik', 444.
79 WW to HR, 2.4.1937.
80 WW memorandum, 24.
81 Stiftsarchiv Heiligengrabe, 'Chronik', 435f. and 442.
82 Ibid., 438 and 440f.
83 Ibid., 442 (WW to Kube), 2.9.1934.
84 Ibid., 444, WW.
85 Ibid., 447.
86 RWA, FW to her aunts, 9.8.1937.
87 WW to HR, 12.12.1934.
88 Goebbels diary, 25.12.1934.
89 Ibid., 2.3.1935.
90 WW to HR, 14.5.1935.
91 Wilhelm Furtwängler, *Briefe*, ed. by Frank Thiess, Wiesbaden, 1965, 81.
92 *Richard Strauss/Clemens Krauss Briefwechsel*, ed. by Günter Brosche, Tutzing, 1997, 191.
93 Ibid., 211, 15.11.1935.
94 Berlin BA, RKK, 23.11.1935.
95 WW to HR, 25.12.1934.
96 WW to AH, 26.12.1934, in Beatrice and Helmut Heiber (eds.), *Die Rückseite des Hakenkreuzes*, Munich, 1993, 14.
97 LS, 2.11.1934.
98 WW to HR, 10.10.1934.
99 WoW, (see note 72), 71.
100 WW to HR, 14.4.1935.

101 LS, 12.3.1935.
102 WW to HR, 14.3.1935.
103 LS, 12.3.1935.
104 WW to HR, 14.3.1935.
105 LS, 12.3.1935.
106 Coburg StA, SKA, Deubzer.
107 LS, 17. and 12.3.1935.
108 Paul Schmidt, *Statist auf diplomatischer Bühne*, Vienna, 1953, 307.
109 LS, 12.3.1935.
110 Hans Severus Ziegler, *Adolf Hitler aus dem Leben dargestellt*, Göttingen, 1964, 179.
111 Schmidt (see note 108), 308.
112 Ziegler (see note 110), 308.
113 WW to HR, 5.4.1935.
114 BStA, SKA, minutes, 49, statement by Deubzer.
115 Jonathan and Catherine Guinness, *The House of Mitford*, London, 1984, 109, 369 and 375.
116 WW to HR, 26.4.1935.
117 Ibid., 21.7.1935.
118 Albert Speer, *Spandauer Tagebücher*, Frankfurt a. M., 1975, 154f.
119 FW (see note 41), 305.
120 WW to HR, 10.9.1935.
121 Helmut Paulus, 'Die "Reichskristallnacht"', in the *Archiv für Geschichte von Oberfranken*, 1998, 428f.
122 LS, 11.10.1935.
123 WW to HR, 8.3.1935.
124 Fritz Kempfler, 'Lebenserinnerungen', typescript, 83.
125 BStA, SKA, minutes, 47, statement by Deubzer.
126 Ibid., 68, statement by Konrad Pöhner.
127 WW memorandum, 51.
128 AH, MK, 127.
129 Statement by Verena Lafferentz, July 2000.
130 WW memorandum, 32.
131 Fritz Wiedemann, *Der Mann, der Feldherr werden wollte*, Velbert, 1964, 71f.
132 BOm, 15.10.1935.
133 RWA, Fritz Böhner, 18.10.1935.
134 Ibid., Gauverlag, 15.1.1936.
135 WW film, 121.
136 Lotte Warburg, *Eine vollkommene Närrin durch meine ewigen Gefühle*, Bayreuth, 1989, 17.7.1936.
137 WW to HR, 9.7.1935.
138 LS, 23.10.1935.
139 WW to HR, 3.1. (1936); see Goebbels diary, 1.1.1936: 'the Wagners are here'.
140 Joachim Fest, *Albert Speer*, Berlin, 1999, 487.
141 WW film, 72.
142 LS, 8.5.1936.
143 Statement by Verena Lafferentz, June 2001.
144 LS, 8.5.1936.

145 WW memorandum, 20.
146 AH, *Monologe im Führerhauptquartier 1941–1944*, ed. by Werner Jochmann, Hamburg, 1980, 28.2./1.3.1942, 308.
147 Berlin, BA, RKK, R55/20172.

10. *LOHENGRIN* AND THE 'THOUSAND-YEAR REICH' (1936–8)

1   *Bayreuther Tagblatt*, 20.7.1936.
2   BOm, 18./19.7.1936.
3   Bayreuth STA, HMB, 4.8.1936.
4   LS, 24.7.1936.
5   WW film, 273.
6   WW (IfZ, ZS 2242), March 1971.
7   BOm, 28.7.1941.
8   Thomas Mann, *Tagebücher*, ed. by Peter de Mendelssohn, Frankfurt a. M., 1978, 16.7.1936.
9   Christa Schroeder, *Er war mein Chef*, Munich, 1985, 277.
10 Statement by Wolfgang Wagner, February 1998.
11 Goebbels diary, 25.7.1936.
12 According to an eyewitness, Dr Dieter Starck.
13 And of Bodo Lafferentz, according to a statement by his widow, Verena.
14 Goebbels diary, 27. and 28.7.1936.
15 WW film, 61.
16 Berta Geissmar, *Taktstock und Schaftstiefel*, Cologne, 1996, 265.
17 Ibid., 253.
18 Ibid., 265 and 241.
19 Ibid., 264 and 266.
20 Ibid., 268 and 265.
21 Goebbels diary, 19. and 20.6.1936.
22 Bella Fromm, *Als Hitler mir die Hand küsste*, Hamburg, 1993, 272.
23 LS, 8.5.1936.
24 NTh, FW, manuscript for radio, n.d. (1940).
25 WW to HR, 8.3.1935.
26 FW, *Nacht über Bayreuth*, Cologne, 3rd edition, 1997, 310.
27 AH, speech, 9.9.1936, in Max Domarus, *Hitler, Reden und Proklamationen 1932–1945*, Wiesbaden, 1973, 637f.
28 WW to HR, 11.9.1936.
29 Goebbels diary, 14.11.1936.
30 WW to HR, 23.11.1936.
31 GSt, 13.11.1940.
32 Ibid., 17.6.1941, statement by Kurt Overhoff.
33 Ibid., 27.8.1941.
34 WW to HR, 28.3.1936.
35 NTh, HT to FW, 24.11.1936.
36 Ibid.
37 WW to Wolfgang Hermann, 1.5.1976
38 NTh, HT to FW, 24.11.1936.

39 WW to HR, 29.1.1938.
40 Statement by Lieselott Tietjen, 1999.
41 WW to HR, 28.3.1936.
42 Ibid., 25.12.1936.
43 WoW, AH to WW, no date or place given, copied out in 1945 by WW for the CIC.
44 LS, 29.1.1937.
45 BStA, SKA, minutes, 47, statement by Wolfgang Deubzer.
46 NTh, LS to FW, Bayreuth, 24.2.1938.
47 BStA, SKA, minutes, statement by Deubzer.
48 Ibid., WW to Heinrich Himmler, 8.5.1938.
49 Ibid., WW to AH, 8.5.1938.
50 Ibid., minutes, 48, interrogation of Deubzer.
51 Ibid., 541f., statement by Körber.
52 Ibid., interrogation of Deubzer.
53 Ibid., WW list of defence witnesses.
54 Maria-Elisabeth Ranft, 'Eva Hauptmann zum 100 Geburtstag'. Programme of a memorial concert on 27.11.1994, Hochschule für Musik, Hamburg.
55 BStA, SKA, statement by Paul Ottenheimer.
56 Frida Leider, *Das war mein Teil*, Berlin, 1981, 168.
57 BStA, SKA, minutes, statement by Konrad Pöhner.
58 WW to HR, 2.11.1937.
59 Goebbels diary, 3.7.1937.
60 BStA, SKA, 3.9.1946, to the CIC, copy.
61 *Fränkische Presse*, 2.12.1948, WW appeal court hearings.
62 BStA, SKA.
63 WW to HR, 2.11.1936.
64 Goebbels diary, 29.7.1937.
65 Ibid., 27. and 29.7.1937.
66 BStA, SKA, letter from the *Land* bishop of the Thuringian Protestant church, 22.3.1946.
67 14.5.1938, Nike Wagner's copy.
68 WW to HR, 2.11.1936.
69 LS, 7.2.1936.
70 WW to Gerdy Troost, 8.9.1975.
71 WoW, Bayreuth, 4.7.1939, to Albert Wetzel.
72 This and following information from Berlin BA, R55/264, 12.6.1937.
73 Goebbels diary, 23.6.1937.
74 LS, 29.6.1937.
75 WW to HR, 17.6.1937.
76 LS, 2.7.1937.
77 GSt, 14.11.1946.
78 AdK, N. Tietjen, Preetorius interview, Bayerischer Rundfunk, after 1945.
79 RWA, FW to the aunts, 9.8.1937.
80 WW to HR, 8.11.1937.
81 Bayreuth STA, situation report by the mayor, 1.8.1937.
82 Hans Severus Ziegler, *Adolf Hitler aus dem Leben dargestellt*, Göttingen, 1964, 157.
83 Goebbels diary, 26.7.1937.

84 LS, 28.7.1937.
85 Communication from Gertrud Rosvaenge.
86 Goebbels diary, 11.11.1937.
87 AdK, Tietjen, Preetorius to HT, 3.7.1947.
88 Fred A. Prieberg, *Kraftprobe*, Wiesbaden, 1986, 291, HT to FW, 16.11.(1937).
89 WW, 4.5.1976.
90 Goebbels diary, 24.7.1937.
91 Arno Breker, *Im Strahlungsfeld der Ereignisse*, Preussisch-Oldendorf, 1972, 134.
92 IfZ, ZS 2242, WW, 13.3.1971.
93 Goebbels diary, 25.7.1937.
94 WoW, *Lebens-Akte*, Munich, 1994, 76.
95 BOm, 26.7.1937.
96 BTb, 26.7.1937.
97 Beatrice and Helmut Heiber (eds.), *Die Rückseite des Hakenkreuzes*, Munich, 1993, 40–45.
98 Goebbels diary, 26.7.1937.
99 Albert Speer, *Spandauer Tagebücher*, Frankfurt a. M., 1975, 144ff.
100 Kempfler, 'Erinnerungen', typescript, 123.
101 WW film, 69ff.
102 All in LS, 22.8.1937.
103 Ziegler (see note 82), 176f.
104 WW to Weckherlin, 9.6.1976.
105 WW to HR, 11.9.1937.
106 WW to Albert Knittel, 15.9.1937.
107 WW to HR, 15.9.1937.
108 AH, *Monologe im Führerhauptquartier 1941–1944*, ed. by Werner Jochmann, Hamburg , 1980, 225, 24./25.1.1942.
109 Max Domarus, *Mussolini und Hitler*, Würzburg, 1977, 212.
110 WW to HR, 8.10.1937.
111 Goebbels diary, 23.10.1937.
112 Ibid., 3.11.1937.
113 Prieberg (see note 88), 289, Wilhelm Furtwängler to WW, 15.11.1937.
114 Goebbels diary, 20. and 27.11.1937.
115 WW to HR, 10.12.1937.
116 WoW to HR, 27.11.1937.
117 Coburg StA, SKA, Treuter, statement by WW, 11.9.1946.
118 WW to HR, 10.12.1937.
119 BStA, SKA, minutes, 50, statement by Deubzer.
120 WW to HR, 29.1.1938.
121 Statement by Betty Weiss, née Steinlein, October 2001.
122 LS, 11.3.1938.
123 Ibid., 14.3.1938.
124 WW to HR, 24.3.1938.
125 LS, 24.3.1938.
126 Ibid., 10.4.1938.

11. TOWARDS WAR (1938–9)

1 WW to HR, 29.1.1934.
2 Bayreuth STA, WW to Margarethe Strauss, 6.7.1932.
3 WW to Albert Knittel, 19.8.1935.
4 Purchase price mentioned in WW to HR, 12.10.1930.
5 *Cosima Wagner/Richard Strauss Briefwechsel*, ed. by Franz Trenner, Tutzing, 1978, 296 and 300, 27.4.1933 and 4.8.1934.
6 WW to HR, 2.4.1937.
7 HT to Knittel, 25.11.1935.
8 WW to Gerdy Troost, 24.1.1969.
9 According to matching statements by Wolfgang Wagner, Verena Lafferentz and Knittel's granddaughter Countess Verena von Rittberg, August 1999.
10 WW to HR, 14.4.1938.
11 Ibid., 21.4.1938.
12 Ibid., 26.4.1938.
13 WW to Troost, 24.1.1969.
14 Knittel to Max Wiskott, 23.8.1937.
15 FW, *Nacht über Bayreuth*, Cologne, 3rd edition, 1997, 297f.
16 WW to HR, 7.7.1938.
17 Ibid., 16.1.1938, from Bordighera.
18 WW to 'my dear both of you', 14.5.1938, Nike Wagner's copy.
19 Boblenz BA, Neue Reichskanzlei, WW to Martin Bormann.
20 WW to HR, 7.7.1938.
21 Michael Karbaum, *Studien zur Geschichte der Bayreuther Festspiel (1876–1976)*, Regensburg, 1976, 119f.
22 WW to HR, 29.12.1932.
23 Vienna ThM, N. Bahr-Mildenburg, Bayreuth, 6.9.1938.
24 GSt, 6.11.1946.
25 Ibid., 27.3.1947.
26 Autograph catalogue of Hauswedell & Nolte, May 1999, No. 2186, WW, SW, Helena Wallem to Anna Jacobson et al.
27 WW to Knittel, 16.9.1935.
28 BStA, SKA, Otto Strobel, 30.11.1948.
29 Ibid., minutes, 21, evidence from Bernhard Erkelenz.
30 Ibid., Bormann, 25.4.1938.
31 WoW, WW to Bormann. 30.4.1938.
32 Heinz Boberach (ed.), *Meldungen aus dem Reich 1938–1945*, Herrsching, 1984, 117.
33 WW memorandum, 35.
34 Hans Severus Ziegler, *Adolf Hitler aus dem Erleben dargestellt*, Göttingen, 1964, 171.
35 WW to HR, 8.10.1937; similarly to Knittel, 29.9.1937.
36 Lucerne STA, Adolf Zinsstag to Landolt, 5.5.1938.
37 WW to HR, 7.7.1938.
38 WW to WieW and WoW, 14.5.1938, Nike Wagner's copy.
39 Fritz Kempfler, 'Lebenserinnerungen', typescript, 87.
40 FW, *Nacht über Bayreuth*, Cologne, 3rd edition, 1997, 310.

41 Kempfler (see note 39), 92.
42 Ibid., 93.
43 Ibid., 94.
44 WW to HR, 3.8.1938.
45 Bernd Mayer, 'Ärzte-Affäre', in *Heimat-Kurier Bayreuth*, 3.1997.
46 Goebbels diary, 26.7.1938.
47 Berlin BA, BDC, Heinz Tietjen file, statement by Franz Stassen, 14.10.1946.
48 Kempfler (see note 39), 98.
49 WW film, 130.
50 Kempfler (see note 39), 97.
51 Nicole Casanova, *Isolde 1939. Germaine Lubin*, Paris, 1974, 139f. and 153.
52 Berlin BA, BDC.
53 WW to HR, 26.4.1938.
54 FW (see note 40), 306f.
55 Jonathan and Catherine Guinness, *The House of Mitford*, London, 1948, 416.
56 WW to Hermann Ernst, 2.11.1971.
57 HT to Gertrud Beckel, n.d. (after 1947).
58 Frida Leider, *Das war mein Teil*, Berlin, 1981, 170f.
59 HT to Gertrud Beckel, n.d. (after 1947).
60 RWA, FW to her aunts, 14.9.1938.
61 Lucerne STA, Daniela Thode to Adolf Zinsstag, 28.9.1938.
62 WW to HR, 28.9.1938.
63 Joint declaration of 30.9.1938.
64 Nevile Henderson, *Wasser unter den Brücken*, Zurich, 1949, 314.
65 WW to HR, 10.10.1938.
66 RWA, FW to ECh, 10.10.1938.
67 Helmut Paulus, 'Die "Reichskristallnacht"', in *Archiv für die Geschichte von Oberfranken*, 1998, 404f.
68 Kempfler (see note 39), 87 and 112.
69 Paulus (see note 67), 408f.
70 Mayer (see note 45), 42.
71 Rabbi Josef Gothart, 9.11.1988.
72 Kempfler (see note 39), 87.
73 WoW, *Lebens-Akte*, Munich, 1994, 77.
74 Paulus (see note 67), 440 and 430f.
75 Richard Strauss to HT, 17.12.1938 and 9.1.1939, in Dagmar Wünsche, 'Richard Strauss und Heinz Tietjen', *Richard Strauss-Blätter*, Tützing, 1980.
76 Paulus (see note 67), 434f.
77 Thomas Mann, *Tagebücher*, ed. by Peter de Mendelssohn, Frankfurt a. M., 1978, 25.7.1939.
78 Klaus Pringsheim Jr/Victor Boesen, *Wer zum Teufel sind Sie?*, Bonn, 1995, 281.
79 Wien ThM, Roller papers, Nussdorf, n.d.
80 Ziegler (see note 34), 185.
81 Kempfler (see note 39), 91.
82 IfZ, ZS 2238, Henriette von Schirach, 28.7.1986.
83 WW to Albert Speer, 17.9.1973.
84 Compiled by Otto Strobel, 1.10.1951, Nike Wagner's copy.
85 Albert Speer, *Spandauer Tagebücher*, Frankfurt a. M., 1975, 157.

86 IfZ, ZS 2238, Schirach.
87 VB, 27.7.1939.
88 AdK, Tietjen papers, typescript of a Preetorius interview with the Bayerischer Rundfunk, n.d.
89 BOm, 27.7.1939.
90 BTb, 2.8.1939; front cover title 'Japan's Position in the Pacific'.
91 Speer (see note 85), 165.
92 Kempfler (see note 39), 128.
93 Arno Breker, *Im Strahlungsfeld der Ereignisse*, Preussisch Oldendorf, 1972, 235.
94 VB, 27.7.1939.
95 Kempfler (see note 39), 127.
96 Ibid., 124.
97 Statement by Verena Lafferentz, 1999.
98 Ibid., June 2001.
99 Otto Dietrich, *12 Jahre mit Hitler*, Munich, 1955, 59f.
100 Henderson (see note 64), 309.
101 Berlin BA, BDC, Tietjen file, statement by Stassen, 14.10.1946.
102 BStA, SKA, CIC interrogation, 14.9.1946.
103 Nevile Henderson, *Failure of a Mission*, London, 1940, 241.
104 Dietrich (see note 99), 58.
105 BTb, 30.7.1939.
106 VB, 26.7.1925.
107 Kempfler (see note 39), 126.
108 Ibid.
109 Brigitte Hamann, *Hitlers Wien*, Munich/Zurich, 1996, 195ff.
110 August Kubizek, *Adolf Hitler. Mein Jugendfreund*, Graz, 1953, 338–43.
111 Speer (see note 85), 136.
112 BOm, 17.8.1939.
113 NTh, WW to FW, 10.9.1939.
114 RW, FW to her aunts, 6.6.1937.
115 Ibid., 4.4. and 12.2.1938.
116 Ibid., 4.10.1937.
117 WW to HR, 29.1.1938.
118 FW (see note 40), 294.
119 RWA, letters, FW to her aunts, WW to Daniela Thode.
120 Communication from Verena Lafferentz, November 1998.
121 NTh, WW to FW, 10.9.1939.
122 WoW, Christian Ebersberger, 'Three generations in Villa Wahnfried', Supplement, 4.
123 *Neue Zürcher Zeitung*, 1.9.1939, 1.
124 WW memorandum, 18.
125 WW film, 83.
126 John Russell, *Erich Kleiber*, Munich, n.d. (1959), 205.
127 Kempfler (see note 39), 130.
128 WW to Troost, 7.12.1962.
129 WoW (see note 73), 109.
130 Statement WoW, January 2000.
131 Communication from Rudolf Pfeiffer.

12. WARTIME FESTIVALS (1940–42)

1   WW to Trudi Beckel, 8.9.1939.
2   Ibid., 21.9.1939.
3   Related in WoW, *Lebens-Akte*, Munich, 1994, 110f.
4   NTh, WW to FW, 7.10.1939.
5   Ibid., Berlin, 10.10.1939.
6   Ibid., 10.9.1939.
7   WW film, 96.
8   NTh, WW to FW, 6.1.1940.
9   WW to Trudi Beckel, letter of thanks, 25.12.1939.
10   Ibid., n.d. (1940).
11   NTh, WW to FW, 25.1.1940.
12   Ibid., WieW to FW, 26.1.1940.
13   Lucerne StA, Adolf Zinsstag to FW, 6.2.1940.
14   FW, *Nacht über Bayreuth*, Cologne, 3rd edition, 1997, 326.
15   NTh, WW to FW, Berlin, 31.1.1940.
16   FW (see note 14), 333. FW wrote her memoirs in collaboration with the American journalist Page Cooper, as anti-Hitler propaganda; hence the facts were often distorted.
17   Ibid., 335.
18   NTh, FW to WW, 29.2.1940; copy.
19   Ibid., 18.3.1940; copy.
20   Ibid., WW to FW, 5.7.1947.
21   Lucerne STA, WW to Jakob Zimmerli, 27.3.1940.
22   Fritz Kempfler, 'Lebenserinnerungen', typescript, 89.
23   NTh, FW, ms. in the original German.
24   Ibid., FW, 'A Sex-Murderer Teaches Hitler', ms. for radio talk, n.d. (1940?).
25   WW film, 96.
26   Goebbels diary, 6.6.1940.
27   BStA, SKA, Karl Brandt to WW, 31.1.1947.
28   Statement by Verena Lafferentz, November 1988.
29   *Fränkische Presse*, 2.12.1948, WW to de-nazification court.
30   GSt, 20.5.1942.
31   Philipp Hausser, *Die Geschichte eines Hauses*, Bayreuth, 1963, 95.
32   BStA, SKA.
33   Ibid., statement by Philipp Hausser.
34   Hausser (see note 31), 95.
35   DRWG, Otto Daube, 'Begegnungen eines Neunzigjährigen', typescript, 446.
36   Heinz Boberach (ed.), *Meldungen aus dem Reich 1938–1945*, Herrsching, 1984, 644, 15.1.1940.
37   BStA, SKA, WW to HT, 6.1.1940.
38   WW memorandum, 27.
39   WW film, 63.
40   Berlin BA, DFA, 'Archiv der Persönlichkeiten', Winifred Wagner, 10.7.1943.
41   WW memorandum, 27f.
42   WW to Gertrud Beckel, 9.5.1940.
43   BStA, SKA, interrogation of WW, 90f.

44   GSt, 1.8.1941.
45   Ibid.
46   BStA, SKA, report by Wilhelm Hieber, 2.12.1948.
47   Vienna ThM, Roller papers, 10.6.1940.
48   GSt, 2.9.1940.
49   Address by Tietjen to colleagues at the beginning of rehearsals on 31.6.1940; 1.7.1940 according to BOm.
50   GSt, 7.7.1940.
51   Kempfler (see note 22), 134.
52   WW film, 67.
53   BOm, 18.7.1940.
54   Ibid., 23.7.1940.
55   GSt, 19.7.1940.
56   Ibid., 23.7.1940.
57   BStA, SKA, minutes, 48ff. Statement by Wolfgang Deubzer.
58   WW to Germaine Lubin, 12.10.1940, in Nicole Casanova, *Isolde 1939. Germaine Lubin*, Paris, 1974, 166.
59   WW film, 208.
60   First-hand account from Verena Lafferentz, June 2000.
61   Hans Severus Ziegler, *Adolf Hitler aus dem Erleben dargestellt*, Göttingen, 1964, 179.
62   GSt, 13.1.1941. The letter was addressed to Theodor Uhlig's widow.
63   August Kubizek, *Adolf Hitler. Mein Jugendfreund*, Graz, 1953, 345ff.
64   Berta Geissmar, *Taktstock und Schaftstiefel*, Cologne, 1996, 344.
65   WW memorandum, 51.
66   Ibid., 43.
67   BStA, SKA, WW for CIC, 3.9.1946.
68   WW to HR, 1.3.1944.
69   GSt, 17.2.1940.
70   Ibid., 13.11.1940 and 1.1.1941.
71   Ibid., 13.1.1941.
72   WW to HR, 27.2.1943.
73   Goebbels diary, 1.4.1941.
74   GSt, 27.4.1941.
75   Kempfler (see note 22), 140.
76   GSt, 30.4.1941.
77   WW to Troost, 3.3.1963.
78   Arno Breker, *Im Strahlungsfeld der Ereignisse*, Preussisch Oldendorf, 1972, 148.
79   WW to Troost, 17.11.1971.
80   BOm, 26./27.7.1941.
81   Ilse Hess, *Ein Schicksal in Briefen*, Leoni (1952), Rudolf to Ilse Hess, 31.7.1949.
82   Goebbels diary, 13.5.1941.
83   WW to Ilse Hess, 11.11.1952.
84   WW to unknown correspondent, 14.5.1941, Nike Wagner's copy.
85   BStA, SKA, letter from E. Caspari, 15.4.1947.
86   Ibid., 31.3.1947.
87   Communication from Verena Lafferentz.
88   Reinhold P. Kuhnert, 'Geschichte der "Hans Schemm-Gartenstadt"', in Vol. 80 of the 'Historischer Verein für Oberfranken', 434.

89 Albert Speer, *Spandauer Tagebücher*, Frankfurt a. M., 1975, 156.
90 Boberach (see note 36), 2533.
91 GSt, 29., 30.6. and 1.7.1941.
92 Ibid., 15. and 16.7.1941.
93 Goebbels diary, 26.7.1941.
94 Kempfler (see note 22), 140f.
95 BOm, 16.7.1941.
96 GSt, 3.1.1940 and 1.8.1941.
97 Ibid., 11.10.1941.
98 Ibid., 1.12.1941.
99 Ibid., 9.12.1941 and 6.2.1942.
100 Vienna, Archiv der Republik, directorate of the State Opera, letter of 23.10.1940.
101 Statement by Roller's brother, Professor Dietrich Roller, March 1998.
102 IfZ, ZS 2242, WW, 13.3.1971.
103 AH, *Monologe im Führerhauptquartier 1941–1944*, ed. by Werner Jochmann, Hamburg, 1980, 295, 24.2.1942.
104 Goebbels diary, 20.3.1942.
105 Vienna ThM, Roller papers, n.d. (January 1942).
106 Ibid., 13.6.1939 and n.d. (January 1942).
107 Max Domarus, *Hitler, Reden und Proklamationen 1932–1945*, Wiesbaden, 1973, 1799f.
108 GSt, 4.12.1941.
109 AH (see note 103), 225, 24./25.1.1942.
110 Speer (see note 89), 156.
111 AH (see note 103), 308, 28.2./1.3.1942.
112 Communication from Marlene von Exner, 1995.
113 Kurt Overhoff, 'Neu-Bayreuth', in *Staatsbriefe 6–7*, Munich, 1991, 31.
114 Renate W. Schostack, *Hinter Wahnfrieds Mauern*, Hamburg, 1998, 176.
115 WoW, HT, 21.8.1941.
116 GSt, 19.6.1941.
117 Ibid., 1.8.1941.
118 Ibid., 19.7.1941.
119 Overhoff (see note 113), 30ff.
120 GSt, 17.8.1941.
121 Overhoff (see note 113), 32.
122 GSt, 24.8.1941.
123 Statement by Gertrud Rosvaenge, August 1999.
124 WW film, 101.
125 Berlin BA, RKK, Tietjen, supplement to SKA.
126 WoW, HT, 21.8.1941, also statement by Hofmann in Berlin BA, RKK, Tietjen file.
127 Overhoff (see note 113), 32.
128 Berlin BA, RKK, Tietjen, 14.3.1947.
129 Statement by Trudi Beckel, to whom HT told this a few days later.
130 Berlin BA RKK, statutory declaration, 1.3.1947.
131 GSt, 25.12.1941.
132 Frankfurt, Deutsches Rundfunkarchiv.

133 NTh, SS-Oberführer A. I. Berndt to WW, 20.2.1942 and 1.3.1942.
134 Goebbels diary, 23.11.1942.
135 WW to HR, 29.1.1942.
136 WW to AH, 12.2.1942, Nike Wagner's copy.
137 Goebbels diary, 24.12.1941.
138 Munich BSA, SKA, minutes, 81, auditor Wilhelm Hieber, 2.12.1948.
139 GSt, 5. and 9.3.1942.
140 Ibid., 23.3.1942.
141 Ibid.
142 WW memorandum, 24.
143 Goebbels diary, 21.7.1936 and 22.11.1941.
144 GSt, 9.4.1942.
145 Ibid., 25.12.1941.
146 Ibid., 15.6.1942.
147 Ibid., 9.4 and 15.6.1942.
148 Henry Picker, *Hitlers Tischgespräche*, Frankfurt a. M., 1951, 372, 10.6.1942.
149 GSt, 26.6.1942.
150 Ibid., 1.7.1942.
151 Munich BSA, SKA, minutes, 28.
152 GSt, 1.7.1942.
153 BOm, 13.8.1942.
154 DRWG, Lt. M. A. Schuch, 'Eindrücke und Erlebnisse meiner Bayreuth-Fahrt im 3. Kriegsjahr 1942', 11f.
155 BOm, 17.8.1942.
156 Lotte Warburg, *Eine vollkommene Närrin durch meine ewigen Gefühle*, Bayreuth, 1989, 330f., 17.7.1942.
157 GSt, 25.8.1942.
158 Schostack (see note 114), 191.
159 GSt, 9.1.1943.
160 Ibid., 29.10.1942.
161 Goebbels diary, 24.11.1942.
162 Ibid., 8.12.1942.
163 GSt, 17.12.1942.
164 Emil Preetorius to Thomas Mann, 10.6.1946, in Hans Wysling, 'Aus dem Briefwechsel Thomas Mann–Emil Preetorius', in *Blätter der Thomas Mann-Gesellschaft*, Zurich, 1963, No. 4, 14f.
165 IfZ, Amt Musik Dr Gk/Lu Berlin, 8.2.1943, confidential note on file relating to Preetorius, MA 45, files of the Reich directorate, 1942–5.

13. THE LONG ENDING (1943–5)

1 Helmut Paulus, 'Die "Reichskristallnacht"', in Archiv für Geschichte von Oberfranken, 1998, 451.
2 Hübschmann, Paulus, and Pokorny, *Physische und behördliche Gewalt*, Bayreuth, 2000, 220f.
3 Paulus (see note 1), 446.
4 WW memorandum, 41f.

5 BStA, SKA, minutes, 90.
6 Elsa Bernstein, *Das Leben als Drama. Erinnerungen an Theresienstadt*, Dortmund, 1999, 174.
7 Ruth Bondy, 'Prominent auf Widerruf', in *Theresienstädter Studien und Dokumente*, Prague, 1995, 139.
8 Bernstein (see note 6), 58.
9 WW memorandum, 37.
10 Bondy (see note 7), 140.
11 BStA, SKA, minutes, 61–4, interrogation of Paul and Susi Ottenheimer.
12 Ibid.
13 WW memorandum, 42f.
14 Helene Grandel-Winternitz to WW, WW memorandum, 39f.
15 Statement of WW at the Kempfler trial, with thanks to Gerdi Kempfler.
16 Information from Klaus von Schirach, December 2000.
17 WW memorandum, 19.
18 Communication from Richard and Dr Franz Strauss, Garmisch-Partenkirchen, November 2000.
19 Vienna Jewish Museum, WW to Melanie Adler, 17.1.1941, with thanks to Nikolaus Vielmetti.
20 Vienna STLA, account of the estate of Professor Guido Adler. Report of valuer Carl Borufka, 19.6.1941.
21 WW memorandum, 36.
22 Vienna Dokumentationsarchiv für den Österreichischen Widerstand, Rudolf von Ficker, 22.10.1945.
23 Ibid., statement by Ficker.
24 Vienna STLA, witness statement pertaining to Melanie Adler's death certificate, by the language teacher Carola Fischmann, who survived the war by going underground.
25 BStA, SKA, WW to CIC, 3.9.1946.
26 Fritzler Kempfler, 'Lebenserinnerungen', typescript, 139.
27 WW memorandum, 13 and 64.
28 Henriette von Schirach, *Der Preis der Herrlichkeit*, Wiesbaden, 1956, 220ff.
29 Hans Baur, *Ich flog Mächtige der Erde*, Kempten, 1956, 136.
30 Kempfler (see note 26), 88.
31 WW to HR, 29.1.1944.
32 Communication from his widow Eva W., née Pöhner.
33 Kempfler (see note 26), 142 and 155.
34 GSt, 22.1.1943 and 3.2.1943.
35 Heinz Boberach (ed.), *Meldungen aus dem Reich 1938–1945*, Herrsching, 1984, 4208.
36 WW to HR, 22.2.1943.
37 WW film, 180.
38 WW to HR, 15.3.1943.
39 WW to AH, 8.3.1943, Nike Wagner's copy.
40 GSt, 21.3.1943.
41 BDtA, SKA, minutes, 64ff., interrogation of Willi and Betty Wagner.
42 Kurt Overhoff, 'Neu-Bayreuth', in *Staatsbriefe 6–7*, Munich, 1991, 32.
43 Statement by Verena Lafferentz, June 2000.

44 Hans Severus Ziegler, *Hitler aus dem Erleben dargestellt*, Göttingen, 1964, 173.
45 Overhoff (see note 42), 32f.
46 Geoffrey Skelton, *Wieland Wagner, the Positive Sceptic*, New York, 1971, 71.
47 WoW to HR and August Roesener, 20.4.1943.
48 WW to HR, 15.5.1943.
49 Ibid., 22.2.1943.
50 GSt, 17. and 20.5.1943.
51 WW to HR, 22.2.1943.
52 Ibid., 15.5.1943.
53 Obb. Liebel to WW, 3.3.1943, Nike Wagner.
54 Bayreuth STA, reference point 'Residents Bureau 1947', with thanks to Christine Bartholomäus.
55 WW to Trudi Beckel, 28.6.1943.
56 GSt, 11.2.1943.
57 Elisabeth Furtwängler, *Über Wilhelm Furtwängler*, Wiesbaden, 1979, 1943.
58 GSt, 11.2.1943.
59 Ibid., 12. and 14.8.1943.
60 Richard Wilhelm Stock, *Richard Wagner und seine Meistersinger*, Nuremberg, 1943, Preface and 11. The book was a reprint of the souvenir copy given to guests at the Nazi party rally in 1938, but now on poor-quality wartime paper, and with political welcoming speeches added.
61 Boberach (see note 35), 5807ff.
62 Berlin BA, DFA, 'Archiv der Persönlichkeiten', Winifred Wagner.
63 Georg Marischka, 'Erinnerungen', ms., n.d., with thanks to Nicole Marischka.
64 Communication from Georg Marischka, survivor of a variety of prisons in Hitler Germany.
65 Michael Karbaum, *Studien zur Geschichte der Bayreuther Festspiele (1876–1976)*, Regensburg, 1976, 121.
66 Ibid., 122f., Goebbels to Lammers, 19.11.1943.
67 Ibid., 123, Rust to Lammers, 18.3.1944.
68 Ibid., note on Lammers file, 29.4.1944.
69 NTh, WW to FW, 7.4.1946.
70 WW to HR, 11.12.1943.
71 Ibid., 15.11.1943.
72 Ibid., 21.11.1943.
73 Berlin BDC, Lafferentz file.
74 BStA, SKA, minutes, 73ff. and 137.
75 WW memorandum, 31f.
76 WW to HR, 7.1.1943.
77 Ibid., 16.3. and 7.2.1944.
78 WW memorandum, 63.
79 WW to HR, 7.1.1944.
80 WW to Fritz Kempfler, RW-Frauenverband and Bayreuther Bund, 12.2.1944, Nike Wagner's copy.
81 Kempfler (see note 26), 160.
82 Ibid., 162.
83 WW to HR, 28.2.1944.

84 WW memorandum, 56f.
85 Bamberg StA, 30, weekly report of the *Kreis* office to the office of the Bayreuth Gauleiter, 10.8.1944.
86 DRWG, Otto Daube, 'Begegnungen eines Neunzigjährigen', typescript, 450.
87 WW to Gerdy Troost, 21.10.1977.
88 Kempfler (see note 26), 162.
89 Nicole Casanova, *Isolde 1939. Germaine Lubin*, Paris, 1974, 211.
90 WW to Troost, 3.3.1963.
91 Casanova (see note 89), 155, after interviewing WW, *c.* 1973.
92 WW to HR, 17.1.1944.
93 Albrecht Bald, 'Das Aussenlager Bayreuth des KZs Flossenbürg', unpublished typescript, 26.
94 On this satellite camp, see Hans Mommsen and Manfred Grieger, *Das Volkswagenwerk und seine Arbeiter im Dritten Reich 1933–1948*, Düsseldorf, 1997, 910ff.
95 Berlin BDC, Lafferentz. This decoration, awarded on 14.1.1944, was not unusual after three years' service in the SS.
96 Goebbels diary, 17.1.1944.
97 Jörg Skriebeleit, 'Das Aussenlager Bayreuth des KZ Flossenbürg in der neuen Baumwollspinnerei', unpublished manuscript, 7f.
98 Peter Engelbrecht, 'Aussenlager Bayreuth', NbK, 1.12.2000.
99 Bayreuth STA, construction files, with thanks to Walter Bartl.
100 Skriebeleit (see note 97), 14.
101 Skelton (see note 46), 78f.
102 WoW, *Lebens-Akte*, Munich, 1994, 117.
103 Bald (see note 93).
104 Engelbrecht (see note 98).
105 Bald (see note 93), 26; based on reports by Hans Imhof.
106 Skriebeleit (see note 97), 12f.
107 GSt, 3.12.1944.
108 Renate W. Schostack, *Hinter Wahnfrieds Mauern*, Hamburg, 1998, 204.
109 GSt, 6.11.1944.
110 Skriebeleit (see note 97), 18f. and 23.
111 Anton Joachimsthaler, *Hitlers Ende*, Munich, 1995, 104f.
112 Munich BStA, SKA, minutes, 86, statement by Lydia Beil.
113 WW to Ilse and Hermann Ernst, 18.12.1970.
114 WW, draft, 16.10.1944, Nike Wagner's copy.
115 GSt, 25.10.1944.
116 Ibid., 6.11.1944.
117 Ibid., 5.12.1944.
118 Ibid., 22.1.1944.
119 This and following information from a statement by Verena Lafferentz.
120 IfZ, ZS 2242, WW, 13.3.1971.
121 GSt, 11.12.1946.
122 New York Public Library, WieW to WW, 22.12.1944, English translation by CIC officer Joseph Stein.
123 GSt, 22.12.1944.
124 WoW, HT to WW, 17.12.1944.

125 GSt, 22.12.1944.
126 Ibid., 14.12.1944.
127 Statement by WW, SKA, Kempfler, Regensburg, with thanks to Gerdi Kempfler.
128 New York Public Library (see note 122).
129 GSt, 8.1.1944.
130 Statement by Wolfgang Wagner.
131 GSt, 18.1.1942.
132 Ibid., 9 and 10.1.1945.
133 Schostack (see note 108), 207, WW to Kurt Overhoff, 15.1.1945.
134 BStA, SKA, report by Wilhelm Hieber, 2.12.1948.
135 Coburg StA, SKA, Treuter, 13.9.1946.
136 GSt, 17.11.1942.
137 Ibid., 27.1.1945.
138 Coburg StA, SKA, Treuter, 13.9.1946.
139 Ibid., statement by Kempfler, 27.8.1948.
140 Ibid., 3.11.1947.
141 Kempfler (see note 26), 88.
142 Statement by Pöhner's daughter Brigitte, 31.1.2001, for ZDF.
143 GSt, 7.2.1945.
144 Schostack (see note 108), 208.
145 Coburg StA, SKA, Treuter, statement by Oswald Rothaug, 3.11.1947.
146 GSt, 16.3.1945.
147 Graz UB mss., WW to Fred Fritsch, 9.1.1945.
148 GSt, 4.6.1943.
149 Ibid., 9. and 10.1.1945.
150 Ibid., 12.1.1945.
151 Ibid., 4.1.1945.
152 Kempfler (see note 26), 164.
153 GSt, 18.1.1945.
154 Werner Meyer, *Götterdämmerung. April 1945 in Bayreuth*, Percha, 1975, WW to Meyer.
155 Communication from Verena Lafferentz.
156 GSt, 16.2.1945.
157 BSt, SKA, Friedrich Ernst von Seherr-Thoss, 2.6.1946.
158 GSt, 6. and 7.2.1945.
159 Statement by Verena Lafferentz, July 2000.
160 GSt, 28.2.1945.
161 Statement by Verena Lafferentz, July 2000.
162 Gerhard Schulze-Pfaelzer, *Kampf um den Kopf*, Berlin, 1977, 234.
163 Lisa de Boor, *Tagebuchblätter, 1938–1945*, Munich, 1963, 1.3.1945, 233.
164 Statement by Ursula de Boor's son Helmut Seemann, 3.11.2001.
165 WW memorandum, 58.
166 Kempfler (see note 26), 170.
167 Baur (see note 29), 258.
168 Kempfler (see note 26), 172 and 177.
169 Meyer (see note 154), 63ff.
170 WW to unknown woman, 30.3.1945; with thanks to Manfred Eger.

171 WW to Ursel Gossmann, 2.4.1945.
172 Meyer (see note 154), 97f.
173 Ibid., 44.
174 Ibid., 46ff.
175 In Meyer (ibid.), 50, from GSt.
176 WW to Ursel Gossmann, 15.1.1945.
177 WoW (see note 102), 118.
178 Kempfler (see note 26), 187.
179 Ibid., 188.
180 Skriebeleit (see note 97), 20.
181 WW film, 158.
182 Statement by Verena Lafferentz.
183 Communication from Dr Helmut Seemann.
184 NTh, WW to FW, 17.9.1945.
185 Ibid., 13.6.1947.
186 NTh, WW to FW, 12.10.1945.
187 Ibid., 10.10.1946.
188 Schostack (see note 108), 214.
189 GSt, 13.4.1946.
190 NTh, Ellen Beerli to FW, 28.9.1945.
191 WW film, 135.

14. DE-NAZIFICATION (1945–9)

1   WW film, 172.
2   GSt, 14.4.1946.
3   Lucerne RWM, WW to Olly Rothenfelder, 10.12.1947.
4   GSt, 13.11.1946.
5   Kurt Overhoff, 'Manipulationen. Die mit Dokumenten belegte Geschichte meines Lebens', typescript, 108.
6   Bayreuth STA, WW to the search department, Population Office, 18.2.1947. A new search instigated by the author through the International Red Cross yielded no results.
7   HT to Gertrud Beckel, n.d. (after May 1945).
8   Hübschmann, Paulus, and Pokorny, *Physische und behördliche Gewalt*, Bayreuth, 2000, 79.
9   WW film, 79.
10 Ibid., 79f.
11 Klaus Mann, *Der Wendepunkt*, Hamburg, 1993, 501f.
12 Marbach, WW to Hans Grimm, 19.10.1954.
13 NTH, FW to Ellen Beerli, n.d. (April 1946).
14 For example, NTh, *New York Journal American*, 23.10.1935.
15 NTh, Beerli to FW, 28.9.1945.
16 Ibid., FW to Beerli, 19.9.1945.
17 Ibid., FW to WieW, 5.11.1945.
18 Ibid., WW to Fiori, 3.8.1945.

19 Koblenz BA, N. Speer, WW to Albert Speer, 1.12.1966.
20 BStA, SKA, CIC minutes, 14.9.1946.
21 Christa Schroeder, *Er war mein Chef*, Munich, 1985, 79.
22 BStA, SKA, CIC minutes, 14.9.1946.
23 NTh, WW to FW, 3.3.1960.
24 Ibid., 3.3.1960.
25 BStA, SKA, WW supplement, 3.9.1946, to the CIC.
26 WW to HR, 22.8.1948.
27 GSt, 15.4.1947.
28 Hans Wysling, 'Aus dem Briefwechsel Thomas Mann – Emil Preetorius', in *Blätter der Thomas Mann-Gesellschaft*, Zurich, 1963, No. 4, 7.
29 Emil Preetorius to Thomas Mann, 8.9.1945, ibid., 9.
30 Ibid., 10.6.1946, 14f.
31 Mann to Preetorius, 30.12.1946, ibid., 16.
32 Elisabeth Furtwängler, *Über Wilhelm Furtwängler*, Wiesbaden, 1979, 133f.
33 NTh, FW to Beerli, Hotel Ansonia, New York, 2.9.1945.
34 Ibid., WW to FW, 17.9.1945.
35 Vienna, ÖNB Mslg, WW to Erich Müller von Asow, 4.1.1946.
36 NTh, WW to FW, 12.10. and 17.9.1945.
37 Ibid., WieW to FW, 29.9.1945.
38 Ibid., WieW to Toscanini, 31.9.1945.
39 Ibid., FW to WieW, 5.11.1945.
40 Ibid., Meyer to FW, 9.7.1946, referring to an invitation 'of some months ago'.
41 Overhoff (see note 5), appendix, 5, WieW to Overhoff, early March 1946.
42 WoW, WoW to WieW, 27.8.1946.
43 GSt, 3.9.1946.
44 NTh, Meyer to FW, 9.7.1946.
45 According to Neill Thornborrow, May 2000.
46 NTh, FW to WieW, 5.11.1945.
47 Marbach, WW to Anton Kippenberg, 22.11.1946.
48 WW film, 159f.
49 WW to August Roesener, 7.3.1947.
50 WoW, WW to Dr Schultz, 8.12. and 1.11.1948.
51 WW to Gertrud Beckel, 30.6.1948.
52 WoW, excerpts from WW's letters to Schultz, in this case 29.10.1947.
53 Vienna, ÖNB Mslg., WW to Müller von Asow, 26.4.1946.
54 Overhoff (see note 5); WieW to Overhoff, 6.5.1946, Appendix, 6.
55 WW to Ilse Ernst, 6.1.1947.
56 DRWG, Otto Daube, 'Begegnungen eines Neunzigjährigen', typescript, 68, WW to Daube, 24.3.1946.
57 Ibid., 490ff., WW to Joachim Schäfer, 31.8.1946.
58 NTh, WW to FW, 6.8.1947.
59 WW to FW, 26.6.1948.
60 ZDF, 'Hitler's Women', WW, interview notes Betty Weiss.
61 WW to FW, 7.4.1946.
62 Daube (see note 56), 68, WW to Daube, 24.3.1946.
63 Ibid., 493ff., WW to Schäfer, 31.8.1946.
64 WoW, WW to Meyer, 24.5.1947.

65 GSt, 4.4.1946.
66 WW memorandum, 40f.; checked in the files of the Austrian 'Underground' Association, with thanks to Brigitte Ungar-Klein.
67 Lucerne RWM, WW to Rothenfelder, 6.1.1947.
68 GSt, 5.9.1946.
69 WW to FW, 10.10.1946.
70 WW memorandum, 7 and 18.
71 Ibid., 19f.
72 Ibid., 47.
73 Ibid., 19.
74 Coburg StA, SKA, Treuter, statement by Albert Angerer, 28.7.1946.
75 Ibid., 18.4.1949.
76 NTh, WW to FW, 13.6.1947.
77 Coburg StA, SKA, Treuter, statement by refugee Liebner, 5.11.1946.
78 Ibid., Angerer, letter from Lotte Meyer-Viol to the court, 3.7.1947, and Paula Schwabacher.
79 Marbach, WW to Kippenberg, 22.11.1946.
80 GSt, 30.10.1946.
81 WoW, minutes of meeting, 11.1.1947.
82 NTh, WW to FW, 8.5.1947.
83 GSt, 16.12.1946.
84 Franz Wilhelm Beidler, *Cosima Wagner–Liszt*, ed. by Dieter Borchmeyer, Bielefeld, 1997, 354.
85 Ibid., 351ff., Beidler to Thomas Mann, 9.1.1947.
86 Ibid., 354f.
87 WW to August Roesener, 7.3.1947.
88 NTh, WW to FW, 7.4.1946.
89 Ibid., 20.5.1946.
90 WoW, WoW to WieW, 9.11.1946.
91 WW to Roesener, 7.3.1947.
92 WoW, WoW to WieW, 5.4.1947.
93 WW to Roesener, 7.3.1947.
94 WW to FW, 16.3.1947.
95 NTh, WW to FW, 6.8.1947.
96 FW, *Nacht über Bayreuth*, Cologne, 3rd edition, 1997, 300.
97 NTh, WW to FW, 8.5.1947.
98 WoW, Pree to WW, 13.5.1947.
99 HT to Gertrud Beckel, 16.3.1947.
100 NTh, WW to FW, 13.6.1947.
101 WoW, WW to Meyer, 25.5.1947.
102 WW film, 167f.
103 Communication from Regine von Schenck zu Schweinsberg, November 2001.
104 GSt, 28.5.1947.
105 NTh, WW to FW, 3.6.1947.
106 NTh, telegram FW to Fritz Meyer.
107 WW to Ursel Gossmann, 21.6.1946.
108 NTh, WW to FW, 5.7.1947.
109 WW to Ilse Ernst, 20.11.1947.

110 WoW, WoW to WieW, 19.5.1947.
111 BStA, SKA, minutes, 24, witness Spitzer.
112 Ibid., witness Gustav Kröniger.
113 Ibid., 31f., witness Zimmermann.
114 Ibid., 33f., witness Hochgesang.
115 Ibid., 37 and 44, statement by Körber.
116 Ibid., 44–6, statement by Körber.
117 WW film, 78.
118 BStA, SKA, minutes, 52–7.
119 Ibid., annexe, 1.
120 Ibid., minutes, 58f.
121 Ibid., 62f.
122 Rainer Maria Kiel, Postscript to Karl Würzburger, *Im Schatten des Lichts*, Bayreuth, 1997, 352.
123 Bayreuth UB, N. Würzburger, 'Der Fall Wagner', with thanks to Albrecht Bald.
124 BStA, SKA, minutes, 87.
125 Bayreuth UB (see note 123).
126 BStA, SKA, minutes, 109.
127 Reported by Verena Lafferentz, August 1999.
128 BStA, SKA, verdict, 2.7.1947.
129 GSt, 2.7.1947.
130 WW to FW, 5.7.1947.
131 Bayreuth UB (see note 123).
132 GSt, 4.7.1947.
133 WoW, FW to WoW, 11.7.1947.
134 Lucerne RWM, WW to Rothenfelder, 31.1.1948.
135 Ibid., 10.11.1953.
136 Ibid., 10.12.1947.
137 WW to Alice Strauss, 24.4.1948.
138 HT to Beckel, 16.9.1948.
139 BStA, SKA, Brandt, 31.3.1947.
140 NTh, WW to FW, 2.9.1947.
141 WW to Ilse Ernst, 11.12.1947 and 26.3.1948.
142 HT to Beckel, 4.1.1948.
143 Nike Wagner, *Wagner Theater*, Frankfurt a. M. 1998, 340; translated by Ewald Osers and Michael Downes, as *The Wagners: The Dramas of a Musical Dynasty*, London, 2000, 240.
144 Renate W. Schostack, *Hinter Wahnfrieds Mauern*, Hamburg, 1998, 298.
145 Ibid., 225, WieW to Maria Dernburg, 1946.
146 GSt, 20. and 27.11.1947.
147 NTh, WW to Beerli, 31.3.1947.
148 Overhoff (see note 5), WieW to Overhoff, early March 1946, documents, 5.
149 GSt, 26.4.1946.
150 WW to WieW and Gertrud Wagner, 16.1.1948.
151 AdK, N. Tietjen, Pree to HT, 22.2.1948.
152 RWA, copy, WW to Maude Williams, 7.11.1947, in English.
153 Ibid., 5.12.1947.

154 WoW, WW to Schultz, 27.1.1948.
155 WW to Daube, 31.3.1948.
156 Helmut Paulus, 'Die "Reichskristallnacht"', in the Archiv für die Geschichte von Oberfranken, 1998, 410.
157 Coburg StA, SKA, von Eberhardt, Hans and Adolf Reissinger, Otto Strobel.
158 WW to FW, 1.5.1948.
159 WoW, WoW to WieW, 15.6.1948.
160 Lucerne RWM, WW to Rothenfelder, 22.5.1948.
161 WW to HR, 22.8.1948.
162 WW to Daube, 16.10.1948.
163 WW to HR, 22.8.1948.
164 Ibid., November 1948.
165 BStA, SKA, minutes, 80, statement by Wilhelm Hieber.
166 Unfortunately, there is no record of these cases in the Munich de-nazification court files.
167 BStA, SKA, ruling of the Ansbach appeal court, 8.12.1948.
168 WW to FW, 14.12.1948.
169 Coburg StA, SKA, WieW.
170 AdK, Tietjen papers, HT to Preetorius, 17.12.1948.
171 WW film, 216f.
172 WW to Troost, 6.6.1949.
173 WW to FW, 14.12.1948.
174 DRWG, Curt von Westernhagen, 'Erinnerungen', 6, WW to Westernhagen, 1948.

15. SUPERANNUATION (1949–73)

1 WoW, WW, 21.1.1949.
2 WW to Ilse Ernst, 16.3.1949; there is a similar letter of the same date to Olly Rothenfelder.
3 Ibid., 23.4.1950, copy.
4 VL to WW, 12.6.1950, Nike Wagner's copy.
5 WW to HR, 20.12.1951.
6 BStA, SKA, copy.
7 WW to Ilse Hess, 26.6.1949.
8 WW film, 227.
9 DRWG, notes by Ursula Kröll.
10 WW to Gerdy Troost, 13.1.1966.
11 AdK, Pree to HT, 15.5.1949.
12 Mannheim, Reger-Archiv, Fritz Busch to Liholm, 12.12.1949 and 30.1.1950.
13 WoW, Financial plan, 14.9.1949.
14 WW to HR, 14.2.1952.
15 WW to Ilse Ernst, 23.4.1950.
16 WoW, Konrad Pöhner to Otto Strobel, 1.3.1949.
17 NbK, 10.3.1971, 'Zum 80. Geburtstag Dr. Würzburgers'.
18 Rainer Trübsbach, Geschichte der Stadt Bayreuth, Bayreuth, 1993, 354.
19 WW to Ilse Hess, 3.2.1950.
20 Renate W. Schostack, Hinter Wahnfrieds Mauern, Hamburg, 1998, 276.

21 Marbach, WW to Will Vesper, 25.5.1951.
22 WW to HR, 11.7.1951.
23 Alan Jefferson, *Elisabeth Schwarzkopf*, Munich, 1996, 168.
24 WoW, *Lebens-Akte*, Munich, 1994, 170.
25 Graz UB, WW to Fritsch, 10.4.1951.
26 WW film, 55.
27 AdK, Pree to HT, 11.8.1951.
28 WW to Tilly Kallmeyer, 18.11.1951.
29 AdK, Pree to HT, 23.9.1952.
30 Lucerne RWM, WW to Rothenfelder, 4.9.1953.
31 IfZ, WW to Freda Rössler, 17.1.1955.
32 WW to HR, 5.8.1953.
33 WW to Walter Clauss, 25.11.1953.
34 WW to HR, 3.9.1954.
35 WW to Lisa Gleissner, 16.4.1958.
36 WW to Ilse Ernst, 25.12.1959.
37 WW to Kallmeyer, 19.6.1950.
38 WW to HR, 19.10.1951.
39 Statements by Neill Thornborrow and Gottfried von Einem's widow, Lotte Ingrisch.
40 WW to HR, 5.8.1953.
41 ZDF, 'Hitlers Frauen', interview with Daphne Wagner, 24.1.2001.
42 WW to Kallmeyer, 6.10.1953.
43 Ibid.
44 WW to HR, 4.6.1953.
45 WW to Kallmeyer, 6.10.1953.
46 RWA, WW to her half-sister Maude, 10.1.1954, in English.
47 WW to HR, 22.1.1959.
48 WW film, 110.
49 WoW, copied from WW's letters to Dr Schultz, in this case 27.6. and 9.11.1959.
50 WW to Gerdy Troost, 25.6.1962.
51 WW to Kallmeyer, 6.6.1959.
52 WW to HR, 7.6.1959.
53 NTh, Lotte Lehmann to FW, 22.12.1958.
54 WW to Ilse Ernst, 9.11.1961.
55 WW to Ilse Hess, 3.2.1950.
56 WW to Ilse Ernst, 23.4.1950.
57 Information from the RW Museum in Graupa.
58 *Echo der Woche*, 26.4.1952.
59 Ibid., 'Winifred Wagner und die Sowjetzone'.
60 BStB mss., WW to Troost, 18.2.1968.
61 WW to Troost, 18.2.1963.
62 Lucerne RWM, WW to Rothenfelder, 1968.
63 WW to Fritz Kempfler, 3.1.1968.
64 Ibid., 25.6.1974.
65 AdK, Pree to HT, 6.11.1949.
66 Kurt Overhoff, 'Manipulationen. Die mit Dokumenten belegte Geschichte meines Lebens', typescript, 61.

67 Kurt Overhoff, 'Neu-Bayreuth', in *Staatsbriefe 6–7*, Munich, 1991, 16.
68 WW to Dr Dingeldey, n.d.
69 Communication from Nike and Daphne Wagner, 2001.
70 Kröll (see note 9).
71 Walter Erich Schäfer, *Bühne eines Lebens*, Stuttgart, 1975, 190.
72 WW to Lisa Gleissner, 12.4.1957.
73 WW to Ilse Ernst, 18.5.1957.
74 WW to Troost, 15.9.1962.
75 WW to HR, 18.1.1958.
76 WW to Ilse Ernst, 22.8.1955.
77 WW to Dingeldey, 12.7.1959.
78 WW to Ilse Ernst, 9.11.1961.
79 Kröll (see note 9).
80 WW film, 54.
81 WW to Ilse Ernst, 28.9.1960.
82 Marbach, WW to Hans Grimm, 8.7.1950.
83 WW to Ilse Ernst, 11.11.1968.
84 WW to Troost, 15.8.1969.
85 WW to HR, 31.10.1951.
86 WW to Troost, 15.9.1962.
87 Ibid., 14.1.1974.
88 WW to Ilse Hess, 14.9.1953.
89 WW to Dingeldey, 6.9.1960.
90 Hermann Weiss (ed.), *Biographisches Lexikon zum Dritten Reich*, Frankfurt a. M., 1998, 494f.
91 WW to Troost, 30.1.1963.
92 WW to Ilse Hess, 3.2.1950.
93 Ilse Hess to WW, 29.1.1950.
94 WW to Ilse Hess, 11.11. and 8.5.1952.
95 WW to Ilse Ernst, 28.1.1958.
96 WW to Troost, 6.9.1962.
97 WW to Ilse Hess, 3.2.1950.
98 WW to Ilse Ernst, 5.3.1970.
99 WW to Troost, 1.11.1973 and 11.11.1969.
100 WW to Fritz Kempfler, 3.1.1968.
101 WW to Troost, 5.11.1968.
102 IfZ, WW to Freda Rössler, 17.1.1955.
103 WW to Lisa Gleissner, 1955.
104 Marbach, WW to Will Vesper, 25.5.1951.
105 WW to HR, 21.11.1950.
106 IfZ, ZS 2242, WW interview with David Irving, 13.3.1971.
107 Marbach, WW to Grimm, 19.10.1954.
108 RWA; an excerpt from this letter has been pasted into the archive copy of Ziegler's book.
109 WW to HR, 13.8.1964.
110 WoW (see note 16), 181f., also Schostack (see note 20), 425.
111 WW film, 181f.
112 Schostack (see note 20), 360ff.

113 WW to Gossmann, 3.2.1962.
114 Nike Wagner, *Wagner Theater*, Frankfurt a. M., 1998, 367; English version, *The Wagners. The Dramas of a Musical Dynasty*, translated by Ewald Osers and Michael Downes, London, 2000, 261.
115 WW to Troost, 11.6.1973.
116 Walter Legge and Elisabeth Schwarzkopf, *Gehörtes, Ungehörtes*, Munich, 1982, 97.
117 WoW, excerpts from WW letters to Schultz, in this case 2.11.1965.
118 WW to HR, 26.10.1960.
119 Zurich ZB MSlg., WieW to Taubmann, 14.7.1966.
120 WW to HR, 15.10.1965.
121 Anja Silja, *Die Sehnsucht nach dem Unerreichbaren*, Berlin, 1999, 164ff.
122 WW to Troost, 7.7.1966.
123 Zurich ZB, mss., WieW to Taubmann, 14.7.1966.
124 Communication from Anja Silja, 18.1.2002.
125 WW to Troost, 15.10.1966.
126 Nike Wagner (see note 114), 383.
127 WW to Troost, 23.10.1966.
128 WW to Ilse Ernst, 20.2.1967.
129 Wagner (see note 114), 377; Osers and Downes (transl.), 269.
130 WW to Troost, 23.11.1966.
131 NbK, 11.3.1980.
132 WW to Ilse Ernst, 6.12.1967.
133 WW to Troost, 4.12.1966.
134 WW to Ilse Ernst, 10.4.1967.
135 WoW, WW, 13.2.1967, ms.
136 Lucerne RWM, WW to Rothenfelder, 28.6.1970.
137 WW to Troost, 24.1.1969. Daphne was soon divorced from him. In 1991, Proksch was convicted of murdering six people in connection with an insurance scam, and received a twenty-year gaol sentence. He died in prison in 2001.
138 *Quick*, 19.6.1968.
139 WW to Ilse Ernst, 11.1.1968.
140 WoW to FW, 1.7.1968, Nike Wagner's copy.
141 WW to Ilse Ernst, 25.8.1965.
142 Bayreuth STA, *Frankenpost*, Hof, 16.1.1969.
143 Ibid.
144 WW to Troost, 16.1.1969.
145 Troost to WW, 23.1.1969.
146 Troost to WW, 1.10.1969.
147 WW to Kempfler, 26.6.1971.
148 WW to Ilse Ernst, 10.4.1967.
149 DRWG, Ursula Kröll's notes, 23.1.1963.
150 Statement by Verena Lafferentz, August 1999.
151 WW to Troost, 19.9.1972.
152 Ibid., 9.12.1971.
153 DRWG, WW to Daube, 9.2.1965. Similarly, WW to Troost, 8.2.1965.
154 RWA, Marietta Coudenhove to WW, 17.12.1936.
155 WW to Troost, 21.12.1963.

156 Zdenko von Kraft, *Der Sohn. Siegfried Wagners Leben und Umwelt*, Graz, 1969, 255f.
157 Ibid., 307.
158 WW to Kempfler, 30.6.1969.
159 WW to Ilse Ernst, 19.7.1969.
160 Nike Wagner (see note 114), 383.
161 WW to Troost, 7.7.1972.
162 WW in the Festival programme, 1972.
163 WW to Ilse Ernst, 2.7.1971.
164 WW to Troost, 11.6.1973.
165 Ibid., 28.6.1973.
166 Ibid., 18.12.1973.
167 WW to Kempfler, 25.6.1974.

16. AT THE END, A FILM (1974–80)

1   WW to Ilse Ernst, 1.12.1976.
2   Nth, WW to FW, 22.4.1975.
3   WW to August Roesener, 18.8.1975.
4   Syberberg, *Zeitmagazin*, 23.4.1975.
5   Syberberg, *Filmbuch*, Munich, 1976, 271.
6   Syberberg (see note 4), 5.
7   Communication from Gottfried Wagner, 2001.
8   Syberberg (see note 5).
9   Ibid., 257f.
10 WW to Overhoff, 2.9.1976.
11 Syberberg (see note 5), 252.
12 Gottfried Wagner, *Wer mit dem Wolf heult*, Cologne, 1997, 128.
13 This and other quotations from WW are taken from the transcript of the tape made during and between filming, and meant to form the basis of a book (WoW).
14 WW to Gerdy Troost, 15.4.1975.
15 WW to Ilse Ernst, 14.6.1975.
16 *Die Zeit*, 18.7.1975
17 *Neue Rhein Ruhr Zeitung*, 12.6.1975.
18 WW to Roesener, 18.8.1975.
19 WW to Kurt Overhoff, 2.9.1976.
20 Syberberg (see note 5), 261.
21 Statement by Ingrid Brenner, August 2001.
22 BStB mss., WW to Herr and Frau Köster, 19.8.1975.
23 WW to Troost, 27.7.1975.
24 WW to Kempfler, 4.12.1975.
25 BStB mss., WW to the Kösters, 29.6.1976.
26 WW to Weckherlin, 9.6.1976.
27 WW film, 216.
28 NTh, WW to FW, 13.12.1976.
29 WW to Troost, 8.2.1977.

30 NTh, WW to FW, 22.2.1977.
31 WW to Troost, 30.3.1976.
32 NTh, WW to FW, 20.1.1974.
33 BStB mss., WW to the Kösters, 29.6.1976.
34 WW to Kempler, 25.6.1974.
35 Numerous attempts to contact Frau Amélie Hohmann both by telephone and in person, and at least raise a few important questions, have been unsuccessful.
36 NTh, WW to FW, 11.10.1977.
37 Nike Wagner, *Wagner Theater*, Frankfurt a. M., 1998, 380.
38 WW to Herr and Frau Brenner, 26.5.1976.
39 First-hand report by Oswald Georg Bauer.
40 Interview in *Spiegel* magazine, 25.9.1967.
41 NTh, WW to FW, 21.7.1976.
42 WW to Kempfler, 6.12.1976.
43 WW to Ilse Ernst, 6.10.1977.
44 WW to the Brenners, 1.12.1976.
45 WW to Kempfler, 3.12.1977.
46 WW to Troost, 1.8.1977.
47 WW to Rüdiger Pohl, 5.8.1978.
48 Communication from Gottfried Wagner, 2001.
49 WW to Hermann Ernst, 2.11.1971.
50 Ernst Günther Schenck, *Patient Hitler*, new edition Augsburg, 2000.
51 WW to Ilse Ernst, 27.1.1977.
52 Records of the Richard Wagner Society, Linz, 14.9.1977.
53 WW to Troost, 8.5.1977.
54 Statement by Ingrid Brenner, Altaussee, 1.8.2001.
55 Lotte Pfeiffer-Bechstein to WW, 15.7.1975, enclosed with WW's letters to Gerdy Troost.
56 *The National Socialist*, Fall 1980, 2, 5f., with thanks to María Infiesta, Barcelona.
57 WW to Troost, 26.2.1976.
58 James King, *Nun sollt Ihr mich befragen*, Berlin, 2000, 173.
59 WW to Hermann Ernst, 1. and 3.2.1978.
60 WW to Ilse Hess, 21.4.1978.
61 Eva Wagner-Pasquier to WW, 10.9.1978.
62 WW to Kempfler, 6.12.1979.
63 Statement by Betty Weiss, 16.11.2001.
64 *Deutsche Nationalzeitung*, 14.3.1980, 4.
65 Gerhard R. Koch, *Frankfurter Allgemeine Zeitung*, 5.3.1980.
66 Statement of an anonymous witness, Bayreuth, 23.7.1998.
67 WW to Troost, 1.10.1979.
68 Ibid., 23.10.1979.

INDEX

All musical compositions are indexed at the end of the entry for their composer; 'Festival' refers to the Bayreuth Festival; 'Wagner' refers to Richard Wagner.